Problem Solving, Abstraction, and Design Using C++

SECOND EDITION

FRANK L. FRIEDMAN
ELLIOT B. KOFFMAN

Temple University

 **ADDISON-WESLEY**

An imprint of Addison Wesley Longman, Inc.

Reading, Massachusetts • Harlow, England • Menlo Park, California
Berkeley, California • Don Mills, Ontario • Sydney • Bonn • Amsterdam
Tokyo • Mexico City

Sponsoring Editor	Susan Hartman
Editorial Assistant	Julie Dunn
Production Manager	Karen Wernholm
Editorial Production Services	Amy Willcutt
Compositor	Michael Wile
Text Designer	Joyce Weston
Cover Designer	Diana Coe
Senior Manufacturing Coordinator	Judith Sullivan

Library of Congress Cataloging-in-Publication Data

Friedman, Frank L.
    Problem solving, abstraction, and design using C++ / Frank L.
Friedman, Elliot B. Koffman. — 2nd ed.
        p.   cm.
    Includes index.
    ISBN 0-201-88337-6
    1. C++ (Computer program language) I. Koffman, Elliot B.
II. Title.
QA76.73.C153F75 1996
005.13'3—dc20   96-43063
                                                      CIP

Access the latest information about Addison-Wesley titles from our World Wide Web page:
http://www.awl.com/cseng

The programs and applications presented in this book have been included for their instructional value. They have been tested with care but are not guaranteed for any particular purpose. The publisher does not offer any warranties or representations, nor does it accept any liabilities with respect to the programs or applications.

1 2 3 4 5 6 7 8 9 10-MA-99989796

Preface

This is a textbook for a one- or two-semester course in problem solving and program design. It is suitable for use by students with no programming background as well as those who may have had the equivalent of up to a one-semester course in another programming language. Students' backgrounds will determine the time required to cover the earlier chapters of the text and the extent of coverage possible for later chapters.

The second edition of this book represents the culmination of an eight-year effort, partially sponsored by the National Science Foundation,[1] to define an introductory-level course combining the presentation of rudimentary principles of software engineering and object-oriented programming with an introduction to the C++ programming language. Our primary goal is to motivate and introduce sound principles of program engineering in a first programming course. Topics such as program style, documentation, algorithm and data structuring, procedure- and data-oriented modularization, component reuse, and program verification are introduced early. The focus throughout is on the problem solving/software construction process, from problem analysis to program design and coding.

Early Coverage of Classes and Objects

Object-oriented concepts are introduced at the beginning of the book and further developed in succeeding chapters. Chapter 2 begins with an emphasis on the reuse of existing classes: the new C++ string class (variable-length strings), the iostream class, and a user-defined money class. The importance of data modeling in the programming process is stressed from the start. Emphasis is placed on identifying the entities to be manipulated in solving a problem and extracting their essential features in building a new model, or selecting an existing one, to represent each entity in the program. The importance of using the most accurate, representative model (data type) for each entity is illustrated through the repeated reuse of such models in examples and case studies.

Balancing Object-Oriented and Procedural Approaches

The definition of classes is first introduced in Chapter 11. The benefits of being able to define new data types as models of problem domain entities and

[1]NSF Instrumentation and Laboratory Improvement (ILI) Grant Number USE-9250254 and NSF Undergraduate Curriculum Course Development (UCCD) Grant Number USE-9156079

to write programs in terms of objects of these types is first presented in Chapters 2 and 3. These benefits are now further emphasized and illustrated, as students are shown how to define their own classes based upon the analyses of a problem and the selection of reasonable models of the entities to be manipulated in solving the problem. The importance of encapsulation (of data stores and operations) in limiting the scope of access to information, and in the separation of implementation details based upon the properties of and required operations on problem domain entities is explained and illustrated. Faculty who want their students to write class definitions earlier can cover most of the material in Chapter 11 anytime after Chapter 7.

We continue to emphasize the design of classes and data modeling in Chapter 12, which introduces template classes, an indexed-list class, a stack class, friend functions, and operator overloading. We also use template classes in Chapter 14 where we discuss dynamic data structures: lists, stacks, queues, and trees. An illustration of the C++ inheritance and virtual function mechanisms is provided in Appendix E.

We have done our best to follow a balanced path between the strictly objects-first and totally procedure-focused programming metaphors. We agree with the objects-first concept, but not at the expense of the fundamentals of algorithm organization and design. Students in a first course can and should be taught the basic elements of procedural design. Our task is to do so within the context of an early focus on the importance of data modeling, reuse, and other fundamental principles of good software development.

Software Engineering and Object-Oriented Concepts

Many fundamental software engineering and object-oriented concepts are illustrated in the text: user-defined types, modeling problem domain entities and their relationships, minimal interfaces, high-level cohesion, information hiding, separation of concerns, parameterized components, and (in an appendix) type hierarchies, and inheritance. Abstraction is stressed from the start. Numerous complete case examples are provided throughout the text, consistent with the notion that there is much to be learned by studying such examples, from the analysis of the specification of a problem to a first stage of design to the final coding.

Issues of program style are presented throughout in special displays. The concept of a program as a sequence of control structures is introduced in Chapter 3 and discussed in more detail in Chapters 4 (on selection structures) and 5 (repetition structures). The text embodies many of our choices for software engineering concepts to be introduced in the first-year course. We have introduced functions and classes as early as possible at the introductory level—functions in Chapters 3 and 6, and the use and definition of classes in

Chapters 3 and 11 respectively. We also provide several sections that discuss testing, debugging, and program verification.

Outline of Contents

Conceptually, the text may be partitioned into three sections. Chapters 1 through 6 provide introductory material on functions and top-down design; detailed coverage of selection and repetition structures and program design strategies for using these structures are presented here. The connection between good problem-solving skills and effective software development is established early in the first three chapters. Included in the first two chapters are sections on problem solving and an introduction to software development methodologies based on a systematic approach to problem solving. The problem-solving approach outlined in these chapters is also used to solve the first case study and is applied consistently to all other case studies in the text. Chapter 2 also contains an introduction to the basic elements of C++, including two sections in which we discuss abstraction, data modeling, and object-oriented programming. In Chapter 3, we continue the emphasis on basic problem-solving skills with a discussion of top-down design, divide and conquer, solution by analogy, and solution by generalization. The reuse of program components is discussed and additional detail is provided on the money and string classes and their member functions.

Top-down procedural decomposition is further illustrated throughout Chapters 4 through 6. Decision structures are introduced in Chapter 4, and repetition structures are presented in Chapter 5. In Chapter 6, we revisit the C++ function, introducing functions with output arguments and providing a complete case study illustrating much of what has been learned to this point. An optional section on recursion is also included at the end of Chapter 6.

Chapters 7 through 9 cover simple data types, input and output, and structured data types (arrays and structs). Chapter 7 contains a more detailed discussion of simple data types, including additional commentary on data abstraction as well as a description of the internal and external distinctions among the simple types. In Chapter 9, the structured types (arrays and structs) are first introduced. Simple searching and sorting algorithms are discussed and the use of structured types as function arguments is illustrated.

Chapter 8 provides an introduction to external file input/output. Although studying external files may seem premature at this point, we believe it is appropriate. Programs do not exist in a vacuum; they manipulate data that often come from external sources and they produce results that may subsequently be manipulated by other programs. It is therefore important for students to gain a relatively early exposure to some fundamental concepts related to file input and output, as long as this exposure does not disrupt the presentation of other essential ideas. Of course, by the time Chapter 8 is reached, students will have already been introduced to the basics of stream input and output, including a minimal use of formatting functions and input/output manipulators (Chapter 5).

For students with the equivalent of a one-semester programming course in another language, Chapters 1 through 9 can be covered fairly quickly, perhaps in as little as five or six weeks. For students with little or no background, this coverage may take ten to twelve weeks.

Chapters 10 through 12 cover intermediate-level concepts. Chapter 10 begins with an introduction to the idea of programming in the large followed by a review of procedural abstraction, illustrations of the use of function templates, and a discussion of separate compilation. Program verification (with a focus on assertions and loop invariants) and algorithm analysis and big-O notation are also introduced. Additional commentary in Chapter 10 on software engineering and data abstraction sets the stage for Chapters 11 and 12, which describe the definition and use of classes and class instances (objects). Chapter 12 focuses on data modeling. We begin with a discussion of multidimensional arrays and arrays of structs and classes, and then extend our modeling capability with illustrations of the use of class templates.

Chapters 13 and 14 cover more advanced topics in some depth: recursion (Chapter 13), and linked lists, stacks, queues, and trees (Chapter 14). This material will be covered in the second semester of the first-year sequence.

Coverage of Pointers

Pointers are introduced only where they really belong—in the discussion of dynamic data structures (Chapter 14). The pointer is one of the more dangerous, relatively unprotected aspects of the C++ language and need not be an essential part of an introductory text. Use of the `new` and `delete` operators and the allocation and deallocation of memory cells in the heap are discussed at the beginning of Chapter 14. Dynamic data structures such as simple linked lists, stacks and queues, and binary trees are used to provide a number of illustrations of the manipulation of dynamic data structures.

Pedagogical Features

Several pedagogical features also enhance the usefulness of the text as an instructional tool. These include the following:

- Consistent use of analysis and design aids such as data requirements tables and program structure charts
- End-of-section self-check and programming exercises (answers to the odd number self-check exercises are provided in the text)

- End-of-chapter self-check exercises (answers are provided)
- End-of-chapter programming projects
- Numerous examples and case studies carried through from analysis and design to implementation
- Syntax displays containing the syntax and semantics of each new C++ feature introduced
- Program style and design guideline displays
- Detailed syntax and run-time error discussions at the end of each chapter
- Chapter reviews and review questions

Appendixes and Special Supplements

Separate appendixes are provided, summarizing information about character sets, C++ reserved words, C++ operators, and function libraries (with descriptions and specific page numbers). The last appendix contains an introductory example illustrating inheritance and virtual functions.

The instructor's manual includes the following features:

- A statement of objectives for each chapter and a section-by-section guide for coverage of material based upon student backgrounds and needs
- Answers to even-numbered self-check exercises
- Answers to review questions
- Commentary on the analysis and design of selected programming projects

To order the IM, please contact your local A-W sales representative.

The following can be obtained electronically through Addison-Wesley's web site: http://www.aw.com/cseng/authors/friedman/probsol2e/probsol2e.html

- All programs, functions, and classes from the text
- Answers to all end-of-section programming exercises
- The implementation of selected programming projects
- Supplementary examples that were not included in the text
- Sample exam questions
- A money class
- A string class

Acknowledgements

Many people helped with the development of this book. Primary contributors to the first edition included Paul LaFollette, Paul Wolfgang, and Rajiv Tewari of Temple University. Temple graduate students Donna Chrupcala, Bruce

Weiner, and Judith Wilson also contributed significantly to the development of the first edition. Steve Vinoski provided detailed comments concerning the C++ material in many of the later chapters.

The principal reviewers and class testers were enormously helpful in suggesting improvements and finding errors. For the first edition, these included Allen Alexander (Delaware Technical and Community College), Ruth Barton and Richard Reid (Michigan State University), Larry Cottrell (University of Central Florida), H. E. Dunsmore and Russell Quong (Purdue University), Donna Krabbe (College of Mount St. Joseph), Sally Kyvernitis (Neumann College), Xiaoping Jia (DePaul University), Xiannong Meng and Rick Zaccone (Bucknell), Jeff Buckwalter and Kim Summerhays (University of San Francisco), and Jo Ellen Perry (University of North Carolina). Valuable proofreading and editing assistance were provided by Sally Kyvernitis, Donna Skalski, and Frank Friedman's daughters Dara and Shelley.

We are also very grateful to the principal reviewers of this edition for their hard work and timely responses. They include: William E. Bulley (Merit Network, Inc.), Greg Comeau (Comeau Computing), Bruce Gilland (University of Colorado at Boulder), William I. Grosky (Wayne State University), Bina Ramamurthy (SUNY at Buffalo), and W. Brent Seales (University of Kentucky). Our thanks, also, to Temple student Ayish Mertens, who tested the programs appearing in this edition.

We would also like to thank Conrad Weisert (Information Disciplines, Inc.) for permission to use the money class and for providing the code for this class for users of the text (see special supplements).

Frank Friedman is particularly indebted to several members of the staff at the Software Engineering Institute (Pittsburgh), particularly Mary Shaw, Norm Gibbs (now at Guilford College), and Gary Ford, for their support during the year in which the seeds that lead to this book were sown.

As always, it has been a pleasure working with the people of Addison-Wesley throughout this endeavor. Susan Hartman, computer science editor, was closely involved in all phases of the development of the manuscript, and provided friendship, guidance, and encouragement. Julie Dunn, editorial assistant, provided timely assistance at a moment's notice. Amy Willcutt coordinated the conversion of the manuscript to a finished book, Stephanie Magean thoroughly copyedited the manuscript, Sarah Corey proofread the page proofs, and Mike Wile handled the production of the book.

Philadelphia, PA   F. L. F.
                                                                            E. B. K.

Contents

4 ──── SELECTION STRUCTURES: `if` AND `switch` STATEMENTS   155

5 ──── REPETITION: `while`, `for`, AND `do-while` STATEMENTS   211

6 _____ PROGRAM DESIGN AND FUNCTIONS REVISITED   277

7 _____ SIMPLE DATA TYPES   325

8 _____ FORMATTING AND FILES   365

12 _____ MODELING DATA WITH ARRAYS, STRUCTS, AND CLASSES   539

13 _____ RECURSION   601

14 _____ POINTERS AND DYNAMIC DATA STRUCTURES   631

APPENDIXES

ANSWERS   A-1

INDEX   I-1

1

Introduction to Computers, Problem Solving, and Programming

Since the 1940s—a period of little more than 50 years—the development of the computer has spurred the growth of technology into realms only dreamed of at the turn of the century. Computers have changed the way we live and how we do business. Today computers are used to present instructional material in school, print transcripts, prepare bills and paychecks, send and receive electronic mail, launch rockets into space, reserve airline and concert tickets, and help us write term papers and even books. Computers are a key component of automatic teller machines and embedded or hidden computers help control the ignition, fuel, and transmission systems of modern automobiles. At the supermarket, computers record information scanned from the bar codes on packages, total your purchases, and help manage the store's inventory. Even a microwave oven has a special-purpose computer built into it.

Although we often are led to believe otherwise, computers cannot reason as we do. Basically, computers are devices for performing computations at incredible speeds (more than one million operations per second) and with great accuracy. To accomplish anything useful, however, a computer must be provided with a *program*—that is, a list of instructions. Programs are usually written in special computer programming languages such as C++, the subject of this book and one of the most versatile programming languages available today.

In this chapter, we introduce the computer and its components and then present an overview of programming languages. Finally, we describe how to use the C++ language system for a commonly used personal workstation.

1.1 —— ELECTRONIC COMPUTERS: THEN AND NOW

In everyday life, you probably come in contact with computers frequently. You may have used computers for word processing or even studied programming in high school. But it was not always this way. Not long ago, most people considered computers to be mysterious devices whose secrets were known only by a few computer wizards.

If we take the literal definition for a *computer* as "a device for counting or computing," then we could consider the abacus to have been the first computer. The first electronic digital computer was designed in the late 1930s by Dr. John Atanasoff at Iowa State University. Atanasoff designed his computer to assist graduate students in nuclear physics with their mathematical computations.

The first large-scale, general-purpose electronic digital computer, called the ENIAC, was completed in 1946 at the University of Pennsylvania with funding from the U.S. Army. The ENIAC weighed 30 tons and occupied a 30-by 50-foot space (see Fig. 1.1). It was used to compute ballistics tables, to predict the weather, and to make atomic energy calculations.

Figure 1.1 The ENIAC computer (Photo courtesy of Unisys Corporation)

To program the ENIAC, engineers had to connect hundreds of wires and arrange thousands of switches in a certain way. In 1946, Dr. John von Neumann of Princeton University proposed the concept of a *stored-program computer*—a computer whose program was stored in computer memory rather than being set by wires and switches. Von Neumann knew that the data stored in computer memory could easily be changed by a program. He reasoned that programs, too, could be stored in computer memory and changed as required far more easily than connecting wires and setting switches. Von Neumann designed a computer based on this idea. His design was a success and greatly simplified computer programming. The *von Neumann architecture* is the basis of the digital computer as we know it today.

A Brief History of Computing

Table 1.1 lists some of the milestones along the path from the abacus to modern-day computers and programming languages. The entries before 1890 illustrate some of the earlier attempts to develop mechanical computing devices. In

Table 1.1   Milestones in Computer Development

DATE	EVENT
2000 B.C.	The abacus is first used for computations.
1642 A.D.	Blaise Pascal creates a mechanical adding machine for tax computations. It is unreliable.
1670	Gottfried von Liebniz creates a more reliable adding machine that adds, subtracts, multiplies, divides, and calculates square roots.
1842	Charles Babbage designs an analytical engine to perform general calculations automatically. Ada Augusta (a.k.a. Lady Lovelace) is a programmer for this machine.
1890	Herman Hollerith designs a system to record census data. The information is stored as holes in cards that are interpreted by machines with electrical sensors. Hollerith starts a company that will eventually become IBM.
1939	John Atanasoff, with graduate student Clifford Berry, designs and builds the first electronic digital computer. His project was funded by a grant for $650.
1946	J. Presper Eckert and John Mauchly design and build the ENIAC computer. It used 18,000 vacuum tubes, and cost $500,000 to build.
1946	John von Neumann proposes that a program be stored in a computer in the same way that data are stored. His proposal, called the "von Neumann architecture," is the basis for modern computers.
1951	Eckert and Mauchly build the first general-purpose commercial computer, the UNIVAC™.
1957	An IBM team, led by John Backus, designs the first successful high-level programming language, FORTRAN, for solving engineering and science problems.
1958	The first computer to use the transistor as a switching device, the IBM 7090, is introduced.
1964	The first computer to use integrated circuits, the IBM 360, is announced.
1965	The CTSS (Compatible Time-Sharing System) operating system is introduced. It allows several users to simultaneously use, or share, a single computer.
1970	A first version of the UNIX™ operating system is running on the DEC PDP-7.
1971	Nicklaus Wirth designs the Pascal programming language as a language for teaching structured programming concepts.
1972	Dennis Ritchie of Bell Laboratories in New Jersey develops the language C.
1973	Part of the UNIX operating system is implemented in C.
1975	The first microcomputer, the Altair, is introduced.
1976	The first supercomputer, the Cray-1, is announced.

(continued)

Table 1.1 *(continued)*

DATE	EVENT
1976	Digital Equipment Corporation introduces its popular minicomputer, the DEC VAX 11/780.
1977	Steve Wozniak and Steve Jobs found Apple Computer.
1978	Dan Bricklin and Bob Frankston develop the first electronic spreadsheet, called VisiCalc, for the Apple computer.
1979–82	Bjarne Stroustrup of Bell Laboratories in New Jersey introduces "C with Classes."
1981	IBM introduces the IBM PC.
1983–85	C with Classes is redesigned and reimplemented as C++.
1984	Apple introduces the Macintosh, the first widely available computer with a "user-friendly" graphical interface using icons, windows, and a mouse device.
1988	Work on standardization of C++ begins.
1989	Microsoft Corporation introduces Windows for IBM compatible computers.
1989	The American National Standards Institute (ANSI) publishes the first standard for the C programming language.
1993	Intel Corporation develops the Pentium Processor.
1995	Microsoft Corporation introduces Windows 95.
1996	The C++ standardization committee distributes a proposed C++ standard for review.

1890, the first special-purpose computer that used electronic sensors was designed; this invention eventually led to the formation of the computer industry giant called International Business Machines Corporation (IBM).

A number of important events in the development of programming languages and environments are listed in the table, including FORTRAN (1957), CTSS (1965), C (1972), VisiCalc (1978), C++ (1983), and Windows (1989). As we look at the table from 1939 on, we see also a variety of new computers introduced. Early computers used the vacuum tube as their basic electronic component. Technological advances in the design and manufacture of electronic components led to new generations of computers that were considerably smaller, faster, and less expensive than their predecessors (see Table 1.2).

Using today's VLSI (Very-Large-Scale Integration) technology, a computer can be packaged in a single electronic component called a *computer chip*, which is about the size of a postage stamp. Because of their affordability and small size, computer chips can be installed in watches, pocket calculators, cameras, home appliances, automobiles, and, of course, computers.

Table 1.2 Computer Generations

GENERATION	YEARS	ELECTRONIC COMPONENT
First	1930–1957	vacuum tubes
Second	1958–1963	transistors
Third	1964–1974	integrated circuits
Fourth	1975–1990	Large-Scale Integrated circuits (LSI)
Fifth	1990–present	Very-Large Scale Integrated circuits (VLSI)

Today, a common sight in offices and homes is the personal computer, which can cost less than $2000 and sit on a desk, and yet have as much computational power as the giants of 20 years ago that cost more than $100,000 and filled a 9-by-12-foot room. Even smaller computers can fit inside a briefcase (Fig. 1.2a and b).

The computers of today are categorized according to their size and performance. *Microcomputers*, shown in Fig. 1.2, are used by a single person at a time. The largest of the microcomputers shown is called a *workstation* (Fig. 1.2c). Business and research laboratories also use larger and faster computers, called *minicomputers* and *mainframes*, which can be used by many people simultaneously. *Supercomputers*, the most powerful mainframe computers, can perform in seconds computations that might take hours or even days on other computers.

A computer system consists of two major components: hardware and software. *Hardware* is the equipment used to perform the necessary computations and includes the central processing unit (CPU), monitor, keyboard, and printer. The *software* is the set of *programs* that enable the user to solve problems with a computer by providing it with a list of instructions to perform.

Programming a computer has undergone significant changes over the years. Initially, the task was very difficult, requiring programmers to write their program instructions as long *binary numbers* (a number whose digits are sequences of 0s and 1s). Today, programming languages such as C++ make programming much easier.

EXERCISES FOR SECTION 1.1

Self-Check   1. Is a computer program a piece of hardware or software?
2. Which do you think is the major source of computer errors, faulty computer hardware or incorrect software?

(a)

(b)

(c)

Figure 1.2   (a) Notebook computer; (b) personal digital assistant; (c) workstation

1.2 ——— AN INTRODUCTION TO COMPUTER HARDWARE

Despite significant variations in cost, size, and capabilities, modern computers resemble each other in many basic ways. Essentially, most consist of the following components:

- Main memory
- Secondary memory, which includes storage devices such as hard disks and floppy disks
- Central processing unit
- Input devices, such as a keyboard and mouse
- Output devices, such as monitors and printers

Figure 1.3 shows how these components interact in a computer with the arrows connecting the components showing the direction of information flow. The program must first be transferred from secondary memory to main memory before it can be executed. Normally the person using a program must

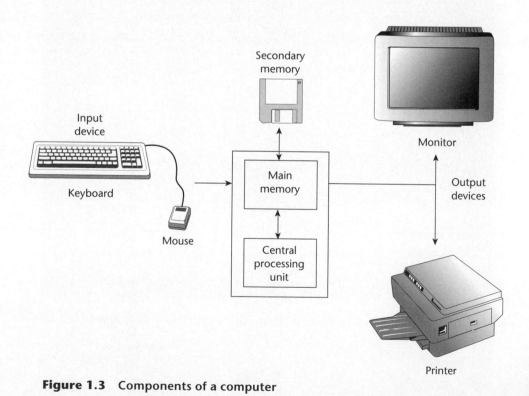

Figure 1.3   **Components of a computer**

supply some data to be processed. These data are entered through an input device and are stored in the computer's main memory where they can be accessed and manipulated by the central processing unit. The results of this manipulation are stored back in main memory. Finally, the information in main memory may be displayed through an output device. In the remainder of this section, we describe these components in more detail.

Memory

Memory is an essential component in any computer. It retains information that has been entered through an input device or previously computed so that it may be made available for processing or for output. Let's first look at what constitutes memory and how it is used in a computer.

Anatomy of Memory

Imagine the memory of a computer as an ordered sequence of storage locations called memory cells (see Fig. 1.4). To store and access information, the computer must have some way of identifying the individual memory cells. Therefore each memory cell has a unique address that indicates its relative position in memory. Figure 1.4 shows a portion of computer memory consisting of 1024 memory cells with addresses 0 through 1023. Most computers have millions of individual memory cells, each with its own address.

The data stored in a memory cell are called the *contents* of the cell. Every memory cell always has some contents; no cell is ever empty. In Fig. 1.4, the

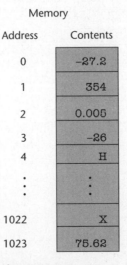

Figure 1.4 A portion of main memory

contents of memory cell 3 is the number −26 and the contents of memory cell 4 is the letter H.

Although not shown in Fig. 1.4, a memory cell can also contain a program instruction. The ability to store programs as well as data is called the *stored-program concept:* a program's instructions must be stored in main memory before they can be executed. We can change the computer's operation by storing a different program in memory.

Bytes and Bits   A memory cell is actually a grouping of smaller units called bytes. A *byte* is the amount of storage required to store a single character, such as the letter H used in Fig. 1.4. The number of bytes a memory cell may contain varies from computer to computer.

A byte is composed of even smaller units of storage called bits (see Fig. 1.5). The term *bit* derives from the words *bi*nary dig*it* and is the smallest element a computer can deal with. A bit is either a 0 or a 1. Generally there are eight bits to a byte.

Storage and Retrieval of Information in Memory   Each value in memory is represented by a particular pattern of 0s and 1s. A computer can either store or retrieve a value. To *store* a value, the computer sets each bit of a selected memory cell to either 0 or 1, destroying the previous contents of the cell in the process. To *retrieve* a value from a memory cell, the computer copies the pattern of 0s and 1s stored in that cell to another storage area for processing; the copy operation does not destroy the contents of the cell whose value is retrieved. The process described above is the same regardless of the kind of information—character, number, or program instruction—to be stored or retrieved.

Main Memory   Main memory stores programs, data, and results. In most computers, there are two types of main memory: *random access memory (RAM),* which provides temporary storage of programs and data, and *read-only memory (ROM),* which stores programs or data permanently.

Programs may be temporarily stored in RAM while they are being executed (carried out) by the computer. Data such as numbers, names, and even pictures may also be stored in RAM while a program is manipulating them.

Figure 1.5   The relationship between a byte and a bit

RAM is usually *volatile memory*, which means that when you switch off the computer, you will lose everything in RAM unless you first store it in secondary memory, which provides for semipermanent storage of data.

ROM, on the other hand, may be used to permanently store information in the computer. The computer can retrieve (or read) information in ROM but cannot store (or write) information in ROM—hence its name, read-only. Because ROM is not volatile, the data stored there do not disappear when the computer is switched off. Usually ROM is used to store the instructions needed to get the computer running when you first switch it on. In most computers, RAM memory capacity is much greater than ROM and RAM often can be increased (up to a specified maximum, such as 64 million bytes), whereas the amount of ROM is usually fixed. When we refer to main memory in this text, we mean RAM because that is the part of main memory that is normally accessible to a program.

Secondary Memory and Secondary Storage Devices

Secondary memory, accessed through secondary storage devices, provides semipermanent data storage capability. A common secondary storage device is a *disk drive*, which is used to store and retrieve data and programs on a storage medium called a *disk*. A disk is considered semipermanent instead of permanent because its contents can be changed, rather like a cassette tape that contains music that can be played over and over but can be erased and recorded over.

There are two kinds of disks: *hard* (also called fixed) and *floppy*. Most computers contain one hard disk which cannot be removed from its disk drive and so provides a storage area to be shared by all users of the computer. Normally the programs that are needed to operate the computer system are stored on its hard disk. Each computer user can have one or more floppy disks that can be inserted into a computer's floppy disk drive. A floppy disk is a plastic sheet with a magnetic coating and a diameter of 3.5 or 5.25 inches housed in a thin square container. These floppy disks can be used to store an individual user's programs and personal data.

A hard disk can store much more data than a single floppy disk. For example, hard disk drives capable of storing over 500 million bytes of memory are commonplace today, whereas most floppy disks can store on the order of 1.4 million bytes of data. Furthermore, the CPU can access the data on a hard disk much more quickly. Each user can have an unlimited number of floppy disks. Floppy disks, unlike most hard disks, are *portable*, which means they can be used with many different computers as long as they are all compatible.

Information stored on a disk is organized into separate collections called *files*. One file may contain a C++ program. Another file (a *data file*) may contain the data to be processed by that program. A third file (an *output file*) may contain the results generated by a program.

An increasingly common secondary storage device is a CD-ROM drive. This drive accesses information stored on plastic disks that resemble the CDs used in a CD player. The ROM in CD-ROM indicates that currently most drives can only read the data stored on a CD and cannot write new information to the CD.

Comparison of Main and Secondary Memory

The computer processor cannot manipulate data that are stored on secondary storage devices. Therefore data stored in secondary memory, including program instructions, must be transferred into main memory before they can be processed. A fixed disk has much more storage capacity than does main memory. On most computers, you can increase the size of main memory by installing additional memory chips. You can also increase the size of secondary memory by purchasing additional floppy disks or installing another hard disk. However, main memory is considerably more expensive than secondary memory. Data in main memory are volatile and disappear when you switch off the computer, whereas data in secondary memory are semipermanent and do not disappear when the computer is switched off. Therefore, you will want to store all your programs as files in secondary memory and transfer a program file into main memory when you want it executed.

Central Processing Unit

The *central processing unit (CPU)* has two roles: coordinating all computer operations and performing arithmetic and logical operations on data. The CPU follows the instructions contained in a computer program to determine which operations should be carried out and in what order. It then transmits coordinating control signals to the other computer components. For example, if the instruction requires reading a data item, the CPU sends the necessary control signals to the input device.

To process a program stored in main memory, the CPU retrieves each instruction in sequence (called *fetching an instruction*), interprets the instruction to determine what should be done, and then retrieves any data needed to carry out that instruction. Next, the CPU performs the actual processing of the data it retrieved. The CPU stores the results in main memory.

The CPU can perform such arithmetic operations as addition, subtraction, multiplication, and division. The CPU can also compare the contents of two memory cells (for example, it can determine which contains the larger value or whether the values are equal) and make decisions based on the results of that comparison.

Input/Output Devices

We use *input/output (I/O) devices* to communicate with the computer. Specifically, they allow us to enter data for a computation and to observe the results of that computation.

The *keyboard* (see Fig. 1.6) is used as an input device and the *monitor* (display screen) as an output device. When you press a letter or digit key on a keyboard, that character is sent to main memory and is also displayed on the monitor at the position of the *cursor,* a moving place marker (normally a blinking underscore symbol). A computer keyboard resembles a typewriter keyboard except for some extra keys for performing special functions. For example, on the computer keyboard shown in Fig. 1.6, the 12 keys in the top row labeled F1 through F12 are *function keys.* The activity performed when you press a function key depends on the program currently being executed; that is, pressing F1 in one program will usually not produce the same results as pressing F1 in another program. Other special keys enable you to delete characters, move the cursor, and "enter" a line of data you typed at the keyboard (see the highlighted keys in Fig. 1.6).

Another common input device is a mouse. A *mouse* is a hand-held, pointing device used to select an operation. When you move the mouse around on your desktop, a rubber ball on the bottom of the mouse rotates. As the ball moves, so does the *mouse cursor* (normally a small rectangle or an arrow) displayed on the monitor's screen. You can use the mouse to select an operation by moving the mouse cursor to a word or picture that represents the computer operation you wish to perform. You then press or click the appropriate mouse button to activate the operation selected.

A monitor provides a temporary display of the information that appears on its screen. Once the image disappears from the monitor screen, it is lost. If you

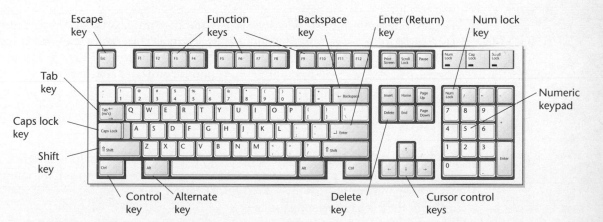

Figure 1.6   **Keyboard for IBM-compatible computers**

want *hard copy* (a printed version) of some information, you must send that information to an output device called a *printer*.

Computer Networks

Until now we have talked about the components of individual computers. Often several computers are interconnected to form a *computer network,* a system that allows each computer to access a large, shared hard disk and high-quality printers. The computer that controls access to the shared disk is called the *file server*. Each computer in the network also has its own keyboard, monitor, and disk drives. Many computer laboratories now arrange their computer hardware in a network.

EXERCISES FOR SECTION 1.2

Self-Check
1. What is the contents of memory cells 0 and 1023 in Fig. 1.4? What memory cells contain the letter X and the fraction 0.005?
2. Explain the purpose of main memory, secondary memory, CPU, and the disk drive and disk. What input and output devices will be used with your computer? What is a computer network and what is a file server?
3. List the following in order of smallest to largest: byte, bit, main memory, memory cell, secondary memory.

1.3 ——— AN OVERVIEW OF PROGRAMMING LANGUAGES

We use programming languages to write computer programs. Although there are many different programming languages, the most commonly used today are called high-level languages. To understand the advantage of-high-level languages, it is necessary to first understand how a computer communicates.

Machine Language

The native tongue of a computer is *machine language*. Each machine language instruction is a binary string of 0s and 1s that specifies an operation and identifies the memory cells involved in that operation. For example, if we wanted to represent the algebraic formula

cost = price + tax

in a machine language program, we might need a sequence of instructions such as the following:

```
0010 0000 0000 0100
0100 0000 0000 0101
0011 0000 0000 0110
```

In each machine language instruction, the operation to be performed and the address of the data to be manipulated are written as binary numbers. Although the computer would have no difficulty understanding the three machine language instructions above, they are unintelligible to most people.

High-Level Languages

When you write programs in a *high-level language,* you use instructions that resemble human language. In C++, you would use the instruction

```
cost = price + tax;
```

which closely resembles the original formula. This statement means "Add the value of `price` to the value of `tax` and store the result as `cost`." When writing a program in a high-level language, you can reference data stored in memory using descriptive names—for example, `price`, `cost`, `tax`—rather than numeric memory cell addresses. We can also use familiar symbols (such as +) to describe operations we want performed.

Common high-level languages include Ada, Pascal, BASIC, COBOL, FORTRAN, Lisp, C, and C++. Each language was designed with a specific purpose in mind. The development of Ada was driven largely by the U.S. Department of Defense, which sought a single high-level language to be used in the specialized program applications area known as *real-time, distributed systems.* BASIC (Beginners All-purpose Symbolic Instruction Code) was designed to be easily learned and used by students. COBOL (COmmon Business-Oriented Language) is used primarily for business data-processing operations. FORTRAN (FORmula TRANslator) is primarily used by engineers and scientists. Lisp (LISt Processing) is a language used primarily in artificial intelligence applications. Pascal was developed primarily for teaching introductory programming by following a particular approach often referred to as *structured programming.*

The C language, developed in 1972 by Dennis Ritchie of Bell Laboratories, is a highly versatile language that has been used in a wide variety of applications, from operating systems implementation (such as UNIX) to database and large-scale, numeric-processing applications. C++ is based on C; it is also a versatile programming language that is rapidly gaining wide acceptance in the computing field. It is becoming increasingly popular for teaching programming concepts, partly because it provides powerful features useful for practicing modern approaches to software development.

Many high-level languages have a *language standard* that describes the grammatical form (syntax) of the language. Every high-level language instruction must conform to the syntax rules specified in the language standard. These rules are very precise—no allowances are made for instructions that are *almost* correct. Programs that conform to these rules are *portable*, which means that they can be used without modification on many different types of computers. A machine-language program, on the other hand, may be used on only one type of computer.

The C programming language has a standard approved in 1990 by the American National Standards Institute (ANSI). C++ has a proposed standard, which was undergoing the ANSI review and approval process at the time this book was being written. This lack of a standardization leaves open the possibility of some variation in the syntax rules for versions of C++ produced by different companies. However, the language is close enough to standardization at this point that you will rarely notice these differences even if you move C++ programs from one computer to another.

Because a computer can only understand programs written in machine language, each instruction in a high-level language program must first be translated into machine language before it can be executed. The original high-level language program is called the *source program*; the machine-language translation is called the *object program*. The next section discusses the steps required to process a high-level language program.

EXERCISES FOR SECTION 1.3

Self-Check

1. What do you think the four high-level language statements below mean? Assume the symbol ; marks the end of each statement.

```
x = a + b + c;
x = y / z;
d = c - b + a;
z = z + 1;
kelvin = celsius + 273.15;
```

2. Which high-level language was designed for teaching how to program? Which was designed for business applications? Which was designed for translating scientific formulas?

1.4 ____ PROCESSING A HIGH-LEVEL LANGUAGE PROGRAM

Before a computer can execute a high-level language program, it must be entered into the computer and saved on a disk as a *program file* or *source file*. The program must then be stored in executable form in main memory. Several

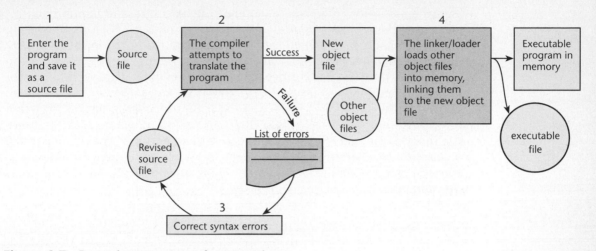

Figure 1.7   **Preparing a program for execution**

system programs assist with this task. We describe the role of these programs next. The entire process is summarized in Fig. 1.7.

The following steps can be followed to prepare a program for execution:

1. Use the *editor* program to enter each line of the source program into memory and to save it on disk as a source file.
2. Use a *compiler* program to translate the source program into machine language. If there are any *syntax errors* (errors in grammar), the compiler displays these errors on the monitor.
3. Use the editor program to correct the errors by editing and resaving the source program. When the source program is error free, the compiler saves its machine language translation as an object file.
4. Use the *linker/loader* program to combine the object file with additional object files that may be needed for the program to execute (for example, programs for input and output). The final machine language program is stored in memory, ready for execution. The linker/loader can also save the final machine language program as an *executable file* on disk. Often the linker/loader is written as two separate system programs.

Executing a Program

To execute a machine-language program, the CPU must examine each program instruction in memory and send out the command signals required to carry out the instruction. Although the instructions are normally executed in sequence, as we will discuss later, it is possible to have the CPU skip over some instructions or execute some instructions more than once.

During execution, data can be entered into memory and manipulated as specified in the program. Special instructions are used for entering or reading a program's data (called *input data*) into memory. After the input data have been processed, instructions for displaying or printing values in memory can be executed to display the program results. The lines displayed by a program are called the *program output.*

Let's use the situation described in Fig. 1.8—executing a payroll program stored in memory—as an example. Step 1 of the program enters into memory data that describe the employee's hours worked and pay rate. In step 2, the program manipulates the employee data and stores the results of the computations in memory. In the final step, the computation results are displayed as payroll reports or employee payroll checks.

EXERCISES FOR SECTION 1.4

Self-Check   1. Would a syntax error be found in a source program or an object program? What system program would find a syntax error if one existed? What system program would you use to correct it?
2. What is the role of a linker/loader?
3. Explain the difference between the source program, object program, and an executable program. Which do you create, and which does the compiler create? Which does the linker/loader create?

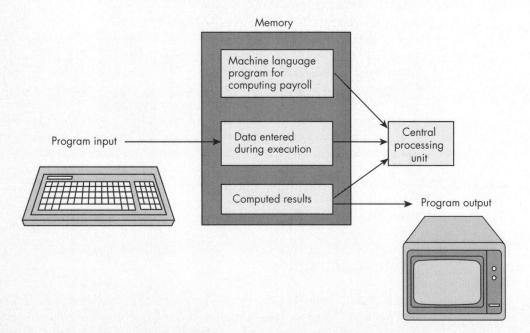

Figure 1.8   Flow of information during execution of a payroll program

1.5 ——— THE SOFTWARE DEVELOPMENT METHOD

A Problem-Solving and Programming Strategy

You may be tempted to rush to the computer laboratory and start entering your program as soon as you have some idea of how to write it, but you should in fact try to resist such a move. Instead, think carefully about the problem and its solution before you write any program instructions. When you have a potential solution in mind, plan it out beforehand, check it over to see that it addresses the problem at hand, and modify the solution if necessary.

The process of planning and organizing a solution to a problem is similar to that of writing a term paper. In the case of the latter, larger projects require much more planning, beginning with an outline drafted before any substantial writing is done. The same is true in programming. As problems increase in size and complexity, considerable planning and organizing of the solution is required. *Program engineering* involves the consistent application of an organized and well thought out approach. The approach begins with a thorough analysis of the problem to be solved. An outline or high-level design of the solution to the problem is worked out next. Then, additional details are added to this outline, providing a clearer, lower-level view of the problem solution. Once sufficient detail has been provided, the outline may be used to write the desired program. Finally, the program is tested to verify that it behaves as intended.

These steps are illustrated in Fig. 1.9 and described in more detail in the next section.

Software Development Method

1. **Problem Analysis:** The first step in solving a problem is to gain a clear understanding of the *problem specification:* what is given and what is required for the problem solution. Although this step sounds easy, it can be the most critical part of problem solving. You must study the problem carefully then eliminate aspects that are unimportant and focus on the essential aspects of the problem. If the problem is not clearly and completely defined, you should request clarifications or additional information from the individuals posing the problem.

   As was indicated in Fig. 1.9, we use a software development approach that stresses the importance of data in designing the solution to a problem. We focus first on the identification of the *data objects* to be manipulated by the program. Our goal is to build a description (*model*) of the essential properties of each object and the operations to be performed on them. We begin by identifying the *problem input data* (the data objects we are given to work with), the *problem output data* (the desired results), and any additional

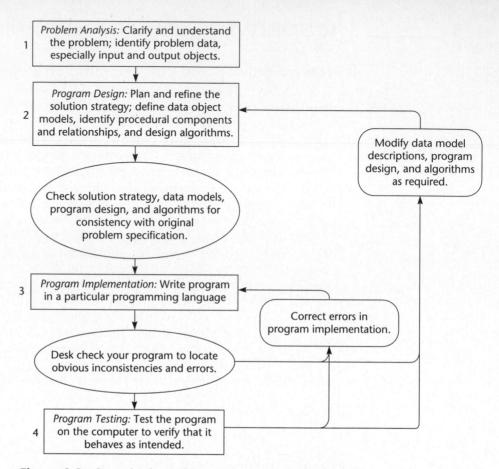

Figure 1.9   Steps in the Software Development Method

data objects, formulas, requirements, or constraints on the problem solution. Then we determine the required form and units in which the results should be displayed (for example, as a table with specific column headings).

These first steps are most critical; if they are not done properly, you will be trying to solve the wrong problem. Read each problem statement carefully, first, to obtain a clear idea of the problem and, second, to determine the input and output data objects. You may find it helpful to underline phrases in the problem statement that identify these input and output objects as shown next.

Problem: Determine the <u>total cost of apples</u> given the number of <u>pounds of apples</u> purchased and the <u>cost per pound</u> of apples.

Next, summarize the information contained in the underlined phrases:

Problem Input:

Quantity of apples purchased (in pounds)
Cost per pound of apples (in dollars per pound)

Problem Output:

Total cost of apples (in dollars)

Once you know the problem input and output, you should then develop a list of formulas that specify relationships between them. The general formula

Total cost = Unit cost × Number of units

computes the total cost of any item purchased. Substituting the data objects for our particular problem, yields the following formula:

Total cost of apples = Cost per pound × Pounds of apples

In some situations, you may have to make certain assumptions or simplifications in order to derive these relationships. This process of extracting the essential variables and their relationships from the problem statement is called *abstraction.*

2. **Program Design:** The first steps of the program design process involve the decomposition of the original problem into smaller subproblems. The main motivation behind this breakdown is the production and organization of smaller, relatively independent subproblems, each of which is considerably easier to solve than the original. In this way, we are better able to *manage the complexity* of a problem, separately solving each subproblem and progressively adding more details to these smaller pieces.

Designing an algorithm to solve a problem requires you to write a list of steps—the *algorithm*—and then verify that these procedures solve the problem as intended. Writing an algorithm is not easy, especially if you attempt to handle all of the algorithm details at the same time. Don't attempt to solve every last detail of the problem at the beginning; instead, discipline yourself to use *top-down design* (also called *divide and conquer*). In top-down design, you first list the major steps, or subproblems, that need to be solved, then solve the original problem by solving each of its subproblems. The algorithm for a typical programming problem would consist of at least the following subproblems:

1. Read the data.
2. Perform the computations.
3. Display the results.

Once you know the subproblems, you can attack each one individually. In the above example, Step 2 is the most difficult and may need to be broken down into a more detailed list of steps called *algorithm refinements.*

Desk checking is an important but often overlooked part of algorithm design. To desk check an algorithm, perform each algorithm step (or its refinements) just as a computer would and verify that the algorithm works as intended. You'll save time and effort if you locate algorithm errors at this early stage in the problem solving rather than later.

3. **Program Implementation:** Step 3 in Fig. 1.9 involves writing the algorithm as a program. To do this, you must be familiar with a particular programming language and able to convert each algorithm step into one or more statements in that language.

4. **Program Testing:** Testing and verifying the program requires that you verify whether the completed program works as desired. Don't rely on just one test case; run the program several times using different sets of data, making sure that it works for every situation provided for in the algorithm. Performing such an exhaustive test of each path through a program is as much a science as an art. In industry, the testing phase is often carried out by individuals who do not know programming but who specialize in developing good tests of programs. Program testing suggestions are included in most of the case studies we examine in this text. Testing strategies are described in more detail in Chapter 10.

Program Maintenance and Documentation

Maintaining and updating a program involves modifying the program to remove previously undetected errors and keep it up to date as required by the user. Many organizations maintain a program for five years or more, often after the programmers who originally coded it have moved on to other positions. Readable, highly modularized, and easy to understand programs therefore are critically important for the success of a project over a long period of time.

Documentation is an important part of a software development project. It includes a written description of the problem to be solved and a discussion of the solution design approach. An explanation of the organization and structure of the problem solution also should be included. Since most larger programs are the product of the work of many different people working over a long period of time, documentation must be maintained as carefully as the program itself. It must be readable and understandable to everyone associated with the software project.

An equally important component of documentation is a user manual describing how a software product is to be used. User manuals are often read by people who are familiar with the problem but not with the technical aspects of computing. The manuals therefore usually contain step-by-step instructions as to how to use the software.

On-line documentation is also an important part of the information about a program. This documentation ranges from comments embedded in a program and intended for those working on the program to "help documentation" available to the program users. This information is stored on the computer and is directly accessible at the workstations of programmers and users.

Object-Oriented and Structured Programming

We will use the software development method just described throughout the text. We will focus as much on abstracting and describing the essential features of the problem data objects as on the construction of correct algorithms for solving a problem, because we believe that the mastery of both processes is important for the beginning programmer. In the earlier chapters, we will use data abstractions that are provided as part of the C++ language. Later, we will show how to define our own abstractions, called *classes*, for modeling problem data.

In working with both data abstractions and algorithms, we follow the same basic software design approach. Among other things, this approach yields consistent documentation of the data abstractions and algorithms we select. It also makes it easier for us to identify and reuse some ideas that are fundamental to solving problems using the computer.

The focus on the data objects in the problem domain and the development of abstract models of these objects has lead to the use of the term object-oriented programming. *Object-oriented programming* is a disciplined approach to programming that results in programs that are easy to read and understand and less likely to contain errors. Programs are constructed from well designed, largely independent *data and procedural components* that provide natural models of the properties and behaviors of the problem data objects. These components are largely independent of one another and may be more easily designed, implemented, and tested separately. If designed and implemented properly, these components are also highly reusable.

The algorithms forming the basis for our procedural components are also developed in a highly structured manner, using a top-down, step-wise refinement approach often referred to as *structured programming*. In the following chapters, we knit together some of the fundamental ideas of object-oriented and structured programming in a coherent, consistent software development method. In the process, we will introduce some simple tools for documenting the data modeling and algorithm design decisions that are made during the problem-solving process.

EXERCISES FOR SECTION 1.5

Self-Check
1. List the steps of the software development method.
2. What would the data requirements and formulas look like for a computer program that converts a weight in pounds to a weight in kilograms?

3. What is the difference between the design and implementation stages of the software development method?
4. At which stage of the software development method is the algorithm for a solution developed?
5. What is an algorithm? How does it differ from a program?
6. What is object-oriented programming?

1.6 _____ USING A COMPUTER SYSTEM

The mechanics of entering a program as a source file, translating it to machine language, and executing a machine language program differ on each computer system. We will not give specific details for a particular computer system in this section. Instead, we will describe the general process involved for several different kinds of common *integrated computer system environments*, including a single-user (or stand-alone) personal computer or workstation, a timeshared system, and a network of personal computers or workstations. At home, you may use a stand-alone computer, not connected in any way to other computing facilities. However, laboratories of such single-user, unconnected computers in colleges and universities and in the workplace are rapidly being replaced by networked systems. Even home computer users are often linked by phone to other computing facilities. The information on the use of computer networks, therefore, may be most relevant for you.

Operating Systems

Regardless of the computing system that you use, you will need to interact with a supervisory program called the *operating system*. MS-DOS™, Microsoft Windows 95™, Solaris™, and UNIX are all examples of computer operating systems. The tasks performed by an operating system include the following:

- validating user identification and account number;
- allocating memory and processor time;
- ensuring the security of each user's files and program execution;
- managing the input and output devices connected to a computer;
- managing (saving and retrieving) files of information;
- making the editor, compiler, linker, and loader programs as well as entire libraries of other programs available to users.

In general, performance of the first two of these tasks is not required of the operating system for a stand-alone computer.

Many of you will be using a personal computer. This is the simplest computing environment. In general, except for the sharing of a hard disk (used for secondary storage), the operating system for such a computer need not be concerned about the sharing, allocation, or protection of other resources such as main memory, CPU, or input/output devices among multiple users.

Some of you will be using a *timeshared computer*. In a timeshared environment, many users are connected by terminals or workstations to one central computer, and all users share the central facilities, including secondary and main memory, the CPU, and the input/output devices. In a timeshared environment, users need an account number and password to be able to access the system. The operating system controls the allocation of resources to all of the users, determining such things as how much memory each user gets and who controls the CPU at any given time. With a timeshared system, all files are stored on central secondary storage devices and all programs execute on the same shared CPU. Timeshared system users also have the capability to communicate with one another using electronic mail.

From the point of view of the user, a networked system of personal computers or workstations looks much like a timeshared system. Users usually need special account numbers and passwords to be able to use the system. They also may communicate with each other, and share a central secondary memory device (such as a large, hard disk drive) often referred to as a *network server*. Here, the similarity ends, however, as the computers attached to the network usually have the full capability of a personal computer or workstation—their own *local memory* (secondary and main memory), their own CPU, and perhaps even their own input/output devices (in addition to a keyboard and a screen). Users sometimes may be able to store some of their own files locally and download other files from the server for local use or execution. In some cases, network users also may be able to upload local files for saving on the central server.

Each of the computing environments just discussed has its own special control language for communicating with its operating system. We will not discuss the specifics of these languages here; your instructor will provide the specific control language commands for your system. Instead, we will provide an introductory discussion intended to provide a general idea of how to access each of the three computing environments just described.

Booting a Single-User Personal Computer or Workstation

Before you can use a single-user personal computer or workstation, you first need to *boot up* the computer. Booting involves switching on the computer, which causes the operating system to be loaded into main memory (usually from a hard disk drive). Once booted, the operating system displays a prompt (for example, C:\>) to indicate that it is ready to accept commands. One command is usually sufficient to put you in a windowing environment, such as X

Windows (used with UNIX) or Microsoft Windows. Once in such an environment, virtually all activity, such as typing in your program, compiling and correcting it, and finally executing it, is controlled by moving a mouse pointer (on your screen) to point to small symbols (*icons*) or *bars* in a *pull-down menu.* Aside from typing in your program and test data, very little typing is needed to tell the computer what to do next. Your instructor should be able to provide you with specific steps for using the windows system available on your computer.

Using a Timeshared System

Before you can use a timeshared computer, you must *log on,* or connect, to the computer. To log on, enter your account name and password (given to you by your instructor). For security reasons, your password is not displayed. Figure 1.10 illustrates this process for a Sun Microsystems workstation. The computer user enters the characters that are in color; the other characters are those that the operating system displays. The timeshared operating system shown, SunOS UNIX, displays the symbol > as a prompt.

Using a Network of Computers

To access a networked system of computers, you must first gain access to the network and to the server disk. This is usually accomplished by booting your personal computer or workstation and then entering a few special network commands. You then need to log on to the network using the unique user identification and password given to you by your instructor. Once you have logged on, all of the software that you are allowed to use should be accessible from the server in much the same way as it would be if you were operating from a stand-alone computer.

Figure 1.10   Logging on to a timeshared computer

```
SunOS UNIX (yoda)

login: stafford
Password: idunno

Last login: Sat Apr 25 09:57:55 from
jedi.temple.edu
SunOS Release 4.1.3 (YODA) #1:
Tue Nov 7 20:39:13 EST 1995

>
```

Creating a Program File

Once you have booted your personal computer or workstation or logged on to a timeshared or networked system, you can begin to create your C++ program. In most cases, you will use a special program called an *editor* for this purpose. After accessing the editor, you can start typing in your C++ instructions. If you want a record of the program once it is entered, you must save it as a permanent file on disk; otherwise, your program disappears when your session with the editor is over. Four general steps can be followed to create and save a program file:

1. Access the editor program on your system, and indicate that you are creating a new file. (You may be able to specify the file name at this point.)
2. Enter each line of the program file.
3. Name your program file (if not named in Step 1), and save it as a permanent file in secondary memory.
4. Exit from the editor.

After you have created your program and are satisfied that each line is typed correctly, you can attempt to compile, link, and execute the program. On some systems, you must give at least two separate commands (such as COMPILE and RUN) to accomplish these tasks; on other systems, one command, such as RUN or the name of the load file, initiates this sequence of operations.

If your program will not compile because it contains syntax errors, you must correct and recompile it following these general steps:

1. Access the editor program again, and have it display your program file for editing.
2. Correct the statements containing syntax errors.
3. Save your edited program file.
4. Compile, link, and execute the new program file.

Many modern computer systems provide special C++ integrated environments that make it easier to perform all of these tasks. Once you enter such an environment, switching from one task to another (for example, from edit to compile or compile to run) is accomplished simply by moving a mouse pointer to a particular icon or menu bar and clicking a button on the mouse. You can switch from one window to another to view all that needs to be seen concerning the current activity in the computer. The screen shown in Fig. 1.11 provides a sample illustration of such an environment (the Borland C++, Version 5.0 environment). The upper window shows a very small program (with a syntax error) that has just been compiled. The errors (just detected by the compiler) are shown in the Message window at the bottom of the screen.

```
Borland C++ - hellotst                                                  _ □ ×
File  Edit  Search  View  Project  Script  Tool  Debug  Options  Window  Help

D:\BC5\BIN\HELLOTST.CPP
   // File: Hello.cpp
   // DISPLAYS A USER'S NICKNAME

   #include <iostream.h>

   void main ()
   {
      // Local data ...
      char letter1, letter2, letter3;      // input: 3 letters to display

      //Enter letters and display message.
      cout << "Enter a three letter nickname and press return: ;
      cin >> letter1 >> letter2 >> letter3;
      cout << "Hello " << letter1 << letter2 << letter3 << ". " << endl;
   }

Message                                                                  _ □ ×
  ⊟ ▪  Compiling D:\BC5\BIN\hellotst.cpp
     !  hellotst.cpp(12,13):Unterminated string or character constant
     !  hellotst.cpp(13,7):Statement missing ;
     ⚲  hellotst.cpp(14,70):Possible use of 'letter1' before definition
     ⚲  hellotst.cpp(14,70):Possible use of 'letter2' before definition
     ⚲  hellotst.cpp(14,70):Possible use of 'letter3' before definition
 Buildtime / Runtime / Script /

                    12:13          Modified       Insert       5:18:14 PM
```

Figure 1.11   **Program and error message windows (Borland C++—Version 5.0)**

In the programming environment illustrated, the lines in the program are not numbered. We identify the C++ statement causing a particular error message by moving the mouse pointer to the message shown in the error message window. Clicking the mouse button highlights the error message. At the same time, in the program window, the statement containing the error is highlighted, thereby assisting in locating the cause of the error (in this case, a missing closing double quote, ", just before the semicolon in the first line beginning with cout). We can now move the mouse pointer back to the program window, click the button, correct the program, and try again (see Self-Check Exercise 2 at the end of this section). All work—editing, compiling, error correction, etc.—is done by pulling down menus and moving the mouse pointer to one of the windows displayed. Once the program compiles correctly, we can execute it by pulling down the Debug menu and clicking on the Run bar. The output from the program may be viewed in the output window, as shown at the bottom of Fig. 1.12.

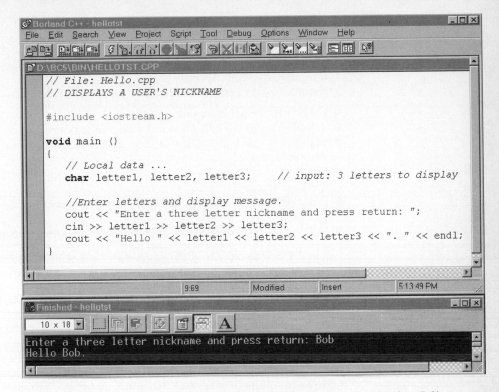

Figure 1.12   Program and output windows (Borland C++—Version 5.0)

EXERCISES FOR SECTION 1.6

Self-Check
1. Explain one or two distinguishing factors among stand-alone, timesharing, and networked computer systems. Which are you using for this course?
2. Try following the steps outlined in this section for entering, compiling, and correcting (and recompiling) the program shown on the screen in Fig. 1.11. (Be sure you have a detailed list of the specific steps required for your computer system before attempting this.) If you can get your program to compile with no errors, try to execute it. The program should pause after the "three letter" prompt. At this point, type in three letters and press the key. Write down a description of what happened next.
3. Modify the Hello program shown in Fig. 1.11 to display the message

   ```
   Hello, <<your name>>
   ```

   rather than just

   ```
   Hello
   ```

   (The notation <<your name>> is used to indicate that you should enter your own name in the message.)

CHAPTER REVIEW

1. The basic components of a computer are main and secondary memory, the CPU, and input and output devices.
2. Main memory is organized into individual storage locations—memory cells.

   - Each memory cell has a unique address.
   - A memory cell is a collection of bytes; a byte is a collection of eight bits.
   - A memory cell is never empty, but its initial contents may be meaningless to your program.
   - The current content of a memory cell is destroyed whenever new information is stored in that cell.
   - Programs *must* be copied into the memory of the computer before they can be executed.
   - Data cannot be manipulated by the computer until they are first stored in memory.

3. Information in secondary memory is organized into files: program files and data files. Secondary memory stores information in semipermanent form and is less expensive than main memory.
4. A computer cannot think for itself; a programming language is used to instruct it in a precise and unambiguous manner to perform a task.
5. Two categories of programming languages are machine language (meaningful to the computer) and high-level language (meaningful to the programmer). Several system programs are used to prepare a high-level language program for execution. An editor enters a high-level language program into memory. A compiler translates a high-level language program (the source program) into machine language (the object program). The linker/loader links this object program to other object files, creating an executable program, and loads the executable program into memory.
6. Programming a computer can be fun, if you are patient, organized, and careful. An outline of a software development method for solving problems using a computer can be of considerable help in your programming work. Four major steps in the problem-solving process must be emphasized:

   - problem analysis
   - program design
   - program implementation
   - program testing

   Documentation was also discussed as an important product of the software development process.
7. Through the operating system, you can issue commands to the computer and manage files.

✔ QUICK-CHECK EXERCISES

1. The _____ translates a(n) _____ language program into _____.
2. After a program has been executed, all program results are automatically displayed. True or false?

3. Specify the correct order for these operations: execution, translation, linking/loading.
4. A high-level language program is saved on disk as a(n) _____ file.
5. The _____ finds syntax errors in the _____ file.
6. Before linking, a machine-language program is saved on disk as a(n) _____ file.
7. After linking, a machine-language program is saved on disk as a(n) _____ file.
8. The _____ program is used to create and save the source file.
9. Computers are becoming (more/less) expensive and (bigger/smaller) in size.
10. List the four primary components of the software development method outlined in this chapter.
11. Determine whether each characteristic below applies to main memory or secondary memory.

    a. faster to access
    b. volatile
    c. may be extended almost without limit
    d. less expensive
    e. used to store files
    f. central processor accesses it to obtain the next machine-language instruction for execution
    g. provides semipermanent data storage

Answers to Quick-Check Exercises

1. compiler, high-level, machine language
2. false
3. translation, linking/loading, execution
4. source
5. compiler, source
6. object
7. executable
8. editor
9. less, smaller
10. analysis, design, implementation, testing
11. main (a, b, f), secondary (c, d, e, g)

REVIEW QUESTIONS

1. List at least three kinds of information stored in a computer.
2. List two functions of the CPU.
3. List two input devices, two output devices, and two secondary storage devices.
4. A computer can think. True or false?
5. List two categories of programming languages.
6. Describe two advantages of programming in a high-level language such as C++.

7. What processes are needed to transform a C++ program to a machine language program that is ready for execution?
8. Explain the relationship between memory cells, bytes, and bits.
9. Name two operating systems for IBM compatible computers. Which are you using?
10. Name three high-level languages and describe their main usage.
11. What are the differences between RAM and ROM?

2

Overview of C++

Programming is a problem-solving activity. So, if you are a good problem solver, you are likely to become a good programmer. One important goal of this book is to help you improve your problem-solving ability. We believe it is beneficial to approach each programming problem in a systematic and consistent way. Therefore, in this book we focus on the description and illustration of a number of techniques that should prove useful in developing solutions to programming problems. We begin our discussion of these topics in this chapter.

This chapter also introduces the high-level language C++. Our focus will be on the C++ features for entering data, performing simple computations, and displaying results. In addition, we describe how to run C++ programs interactively and in batch mode. In interactive programming, the program user enters data during program execution; in batch mode, the program user must prepare a data file before program execution begins. We begin our introduction to C++ by presenting a case study that concludes with a complete C++ program.

2.1 —— APPLYING THE SOFTWARE DEVELOPMENT METHOD

Throughout this text, we use the software development method described in Section 1.5 to solve programming problems. These problems, presented as case studies, begin with a problem statement or *specification*. As part of the problem analysis, we identify the data objects to be manipulated in solving the problem. We develop a *data requirements table* in which we list and describe the relevant *problem domain data elements*—the input and output data, as well as other information pertinent to the problem solution. Next, we define an *initial algorithm* and then refine this algorithm until sufficient detail has been provided for the implementation of the complete algorithm as a C++ program. We also provide a sample execution of the program and discuss how to *test* the program.

We walk you through a sample case study next. In this example, we provide a running commentary on the problem-solving and programming process being followed so that you will be able to apply it to other situations.

CASE STUDY: CONVERTING UNITS OF MEASUREMENT

Problem Statement

You work in a store that sells imported fabric. Most of the fabric you buy is measured in square meters, but your customers want to know the equivalent amount in square yards. Write a program that performs this conversion.

Problem Analysis

The first step in understanding this problem is to determine what you are being asked to do. You must convert from one system of measurement to another, but are you supposed to convert from square meters to square yards, or vice versa? The problem states that you buy <u>fabric measured in square meters</u>, so the problem input is *fabric size in square meters.* Your customers want the <u>equivalent amount in square yards</u>, so the problem output is *fabric size in square yards.* To write the program, you need to know the relationship between square meters and square yards. Consulting a metric table shows that one square meter equals 1.196 square yards.

We summarize the data requirements and relevant formulas in the data requirements table shown below. To each problem domain data element identified at the beginning of our analysis, we associate an *identifier* (a name). We use the identifier `size_in_sqmeters` to represent the locations in computer memory that will contain the problem input, and the identifier `size_in_sqyards` to represent the locations that will contain the program result or the problem output. We use names such as these from now on to represent memory locations containing information. Our goal is to become accustomed to thinking in terms of these problem-oriented *descriptive names*, rather than the *machine-oriented* memory locations they represent.

DATA REQUIREMENTS

> *Problem Constant*
>
> `meters_to_yards = 1.196`   — conversion constant
>
> *Problem Input*
>
> `size_in_sqmeters (float)`   — the fabric size in square meters
>
> *Problem Output*
>
> `size_in_sqyards (float)`   — the fabric size in square yards

FORMULAS

> 1 square meter = 1.196 square yards

Program Design

Next, we formulate the algorithm that solves the problem. We begin by listing the three major steps, or subproblems, of the original problem.

INITIAL ALGORITHM

1. Read the fabric size in square meters.
2. Convert the fabric size to square yards.
3. Display the fabric size in square yards.

We now must decide whether any steps of the algorithm need further *refinement* (additional details) or whether they are perfectly clear as stated. Step 1 (reading data) and step 3 (displaying a value) are basic steps and require no refinement. Step 2 is fairly straightforward, but some detail might help.

Step 2 Refinement

2.1. The fabric size in square yards is 1.196 times the fabric size in square meters.

The complete algorithm with refinements is listed next to show how it all fits together. The algorithm resembles an outline for a paper. The refinement of step 2 is numbered as step 2.1 and is indented under step 2.

REFINED ALGORITHM

1. Read the fabric size in square meters.
2. Convert the fabric size to square yards.
    2.1 The fabric size in square yards is 1.196 times the fabric size in square meters.
3. Display the fabric size in square yards.

Let's desk check the algorithm before going further. If step 1 reads in a fabric size of 2.0 square meters, step 2.1 should convert it to 1.196×2.0, or 2.392 square yards. This correct result would be displayed by step 3.

Program Implementation

To implement the solution, we must convert the algorithm to a C++ program. We first tell the C++ compiler about the problem data requirements by listing the identifiers associated with each element together with information about the kind of data to be stored in the memory associated with the identifier. We then convert each algorithm step into one or more C++ statements. If an algorithm step needs refinement (for example, step 2.1), we convert the refinements, not the original step, into C++ statements.

Figure 2.1 shows the C++ program along with the output from a sample execution (the last two lines of the figure). For ease of identification, the input data typed in by the program user is shown in boldface type. Don't worry about understanding the details of this program yet. We will explain the program in more detail in the following sections.

Program Testing

It is always important to examine program results carefully to be sure they are correct. In the program output shown in Fig. 2.1, a fabric size of 2.0 square meters is converted to 2.392 square yards as it should be. To verify that the program works properly, we should enter a few more test values of square meters. We really don't need to try more than a few test cases to verify that a simple program like this is correct.

Figure 2.1   Metric conversion program

```
// FILE: Metric.cpp
// CONVERTS FABRIC MEASURES IN SQUARE METERS TO SQUARE YARDS

#include <iostream.h>

void main ()
{
    // Local data ...
    const float meters_to_yards = 1.196; // conversion constant
    float size_in_sqmeters; // input: fabric size in square meters
    float size_in_sqyards;  // output: fabric size in square yards

    // Read the fabric size in square meters.
    cout << "Enter the fabric size in square meters: ";
    cin  >> size_in_sqmeters;

    // Convert the fabric size to square yards.
    size_in_sqyards = meters_to_yards * size_in_sqmeters;

    // Display fabric size in square yards.
    cout << "The fabric size in square yards is "
        << size_in_sqyards << endl;
}
```

————— Program Output —————

```
Enter the fabric size in square meters: 2.0
The fabric size in square yards is 2.392
```

EXERCISES FOR SECTION 2.1

Self-Check
1. List the steps of the software development method.
2. What would the data requirements and formulas look like for a computer program that converts a weight in pounds to a weight in kilograms?
3. What is the difference between the design and implementation stages of the software development method?
4. At which stage of the software development method is the algorithm for a solution developed?
5. What is a data requirements table? How is it used in the software development process?
6. What is an algorithm? How does it differ from a program?

2.2 ——— C++ LANGUAGE ELEMENTS

In the remainder of this chapter, we provide a description of some basic features of the C++ programming language. We begin with a discussion of the program just shown in Fig. 2.1, then we proceed to another short example.

With each of the remaining sections of this chapter, we describe additional features of the example programs illustrated. By the end of the chapter, all of the features of C++ shown in these programs will have been discussed. So please be patient.

The General Form of a C++ Program

The program shown in Fig. 2.1 consists of a single C++ function named `main` and has the general form shown in Fig. 2. 2. A *function* is the basic unit of computer instructions in C++; it contains a collection of related statements all under one name. Our function begins with optional comments that identify the name of the file in which it is stored along with a brief description of the purpose of the program. The identifier `main` is required; all C++ programs contain one or more functions with the requirement that exactly one be called `main`. We refer to this function as the main program, or sometimes, just the program.

The main function begins with the *function header line*

```
void main ()
```

The word `void` indicates that the main function does not return a value to the operating system. The word `main` must be typed in lowercase letters and followed by a pair of parentheses.

Anything typed within the braces { } is part of the *function body.* The main function body consists of two kinds of statements: *declaration statements* and *executable statements.* Although not required in C++, we will usually write declaration statements in a separate section appearing before the executable statements.

Figure 2.2   General form of a C++ program

```
// FILE: filename
// PROGRAM DESCRIPTION

#include directives

void main ()
{
   declarations section

   executable statements section
}
```

Declarations

Declaration statements tell the compiler what data are needed in the program. These statements are based on the problem data requirements identified during the problem analysis. Every identifier associated with a problem data element must be declared exactly once in the declaration section. All identifiers must be declared before they are used. The comma is used to separate identifiers if more than one appears in the same declaration. In our program, the conversion constant `meters_to_yards` (value is 1.196) and the identifiers `size_in_sqmeters` and `size_in_sqyards` are declared.

Two other undeclared identifiers—`cin` and `cout`—appear in our program. These are names of special data elements called streams; `cin` represents the *input stream* and `cout` represents the *output stream*. These data elements are declared in the library header file `iostream.h` and therefore do not have to be declared in our program.

Comments in Programs

One thing you might notice in the metric conversion program is a number of lines that begin with a double slash, such as

```
// CONVERTS FABRIC MEASURES IN SQUARE METERS TO SQUARE YARDS.
```

In C++, a double slash denotes a *program comment*. A program comment is like a parenthetical remark in a sentence—it is intended to make the program easier to understand by describing its purpose (see the second comment line in Fig. 2.1). Comments are also used to describe the use of identifiers and the purpose of each program step. As shown in Fig. 2.1, a comment can appear by itself on a program line or at the end of a line after a statement. Comments are an important part of the *documentation* of a program because they help others read and understand the program. The compiler, however, ignores comments; they are not translated into machine language.

The double slash `//` can be used only when a comment fits on a single line or when the remainder of a line is a comment. The double slash marks the beginning of a comment that is then assumed to terminate at the end of the line. Another form of comment, the slash-asterisk combination `/* */`, can stand alone or can be embedded in the middle of a statement. The slash-asterisk combination encloses a comment, marking both the beginning and the end, as shown in Fig. 2.3. A comment that begins with `/*` may extend over any number of lines until it closes with `*/`. The `/*` and `*/` are additional examples of special character pairs; no character, not even a blank, can come between the `*` and `/`. The next syntax display box describes the use and syntax of comments. We use this stylistic form throughout the text to summarize the characteristics of each feature of the C++ language to be introduced.

Figure 2.3 Two multiline comments using both styles

```
// FILE: MyProg1.cpp
// THIS PROGRAM DOES LOTS OF THINGS AND NEEDS SEVERAL LINES OF
//    EXPLANATION

/* Here are the
     several lines
          of explanation

   Written by Dara and Shelley Friedman
   June 1, 1996
*/
```

C++ SYNTAX

Comment

Form: // comment
 /* comment */

Example: // This is a comment
 /* and so is this */

Interpretation: A double slash indicates the start of a comment. Alternatively, the symbol pair /* may be used to mark the beginning of a comment that is terminated by the symbol pair */. Comments are listed with the program but are otherwise ignored by the C++ compiler. ∎

Comments make a program more readable by describing the purpose of the program and by describing the use of each identifier, as shown in the line

```
float size_in_sqmeters; // input: fabric size in square meters
```

which describes the use of identifier `size_in_sqmeters`.

Also, you should use comments within the executable section of a program to describe the purpose of each major algorithm step. Such comments should describe what the step does rather than simply restate the step in English. For example, the comment

```
// Converts fabric measures in square meters to square yards.
   size_in_sqyards = meters_to_yards * size_in_sqmeters;
```

is more descriptive and hence preferable to

```
// Multiply meters_to_yards by size_in_sqmeters and save the
//    result in size_in_sqyards.
   size_in_sqyards = meters_to_yards * size_in_sqmeters;
```

The C++ code for each step in the initial algorithm should be preceded by a comment that summarizes the purpose of the algorithm step. Carefully chosen identifier names should provide sufficient information about the individual statements, thereby eliminating the need to comment on every line.

Each program you write should begin with a header section that consists of a series of comments specifying the following:

- Name of the file in which the program is saved
- Brief description of what the program does
- Programmer's name
- Date of the current version

If you write a program for a class assignment, you should also list the class identification and your instructor's name.

```
/* FILE: assignmt.cpp
   This program reads a value in square meters and converts it
   to square yards.

   Programmer:  Ayisha Mertens   Date completed: August 15, 1996
   Instructor:  Dr. Elliot Koffman   Class:  CIS67
*/
```

The `include` Compiler Directive

The line beginning with #include represents a different kind of C++ statement called a *compiler directive*. A compiler directive is a statement that is processed at compilation time, when the program is translated to machine language (as opposed to execution time, when the translated program statements are executed by the CPU). The #include directive instructs the compiler to insert the indicated C++ instructions into your program in place of the directive. In this case, iostream.h is the name of a C++ library *header file* whose contents are inserted in place of the #include line during compilation. The iostream.h file is one of the many *library files* that are included with the C++ programming system. This type of file name should be enclosed by the symbol pair < >. The use of libraries can help us to *reuse* C++ code that has already been written and tested. This saves us from having to type many extra, complex lines of code. There may be many #include, and possibly other compiler directives, in each program that you write.

Compiler Directive `#include`

Form: `#include` *<filename>*

Example: `#include <iostream.h>`

Interpretation: This line is a *compiler directive* that is replaced during translation by the named C++ library header file. The library `iostream.h` is required in order to be able to use the stream input/output facilities provided by `cin`, `cout`, and `endl`. It is stylistically preferred that compiler directives, such as `#include`, be listed first, but they will work as long as they appear before they are used.

Note: A compiler directive should not end with a semicolon.   ∎

Reserved Words, Identifiers, and Special Symbols

Each line of the program in Fig. 2.1 contains a number of different *syntactic elements,* such as reserved words, identifiers, and special character symbols. The reserved words and identifiers used in Fig. 2.1 are listed in Table 2.1. The *reserved words* have a specific meaning unique to C++ and they cannot be used for other purposes.

The identifiers appearing in Fig. 2.1 (for example, `meters_to_yards`, `size_in_sqyards`, and `cout`) are used to name the problem data elements to be manipulated by a program. You have quite a bit of freedom in selecting the identifiers that you use as long as you follow these syntactic rules:

1. An identifier should always begin with a letter.
2. An identifier must consist of letters, digits, or underscores only.
3. You cannot use a C++ reserved word as an identifier.

Some valid and invalid identifiers are listed below.

- *Valid identifiers*

```
letter1, Letter1, letter2, inches, cent, CentPerInch,
cent_per_inch, hello
```

- *Invalid identifiers*

```
1Letter, const, two*four, two-dimensional, Joe's, float
```

It is very important to pick meaningful names for identifiers; meaningful identifiers make it easier to understand the purpose of each identifier, which in turn can make an entire program easier to read and understand. For example, the

Table 2.1 Reserved Words and Identifiers Illustrated to This Point

RESERVED WORDS	IDENTIFIERS	
const	meters_to_yards	cin
float	size_in_sqmeters	cout
void	size_in_sqyards	

identifier `salary` would be a good name for a variable used to store a person's salary; the identifiers `s` and `bagel` would be bad choices.

Identifiers may be up to 127 characters long. It is difficult to form meaningful names using fewer than three letters, but, on the other hand, excessively long identifiers are more prone to typing errors. As a reasonable rule of thumb, use names that are readable and sufficiently unique.

If you incorrectly type an identifier, the compiler will usually detect this as a syntax error and display an *undefined identifier* error message during program translation. Sometimes, incorrectly typed identifiers resemble other identifiers, so it is best to avoid picking names that are very similar to each other. Try not to choose two names that are identical except for their use of case because, although the compiler will be able to distinguish between them, you might inadvertently get them mixed up and attempt to use them interchangeably.

Some symbols and symbol pairs (e.g., =, *, ;, ", { }, ( ), //, <<, >>) have a special meaning in C++, and there are specific rules governing their use. As we proceed through the book, we will encounter many more reserved words and special character symbols, and we will learn the rules for using them. Appendix B contains a complete list of C++ reserved words as well as lists of special characters and special character pairs used in the text.

Executable Statements

The executable statements cause some kind of action to take place when a program is executed. When an executable statement begins with the output stream name `cout` (pronounced c–out), it causes output to be displayed to the *standard output device* (generally, a monitor or screen). The first such line

```
cout << "Enter the fabric size in square meters: ";
```

displays the first output line in the sample execution. This *program prompt* tells the user to type in a fabric size value in square meters. The next line

```
cin >> size_in_sqmeters;
```

causes the data value (2.0), typed by the user from the *standard input device* (usually the keyboard), to be read into the variable `size_in_sqmeters`. (`cin` is pronounced c–in.) The statement

```
size_in_sqyards = meters_to_yards * size_in_sqmeters;
```

computes the equivalent fabric size in square yards by multiplying the size in square meters by 1.196; the product is stored in the memory cell `size_in_sqyards`.

Finally, the statement

```
cout << "The fabric size in square yards is "
     << size_in_sqyards << endl;
```

displays the *character string* (the text enclosed in double quotes) together with the value contained in `size_in_sqyards`. The value of `size_in_sqyards` is displayed as a floating-point number—that is, a number with a decimal point and a fractional part. `endl` stands for "endline" and causes a screen display or printer to advance to the beginning of a new line of output. The last line of the program in Fig. 2.1 is a right brace, `}`, denoting the end of the main function.

Some punctuation marks—or *punctuators*, for short—appear in Fig. 2.1: Double slashes begin several lines; a semicolon appears at the end of each C++ statement, parentheses and braces are present; and many *pairs of special characters* such as the less-than or greater-than symbol are interspersed. As we progress through this chapter, we will provide descriptions for the use of these symbols.

A C++ statement can extend over more than one line, but it should not be split in the middle of an identifier a special character pair, number, or string.

Example 2.1   Figure 2.4 contains a C++ program and output from a sample execution (the last two lines of the figure). The program displays a personalized message to the program user.

The line starting with `char` is followed by two identifier names (`letter1`, `letter2`) used to store the first two initials of the name of the program user. The line beginning with `string` is followed by the identifier `last_name` used to store the last name of the user. The instruction

```
cin >> letter1 >> letter2 >> last_name;
```

reads the two letters, `E` and `B`, and the last name, `Koffman`, all typed by the program user and stored in memory cells as indicated by the three identifiers listed. The next line

```
cout << "Hello " << letter1 << ". " << letter2 << ". "
     << last_name << "! ";
```

Figure 2.4   Printing a welcoming message

```
// FILE: Hello.cpp
// DISPLAYS A USER'S NAME

#include <iostream.h>
#include <string>

void main ()
{
   // Local data ...
       char letter1, letter2;      // input and output: first two initials
       string last_name;           // input and output: last name

   // Enter letters and print message.
   cout << "Enter first two initials and last name (no spaces) and press return: ";
   cin >> letter1 >> letter2 >> last_name;
   cout << "Hello " << letter1 << ". " << letter2 << ". " << last_name << "!  ";
   cout << "We hope you enjoy studying C++." << endl;
}
```

──────────────── Program Output ────────────────

```
Enter first two initials and last name (no spaces) and press return: EBKoffman
Hello E. B. Koffman! We hope you enjoy studying C++.
```

displays E. B. Koffman after the message string "Hello ". The string ". " causes a period and one blank space to be displayed after each initial. Finally the last cout line displays the rest of the second line shown in the program output. ∎

Use of Uppercase and Lowercase in C++ Programs

C++ is a case-sensitive language; the compiler differentiates between uppercase and lowercase letters. This means that you cannot write const as CONST or cin as CIN.

Identifiers can be any mixture of uppercase and lowercase, such as SizeInSqMeters. In this book we use all lowercase letters with an underline symbol "_" between multiple words (e.g., size_in_sqmeters). Your instructor may have a different preference that will work just as well. Whatever convention you adopt, you should use it consistently. Remember that C++ considers Size_in_sqmeters and size_in_sqmeters to be different identifiers, so a lack of consistency in choosing identifier names can be quite harmful.

Some Issues of Programming Style

Throughout the book, issues of good programming style will be presented, often in syntax displays such as the one shown below. Programming style displays will provide guidelines for improving the appearance and readability of programs. Most programs that you write will be examined, studied, and modified by someone else. A program that follows some consistent style conventions will be easier to read than one that is sloppy or inconsistent. Although these conventions make it easier for humans to understand programs, they have no effect on the C++ compiler or the steps specified to be carried out by the computer.

PROGRAM STYLE

Blank Spaces

The consistent and careful use of blank spaces can significantly enhance the style of a program. A blank space is required between words in a program line (for instance, between `const`, `float`, and `meters_to_yards` in Fig. 2.1).

The compiler ignores extra blanks between words and symbols. You may insert space to improve the style and appearance of a program. As illustrated in Figs. 2.1 and 2.4, you should always leave a blank space after a comma and before and after operators such as `*`, `-`, `=`, and `<<` or `>>`. Remember to indent each line of the program except for the braces that mark the beginning and end of `main`. All lines between the `{ }` are indented three or more spaces. Finally, use blank lines between sections of the program.

Be careful not to insert blank spaces where they do not belong. For example, there cannot be a space between the characters `<` and `<` when they form the output operator `<<`. Also, the identifier `start_salary` cannot be written as `start salary`. ∎

EXERCISES FOR SECTION 2.2

Self-Check
1. What is the purpose of the special character pair of symbols `//`?
2. Explain what is wrong with the comments below.

```
// This is a comment? */
/* How about this one /* it seems like a comment
*/ doesn't it? */
```

3. Why are comments important in a computer program? When should they be used?
4. What is the purpose of the `#include`?
5. Can reserved words be used as identifiers?
6. Why is it important to use consistent programming style?
7. Indicate which of the symbols below are C++ reserved words, or valid or invalid identifiers.

main	cin	Bill	Sue's	rate	start
const	xyz123	123xyz	'MaxScores'	int	return
y=z	Prog#2	ThisIsALongOne	so_is_this_one	two-way	go

2.3 ———— ABSTRACTION, DATA TYPES, AND DECLARATIONS

Abstraction

An *abstraction* is a model or simplification of a physical object or concept. We frequently use abstractions in problem solving and programming. For example, in problem solving, we sometimes make simplifying assumptions that enable us to solve a limited version of a more general problem.

Abstraction is an important concept in programming. The programs we write present an abstract view of *problem domain elements* (such as money or students), their *attributes* (such as dollars and cents for money or the names, addresses, and grade point averages for students), and a collection of meaningful *operations* (such as computing a student's pay for the week, or modifying a student's grade point average) that can be performed on them. These views of problem domain data elements are often referred to as *data abstractions*. The operations are expressed in terms of sequences of *control abstractions*. The programs also describe any relationships among the entities that might be relevant to the problem we are trying to solve.

Relevance is the key here, for the software development method is a step-by-step process of focusing on what we need to know, ignoring irrelevant details. At each *level of refinement*, we continue to add detail until we finally reach a level with which we are sufficiently comfortable to write our program. Thus, programming is a process of building multiple levels of both data and control abstraction; we begin with abstractions related to problem domain elements and processes and end with those related to programming language elements and operations.

We use abstraction in problem solving throughout this book, introducing features of C++ that are useful in the abstraction process. C++ has a wealth of such features. In the next section, we introduce some of the most elementary and most often used data abstractions.

Data Types in C++

How a particular value is represented in memory is determined by the data type of that value. A *data type* provides a method of modeling or representing a particular set of values and determines what operations can be performed on those values. The C++ language has a number of *language-defined types* (sometimes called *predefined data types*) and the C++ libraries provide a large number of additional types, called *system-defined data types*. In addition to these types, C++ programmers have the capability of constructing their own data types, called *user-defined data types*. In this section, we introduce four language-defined types: float (for real numbers), int (for integers), char (for single character values), and bool (for the Boolean values true and false). Two system-defined types are also described: stream, which provides the program mechanism for entering and displaying data; and string, which facilitates the processing of sequences of characters (for example, a person's name or address). Finally, we will examine an example of a user-defined type, one related to the all-important commodity of money.

Each data type has its own set of values and of operations that can be performed on those values. We will describe the correct form to be used when writing the values of each data type as *literals*—that is, when writing these values *in-line* in a program or entering them as data to be read by a program. We also list some of the typical operations that can be performed on the values of each type. Further details on C++ data types will be covered later in this chapter, and in Chapters 7 and 11.

int Data Type

From a mathematical point of view, integers are positive or negative whole numbers. A number without a sign is assumed to be positive. The int data type is used to model integers in C++. These integers might represent a person's age (in years), the term of a loan (in months), or the number of students enrolled in a course.

Because of the memory cell's finite size, not all integers can be represented. Although the range of integers depends on the version of C++ you are using, there is a predefined constant named INT_MAX whose value represents the largest positive integer for your C++ compiler. An integer cannot contain a comma or a decimal point, so we use integers to model numeric values that do not have a fractional part. The following are some valid integer literals:

```
-10500  435  15  -25  0  32767  (2^16 − 1, often the value of INT_MAX)
```

We can read and display integers in C++ and perform the common arithmetic operations (add, subtract, multiply, and divide). We discuss these operations in more detail later in this chapter.

float Data Type

In C++, we use the basic data type float as an abstraction for the real numbers (in the mathematical sense), or numbers that consist of an integral part and a fractional part, separated by a decimal point. The float data type is used for storing and manipulating real numbers. A float literal can have an integral part and a fractional part with a decimal point in between. Either the integral part or the fractional part, but not both, may be missing. Examples of type float data are

```
64.0   -18.   16.5   .4   22.87603
```

As with integers, we can read and display type float data and perform addition, subtraction, multiplication, and division on these data.

We can use scientific notation to represent very large and very small type float values. In normal scientific notation, the real number 1.23×10^5 is equivalent to 123000.0 where the exponent 5 means move the decimal point 5 places to the right. In C++ scientific notation, we write this number as 1.23E5 or 1.23E+5. If the exponent has a minus sign, the decimal point is moved to the left (e.g., 0.34E-4 is equivalent to 0.000034). Table 2.2 shows examples of valid and invalid float literals. The last valid example shows we can write a float literal in C++ scientific notation without using a decimal point. We can read and display type float values in C++ and perform the common arithmetic operations (add, subtract, multiply, and divide). These operations are described in detail in Section 2.6.

The data type float is an abstraction because it does not include all the real numbers. Some real numbers are too large or too small, and some cannot be represented precisely because of the finite size of a memory cell (more on this in Chapter 7). However, we can certainly represent enough of the real numbers in C++ to carry out most of the computations we wish to perform with sufficient accuracy.

The float and int data types differ in one basic way: Type float data represent values with a decimal point and a fractional part, whereas type int data represent integral values only. For this reason, type int data are more restricted in their use. We often use integers to represent a count of items (for example, the number of children in a family) because a count must always be an integer. Type float data, on the other hand, can be used to model fabric measurements (in yards or meters), rainfall (to the nearest hundredths of an inch), or a student's grade point average (measured to the nearest tenth or hundredth).

char Data Type

The data type char represents an individual character value—a letter, a digit, or a special symbol. Each type char literal is enclosed in apostrophes (single quotes) as shown below:

'A'   'z'   '2'   '9'   '*'   ':'   '"'   ' '

Table 2.2 Valid and Invalid Type float Literals

VALID float LITERALS		INVALID float LITERALS
3.14159		150 (no decimal point)
.005		245e (no exponent)
12345.		-15e-0.3 (0.3 is invalid exponent)
15.0e-04	(value is 0.0015)	12.5e.3 (.3 is invalid exponent)
2.345e2	(value is 234.5)	
1.15e-3	(value is 0.00115)	
12E+6	(value is 12000000.0)	

The next to last literal preceding list represents the double quote character "; the last literal represents the blank character, which is written by pressing the apostrophe key, the space bar, and the apostrophe key.

Although a type `char` literal in a program requires the use of the apostrophe as a *delimiter*, this delimiter character is not used when entering `char` data or when `char` data is displayed. When entering the letter z as a character data item to be read by a program, press the z key instead of the sequence `'z'`.

Although it is not prohibited in C++, you should not perform arithmetic operations on type `char` data. There is little programming that we will do for which `'3' + '5'` is meaningful. However, we can compare characters and read and display them.

`bool` Data Type

Unlike the other data types, the `bool`[1] data type has just two possible values: `true` and `false`. We can use this data type to represent conditional values so that a program can make decisions. We can compare type `bool` values and we can perform logical operations on them. More about this in Chapter 4.

Ordinal Types

The data types `int`, `char`, and `bool` have one property in common that is not shared by the data type `float`. We can list all of the values of these types that can be represented in a particular version of C++. However, we cannot list all of the values of type `float` that may be represented. For example, if we attempt to list all the floating-point numbers and we have 3.14 and 3.15 in our list, then someone could say that we omitted 3.141, 3.142, and so on. If we include these numbers, then someone could say that we left out 3.1411, 3.1412, and so on. A data type whose values can be listed is called an *ordinal type*. We will examine another kind of ordinal type called an enumeration in Chapter 7.

The data types just described represent four of the most common models of data used in programming. Similar data types are predefined to many programming languages. We now turn our attention to two other data types that will be are used frequently in this book: `string` and `stream`. These types are not predefined but are rather user-defined types defined in our C++ libraries using the C++ *class* construct (see Section 2.4).

`string` Data Type

A string literal is a sequence of characters enclosed in double quotes; the next line contains four string literals.

```
"ABCDE"   "1234"   "true"   "Enter the fabric size in square meters >"
```

---

[1]The `bool` data type is named after the English mathematician George Boole (1815–1864) who invented a two-valued algebra. This data type is part of the proposed C++ standard but may not be available on all compilers.

Note that the string `"1234"` is not stored the same way as the integer `1234`; the use of strings with the arithmetic operators should therefore be avoided as the results will be meaningless. The string "`true`" is also stored differently from the `bool` value `true`.

In C++, string objects may be read, stored in memory, compared, and displayed; `string` values are entered and displayed without the double quote delimiter.

`stream` Data Type

The majority of programs you write will perform input and output operations involving some of your data. These operations are performed on objects (defined in the `iostream.h` library) consisting of streams of characters that are external to your program, often entered at the keyboard and displayed at your workstation. The standard input and output stream objects, `cin` and `cout` respectively, do not need to be declared in your program. They are already defined in `iostream.h`.

Purpose of Data Types— Constants, Variables, and Objects

The reason for having different data types is so that the compiler knows what operations are valid for each data element used in a program. If you try to manipulate a literal or a value in memory in an incorrect way (for example, add two `char` values, or read data from a `float` variable rather than a `stream` object), the C++ compiler displays an error message telling you that this is an incorrect operation. Similarly, if you try to store the wrong kind of value in a memory cell (for example, a string in a memory cell that is type `int`), you get an error message. Detecting these errors keeps the computer from performing operations that make no sense. In the next section, we discuss how to tell the C++ compiler the data type associated with the identifiers used in your programs.

In the problem solving process described at the beginning of this chapter, the choice of an appropriate data type to use in modeling each problem domain data element is made after each such element has been identified and named. In the fabric measurement problem, this was a fairly easy decision since all of our measurements needed to accommodate a fractional part— hence the use of the `float` data type. As shown in the solution to this problem, it is customary to associate the name of the type chosen to model each data element in the data requirements table.

As we progress through the book, we will see that the choice of data types is often far more difficult, and often results in the use of new user-defined data types for modeling the data elements to be manipulated. Rarely, if ever, will all the data used in a program be modeled by the same type of data, as was the case in the fabric measurement problems.

Declarations

We tell the C++ compiler the names of the memory cells used in a program and the types associated with these names through the use of *constant, variable,* and *object declarations.*

Constant Declarations

It is often convenient to associate meaningful names with special program constants, such as 1.196 in the metric conversion program. This association may be done using a constant declaration. The *constant declaration*

```
const float meters_to_yards = 1.196;
```

specifies that the identifier `meters_to_yards` will be associated with the program constant 1.196; the identifier `meters_to_yards` is called a *constant* and should be used in the program in place of the value 1.196. Only data values that never change (e.g., the number of square yards in a square meter, which is always 1.196) should be associated with an identifier that is a constant. You cannot write instructions that attempt to change the value of a constant.

C++ SYNTAX

Constant Declaration

Form: const *type constant-identifier = value*;

Example: const float pi = 3.14159;

Interpretation: The specified value is associated with the constant identifier. This value cannot be changed at any time by the program. More than one constant declaration may be listed. A semicolon appears at the end of each declaration.

Note: By convention, we place constant declarations before any variable or object declarations in a C++ program.

Variable Declarations

In the programs illustrated in Figs. 2.1 and 2.4, we used identifiers to represent the memory cells or *data stores* used to store the values of the problem domain data. We introduce two such data stores—variables and objects—and illustrate how to tell the C++ compiler the type of the data that is to be stored in the designated memory cells.

The predefined data types just described represent four of the most common models of data used in programming. Similar data types are predefined in many programming languages. Identifiers associated with memory cells of a predefined type used for storing program input data or computational results are called *variables* (the values stored in these cells are changeable as the program executes). The *variable declarations*

```
float size_in_sqmeters;    // input: fabric size in meters
float size_in_sqyards;     // output: fabric size in yards
```

in Fig. 2.1 give the names of two variables used to store floating-point numbers (for example, 30.0, 562.57). The variable declaration

```
char letter1, letter2;
```

in Fig. 2.4 gives names of two variables used for storing individual characters.

C++ SYNTAX

Variable Declaration

Form: *type variable-identifier-list;*

Example: `float x, y;`
                 `int me, you;`

Interpretation: One or more bytes of computer memory (a data store) is allocated for each identifier in the *variable-identifier-list*. The *type* of data (`float`, `int`, etc.) to be stored in each variable is specified. Commas are used to separate the identifiers in the *variable list*. More than one list of variables may be declared; each declaration must be terminated by a semicolon. ∎

Object Declarations

We now turn our attention to two other data types which are used frequently in this book: `string` and `stream`. These types are not part of the C++ language (they are not language-defined), but they are defined instead in the *class libraries* that accompany the C++ language system. The C++ construct used to define these *system-defined types* is called a *class*. The data stores associated with system-defined types are called *objects*.

Object declarations look like variable declarations. Indeed, both object and variable declarations associate identifiers of a given type with memory cells used to store values of this type. We will have more to say about the distinction between variables, objects, and classes in the next section.

C++ SYNTAX

Object Declaration

Form: *type object-identifier-list;*

Example: `string last_name, address;`

Interpretation: One or more bytes of computer memory (a data store) is allocated for each identifier in the *object-identifier-list*. The *type* of data (`string`, stream, etc.) to be stored in each object is specified. Commas are used to separate the identifiers in the *object-identifier-list*. More than one list of objects may be declared; each declaration must be terminated by a semicolon. ∎

EXERCISES FOR SECTION 2.3

Self-Check
1. Why should the value of pi (3.14159) be stored in a constant?
2. What is the purpose of data types in C++?
3. Distinguish between (a) the int and float data types, and (b) the int and char data types.
4. What is a literal?
5. What is the difference between a string literal and a character literal? How would you write a character string of length one in a C++ program—for example, a character string consisting solely of an exclamation point.
6. a. Write the following numbers in normal decimal notation:

    103E-4 1.2345E+6 123.45E+3

   b. Write the following numbers in C++ scientific notation:

    1300 123.45 0.00426

7. Write the declaration for a program designed to manipulate objects named triangle, rectangle, and circle, all of the user-defined data type shape.
8. What is the purpose of a declaration?

Programming
1. Write the constant and variable declarations for a program that has variables radius, area, and circum (all type float) and a constant pi (3.14159).

2.4 OBJECT-ORIENTED PROGRAMMING: CLASSES AND OBJECTS

As we have seen, the C++ language provides predefined data types, such as those used for processing numeric data (for example, int and float), characters (char), and logical data (bool). These data types provide mechanisms for representing certain data elements in the memory of the computer and for performing operations on this data. However, these models have substantial limitations. For example, the int data type can be used to model only a subset of the integers (for example, those ranging from -32767 to 32767). The float type allows us to model a far larger range of real numbers, but not all of the numbers in this range can be modeled precisely.

Because of these limitations and other factors, we find that the predefined data types by themselves are not always sufficient for modeling the problem domain data elements to be manipulated by our programs. We need new data types in order to obtain more meaningful and accurate models for our programs. For example, a word processor is constantly manipulating strings of characters of varying (and sometimes very large) sizes. Even a simple mailing label program has a need to store such data elements (e.g., student names and addresses) and to perform manipulations such as input and output, copy, and comparison, and substring searches, insertions, deletions, and replacements.

Let's consider another example: a payroll program or a banking program. Both programs deal with quantities of money, so it would be nice to have a data type to represent monetary values. Although we could use data type `float` for a payroll program, some money amounts are not represented precisely (to the exact penny) as type `float` numbers. This inaccuracy might become significant in banking or financial applications.

To allow for precise representation, we need a data type that stores a money amount as a pair of components or *data members:* dollars [an integer with possible negative (for debits), zero, or positive (for credits) values], and cents (an integer between 0 and 99 inclusive). We also need operators for money objects such as an addition operator that will allow us to add two money objects obtaining a money object as a result, and a multiplication operator that allows us to multiply a money object by some nonmoney value (perhaps of type `int` or type `float`) obtaining another money object.

These two operators should have some special properties. For example, when we add two money amounts, the cents part of the result must always be non-negative and less than 100. Therefore, our add operator algorithm should contain steps to ensure this is always the case. When we multiply a money amount by some value (e.g., a person's hourly pay rate modeled using the `money` type multiplied by the number of hours worked modeled as type `float`), we must ensure a money amount result (accurate to the nearest cent). Thus, the product of $4.55 and the value 13.75 is 62.5625 which should be rounded to $62.56. Our multiplication operation should ensure that this rounding is always done.

C++ allows us to define our own data types to model problem domain data elements and to use data types defined by others as well. Such user-defined data types are called *classes.* A variable whose type is a class is called a *class instance* or, more simply, an *object.* If we define a class named `money`, the statement

```
money balance, deposit, withdrawal;
```

declares three objects of type `money` with sufficient memory for storing both dollars and cents (both perhaps as data elements of type `int`). We would also need to provide descriptions of some of the common operations, such as addition and multiplication (as just described) to be performed on money quantities. Note carefully that the addition and multiplication operations defined in the `money` class are not the same as the addition and multiplication defined for type `int` or for type `float` data. Among other things, the addition operator for money would have to ensure that the cents component of the addition result was always less than 100. The multiplication operation would have to ensure a result rounded to the nearest cent.

We will have more to say about this distinction between operations later in the text, and we will learn much more about user-defined data types, objects, classes, and object-oriented programming in later chapters. The diagram in Fig. 2.5 depicts what we have discussed so far.

Figure 2.5   Data abstractions, data types, and data stores

Data Abstractions

| real number | money | integer | shape | character string |
| student | textbook | stream | line | faculty member |

Data Types Defined Using C++ Classes

(Models of data abstractions specified in C++ using classes)

Three different kinds of C++ data types

Language-defined: built into the C++ language definition (predefined)
C++ examples: `float, int, char, bool`

System-defined: defined in a C++ class library
C++ examples: `ifstream, ofstream, string`

User-defined: defined by a programmer
Examples: `money, shape, student, faculty_member, line`

Data Stores

(Instances of data type in which data can be stored)

Variables: instances of language-defined data types

C++ examples:
```
float size_in_sqmeters, rainfall, circumference;
int age, size_of_class, loan_period;
bool error_flag, io_status;
char first_initial, letter_grade;
```

Objects: instances of system-defined and user-defined data types (also called class instances)

Examples (illustrated in C++ declarations):
```
money hourly_rate, gross_pay, interest_amount;
string first_name, last_name, address;
ifstream student_data, school_course_data;
shape rectangle, circle, triangle, pentagon;
```

Some Benefits of Using Classes

Abstraction and Reuse through Classes

There are several advantages to using classes and objects. First, as we have mentioned, we can build better models (abstractions) for real-world items. For example, a payroll program might involve a collection of hourly employees (the people to be paid). To build a useful model of one such hourly employee, we need to decide what are the essential characteristics (attributes) of such a person and what are the operations we might associate with this person. In C++, we refer to the attributes as *the data members of the class.* An `hourly_employee` class might include the following data members:

Data members for class `hourly_employee`

- `name`: a sequence of characters
- `id`: a sequence of 11 digit characters
- `address`: a sequence of characters
- `num_dependents`: an integer
- `job_title`: a sequence of characters
- `weekly_hours`: a real number
- `hourly_rate`: type `money`
- `weekly_gross`: type `money`
- `weekly_net`: type `money`

Right away, we see an important advantage of the use of classes: *reusability.* We can reuse the class `money` as the data type for data members that are money quantities.

Besides the data members, we must determine what operators should be provided for this class. It makes no sense to provide arithmetic operators like +, −, *, and so on for objects of this class. However, we might want an operator that computes an employee's weekly gross pay and one that computes an employee's weekly net pay. We also need an operator to read the data for an employee and one to display an employee's data. Finally, we may need to change an employee's address or other information or simply access the value of a particular employee attribute such as `job_title` or `weekly_net`. We provide these operators (called *member functions* of the class) with names that are valid C++ identifiers and that describe the operation they perform.

Member functions for class `hourly_employee`

- `compute_gross_pay`
- `compute_net_pay`
- `read`
- `display`
- `set_address`
- `set_num_depend`

- `set_job_title`
- `set_hourly_rate`
- `set_weekly_hours`

At this point, we have a reasonable model for the class `hourly_employee` that we can use in a payroll program and perhaps in other programs just as we reused the class `money`. Later we will learn how to code this model in C++ and how to use it in programs.

Importance of Reuse   You may be wondering why reuse is so important in programming. To answer this question, consider what happens when you decide to purchase a stereo system from components. To "design" your system, you must decide which kind of CD player you want, select a receiver, and then choose speakers that fit your budget. To "build" your system, you only need to connect the components using standard cables.

Besides simplifying the task of installing your initial system, you also have the capability to modify your system without much effort. If you later decide to upgrade to a new CD changer, you only need to unplug the old CD player and plug in the changer. You can also add new functionality, such as a record turntable, very easily. Without the use of components, you would need to buy a completely new system if you wanted to make changes or additions.

In the not too distant past, most software development was done without the use of reusable components. If a payroll system needed upgrading, it was often easier to program a new system from scratch rather than to reuse pieces of the old system, or to modify a similar system designed for another company. Object-oriented programming promotes software reuse, thereby reducing the cost and time required for initial software development and making it much easier to upgrade existing systems.

Two Classes from the C++ Class Library

In Example 2.1, we illustrated the declaration and use of objects of two of the most commonly used classes in C++, the `stream` and `string` classes. Because the manipulation of stream and string objects is so important in C++ programming, these classes have been included as part of the C++ collection of class libraries—the `stream` class is defined in the C++ *library header file* `iostream.h`; the string class is defined in the library header file `string` (`cstring.h` on some systems).

Stream Objects   In C++, a *stream* is a sequence of characters associated with an input device, an output device, or a disk file. In Section 2.5, we describe input and output using cin and cout and the *input operator* >> and *output operator* <<. Both cin and cout are objects. Object cin is an instance of the class istream, and object cout is an instance of the class ostream. The input operator >> is a member function of the class istream; the output operator << is a member function of the class ostream. Both classes are derived from the parent class stream.

The header file iostream.h also contains declarations for cin and cout:

```
istream cin;     // cin is type istream (input stream)
ostream cout;    // cout is type ostream (output stream)
```

These declarations enable us to reference and use cin and cout and the operators >> and << in our programs without error.

String Objects   If you have ever used a word processor, you are familiar with the kinds of operations performed on string data. For example, we frequently want to insert one or more characters into an existing string, delete a portion of a string, overwrite or replace one substring of a string with another, search for a target substring, or join two strings together to form a longer string. C++ provides a string class, accessed by using the compiler directive

```
#include <string>
```

The attributes of this class include the actual sequence of characters stored in a string object and the length of the object (number of characters in the string). The member functions of the string class enable us to read, display, and compare string objects as well as to perform all of the operations listed in the preceding paragraph. Chapter 3 will discuss how to use these functions. For now, we will focus on reading and storing data in string objects.

In Fig. 2.4, the declaration

```
string last_name;                     // input and output: last name
```

allocates storage for a string of characters. The statement

```
cin >> last_name;
```

reads the characters typed at the keyboard up to but not including the first blank or carriage return. This string of characters is then stored in the string object last_name. The statement

```
cout << last_name << endl;
```

displays the sequence of characters in last_name.

EXERCISES FOR SECTION 2.4

Self-Check
1. Distinguish between variables and objects.
2. What is the purpose of using classes in C++ (and what are some of the benefits)?
3. What is a class member function? What is a class data member?
4. List two data members for a class designed to model a two-dimensional shape. (What are some of the most common properties of a two-dimensional shape?) List one additional member for a class designed to model a circle. Note that a circle is a specialized shape that may be derived from the class shape.

Programming
1. Write out the algorithm for multiplying an object of type money times a variable of type float (for example, the number of hours you worked this week—perhaps 8.75 hours).

2.5 ——— EXECUTABLE STATEMENTS

A common use for a computer is to perform arithmetic computations and display the results. These operations are specified by the *executable statements* of a C++ program. Executable statements cause some kind of action to occur when a program is run. Each executable statement is translated by the C++ compiler into one or more machine language instructions, which are copied to the object file and later executed.

Programs in Memory

Before examining each kind of executable statement in Figs. 2.1 and 2.4 in detail, let's see what computer memory looks like after a program is loaded into memory (but before it executes), and then again after that program executes. Figure 2.6(a) shows the metric conversion program and the space allocated for its variables in memory before execution. The question marks in memory cells size_in_sqmeters and size_in_sqyards indicate that these variables are undefined (value unknown) before program execution begins. During execution, the data value 2.0 is read into the variable size_in_sqyards. After the assignment statement

size_in_sqyards = meters_to_yards * size_in_sqmeters;

executes, the variables are defined as shown in Fig. 2.6(b). We introduce the assignment statement next. Our examples will be confined to the use of assignment statements with type float variables, since that is the data type used in the metric conversion problem.

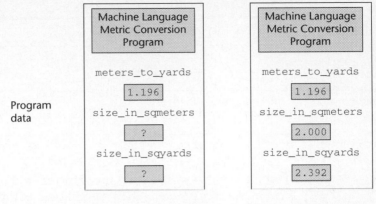

Program
data

(a) Memory before execution   (b) Memory after execution

Figure 2.6   Memory before and after execution of a program

Assignment Statements

The *assignment statement* is used in C++ to specify computations and to indicate where the results of these computations are to be stored. The assignment statement

```
size_in_sqyards = meters_to_yards * size_in_sqmeters;
```

in Fig. 2.1 assigns a value to the variable `size_in_sqyards`. In this case, `size_in_sqyards` is assigned the result of the multiplication (* means multiply) of the constant `meters_to_yards` by the variable `size_in_sqmeters`. This computation will produce a meaningful result only if meaningful information has been stored in both `meters_to_yards` and `size_in_sqmeters` before the assignment statement is executed. As shown in Fig. 2.7, only the variable on the left, `size_in_sqyards`, is affected by the assignment statement; the variables on the right side, `meters_to_yards` and `size_in_sqmeters`, retain their original values.

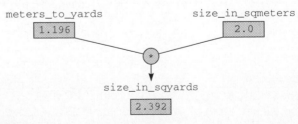

Figure 2.7   Effect of `size_in_sqyards = meters_to_yards • size_in_sqmeters;`

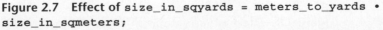

Table 2.3   Some Arithmetic Operators

ARITHMETIC OPERATOR	MEANING
+	Addition
–	Subtraction
*	Multiplication
/	Division
%	Modulus

The symbol = is the *assignment operator* in C++ and should be pronounced "becomes" or "gets" or "takes the value of" rather than "equals." The general form of the assignment statement is shown in the next display.

C++
SYNTAX

Assignment Statement (arithmetic)

Form: *result = expression;*

Example: x = y + z + 2.0;

Interpretation: The variable or object specified by *result* is assigned the value of *expression*. The previous value of *result* is destroyed. The *expression* may be a single variable or object, or a single constant, or it may involve variables and constants, and the arithmetic operators listed in Table 2.3. ∎

Example 2.2   In C++, you can write assignment statements of the form

```
sum = sum + item;
```

where the variable sum is used on both sides of the assignment operator. This is obviously not an algebraic equation, but it illustrates a common programming practice. This statement instructs the computer to add the value of item to the current value of the variable sum and store the result back into sum. The previous value of sum is destroyed in the process, as illustrated in Fig. 2.8; however, the value of item is unchanged. ∎

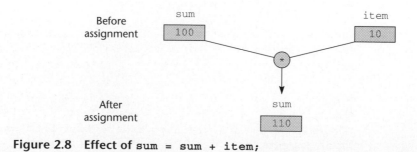

Figure 2.8   Effect of sum = sum + item;

Keep in mind that the assignment operator = may be applied to many other types of data, not just type `float`. The addition and multiplication operators, + and *, respectively, may also be applied to other data types—for example, type `int` data.

Input/Output Operations

Data can be stored in memory in two different ways: through assignment to a variable or object or through an input statement. We have already discussed the first method. The second method, using an input statement to read data into a variable, is necessary if you want the program to manipulate different data each time it executes. Reading data into memory is called an *input operation*.

As a program executes, it performs computations and assigns new values to variables and objects. These program results can be displayed to the program user by an *output operation*.

Among other things, the C++ libraries provide instructions for performing input and output. In this section, we will discuss how to use the input/output operations associated with the C++ stream objects `cin` and `cout` defined in the `iostream.h` library.

Program Input

The input statement

```
cin >> size_in_sqmeters;
```

in Fig. 2.1 indicates that the next data value entered by the program user is *extracted from* `cin` and *directed to* the input variable `size_in_sqmeters`. The *input operator* >> directs the input to be placed into `size_in_sqmeters`. Where do the data extracted from `cin` come from? C++ normally associates the input stream `cin` with the *standard input device* (usually the keyboard). Consequently, the previous statement causes the computer to extract a data value typed by the program user from the *keyboard input stream* and then to attempt to store this data in `size_in_sqmeters`. Because `size_in_sqmeters` is declared as type `float`, the input operation will proceed correctly only if the program user types in a number. The number should contain a decimal point, but the operation will work if an integer value, such as 16.0, is entered without the decimal point (as 16, for example). The program user should press the key labeled RETURN (or ENTER) after typing the value. The effect of this input statement is shown in Fig. 2.9. Any blanks preceding the number entered (2.0) will be ignored during the input operation. This is true for the input of type `int`, `float`, `char`, `bool`, and `string` values.

Figure 2.9 Effect of `cin >> size_in_sqmeters;`

The program in Fig. 2.4 reads a person's first two initials and last name. Each person using the program may have different initials and last name; therefore, the input statement

```
cin >> letter1 >> letter2 >> last_name;
```

causes data to be extracted from the input stream object `cin` and directed to each of the data stores (two variables and an object) listed. One character will be directed to each of the two variables of type `char`. Note that case is important for character data; the letters B and b are not the same. Again, the program user should press the RETURN key after typing in the name to be entered. Figure 2.10 shows the effect of this statement when the name `EBKoffman` is entered.

The number of characters extracted from `cin` by the operator `>>` depends on the type of the variable or object in which the data will be stored. Only one nonblank character is stored for a type `char` variable. For a type `float` or `int` variable, the program continues to read characters until it reaches a character that cannot be part of the number (usually indicated by entering a blank character or pressing the RETURN or ENTER key). This same rule applies to input of string values.

How do we know when to enter the input data and what data to enter? Your program should display a *prompting message* as a signal that informs the program user what data to enter and when. (Prompting messages are discussed in more detail in the next section.) Each character entered is *echoed* on the screen and is also processed by the input operator.

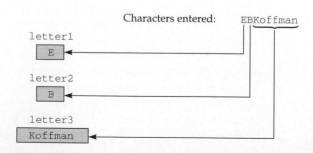

Figure 2.10 Effect of `cin >> letter1 >> letter2 >> last_name;`

C++
SYNTAX

The Input Operator >>

Form: >> *data-store* ;

Example: `cin >> age >> first_initial;`

Interpretation: The input operator >> (also called the *extraction operator*) causes data typed at the keyboard to be read into the indicated *data-store* (variable or object) during program execution. The program extracts one data item for each *data-store* specified. The input operator symbol, represented by the *special-character-pair* >>, precedes each *data-store*.

The order of the data must correspond to the order of the data stores in the input statement. You must insert one or more blank characters between numeric and string data items, and you may insert blanks between consecutive character data items and strings. The input operator >> skips any blanks that precede the data value to be read. This operator stops reading when a character (normally a blank) that cannot legally be a part of the value being read in is encountered. Press the RETURN key after entering all data items. Note that the >> operator must appear with no blanks (or other characters) in between.

Program Output

In order to see the results of a program execution, we must have some way of specifying what data values should be displayed. In Fig. 2.1, the output statement

```
cout << "The fabric size in square yards is "
     << size_in_sqyards << endl;
```

displays a line of program output containing two data elements: the string literal "The fabric ... is " and the type `float` value of `size_in_sqyards`. The string of characters inside the quotes are displayed, but the quotes are not. The *output operator* << (also called the *insertion operator*) causes the data on the right of each occurrence of the operator to be *inserted into* the output stream object `cout`. Thus, the previous output statement causes the line

```
The fabric size in square yards is 2.392
```

to be displayed. In Fig. 2.4, the line

```
cout << "Hello " << letter1 << ". " << letter2 << ". "
     << last_name << "!  ";
```

displays

```
Hello E. B. Koffman!
```

In this case, three values are printed between the strings `"Hello "` and `"!   "`. Finally, the lines

```
cout << "Enter the fabric size in square meters: ";
cout << "Enter first two initials and last name (no spaces): ";
```

in Figs. 2.1 and 2.4, respectively, display prompts or *prompting messages.* You should always display a prompting message just before an input statement to remind the program user to enter data. The prompt should always provide a description of the data to be entered, for example, `fabric size in square meters`, `account balance in dollars and cents`, or `three letter nickname`. Failure to precede each input statement with a prompt will leave the program user with no idea that the program is waiting for data or what data to enter when the input statement is executed.

Unless you specify otherwise, information displayed at your workstation using the output operator is shown on a single line. This is often desirable after a prompt, when you might wish to have the response to the prompt appear immediately following on the same line as the prompt (such as after `Enter the size in square meters: `). It is also sometimes desirable when you use more than one output statement to display a single line. This was done in the Hello Program, where two output statements were used to display the line

```
Hello E. B. Koffman! We hope you enjoy studying C++.
```

But there are also many times when we would like to explicitly indicate where one line ends and a new one starts. This is accomplished by inserting `<< endl` at the end of an output statement.

Example 2.3   Inserting Blank Lines

The statements

```
cout << "The fabric size in square yards is "
     << size_in_sqyards << endl << endl;
cout << "Metric conversion completed." << endl;
```

display the lines

```
The fabric size in square yards is 2.392

Metric conversion completed.
```

A blank line occurred because endl appeared twice in succession. Typing endl always causes the display to be advanced to the next line. If there is nothing between the two endls, a blank line appears in the program output. It is wise to get in the habit of inserting endl after your last cout statement to ensure that anything displayed on the screen immediately following your program run will appear beginning at the left margin on the next line. ∎

C++ SYNTAX

The Output Operator <<

Form: << *data-element;*

Example: cout << "My height in inches is " << height
                    << endl;

Interpretation: The *data-element* can be a variable, object, constant, or literal (such as a string or float literal). Each data-element must be preceded by the output operator. The output operator causes the value of the data-element that follows it to be displayed. Each value is displayed in the order in which it appears. An endl at the end of the output statement advances the display to the next line. A string is printed without the quotes.

If no endl appears, the display will not advance to the next line, even after completing the requested output. It will remain at the position just after the last character that was output.

The two cout lines

```
cout << "The fabric size in square yards is ";
cout << size_in_sqyards << endl;
```

display the same output as the single cout line

```
cout << "The fabric size in square yards is "
     << size_in_sqyards << endl;
```

It is generally more convenient to use the latter form.

EXERCISES FOR SECTION 2.5

Self-Check   1. Show the output displayed by the program lines below when the data entered are 5.0 and 7.0.

```
cout << "Enter two numbers: ";
cin >> a >> b;
```

```
a = a + 5.0;
b = 3.0 * b;
cout << "a = " << a << endl;
cout << "b = " << b << endl;
```

2. Show the contents of memory before and after the execution of the program lines shown in Self-Check Exercise 1.
3. Show the output displayed by the lines below.

```
cout << "My name is: ";
cout << "Doe, Jane" << endl;
cout << "I live in ";
cout << "Ann Arbor, MI ";
cout << "and my zip code is " << 48109 << endl;
```

Programming 1. Write the C++ instructions that first ask a user to type three integers and then read the three user responses into the variables first, second, and third.
2. Write a C++ statement that displays the value of x as indicated in the line below.

```
The value of x is _____
```

3. Write a program that will ask the user to enter the radius of a circle and will compute and display the circle's area and circumference. Use the formulas

$$area = \pi r^2$$
$$circumference = 2\pi r$$

where r is radius and π is the constant pi: 3.14159.

2.6 ——— ARITHMETIC ASSIGNMENT STATEMENTS AND EXPRESSIONS

Focus on Integer Arithmetic

We can use four of the arithmetic operators listed in Table 2.3 (+, −, *, /) and the assignment, input, and output operators with type int data as well as with data of type float. The *modulus* operator, %, may be used only with type int operands. Because these operands have no fractional part, some care must be exercised in the use of the division and modulus operators. For now, you need simply remember the descriptions of these operators given in the box on the next page.

Division and Modulus Operators with Integer Operands

- When used with two integer operands, the division operator always yields the *integral part* of the result of dividing its first operand by its second and truncates the fractional part. If either or both of the operands are negative, the sign of the remainder is implementation-dependent. As can be expected, division by zero is undefined.

$$15 \: / \: 3 = 5 \qquad\qquad 15 \: / \: 0 \text{ is undefined}$$
$$15 \: / \: 2 = 7 \qquad\qquad -19 \: / \: 5 = -3 \text{ or } -4$$
$$0 \: / \: 15 = 0$$

- The modulus operator must be used only with integer operands and always yields the *integer remainder* of the result of dividing its first operand by its second. If either one of the operands is negative, the sign of the result is machine-dependent. As with /, the result is undefined when the second operand of % is zero. For example,

$$7 \: \% \: 2 = 1 \qquad\qquad -5 \: \% \: 4 = +1 \text{ or } -1$$
$$299 \: \% \: 100 = 99 \qquad\qquad 15 \: \% \: -7 = +1 \text{ or } -1$$
$$49 \: \% \: 5 = 4 \qquad\qquad 15 \: \% \: 0 \text{ is undefined}$$

The magnitude of $m \: \% \: n$ must always be less than the divisor n; for example, if m is positive, the value of $m \: \% \: 100$ must be between 0 and 99. The formula

$$m = (m \: / \: n) * n + (m \: \% \: n)$$

defines the relationship between the operators / and % for a dividend of m and a divisor of n (not equal to zero). We can see that this formula holds for two of the examples discussed earlier by substituting values for m, n, $m \: / \: n$, and $m \: \% \: n$. In the first line below, m is 7 and n is 2; in the second line below, m is 299 and n is 100.

```
7 = (7 / 2) * 2 + (7 % 2) = 3 * 2 + 1 = 7
299 = (299 / 100) * 100 + (299 % 100) = 2 * 100 + 99 = 299
```

Example 2.4 The following examples illustrate some of the computations shown in the previous display, using long division. The top row shows that the remainder (1, 2, and -2) is lost when the / operator is used; the bottom row shows that the quotient (3, 2, and 9) is lost when the % operator is used.

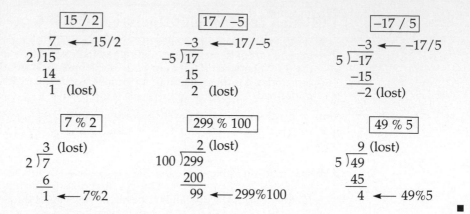

Example 2.5   If you have p people and b identical boats, the expression

```
p / b
```

tells you how many people to put in each boat. For example, if p is 18 and b is 4, then 4 people would go in each boat. The formula

```
p % b
```

tells you how many people would be left over (18 % 4 is 2).   ∎

Using Integer Data

The following case study provides an example of manipulating type int data in C++.

CASE STUDY: FINDING THE VALUE OF A COIN COLLECTION

Problem Statement

Your little sister, who has been saving nickels and pennies, is tired of lugging around her piggy bank when she goes shopping. She wants to exchange her coins at the bank, so she needs to know the value of her coins in dollars and cents.

Program Analysis

In order to solve this problem, we need a count of nickels and a count of pennies in the collection. From those counts, we determine the total value of coins in cents. With this figure, we can do an integer division using 100 as the divisor to get the dollar value; the remainder of this division will be the loose change that she should receive. In the data requirements table below, we list the total value in cents (`total_cents`) as a *program variable* because it is needed as part of the computation process but is not a required problem output.

DATA REQUIREMENTS

Problem Input

`name` (string)	— your sister's first name
`nickels` (int)	— the count of nickels
`pennies` (int)	— the count of pennies

Problem Output

`dollars` (int)	— the number of dollars she should receive
`change` (int)	— the loose change she should receive

Additional Program Variable

`total_cents` (int)	— the total number of cents

FORMULAS

one dollar equals 100 pennies
one nickel equals 5 pennies

Program Design

The algorithm is straightforward and is presented next.

INITIAL ALGORITHM

1. Prompt for your sister's last name.
2. Read in the count of nickels and pennies.
3. Compute the total value in cents.
4. Find the value in dollars and loose change.
5. Display the value in dollars and loose change.

Steps 3 and 4 require further refinement.

Step 3 Refinement

3.1. `total_cents` is 5 times `nickels` plus `pennies`.

Step 4 Refinement

    4.1. `dollars` is the integer quotient of `total_cents` and 100.
    4.2. `change` is the integer remainder of `total_cents` and 100.

Program Implementation

The program is shown in Fig. 2.11. The statement

```
total_cents = 5 * nickels + pennies;
```

implements algorithm step 3.1. The statements

```
dollars = total_cents / 100;
change = total_cents % 100;
```

use the `/` and `%` operators to implement algorithm steps 4.1 and 4.2, respectively.

Program Testing

To test this program, try running it with a combination of nickels and pennies that yields an exact dollar amount with no change left over. For example, 35 nickels and 25 pennies should yield a value of 2 dollars and no cents. Then increase and decrease the amount of pennies by 1 (26 and 24 pennies) to make sure that these cases are also handled properly. ∎

Type of an Expression Involving `int` and `float` Data

The data type of each data store must be specified in its declaration, but how does C++ determine the type of an expression? The data type of an expression depends on the type of its operands. For example, the expression

```
ace + bandage
```

is type `int` if both `ace` and `bandage` are type `int`; otherwise, it is type `float`. A C++ expression is type `int` only if all its operands are type `int`, and a C++ expression is type `float` if any of its operands are type `float`. For example, `5 / 2` is type `int`, but `5 / 2.0` is type `float`. The latter expression, containing an integer and a floating-point operand, is called a *mixed-type expression*. The type of a mixed-type expression involving integer and floating-point data must be `float`.

Figure 2.11   Value of a coin collection

```cpp
// FILE: Coins.cpp
// DETERMINES THE VALUE OF A COIN COLLECTION

#include <iostream.h>
#include <string>

void main ()
{
   // Local data ...
   string name;              // input: sister's first name
   int pennies;              // input: count of pennies
   int nickels;              // input: count of nickels
   int dollars;              // output: value of coins in dollars
   int change;               // output: value of coins in cents
   int total_cents;          // total cents represented

   // Prompt sister for name.
   cout << "Enter your first name and press return: ";
   cin >> name;

   // Read in the count of nickels and pennies.
   cout << "Enter the number of nickels and press return: ";
   cin >> nickels;
   cout << "Enter the number of pennies and press return: ";
   cin >> pennies;

   // Compute the total value in cents.
   total_cents = 5 * nickels + pennies;

   // Find the value in dollars and change.
   dollars = total_cents / 100;
   change = total_cents % 100;

   // Display the value in dollars and change.
   cout << "Good work " << name << '!' << endl;
   cout << "Your collection is worth " << dollars << " dollars and "
        << change << " cents." << endl;
}
```

───────────── Program Output ─────────────

```
Enter your first name and press return: Sally
Enter the number of nickels and press return: 30
Enter the number of pennies and press return: 77

Good work Sally!
Your collection is worth 2 dollars and 27 cents.
```

Expressions with Multiple Operators

In our programs so far, most expressions have involved a single operator; however, expressions with multiple operators are common in C++. To understand and write such expressions, we need to know the C++ rules for evaluating expressions. For example, in the expression 10 + 5 / 2, is + performed before /, or vice versa? Is the expression 10 / 5 * 2 evaluated as (10 / 5) * 2 or 10 / (5 * 2)? Verify for yourself that the order of evaluation does make a difference. In both these expressions, the / operator is evaluated first. The reasons for this are explained in the C++ rules for expression evaluation, which are based on familiar algebraic rules.

The C++ Rules for Expression Evaluation

a. All parenthesized subexpressions must be evaluated separately. Nested parenthesized subexpressions must be evaluated inside out, with the innermost subexpression evaluated first.

b. *The operator precedence rule:* Operators in the same subexpression are evaluated in the following order:

*, /, %	first
+, –	last

c. *The left associative rule:* Operators in the same subexpression and at the same precedence level (such as + and –) are evaluated left to right.

d. *Remember:* In an assignment statement, the entire expression to the right of the assignment operator is evaluated first before being assigned to the variable on the left.

Knowledge of these rules will help you understand how C++ evaluates expressions. Use parentheses as needed to specify the order of evaluation. Often, it is a good idea to use extra parentheses to document clearly the order of operator evaluation in complicated expressions. For example, the expression

```
x * y * z + a / b - c * d
```

can be written in a more readable form using parentheses:

```
(x * y * z) + (a / b) - (c * d)
```

Example 2.6   The formula for the area of a circle

$$a = \pi r^2$$

may be written in C++ as

```
area = pi * radius * radius;
```

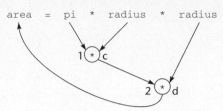

Figure 2.12   Evaluation tree for `area = pi * radius * radius;`

where `pi` is the constant 3.14159. Figure 2.12 shows the *evaluation tree* for this formula. In this tree, the lines connect each operand with its operator. The order of operator evaluation is shown by the number to the left of each operator, the rules that apply are shown to the right.   ∎

Example 2.7   The formula for the average velocity, *v*, of a particle traveling on a line between points p_1 and p_2 in time t_1 to t_2 is

$$v = \frac{p_2 - p_1}{t_2 - t_1}$$

This formula can be written and evaluated in C++ as shown in Fig. 2.13.   ∎

Example 2.8   Consider the expression

```
z - (a + b / 2) + w * y
```

containing integer variables only. The parenthesized subexpression `(a + b / 2)` is evaluated first (Rule a) beginning with `b / 2` (Rule b). Once the value of `b / 2` is determined, it can be added to `a` to obtain the value of `(a + b / 2)`. Next, the multiplication operation is performed (Rule b) and the value for `w * y` is determined. Then, the value of `(a + b / 2)` is subtracted from `z` (Rule c). Finally, this result is added to `w * y` (see Fig. 2.14).   ∎

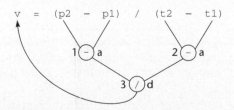

Figure 2.13   Evaluation tree for `v = (p2 - p1) / (t2 - t1);`

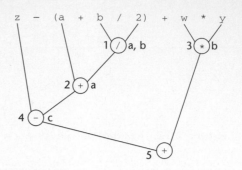

Figure 2.14   Evaluation tree for `z - (a + b / 2) + w * y;`

Mixed-Type Assignment Statement

When an assignment statement is executed, the expression is first evaluated and then the result is assigned to the data-store listed to the left of the assignment operator (=). C++ allows any mixture of type `float` or `int` in such an assignment expression. This kind of flexibility can be very useful, but it is also quite error-prone. Be careful that you say what you mean. All assignment statements below are valid, assuming that a, b, and x are type `float` and m and n are type `int`.

```
a = 10;     // the constant 10 (int) is converted to 10.0 (float)
            //    and then assigned to a
b = 5;      // 5 is converted to 5.0 and then assigned to b
m = 3.0;    // 3.0 is converted to 3 and then assigned to m
n = 2.5;    // 2.5 is converted to 2 and then assigned to n
x = m / n;  // the division result of 1 (type int) is converted
            //    to 1.0 and assigned to x
```

In the next to last statement above, the decimal portion of 2.5 is lost when it is assigned to the integer variable n. This may not always be desirable, and care must be taken because, according to C++, this is not an error. In the last statement, the expression m / n evaluates to the integer 1 because both operands, m = 3 and n = 2, are of type `int`. This value is converted to type `float` (1.0) before it is stored in x.

Example 2.9   The evaluation of multiple operator expressions containing both type `int` and `float` values can be quite tricky to follow, even though the principle of evaluation is quite simple—the final result is determined by examining the *intermediate results* of each operand-operator-operand subexpression, as shown in Fig. 2.15, with x = 5.5 (type `float`), k = 5 (type `int`), and m (type `int`).

First, k / 2 is evaluated (Rule b). Because both k and 2 are type `int`, the result is type `int` as well (k / 2 = 2). Next, x + 2 is evaluated. Because x

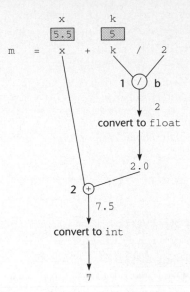

Figure 2.15 Evaluation tree for m = x + k / 2;

is type float. 2 is first converted to 2.0 so that the triple 5.5 + 2.0 is evaluated. The result 7.5 is then truncated to 7 before it is assigned to the type int variable m. ∎

Writing Mathematical Formulas In C++

You may encounter two problems when writing mathematical formulas in C++: The first concerns multiplication, which is often implied in a mathematical formula by writing the two multiplicands next to each other; for example, $a = bc$. In C++, however, you must always use the * operator to indicate multiplication, as in

```
a = b * c;
```

The other difficulty arises in formulas using division in which we normally write the numerator and denominator on separate lines:

$$m = \frac{y - b}{x - a}$$

In C++, however, all assignment statements must be written in a linear form. Consequently, parentheses are often needed to separate the numerator from the denominator and to clearly indicate the order of evaluation of the operators in the expression. The formula above would thus be written in C++ as

```
m = (y - b) / (x - a);
```

Example 2.10   This example illustrates how several mathematical formulas can be written in C++.

Mathematical Formula	C++ Expression
1. $b^2 - 4ac$	`b * b - 4 * a * c`
2. $a + b - c$	`a + b - c`
3. $\dfrac{a + b}{c + d}$	`(a + b) / (c + d)`
4. $\dfrac{1}{1 + y^2}$	`1 / (1 + y * y)`
5. $a \times -(b + c)$	`a * (-(b + c))` ∎

The points illustrated are summarized as follows:

- Always specify multiplication explicitly by using the operator * where needed (1, 4).
- Use parentheses when required to control the order of operator evaluation (3, 4).
- Avoid writing two arithmetic operators in succession; adjacent arithmetic operators should be separated by an operand or an open parenthesis (see formula 5). (This is not required in C++ but is suggested for the purpose of clarity.)

The fifth C++ expression in Example 2.10 involves the use of a unary minus to negate the value of (b + c) before performing the multiplication. The *unary minus* has only one operand, and it has a higher precedence than the subtraction operator.

EXERCISES FOR SECTION 2.6

Self-Check   1. Correct the syntax errors in the program below, and rewrite it so that it follows the style conventions used in the text. What does each statement of your corrected program do? What values are printed?

```
include iostream.h FLOAT x, y, z:
MAIN() {   y = 15.0,
z = y + 3.5;   y + z = x;
cout >> x; y; z; }
```

2. Evaluate the following expressions with 7 and 22 as operands:

   a. 22 / 7   7 / 22   22 % 7   7 % 22

   Repeat this exercise for the pairs of integers:

   b. 15, 16   c. 3, 23   d. −4, 16

3. Show that the formula $m = (m / n) * n + (m \% n)$ holds when $m = 45$ and $n = 5$ (both of type int).

4. Draw the evaluation trees for the expressions below.

   ```
   1.8 * celsius + 32.0
   (salary - 5000.00) * 0.20 + 1425.00
   ```

5. Given the declarations

   ```
   const float pi = 3.14159;
   const int max_i = 1000;
   float x, y;
   int a, b, i;
   ```

   indicate which C++ statements below are valid and find the value of each valid statement. Also, indicate which are invalid and why. Assume that a is 3, b is 4, and y is −1.0.

a. i = a % b;	b. i = (max_i - 990) / a;
c. i = a % y;	d. i = (990 - max_i) / a;
e. i = pi * a;	f. x = pi * y;
g. x - pi / y;	h. i = (max_i - 990) % a;
i. x = a % (a / b);	j. i = a % 0;
k. i = b / 0;	l. i = a % (max_i - 990);
m. x = a / y;	n. i = a % (990 - max_i);
o. x = a / b;	

6. What values are assigned by the legal statements in Exercise 5 above, assuming a is 5, b is 2, and y is 2.0?

7. Assume that you have the following variable declarations:

   ```
   int color, lime, straw, yellow, red, orange;
   float black, white, green, blue, purple, crayon;
   ```

   Evaluate each of the statements below given the values: color is 2, black is 2.5, crayon is −1.3, straw is 1, red is 3, and purple is 0.3e+1.

   a. white = color * 2.5 / purple;
   b. green = color / purple;
   c. orange = color / red;
   d. blue = (color + straw) / (crayon + 0.3);
   e. lime = red / color + red % color;
   f. purple = straw / red * color;

8. Let a, b, c, and x be the names of four type float variables, and let i, j, and k be the names of three type int variables. Each of the statements below contains a

violation of the rules for forming arithmetic expressions. Rewrite each statement so that it is consistent with these rules.

a. `x = 4.0 a * c;`   b. `a = ac;`
c. `i = 5j3;`   d. `k = 3(i + j);`
e. `x = 5a / bc;`

Programming   1. Write an assignment statement that might be used to implement the equation below in C++.

$$q = \frac{ka(t_1 - t_2)}{b}$$

2. Write a program that stores the values `'x'`, `'0'`, and `1.345e10` in separate variables. Your program should input the three values as data items.
3. Extend the program in Fig. 2.11 to handle dimes and quarters as well as nickels and pennies.

2.7 ———— CHARACTERS AND STRINGS— AN INTRODUCTION

Type `char` variables can be used to store any single character value. A type `char literal` must be enclosed in single quotes (for example, `'A'`); however, quotes should not be used when typing character data at a keyboard. When `cin` reads character data into a type `char` variable, the next nonblank character you enter at the keyboard is stored in that variable. Any blanks that you enter (by pressing the space bar) preceding this nonblank will be ignored. This is consistent with the mechanics for reading numeric values, when leading blanks (those that precede the number) are ignored.

Example 2.11   The program in Fig. 2.16 first reads and echoes three characters entered at the keyboard. Next, it prints them in reverse order enclosed in asterisks. Each character is stored in a variable of type `char`; the character value `'*'` is associated with the character constant `border`.
   The statement

```
cout << border << third << second << first << border << endl;
```

displays the three characters in reverse order. As shown in the program output, each character value takes up a single print position. Blanks between the letters are ignored (see Program Output 2).   ■

   In Fig. 2.16, the string `"Enter 3 characters: "` is displayed as a prompt. In this example and in other earlier examples, we have used strings enclosed in double quotes, `" "`, as prompts and to clarify program

Figure 2.16 Program for Example 2.11

```
// FILE: Mirror.cpp
// READS 3 CHARACTERS AND DISPLAYS THEM IN REVERSE ORDER

#include <iostream.h>

void main ()
{
    // Local data ...
    const char border = '*';        // encloses 3 characters
    char first, second, third;      // input/output: 3 characters

    cout << "Enter 3 characters: ";
    cin  >> first >> second >> third;
    cout << border << third << second << first << border << endl;
}
```

——————— Program Output 1 ———————

Enter 3 characters: **EBK**
KBE

——————— Program Output 2 ———————

Enter 3 characters: **D G   F**
FGD

output. Only single characters (enclosed in single quotes), not strings, can be stored in type char variables; we will see how to process strings in Section 3.7.

In addition to the characters that we are accustomed to seeing on the screen and keyboard, there are additional characters in the C++ character set. These characters, three of which are shown in Table 2.4, are represented using the *escape symbol* '\', the backslash character.

As shown in Table 2.4, the backslash, followed immediately by a particular letter, represents a single, nonprintable character. When written in a program output line, these characters cause a specific action to occur. Example 2.12 demonstrates the use of these characters in a slightly revised version of the Hello Program, which appeared in its original form in Fig. 2.4.

Table 2.4 Some Escape Sequences

CHARACTER	MEANING
\a	alert (bell)
\n	newline
\t	horizontal tab

Example 2.12   The Hello Program Revised

The output statement shown below is a slightly revised version of the statement in the Hello Program (see Fig. 2.4):

```
cout << "\tHello " << letter1 << letter2 << last_name
     << "!\n\a\a";
```

This line now causes the following things to happen:

- The character \t causes a tab to be placed in the output line before the string "Hello ".
- The two characters and the string just entered, EBKoffman, are displayed with an exclamation point at the end.
- The character \n causes the display to go to the next line.
- The two consecutive occurrences of \a cause two beeps to be heard.   ■

EXERCISES FOR SECTION 2.7

Self-Check   1. Indicate which of the following constants are legal in C++ and which are not. Identify the data type of each valid value.

```
15     'XYZ'    '*'     $     25.123    15.   -999     .123     'x'
"x"    '9'     '-5'    'x'   $4.79     6.3E-2         .0986E3.0
```

2.8 ——— INTERACTIVE MODE, BATCH MODE, AND DATA FILES

There are two basic modes of computer operation: interactive and batch. The programs we have written so far are intended to be run in *interactive mode*. In this mode, the program user can interact with the program and enter data while the program is executing. In batch mode, all data must be supplied beforehand and the program user cannot interact with the program while it is executing. Batch mode is an option on most computers.

If you use batch mode, you must prepare a batch data file before executing your program. On a timeshared or personal computer, a batch data file is created and saved in the same way as a program or source file.

Input Redirection

Figure 2.17 shows the metric conversion program rewritten as a batch program. We assume that the input is associated with a batch data file instead of the keyboard. In most systems this can be done relatively easily through

Figure 2.17 Batch version of metric conversion program

```
// FILE: Metbatch.cpp
// CONVERTS FABRIC MEASURES IN SQUARE METERS TO SQUARE YARDS

#include <iostream.h>

void main ()
{
    // Local data ...
    const float meters_to_yards = 1.196; // conversion constant
    float size_in_sqmeters; // input: fabric size in square meters
    float size_in_sqyards;  // output: fabric size in square yards

    // Read in fabric size in square meters.
    cin >> size_in_sqmeters;
    cout << "The fabric size in square meters is "
         << size_in_sqmeters << endl;

    // Convert the fabric size to square yards.
    size_in_sqyards = meters_to_yards * size_in_sqmeters;

    // Display the fabric size in square yards.
    cout << "The fabric size in square yards is "
         << size_in_sqyards << endl;
}
```

———————————— Program Output ————————————

```
The fabric size in square meters is 2
The fabric size in square yards is 2.392
```

input/output redirection using operating system commands. For example, in the UNIX and MS-DOS operating systems, you can instruct your program to take its input from file `mydata` instead of the keyboard, by placing the symbols

```
< mydata
```

at the end of the command line that causes your compiled and linked program to execute. If you normally used the UNIX or MS-DOS command line

```
metric
```

to execute this program, your new command line would be

```
metric < mydata
```

Echo Prints versus Prompts

In Fig. 2.17, the statement

```
cin >> size_in_sqmeters;
```

reads the value of `size_in_sqmeters` from the first (and only) line of the data file. Because the program input comes from a data file, there is no need to precede this statement with a prompt. Instead we follow the input statement with the statement

```
cout << "The fabric size in square meters is "
     << size_in_sqmeters << endl;
```

which *echo prints*, or displays, the value just read into `size_in_sqmeters`. This statement provides a record of the data to be manipulated by the program; without it, we would have no easy way of knowing what value was read. Whenever you convert an interactive program to a batch program, make sure you replace each prompt with an echo print that follows each input statement.   ■

Output Redirection

You can also redirect program output to a disk file instead of the screen. Then you could send the output file to the printer (using an operating system command) to obtain a printed version of the program output. In UNIX or MS-DOS, you would type

```
> myoutput
```

to redirect output from the screen to file `myoutput`. The command

```
metric > myoutput
```

executes the compiled and linked code for the metric conversion program, reading program input from the keyboard and writing program output to the file `myoutput`. However, it would be difficult to interact with the running program because all program output, including any prompts, are sent to the output file. It would be better to use the command

```
metric < mydata > myoutput
```

which reads program input from the data file `mydata` and sends program output to the output file `myoutput`.

EXERCISES FOR SECTION 2.8

Self-Check
1. Explain the difference in placement of cout statements used to display prompts and cout statements used to echo data. Which are used in interactive programs and which are used in batch programs?
2. How are input data provided to an interactive program? How are input data provided to a batch program?

Programming
1. Rewrite the program in Fig. 2.11 as a batch program. Assume data are read from the file mydata.

2.9 ——— COMMON PROGRAMMING ERRORS

Beginning programmers soon discover that a program rarely compiles, links, and executes correctly on the first try. Murphy's law, "If something can go wrong, it will," seems to have been written with the computer program in mind. In fact, errors are so common that they have their own special name—*bugs*—and the process of correcting them is called *debugging a program.* (According to computer folklore, the first hardware error was caused by a large insect found inside a computer component.) To alert you to potential problems, we will provide a section on common errors at the end of each chapter.

When the compiler detects an error, it displays an *error message* indicating you have made a mistake and what the likely cause of the error might be. Unfortunately, error messages are often difficult to interpret and are sometimes misleading. They also vary from compiler to compiler. As you gain some experience, you will become more proficient at understanding them. Our goal in the Common Programming Errors section of each chapter is to describe the most common kinds of errors that can occur and to suggest appropriate corrections for these errors.

Three kinds of errors—syntax errors, run-time errors, and logic errors—can occur. Each of these is discussed in the following sections.

Syntax Errors

A compilation, or *syntax error*, occurs when your code violates one or more of the grammar rules of C++. Such errors are detected and displayed by the compiler as it attempts to translate your program. If a statement has a syntax error, it cannot be completely translated, and your program will not execute.

Figure 2.18 shows a listing of the metric conversion program with errors introduced. A *compiler listing* is a listing of your program printed by the compiler during program translation. The listing shows each line of the source program preceded by a line number and any syntax errors detected by the

Figure 2.18 Compiler listing of a program with syntax errors

```
1 // FILE: Metric.cpp
2
3 // CONVERTS FABRIC MEASURES IN SQUARE METERS TO SQUARE YARDS
4
5 #include <iostream.h>            // necessary for cout and cin
6
7 void main ();
8 {
9    // Local data ...
10   const float meters_to_yards = 1.196;  // conversion constant
11   float size_in_sqmeters   input: fabric size in square meters
12
13   Read in fabric size in square meters.
14   cout << "Enter the fabric size in square meters: ;
15   cin  >> size_in_sqmeters;
16
17   // Convert the fabric size to square yards.
18   meters_to_yards * size_in_sqmeters = size_in_sqyards;
19
20   // Display the fabric size in square yards.
21   cout << "The fabric size in square yards is "
22        << size_in_sqyards << endl;
23 }
```

```
 8: Declaration was expected
12: , expected
12: Declaration missing ;
13: Expression syntax
13: Undefined symbol 'Read', Undefined symbol 'in', etc.
14: Unterminated string or character constant
14, 15, 18, 21: Type name expected
15: Expression syntax
18: Lvalue required
18, 22: Undefined symbol 'size_in_sqyards'
```

compiler. The error messages shown in Fig. 2.18 were generated separately, one for each error, but are grouped together in one listing for illustration purposes. The errors are summarized at the bottom of the compiler listing. The program contains the following syntax errors:

- Semicolon not expected after the main header (line 7)
- Missing semicolon after the variable declaration (line 11)
- Missing double slash preceding a comment (lines 11 and 13)
- Missing double quote at the end of a string (line 14)
- Missing declaration for variable `size_in_sqyards` (lines 18 and 22)
- Assignment statement with transposed variable and expression part (line 18)

The actual format of the listing and error messages produced by your compiler may differ from those shown in Fig. 2.18. In some systems, whenever an error is detected the compiler displays a list of errors in a separate message window (see Chapter 1, Fig. 1.11). Each line of this display contains the program file name and line number where the compiler detected a mistake, and a brief error message. Some systems also have a help feature that further explains the short message in greater detail. As you highlight a particular line in the message box, the corresponding line containing the error is highlighted simultaneously in your code. At times, a separate block cursor also is placed on the character where the compiler first detects the error.

To understand how this works, look at the first error in the program, which was detected when the opening brace { in line 8 was processed by the compiler. At this point, the compiler recognized that a semicolon was inserted (after the main header) and indicated this by printing the error message

```
Declaration was expected
```

In this case, both the error message and the indicated line number are misleading. Unfortunately, the compiler could not detect the error in line 7 until it started to process line 8. At this point, because of the extraneous semicolon, the compiler expected to find a declaration rather than a brace as it indicated with the error message.

There is also a missing semicolon after the declaration in line 11; however, this time the compiler prints several error messages

```
, expected
Declaration missing ;
Expression syntax
Undefined symbol
```

Since line 11 was not properly terminated, the compiler continues to look for another `float` type variable after `size_in_sqmeters`. Because it does not expect or recognize any of the symbols that follow on this line or the next one, it continues to display additional error messages. At least some of these messages could have been eliminated had the comment symbol // been used as required in lines 11 and 13.

The transposed assignment statement in line 18 causes the error

```
Lvalue required
```

to be displayed; the compiler is looking for only one variable on the left side of the assignment operator and detects an error when it reaches this operator.

An undefined symbol error occurs if the compiler cannot find the declaration for an identifier referenced in the program body. This can happen because the programmer forgot the declaration or misspelled the name of the identifier. In Fig. 2.18, omitting the declaration for variable `size_in_sqyards` in line 12 causes the display of the error message

```
Undefined symbol
```

in lines 18 and 22.

One syntax error often leads to the generation of multiple error messages. For example, forgetting to declare variable `size_in_sqyards` will cause an error message to be printed each time `size_in_sqyards` is used in the program. Then again, some C++ compilers will display the error only once and state that such errors will not be repeated. For this reason, it is often a good idea initially to concentrate on correcting the errors in the declaration part of a program and then recompile rather than attempt to fix all the errors at once. Many later errors will disappear once the earlier ones are corrected.

Syntax errors are often caused by the improper use of double quote marks with strings, or the accidental use of single quotes rather than double quotes. Make sure that you always use double quotes to begin and end a string. Single quotes are used only in writing single-character constants (such as `'c'` or `'\n'`); they cannot be used with strings. A string should begin and end on the same line.

Another common syntax error involves the omission of one of the double quote marks when writing a string of characters. If the quote mark at the end is missing (as in line 14, Fig. 2.18), the compiler will assume that whatever follows is part of the character string, rather than part of your executable statements. It will continue with this assumption until another double quote is found or the end of your program is encountered.

If the opening `/*` is missing in a comment, or if you forget to precede a comment with `//`, the compiler will not recognize the beginning of the comment and will attempt to process it as a C++ statement (for example, line 13, Fig. 2.18). This should cause a syntax error (or a number of syntax errors). If the closing `*/` in a `/* ... */` comment is missing, the comment will simply be extended to include the program statements that follow it. If the comment is not terminated, the rest of the program will be considered a comment, and a syntax error, such as

```
Unexpected end of file in Comment
Compound statement missing }
```

will be printed.

Run-Time Errors

There are two types of *run-time errors*: those that are detected by the C++ *run-time system* and those that allow your program to run to completion but give incorrect results.

A run-time error can occur as a result of the user directing the computer to perform an illegal operation, such as dividing a number by zero or manipulating undefined or invalid data. When this type of run-time error occurs, the computer will stop executing your program and a diagnostic message, such as

```
Divide error, line number nnn
```

may be printed.

If you attempt to manipulate undefined or invalid data, your output may contain strange results. *Arithmetic overflow* can occur when a program attempts to store a number that is larger than the maximum size that can be accommodated by your computer.

The program in Fig. 2.19 compiles successfully but contains no statement assigning a value to variable x before the assignment statement

```
z = x + y;
```

executes, causing a run-time error. Some compilers may give you a warning message but will still compile your program and allow you to run it.

Figure 2.19 A program with a run-time error

```
1   // FILE: Test.cpp
2   // PROGRAM TO TEST RUN-TIME ERRORS
3
4   #include <iostream.h>
5
6   void main ()
7   {
8       // Local data ...
9       float x, y, z;
10
11      y = 5.0;
12      z = x + y;
13      cout << "x = " << x << endl << "y = " << y << endl
14           << "z = " << z << endl;
15  }
```
─────────── Program Output ───────────
```
x = 6.111804e-09
y = 5.0
z = 5.0
```

However, the program will produce incorrect results. In this case, because we did not assign a specific value to x, it will contain an unpredictable value and the result of the addition will be unpredictable. Many compilers initialize variables to zero automatically, making it more difficult to detect the omission when your program is transferred to another compiler that does not. Therefore, it is essential that you hand-check your results to make sure that your program does what you intend.

Data entry errors are common run-time errors caused by reading the wrong data into an input variable or object. Sometimes data of the wrong type are read into a data store, and other times the wrong data value may be read.

Logic Errors

Logic errors occur when a program follows a faulty algorithm. Because logic errors usually do not cause run-time errors and do not display error messages, they are the most difficult to detect because the program appears to run without mishap. The only sign of a logic error may be incorrect program output. The statement

```
size_in_sqmeters = meters_to_yards * size_in_sqyards;
```

is a perfectly legal C++ statement, but it does not perform the computation specified by the metric conversion problem. The compiler cannot know what you really meant to compute. It simply translates what you give it.

You can detect logic errors by testing the program thoroughly, comparing its output to calculated results. You can prevent logic errors by carefully desk-checking the algorithm and then the program before you type it in.

Because debugging a program can be very time-consuming, plan your program solutions carefully and desk-check them to eliminate bugs early. If you are unsure of the syntax for a particular statement, look it up in the text. You may find it to be particularly frustrating as you begin learning to use C++. Providing meaningful compiler diagnostics for any programming language is a challenge. But for a powerful and somewhat complicated language, such as C++, this is even more so the case. Sometimes, even the simplest of errors will produce a number of seemingly incomprehensible diagnostics, some containing terminology beyond the scope of this book.

As you gain more familiarity with the language and the C++ diagnostics, you will notice considerable improvement in your ability to understand what you may have done to cause these messages. If all else fails, ask someone for help. The computer is a wonderful tool for many things.

However, when you need help, there is no substitute for knowing the people who can assist you. Get to know the right people, and learn to ask questions.

CHAPTER REVIEW

This chapter began with an illustration of the use of the software development method in solving problems with the computer. Four major steps in the problem solving process were emphasized: (1) problem analysis, (2) program design, (3) program implementation, and (4) program testing. The importance of checking your design and desk-checking your algorithm and program as the process progressed was also stressed.

We focused considerable attention on the importance of identifying and modeling entities in the problem domain that needed to be manipulated as part of a problem solution. Abstraction in software design, algorithm construction, and data modeling was a key idea throughout this discussion. The end product of our illustration was a short but complete C++ program.

We introduced some additional sample C++ programs and discussed in detail each C++ feature used in these programs. We illustrated how to use the C++ programming language to instruct the computer to perform some fundamental operations: to read information into memory, to perform some simple computations, and to print the results of the computation. All of this was done using symbols (punctuators, variable names, and operators, such as +, -, ^, and /) that are familiar, easy to remember, and easy to use.

As part of this discussion, we returned once again to the concept of data abstraction and its importance in programming. The predefined types `float`, `int`, `char`, and `bool` were introduced, and the use of the arithmetic operators on `int` and `float` data was described. Two user-defined data types, `string` (for modeling strings of characters) and `stream` (for modeling input and output data) were also introduced. Variables (representing data stores for predefined type information) and objects (representing data stores for system-defined and user-defined data types) were introduced and their differences noted.

In the remainder of this book, you will learn more about abstraction and programming and about many more features of the C++ language along with rules for using these features. You must remember throughout that, unlike the rules of English, the rules of C++ are precise and allow no exceptions. The compiler will be unable to translate C++ instructions that violate these rules. Remember to declare every identifier used as a constant or variable and to terminate program statements with semicolons.

Table 2.5   Summary of New C++ Constructs

CONSTRUCT	EFFECT
Compiler Directive `#include <iostream.h>`	A compiler directive that causes the contents of file `iostream.h` to be placed in the program where the directive appears.

Constant Declaration
`const float tax = 25.00;`
`const char star = '*';`
	Associates the constant identifier `tax` with the floating-point constant `25.00` and the constant identifier `star` with the character constant `'*'`.

Variable Declaration
`float x, y, z;`
`int me, it;`
	Allocates memory cells named `x`, `y`, and `z` for storage of floating-point numbers and cells named `me` and `it` for storage of integers.

Assignment Statement `distance = speed * time;`	Assigns the product of `speed` and `time` as the value of `distance`.
`cin` *Statement* `cin >> hours >> rate;`	Enters data into the variables `hours` and `rate`.
`cout` *Statement* `cout << "Net = " << net << endl;`	Displays the string `"Net = "` followed by the value of `net`. `endl` advances the output to the left margin of a new line after this information is displayed.

Table 2.5 describes the new C++ constructs introduced in this chapter.

✔ QUICK-CHECK EXERCISES

1. What value is assigned to x by the following statement?

   `x = 25.0 * 3.0 / 2.5;`

2. What value is assigned to x by the statement below assuming x is 10.0?

   `x = x - 20.0;`

3. Show the form of the output line displayed by the following `cout` lines when `total` is 352.74.

```
cout << "The final total is: " << endl << endl;
cout << "$" << total << endl;
```

4. Show the form of the output line displayed by the following `cout` line when `total` is 352.74.

```
cout << "The final total is $" << total << endl;
```

5. Indicate which type of data you use to represent the following items: number of children at school; a letter grade on an exam; your full name; the average numeric score of all students who took the last computer science exam.
6. In which step of the software development method are the problem input and output data identified?
7. In reading two integers using the input operator >>, what character should be entered following the first value? What should be entered after the second number?
8. When reading two characters using the input operator >>, does it matter how many blanks (if any) appear
   a. before the first character?
   b. between the first and second characters?
   c. after the second character?
9. How does the compiler determine how many and what type of data values are to be entered when an input statement is executed?
10. What is the syntactic purpose of the semicolon in a C++ program?
11. Does the compiler listing show syntax or run-time errors?

Answers to Quick-Check Exercises

1. 30.0
2. −10.0
3. The final total is:

   $352.74

4. The final total is $352.74
5. `int`, `char`, `string`, `float`
6. problem analysis
7. a blank, RETURN key
8. For (a) and (b), the number of blanks is irrelevant; any number is allowed, even none, since the input operator skips all leading blanks and stops reading after the first nonblank is read. For (c), there is no need for any blanks; press RETURN key after the entering the second character.
9. The number of values to be entered depends on the number of variables in the input list.
10. It terminates a C++ statement.
11. syntax errors

REVIEW QUESTIONS

1. What type of information should be specified in the program header section comments?

2. Place a checkmark next to those variables below that are syntactically correct.

income ____	two fold ____	hours*rate ____	myprogram ____
1time ____	C3PO ____	read_line ____	program ____
const ____	income#1 ____	main ____	MAIN ____
Tom's ____	item ____	variable ____	pi ____

3. What is illegal about the following declarations and assignment statement?

   ```
   const float pi = 3.14159;
   float c, r;


   pi = c / (2 * r * r);
   ```

4. What do the following statements do?
   a. `float cell;`
   b. `string name;`
   c. `const year = 1996;`

5. List and define the rules of order of evaluation for arithmetic expressions.

6. Write the data requirements, necessary formulas, and algorithm for Programming Project 6.

7. If the average size of a family is 2.8 and this value is stored in the variable `family_size`, provide the C++ statement to display this fact in a readable way (leave the display on the same line).

8. List three basic data types of C++.

9. Convert the program statements below to read and echo data in batch mode.

   ```
   cout << "Enter three numbers separated by spaces: " << endl;
   cin >> x >> y >> z;
   cout << "Enter two characters: ";
   cin >> ch1 >> ch2;
   ```

10. Write an algorithm that allows for the input of an integer value, doubles it, subtracts 10, and displays the result.

11. Assuming a and b are type int variables, what are the types of the results of the following expressions:

    a. `a / b`   b. `a % b`   c. `a * b`   d. `a + b`

12. Assuming A and B are type int variables, which of the following expressions evaluate to the same value?

    a. `a + b * c`   b. `(a + b) * c`   c. `a + (b * c)`

13. Differentiate among syntax errors, run-time errors, and logic errors.

PROGRAMMING PROJECTS

1. Write a program to convert a temperature in degrees Fahrenheit to degrees Celsius.

    DATA REQUIREMENTS

    Problem Input

    `fahrenheit (int)` — temperature in degrees Fahrenheit

    Problem Output

    `celsius (float)` — temperature in degrees Celsius

    FORMULA

    $celsius = (5/9) * (fahrenheit - 32)$

2. Write a program to read two data items and print their sum, difference, product, and quotient.

    DATA REQUIREMENTS

    Problem Input

    `x, y (int)`   — two items

    Problem Output

    `sum (int)`   — sum of x and y
    `difference (int)`   — difference of x and y
    `product (int)`   — product of x and y
    `quotient (float)`   — quotient of x divided by y

3. Write a program to read in the weight (in pounds) of an object, and compute and print its weight in kilograms and grams. (*Hint:* One pound is equal to 0.453592 kilograms or 453.59237 grams.)

4. Write a program that prints your first initial as a block letter. (*Hint:* Use a 6 × 6 grid for the letter and print six strings. Each string should consist of asterisks (*) interspersed with blanks.)

5. Write a program that reads in the length and width of a rectangular yard and the length and width of a rectangular house situated in the yard. Your program should compute the time required to cut the grass at the rate of 2 square meters per second.

6. Write a program that reads in the numerators and denominators of two fractions. The program should print the product of the two fractions as a fraction and as a percent.

7. Write a program that reads the number of years ago that a dinosaur lived and then computes the equivalent number of months, days, and seconds ago. Use 365.25 days per year. Test your program with a triceratops that lived 145 million years ago and a brontosaurus that lived 182 million years ago.

8. Arnie likes to jog in the morning. As he jogs, he counts the number of strides he makes during the first minute and then again during the last minute of his jogging. Arnie then averages these two and calls this average the number of strides he

makes in a minute when he jogs. Write a program that accepts this average and the total time Arnie spends jogging in hours and minutes and then displays the distance Arnie has jogged in miles. Assume Arnie's stride is 2.5 feet. There are 5280 feet in a mile.

9. Write a program that reads a number of seconds between 0 and 18,000 (5 hours) and displays the hours, minutes, and seconds equivalent.

10. Redo Programming Project 6, only this time, compute the sum of the two fractions.

11. The Pythagorean theorem states that the sum of the squares of the sides of a right triangle is equal to the square of the hypotenuse. For example, if two sides of a right triangle have lengths 3 and 4, then the hypotenuse must have a length of 5. The integers 3, 4, and 5 together form a Pythagorean triple. There is an infinite number of such triples. Given two positive integers, m and n, where $m > n$, a Pythagorean triple can be generated by the following formulas:

$$side1 = m^2 - n^2$$
$$side2 = 2mn$$
$$hypotenuse = \sqrt{side1^2 + side2^2}$$

Write a program that reads in values for m and n and prints the values of the Pythagorean triple generated by the formulas above.

3 Top-Down Design with Functions and Classes

Programmers who use the software development method to solve problems seldom tackle each new program as a unique event. Information contained in the problem statement and amassed during the analysis and design phases helps programmers plan and complete the finished program. Programmers also use segments of earlier program solutions as building blocks to construct new programs.

In the first section of this chapter, we demonstrate how programmers can tap existing information and code in the form of predefined functions to write programs. In addition to using existing information, programmers can use top-down design techniques to simplify the development of algorithms and the structure of the resulting programs. To apply top-down design, the programmer starts with the broadest statement of the problem solution and works down to more detailed subproblems.

We also introduce the structure chart that documents the subordinate relationships among subproblems. We illustrate the use of procedural abstraction to develop modular programs using separate functions to implement each subproblem solution. Finally, we continue our discussion of data abstraction and provide further detail on classes `string` and `money` and their member functions.

3.1 —— BUILDING PROGRAMS FROM EXISTING INFORMATION

Programmers seldom start off with a blank slate (or empty screen) when they develop a program. Often some—or all—of the solution can be developed from information that already exists or from the solution to another problem, as we demonstrate for the metric conversion program.

Carefully following the software development method generates important system documentation before program coding begins. Such documentation, consisting of a description of a problem's data requirements (developed during the analysis phase) and its solution algorithm (developed during the design phase), summarizes intentions and thought processes of the programmer.

You can use this documentation as a starting point in coding your program. For example, first edit the problem data requirements below to conform to the C++ syntax for constant and variable declarations (Fig. 3.1).

Problem Constant

```
meters_to_yards = 1.196            — conversion constant
```

Problem Input

```
size_in_sqmeters (float)           — fabric size in square meters
```

Figure 3.1   Declarations after editing

```
// FILE: Metric.cpp
// CONVERTS FABRIC MEASURES IN SQUARE METERS TO SQUARE YARDS
//     DECLARATIONS ...

void main()
{
   // Local data ...
   const float meters_to_yards = 1.196;      // conversion constant

   float size_in_sqmeters; // input: fabric size in square meters
   float size_in_sqyards;  // output: fabric size in square yards
}
```

Problem Output

```
size_in_sqyards (float)          — fabric size in square yards
```

This approach is especially helpful if the documentation was created with a word processor and is in a file that you can edit.

To develop the executable statements, write the initial algorithm and its refinements as program comments. The comments describe each algorithm step and provide program documentation that guides your C++ code. Figure 3.2 shows how the program will look at this point. After the comments are in place in the program body, you can begin to write the C++ statements. Place the C++ code for an unrefined step directly under that step. For a step that is refined, edit the refinement to change it from English to C++ (Fig. 3.3). We illustrate this entire process in the next case study.

Figure 3.2   Using refined algorithm as program framework

```
// FILE: Metric.cpp
// CONVERTS FABRIC MEASURES IN SQUARE METERS TO SQUARE YARDS.
//     ANALYSIS STAGE ...

void main()
{
   // Local data ...
   const float meters_to_yards = 1.196; // conversion constant

   float size_in_sqmeters; // input: fabric size in square meters
   float size_in_sqyards;  // output: fabric size in square yards


   // 1. Read the fabric size in square meters.
   // 2. Convert the fabric size to square yards.
   //    2.1   The fabric size in square yards is 1.196 times the
   //          fabric size in square meters.
   // 3. Display the fabric size in square yards.
}
```

Figure 3.3   Final edited program

```
// FILE: Metric.cpp
// CONVERTS FABRIC MEASURES IN SQUARE METERS TO SQUARE YARDS
#include <iostream.h>

void main ()
{
   // Local data ...
   const float meters_to_yards = 1.196; // conversion constant

   float size_in_sqmeters;    // input: fabric size in square meters
   float size_in_sqyards;     // output: fabric size in square yards

   // Read the fabric size in square meters.
   cout << "Enter the fabric size in square meters: ";
   cin  >> size_in_sqmeters;

   // Convert the fabric size to square yards.
   size_in_sqyards = meters_to_yards * size_in_sqmeters;

   // Display the fabric size in square yards.
   cout << "The fabric size in square yards is "
        << size_in_sqyards << endl;
}
```

CASE STUDY: FINDING THE AREA AND CIRCUMFERENCE OF A CIRCLE

Problem Statement

Given the radius of a circle, compute and print its area and its circumference.

Problem Analysis

The problem input is the circle radius. Two output values are requested: the circle's area and circumference. These data should be represented as type float because each element may contain a fractional part. The geometric relationship between a circle's radius and its area and circumference are listed next along with the data requirement.

DATA REQUIREMENTS

> *Problem Constant*
>
> pi = 3.14159
>
> *Problem Input*
>
> radius (float)   — radius of a circle

Problem Output

area (float)	— area of a circle
circum (float)	— circumference of a circle

FORMULAS

area of a circle = π * radius^2
circumference of a circle = 2π * radius

Program Design

After identifying the problem inputs and outputs, list the steps necessary to solve the problem. Pay close attention to the order of the steps. The initial algorithm follows.

INITIAL ALGORITHM

1. Read radius of circle.
2. Compute area of circle.
3. Compute circumference of circle.
4. Display area and circumference.

ALGORITHM REFINEMENTS

Next, refine any steps that do not have an obvious solution (steps 2 and 3).

Step 2 Refinement

2.1. Assign pi * radius * radius to area.

Step 3 Refinement

3.1. Assign 2 * pi * radius to circum.

Program Implementation

Figure 3.4 shows the C++ program so far. Function main consists of the initial algorithm with its refinements.

To write the final program, convert the refinements (steps 2.1 and 3.1) to C++, write C++ code for the unrefined steps (steps 1 and 4), and delete the step numbers from the comments. Figure 3.5 shows the final program.

Figure 3.4   Outline of area and circumference program

```
// FILE: Circle.cpp
// COMPUTES AND PRINTS THE AREA AND CIRCUMFERENCE OF A CIRCLE
//     ANALYSIS STAGE ...

void main ()
{
```

(continued)

Figure 3.4   *(continued)*

```
      // Local data ...
      const float pi = 3.14159;

      float radius;              // input: radius of circle
      float area;                // output: area of circle
      float circum;              // output: circumference of circle

      // 1. Read radius of circle.
      // 2. Compute area of circle.
      //    2.1 Assign pi * radius * radius to area.
      // 3. Compute circumference of circle.
      //    3.1 Assign 2 * pi * radius to circum.
      // 4. Display area and circumference.
}
```

Figure 3.5   Finding the area and circumference of a circle

```
// FILE: Circle.cpp
// COMPUTES AND PRINTS THE AREA AND CIRCUMFERENCE OF A CIRCLE

#include <iostream.h>

void main ()
{
      // Local data ...
      const float pi = 3.14159;

      float radius;              // input: radius of circle
      float area;                // output: area of circle
      float circum;              // output: circumference of circle

      // Read radius of circle.
      cout << "Enter the circle radius: ";
      cin >> radius;

      // Compute area of circle.
      area = pi * radius * radius;

      // Compute circumference of circle.
      circum = 2 * pi * radius;

      // Display area and circumference.
      cout << "The area of the circle is " << area << endl;
      cout << "The circumference of the circle is " << circum << endl;
}
```

──────────── Program Output ────────────

```
Enter the circle radius: 5.0
The area of the circle is 78.539749
The circumference of the circle is 31.415901
```

Program Testing

The program output in Fig. 3.5 provides a good test of the solution because it is relatively easy to compute by hand the area and circumference for a radius value of 5.0. The radius squared is 25.0, so the value of the area is correct. The circumference should be ten times π, which is also an easy number to compute by hand.

EXERCISES FOR SECTION 3.1

Self-Check

1. For a Simple Payroll Problem, describe the problem input and output and algorithm for computing an employee's gross salary given the hours worked and hourly rate.
2. Write a program outline from the algorithm you developed in Exercise 1. Use Fig. 3.4 as a model for your outline.

Programming

1. Add refinements to the program outline shown below and write the final C++ program.

```
// COMPUTES AND PRINTS THE SUM AND AVERAGE OF TWO NUMBERS
//     ANALYSIS STAGE ...
void main()
{
    // Local data ...
    // Any local constants and variables you need will go here.

    // 1. Read two numbers.
    // 2. Compute the sum of the two numbers.
    // 3. Compute the average of the two numbers.
    // 4. Display sum and average.
}
```

2. Write a complete C++ program for Self-Check Exercise 1.

3.2 ___ FUNCTIONS AS PROGRAM BUILDING BLOCKS: C++ LIBRARIES

A primary goal of structured programming is to write error-free code. One way to accomplish this is to reuse whenever possible code that has already been written and tested. This feature is call *reusability*. Stated more simply, this means that we do not have to reinvent the wheel for each new project.

One of the nice things about C++ and most other high-level languages is that they provide access to a large collection of previously written and tested functions and other program components, ready to be used in your work. In C++, these functions are organized in *libraries*, a few of which are described in Table 3.1.

Table 3.1   Summary of Libraries Accessible in Your C++ System

LIBRARY NAME	DESCRIPTION
assert	Provides facilities for adding assertions about the expected behavior of a program and for generating diagnostics if these assertions fail.
ctype	Contains functions for case conversion and for testing characters (for example, checking for uppercase or lowercase letters or for special characters or blanks).
float	Contains definitions of various type `float` and `double` limits for your computer system (for example, the maximum integer n such that 10^n is representable in your computer).
iostream	The library containing operations (such as << and >>) for performing stream input/output.
limits	Contains definitions of various type integer and character limits for your computer system (for example, the largest and smallest integers that can be stored and manipulated).
math	Contains mathematical functions such as square root and trigonometric, logarithmic, and exponentiation functions.
stdlib	Contains functions for number conversion (such as `atoi`), memory allocation (`free`), sorting (`qsort`), searching (`bsearch`), random-number generation (`rand`, `srand`), and program termination (`exit`).
string	Contains the string manipulation functions. Included are functions for comparing, concatenating, and copying strings, and for testing strings for the presence of specific characters or substrings.
time	Contains functions for manipulating date and time.

As we progress through the book, we will introduce functions in several C++ libraries listed in this table. Also, Appendix C will present a more complete description of C++ libraries and the functions that are in them. You can also refer to other reference material for your version of C++.

Mathematical Functions in Library `math`

In this section, we introduce some of the functions in the `math` library which can be used to perform mathematical computations (see Table 3.2). Some of these functions may be familiar from earlier courses in mathematics (`sqrt`, `cos`, `sin`, `asin`, `log`, `log10`), but some will be new (`fabs`, `floor`, `ceil`).

Table 3.2 Some Mathematical Functions in the `math` Library

FUNCTION	PURPOSE
acos (x)	Inverse cosine—returns the angle y in radians satisfying $x = \cos(y)$. $-1 \le x \le 1$; $0 \le y \le \pi$
asin (x)	Inverse sine—returns the angle y in radians satisfying $x = \sin(y)$. $-1 \le x \le 1$; $-\pi/2 \le y \le \pi/2$
atan (x)	Inverse tangent—returns the angle y in radians satisfying $x = \tan(y)$. $-\pi/2 \le y \le \pi/2$
ceil (x)	Smallest integer not less than x.
cos (x) sin (x) tan (x)	Cosine, sine, and tangent of x, respectively. Result is returned in radians.
exp (x)	e^x, where $e = 2.71823$
fabs (x)	Absolute value, $\lvert x \rvert$
floor (x)	Largest integer not greater than x.
log (x)	$\ln(x)$—the natural log of x (base e) for $x > 0$.
log10 (x)	$\log_{10}(x)$—base 10 log of x for $x > 0$.
pow (x, y)	x^y. An error will occur if $x = 0$ and $y \le 0$, or $x < 0$ and y is not an integer.
sqrt (x)	The positive square root of x, $\sqrt{x}$. $x \ge 0$.

Consider the function `sqrt`, which performs the square root computation. The expression part of the assignment statement,

```
y = sqrt (x);
```

Function name   *Function argument*

activates the code for function `sqrt`, passing the *argument* x to the function. A function is activated by a *function call* or *function reference* (`sqrt (x)`). After the function executes, the function result is substituted for the function reference in the expression and is assigned to the variable y. If x is 16.0 (`sqrt` takes a type `float` argument), the assignment statement is evaluated as follows:

1. x is 16.0, so function `sqrt` computes the square root of 16.0, or 4.0.
2. The function result 4.0 is assigned to y.

A function can be thought of as a "black box" that is passed one or more input values and automatically returns a single output value. Figure 3.6 illustrates

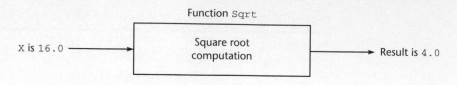

Figure 3.6   Function **sqrt** as a "black box"

this for the call to function sqrt. The value of x (16.0) is the function input, and the function result, or output, is the square root of 16.0 (result is 4.0).

As another example, if w is 9.0, C++ evaluates the assignment statement

```
z = 5.7 + sqrt (w);
```

as follows:

1. w is 9.0, so function sqrt computes the square root of 9.0, or 3.0.
2. The values 5.7 and 3.0 are added together.
3. The sum, 8.7, is stored in z.

Example 3.1   The program in Fig. 3.7 displays the square root of two numbers provided as input data (first and second) and the square root of their sum. To do so, we must call the function sqrt three times:

```
answer = sqrt (first);
answer = sqrt (second);
answer = sqrt (first + second);
```

All arguments must be nonnegative or the function will not work correctly (see Programming Exercise 2 at the end of this section).

For the first two calls, the function arguments are variables (first and second). The third call shows that a function argument can also be an expression (first + second). For all three calls, the result returned by function sqrt is assigned to variable answer. Notice that you must insert the statement

```
#include <math.h>                    // sqrt function
```

before the main function.

Figure 3.7   Illustration of the use of the C++ sqrt function

```
// FILE: SqreRoot.cpp
// PERFORMS THREE SQUARE ROOT COMPUTATIONS

#include <iostream.h>        // i/o functions
#include <math.h>            // sqrt function
```

(continued)

Figure 3.7 *(continued)*

```
void main ()
{
    // Local data ...
    float first;              // input:  one of two data values
    float second;             // input:  second of two data values
    float answer;             // output: a square root value

    // Get first number and display its square root.
    cout << "Enter the first number: ";
    cin >> first;
    answer = sqrt (first);
    cout << "The square root of the first number is " << answer
         << endl;

    // Get second number and display its square root.
    cout << "Enter the second number: ";
    cin  >> second;
    answer = sqrt (second);
    cout << "The square root of the second number is " << answer
         << endl;

    // Display the square root of the sum of first and second.
    answer = sqrt (first + second);
    cout << "The square root of the sum of both numbers is "
         << answer << endl;
}
```

————————— Program Output —————————

```
Enter the first number: 9
The square root of the first number is 3
Enter the second number: 16
The square root of the second number is 4
The square root of the sum of both numbers is 5
```

∎

Example 3.2   *Roots of Quadratic Equations.* We can use the C++ functions sqrt and pow to compute the roots of a quadratic equation in *x* of the form

$$ax^2 + bx + c = 0.$$

These two roots are defined as

$$\text{root}_1 = \frac{-b + \sqrt{b^2 - 4ac}}{2a}, \qquad \text{root}_2 = \frac{-b - \sqrt{b^2 - 4ac}}{2a},$$

whenever the *discriminant* ($b^2 - 4ac$) is greater than zero. If we assume that this is the case, we can use the following assignment statements to assign values to root1 and root2.

```
// Compute two roots, root1 & root2, for discriminant values > 0.
disc = pow(b, 2) - 4.0 * a * c;
root1 = (-b + sqrt (disc)) / (2.0 * a);
root2 = (-b - sqrt (disc)) / (2.0 * a);
```

■

Example 3.3   *The Length of the Third Side of a Triangle.* If we know the length of two sides (*b* and *c*) of a triangle and the angle between them in degrees (*alpha*) (see Fig. 3.8), we can compute the length of the third side, *a*, by using the formula

$$a^2 = b^2 + c^2 - 2bc(\cos(alpha)).$$

To use the C++ cosine function, we must express its argument angle in radians instead of degrees. The following C++ assignment statement computes the unknown side length where the function convert_to_radians performs the conversion from units in degrees to units in radians (see Programming Exercise 1 at the end of this section).

```
a = sqrt (pow (b, 2) + pow (c, 2)
     - 2.0 * b * c * cos (convert_to_radians (alpha)));
```
■

Predefined Functions and Reusability

The computations carried out by the functions in the math library are quite complicated. The ease with which we may reuse these functions in our own programs offers a sizable advantage in that it frees us from concern with the considerable detail involved in these calculations. This reuse will be emphasized throughout the remainder of this book because it is one way we can manage and reduce the complexity of writing programs.

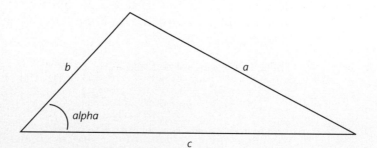

Figure 3.8   Triangle with unknown side *a*

A Look Ahead

Besides calling library functions from main, we can also write and call our own functions. Let's assume that we have already written functions compute_area and compute_circum:

- Function compute_area (r) returns the area of a circle with radius r.
- Function compute_circum (r) returns the circumference of a circle with radius r.

We can reuse these functions in the circle program shown earlier in this chapter. The program in Fig. 3.5 displays the area and the circumference of a circle whose radius is provided as input data. Figure 3.9 shows a revised main function that calls the functions compute_area and compute_circum through the assignment statements

```
area = compute_area (radius);
circum = compute_circum (radius);
```

The expression part of each assignment statement is a function reference with argument radius (the circle radius). The result returned by each function execution is stored in an output variable for the program (area or circum). We will complete the functions and the program in Section 3.5.

Figure 3.9 Revised main function for area and circumference problem

```
void main ()
{
   // Local data ...
   float radius;              // input: radius of circle
   float area;                // output: area of circle
   float circum;              // output: circumference of circle

   // Read radius of circle.
   cout << "Enter the circle radius: ";
   cin  >> radius;

   // Compute area of circle.
   area = compute_area (radius);

   // Compute circumference of circle.
   circum = compute_circum (radius);

   // Display area and circumference.
   cout << "The area of the circle is " << area << endl;
   cout << "The circumference of the circle is " << circum
        << endl;
}
```

Besides the advantage of reusing "tried and true" code, using functions `compute_area` and `compute_circum` frees us from having to be concerned with the details of computing a circle's area or circumference when we write the `main` function. This is another way we can manage and reduce the complexity of writing programs.

EXERCISES FOR SECTION 3.2

Self-Check

1. Rewrite the following mathematical expressions using C++ functions.
   a. $\sqrt{u + vw^2}$
   b. $\log_{10}(x^y)$
   c. $\sqrt{(x-y)^2}$
   d. $|xy - w/z|$

2. Evaluate the following function calls.
   a. `sqrt (fabs (-15.8))`
   b. `ceil (-3.5)`
   c. `ceil (3.5)`
   d. `floor (3.5)`
   e. `pow (2.5, 3.0)`

3. Let a = 3.0, b = 25.0, and c = 1.0. Evaluate the following pairs of expressions. If the results of the evaluation are different for each expression in the pair, explain why.
   a. `disc = pow (b, 2) - 4.0 * a * c;`
      `disc = pow (b, 2) - (4.0 * a) * c;`
   b. `x1 = (-b + sqrt (disc)) / (2.0 * a);`
      `x1 = (-b + sqrt (disc)) / 2.0 * a;`
   c. `x2 = (-b - sqrt (disc)) / (2.0 * a);`
      `x2 = -b - sqrt (disc) / (2.0 * a);`

Programming

1. Write function `convert_to_radians` for example 3.3. To convert an angle from degrees to radians, we multiply the angle by $\pi/180$.
2. Modify the `main` function in Fig. 3.7 to ensure that nonnegative values are passed to function `sqrt` before the square root calculations are performed. Use function `fabs`.
3. Write a C++ function `compute_distance` with four formal arguments representing the Cartesian coordinates of two points (x_1, y_1) and (x_2, y_2). Your function should compute the distance between these points using the formula

$$distance = \sqrt{(x_1 - x_2)^2 + (y_1 - y_2)^2} .$$

3.3 ——— TOP-DOWN DESIGN AND STRUCTURE CHARTS

Often the algorithm needed to solve a problem is more complex than those we have seen so far and the programmer has to break up the problem into subproblems to develop the program solution. In attempting to solve a subproblem at one level, we introduce new subproblems at lower levels. This process, called *top-down design,* proceeds from the original problem at the top level to the subproblems at each lower level. The splitting of a problem into its related subproblems is analogous to the process of refining an algorithm. The following case study introduces a documentation tool—the *structure chart*—that will help you to keep track of the relationships among subproblems.

CASE STUDY: DRAWING SIMPLE FIGURES

Problem Statement

You would like to write a program that will draw some simple diagrams on your printer or screen. Two examples are the diagrams shown in Fig. 3.10.

Problem Analysis

The house is formed by displaying a triangle without its base on top of a rectangle. The stick figure consists of a circular shape, a triangle, and a triangle without its base. We can draw both figures with four basic graphical components:

- a circle
- a base line
- parallel lines
- intersecting lines

Program Design

To create the stick figure, you can divide the problem of drawing this figure into three subproblems.

INITIAL ALGORITHM

1. Draw a circle.
2. Draw a triangle.
3. Draw intersecting lines.

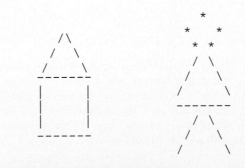

Figure 3.10 A house and stick figure diagram

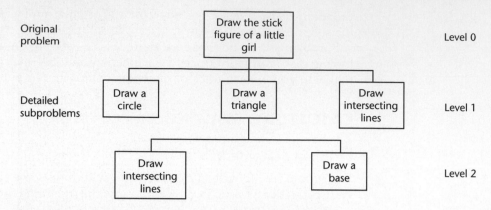

Figure 3.11   Structure chart for drawing a stick figure

ALGORITHM REFINEMENTS

Because a triangle is not a basic component, you must refine step 2.

Step 2 Refinement

2.1. Draw intersecting lines.
2.2. Draw a base line.

You can use a structure chart to show the relationship between the original problem and its subproblems, as in Fig. 3.11, where the original problem (level 0) is connected to its three subordinate subproblems shown at level 1. The subproblem "Draw a triangle" has its own subproblems (shown at level 2).

The subproblems appear in both the algorithm and the structure chart. The algorithm, not the structure chart, shows the order in which you carry out each step to solve the problem. The structure chart simply illustrates the subordination of subproblems to each other and to the original problem.

EXERCISES FOR SECTION 3.3

Self-Check

1. Draw the structure chart for the subproblem of drawing the house (see Fig. 3.10) in the simple figures case study.
2. Draw the structure chart for the complete simple figures case study. You need not redraw any parts of the chart that have already been completed.
3. Draw the structure chart for the problem of drawing a triangle and a rectangle with a circle in between.

4. Draw the structure chart for the problem of drawing the rocket ship shown below.

3.4 ——— FUNCTIONS WITHOUT ARGUMENTS

Programmers use functions to implement top-down design in their programs. They will often write one function for each subproblem in the structure chart. Function main can call these functions in the same way that it calls functions defined in a C++ library.

Note that main itself is just a function, but it is called by the operating system rather than by a particular program. Thus, we can view each C++ program that we write as made up of a collection of one or more functions. Exactly one of these functions, the one corresponding to the top-level block in a structure chart, must be named main. Because of its position relative to the called functions in the structure chart, we sometimes refer to the calling function as the *parent*, and we refer to the lower-level functions as *subordinate functions*.

As an example of top-down design with functions, you could use the main function in Fig. 3.12 to draw the stick figure in the case study. The three algorithm steps in Fig. 3.12 are coded as calls to three C++ functions. For example, the statement

```
// Draw a triangle.
draw_triangle ();
```

calls a function (draw_triangle) to implement the algorithm step *Draw a Triangle*. We will show the functions later.

Figure 3.12 Function prototypes and `main` function for drawing a stick figure

```
// FILE: StkFigMn.cpp
// DRAW A STICK FIGURE (Main function only)

#include <iostream.h>

// Functions used ...
// DRAWS A CIRCLE
void draw_circle ();

// DRAWS A TRIANGLE
void draw_triangle ();

// DRAWS INTERSECTING LINES
void draw_intersect ();

// DRAWS A HORIZONTAL LINE
void draw_base ();

void main ()
{
   // Draw the figure.
   // Draw a circle.
   draw_circle ();

   // Draw a triangle.
   draw_triangle ();

   // Draw intersecting lines.
   draw_intersect ();
}

// Insert definitions for functions draw_circle, draw_triangle,
// draw_intersect and draw_base.
```

Function Declarations

You must declare every subordinate function before its first reference. The lines

```
// Functions used ...
// DRAWS A CIRCLE
void draw_circle ();

// DRAWS A TRIANGLE
void draw_triangle ();

// DRAWS INTERSECTING LINES
void draw_intersect ();
```

declare the three functions called by the parent function `main`. The lines beginning with the reserved word `void` are C++ *function prototypes*.

Function Prototype (syntax for function without arguments)

Form: *type fname* `()` ;

Example: `// SKIPS THREE LINES`
`            void skip_three ();`

Interpretation: A function prototype begins with the *type specification, type* (for example, `int`, `char`, or `float`) associated with the function. (The meaning of this type association will be discussed later in this chapter.) If no type is associated with the function, the reserved word `void` is used as the type specification. The identifier *fname* is declared as the name of a function. The empty parentheses after the function name indicate that the function has no arguments. The prototype provides all of the information that the C++ compiler needs to know to translate calls to the function correctly.

For reasons that we will explain later, we recommend that you place all function prototypes just before the `main` function. A descriptive comment, indicating in English what the function does, should precede each prototype declaration. C++ requires the use of a prototype for each function referenced in a parent function. In the case of multiple prototypes, it makes no difference which function you declare first.   ■

Function Calls

The function `main` shown in Fig. 3.12 contains three function calls. They look like the calls to the `math` library functions discussed earlier, except they are not part of an expression or an assignment statement. The empty parentheses after the function name indicate that the function has no arguments.

Function Call

Form: *fname* `()` ;

Example: `draw_circle ();`

Interpretation: The function call initiates the execution of function *fname*. After *fname* has finished executing, the next statement in the parent function will be executed.   ■

Defining Functions

Let's now try to describe or *define* what each function is to do. We define other functions in a program in the same way that we define the function main. A *function definition* describes the sequence of steps to be carried out by a function. The details of what must be included in a function definition are summarized next.

C++
SYNTAX

Function Definition

Form: *type fname* ()   — function header
            {
            local-declarations   — function body
            executable-statements
            }

Example: `// DRAWS A TRIANGLE`
            `void draw_triangle ()`
            `{`
            `    // Draw a triangle.`
            `    draw_intersect ();`
            `    draw_base ();`
            `}   // end draw_triangle`

Interpretation: A function consists of two parts: a *function header* and a *function body*. A function body consists of *local-declarations* (optional) and *executable-statements.* The form of the function header is very similar to that of the function prototype described earlier. The one notable exception is that a prototype must be terminated by a semicolon, just as any other declaration in a C++ program.

A function header begins with a *type specification* (such as int, float, char, or void) followed by the function name, *fname,* and left and right parentheses. The function header is followed by the *function body.* The function body always starts with a left brace and ends with a right brace. We will adopt the convention of starting every function definition with a comment describing the purpose of the function, although this is not required by C++.

Any identifiers (constants or variables) declared in the *local-declarations* are defined only during the execution of the function and can be referenced only within the function. In fact, these identifiers have no meaning outside the function in which they are declared.

The *executable-statements* describe the data manipulation to be performed by the function.   ■

You should provide each function definition separately, and you should place the subordinate functions after the definition of function `main`. Except for `main`, you can define the functions in any order.

Figure 3.13 shows the definitions for all functions used in `main`, and for function `draw_base` (called by `draw_triangle`). The body of function `draw_circle` contains three lines beginning with `cout`. These lines cause the computer to draw a shape that resembles a circle. The function call

```
draw_circle ();
```

in `main` causes these lines to execute.

If you examine Fig. 3.13 carefully, you will notice several occurrences of the pair of characters \ \. Recall from Section 2.7 that the backslash character ' \ ' is used as an *escape character* in C++. That is, it is used to indicate special characters, such as the *newline* character ' \n ', that have no single character

Figure 3.13 Functions used to draw a stick figure

```
// DRAWS A CIRCLE
void draw_circle ()
{
    cout << "     ^     " << endl;
    cout << "  *     *" << endl;
    cout << "     * *  " << endl;
}   // end draw_circle


// DRAWS A TRIANGLE
void draw_triangle ()
{
    // Draw a triangle.
    draw_intersect ();
    draw_base ();
}   // end draw_triangle


// DRAWS INTERSECTING LINES
void draw_intersect ()
{
    cout << "    / \\  " << endl;
    cout << "   /   \\ " << endl;
    cout << "  /     \\" << endl;
}   // end draw_intersect


// DRAWS A HORIZONTAL LINE
void draw_base ()
{
    cout << " -------" << endl;
}   // end draw_base
```

representation. Because of this special use of '\', if we wish to use this character in a character string (see function `draw_intersect`), it is necessary to indicate this using the pair of characters \\.

PROGRAM
STYLE

Use of Comments in Function Declarations and Definitions

Fig. 3.13 includes several comments. Each function (and its prototype in Fig. 3.12) begins with a comment that describes its purpose. For clarity, the right brace at the end of each function is followed by a comment, such as

```
// end fname
```

identifying that function.   ∎

Order of Execution of Functions

In the stick figure subproblem, we wrote the `main` function as a sequence of calls to other functions before we specified the details of these functions. For each function called in `main`, we needed to specify only the prototype of the function and a comment (to indicate its purpose). The details of implementation of each of these functions (the function definitions) were handled separately.

Once we have completed the implementation details, we can compile all of the functions that we have written. The compiler translates a function call as a *transfer of control* to the called function. At the end of a function, the compiler inserts a transfer of control back to the calling function.

Figure 3.14 shows the main function and function `draw_circle` of the stick figure program in separate areas of memory. Although the C++ statements are shown in Fig. 3.14, it is actually the object code corresponding to each statement that is stored in memory.

When execution of function `main` begins, the first statement executed is the call to `draw_circle`. When the computer carries out this function call, it

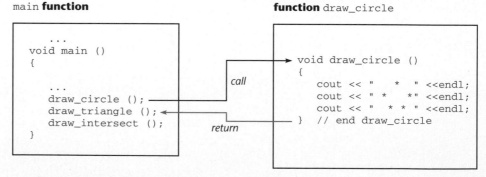

main **function**   **function** draw_circle

```
      ...
   void main ()
   {

      ...
      draw_circle ();                call      void draw_circle ()
      draw_triangle ();                        {
      draw_intersect ();                           cout << "   *   " <<endl;
   }                                return      cout << "  * *  " <<endl;
                                                 cout << " * * * " <<endl;
                                             }  // end draw_circle
```

Figure 3.14 Flow of control between functions

transfers control to the referenced function (indicated by the top arrow in Fig. 3.14). The computer then executes the body of function `draw_circle`. After the last statement in function `draw_circle` is executed, control is returned to `main` (indicated by the bottom arrow in the figure). After the return, the next statement in `main` is executed (the call to `draw_triangle`).

Advantages of Using Functions

Functions as Separate Units

There are many advantages to using functions. Their availability changes how an individual programmer organizes the solution to a programming problem. For a team of programmers working together on a large program, functions simplify the apportioning of programming tasks; each programmer will be responsible for a particular set of functions.

Each function definition is treated as a separate unit (each unknown to the other) by the compiler. They are connected only through the name by which one function references another during execution. Yet, when it translates a calling function, it is important for the compiler to know about this connection so that it can verify that a function call is consistent. The information required for the compiler to perform this *consistency check* is provided through the function prototypes.

Procedural Abstraction and Information Hiding

The top-down approach to program design involves *procedural abstraction*. It enables us to associate meaningful names with more complicated algorithm steps, reference these steps by name, and defer their implementation details until later. We then can write our programs using logically independent sections in the same way that we develop the solution algorithm. Focusing on one function at a time is much easier than trying to write the complete program all at once. Also, use of these logically independent program sections enables us to hide the details of subproblem implementations from one another. This feature of *information hiding* is important in all stages of the program development process.

Reuse of Functions

Another advantage of using functions is that functions can be executed more than once in a program. For example, `draw_intersect` is called twice in the stick figure program (once by `draw_triangle` and once by the `main` function). Each time `draw_intersect` is called, the statements in its function body draw a pair of intersecting lines. Without functions, the statements that draw the lines would have to be listed twice in the main program, thereby increasing the main program's length and the chance of error.

Finally, once you have written and tested a function, you can use it in other programs. For example, the functions for the stick figure program could easily be used in programs that draw other diagrams.

Figure 3.15   Function `draw_rectangle`

```cpp
// FILE: DrawRect.cpp
// FUNCTION TO DRAW A RECTANGLE

// DRAWS A RECTANGLE
void draw_rectangle ()
{
   // Draw the rectangle.
   draw_base ();
   draw_parallel ();
   draw_base ();
} // end draw_rectangle
```

Example 3.4   Many figures contain triangles and rectangles. We have seen how to use the functions `draw_intersect` and `draw_base` to define a new function, `draw_triangle`. Similarly, we can use two functions `draw_parallel` and `draw_base` to define the new function `draw_rectangle`, as shown in Fig. 3.15.   ∎

Local Declarations in Functions

Identifiers declared within a function are called *local identifiers* because they can be referenced only within the function. Figure 3.16 shows another version of the function `draw_circle` with a local symbol named `print_symbol`. The output statements in the function body display `print_symbol` at various locations in order to draw a shape that resembles a circle. The advantage of using this local constant is that we can easily change the appearance of the circle being displayed just by changing the line that defines the value of

Figure 3.16   Function to draw a circle

```cpp
// FILE: DrawCirc.cpp
// DRAWS A CIRCLE USING A CONSTANT CHARACTER SYMBOL

void draw_circle ()
{
   // Local data ...
   const char print_symbol = '@';

   // Draw the circle.
   cout << "     " << print_symbol << endl;
   cout << "   " << print_symbol << "     " << print_symbol << endl;
   cout << "     " << print_symbol << " " << print_symbol << endl;
} // end draw circle
```

`print_symbol`. The circle displayed by the version of the function shown in Fig. 3.16 is shown below.

```
  @
@   @
 @ @
```

Note that the detail of what symbol is displayed for the circle is hidden from the view of any parent functions that might use `draw_circle`. Among other things, using a local constant here would enable us to change this symbol without worrying about the effect of the change on any of the other functions in our program.

Displaying User Instructions

Functions, as we have described them up to this point, have very limited utility because we do not yet know how to transmit, or *pass*, information into or out of a function that we write. Until we have this capability, we will use functions only to display information or instructions to a program user, as shown in the next example.

Example 3.5   The function in Fig. 3.17 displays instructions to a user of the area and circumference program shown in Fig. 3.5. You can begin the main function body with the function call

```
instruct_user ();
```

Figure 3.17   Function `instruct_user`

```cpp
// FILE: DispInst.cpp
// DISPLAYS INSTRUCTIONS TO THE USER OF AREA/CIRCUMFERENCE
// PROGRAM

void instruct_user ()
{
    cout << "This program computes the area and " << endl;
    cout << "circumference of a circle. " << endl << endl;
    cout << "To use this program, enter the radius of the "
        << endl;
    cout << "circle after the prompt" << endl; endl;
    cout << " Enter the circle radius: " << endl << endl;
    cout << "The circumference will be computed in the same "
        << endl;
    cout << "units of measurement as the radius. The area "
        << endl;
    cout << "will be computed in the same units squared."
        << endl << endl;
}   // end instruct_user
```

Figure 3.18   Output lines displayed by function `instruct_user`

Program Output

```
This program computes the area and
circumference of a circle.

To use this program, enter the radius of the
circle after the prompt

Enter the circle radius:

The circumference will be computed in the same
units of measurement as the radius. The area
will be computed in the same units squared.
```

The rest of the `main` function body will consist of the executable statements shown earlier. Figure 3.18 shows the output displayed by calling function `instruct_user`. Don't forget to place the prototype

`void instruct_user ();`

before function `main`. ∎

EXERCISES FOR SECTION 3.4

Self-Check   1. Assume that you have functions `print_h`, `print_i`, `print_m`, and `print_o` that print 5 × 5 letters, such as the M shown below:

```
M           M
M   M   M   M
M       M   M
M           M
M           M
```

What is the effect of executing the `main` function body below?

```
{
    print_o();
    cout << endl;
    print_h();
    skip_three (); // see Programming Exercise Number 2

    print_h();
    cout << endl;
    print_i();
    cout << endl;
    print_m();
}
```

2. Why is it better to place the user instructions in a separate function rather than to insert the necessary statements in the `main` function body itself?

Programming

1. Write the function `draw_parallel` to draw two horizontal, parallel lines, each 5 spaces in length and 3 lines apart.
2. The line

   ```
   cout << endl << endl << endl;
   ```

   may be used to cause three blank lines to be inserted into your printed output. Write a function `skip_three` that uses this line to insert three blank lines into your output. Write `draw_parallel` using `skip_three`.
3. Write a program to print "HI HO" in block letters. First, provide a structure chart for this problem.
4. Provide functions `print_h`, `print_i`, `print_m`, and `print_o` for Self-Check Exercise 1.
5. Show the revised `main` function for the area and circumference problem (see Fig. 3.5) with the `instruct_user` prototype and the call to `instruct_user`.
6. Rewrite the metric conversion program shown in Fig. 3.3 so that it includes a function that displays instructions to its user. Write the function, the prototype, and the call for `instruct_user`.

3.5 ──── FUNCTIONS WITH INPUT ARGUMENTS AND RETURN VALUES

Programmers use functions like building blocks to construct large programs, a process that is analogous to constructing a stereo system. Each stereo component is an independent device that performs a specific function. The tuner and amplifier may contain similar electronic parts, but each component uses its own internal circuitry to perform its required function.

Information in the form of electronic signals is passed back and forth between these components over wires. If you look at the rear of a stereo amplifier, you will find that some plugs are marked input and others are marked output. The wires attached to the input plugs carry electronic signals to the amplifier, where they are processed. (These signals may come from a cassette deck, tuner, or compact disc player.) New electronic signals are generated. These signals come out of the amplifier from the output plugs and go to the speakers or to the back of the tape deck for recording. Thus, the wires are used for the transmission of information (electronic signals) between the components of a stereo system.

Currently, we know a little about how to design the separate components (functions) of a programming system, but we do not know how to pass data between the `main` function and the other functions that we write. In this section, we will learn how to use function return values and argument lists to provide communication paths between two functions.

Example 3.6   *Squaring the Integer* k. The function square_int, shown at the bottom of Fig. 3.19, computes the square of any integer we provide it. This function has a single type int input argument through which the user can indicate which integer is to be squared each time the function is called. The line

```
return k * k;
```

returns the square of the integer, represented by k, to the calling function. ∎

The main function in the middle of Fig. 3.19 uses the statement

```
area = square_int (side);
```

Figure 3.19   Prototype, use, and definition of function **square_int**

```
prototype for function square_int
// Functions used ...
// COMPUTE THE SQUARE OF AN INTEGER
int square_int
    (int);            // IN: represents the integer to be squared

use of the function square_int — compute the area of a square
void main ()
{
    // Local data ...
    int side;       // input: contains the side length of a square
    int area;       // output: contains the area of the square
    ...

    // Compute the area of the square.
    area = square_int (side);
    ...
}

definition of function square_int
// COMPUTE THE SQUARE OF AN INTEGER
int square_int
    (int k)         // IN: represents the integer to be squared
{
    // Compute and return square of the integer represented by k
    return k * k;
}   // end square_int
```

to compute the area of a square whose side length is `side`. This statement causes the following actions:

1. The function `square_int` is called with `side` as the actual argument.
2. `square_int` computes and returns the square of the integer value associated with `side`.
3. The value returned is assigned to `area`.

As part of the function execution, the *actual argument* `side` is substituted for the *formal argument* `k` (both arguments are of type `int`). If `side` happens to have the value 9, the value 81 will be returned by `square_int` and stored in `area`.

In this illustration, the integer input argument is indicated by the *formal argument specification*

```
int k
```

in the header line of the function definition and by the specification

```
int
```

in the function prototype (top of Fig. 3.19). These specifications are required by C++, and they must be consistent, although no identifier name (such as `k`) is required in the prototype. However, the identifier name is optional in the prototype and may be included.

Example 3.7 Figure 3.20 shows a program for computing the area and circumference of a circle using functions. Function `main` uses the assignment statements

```
area = compute_area (radius);
circum = compute_circum (radius);
```

to perform the computation steps. The variable `radius` is the actual argument in each function call.

Figure 3.20 Revised program for area and circumference problem

```
// FILE: AreaMain.cpp
// FINDS AND PRINTS THE AREA AND CIRCUMFERENCE OF A CIRCLE
//     USING FUNCTIONS

#include <iostream.h>

   // global constant ...
   const float pi = 3.14159;
```

(continued)

Figure 3.20   *(continued)*

```
// Functions used ...
// COMPUTES THE AREA OF A CIRCLE
float compute_area
    (float);                    // IN: radius of the circle

// COMPUTES THE CIRCUMFERENCE OF A CIRCLE
float compute_circum
    (float);                    // IN: radius of the circle

// COMPUTES THE SQUARE OF A FLOATING-POINT NUMBER
float square_float
    (float);                    // IN: number to be squared
void main ()
{
    // Local data ...
    float radius;               // input: radius of circle
    float area;                 // output: area of circle
    float circum;               // output: circumference of circle

    // Read radius of circle.
    cout << "Enter the circle radius: ";
    cin  >> radius;

    // Compute area of circle.
    area = compute_area (radius);

    // Compute circumference of circle.
    circum = compute_circum (radius);

    // Display area and circumference.
    cout << "The area of the circle is " << area << endl;
    cout << "The circumference of the circle is " << circum
         << endl;
}

// COMPUTES THE AREA OF A CIRCLE
float compute_area
    (float r)                   // IN: radius of the circle
{
    // Compute and return the area.
    return pi * square_float (r);
}   // end compute_area

// COMPUTES THE CIRCUMFERENCE OF A CIRCLE
float compute_circum
    (float r)                   // IN: radius of the circle
{
```

(continued)

Figure 3.20 *(continued)*

```
    // Compute and return the circumference.
    return 2.0 * pi * r;
}   // end compute_circum

// Insert definition for function square_float.
```

∎

Note that we declare the floating-point constant `pi` (representing the mathematical symbol π), which is required to compute both the area and circumference of a circle before function `main`. Such a constant is said to be *global* to the functions that follow its declaration, so functions `main`, `compute_area`, and `compute_circum` can reference it.

Functions `compute_area` and `compute_circum` are very similar; they both begin with a function header line of the form

```
// COMPUTES THE ____ OF A CIRCLE
float fname
    (float r)              // IN: radius of the circle
```

The function name is represented by *fname*; the type specifier `float` that precedes this name indicates the type of the value to be returned by the function. The *formal argument list* indicates that each function has one floating-point formal argument, `r`. Note that with respect to the function name, return value type, and formal argument types, the function definition headers are completely consistent with the function prototype.

The program also contains a prototype for the function `square_float`, which is similar to the `square_int` function described in Example 3.6. We leave function `square_float` as an exercise (Programming Exercise 2).

The executable part of each function consists of a single statement that computes and returns a value to the calling program. In `compute_area`, the statement

```
return pi * square_float (r);
```

references the constant `pi`, the formal argument `r`, and the function `square_float`. When the function `compute_area` begins executing, this statement causes the following actions:

1. The function `square_float` is called with `r` as the actual argument.
2. `square_float` computes and returns the square of the floating-point value associated with `r`.
3. In `compute_area`, the value returned from `square_float` is multiplied by `pi`.
4. This product (`pi` multiplied by the value returned from `square_float`) is returned from `compute_area` to the calling function.

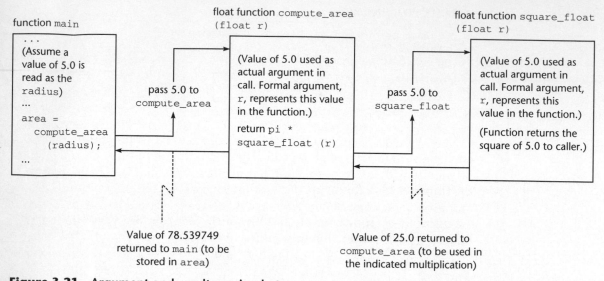

Value of 78.539749
returned to main (to be
stored in area)

Value of 25.0 returned to
compute_area (to be used in
the indicated multiplication)

Figure 3.21   Argument and result passing between **main**, **compute_area**, and **square_float**

This sequence is illustrated in Fig. 3.21. We will assume that the value 5.0 is read as the value of radius.

As shown in the figure, the following sequence of events occurs when the statement

```
area = compute_area (radius);
```

in function main is executed (with radius assumed to be equal to 5.0).

1. The value (5.0) of the radius (the actual argument) is passed to compute_area in correspondence with the formal argument, r.
2. The function compute_area executes; the statement

```
return pi * square_float (r);
```

causes the following sequence of events to occur:
   a. The function square_float is called, and the actual argument, r, which now has the value 5.0, is placed in correspondence with the formal argument in square_float.
   b. square_float is executed and returns a value of 25.0 to compute_area.
   c. In compute_area, the value of the constant pi is multiplied by the returned value, 25.0.
   d. The value of this product (78.539749) is returned to the main function.
3. The value returned by compute_area is assigned to the variable area.

Use of Formal Arguments as Placeholders

Formal argument `r` is used in the functions `compute_area` and `compute_circum` to describe the computations to be performed by these functions. Formal argument `r` acts as a *placeholder* for the actual argument in the function definition because the actual argument is unknown when you write the function definition. Therefore, you must use `r` in place of the actual argument when writing a statement in the function body that processes the function argument.

The function call

```
compute_area (radius);
```

defines a correspondence between the calling function variable `radius` (the actual argument) and the formal argument `r` listed in the header for the function `compute_area`. The value of `radius` is *passed to* the function and used as the value of formal argument `r` wherever this argument appears in the function body. This is summarized in the following two displays.

C++ SYNTAX

Function Prototype (with arguments)

Form: *type fname (formal-argument-type-list)* ;

Example:
```
// COMPUTES THE INVERSE OF THE SUM OF TWO
// FLOATING POINT VALUES
float inverse_sum
    (float,        // IN: first value to be added
     float);       // IN: second value to be added
```

Interpretation: The identifier *fname* is declared as the name of a function returning the indicated *type*. This declaration provides all the information that the C++ compiler needs to know to translate correctly all references to the function. The *formal-argument-type-list* is a list of one or more type specifiers separated by commas.

Note: C++ permits the specification of formal argument names in function prototypes, as in

```
// COMPUTES THE INVERSE OF THE SUM OF TWO FLOATING-POINT VALUES
float inverse_sum
    (float x,      // IN: first value to be added
     float y);     // IN: second value to be added
```

We have chosen not to use names in prototypes, however, because there is no connection between these names and those used as the formal arguments in the function definition or the actual arguments in a function call. ∎

Function Definition (with arguments)

Form: *type fname* (*formal-argument-list*)
{
    local-declarations
    executable-statements } — function body
}

Example:
```
// COMPUTES THE INVERSE OF THE SUM OF TWO
// FLOATING-POINT VALUES
float inverse_sum
   (float x,          // IN: first value to be added
    float y)          // IN: second value to be added
{
   return 1.0 / (x + y);
}  // end inverse_sum
```

Interpretation: The function *fname* is defined. The rules for specifying a function with arguments are the same as for functions without arguments except for the addition of the *formal argument list.* This list is enclosed in parentheses and consists of a sequence of one or more formal argument specifications of the form

type user-defined-identifier

Multiple argument specifications are separated from each other by commas. The parentheses are required even if there are no formal arguments. A formal argument cannot be declared as a local identifier. There is no semicolon following the right parenthesis enclosing the formal argument list.

The *executable-statements* describe the data manipulation to be performed by the function using the formal argument names in the description. When a formal argument is referenced during function execution, the value of the corresponding actual argument is manipulated. ∎

Function Return

Form: `return` *expression*;

Example: `return x * y;`

Unless the function type is `void`, a function must return a single result of the indicated type. This is accomplished through the use of the C++ `return` statement. When a `return` statement executes, the *expression* following `return` is evaluated, and its value is communicated back to the calling function as the function result. Execution continues with the next operation in the calling function. ∎

C++
SYNTAX

Function Call (with arguments)

Form: *fname (actual-argument-list)* ;

Example: `inverse_sum (3.0, z);`

Interpretation: The *actual-argument-list* is enclosed in parentheses. (The parentheses are required even if there are no actual arguments.) An actual argument may be a constant, variable, or an expression; multiple arguments are separated by commas. When function *fname* is called into execution, the first actual argument is placed in correspondence with the first formal argument, the second actual argument with the second formal argument, and so on. The type of each actual argument must be consistent with the corresponding formal argument type. If the use of a function requires that a value be returned, then the function must be written so as to return a value of the expected type. Following the execution of the function, the returned result replaces the reference to the function. Note that a function defined with a *type* of `void` cannot return a value. ■

PROGRAM
STYLE

Writing Formal Argument Lists

```
(float,    // IN: first value to be added
 float);   // IN: second value to be added
```

The formal argument list for function `inverse_sum` is written on two lines to improve readability. In addition, this allows us room to provide a descriptive comment next to the specification of each formal argument. (This comment is not required by C++, but it can provide useful information about the use of each function argument.) The order of the actual arguments in the function call must correspond to the order of the formal arguments in the function prototype (and in the function definition). We will continue with the convention of writing formal argument descriptions on separate lines throughout the remainder of the book. ■

EXERCISES FOR SECTION 3.5

Self-Check

1. What is the purpose of function arguments?
2. Consider the function `cube` shown below:

```
void cube
  (int k)
{
    cout << "k cubed is ";
    cout << k * k * k << endl;
}   // end cube
```

   a. What is displayed when the function call `cube(3)` executes?
   b. If `m` is 5, what happens when the function call `cube(m)` executes?
   c. What is the value of the actual argument `m` after the function cube executes?
   d. Where should `m` be declared and what should its data type be?

2. In the area and circumference program shown in Fig. 3.20, assume that a value of 2.0 is entered in response to the radius prompt. Using the step-by-step analysis illustrated in this section (see Fig. 3.21 and the related discussion), trace
   a. the computation of the area of the circle;
   b. the computation of the circumference.
   Indicate what values would be printed during the execution of the `main` function.
3. Provide a complete structure chart for the revisited version of the area and circumference problem.

Programming
1. Write a function `square_neg_7` that computes and returns the square of the integer −7. Note carefully any differences
   a. between this function and `square_six`;
   b. between this function and `square_int`.
2. Write the function `square_float`. Note any differences between this function and the function `square_int` implemented in Example 3.6.
3. Rewrite functions `main`, `compute_area`, and `compute_circum` in the area and circumference problem with the following changes: Remove the global declaration of the constant `pi` and pass `pi` to `compute_area` and `compute_circum` as the second actual argument.

3.6 —— ARGUMENT LIST CORRESPONDENCE

All the functions in earlier programs (except for `inverse_sum`) have had a single argument. However, a function can have more than one argument. Figure 3.22 provides a diagrammatic view of a function having more than one argument. As shown in this figure, we have now extended the concept of a function from our original view of a "black box" with no information connectors to a "black box" that may have a number of input connectors (arguments) and one output connector (the return value).

A call to a function establishes a pair-wise correspondence between actual and formal arguments. The function call

```
inverse_sum (3.0, z);
```

establishes the correspondence between actual and formal arguments shown below.

ARGUMENT CORRESPONDENCE FOR `inverse_sum (3.0, z)`

Actual Argument	Formal Argument
3.0	x
z	y

The function call

```
inverse_sum (x + 2.0, y);
```

establishes a different correspondence.

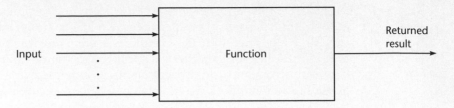

Figure 3.22 **Function with multiple inputs and a single return value**

ARGUMENT CORRESPONDENCE FOR `inverse_sum (x + 2.0, y)`

Actual Argument	Formal Argument
x + 2.0	x
y	y

This correspondence is perfectly fine, as long as x + 2.0 and y are type `float` in the calling function. Note that it is possible for an actual argument to be an expression (such as x + 2.0), although a formal argument must always be an identifier.

Finally, the function call

`inverse_sum (y, x);`

establishes the following correspondence:

ARGUMENT CORRESPONDENCE FOR `inverse_sum (y, x)`

Actual Argument	Formal Argument
y	x
x	y

This, too, is okay according to C++ rules, as long as the calling function declares x and y to be type `float`. However, for obvious reasons, we discourage this type of argument correspondence; it is very prone to mistakes.

Prototypes Revisited: Scope and Functional Independence

An identifier declared within a function has *local scope* within that function. This means that you can reference it anywhere after its declaration up to that function's closing brace. This is true for identifiers declared in function `main` as well. An identifier declared before function main has *global scope* (see the declaration for constant `pi` in Fig. 3.20). This means that you can reference it anywhere after its declaration up to the closing brace of the last function in the program. Our placement of the function prototypes before function `main`, enables any function in our program to call another (except for `main`, which is called by the operating system).

The last correspondence shown in the preceding section may seem confusing at first, but it causes no problems because the compiler separately translates each function. Therefore, the identifiers used in one function have no connection to those used in another except through the positional correspondence between actual and formal arguments as specified in a function call. This applies to all identifiers in a function definition—including formal arguments, local constants, and variables occurring within the *scope of definition* of the function—that is, between the function header up to the function closing brace.

Because the only connection between any two functions is through argument correspondence and return values, it is extremely important that these corresponding values be *type consistent*.

Type Consistency Between Functions

- The *type of a value* returned by a called function must be consistent with the type expected by the caller as indicated in the prototype.
- The *type of an actual argument* in a function call must be consistent with the type of its corresponding formal argument.

You must understand argument substitution in order to use functions effectively. We will provide many examples illustrating how this substitution works. In studying these examples, you should keep the following in mind:

1. The substitution of the value of an actual argument in a function call for its corresponding formal argument is strictly positional. That is, the value of the first actual argument is substituted for the first formal argument; the value of the second actual argument is substituted for the second formal argument, and so on.
2. The names of these corresponding pairs of arguments are of no consequence in the substitution process—the names may be different, or they may be the same.
3. The substituted value is used in place of the formal argument at each point where that argument appears in the called function.

Type inconsistencies between actual and formal arguments and function return values are among the most common programming errors. If not detected by your compiler, they can be very difficult to find during program testing. The function prototype can help in this respect, for it provides all of the information that the compiler needs to check the consistency of the input arguments and of the returned type for our functions. It is still important for you to double-check the consistency of arguments but understand that the compiler also performs this check.

You may have noticed by this time that we have not exactly defined what we mean by "type consistent." For now, we will adopt a very rigid view of type consistency, insisting that there be an identical *type match* between an actual argument in a function call and the corresponding formal argument in the function prototype. In fact, C++ is more tolerant than this, allowing considerable room for differences in these corresponding types. In most instances, when these differences occur, C++ converts the actual argument type to that of the formal argument. If the standard conversion rules used by C++ are not clearly understood, the results produced can be very confusing. So for now, we urge you to ensure that there is always a perfect type match in corresponding argument types in a function call and its prototype. If necessary, to ensure this perfect match, there is a way to do your own explicit conversions using C++ *casting operators* to create a copy of a value of the correct type.

Casting Operators for Type Conversion

Example 3.8   *Casting Operations.* If x is a floating-point variable, the expression

```
int(x)
```

can be used to create a copy of x of type integer. The reserved word int used in this manner is called a *casting operator.* We will see more about casting operators and type conversions in Chapter 7. For now, however, all you need to know is that int may be used as a casting operator to create an integer copy of a floating-point value; float may be used to create a floating-point copy of an integer value. The use of the casting operator will not destroy the original value. Rather, a copy is made and saved. Note that in converting a floating-point value to an integer, the fractional part (the part following the decimal point) is truncated (chopped off) and lost. You need to be careful when performing such conversions to ensure you are getting the desired result. ∎

Problem-Solving Revisited

All of the points just raised regarding the use of functions, prototypes, and arguments fit well with our earlier discussion regarding the separation of concerns and information hiding in designing and implementing computer programs. For example, the top-down problem-solving strategy illustrated in both the area and circumference and the simple figures problems involved a decomposition of problems into subproblems, and a further decomposition of some of these subproblems into still smaller problems. As we indicated at the start of this section, the C++ function enables us to carry this strategy through to the coding stage of the program development process. We can completely implement functions to solve higher-level problems in terms of lower-level functions. To do so, we follow the steps shown in the following box.

The Problem-Solving Process

1. Read the problem carefully and be certain that all aspects are clearly understood.
2. Describe all problem input and output data, the type of the data, and their relevance to the problem.
3. Break the problem into subproblems and begin constructing the program structure chart showing the relationships between the top-level problem and the subproblems at the next level.
4. Be sure you have a clear definition of each subproblem and then develop a top-level algorithm for the main function. Identify any additional information (type and description) required by your algorithm. The algorithm should be written in terms of lower-level functions that will eventually be designed to implement each of the subproblems. Note that to reference a lower-level function, we need to know only what this function is to do and what input arguments and return value are required (if any).
5. Once this information has been determined and your algorithm has been formulated and refined as necessary, you can write the main function. You can also write the prototypes for the lower-level functions, but do not write the lower-level functions yet.
6. Repeat steps 2 through 5 for each subproblem, further developing the structure chart as necessary and designing and coding your algorithms. This process will continue until each of the subproblems is sufficiently straightforward as to not require further development.

EXERCISES FOR SECTION 3.6

Self-Check
1. Discuss the importance of the C++ function prototype declaration
   a. with respect to the top-down design process;
   b. with respect to compile-time type consistency checks on return values and input arguments.

Programming
1. Write a function cube_int to compute the cube, k^3, of an integer, k. Then write a function main that calls cube_int to compute the volume of a sphere with radius r. Test your program for $r = 2$. The formula for computing the volume of a sphere of radius r is

$$volume = (4/3)\pi r^3$$

where π is the constant 3.14159.

3.7 ───── EXTENDING C++ THROUGH CLASSES: money AND string

So far in this chapter we have illustrated the advantages of procedural abstraction and the use of functions as program building blocks. C++ also facilitates data abstraction through its class feature, which enables users to define new data types and their associated operations. In this section we discuss two classes: string and money. The string class is included in the standard for C++ proposed in 1996. If your system does not provide this class, check the preface of this book to see how you can access a comparable string class. Because the money class (discussed in Section 2.4) is a user-defined class that is not part of your C++ system, check the preface of this book to see how you can access it (your instructor may have done this for you).

The money Class

In Section 2.5 we introduced the money class, which can be used to process money objects. A money object has two attributes: dollars and cents. Using this class to process monetary amounts (instead of type float) ensures that all operations on money objects result in values with a cents attribute between 0 and 99. Also, when you display a money object, the value of the cents attribute is displayed using two digits. Figure 3.23 illustrates the money class. Notice that we follow #include with "money.h", not <money.h>, to show that money is a user-defined class, not a system-defined class.

The program allocates storage for four type money objects, initializing one of them, credit_limit, to $5,000.00:

```
money credit_limit = 5000.00;          // credit limit
```

Next the program uses the extraction operator >> to read a monetary amount into money object sale_price.

The first assignment statement

```
tax_amount = sale_price * tax_percent / 100.0;
```

computes and assigns a value to money object tax_amount. Notice that the expression involves one type money object (sale_price), a type float constant (tax_percent), and a type float literal (100.0), and the result is a value of type money. The statement

```
final_cost = sale_price + tax_amount;
```

Figure 3.23 Illustrating money operations

```
// FILE: MoneyOp.cpp
// ILLUSTRATES MONEY OPERATIONS

#include "money.h"                          // user-defined class

void main ()
{
    // Local declarations
    const float tax_percent = 6.25;         // tax percentage

    money credit_limit = 5000.00;           // credit limit
    money sale_price;                       // input - selling price of
                                            // an item
    money tax_amount;                       // output - tax amount
    money final_cost;                       // output - final cost

    // Read price of item.
    cout << "Enter item price: ";
    cin >> sale_price;

    // Compute tax amount
    tax_amount = sale_price * tax_percent / 100.0;

    // Compute final cost
    final_cost = sale_price + tax_amount;

    // Display sales receipt
    cout << "Sales receipt" << endl;
    cout << "Price " << sale_price << endl;
    cout << "Tax   " << tax_amount << endl;
    cout << "Paid  " << final_cost << endl << endl;

    // Compute new credit limit
    cout << "Your initial credit limit is " << credit_limit << endl;
    credit_limit = credit_limit - final_cost;
    cout << "Your new credit limit is " << credit_limit << endl;
}
```

───────────── Program Output ─────────────

```
Enter item price: 345.77
Sales receipt
Price $345.77
Tax   $21.61
Paid  $367.38

Your initial credit limit is $5,000.00
Your new credit limit is $4,632.62
```

stores the sum of two type `money` objects in a third one. The statement

```
credit_limit = credit_limit - final_cost;
```

updates the value of `credit_limit` by subtracting `final_cost`. These statements show that the extraction operator >>, the assignment operator =, and the arithmetic operators (+ , -, *, /) are defined in the `money` class, and they work with `money` objects in the expected way.

Finally, the lines beginning with `cout` use the insertion operator << with `money` objects and strings to display a sales receipt. Notice that all money objects are displayed with a leading dollar sign and with two decimal digits. Also, commas are inserted to make amounts over $999.99 more readable.

The `string` Class

In Section 2.5 we introduced the C++ `string` class, which defines a new data type `string` and many operators for `string` objects. Two attributes of a `string` object are the character sequence it stores and the length of that sequence. Some of the common operators you have seen so far (<<, >>, =, +) can be used with `string` objects. Figure 3.24 illustrates how we use these familiar operators and some new ones with `string` objects as operands. Notice that we must follow `#include` with the class name `string`, not the header file `string.h`, in this program. (Note: Some compilers use `String` instead of `string`; some compilers use the header file `cstring.h`.)

Declaring `string` Objects

The declarations

```
string first_name, last_name;    // inputs - first and last names
string whole_name;               // output - whole name
```

allocate storage for three `string` objects that initially contain empty strings (a string with zero characters). You can store new data in these strings through a string assignment or by reading a string value typed at the keyboard. You can also store data in a `string` object when you declare it. The statement

```
string greeting = "Hello ";    // output - a greeting string
```

stores the string `"Hello "` in the `string` object `greeting`.

Figure 3.24   Illustrating string operations

```cpp
// FILE: StringOp.cpp
// ILLUSTRATES STRING OPERATIONS

#include <string>

void main ()
{
   // Local declarations
   string first_name, last_name;      // inputs - first and last names
   string whole_name;                 // output - whole name
   string greeting = "Hello ";        // output - a greeting string

   // Read first and last names.
   cout << "Enter your first name: ";
   cin >> first_name;
   cout << "Enter your last name: ";
   cin >> last_name;

   // Join names in whole name
   whole_name = first_name + " " + last_name;

// Display results
   cout << greeting << whole_name << '!' << endl;
   cout << "You have " << whole_name.length () - 1 <<
           " letters in your name." << endl;
// Display initials
   cout << "Your initials are " << first_name.at (0) <<
           last_name.at (0) << endl;
}
```

──────────── Program Output ────────────

```
Enter your first name: Judy
Enter your last name: Jones
Hello Judy Jones!
You have 9 letters in your name.
Your initials are JJ
```

Reading and Displaying `string` Objects

In Section 2.5, you saw that the statement

```cpp
cin >> first_name;
```

uses the extraction operator >> to read keyboard data into `first_name`. It stores in `first_name` all data characters up to (but not including) the first blank or return. You must not enclose these characters in double quotes. The statement

```cpp
cout << greeting << whole_name << '!' << endl;
```

displays `string` objects `greeting` and `whole_name` followed by the character value `'!'`.

What if you want to read a data string that contains a blank? For example, you may want to read the characters `Van Winkle` into `last_name`. You can do this using the `getline` function. For example, the statement

```
getline (cin, last_name, '\n');
```

reads all characters typed at the keyboard (stream `cin`) up to (but not including) the first return into `string` object `last_name`.

The third function argument, `'\n'`, specifies that the return character marks the end of the input data. The backslash, followed by the letter n, represents the *newline* or return character.

You can specify another terminator character by changing the third argument. For example, use `'*'` as the third argument to make the symbol * the terminator character. In this case, you can type your data string over multiple lines, and it will not terminate until you enter the symbol *. All data characters entered, including any newline characters (but not the *), will be stored in the `string` object used as the second argument.

String Assignment and Concatenation

The assignment statement

```
whole_name = first_name + " " + last_name;
```

stores in `whole_name` the new string formed by joining the three strings that are operands of the operator +, which means join or *concatenate* when its operands are strings. Notice that we insert a space between string objects `first_name` and `last_name` by joining the string value `" "`, not the character value `' '`. Remember to use double quotes, not single quotes, to enclose string values in C++ statements.

Operator Overloading

Until now, the operator + has always meant addition, but now we see that it means concatenation when its operands are `string` objects. We use the term *operator overloading* to indicate that the meaning of an operator may vary depending on its operands. Operator overloading is a very powerful concept because it allows C++ to give multiple meanings to a single operator; C++ can determine the correct interpretation of the operator from the way we use it.

We should also mention that the operators >> and << are overloaded as well because they can be used with different type operands (for example, characters, strings, numbers, money values). However, the operation performed (read a value, display a value) is the same regardless of the operand type.

Dot notation: Calling Functions `length` and `at`

Figure 3.24 also uses member functions `length` and `at` from the `string` class. To call these functions (and most member functions), we use *dot notation*. Rather than passing an object as an argument to a member function, we write the object name, a dot (or period), and then the function to be applied to this object. The function reference

```
whole_name.length ()
```

applies member function `length` (no arguments) to string object `whole_name`. This call to function `length` returns a value of 10 (`whole_name` contains the 10-character string `"Judy Jones"`); however, we subtract one before printing the result because of the blank character between the first and last names:

```
cout << "You have " << whole_name.length () - 1 <<
        " letters in your name." << endl;
```

The expression

```
first_name.at (0)
```

retrieves the character in `first_name` that is at position 0, where we number the characters from the left, starting with 0 for the first character, 1 for the second, and so on. By this numbering system, the last character in `string` object `whole_name` (the letter s) is at position `whole_name.length () - 1`, or position 9.

Member Functions for Word-Processing Operations

We would like to be able to perform on a `string` object all the operations that are available on most word processors. C++ provides member functions for searching for a string (`find`), inserting a string at a particular position (`insert`), deleting a portion of a string (`remove`), and replacing part of a string with another string (`replace`). We illustrate some simple examples of these functions next.

For the strings `first_name`, `last_name`, and `whole_name` in Fig. 3.24, the expression

```
whole_name.find (first_name)
```

returns 0 (the position of the first character of `"Judy"` in `"Judy Jones"`) and the expression

```
whole_name.find (last_name)
```

returns 5 (the position of the first character of `"Jones"` in `"Judy Jones"`).

The first statement below inserts a string at the beginning of `string` object `whole_name` (at position 0) and the second statement inserts a string in the middle of `whole_name` (at new position 9).

```
whole_name.insert (0, "Ms");          // Change to "Ms. Judy
                                      // Jones"
whole_name.insert (9, "Abigail");     // Change to "Ms. Judy
                                      // Abigail Jones"
```

You can use the following statement to change the middle name from Abigail to Abby:

```
whole_name.replace(9, 7, "Abby");     // Change to "Ms. Judy Abby
                                      // Jones"
```

This statement means: start at position 9 of `whole_name` (at the letter A) and replace the next 7 characters (`Abigail`) with the string `"Abby"`. Finally, you can delete the middle name altogether by using the statement:

```
whole_name.remove (9, 5);      // Change back to "Ms. Judy Jones"
```

which means: start at position 9 and remove 5 characters (`Abby `) from `string` object `whole_name`.

Assigning a Substring to A `string` Object

You can also store a *substring* (portion of a string) in another `string` object using member function `assign`. For example, if `title` is a `string` object, the statement

```
title.assign (whole_name, 0, 3);     // Store "Ms." in title
```

stores the first three characters of `whole_name` in `title`. The content of `whole_name` is not changed.

If you call `assign` with just two arguments (a string and an integer), the substring assigned will begin with the character selected by the second argument and continue to the end of the argument string. For example, the statement

```
name_only.assign (whole_name, 4);     // Store "Judy Jones" in
                                      // whole_name
```

assigns all characters of `whole_name` from the fifth on to the `string` object `name_only`.

Table 3.3 summarizes the member functions described in this section.

Table 3.3 Some Member Functions in the `string` Class

FUNCTION	PURPOSE
`get_line (cin, a_string, '\n')`	Extracts data characters up to (but not including) the first newline character from stream `cin` and stores them in `a_string`. The first newline character is extracted from `cin` but not stored in `a_string`.
`a_string.length ()`	Returns the count of characters (an integer) in `a_string`.
`a_string.at (i)`	Returns the character in position `i` of `a_string` where the leftmost character is at position 0 and the rightmost character is at position `a_string.length () - 1`.
`a_string.find (target)`	Returns the starting position (an integer) of string `target` in `a_string`. If `target` is not in `a_string`, returns a value $\geq$ the length of `a_string`.
`a_string.insert (start, new_string)`	Inserts `new_string` at position `start` of `a_string`.
`a_string.replace (start, count, new_string)`	Starting at position `start` of `a_string`, replaces the next `count` characters with `new_string`.
`a_string.remove (start, count)`	Starting at position `start` of `a_string`, removes the next `count` characters.
`a_string.assign (old_string, start, count)`	Starting at position `start` of `old_string`, assigns the next `count` characters to `a_string`.
`a_string.assign (old_string, start)`	Starting at position `start` of `old_string`, assigns the rest of `old_string` to `a_string`.

EXERCISES FOR SECTION 3.7

Self-Check

1. Explain the effect of each of the following statements:

```
money my_pay = 500.0;
my_pay = my_pay - 777.6873;
cout << my_pay << endl;
```

2. Trace each of the following statements:

```
string author;
author = "John";
author = author + " Steinbeck";
cout << author.length () << endl;
cout << author.at (0) << author.at (4) << endl;
cout << author.at (author.length () - 1) << endl;
```

```
author.find ("n");
author.find ("nb");
author.insert (4, "ny");
author.replace (0, 6, "Jonathon");
author.remove (3, 5);
```

3. Write a statement that stores the strings in `first_name` and `last_name` in `whole_name` in the form *last_name, first_name*.

Programming   1. Write a program that reads three strings and displays the strings in all possible sequences, one sequence per output line. Display the symbol * between the strings on each line.

3.8 _____ COMMON PROGRAMMING ERRORS

- *Semicolons in a Function Header and Prototype:* A missing semicolon at the end of a function prototype may cause a "Statement missing ;" or "Declaration terminated incorrectly" diagnostic (a prototype is a declaration and must be terminated with a semicolon). However, the accidental inclusion of a semicolon separating a function header from its definition will cause numerous compiler errors following the header.
- *Inconsistencies in the Number of Formal and Actual Arguments:* Although we have used arguments only sparingly thus far, experienced programmers know that the omission or incorrect ordering of function arguments is a common programming error. As your programs increase in size and complexity, you will find yourself writing many calls to functions. You must carefully check the number of actual arguments used in each call to ensure that this number is the same as the number of formal arguments in the prototype. If the number of arguments in a function call is not the same as the number in the prototype, your compiler will generate error messages such as the following:

```
"Too few arguments in call to int_power(int, int)."
"Too many arguments in call to int_power(int, int)."
"Incorrect number of arguments in call to int_power(int,
    int)."
"Extra argument in call to int_power (int, int)."
```

As shown above, in most cases the error message lists the function prototype, `int_power(int, int)` in this case, to help you determine the exact nature of the error.

- *Argument Mismatches:* Verify that each actual argument in a function call is in the correct position relative to its corresponding formal argument. You do this by comparing each actual argument to the type and description of its corresponding formal argument in the function prototype. Remember, the actual argument name is not what is important. Rather, it is the positional correspondence that is critical.

Argument list errors may go undetected. For example, consider the function

```
// RAISE FIRST ARGUMENT TO POWER OF SECOND
int int_power
  (int,        // IN: argument to be raised to specified power
   int);       // IN: power (greater than or equal to 0)
```

The call

```
result = int_power (5, 2);
```

would produce the result 25. The call

```
result = int_power (2, 5);
```

would yield the result 32. Clearly, the order of the arguments makes a difference. Yet both are integers, so an accidental reversal of the arguments will not even result in a type mismatch. We simply get the wrong answer.

C++ permits most type mismatches that you are likely to create at this point in your programming work and usually will not generate even a warning message. Instead, the compiler will perform a *standard conversion* on the actual argument (see Section 3.6), converting it to the type specified by the formal argument. In most cases, these conversions will produce incorrect results, which in turn will cause other errors during the execution of your program. The same is often true for mismatches in function return value types. These errors can be extremely difficult to locate during the debugging or testing of a program. The only way to avoid them is to check your arguments carefully, thus minimizing the potential for such mistakes. If actual argument conversions are required to ensure exact argument matching, perform explicit conversion using the casting functions introduced in Section 3.6.

There are two situations in which your compiler may provide help in finding argument list errors. One occurs when floating-point actual arguments are used where character formal arguments are expected. The other occurs when a floating-point value is returned where a character is expected. Even these mismatches are legal, but the results of the standard conversion are so likely to produce an execution error that most compilers will give you a warning diagnostic such as

```
"Float or double assigned to integer or character data type."
```

■ *Function Prototype and Definition Mismatches:* Once a prototype has been specified you can duplicate it, comments and all, when writing the header for the function definition. All that you need to do with the copied header is to provide an identifier for each function argument and to remove the semicolon at the end of the prototype. Conversely, if a function written by you or someone else is to be called, the prototype may be extracted easily from the header of the existing function. Just remove the argument identifiers and put a semicolon at the end. In fact, the argument identifiers are optional, so you can leave them in if you prefer.

Type mismatches between a function prototype and its definition will not be detected by the compiler. In all likelihood, these mismatches will be detected by the linker program for your C++ system, but the linker error message may be unclear:

```
"Undefined symbol int_power (int, int) in module square."
```

The cause of such a message is usually either a missing function definition (such as for function `int_power`) or the use of a function prototype that does not match the function definition (possibly because one or more of the arguments is of a different type, such as `float` instead of `char`). If the arguments in a function prototype do not match those in the definition, the linker assumes that the prototype refers to a different function, one for which there is no definition.

■ *return Statement Errors:* All functions that you write, except for type `void` functions, should terminate execution with a `return` statement which includes a constant, variable, or expression indicating the value to be returned. The data type of the value returned should match the type specified in the function header. Make sure that you do not omit the expression (or even worse, the entire `return` statement). If you forget to specify a return value when one is expected, you will see a message such as

```
"Return value expected."
```

or

```
"Function should return a value..."
```

If you specify a return value for a `void` function, you will see a message such as

```
"Function cannot return a value..."
"Warning: return with a value in function returning void."
```
■ *Missing Object Name in Call to a Member Function:* If you omit the object name in a call to a member function that uses dot notation to determine the object to which it is applied, you will get an error message such as

```
"Call to undefined function"
```

Because the object name is missing, the compiler cannot determine the class library in which the function is defined and assumes the function definition is missing.

■ *Missing #include Line or Incorrect Library Name in #include:* If you forget to include a library header file or write the wrong header (for example, `<string.h>` instead of `<string>`), you will see multiple error messages because the compiler will not be able to access the symbols and functions defined in that library. The error messages will tell you that symbols and functions from that library are undefined.

■ *Argument Mismatch in a Call to a Member Function:* If you have argument type mismatches or an incorrect number of arguments in a call to a member function, you will get an error message that looks like

```
"Could not find a match for getline(string, char)"
```

This message is displayed if you call function `getline` with a `string` and `char` argument instead of a `stream`, `string`, and `char` argument.

■ *Logic Errors in Your Program—Testing a Program and Checking Your Results:* Many errors, such as the incorrect specification of computations (in writing mathematical formulas) may go undetected by the compiler, yet produce incorrect results. For example, if you are given the formula

$$y = 3k^2 - 9k + 7$$

to program, and you write the C++ code

```
y = 9 * int_power (k, 2) - 3 * k + 7
```

(accidentally reversing the coefficients 9 and 3), no error will be detected by the compiler. As far as the compiler is concerned, no mistake has been made—the expression is perfectly legal C++ code, assuming `int_power` is properly defined and that `k` is an integer.

There is usually just one way to find such errors, and that is by testing your program using carefully chosen *test data samples* and verifying, for each sample, that your answer is correct. Such testing is a critical part of the programming process and cannot be omitted. As we proceed through the text, we will have more to say about testing strategies. One example of such a strategy was introduced in this chapter. It involved the decomposition of a problem into subproblems, writing the solutions to the subproblems using separate functions, and then separately testing these functions. This strategy can help simplify the testing process and make it easier for you to perform a more thorough test of your entire program.

CHAPTER REVIEW

This chapter has presented a number of the C++ function libraries and some examples of the use of the functions in library `math`. We indicated that prototypes for the library functions were not needed because the compiler already knew about the types of return values and arguments for these functions. We emphasized the reuse of our own functions, as well as the C++ library functions, as one of the primary means of reducing and managing problem complexity.

We introduced the important concept of procedural abstraction and showed how to divide a problem into subproblems and how to use a structure chart to indicate the relationship between subproblems. We introduced the function as a means of implementing subproblems as separate program units, and indicated that a C++ program is simply a collection of one or more functions, each representing the boxes in a structure chart.

Initially, we presented functions with no connections (no arguments or return values). We discussed the limitations of such functions, and introduced the idea of providing input arguments and return values. We showed how we could use each of these features of C++ to call functions and have them manipulate different data each time, thereby increasing the generality and reusability of the function.

We stressed the importance of ensuring the proper one-to-one correspondence between associated pairs of actual and formal arguments of a function. We indicated that the compiler uses the prototype declaration to check for this compatibility.

Comments play an important role in program documentation, especially pertaining to functions. We have consistently used comments to describe the purpose of each function that we have written. We have also used them to provide a description of the use of the input arguments and local variables of a function, and the purpose of each logical section of code within a function. By now, you should have absorbed several guidelines for using program comments.

Finally we described two classes that are available for performing operations on money amounts (class money) and processing character data (class string). We showed how to perform operations similar to those found on most word processors using string objects and the string member functions.

New C++ Constructs   The new C++ constructs introduced in this chapter are described in Table 3.4.

Table 3.4   Summary of New C++ Constructs

CONSTRUCT	EFFECT
Function Prototype (with comments)	
`// DISPLAYS A DIAMOND OF STARS` `void display ();`	Prototype for a function that has no arguments and returns no result.

`// COMPUTES AVERAGE OF TWO INTEGERS`
`float average`
`   (int, int);  // IN: the input args`
	Prototype for a function with two integer input arguments and a type `float` result.

(continued)

Table 3.4 *(continued)*

CONSTRUCT	EFFECT
Function Call `display ();`	Calls function `display`, causing it to begin execution.When execution is complete, control returns to the statement in the calling function that immediately follows the call.
Member Function Call `cout << whole_name.at (0);`	Calls `string` member function `at`, applying it to object `whole_name`. Displays the first character in `whole_name`.

Function Definition (with comments)

```
// DISPLAYS A DIAMOND OF STARS
void display ()
{
   cout << "    *    " << endl;
   cout << "   * *   " << endl;
   cout << "  *   *  " << endl;
   cout << " *     * " << endl;
   cout << "  *   *  " << endl;
   cout << "   * *   " << endl;
   cout << "    *    " << endl;
}  // end display
```

Definition of a function that has no arguments and returns no result.

```
// COMPUTES AVERAGE OF TWO INTEGERS
float average
   (int, int)  // IN: the input args
{
   return float (m1 + m2) / 2.0;
}  // end average
```

Definition of a function with 2 integer input arguments and a type `float` result.

Returns a type `float` result.

✔ **QUICK-CHECK EXERCISES**

1. Each function is executed in the order in which it is declared in the `main` program. True or false?
2. Describe the ordering of declarations as shown in this book.
3. What is a local declaration?
4. What is a structure chart?
5. Explain how a structure chart differs from an algorithm.

6. What does the function below do?

```
void nonsense ()
{
    cout << "*****" << endl;
    cout << "*   *" << endl;
    cout << "*****" << endl;
}   // end nonsense
```

7. Given the function `nonsense` from Exercise 6, describe the output that is produced when the following lines are executed.

```
{
    nonsense;
    nonsense;
    nonsense;
}
```

8. Explain what dot notation is and how you use it.

9. Trace the statements below:

```
string flower = "rose";
flower = flower + " of Sharon";
cout << flower.at (0) << flower.at (8) << endl;
cout << flower.find ("s") << " " << flower.find ("S")
    << endl;
flower.replace (5, 2, "from");
flower.remove (0, 4);
flower.insert (0, "thorn");
```

Answers to Quick-Check Exercises

1. False
2. We declare global constants and function prototypes before function `main`. Next comes function `main` followed by any other function definitions. Within each function, we declare any local constants and variables.
3. The declaration of a symbol inside the scope of a function and hence accessible only to that function.
4. A structure chart is a diagram used to show an algorithm's subproblems and their interdependence.
5. A structure chart shows the hierarchical relationship between subproblems; an algorithm lists the sequence in which subproblems are performed.
6. It would display a rectangle whenever it was called.
7. It displays three rectangles on top of each other.
8. In dot notation, you write an object name, a dot, and a member function name. You use dot notation to apply the member function to the object that precedes the dot.
9. Allocate a `string` object `flower` and initialize it to `"rose"`.
   Change `flower` to `"rose of Sharon"`.
   Display rS.
   Display 2 8.
   Change `flower` to `"rose from Sharon"`.

Change `flower` to `" from Sharon"`.
Change `flower` to `"thorn from Sharon"`.

REVIEW QUESTIONS

1. Discuss the strategy of divide and conquer.
2. Provide guidelines for the use of comments.
3. Briefly describe the steps you would take to derive an algorithm for a given problem.
4. The diagram that shows the algorithm steps and their interdependencies is called a _____.
5. What are three advantages of using functions?
6. A C++ program is a collection of one or more _____, one of which must be named _____.
7. When is a function executed? Can function definitions be nested?
8. Is the use of functions a more efficient use of the programmer's time or the computer's time? Explain your answer.
9. Write a program that draws a rectangle made up of asterisks. Draw a structure chart for the problem. Use two functions: `draw_sides` and `draw_line`. Discuss the reusability of your functions for drawing rectangles of different sizes.

PROGRAMMING PROJECTS

1. Add one or more of your own unique functions to the stick figure program presented in Section 3.2. Create several more pictures combining the `draw_circle`, `draw_intersect`, `draw_base`, and `draw_parallel` functions with your own. Make any modifications to these functions that you need in order to make the picture components fit nicely.
2. Write functions that display each of your initials in block letter form. Use these functions to display your initials.
3. Write a function that displays a triangle. Use this function to display six triangles on top of each other.
4. Four track stars entered the mile race at the Penn Relays. Write a program that will read the last name and in the race time in minutes and seconds for one runner and compute and print the speed in feet per second and in meters per second after his name. (*Hints:* There are 5280 feet in one mile, and one kilometer equals 3281 feet; one meter is equal to 3.281 feet.) Test your program on each of the times below.

Name	Minutes	Seconds
Deavers	3	52.83
Jackson	3	59.83
Smith	4	00.03
Rivera	4	16.22

Write and call a function that displays instructions to the program user. Write two other functions, one to compute the speed in meters per second and the other to compute the speed in feet per second.

5. A cyclist coasting on a level road slows from a speed of 10 miles/hr to 2.5 miles/hr in one minute. Write a computer program that calculates the cyclist's constant rate of deceleration and determines how long it will take the cyclist to come to rest, given an initial speed of 10 miles/hr. (*Hint:* Use the equation

$$a = (v_f - v_i) / t,$$

where a is acceleration, t is time interval, v_i is initial velocity, and v_f is the final velocity.) Write and call a function that displays instructions to the program user and another function that computes and returns the deceleration given v_f, v_i, and t.

6. In shopping for a new house, you must consider several factors. In this problem the initial cost of the house, estimated annual fuel costs, and annual tax rate are available. Write a program that will determine the total cost after a five-year period for each set of house data below. You should be able to inspect your program output to determine the "best buy." Use the money class where appropriate.

Initial House Cost	Annual Fuel Cost	Tax Rate
$67,000	$2300	0.025
$62,000	$2500	0.025
$75,000	$1850	0.020

To calculate the house cost, add the fuel cost for five years to the initial cost, then add the taxes for five years. Taxes for one year are computed by multiplying the tax rate by the initial cost. Write and call a function that displays instructions to the program user and another function that computes and returns the house cost given the initial cost, the annual fuel cost, and the tax rate.

7. Write a program that reads in a string containing exactly four words separated by one or more blanks. Perform the following operations.
   a. Insert a * symbol between each word and display the string.
   b. Replace the last word with "#!!@1234" and display the string.
   c. Remove each word, starting with the first, and display the string remaining.

8. Write a program that reads in a string containing exactly four words and stores the words in reverse order in another string. Display both strings.

4

Selection Structures: `if` and `switch` Statements

In this book we teach programming as a disciplined technique that results in programs that are easy to read and less likely to contain errors. We emphasize crafting programs in a consistent, clear, and concise fashion, building larger programs from smaller components, and reusing existing and tested components whenever possible.

In Chapters 4 and 5 we focus on the construction of these smaller components. Our approach, often referred to as structured programming, involves the use of a small number of easy-to-understand control structures to describe the steps required to solve a problem. At this point, we have used just one of these control mechanisms, the sequencing of steps in order of execution. In Chapters 4 and 5, we introduce the other two important control structures: selection structures, which enable us to choose from among several alternatives to be carried out, and iteration structures, which enable us to specify repeated execution of steps to be carried out.

As in the previous chapters, we focus on consistency and clarity of expression. We will emphasize commonly accepted guidelines (such as using meaningful names for identifiers) to write code that is adequately documented with comments and is clear and readable. Government organizations and industry are strong advocates of this structured programming approach because structured programs are much more cost effective in the long term.

4.1 ———— CONTROL STRUCTURES

The control structures of a programming language enable us to extend the top-down program development process to the level of specifying the algorithm steps or logic of each function that we write. We begin by expressing the algorithm in terms of the basic control steps required. We can then write the more detailed steps necessary to implement each of these control steps. The completed program component will still retain its higher-level structure as a sequence of control structures with one entry point and one exit point (see Fig. 4.1).

There are three categories of control structures: *sequence, selection,* and *iteration.* So far, we have illustrated sequential control using *compound statements* or blocks in C++. A compound statement is a group of statements bracketed by { and }. Control flows from top to bottom, from $statement_1$ to $statement_n$.

```
{
    statement₁;
    statement₂;
    .
    .
    .
    statementₙ;
}
```

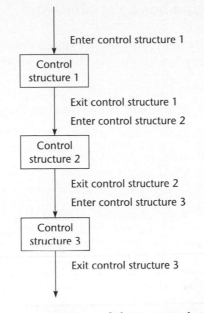

Figure 4.1   A program as a sequence of three control structures

In this chapter we explain how to write algorithms and programs with steps that select from several alternative courses of action. We will see two ways to do this in C++. The first is to use a C++ if control statement with a logical expression; the second is to use the switch control statement. This chapter provides many examples of the use of if and switch statements.

4.2 ——— LOGICAL EXPRESSIONS

A program chooses among alternative steps by testing the value of key variables. For example, different tax rates apply to different salary levels; consequently, an income tax program must select the rate appropriate for each worker's salary. The program selects the rate by comparing the salary value to the maximum salary for a particular income tax bracket. In C++, *logical expressions,* or *conditions,* are used to perform such comparisons. Each logical expression has two possible values, true or false, where true indicates a successful test and false indicates an unsuccessful test.

Type `bool` Variables and Constants

The simplest logical expression is a type `bool` variable or constant. For the type `bool` variable `leap_year`, the assignment statement

```
leap_year = true;
```

specifies that `leap_year` has the value `true`; the statement

```
bool is_found, flag;
```

declares `is_found` and `flag` to be `bool` variables—variables that may be assigned only the values `true` and `false`. Given these declarations, all the following assignment statements are valid.

```
is_found = true;        // is_found gets the value true
flag  = false;          // flag gets the value false
is_found = flag;        // is_found gets the value of flag
```

After these statements execute, both `flag` and `is_found` have the value `false`.

Simple Logical Expressions

Logical expressions may be formed using combinations of three kinds of operators: relational, equality, and logical (see Table 4.1). In the following paragraphs, we describe the permissible forms of C++ expressions using these three kinds of operators. A logical expression must have a type `bool` result.

The following are simple logical expressions with a single relational or equality operator:

```
i < 3
x != 0
y >= 5
```

The relational operators are familiar symbols (< and >= above). The items being compared, or operands, are often two variables or a variable and a constant. If `i` is type `int`, the condition `i < 3` is true when `i` is negative, or `i` is 0, 1, or 2. The two operands of a relational operator should be the same data

Table 4.1 C++ Operators Used in Logical Expressions

RELATIONAL	EQUALITY	LOGICAL
< less than	== equal to	&& and
<= less than or equal to	!= not equal to	|| or
> greater than		! not
>= greater than or equal to		

type (for example, both type int, float, char, bool, money, or string), although C++ does allow some mixing of types.

Be careful not to confuse the assignment operator = with the equality operator ==. The not symbol ! may be used alone as a logical operator or as part of the symbol pair != , meaning "not equal," the opposite of ==. As with all C++ operator pairs, they must appear together with no space between them.

Example 4.1   Individual tax rates depend on a person's salary. Assume single persons who earn less than $24,000 are taxed at a rate of 15 percent, while those who earn more than $24,000 but not more than $58,150 pay 15 percent of the first $24,000 earned and 28 percent of the rest. If taxable income is stored in a type float or type money variable income, the logical expression corresponding to the question "Is annual income less than $24,000?" is

```
income < 24000.00
```

This expression evaluates to true when the answer is "Yes," and it evaluates to false when the answer is "No."   ∎

Example 4.2   Table 4.2 shows the relational and equality operators with some sample conditions. Each condition is evaluated assuming the variable values below.

x	power	max_power	y	item	min_item	mom_or_dad	num	sentinel
−5	1024	1024	7	1.5	−999.0	'm'	999	999

∎

Logical Expressions Involving Logical Operators

We can also use the logical operators—&& (and), || (or), and ! (not)—to combine simpler logical expressions to form more complicated logical expressions:

```
(salary < minimum_salary) || (dependents > 5)
(temperature >= 90.0) && (humidity >= 0.90)
```

Table 4.2   Use of C++ Relational and Equality Operators

OPERATOR	SAMPLE CONDITION	ENGLISH MEANING	TYPE bool RESULT
<=	x <= 0	x less than or equal to 0	true
<	power < max_power	power less than max_power	false
>=	x >= y	x greater than or equal to y	false
>	item > min_item	item greater than min_item	true
==	mom_or_dad == 'm'	mom_or_dad equal to 'm'	true
!=	num != sentinel	num not equal to sentinel	false

Table 4.3   && Operator

OPERAND1	OPERAND2	OPERAND1 && OPERAND2
true	true	true
true	false	false
false	true	false
false	false	false

The first logical expression determines whether an employee is eligible for special scholarship funds. It evaluates to true if *either* condition in parentheses is true. The second logical expression describes an unbearable summer day, with temperature and humidity both in the nineties. The expression evaluates to true only when *both* conditions are true.

The operands (in this case, logical expressions themselves) associated with a logical operator each determine a type bool result (true or false). The resulting logical expression also has a bool result. None of the parentheses included in these expressions are required; they are included just for clarity.

Type bool variables are considered to be the simplest form of a logical expression, so they also can be operands of logical operators. The logical expression

```
winning_record && (!probation)
```

manipulates two bool variables (winning_record, probation). A college team for which this expression is true has a winning record and is not on probation, so it may be eligible for the postseason tournament. Note that the expression

```
(winning_record == true) && (probation == false)
```

is logically equivalent to the one above; however, the first one is preferred because it is more concise and more readable.

Table 4.3 shows that the and operator && yields a true result only when both its operands are true. Table 4.4 shows that the or operator || yields a false result only when both its operands are false. The not operator ! has a

Table 4.4 || Operator

OPERAND1	OPERAND2	OPERAND1 || OPERAND2
true	true	true
true	false	true
false	true	true
false	false	false

Table 4.5 ! Operator

OPERAND1	!OPERAND1
true	false
false	true

single operand; Table 4.5 shows that the not operator yields the logical *complement*, or *negation*, of its operand (that is, if flag is true, !flag is false and vice versa).

Simple expressions such as

```
x == y
x < y
```

can be negated by applying the unary ! operator to the entire expression.

```
!(x == y)
!(x < y)
```

However, using the *logical complement* of the relational operator often works just as well in these situations:

```
x != y
x >= y
```

The best time to use the ! operator is when you want to reverse the value of a long or complicated logical expression that involves many operators. For example, expressions such as

```
(salary < min_salary) || (number_dependents > 5)
```

are most easily negated by enclosing the entire expression in parentheses and preceding it by the ! operator.

```
!((salary < min_salary) || (number_dependents > 5))
```

Remember to use logical operators only with logical expressions.

Operator Precedence

The precedence of an operator determines its order of evaluation in an expression. Table 4.6 shows the precedence of all C++ operators we have learned thus far. As you can see, the ! operator has the highest precedence followed by the arithmetic, relational, equality, and then the binary logical operators. To prevent errors and to clarify the meaning of expressions, use parentheses freely.

Table 4.6   Operator Precedence

OPERATOR	DESCRIPTION
highest (evaluated first)	
`!, +, -`	Logical not, unary plus, unary minus
`*, /, %`	Multiplication, division, modulus
`+, -`	Addition, subtraction
`<, <=, >=, >`	Relational inequality
`==, !=`	Equal, not equal
`&&`	Logical and
`||`	Logical or
`=`	Assignment
lowest (evaluated last)	

Example 4.3   The expression

```
x < min + max
```

involving the `float` variables `x`, `min`, and `max` is interpreted correctly in C++ as

```
x < (min + max)
```

because + has higher precedence than <. The expression

```
min <= x && x <= max
```

is also correct, but providing the extra parentheses

```
(min <= x) && (x <= max)
```

makes the expression clearer.

   Because ! has higher precedence than ==, C++ incorrectly interprets the expression

```
!x == y
```

as

```
(!x) == y
```

Insert the parentheses where needed to avoid this error:

```
!(x == y)
```

■

Writing Conditions in C++

To solve programming problems, you must convert conditions expressed in English to C++. Many algorithm steps require testing to see if a variable's value is within a specified range of values. For example, if `min` represents the

Figure 4.2 Range of true values for `(min <= x) && (x <= max)`

lower bound of a range of values and `max` represents the upper bound (`min` is less than `max`), the expression

```
(min <= x) and (x <= max)
```

tests whether `x` lies within the range `min` through `max`, inclusive. In Fig. 4.2 this range is shaded. The expression is true if `x` lies within this range and false if `x` is outside the range.

Expressions similar to the one just shown are quite common in programming. If `min` represents the lower bound of a range of values and `max` represents the upper bound (`min` is less than `max`), this expression tests whether `x` lies within the range `min` through `max` inclusive.

Example 4.4 The following are all legal logical expressions if `x`, `y`, and `z` are type `float`. The value of each expression, shown on the right, assumes that `x` is 3.0, `y` is 4.0, and `z` is 2.0. Note that not all of the parentheses used in these examples are necessary. Rather, they are included here for clarity.

1. `(x > z) && (y > z)`	true
2. `(x + y / z) <= 3.5`	false
3. `(z > x) || (z > y)`	false
4. `!(y == z)`	true
5. `(x == 1.0) || (x == 3.0)`	true
6. `(z < x) && (x < y)`	true
7. `(x <= z) || (x >= y)`	false
8. `!(x > y) || y + z >= x - z`	true
9. `!((x > y) || ((y + z) >= (x - z)))`	false

Expression 1 gives the C++ form of the relationship "x and y are greater than z." You may be tempted to write this as

```
x && y > z
```

Although such an expression is syntactically correct in C++, it may not produce the desired result because the left operand `x` is not a logical expression. Similarly, expression 5 shows the correct way to express the relationship "x is equal to 1.0 or to 3.0."

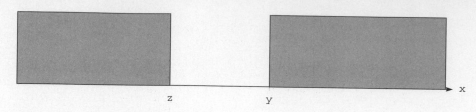

Figure 4.3   Range of true values for (x <= z) || (x >= y)

Expression 6 is the C++ form of the relationship $z < x < y$ (i.e., "x is in the range 2.0 to 4.0)." The boundary values, 2.0 and 4.0, are excluded from the range of x values that yield a true result.

Expression 7 is true if the value of x lies outside the range bounded by z and y. In Fig. 4.3, the shaded areas represent the values of x that yield a true result. Both y and z are included in the set of values that yield a true result.

Finally, expression 8 is evaluated in Fig. 4.4; the values given at the beginning of Example 4.3 are shown above the expression.

The expression in Fig. 4.4 is rewritten below with parentheses to show the order of evaluation. Although these parentheses are not required, they do clarify the meaning of the expression and we recommend their use.

(!(x > y)) || ((y + z) >= (x - z))   ∎

Comparing Characters and Strings

Besides comparing numbers, it is also possible to compare characters and strings of characters using the relational and equality operators. Several examples of such comparisons are shown in Table 4.7.

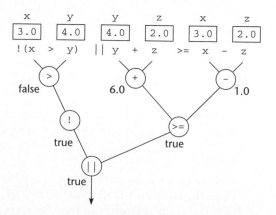

Figure 4.4   Evaluation tree for !(x > y) || y + z >= x - z

Table 4.7 Examples of Comparisons

EXPRESSION	VALUE
`'a' < 'c'`	true
`'X' <= 'A'`	false
`'3' > '4'`	false
`('A' <= ch) && (ch <= 'Z')`	true if ch contains an uppercase letter; otherwise falsefalse
`"XYZ" <= "ABC"`	false (X <= A)
`"acts" > "aces"`	true (t > e)
`"ace" != "aces"`	true (strings are different)
`"ace" < "aces"`	true

In writing such comparisons, you can assume that the uppercase letters appear in alphabetical order. Lowercase letters also appear in alphabetical order, and the *digit characters* are ordered as expected: '0' < '1' < '2' < ... < '9'. For the relationships among other characters (such as '+', '<', '!', etc.) or between two characters not in the same group (for example, 'a' and 'A', or 'B' and 'b', or 'c' and 'A'), see Appendix A.

If you include library `string`, you can compare `string` objects (see the last four examples in Table 4.7). C++ compares two strings by comparing corresponding pairs of characters in each string, starting with the leftmost pair. The result is based on the relationship between the first pair of different characters (for example, for `"acts"` and `"aces"`, the result depends on characters t and e). The last comparison involves a string (`"aces"`) that begins with a shorter *substring* (`"ace"`). The substring `"ace"` is considered less than the longer string `"aces"`. We will say more about character comparisons in Chapter 7.

Boolean Assignment

Assignment statements can be written to provide a type `bool` value to a `bool` variable. If same is type `bool`, the statement

```
same = true;
```

assigns the value `true` to same. Since assignment statements have the general form

variable = expression;

you can use the statement

```
same = (x == y);
```

to assign the value of the logical expression (x == y) to same. The value of same is true when x and y are equal; otherwise, same is false.

Example 4.5   The following assignment statements assign values to two type bool variables, in_range and is_letter. Variable in_range gets true if the value of n is in the range −10 through 10; variable is_letter gets true if ch is an uppercase or a lowercase letter.

```
in_range = (n > -10) && (n < 10);
is_letter = (('A' <= ch) && (ch <= 'Z')) ||
            (('a' <= ch) && (ch <= 'z'))
```

The expression in the first assignment statement is true if n satisfies both the conditions listed (n is greater than −10 and n is less than 10); otherwise, the expression is false. The expression in the second assignment statement uses the bool operators &&, ||. The first subexpression (before ||) is true if ch is an uppercase letter; the second subexpression (after ||) is true if ch is a lowercase letter. Consequently, is_letter gets true if ch is a letter; otherwise, is_letter gets false.   ∎

Example 4.6   Consider the expression

```
even = (n % 2 == 0)
```

If n is an even number, the expression

```
(n % 2 == 0)
```

is true because all even numbers are divisible by 2; otherwise, the expression is false. Therefore, if the remainder of the modulus operation is zero, the variable even will be assigned the bool value true. If the remainder of the modulus operation is not zero, (n % 2 == 0) will evaluate to false, and even will be assigned the bool value false.   ∎

Writing bool Values

Most logical expressions appear in control structures, where they determine the sequence in which C++ statements execute. You will rarely have a need to read bool values as input data or display bool values as program results. If necessary, however, you can display the value of a bool variable using the output operator <<. If flag is false, the statement

```
cout << "The value of flag is " << flag;
```

displays the line

```
The value of flag is 0
```

If you need to read a data value into a type `bool` variable, you can represent the data as an integer: use 0 for false and 1 for true.

If Type `bool` Is Not Implemented on Your C++ Compiler

Not all C++ compilers had implemented type `bool` when this book was written. If this data type is not available on your compiler, you will need to use the `int` data type to model type `bool` data. C++ uses the integer value 0 to represent false and any nonzero integer value (usually 1) to represent true. With this in mind, you can use integers to write logical expressions in the same way that we used type `bool` in this section—with no other difference to be seen. A logical expression that evaluates to 0 is considered false; a logical expression that evaluates to nonzero is considered true.

EXERCISES FOR SECTION 4.2

Self-Check

1. Assuming x is 15.0 and y is 25.0, what are the values of the following conditions?

```
x != y       x < x       x >- (y - x)       x == (y + x - y)
```

2. Evaluate each expression below if a is 5, b is 10, c is 15, and d is 0.

```
a. (c == (a + b)) || (c -- d)
b. (a != 7) && (c >= 6) || ((a + c) <= 20)
c. !(b <= 12) && (a % 2 == 0)
d. !((a > 5) || (c < (a + b)))
```

3. Which of the following logical expressions are incorrect and why? Assume x and y are `float` and p, q, and r are type `bool`.

```
a. x < 5.1 && y > 22.3        b.        p && q || q && r
```

4. Draw evaluation trees for the following:

```
a. a = (b + a - B)
b. (c = (a + b)) or not flag
c. (a <> 7) and (c >= 6) or flag
d. !(b <= 12) && (a % 2 = 0)
e. !((a > 5) || (c < (a + b )))
```

5. Draw the evaluation tree for expression 9 in Example 4.4.

Programming

1. Write a logical expression that is true for each of the following conditions.

a. `age` is from 18 to 21 inclusive.
b. `water` is less than 1.5 and also greater than 0.1.
c. `year` is divisible by 4. (*Hint:* use %.)
d. `speed` is not greater than 55.

2. Write logical assignment statements for the following:

a. Assign a value of `true` to `between` if n is in the range –k and +k, inclusive; otherwise, assign a value of `false`.

  b. Assign a value of true to uppercase if ch is an uppercase letter; otherwise, assign a value of false.
  c. Assign a value of true to divisor if m is a divisor of n; otherwise assign a value of false.

4.3 —— INTRODUCTION TO THE if CONTROL STATEMENT

In C++, the primary selection control structure is an if statement that always contains a logical expression. We can use the if control statement to select from several alternatives of executable statements. For example, the if statement

```
if (gross > 100.00)
    net = gross - tax;
else
    net = gross;
```

selects one of the two assignment statements listed. It selects the statement immediately following the condition (gross > 100.00) if the logical expression is true (i.e., gross is greater than 100.00); it selects the statement following the reserved word else if the logical expression is false (i.e., gross is not greater than 100.00). It is never possible for both statements to execute after testing a particular condition. You must always enclose the condition in parentheses; however, you must not place a semicolon after the condition.

Figure 4.5 provides a graphical description called a *flowchart* for the if control statement above. The figure shows that the condition (gross > 100.00) enclosed in the diamond-shaped box is evaluated first. If the condition is true,

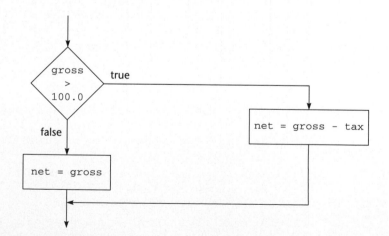

Figure 4.5   Flowchart of if control statement with two alternatives

the arrow labeled true is followed, and the assignment statement in the rectangle on the right is executed. If the condition is false, the arrow labeled false is followed, and the assignment statement in the rectangle on the left is executed.

More if Statement Examples

The if statement above has two alternatives, but only one will be executed for a given value of gross. Example 4.7 illustrates that an if statement can also have a single alternative that is executed only when the condition is true.

Example 4.7   The following if statement has one alternative that is executed only when x is not equal to zero. It causes product to be multiplied by x; the new value is saved in product, replacing the old value. If x is equal to zero, the multiplication is not performed. Figure 4.6 shows a flowchart for this if statement.

```
// Multiply product by a non zero x only.
if (x != 0)
    product = product * x;
```
■

Example 4.8   The following if statement has two alternatives. It displays either "Hi Mom" or "Hi Dad" depending on the character stored in variable mom_or_dad (type char).

```
if (mom_or_dad == 'm')
    cout << "Hi Mom" << endl;
else
    cout << "Hi Dad" << endl;
```
■

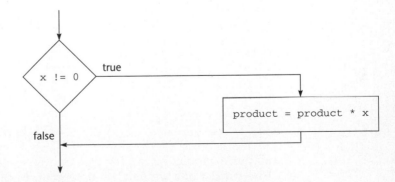

Figure 4.6   Flowchart of if with one alternative

Example 4.9   The following if statement has one alternative; it displays the message "Hi Mom" only when mom_or_dad has the value 'm'. Regardless of whether or not "Hi Mom" is displayed, the message "Hi Dad" is always displayed.

```
if (mom_or_dad == 'm')
    cout <<  "Hi Mom" << endl;
cout << "Hi Dad" << endl;
```
■

Example 4.10   The following if control statement displays the result of a string search operation. The call to string member function find (see Table 3.3) returns to pos_target (type int) the starting position in string test_string of the string target. If target is not found, find returns a value that is not in the allowable range (0 through *k*-1 where *k* is the length of test_string). The if statement tests whether the value returned to pos_target is in range before reporting the search result. If test_string is "This is a string" and target is "his", the if statement would display his found at position 1.

```
pos_target = test_string.find (target);
if ((0 <= pos_target) && (pos_target < test_string.length ()))
    cout << target << " found at position " << pos_target
         << endl;
else
    cout << target << " not found!" << endl;
```
■

Example 4.11   The following if statement replaces one substring (target) with another (new_string). If string target is found in test_string, the true task of the if statement replaces it with new_string. Recall that the three arguments of string member function replace (see Table 3.3) are the starting position of the string to be replaced (targ_pos), the number of characters to be removed (target.length ()), and the replacement string (new_string). If test_string is "This is a string", target is "his", and new_string is "here", test_string will become "There is a string".

```
pos_target = test_string.find (target);
if ((0 <= pos_target) && (pos_target < test_string.length ()))
    test_string.replace (pos_target, target.length (),
                         new_string);
else
    cout << target << " not found - no replacement!" << endl;
```
■

In all our examples so far, the true and false alternatives of an if control structure consist of a single C++ statement. In the next section, we will see how to write true and false alternatives consisting of more than one statement.

PROGRAM STYLE

Format of the if Control Statement

In all the if statement examples, *statement$_T$* and *statement$_F$* are indented. If you use the word else, enter it on a separate line, aligned with the word if. The format of the if statement makes its meaning apparent. Again, we do this solely to improve program readability; the format used makes no difference to the compiler. ∎

C++ SYNTAX

if Control Statement (one alternative)

Form: if (*condition*)
    statement$_T$

Example: if (x > 0.0)
    positive_product = positive_product * x;

Interpretation: If the *condition* evaluates to true, then *statement$_T$* is executed; otherwise, it is skipped. ∎

C++ SYNTAX

if Control Statement (two alternatives)

Form: if (*condition*)
    statement$_T$
  else
    statement$_F$

Example: if (x >= 0.0)
    cout << "Positive" << endl;
  else
    cout << "Negative" << endl;

Interpretation: If the *condition* evaluates to true, then *statement$_T$* is executed and *statement$_F$* is skipped; otherwise, *statement$_T$* is skipped and *statement$_F$* is executed. ∎

EXERCISES FOR SECTION 4.3

Self-Check   1. What do the following statements display?

```
a. if (12 < 12)
      cout << "Never" << endl;
   else
      cout << "Always"  << endl;
b. var1 = 15.0;
   var2 = 25.12;
```

```
if (2 * var1 >= var2)
    cout << "O.K." << endl;
else
    cout << "Not O.K." << endl;
```

2. What value is assigned to x for each segment below when y is 15.0?

   a.
   ```
   x = 25.0;
   if (y != (x - 10.0))
       x = x - 10.0;
   else
       x = x / 2.0;
   ```

   b.
   ```
   if ((y < 15.0) && (y >= 0.0))
       x = 5 * y;
   else
       x = 2 * y;
   ```

3. Trace the execution of the if statement in Example 4.11 for the values of target and new_string below. For each part, assume test_string is "Here is the string" before the if statement executes.
   a. target is "the", new_string is "that"
   b. target is "Here", new_string is "There"
   c. target is "Where", new_string is "There"

Programming

1. Write C++ statements to carry out the steps below.
   a. Store the absolute difference of x and y in z, where the absolute difference is (x - y) or (y - x), whichever is positive. Do not use the abs or fabs function in your solution.
   b. If x is zero, add 1 to zero_count. If x is negative, add x to minus_sum. If x is greater than zero, add x to plus_sum.

4.4 ——— if STATEMENTS WITH COMPOUND ALTERNATIVES

The *statement*$_T$ following the condition to be tested or *statement*$_F$ following the word else may be a single executable statement or a compound statement. Assignment statements, function call statements, or even other if statements may be used in writing these alternatives. Note that in C++, a compound statement is syntactically equivalent to a single statement. Thus, compound statements may be used anywhere the element *statement* appears in our earlier syntax displays. We provide some illustrations of this next.

Example 4.12   In later chapters we will see that it is useful to be able to order a pair of data values in memory so that the smaller value is stored in one variable (say x) and the larger value in another (y). The if statement in Fig. 4.7 rearranges any two values stored in x and y so that the smaller number will always be in x and the larger number will always be in y. If the two numbers are already in the proper order, the compound statement will not be executed.

Figure 4.7 `if` control statement to order **x** and **y**

```
if (x > y)
{                         // exchange values in x and y
   temp = x;              // store original value of x in temp
   x = y;                 // store original value of y in x
   y = temp;              // store original value of x (from temp) in y
}  // end if
```

The variables x, y, and temp should all be the same data type. Although the values of x and y are being switched, an additional variable, temp, is needed for storage of a copy of one of these values.

Table 4.8 provides a step-by-step simulation of the execution of the if control statement when x is 12.5 and y is 5.0. We will *hand trace* through each statement much like the computer would do. The table shows that temp is initially undefined (indicated by ?). Each line of the table shows the part of the if statement that is being executed, followed by its effect. If any variable gets a new value, its new value is shown on that line. The last value stored in x is 5.0, and the last value stored in y is 12.5 as desired. ∎

Example 4.13 As the manager of a clothing boutique, you want to keep records of your financial transactions. The true task in the if statement below processes a transaction (transaction_amount) representing a check written as payment for goods received (in which case, transaction_type is 'c'); the false task processes a deposit made to your checking account. In either case, an appropriate message is printed and the account balance (balance) is updated. Both the true and false statements are compound statements.

```
if (transaction_type == 'c')
{  // process check
   cout << "Check for $" << transaction_amount << endl;
   balance = balance - transaction_amount;
```

Table 4.8 Step-by-Step Hand Trace of `if` Control Statement

STATEMENT PART	x	y	temp	EFFECT
	12.5	5.0	?	
if (x > y)				12.5 > 5.0 is true
{				
temp = x;			12.5	Store x in temp
x = y;	5.0			Store original y in x
y = temp;		12.5		Store original x in y
}				

```
      }
      else
      {   // process deposit
          cout << "Deposit of $" << transaction_amount << endl;
          balance = balance + transaction_amount;
      }   // end if
```

PROGRAM STYLE

Writing if Statements with Compound True or False Statements

Each if statement in this section contains at least one compound statement bracketed by { }. The placement of the braces is a stylistic preference. Your instructor may want the opening { at the end of the same line as the condition. The closing } of a compound if may also appear on the same line as the else:

```
} else {
```

We chose to use the readable style shown in Example 4.13; your instructor may prefer another style. Whatever style you follow, be consistent.

EXERCISES FOR SECTION 4.4

Self-Check

1. Insert the semicolons where needed below to avoid syntax errors. Indent as needed to improve readability.

```
if (x > y)
{
x = x + 10.0
cout << "x bigger" << endl;
}
else
cout << "x smaller" << endl

cout << "y is " << y << endl;
```

2. What would be the effect of removing the braces { } in Self-Check Exercise 1?
3. What would be the effect of placing braces around the last two lines in the same exercise?
4. Correct the following if statement:

```
if (num1 < 0)
    product = num1 * num2 * num3;
    cout << "Product is " << product << endl;
}
else
{
    sum = num1 + num2 + num3;
    cout << "Sum is " << sum << endl;
}
```

Programming
1. Write an `if` statement that might be used to compute the average of a set of n numbers whose sum is `total` when n is greater than 0 and prints an error message when n is not greater than 0. The average should be computed by dividing `total` by n.
2. Write an interactive program that contains a compound `if` statement and may be used to compute the area of a square (area = side^2) or triangle (area = $1/2$ × base × height) after prompting the user to type the first character of the figure name (`t` or `s`).

4.5 ——— DECISION STEPS IN ALGORITHMS

In the case that follows, we will see how to write a payroll program that can be used to compute an employee's gross pay and net pay after deductions.

CASE STUDY: PAYROLL PROBLEM

Problem Statement

Your company pays its hourly workers once a week. An employee's pay is based upon the number of hours worked (to the nearest half hour) and the employee's hourly pay rate. Weekly hours exceeding 40 are paid at a rate of time and a half. Employees who earn over $100 a week must pay union dues of $15 per week. Write a payroll program that will determine the gross pay and net pay for an employee.

Problem Analysis

The relevant employee data include the input data for hours worked and hourly pay and two required outputs, gross pay and net pay. Several constants are also quite important: the union dues ($15), the minimum weekly earnings before these dues must be paid ($100), the maximum hours before overtime must be paid (40), and the overtime rate (1.5 the usual hourly rate for the employee). With this information, we can begin to build the data requirements table for this problem. We can model all data using the `money` (see Section 3.7) and `float` data types. For now, we will not concern ourselves with how to arrive at the gross and net pay figures; we need know only that they must be computed and we will delay consideration of this detail until later.

DATA REQUIREMENTS

Problem Constants

```
max_no_dues = 100.00          — maximum earnings (dollars)
                                without paying union dues
```

```
dues = 15.00                — union dues (dollars) to be paid
max_no_overtime = 40.0      — maximum hours without over-
                              time pay
overtime_rate = 1.5         — time and a half for overtime
```

Problem Input

```
hours (float)              — hours worked
rate (money)               — hourly rate
```

Problem Output

```
gross (money)              — gross pay
net (money)                — net pay
```

Program Design

The problem solution requires that the program read the hours worked and the hourly rate before performing any computations. After reading these data, we need to compute and then display the gross pay and net pay.

The structure chart for this problem (Fig. 4.8) shows the decomposition of the original problem into five subproblems. In order for each subproblem to be solved using a separate function, the function name appears under its box.

We have added to the structure chart *data flow* information that shows the input and output of each program step. The structure chart shows that the step "enter data" provides values for hours and rate as its output (data flow arrow points up). Similarly, the step "compute gross pay" uses hours and rate as input to the function (data flow arrow points down) and provides gross as the function output. We will discuss the relevance of the data flow information after we complete the problem solution.

We can now write the initial algorithm to show the order in which these subproblems are to be carried out.

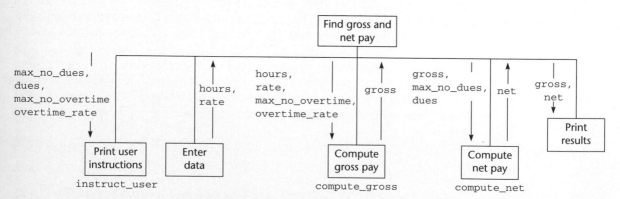

Figure 4.8   Structure chart for payroll problem

INITIAL ALGORITHM

1. Display user instructions (function `instruct_user`).
2. Enter hours worked and hourly rate.
3. Compute gross pay (function `compute_gross`).
4. Compute net pay (function `compute_net`).
5. Display gross pay and net pay.

We now turn our attention to the three lower-level functions listed in parentheses in the algorithm. We begin by defining the interfaces between these functions and the main function.

Analysis for `instruct_user` (step 1)

The constant identifiers, `max_no_dues`, `dues`, `max_no_overtime`, and `overtime_rate` are treated as input arguments so that their values may be referenced in this function. This practice is preferable to just including the constant values inside the function. If values associated with these constants should change in the future, we would need to modify only the main function. We use the prefix `const` before a formal argument's data type to indicate that the function body cannot change the actual argument's value (a constant).

DATA REQUIREMENTS FOR `instruct_user`

Input Arguments

`max no dues (const money)`	— maximum earnings (dollars) before paying union dues
`dues (const money)`	— union dues amount (dollars)
`max_no_overtime (const float)`	— maximum hours without overtime pay
`overtime_rate (const float)`	— time and a half for overtime

Function Return Value

(none—a void function)

FUNCTION PROTOTYPE

```
// DISPLAY USER INSTRUCTIONS
void instruct_user
   (const money,  // IN: max earnings (dollars) before paying
                  //     union dues
    const money,  // IN: union dues (dollars)
    const float,  // IN: max number of hours without overtime pay
    const float); // IN: overtime rate
```

Analysis for `compute_gross` (step 3)

The function `compute_gross` needs to know the hours worked and the hourly rate for the employee. It also needs the values of the constants (`max_no_overtime` and `overtime_rate`) involved in determining the employee's gross pay. (It does not need to know anything about the values required to compute the net pay.)

DATA REQUIREMENTS FOR `compute_gross`

Input Arguments

hours (`float`)	— number of hours worked
rate (`money`)	— hourly pay rate (dollars)
max_no_overtime (`const float`)	— maximum hours without overtime pay
overtime_rate (`const float`)	— time and a half for over-time

Function Return Value

gross (`float`)

FORMULA

gross pay = hours worked $\times$ hourly pay

FUNCTION PROTOTYPE

```
// FIND THE GROSS PAY
money compute_gross
   (float,         // IN: number of hours worked
    money,         // IN: hourly pay rate (dollars)
    const float,   // IN: max number of hours without overtime pay
    const float);  // IN: overtime rate
```

Analysis for `compute_net` (step 4)

Once we have the information provided by `compute_gross`, we are ready to refine step 4 and compute the net pay. It is here that the union dues cutoff value ($100) and the dues ($15) are required.

DATA REQUIREMENTS FOR `compute_net`

Input Arguments

gross (`money`)	— gross pay (dollars)
max_no_dues (`const money`)	— maximum earnings (dollars) before paying union dues
dues (`const money`)	— union dues amount (dollars)

Function Return Value

    net (money)

FORMULA

net pay = gross pay − deductions

FUNCTION PROTOTYPE

```
// FIND THE NET PAY
money compute_net
    (money,             // IN: gross pay (dollars)
     const money,       // IN: maximum earnings (dollars) before
                        //     paying union dues
     const money);      // IN: union dues(dollars)
```

We now write the main function along with the prototypes for the lower-level functions (see Fig. 4.9a). We can then turn our attention to designing and implementing the three lower-level functions required to complete the solution to this problem.

Figure 4.9a   Main function for payroll problem

```
// FILE: Payroll.cpp
// COMPUTES AND PRINTS GROSS PAY AND NET PAY GIVEN AN HOURLY
//    RATE AND NUMBER OF HOURS WORKED.  DEDUCTS UNION DUES OF $15
//    IF GROSS SALARY EXCEEDS $100; OTHERWISE, DEDUCTS NO DUES.


#include <iostream.h>          // needed for cin and cout
#include "money.h"             // needed for money data type

   // Functions used ...
   // DISPLAYS USER INSTRUCTIONS
   void instruct_user
   (const money,       // IN: max earnings (dollars) before paying union dues
    const money,       // IN: union dues (dollars)
    const float,       // IN: max number of hours without overtime pay
    const float);      // IN: overtime rate

   // FIND THE GROSS PAY
   money compute_gross
   (float,             // IN: number of hours worked
    money,             // IN: hourly pay rate (dollars)
    const float,       // IN: max number of hours without overtime pay
    const float);      // IN: overtime rate
```

(continued)

Figure 4.9a *(continued)*

```
// FIND THE NET PAY
money compute_net
(money,              // IN: gross pay (dollars)
 const money,        // IN: max earnings (dollars) before paying union dues
 const money);       // IN: union dues (dollars)

void main ()
{
    // Local data ...
    const money max_no_dues = 100.00;    // max earnings before dues (dollars)
    const money dues = 15.00;            // dues amount (dollars)
    const float max_no_overtime = 40.0;  // max hours before overtime
    const float overtime_rate = 1.5;     // overtime rate

    float hours;                         // input: hours worked
    float rate;                          // input: hourly pay rate (dollars)
    money gross;                         // output: gross pay (dollars)
    money net;                           // output: net pay (dollars)

    // Display user instructions.
    instruct_user (max_no_dues, dues, max_no_overtime, overtime_rate);

    // Enter hours and rate.
    cout << "Hours worked: ";
    cin  >> hours;
    cout << "Hourly rate: ";
    cin  >> rate;

    // Compute gross salary.
    gross = compute_gross (hours, rate, max_no_overtime, overtime_rate);

    // Compute net salary.
    net = compute_net (gross, max_no_dues, dues);

    // Print gross and net.
    cout << "Gross salary is " << gross << endl;
    cout << "Net salary is " << net << endl;
}
// Insert lower-level functions here.
// ...
```

Design for `instruct_user`

This function simply displays a short list of instructions and information about the program for the user. The information includes the values of the four program constants and other information to ensure that the user has an overview of what the program does and how the user should enter the input data.

Design for `compute_gross`

To compute the gross pay, we first need to determine whether any overtime pay is due. If there is, we should compute regular pay and overtime pay and return their sum. If not, we simply compute gross pay as the product of hours and rate. We list the local data needed and refine the algorithm step (step 3) as a *decision step*.

Local data for `compute_gross`

gross (money)   — gross pay (dollars)
regular_pay (money)   — pay for first 40 hours of work
overtime_pay (money)   — pay for hours in excess of 40 (dollars)

Algorithm for `compute_gross`

3.1. If the hours worked exceeds 40.0 (max hours before overtime)
    3.1.1. compute regular_pay.
    3.1.2. compute overtime_pay.
    3.1.3. add regular_pay to overtime_pay to get gross.
  else
    3.1.4. compute gross as hours * rate.

The decision step above is expressed in *pseudocode,* which is a mixture of English and C++ reserved words that is used to describe algorithm steps. In the pseudocode for a decision step, we use indentation and the reserved words `if` and `else` to show the flow of control.

Design for `compute_net`

We simply list the local data needed for `compute_net` and refine the algorithm step (step 4).

Local data for `compute_net`

net (money)   — net pay (dollars)

Algorithm for `compute_net`

4.1. If the gross pay is larger than $100.00 (max earnings before paying dues)
    4.1.1. deduct the dues of $15 from gross pay.
  else
    4.1.2. deduct no dues.

Implementation of Lower-Level Functions

The lower-level functions for the payroll problem are shown in Fig. 4.9b.

Figure 4.9b   Lower-level functions for payroll problem

```cpp
// FILE: Payroll.cpp
// Lower-level functions

// DISPLAYS USER INSTRUCTIONS
void instruct_user
   (const money max_no_dues,       // IN: max earnings (dollars) before paying dues
    const money dues,              // IN: dues amount (dollars)
    const float max_no_overtime,   // IN: max number of hours without overtime pay
    const float overtime_rate)     // IN: overtime rate
{
   cout << "This program computes gross and net salary." << endl;
   cout << "A dues amount of " << dues << " is deducted for" << endl;
   cout << "an employee who earns more than " << max_no_dues << endl << endl;
   cout << "Overtime is paid at the rate of " << overtime_rate << endl;
   cout << "times the regular rate for hours worked over " << max_no_overtime
        << endl << endl;
   cout << "Enter hours worked and hourly rate" << endl;
   cout << "on separate lines after the prompts." << endl;
   cout << "Press <return> after typing each number." << endl << endl;
}  // end instruct_user


// FIND THE GROSS PAY
money compute_gross
   (float hours,                   // IN: number of hours worked
    money rate,                    // IN: hourly pay rate (dollars)
    const float max_no_overtime,   // IN: max number of hours without overtime pay
    const float overtime_rate)     // IN: overtime rate
{
   // Local data ...
   money gross;                    // RESULT: gross pay (dollars)
   money regular_pay;              // pay for first 40 hours
   money overtime_pay;             // pay for hours in excess of 40

   // Compute gross pay.
   if (hours > max_no_overtime)
   {
      regular_pay = max_no_overtime * rate;
      overtime_pay = (hours - max_no_overtime) * overtime_rate * rate;
      gross = regular_pay + overtime_pay;
   }
   else
      gross = hours * rate;

   return gross;
}  // end compute_gross
```

(continued)

Figure 4.9b   *(continued)*

```
// FIND THE NET PAY
money compute_net
  (money gross,                         // IN: gross salary (dollars)
   const money max_no_dues,             // IN: max salary for no deduction (dollars)
   const money dues)                    // IN: dues amount (dollars)
{
   // Local data ...
   money net;                           // RESULT: net pay (dollars)

   // Compute net pay.
   if (gross > max_no_dues)
      net = gross - dues;               // deduct dues amount
   else
      net = gross;                      // no deductions

   return net;
}  // end compute_net
```

Program Testing

To test this program, we need to be sure that all possible alternatives work properly. For example, to test function compute_net, we need three sets of data, one for the if (gross salary greater than $100), one for the else (gross salary less than $100), and one for the pivotal point (gross salary exactly $100). Figure 4.9c shows program output from a sample run.

Figure 4.9c   **Program output for a sample run**

─────────────── Program Output ───────────────

```
This program computes gross and net salary.
A dues amount of $15.00 is deducted for
an employee who earns more than $100.00

Overtime is paid at the rate of 1.5
times the regular rate on hours worked over 40

Enter hours worked and hourly rate
on separate lines after the prompts.
Press <return> after typing each number.

Hours worked: 40
Hourly rate: 5
Gross salary is $200.00
Net salary is $185.00
```

A Reminder About Identifier Scope

Notice that identifier gross is declared as a local variable in functions main and compute_gross, and as a formal argument in function compute_net. The scope of each declaration is the function that declares it. To establish a connection between these independent declarations of the identifier gross, we must use argument list correspondence or the function return mechanism. The variable gross in function main is passed as an actual argument (corresponding to formal argument gross) in the call to compute_net. Function compute_gross returns as its result the value of its local variable gross; the statement in function main that calls compute_gross

```
gross = compute_gross (hours, rate, max_no_overtime,
        overtime_rate);
```

assigns the function result to main's local variable gross.

PROGRAM STYLE

Using Constants to Enhance Readability and Maintenance

The four program constants used in this case are technically not essential to our work. We could just as easily have placed the constant values (40.0, 1.5, 100.00 and 15.00) directly in the code that was written. For example, we could have written the decision in compute_net as

```
if (gross > 100.00)
   net = gross - 15.00;   // deduct amount dues
else
   net = gross;           // no deductions
```

However, the use of constant identifiers rather than constant values has two advantages. First, the original if statement is easier to understand because it uses descriptive names such as max_no_dues rather than numbers, which have no intrinsic meaning. Second, a program written with constant identifiers is much easier to maintain than one written with constant values. For example, if we want to use different constant values in the payroll program in Fig. 4.9, we need to change only the constant declarations in the main function. However, if we had inserted constant values directly in the if statement, we would have to change the if statement and any other statements that manipulate or display the constant values.   ∎

Adding Data Flow Information to Structure Charts

In Fig. 4.8, we added data flow information to the structure chart showing the input and output of each of the top-level problem solution steps. The data flow information is an important part of the program documentation. It shows what program variables are processed by each step and the manner in which these variables are processed. If a step gives a new value to a variable, then the variable is considered an *output of the step*. If a step displays a variable's value or uses it in a computation without changing its value, the variable is considered an *input to the step*. For example, the step "compute net pay" consists of a function that processes variables gross and net. This step uses the value of the variable gross, as well as the constants max_no_dues and dues (its input) to compute net (its output).

Figure 4.8 also shows that a variable may have different roles in different subproblems of the structure chart. When considered in the context of the original problem statement, hours and rate are problem inputs (data supplied by the program user). However, when considered in the context of the subproblem "enter data," the subproblem's task is to deliver values for hours and rate to the main function, so they are considered outputs from this step. When considered in the context of the subproblem "compute gross pay," the subproblem's task is to use hours and rate to compute a value of gross, so they are considered inputs to this step. In the same way, the role of the variables gross and net changes as we go from step to step in the structure chart.

Commentary—The Software Development Method

The sequence of steps taken to solve the payroll problem follows exactly the process outlined for the software development method presented in Chapter 1:

1. Analyze the problem statement to be sure the problem specification is clear and complete.
2. Identify the relevant problem data:
   a. Identify problem domain data elements (including constants, input data, and output requirements) relevant to the problem solution. Construct a data requirements table.
   b. Identify the data types (predefined and, as needed, user-defined) to be used to model data elements listed in the data requirements table.
3. Regarding program design, decompose the main problem into simpler, smaller subproblems and identify the procedural components required for the problem solution. Construct the structure chart, showing the data flow between modules. Write the initial algorithm listing the sequence of steps required for the problem solution.
4. Regarding problems refinements, perform an analysis similar to step 1 for each of the procedural components that have been identified. Construct a data requirements table describing the arguments and return value for each component.

Once steps 1 through 4 have been completed, you can write the main function and the prototypes for the lower-level functions. Next, design each of the subproblems following steps 1 through 4, as was done for the main function. The layered approach to software design will enable you to focus first on the description of the data elements to be modeled and the definition (as needed) of new data types (such as a money type) that are most natural for modeling these elements. The procedural aspects of the problem solution then can be designed strictly in terms of the modeled data and the operations defined on them.

The benefits of this approach will become clearer as problems become more complicated. This is not surprising: the rationale for this method is that it helps us to manage complexity—to design the solution to a complicated problem in terms of smaller and simpler subproblems and program components and then to focus on each component separately as we begin to work out the details necessary for implementation in C++. Most important, however, the software design approach enables us to build a complex system out of largely independent and reusable components, each of which knows only what it needs to know about the rest of the system—no more, no less. Our ability to hide nonessential information about a system from each component and to minimize the connections between each pair of components enables us to write more readable, understandable, and maintainable software. It also makes it easier to test software systems and to identify potential failure points.

EXERCISES FOR SECTION 4.5

Self-Check
1. What are the benefits of using constant identifiers instead of literals in a program?
2. List three benefits of using the software design method applied in solving the payroll problem.
3. List all changes that would have to be made to the payroll program in Fig. 4.9 if the union dues amount were changed from $15 to $17.50.
4. The input arguments to function compute_gross included the employee's hourly rate, hours worked, overtime rate, and the maximum number of hours that could be worked without overtime. Should we have also included the union dues amount and the maximum earnings before union dues had to be paid? Why or why not?

Programming
1. Describe all modifications that would be required in the analysis, design, implementation, and testing of the payroll program if the problem statement were changed to include the requirement to deduct 18 percent in federal income tax if earnings exceeded $250.

4.6 —— CHECKING THE CORRECTNESS OF AN ALGORITHM

A critical step in algorithm design is to verify that the algorithm is correct before you spend extensive time coding it. Often a few extra minutes spent in verifying the correctness of an algorithm saves hours of coding and testing time.

A *hand trace*, or *desk-check*, is a careful, step-by-step simulation on paper of how the computer executes the algorithm. The results of this simulation should show the effect of each step's execution using data that are relatively easy to process by hand. In Section 4.4, we simulated the execution of an `if` statement that switches the values of two variables. We now trace the execution of the refined algorithm for the payroll problem solved in the last section.

Refined Algorithm

1. Display user instructions.
2. Enter hours worked and hourly rate.
3. Compute gross pay.
    3.1. If the hours worked exceeds 40.0 (max hours before overtime)
        3.1.1. compute regular_pay.
        3.1.2. compute overtime_pay.
        3.1.3. add regular_pay to overtime_pay to get gross.
    else
        3.1.4. compute gross as hours * rate.
4. Compute net pay.
    4.1. If the gross pay is larger than $100.00 (max earnings before paying dues)
        4.1.1. deduct the dues of $15.00 from gross pay.
    else
        4.1.2. deduct no dues.
5. Display gross and net pay.

Table 4.9 shows a hand trace of steps 2 through 5 of the algorithm. Each step is listed at the left in the order of its execution. The last column shows the effect of each step. If a step changes the value of a variable, then the table shows the new value. If no new value is shown, the variable retains its previous value.

Table 4.9 Trace of Algorithm for Payroll Problem

ALGORITHM STEP	hours	rate	gross	net	EFFECT
	?	?	?	?	
2. Enter hours and rate	30.0	10.00			Reads the data
3.1. If hours > 40.0					hours > 40 is false
3.1.4. gross gets hours * rate			300.0		Compute gross as hours * rate
4.1. If gross > $100.00					gross > 100.00 is true
4.1.1. Deduct the dues of $15				285.0	Deduct the dues of $15.00
5. Display gross and net					Displays 300.00 and 285.00

For example, the table shows that step 2 stores the data values 30.0 and 10.00 in the variables hours and rate; gross and net are still undefined (indicated by ? in the first table row).

The trace in Table 4.9 shows that 300.0 and 285.0 are stored in gross and net and displayed. To verify that the algorithm is correct, you would need to select other data that cause the two conditions to evaluate to different combinations of their values. Since there are two conditions and each has two possible values (true or false), there are two times two, or four, different combinations that should be tried. (What are they?) An exhaustive hand trace of the algorithm would show that it works for all combinations.

Besides the four cases discussed above, you should verify that the algorithm works correctly for unusual data. For example, what would happen if hours were 40.0 (value of max_no_overtime) or if gross were 100.0 (value of max_no_dues)? Would the algorithm still provide the correct result? To complete the hand trace, you would need to show that the algorithm handles these special situations properly.

In tracing each case, you must be careful to execute the algorithm exactly as the computer would execute it. Often programmers assume how a particular step will be executed and do not explicitly test each condition and trace each step. A trace performed in this way is of little value.

EXERCISES FOR SECTION 4.6

Self-Check   1. Provide sample data that cause both conditions in the payroll problem to be true and trace the execution for these data.
2. If hours = max_hours and gross = max_no_dues, which assignment steps in the algorithm would be performed? Provide a trace.

4.7 ——— NESTED if STATEMENTS AND MULTIPLE-ALTERNATIVE DECISIONS

Until now, we used if statements to implement decisions involving up to two alternatives. In this section, we will see how the if statement can be used to implement decisions involving several alternatives.

A nested if statement occurs when the true or false statement of an if statement is itself an if statement. A nested if statement can be used to implement decisions with several alternatives, as shown in the next examples.

Example 4.14   The following nested if statement has three alternatives. It increases one of three variables (pos_count, neg_count, or zero_count) by one depending on whether x is greater than zero, less than zero, or equal to zero, respectively.

Table 4.10 Trace of if Statement in Example 4.14 for **x** = **-7**

STATEMENT PART	EFFECT
if (x > 0)	-7 > 0 is false
else	
if (x < 0)	-7 < 0 is true
neg_count = neg_count + 1;	add 1 to neg_count

The boxes show the logical structure of the nested if statement: the second if statement is the false task following the else of the first if statement.

```
// Increment pos_count, neg_count, or zero_count
//     depending on the value of x.

if (x > 0)
    pos_count = pos_count + 1;
else
    if (x < 0)
        neg_count = neg_count + 1;
    else  // x == 0
        zero_count = zero_count + 1;
```

The execution of this if statement proceeds as follows: the first condition (x > 0) is tested; if it is true, pos_count is incremented and the rest of the if statement is skipped. If the first condition is false, the second condition (x < 0) is tested; if it is true, neg_count is incremented; otherwise, zero_count is incremented. It is important to realize that the second condition is tested only when the first condition is false.

Table 4.10 traces the execution of this statement when x is −7. Figure 4.10 contains a flowchart that shows the execution of the nested statement. This diagram shows that one and only one of the statement sequences in a rectangular box will be executed. ∎

PROGRAM STYLE

Comparison of the Nested if Statement and a Sequence of if Statements

Beginning programmers sometimes prefer to use a sequence of if statements rather than a single nested if statement. For example, the previous if statement can be rewritten as the following sequence of if statements.

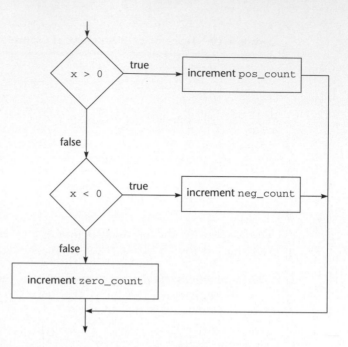

Figure 4.10   Flowchart of nested if statement in Example 4.14

```
if (x > 0)
    pos_count = pos_count + 1;
if (x < 0)
    neg_count = neg_count + 1;
if (x == 0)
    zero_count = zero_count + 1;
```

Although the above sequence is logically equivalent to the original, it is not as readable or as efficient. Unlike the nested if, the sequence does not show clearly that exactly one of the three assignment statements is executed for a particular value of x. With respect to efficiency, the nested if statement executes more quickly when x is positive because the first condition (x > 0) is true, which means that the part of the if statement following the first else is skipped. In contrast, all three of the conditions are always tested in the sequence of if statements. When x is negative, two conditions in the nested if versus three in the sequence of if statements are tested.   ∎

Writing a Nested if as a Multiple-Alternative Decision

Nested if statements may become difficult to read and write. If there are more than three alternatives and indentation is not done consistently, it may be difficult to determine the if to which a given else belongs. (In C++, this is always the closest if without an else.) We find it easier to write the nested if statement in Example 4.14 in the *multiple-alternative decision* form described in the syntax display.

**C++
SYNTAX**

Multiple-Alternative Decision Form

Form:
```
if  (condition1)
    statement₁;
else if  (condition₂)
    statement₂;
        .
        .
        .
else if  (conditionₙ)
    statementₙ;
else
    statementₑ;
// Figuring final grade for lab homework.
```

Example:
```
if (days_late < 0)
    grade = grade + bonus_points;
else if (days_late > 0)
    grade = grade - late_points;
else  // days_late == 0
    cout << "Lab submitted on time, full credit"
        << endl;
```

Interpretation: The conditions in a multiple-alternative decision are evaluated in sequence until a true condition is reached. If a condition is true, the statement following it is executed and the rest of the multiple-alternative decision is skipped. If a condition is false, the statement following it is skipped and the next condition is tested. If all conditions are false, then *statementₑ* following the last else is executed. ∎

**PROGRAM
STYLE**

Writing a Multiple-Alternative Decision

In a multiple-alternative decision, the word else and the next condition appear on the same line. All the words else align, and each *dependent statement* is indented under the condition that controls its execution.

Keep in mind that the multiple-alternative decision form is not a new type of C++ if statement but is simply another way to write nested if statements. ∎

Order of Conditions

Very often the conditions in a multiple-alternative decision are not *mutually exclusive;* in other words, more than one condition may be true for a given data value. If this is the case, then the order of the conditions becomes very important because only the statement following the first true condition is executed.

Example 4.15 Suppose you want to match exam scores to letter grades for a large class of students. The table below describes the assignment of grades based on each exam score.

EXAM SCORE	GRADE ASSIGNED
90 and above	A
80 to 89	B
70 to 79	C
60 to 69	D
Below 60	F

The multiple-alternative decision below prints the letter grade assigned according to this table. If a student has an exam score of 85, the last three conditions would be true; however, a grade of B would be assigned because the first true condition is (score >= 80).

```
// correct grade assignment
if (score >= 90)
   cout << 'A';
else if (score >= 80)
   cout << 'B';
else if (score >= 70)
   cout << 'C';
else if (score >= 60)
   cout << 'D';
else
   cout << 'F';
```

The order of conditions can also have an effect on program efficiency. If we know that low exam scores are much more likely than high scores, it would be more efficient to test first for scores below 60, next for scores between 60 and 69, and so on (see Programming Exercise 1 at the end of this section). ■

Some caution is advised in using multiple-alternative decision structures. For example, it would be incorrect to write the previous decision structure as shown below. All passing exam scores (60 or above) would be incorrectly categorized as a grade of D because the first condition would be true and the rest would be skipped.

```
// incorrect grade assignment
if (score >= 60)
    cout << 'D';
else if (score >= 70)
    cout << 'C';
else if (score >= 80)
    cout << 'B';
else if (score >= 90)
    cout << 'A';
else
    cout << 'F';
```

Example 4.16   You could use a multiple-alternative if statement to implement a *decision table* that describes several alternatives. For instance, let's say you are an accountant setting up a payroll system for a small firm. Each line of Table 4.11 indicates an employee's salary range and a corresponding base tax amount and tax percentage. Given a salary, you can calculate the tax by adding the base tax for that salary range to the product of the percentage of excess and the amount of salary over the minimum salary for that range.

For example, the second line of the table specifies that the tax due on a salary of $2000.00 is $225.00 plus 16 percent of the excess salary over $1500.00 (i.e., 16 percent of $500.00, or $80.00). Therefore, the total tax due is $225.00 plus $80.00, or $305.00.

The if statement in Fig. 4.11 implements the tax table. If the value of salary (type money) is within the table range (0.00 to 15,000.00), exactly one of the statements assigning a value to tax will be executed. A hand trace of the if statement for salary = $2000.00 is shown in Table 4.12. You can see that the value assigned to tax, $305.00, is correct.

Remember not to include symbols such as the dollar sign or commas in a C++ condition. A valid money object may contain digits and a decimal point only (e.g., 15000.00, not $15,000.00).   ∎

Table 4.11   Decision Table for Example 4.16

RANGE	SALARY	BASE TAX	PERCENTAGE OF EXCESS
1	0.00 to 1499.99	0.00	15
2	1500.00 to 2999.99	225.00	16
3	3000.00 to 4999.99	465.00	18
4	5000.00 to 7999.99	825.00	20
5	8000.00 to 15,000.00	1425.00	25

Figure 4.11   if statement for Table 4.12

```
if (salary < 0.00)
   cout << "Error!  Negative salary " << salary << endl;
else if (salary < 1500.00)              // first range
   tax = 0.15 * salary;
else if (salary < 3000.00)              // second range
   tax = (salary - 1500.00) * 0.16 + 225.00;
else if (salary < 5000.00)              // third range
   tax = (salary - 3000.00) * 0.18 + 465.00;
else if (salary < 8000.00)              // fourth range
   tax = (salary - 5000.00) * 0.20 + 825.00;
else if (salary <= 15000.00)            // fifth range
   tax = (salary - 8000.00) * 0.25 + 1425.00;
else
   cout << "Error!  Salary outside table range " << salary
        << endl;
```

PROGRAM STYLE

Validating the Value of Variables

It is important to validate the value of a variable before performing computations using invalid or meaningless data. Instead of computing an incorrect tax amount, the if statement in Fig. 4.11 prints an error message if the value of salary is outside the range covered by the table (0.0 to 15,000.00). The first condition detects negative salaries; an error message is printed if salary is less than zero. Such a condition test is often called a *control structure entry guard,* since it guards the entry to a control structure and prevents its execution on meaningless data.

Within the control structure, all conditions evaluate to false if salary is greater than 15,000.00 and the alternative following else displays an error message. Using control structure entry guards and the else alternative in a multiple-alternative decision is good programming style. ∎

Table 4.12 Trace of if Statement in Fig. 4.11 for salary equals $2000.00

STATEMENT PART	salary	tax	EFFECT
	2000.00	?	
if (salary < 0.00)			2000.00 < 0.00 is false
else if (salary < 1500.00)			2000.00 < 1500.00 is false
else if (salary < 3000.00)			2000.00 < 3000.00 is true
tax = (salary - 1500.00)			Evaluates to 500.00
* 0.16			Evaluates to 80.00
+ 225.00	305.00		Evaluates to 305.00

Short-Circuit Evaluation of Logical Expressions

When evaluating logical expressions, we often employ a technique called *short-circuit evaluation*. This means that we can stop evaluating a logical expression as soon as its value can be determined. For example, if the value of (single == 'y') is false, then the logical expression

```
(single == 'y') && (gender == 'm') && (age >= 18) && (age <= 26)
```

must be false regardless of the value of the other conditions (i.e., false && (...) must always be false). Consequently, there is no need to continue to evaluate the other conditions when (single == 'y') evaluates to false.

Your C++ compiler uses short-circuit evaluation. This means, for example, that evaluation of a logical expression of the form s_1 && s_2 will stop if the subexpression s_1 on the left evaluates to false.

Example 4.17   If x is zero, the if condition

```
if ((x != 0.0) && (y / x > 5.0))
```

is false because (x != 0.0) is false, and false && (...) must always be false. Thus, there is no need to evaluate the subexpression (y / x > 5.0) when x is zero. In this case, the first subexpression *guards* the second and prevents the second from being evaluated when x is equal to 0. However, if the subexpressions were reversed, the expression

```
if ((y / x > 5.0) && (x != 0.0))
```

would cause a "division by zero" run time error when the divisor x is zero. Therefore, the order of the subexpressions in this condition is critical.   ∎

EXERCISES FOR SECTION 4.7

Self-Check
1. Trace the execution of the nested if statements in Fig. 4.11 for salary = 13500.00.
2. What would be the effect of reversing the order of the first two if statements in Fig. 4.11?
3. Evaluate the expressions below, with and without short-circuit evaluation, if x is equal to 6 and y equals 7.
   a. ((x > 10) && (y / x <= 10))
   b. ((x <= 10) || (x / (y - 7) > 3))

Programming
1. Implement the decision table below using a nested if statement. Assume that the grade-point average is within the range 0.0 through 4.0.

GRADE-POINT AVERAGE	TRANSCRIPT MESSAGE
0.0 to 0.99	Failed semester—registration suspended
1.0 to 1.99	On probation for next semester
2.0 to 2.99	(no message)
3.0 to 3.49	Dean's list for semester
3.5 to 4.0	Highest honors for semester

2. Implement the decision table from Programming Exercise 1 without using a nested `if` statement.

4.8 ▬▬▬ THE `switch` CONTROL STATEMENT

The `switch` control statement may also be used in C++ to select one of several alternatives. It is especially useful when the selection is based on the value of a single variable or a simple expression (called the `switch` *selector*). The `switch` selector may be an integer, character, or type `bool` variable or expression.

Example 4.18 The `switch` statement

```
switch (mom_or_dad)
{
    case 'M': case 'm':
        cout << "Hello Mom - Happy Mother's Day" << endl;
        break;
    case 'D': case 'd':
        cout << "Hello Dad - Happy Father's Day" << endl;
        break;
}   // end switch
```

behaves the same way as the `if` statement below when the character stored in mom_or_dad is one of the four letters listed (M, m, D, or d).

```
if ((mom_or_dad == 'M') || (mom_or_dad == 'm'))
    cout << "Hello Mom - Happy Mother's Day" << endl;
else if ((mom_or_dad == 'D') || (mom_or_dad == 'd'))
    cout << "Hello Dad - Happy Father's Day" << endl;
```

The message displayed depends on the value of the `switch` selector mom_or_dad (type `char`). If the `switch` selector value is `'M'` or `'m'`, the first message is displayed. If the `switch` selector value is `'D'` or `'d'`, the second message is displayed. The character constants `'M'`, `'m'` and `'D'`, `'d'` are called *case labels.*

Once a particular case label statement has been executed, the reserved word `break` causes control to be passed to the first statement following the `switch` control statement. ∎

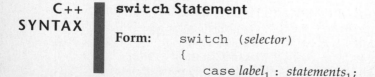

C++
SYNTAX

`switch` Statement

Form: `switch (selector)`
              `{`
                  `case label₁ : statements₁;`

```
                      break;
        case label₂ : statements₂;
                      break;
           .
           .
           .
        case labelₙ: statementsₙ;
                      break;
        default :  statementsₐ; (optional)
    }
```

Example:
```
// Display a musical note
switch (musical_note)
{
    case 'c':
        cout << "do";
        break;
    case 'd':
        cout << "re";
        break;
    case 'e':
        cout << "mi";
        break;
    case 'f':
        cout << "fa";
        break;
    case 'g':
        cout << "sol";
        break;
    case 'a':
        cout << "la";
        break;
    case 'b':
        cout << "ti";
        break;
    default:
        cout << "An invalid note was read." << endl;
}   // end switch
```

Interpretation: The *selector* expression is evaluated and compared to each of the case labels. The selector expression should be an ordinal type (for example, int, char, bool, but not float, money, or string). Each *labelᵢ* is a single, constant value, and each label must have a different value from the others. If the value of the selector expression is equal to one of the case labels—for example, *labelᵢ*—then execution will begin with the first statement of the sequence *statementsᵢ* and continue until a break statement is encountered (or until the end of the switch control statement is encountered).

[Expressions are also allowed as labels, but only if each operand in the expression is itself a constant—e.g., 5 + 7 or x * 13 (the latter is allowed only if x was previously defined as a named constant).] The type of each label should be the same as that of the selector expression.

If the value of the selector is not listed in any case label, none of the options will execute unless a default action is specified. Omission of a default label may create a logic error that is difficult to pinpoint. Although the default label is optional, we recommend its use unless you are absolutely positive that all possible selector values are covered in the case labels. It is not necessary to enclose multiple statements for individual cases in braces; C++ treats the switch statement as one compound statement. ∎

Example 4.19 The switch statement that follows finds the average life expectancy of a standard light bulb based on the bulb's wattage. Since the value of the variable watts controls the execution of the switch statement, watts must have a value before the statement executes. Case labels 40 and 60 have the same effect (also, case labels 75 and 100).

```
// Determine average life expectancy of a standard
// light bulb.
switch (watts)
{
   case 25:
      life = 2500;
      break;
   case 40:
   case 60:
      life = 1000;
      break;
   case 75:
   case 100:
      life = 750;
      break;
   default:
      life = 0;
}        // end switch
cout << "Life expectancy of " << watts << "-watt bulb: "
      << watts << endl;
```
∎

Proper Use of break

The placement of the reserved word break in a switch statement is very important. If the break is omitted following a statement sequence—*statements$_i$*, for example—then when the last statement in *statements$_i$* is executed, execution will continue, or *fall through*, to *statements$_{i+1}$*. There are very few cases in which such a fall-through is desirable. Thus, although the break is not syntactically required in a switch statement, it is almost always necessary to ensure that only one statement sequence is executed. We can selectively leave out a break if multiple cases share the same outcome—for example, case 40 and case 60 in Example 4.19.

Comparison of Nested if Statements and the switch Statement

You can use nested if control statements, a more general control form than the switch statement, to implement any multiple-alternative decision. The switch statement, however, is more readable and should be used whenever practical. Remember that case labels that contain type float values or strings are not permitted.

You will probably find it convenient to use the switch statement when you need to test a series of like types—for instance, a collection of individual integer values. You may want to use nested if statements when there are a large number of situations that require no action to be taken. Also, if the actions to be taken are dependent on the values of more than one variable, then an if statement is more flexible in its ability to combine logical expressions.

PROGRAM STYLE

Positioning Case Labels in a switch Statement

When more than one case label applies to the same statement, the case labels can be written on separate lines, as in Example 4.19, or several labels can be placed on the same line, as in Example 4.18. C++ does not distinguish between the two styles, as long as the punctuation is correct. However, the more case labels you put on one line, the less readable the switch statement becomes; so use good judgment when arranging your alternatives.

The break after the last case label is structurally unnecessary, but we recommend its inclusion. If you decide to add more labels later, there is a good chance you will forget to add a break at that time. We prefer to practice error prevention whenever possible. ∎

Using a switch Statement for Function Calls

As your programs become more complex, you may find your code for some switch alternatives also becoming more complex and lengthy. In such cases, you will usually find it helpful to place this code in a separate function. This leads us to a very common use for the switch statement: selecting a particular function from a group of possible choices, depending on perhaps an interactive question to the user.

Example 4.20   Assume the type char variable edit_op contains a data value that indicates the kind of text edit operation to be performed on string object text_string. We use the next switch statement to call a function that performs the selected operation, passing text_string as a function argument.

```
switch (edit_op)
{
   case 'D': case 'd':              // Delete a substring
      do_delete (text_string);
      break;
   case 'F': case 'f':              // Find a substring
      do_find (text_string);
      break;
   case 'I': case 'i':              // Insert a substring
      do_insert (text_string);
      break;
   case 'R': case 'r':
      do_replace (text_string);     // Replace a substring
      break;
   case 'Q': case 'q':              // Quit
      cout << "Quitting text editor program!" << endl;
      break;
   default:
      cout << "An invalid edit code was entered." << endl;
} // end switch
```

Using this structure, we place the code for each edit operation in a separate function. These functions might prompt the user for specific information, such as a substring to insert, find, or delete, and perform all necessary operations on this input (by calling member functions from the string class).

Program decomposition into separate components is the key here. The details of how our string is processed can be written and modified without affecting the simple *control code* we have written. ∎

EXERCISES FOR SECTION 4.8

Self-Check   1. What will be printed by the following carelessly constructed switch statement if the value of color is 'R'?

```
switch (color)
{
   case 'R': case 'r':
      cout << "red" << endl;
   case 'B': case 'b':
      cout << "blue" << endl;
      case 'Y': case 'y':
      cout << "yellow" << endl;
}
```

2. Write an `if` statement that corresponds to the `switch` statement below.

```
switch (x > y)
{
case 1 :
    cout << "x greater" << endl;
    break;
case 0 :
    cout << "y greater or equal" << endl;
    break;
}
```

3. Why can't we rewrite our nested `if` statement examples from Section 4.7 using `switch` statements?

4. Why is it preferable to include a `default` label in a `switch` statement?

Programming

1. Write a `switch` statement that prints a message indicating whether `next_ch` (type `char`) is an operator symbol (+, -, *, /, %), a punctuation symbol (comma, semi-colon, parenthesis, brace, bracket), or a digit. Your statement should print the category selected.

2. Write a nested `if` statement equivalent to the `switch` statement described in Programming Exercise 1.

3. Guard the `switch` statement described in Programming Exercise 1 by a default label.

4.9 ──── COMMON PROGRAMMING ERRORS

- *Parentheses:* For the most part, the defined precedence levels of C++ will prevent you from making a syntax error. But they will also allow you to do things you may not intend. The rule of thumb is, when in doubt, use parentheses.

- *Operators:* You can use the logical operators, `&&`, `||`, and `!`, only with logical expressions. Remember that the C++ operator for equality is the double symbol `==`. Do not mistakenly use the assignment operator (single `=`) in its place. Your expression will probably compile, but the logic will undoubtedly be incorrect.

- *Compound Statements:* Don't forget to bracket a compound statement used as a true or false task in an `if` control statement with braces. If the `{ }` bracket is missing, only the first statement will be considered part of the task. This can lead to a syntax error or, worse, a logic error that could be very difficult to find. In the following example, the `{ }` bracket around the true task is missing. The compiler assumes that only the statement

```
sum = sum + x;
```

is part of the true task of the `if` control statement. This creates a "misplaced else" syntax error. Of course, the correct thing to do is to enclose the compound statement in braces.

```
if (x > 0)                          // missing { }
    sum = sum + x;
    cout << "Greater than zero" << endl;
else
    cout << "Less than zero" << endl;
```

- *Nested* if *Statement:* When writing a nested if statement, try to select the conditions so that the multiple-alternative form shown in Section 4.7 can be used. If the conditions are not mutually exclusive (i.e., if more than one condition may be true), the most restrictive condition should come first.
- switch *Statements:* When using a switch statement, make sure the switch *selector* and case *labels* are of the same type (int, char, or bool but not float). If the selector evaluates to a value not listed in any of the case labels, the switch statement will fall through without any action being taken. For this reason, it is often wise to guard the switch with a default label. This way you can ensure that the switch executes properly in all situations. Be very careful in your placement of the break statements. Missing break statements will allow control to drop through to the next case label. Don't forget to terminate a switch statement with a closing brace }.

CHAPTER REVIEW

This chapter focused on how to use control structures with one entry point and one exit point to control the flow of execution through a program. The compound statement is a control structure for sequential execution. The if and switch constructs are used to control decisions.

We saw how to express conditions in C++ through logical expressions using the following:

- Type bool variables or constants
- Relational operators (<, <=, >, >=) and equality operators (==, !=) to compare variables and constants of the same data type
- Logical operators (&&, ||, !) with type bool operands

It is useful to perform a hand trace of an algorithm to verify whether it is correct and to help discover any errors in logic. Hand tracing an algorithm before coding it as a program saves time in the long run.

Nested if statements are common in programming and are used to represent decisions with multiple alternatives. Programmers use indentation and the multiple-alternative decision form to make nested if statements easier to read and understand.

A second selection structure, the switch statement, implements decisions with several alternatives. The particular alternative chosen depends on the value of a variable or simple expression (the *case selector*). The *case selector* can be type int, char, or bool, but not type float or string.

New C++ Constructs   We continue to stress the rigorous use of the software design method first discussed in Chapter 1, leading to the development of highly modularized programs that are easier to read, understand, modify, and test. The new C++ constructs introduced in this chapter are presented in Table 4.13.

Table 4.14   Summary of New C++ Constructs

CONSTRUCT	EFFECT

if Control Statement

One Alternative

```
if (y != 0)
   result = x / y;
```
Divides x by y only if y is nonzero.

Two Alternatives

```
if (x >= 0)
   cout << x << " is positive" << endl;
else
   cout << x << " is negative" << endl;
```
If x is greater than or equal to 0, display " is positive"; otherwise, display the message " is negative".

Several Alternatives

```
if (x < 0)
{
   cout << "Negative" << endl;
   abs_x = -x;
}
else if (x == 0)
{
   cout << "Zero" << endl;
   abs_x = 0;
}
else
{
   cout << "Positive" << endl;
   abs_x = x;
}
```
One of three messages is printed, depending on whether x is negative, positive, or zero. abs_x is set to represent the absolute value or magnitude of x.

switch Statement

```
switch (next_ch)
{
   case 'A': case 'a':
      cout << "Excellent" << endl;
      break;
```
Prints one of five messages based on the value of next_ch (type char). If next_ch is 'D', 'd' or 'F', 'f', the student is put on probation.

(continued)

Table 4.14   *(continued)*

CONSTRUCT	EFFECT

```
case 'B': case 'b':
   cout << "Good" << endl;
   break;
case 'C': case 'c':
   cout << "Fair" << endl;
   break;
case 'D': case 'd':
case 'F': case 'f':
   cout << "Poor, student is"
        << " on probation" << endl;
   break;
default :
   cout << "Invalid grade entered."
        << endl;
}  // end switch
```

✔ QUICK-CHECK EXERCISES

1. An if statement implements _____ execution.
2. What is a compound statement?
3. A switch statement is often used instead of _____.
4. What values can a logical expression have?
5. The operator ! = means _____.
6. A hand trace is used to verify that a(n) _____ is correct.
7. Correct the syntax errors below.

```
if x > 25.0
   y = x
else
   y = z;
```

8. What value is assigned to fee by the if statement below when speed is 75?

```
if (speed > 35)
   fee = 20.00;
else if (speed > 50)
   fee = 40.00;
else if (speed > 75)
   fee = 60.00;
```

9. Answer Exercise 8 for the if statement below. Which if statement is correct?

```
if (speed > 75)
   fee = 60.00;
else if (speed > 50)
```

```
      fee = 40.00;
   else if (speed > 35)
      fee = 20.00;
```

10. What output line(s) are displayed by the statements below (a) when grade is
    'I'? (b) When grade is 'B'? (c) When grade is 'b'?

    ```
    switch (grade)
    {
       case 'A':
          points = 4;
          break;
       case 'B':
          points = 3;
          break;
       case 'C':
          points = 2;
          break;
       case 'D':
          points = 1;
          break
       case 'F':
       case 'I':
       case 'W':
          points = 0;
          break;
    }  // end switch

    if (('A' <= grade) && (grade <= 'D'))
       cout << "Passed, points earned = " << points << "."
             << endl;
    else
       cout << "Failed, no points earned." << endl;
    ```

11. Explain the difference between the statements on the left and the statements on the
    right below. For each of them, what is the final value of x if the initial value of x is 0?

    ```
    if (x >= 0)            if (x >= 0)
       x = x + 1;             x = x + 1;
    else if (x >= 1)       if (x >= 1)
       x = x + 2;             x = x + 2;
    ```

Answers to Quick-Check Exercises

1. conditional
2. a block that combines one or more statements into a single statement
3. nested if statements or a multiple-alternative if statement
4. true or false
5. not equal
6. algorithm
7. Add parentheses around test condition and insert a semicolon before else.

8. 20.00, first condition is met
9. 40.00; the one in Exercise 9
10. (a) when grade is 'I': Failed, no points earned.
    (b) when grade is 'B': Passed, points earned = 3.
    (c) when grade is 'b': Failed, no points earned.
11. A nested if statement is on the left; a sequence of if statements is on the right. x becomes 1 on the left; x becomes 3 on the right.

REVIEW QUESTIONS

1. A decision in C++ is actually an evaluation of a(n) _____ expression.
2. How does a relational operator differ from a logical operator?
3. What is short-circuit logical evaluation? What are its benefits?
4. Trace the following program fragment and indicate which function will be called if a data value of 27.34 is entered.

```
cout << "Enter a temperature: ";
cin >> temp;
if (temp > 32.0)
    not_freezing ();
else
    ice_forming ();
```

5. Write a nested if statement to display a message indicating the educational level of a student based on his or her number of years of schooling (0, none; 1 through 6, elementary school; 7 through 8, middle school; 9 through 12, high school; >12, college). Print a message to indicate bad data as well.
6. Write a switch statement to select an operation based on the value of inventory. Increment total_paper by paper_order if inventory is 'b' or 'c'; increment total_ribbon by 1 if inventory is 'e', 'f', or 'd'; increment total_label by label_order if inventory is 'a' or 'x'. Do nothing if inventory is 'm'.
7. Implement a decision structure for the following computation:

   • If your taxable income is less than $24,000, pay taxes at a rate of 18 percent.
   • If your taxable income is greater than $24,000 but less than or equal to $58,150, pay taxes at the rate of 18 percent on the first $24,000 and 28 percent on the amount in excess of $24,000.
   • If your taxable income is greater than $58,150 but less than or equal to $121,300, pay taxes at the rate of 28 percent on the first $58,150 and 31 percent on the amount in excess of $58,150.
   • If your taxable income is greater than $121,300 but less than or equal to $263,750, pay taxes at the rate of 31 percent on the first $121,300 and 36 percent on the amount in excess of $263,750.
   • If your taxable income is greater than $263,750, pay taxes at a rate of 36 percent on the first $263,750 and 39.6 percent on the amount in excess of $263,750.

PROGRAMMING PROJECTS

1. Write functions to draw a circle, square, and triangle. Write a program that reads a letter C, S, or T and depending on the letter chosen draws either a circle, square, or triangle.
2. Write a program that reads in four words (as character strings) and displays them in increasing alphabetic sequence and also in decreasing alphabetic sequence.
3. Write a program that reads in a room number, its capacity, and the size of the class enrolled so far and prints an output line showing the classroom number, capacity, number of seats filled, number of seats available, and a message indicating whether the class is filled. Call a function to display the following heading before the first output line:

```
Room    Capacity    Enrollment    Empty Seats    Filled/
                                                 Not Filled
```

Display each part of the output line under the appropriate heading. Test your program with the following classroom data:

ROOM	CAPACITY	ENROLLMENT
426	25	25
327	18	14
420	20	15
317	100	90

4. Write a program that displays a "message" consisting of three block letters where each letter is an X or an O. The program user's data determines whether a particular letter will be an X or O. For example, if the user enters the three letters XOX, the block letters X, O, and X will be displayed.
5. Write a program to simulate a state police radar gun. The program should read an automobile speed and print the message "speeding" if the speed exceeds 55 mph.
6. While spending the summer as a surveyor's assistant, you decide to write a program that transforms compass headings in degrees (0 to 360) to compass bearings. A compass bearing consists of three items: the direction you face (north or south), an angle between 0 and 90 degrees, and the direction you turn before walking (east or west). For example, to get the bearing for a compass heading of 110.0 degrees, you would first face due south (180 degrees) and then turn 70.0 degrees east (180.0 − 110.0). Be sure to check the input for invalid compass headings.
7. Write a program that will determine the additional state tax owed by an employee. If the state charges a 4 percent tax on net income, determine net income by subtracting a $500 allowance for each dependent from gross income. Your program will read gross income, number of dependents, and tax amount already deducted. It will then compute the actual tax owed and print the difference between tax owed and tax deducted followed by the message "SEND CHECK" or "REFUND" depending on whether this difference is positive or negative.

8. The New Telephone Company has the following rate structure for long-distance calls:

- The regular rate for a call is $0.40 per minute.
- Any call started at or after 6:00 P.M. (1800 hours) but before 8:00 A.M. (0800 hours) is discounted 50 percent.
- Any call longer than 60 minutes receives a 15 percent discount on its cost (after any other discount is subtracted).
- All calls are subject to a 4 percent federal tax on their final cost.

Write a program that reads the start time for a call based on a 24-hour clock and the length of the call. The gross cost (before any discounts or tax) should be printed, followed by the net cost (after discounts are deducted and tax is added). Use separate functions to print instructions to the program user and to compute the net cost.

7. Write a program that will calculate and print out bills for the city water company. The water rates vary, depending on whether the bill is for home use, commercial use, or industrial use. A code of h means home use, a code of c means commercial use, and a code of i means industrial use. Any other code should be treated as an error. The water rates are computed as follows:

- Code h: $5.00 plus $0.0005 per gallon used
- Code c: $1000.00 for the first 4 million gallons used and $0.00025 for each additional gallon
- Code i: $1000.00 if usage does not exceed 4 million gallons; $2000.00 if usage is more than 4 million gallons but does not exceed 10 million gallons; and $3000.00 if usage exceeds 10 million gallons

Your program should prompt the user to enter an account number (type int), the code (type char), and the gallons of water used (type float). Your program should echo the input data and print the amount due from the user.

8. Write a program to control a bread machine. Allow the user to input the type of bread as W for White and S for Sweet. Ask the user if the loaf size is double and if the baking is manual. The program should fail if the user inputs are invalid. The table below is a time chart for the machine used for each bread type. Print a statement for each step. If the loaf size is double, increase the baking time by 50 percent. If baking is manual, stop after the loaf shaping cycle and instruct the user to remove the dough for manual baking. Use a function to print program instructions.

Time Chart for Making Bread

OPERATION	WHITE BREAD	SWEET BREAD
Primary kneading	15 mins	20 mins
Primary rising	60 mins	60 mins
Secondary kneading	18 mins	33 mins
Secondary rising	20 mins	30 mins

Time Chart for Making Bread *(continued)*

OPERATION	WHITE BREAD	SWEET BREAD
Loaf shaping	2 seconds	2 seconds
Final rising	75 mins	75 mins
Baking	45 mins	35 mins
Cooling	30 mins	30 mins

9. Write a program that determines the day number (1 to 366) in a year for a date that is provided as input data. As an example, January 1, 1994 is day 1. December 31, 1993 is day 365. December 31, 1996 is day 366 since 1996 is a leap year. A year is a leap year if it is divisible by four, except that any year divisible by 100 is a leap year only if it is divisible by 400. Your program should accept the month, day, and year as integers.

5

Repetition: `while`, `for`, and `do-while` Statements

In the programs studied so far, the executable statements have executed only once. In most commercial software, however, sequences of instructions can be repeated many times. For example, most companies have more than one employee and would need a modified version of the Chapter 4 payroll program—one that repeated the executable steps once for each employee, for possibly dozens, hundreds, or thousands of them.

Repetition, you'll recall, is the third type of program control structure (*sequence, selection, repetition*), and the repetition of a sequence of steps in a program is called a *loop*. Almost all computer applications require repeated executions of parts of programs. The real power of the computer lies in its ability to perform these repetitive operations at extremely high speeds, far faster than could possibly be achieved by people. It is important, therefore, that a programming language provide a convenient and powerful set of constructs for specifying repetition in a program.

In this chapter, we discuss three C++ control structures for repetition—while, for, and do-while—and the advantages of each. We show how to specify the repetition of a group of program statements and explain when to use each control structure. As with if statements, loops can be nested, and this chapter shows how to write and use nested loops in your programs.

5.1 ——— THE while STATEMENT

Our study of loops begins with the most versatile loop control statement, the while statement. The program segment shown in Fig. 5.1 uses the while statement to compute and display the weekly pay for each of seven employees (assuming no overtime pay). The variables rate and pay are assumed to be of the user-defined type money. The loop body (steps that are repeated) starts

Figure 5.1   Loop to process seven employees

```
employee_count = 0;  // no employees processed yet
while (employee_count < 7)
{   // test value of the employee count
    cout << "Hours: ";
    cin >> hours;
    cout << "Rate : ";
    cin >> rate;
    pay = hours * rate;
    cout << "Weekly pay is " << pay << endl;
    employee_count++; // increment count of employees
} // end while

cout << "All employees processed" << endl;
```

on the line beginning with `while`. Inside the loop body, an employee's payroll data are read and the employee's gross pay is computed and displayed. After the loop body has been executed seven times and seven weekly pay amounts are displayed, the last statement displays the message `All employees processed`.

There are three lines that control the looping process. The first statement

```
employee_count = 0;     // no employees processed yet
```

stores an initial value of 0 in the variable `employee_count`, representing the count of employees processed so far. The next line

```
while (employee_count < 7)
```

evaluates the condition in parentheses. If it is true, the loop body is executed, causing a new pair of data values to be read and a new pay to be computed and displayed. The last statement in the loop body,

```
employee_count++;       // increment count of employees
```

is a feature of C++ that is widely used in counter-controlled loops. This is shorthand for and identical to the familiar longer statement

```
employee_count = employee_count + 1;
```

which increments the value of `employee_count` by one. We will have more to say about the *increment operator*, ++, and the associated *decrement operator*, --, later in this section.

After executing the last step in the loop body, control returns to the line beginning with `while`, and the logical expression is reevaluated for the next value of `employee_count`. The loop body will be executed once for each value of `employee_count` from 0 to 6. Eventually `employee_count` will become 7, and the logical expression will evaluate to false. When this happens, the loop body is not executed, and control passes to the display statement that follows the loop body.

The logical expression following the reserved word `while` is called the *loop repetition condition*. The loop is repeated when this condition is true. We say that the loop is exited when this condition is false.

The flowchart of the `while` loop in Fig. 5.2 summarizes what we have learned about `while` loops. It shows that the expression in the diamond-shaped box is evaluated first. If it is true, the loop body is executed, and the process is repeated. The `while` loop is exited when the expression becomes false.

Make sure you understand the difference between the `while` statement in Fig. 5.1 and the following `if` statement:

```
if (employee_count < 7)
{
   ...
}  // end if
```

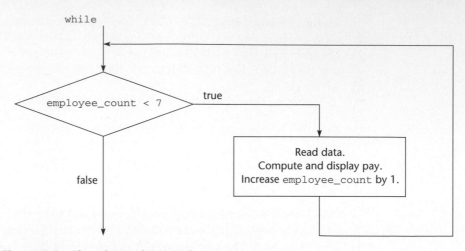

Figure 5.2   Flowchart of while loop

The compound statement of an if statement executes at most one time. In a while statement, the compound statement (loop body) may execute more than one time.

Syntax of the while Statement

In Fig. 5.1, variable employee_count is called the *loop control variable* (*lcv*) because its value determines whether or not the loop body is repeated. There are three critical steps in loop control involving the lcv employee_count.

1. **Initialize:** employee_count is set to a starting value of 0 before the while statement is reached.
2. **Test:** the value of employee_count is tested before the start of each loop repetition (called an *iteration* or a *pass*).
3. **Update:** employee_count is updated (its value increases by 1) during each iteration.

Steps similar to these must be performed for every while loop. If the first step is missing, the initial test of employee_count will be meaningless. If the test step is missing, we will have no way of stopping the loop repetition; thus an *infinite loop* will be created. The last step ensures that we make progress toward the final goal (employee_count >= 7) during each repetition of the loop. If this update is missing, the value of employee_count cannot change, so the loop will execute "forever," again creating an *infinite loop*. The syntax display for the while statement follows.

**C++
SYNTAX**

while Statement

Form: while (*logical expression*)
              statement

Example: // display n asterisks
```
count_star = 0;
while (count_star < n)
{
    cout << "*";
    count_star++;
} // end while
```

Interpretation: The *logical expression* (a condition to control the loop process) is tested; if it is true, the *statement* is executed and the *logical expression* is retested. The *statement* is repeated as long as (while) the *logical expression* is true. When the *logical expression* is tested and found to be false, the while loop is exited and the next program statement after the while statement is executed.

Notes: If the *logical expression* evaluates to false the first time it is tested, the *statement* will not be executed at all.

You must be careful with the placement of semicolons in a while statement. Make sure you do not place a semicolon after the *logical expression* on the first line of a while loop. If you make this mistake, the C++ compiler will assume that you have an *empty statement* for your loop body and execute this statement (which does nothing) forever or until your patience or time limit expires. For clarity, we will indent the body of a while loop. If the loop body is a compound statement enclosed in braces, we will terminate it with the comment // end while after the closing }. ∎

Increment and Decrement Operators

The *increment operator* ++ is used here for the first time in the text. It is discussed along with its companion *decrement operator* in the following display and example. As we will see throughout this chapter, these operators are especially useful when writing loops.

**C++
SYNTAX**

The Unary Operators Increment (++) and Decrement (−−)

Form: These operators may be applied to any single integer-valued variable, simply by writing the operator as either a prefix or a postfix to the variable.

Example: ++i   i++   --i   i--

Interpretation: The first and third examples illustrate the *prefix* use of the increment and decrement operators. The second and fourth examples illustrate the *postfix* use of the operators. The differences between the prefix and postfix forms are illustrated in the next example.   ∎

Example 5.1   *Prefix and Postfix Forms of ++ and --.* If `i` is an integer variable containing the value 3, then each comment below describes the assignment on its left

```
k = i++; // assigns the value 3 to k and 4 to i
k = ++i; // assigns the value 5 to k and 5 to i
k = i--; // assigns the value 5 to k and 4 to i
k = --i; // assigns the value 3 to k and 3 to i
```

These examples illustrate an important difference between the postfix and prefix forms of the increment and decrement operators:

- When the postfix versions of these operators are used, the increment (or decrement) takes place after the current value of the variable has been used.
- When the prefix versions of these operators are used, the increment (or decrement) takes place first and the new value of the variable is then used as prescribed.

Thus, if `i` contains 3,

```
cout << "Value of i is " << i;
cout << "Value of i++ is " << i++;   // displays 3, increments i
                                     // to 4
cout << "Value of --i is " << --i;   // decrements i to 3,
                                     // displays 3
```

the output produced would be

```
Value of i is 3
Value of i++ is 3
Value of --i is 3
```
    ∎

EXERCISES FOR SECTION 5.1

Self-Check   1. What will happen in the execution of the loop in Fig. 5.1
  a. if the increment statement

```
employee_count++;
```

   is omitted?
  b. if the initialization statement

```
employee_count = 0;
```

   immediately preceding the loop is omitted?
2. If the integer m has the value 3,
  a. what is the result of the execution of the statement

```
k = ++m + 1;
```

b. what is the result of the execution of the statement

```
k = m++ + 1;
```

3. How many times is the loop body below repeated? What is printed during each repetition of the loop body?

```
x = 3;
count = 0;
while (count < 3)
{
    x = x * x;
    cout << setw (5) << x;
    count++;
} // end while
```

4. Answer Self-Check Exercise 3 if the last statement in the loop is

```
count = count + 2;
```

5. Answer Self-Check Exercise 3 if the last statement in the loop body is omitted.

Programming
1. Write a `while` loop that displays each integer from 1 to 5 together with its square. Have each pair print on a separate line.
2. Write a `while` loop that displays each integer from −2 to 3 on a separate line. Display the values in the sequence −2, −1, 0, and so on.

5.2 ——— ACCUMULATING A SUM OR PRODUCT IN A LOOP

We often use loops to accumulate a sum or a product by repeating an addition or multiplication operation. The next example uses a loop to accumulate a sum.

Example 5.2   The program in Fig. 5.3 has a `while` loop similar to the loop of Fig. 5.1. Besides displaying each employee's weekly pay, it accumulates the total payroll (`total_pay`) for a company. The assignment statement

```
total_pay += pay;                    // add next pay
```

is shorthand for

```
total_pay = total_pay + pay;
```

and adds the current value of `pay` to the sum being accumulated in `total_pay`. Figure 5.4 traces the effect of repeating this statement for the three values of `pay` shown in the sample run.

Prior to loop execution, the statement

```
total_pay = 0.0;
```

Figure 5.3 Computing company payroll program

```cpp
// FILE: CompPay.cpp
// COMPUTES THE PAYROLL FOR A COMPANY

#include <iostream.h>
#include "money.h"

void main ()
{
    // Local data ...
    int number_employees;          // number of employees
    int employee_count;            // current employee number
    float hours;                   // hours worked
    money rate;                    // hourly rate
    money pay;                     // weekly pay
    money total_pay;               // company payroll

    // Get number of employees from user.
    cout << "Enter number of employees: ";
    cin >> number_employees;

    // Compute each employee's pay and add it to the payroll.
    total_pay = 0.0;
    employee_count = 0;
    while (employee_count < number_employees)
    {
        cout << "Hours: ";
        cin >> hours;
        cout << "Rate : $";
        cin >> rate;
        pay = hours * rate;
        cout << "Pay is "  << pay << endl << endl;
        total_pay += pay;        // accumulate total pay
        employee_count++;
    }  // end while

    cout << "Total payroll is " << total_pay << endl;
    cout << "All employees processed." << endl;
}
```

———————— Program Output ————————

```
Enter number of employees: 3
Hours: 5
Rate : $4
Pay is $20.00

Hours: 6
Rate : $5
Pay is $30.00

Hours: 1.5
Rate : $10
Pay is $15.00

Total payroll is $65.00
All employees processed.
```

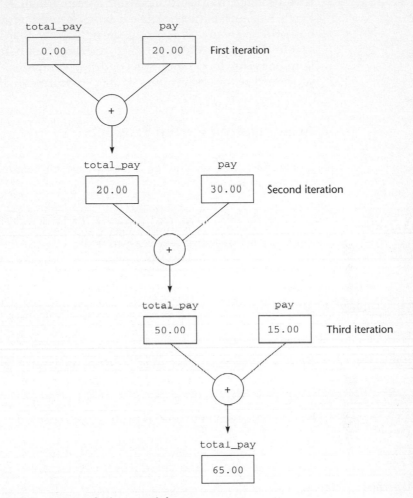

Figure 5.4   Accumulating partial sums

initializes the value of total_pay to zero. This step is critical; if it is omitted, the final sum will be off by whatever value happens to be stored in total_pay when the program begins execution.   ■

Generalizing a Loop

The first loop shown in Fig. 5.1 has a limited utility: It can be used only when the number of employees is exactly 7. If we want to reuse this program for a different number of employees, we would first have to change the loop repetition test to reflect this number rather than 7. The program segment in Fig. 5.3 is much better because it can be reused without change for any number of employees. This program begins by reading the total number of employees into variable `number_employees`. Before each execution of the loop body, the loop repetition condition compares the number of employees processed so far (`employee_count`) to `number_employees`.

Accumulating Partial Products

In a similar way, we can use a loop to accumulate a product, as shown in the next example.

Example 5.3   The loop below accumulates and displays the product of its data items as long as this product is less than 10,000.

```
// Display partial products less than 10000.
product = 1;
while (product < 10000)
{
    cout << product << endl; // display partial product
    cout << "Enter data item: ";
    cin >> item;
    product *= item;     // compute next product
}   // end while
```

It computes each new partial product by repeated execution of the statement

```
product *= item;        // compute next product
```

which is the shorthand version of the statement

```
product = product * item;
```

Figure 5.5 shows the change in the value of `product` with each execution of the above statement. If the data items are 10, 500, and 3, the partial products 1, 10, and 5000 are displayed.

Loop exit occurs when the value of `product` is greater than or equal to 10,000. Consequently, the last value assigned to `product` (15,000 in Fig. 5.5) is not displayed. ∎

The loop in Fig. 5.5 differs from the other loops in this section. Its repetition condition involves a test of the variable `product`. Besides controlling loop repetition, the variable `product` also is used to store the result of the computation being performed in the loop. The other loops involve a test of a variable such as `employee_count` that is not directly involved in the computation being performed in the loop. These variables instead serve a

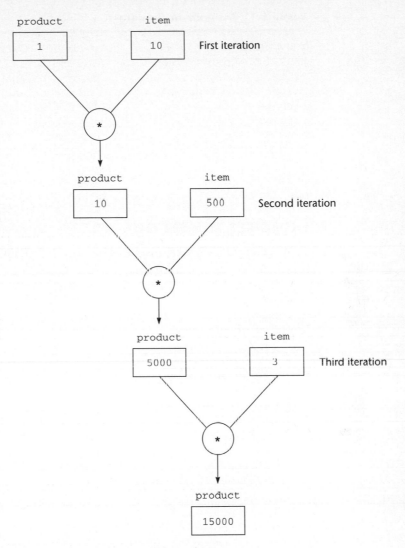

Figure 5.5 **Accumulating partial products**

single purpose—they are used only to count the number of loop repetitions. We will discuss these differences further in the next section.

More Assignment Operators

In Example 5.2, we introduced the *assignment operator*, +=. This shorthand form can be applied to any single binary arithmetic operator. They all work in a similar fashion, as shown in Table 5.1.

Table 5.1 Assignment Operators

SHORTHAND NOTATION	EQUIVALENT NOTATION
`balance += deposit;`	`balance = balance + deposit;`
`balance -= withdrawal;`	`balance = balance - withdrawal;`
`rabbits *= 4;`	`rabbits = rabbits * 4;`
`total /= (x + y * z);`	`total = total / (x + y * z);`
`hour %= 13;`	`hour = hour % 13;`

EXERCISES FOR SECTION 5.2

Self-Check

1. What output values are displayed by the `while` loop below for a data value of 5?

```
cout << "Enter an integer: ";
cin >> x;
product = x;
count = 0;
while (count < 4)
{
    cout << product << endl;
    product *= x;
    count++;
}   // end while
```

2. What values are displayed if the `cout` line comes at the end of the loop instead of at the beginning?

3. In the C++ instructions shown below, insert the opening and closing braces where needed, add the proper indentation, and correct the errors. The corrected segment should read exactly five numbers and display their sum.

```
count = 0;
while (count <= 5)
cout << "Enter data item: ";
cin >> item;
item += sum;
count++;
cout << count << " data items were added;" << endl;
cout << "their sum is " << sum << endl;
```

4. How would the program in Fig. 5.3 need to be modified to display the average employee salary in addition to the total payroll amount?

5. What would happen in the execution of the loop in Fig. 5.3 if the value of `number_employees` were entered as 0?

Programming

1. Write a program segment that computes and displays $1 + 2 + 3 + \ldots + (n - 1) + n$, where n is a data value.

5.3 ——— COUNTING LOOPS AND CONDITIONAL LOOPS

The `while` loop shown in Fig. 5.3 is called a *counter-controlled loop* (or *counting loop*) because its repetition is controlled by a *loop control variable* (the lcv) whose value represents a count. A counter-controlled loop follows the general form shown next.

> Set lcv to an appropriate initial value (usually 0).
> While lcv < final value
>   Perform loop processing.
>   Increase lcv (usually by 1).

We use a counter-controlled loop when we can determine prior to loop execution exactly how many loop repetitions will be needed to solve a problem. The lcv should be incremented as the final line of the `while` loop.

Conditional Loops

In many programming situations, we cannot determine the exact number of loop repetitions before loop execution begins. The number of repetitions may depend on some aspect of the data that is not known before the loop is entered but that usually can be stated by a condition. For example, we may want to continue writing checks as long as our bank balance is positive, as shown next:

> While balance is still positive
>   Read in next transaction.
>   Update and print balance.

The actual number of loop repetitions performed depends on the type of each transaction (deposit or withdrawal) and its amount.

Example 5.4   The program in Fig. 5.6 traces the progress of an Olympic swimmer as she approaches the opposite side of the pool. Each time she moves, the swimmer cuts the distance between herself and the goal by two-thirds her own body length until she is close enough to touch the edge (and hopefully win a gold medal). A `while` loop is the correct looping structure to use because we have no idea beforehand how many moves are required for the swimmer to reach the other end of the pool.

Let's take a close look at the `while` loop in Fig. 5.6. The assignment statement just before the loop initializes the variable `distance` to the starting distance (75), which was previously read into `initial_distance`.

Figure 5.6   The progress of an Olympic swimmer

```cpp
// FILE: Swimmer.cpp
// PRINTS DISTANCES BETWEEN A SWIMMER AND THE FAR SIDE OF THE POOL
// The swimmer keeps cutting the distance by 2/3 her body length
//      on each stroke, until she is close enough to touch the edge
//      of the pool.

#include <iostream.h>

void main ()
{
    // Local data ...
    const float body_length = 5.8;    // swimmer body length in feet

    float initial_distance;           // starting distance of swimmer
    float distance;        // distance between swimmer and other side

    cout << "Enter the initial distance of the swimmer from "
         << endl;
    cout << "the opposite side of the pool in feet: ";
    cin >> initial_distance;

    // Cut the distance between the swimmer and the opposite side
    //      by 2/3 the swimmer's body length until she is close
    //      enough to touch the edge.
    cout.setf (ios::showpoint);
    cout.setf (ios::fixed);
    cout.precision (2);
    distance = initial_distance;
    while (distance >= body_length)
    {
        cout << "The distance is " << distance << endl;
        distance -= body_length / 1.5;    // reduce distance
    }  // end while

    // Print final distance before touching the opposite edge.
    cout << endl;
    cout.precision (1);
    cout << "The last distance before the swimmer touches the edge"
         << endl;
    cout << "on the opposite side of the pool is " << distance
         << endl;
}
```

───────────── Program Output ─────────────

```
Enter the initial distance of the swimmer from
the opposite side of the pool in feet: 75
The distance is 75.00
The distance is 71.13
The distance is 67.27
```

(continued)

Figure 5.6   *(continued)*

```
The distance is 63.40
The distance is 59.53
The distance is 55.67
The distance is 51.80
The distance is 47.93
The distance is 44.07
The distance is 40.20
The distance is 36.33
The distance is 32.47
The distance is 28.60
The distance is 24.73
The distance is 20.87
The distance is 17.00
The distance is 13.13
The distance is 9.27

The last distance before the swimmer touches the edge
on the opposite side of the pool is 5.4
```

Next, the loop header is reached and the *loop repetition condition* (or while condition)

```
distance >= body_length
```

is evaluated. Because this condition is true, the loop body enclosed in braces is executed. The loop body displays the value of distance, and the statement

```
distance -= body_length / 1.5;        // reduce distance
```

reduces the value of distance by two-thirds of a body length, thereby bringing the swimmer closer to the opposite edge of the pool. The loop repetition condition is retested with the new value of distance (71.13); because 71.13 >= 5.8 is true, the loop body displays distance again, and distance becomes 67.27. The loop repetition condition is tested a third time; because 67.27 >= 5.8 is true, the loop body displays distance again, and distance becomes 63.4. The loop repetition condition continues to be tested again and again until we reach distance equal to 5.4. Because 5.4 >= 5.8 is false, loop exit occurs, and the statements following the loop end are executed.

It is important to realize that the loop is not exited at the exact instant that distance becomes 5.4. If more statements appeared in the loop body after the assignment to distance, they would be executed. Loop exit does not occur until the loop repetition condition is retested at the top of the loop and found to be false.

Just as in the counting loop shown earlier, there are three major steps in Fig. 5.6 that involve the loop control variable `distance`.

1. Initialize: `distance` is initialized to `initial_distance` before the loop header is reached.
2. Test: `distance` is tested before each execution of the loop body.
3. Update: `distance` is updated (reduced by approximately 3.87) during each iteration.

Remember that steps similar to these must appear in every loop that you write.   ∎

An Introduction to Formatted Output

Until now, we have exercised very little control over the appearance of an output line. The program in Fig. 5.6 provides our first illustration of the use of C++ constructs for controlling the format of program output. Among other things, this includes the ability to specify the following:

- the width (number of positions) of a *field of characters* to be used to display a value;
- the form to be used to display a floating point value (scientific or fixed notation);
- whether or not to show the decimal point when displaying floating-point values having a fractional part of 0;
- the number of decimal places to be used in printing a floating-point value.

To gain such control over a program's output, we can use special functions defined on output stream object `cout` (and, in fact, on any other output stream object that we might use). These functions are all specified as part of the definition of the C++ output stream class `ostream` (located in the `iostream.h` library header).

Example 5.5   The following C++ library function calls were used to display the floating-point variables in the swimmer program (Fig. 5.6) in fixed point notation and accurate to two decimal places.

```
cout.setf (ios::showpoint);
cout.setf (ios::fixed);
cout.precision (2);
```

These calls appeared in the program prior to the appearance of the output statements to be affected by the functions. They are calls to member functions (`setf` and `precision`) of class `iostream`, and therefore must be written using dot notation.

The first two lines in our example call the function `setf` to turn on the two *format flags* `showpoint` and `fixed`. Turning on these two flags ensures two features for floating-point values:

1. A decimal point is always shown even if the value displayed has a fractional part of zero.
2. All values are displayed in *fixed* notation rather than in *scientific* notation.

If the `showpoint` format flag is not turned on, trailing zeros to the right of the decimal point will not be displayed. Thus, values such as thirteen or thirteen and a half would appear as 13 and 13.5, respectively. This is not wrong, but it can be disconcerting in situations such as the display of dollars and cents, a baseball pitcher's earned run average, or rainfall measurements (in inches), where we might normally expect to see a decimal point and two digits to the right of the decimal point.

Setting the C++ format flag `fixed` ensures that all values printed by the swimmer program, regardless of magnitude, appear in the fixed format we are accustomed to seeing. If this flag is not set, some of the larger floating-point values would be displayed in scientific notation, such as 1.738964e+06. Setting the format flag to `scientific` (by specifying `ios::scientific` in the call to `setf`) ensures that all floating-point values are displayed in scientific notation.

The function `precision` called in the third line ensures that all floating values are displayed accurate to two decimal places even if the fractional part is zero.   ■

The settings carried out by the `setf` function can be undone later in the program by calling the function `unsetf`, as in

```
cout.unsetf (ios::showpoint); // turn off the showpoint flag
```

or by calling `setf` at a later point in the program, as in

```
cout.setf (ios::scientific); // show all float values in
                             // scientific form
```

The `precision` function may also be called later in the program if a change is desired in the precision of a displayed value:

```
cout.precision (1);    // display float values accurate to 1
                       // place
```

One additional function, the `width` function, can be used to control the width (total number of characters) of a field to be used to display a value. The value is normally displayed right adjusted in the field with blank characters used to pad the field on the left. If x = −25.64, the instructions

```
cout.width (12); // display the next value in a field of width
                 //    12
cout >> x;       // value affected by the previous call to width
```

will cause the value of x to appear as follows:

□□□□□□-25.64

The character □ is being used to indicate a blank. The width of the field (number of characters) used to display the value is 12. The value itself takes up six characters (displayed on the right side of the field) and the remaining part of the field is filled with blanks (called *blank fill* or *blank padding*). The width function is useful for displaying multiple lines of data in the form of a table, with each column neatly aligned. Examples of this are illustrated later in this chapter.

The `setf`, `precision`, and `width` functions are summarized below. We will discuss these and other I/O functions and flags in more detail in Chapter 8.

STREAM MEMBER FUNCTION	EXAMPLE USE	EXPLANATION
setf	cout.setf (ios::showpoint); cout.setf (ios::fixed);	Sets designated I/O flags. Setting remains in effect until next change or until `unsetf` is called.
precision	cout.precision (2);	Specifies number of decimal places of accuracy for floating-point value. Setting remains in effect until next change.
width	setw (7)	Specifies field width of next item to be displayed. Affects only the next item to be displayed.

EXERCISES FOR SECTION 5.3

Self-Check
1. What is the least number of times that the body of a `while` loop may be executed?
2. a. What is displayed by the segment below?

```
sum = 0;
while (sum < 100)
    sum += 5;
cout << sum << endl;
```

   b. Rewrite the loop so that it prints all multiples of 5 from 0 through 100, inclusive.
3. a. What values are displayed if the data value in the sample run of the program in Fig. 5.6 is 9.45?
   b. What values would be displayed by this program if the order of the statements in the loop body were reversed?

4. a. How would you modify the loop in Fig. 5.6 so that it also determines the number of strokes (`count_strokes`) made by the swimmer before arriving at the opposite side of the pool?

   b. In your modified loop, which is the loop control variable, `distance` or `count_strokes`?

5. Assuming the statements

```
cout.setf (ios::showpoint);
cout.setf (ios::fixed);
cout.precision (6);
```

have already been executed, how will the data displayed in the following two examples appear? (Show all blanks precisely.)

   a. if radius = 4.5:
```
cout << "The value of pi is " << pi << endl;
cout << "The value of radius is " << radius << endl;
```

   b. (assume `precision (6)` was never put into effect) if x - 4, x_square = 16, y = 10, y_square = 100:
```
cout << x << x_square;
cout << y << y_square;
```

6. a. Write the C++ statements to display a floating-point value accurate to three decimal places.

   b. Write the C++ statements to display a floating-point value accurate to one decimal place and in scientific notation.

Programming   1. There are 9870 people in a town whose population increases by 10 percent each year. Write a loop that determines how many years it will take for the population to exceed 30,000.

5.4 ——— LOOP DESIGN

It is one thing to be able to analyze the operation of a loop (such as the loop in Fig. 5.6) and another to design our own loops. We will use two approaches to attack this problem: The first is to analyze the requirements for a new loop to determine what initialization, test, and update of the loop control variable are needed. The second is to develop *structural patterns* for loops that frequently recur and to use this as the basis for the new loop. We will discuss structural loop patterns later in this section.

To gain some insight into the design of the loop needed for the swimmer problem, we should study the comment in Fig. 5.6 that summarizes the goal of this loop.

```
// Cut the distance between the swimmer and the opposite
//    side by 2/3 the swimmer's body length until she is close
//    enough to touch the edge.
```

In order to accomplish this goal, we must concern ourselves with loop control and loop processing. Loop control involves making sure that loop exit occurs when it is supposed to; loop processing involves making sure the loop body performs the required operations.

To help us formulate the necessary loop control and loop processing steps, it is useful to list what we know about the loop. In this example, if `distance` is the distance of the swimmer from the edge of the pool, we can make the following observations:

a. `distance` must be equal to `initial_distance` just before the loop begins.
b. `distance` during pass i must be less than the value of `distance` during pass i−1 by two-thirds the body length of the swimmer.
c. `distance` must be between 0 and the swimmer's body length just after loop exit.

Statement (a) indicates that `initial_distance` is the same as the distance of the swimmer from the opposite side of the pool. Statement (b) says that the distance of the swimmer from the far edge must be cut by two-thirds of the swimmer's body length during each iteration. Statement (c) derives from the fact that the swimmer must be close enough to touch the edge on her next move right after loop exit. Therefore, after loop exit, the swimmer's distance from the edge must be less than her body length. Because the swimmer has not yet touched the edge, the distance cannot be negative.

Statement (a) by itself tells us what initialization must be performed. Statement (b) tells us how to process `distance` within the loop body (that is, subtract two-thirds the body length). Finally, statement (c) tells us when to exit the loop. Because `distance` is decreasing, loop exit should occur when `distance < body_length` is true. These considerations give us the outline below, which is the basis for the `while` loop shown in Fig. 5.6. The loop repetition condition, `distance >= body_length`, is the opposite of the exit condition, `distance < body_length`. The structural pattern for the `while` loop used in the swimmer problem is as follows:

1. Initialize `distance` to `initial_distance`.
2. While `distance` is greater than or equal to `body_length`
    2.1. Display `distance`.
    2.2. Reduce `distance` by 2/3 `body_length`.

`while` Loops with Zero Iterations

The body of a `while` loop is not executed if the loop repetition test fails (evaluates to false) when it is first reached. To verify that we have the initialization steps correct, we should make sure that a program still generates the correct results for zero iterations of the loop body. If `body_length` is greater than the value read into `initial_distance` (say, 3.4), the loop body in Fig. 5.6 would not execute and the lines below would be correctly displayed.

```
Enter the initial distance of the swimmer from
the opposite side of the pool in feet: 3.4

The last distance before the swimmer touches the edge
on the opposite side of the pool is 3.4
```

Determining Loop Initialization

It is not always so easy to come up with the initialization steps for a loop. In some cases, we must work backward from the results that we know are required in the first pass to determine what initial values will produce these results.

Example 5.6   Your young cousin is learning the binary number system and has asked you to write a program that displays all powers of 2 that are less than a certain value (say, 10,000). Assuming that each power of 2 is stored in the variable power, we can make the following observations about the loop:

a. power during pass i is twice power at pass $i-1$ (for $i > 1$).
b. power must be between 10,000 and 20,000 just after loop exit.

Statement (a) follows from the fact that the powers of 2 are all multiples of 2; statement (b) follows from the stipulation that only powers less than 10,000 are to be displayed. From statement (a) we know that power must be multiplied by 2 in the loop body. From statement (b) we know that the loop exit condition is power >= 10000, so the loop repetition condition is power < 10000. These considerations lead us to the following loop outline:

1. Initialize power to ___.
2. While power < 10000
    2.1. Display power.
    2.2. Multiply power by 2.

One way to complete step 1 is to ask what value should be displayed during the first loop repetition. The value of n raised to the power 0 is 1 for any number n. Therefore, if we initialize power to 1, the value displayed during the first loop repetition will be correct.

1. Initialize power to 1   ∎

Sentinel-Controlled Loops

Frequently, we will not know exactly how many data items a loop will process before it begins execution. This may happen because there are too many data items to count beforehand or because the number of data items to be processed depends on how the computation proceeds.

One way to handle this situation is to instruct the user to enter a unique data value, called a *sentinel value,* as the last data item. The loop condition then tests each data item and terminates when the sentinel value is read. The sentinel value should be carefully chosen and must be a value that cannot possibly occur as data.

Example 5.7   The following statements (a and b) must be true for a sentinel-controlled loop that accumulates the sum of a collection of exam scores where each data item is read into the variable score. The sentinel value must not be included in the sum.

   a.   sum is the total of all scores read so far.
   b.   score contains the sentinel value just after loop exit.

From statement (a) we know that we must add each score to sum in the loop body, and that sum must initially be zero in order for its final value to be correct. From statement (b) we know that loop exit must occur after the sentinel value is read into score.

A solution is to read the first score as the initial value of score before the loop is reached, then perform the following steps in the loop body:

- add score to sum.
- read the next score.

The algorithm outline for this solution is shown next.

1. Initialize sum to zero.
2. Read first score into score.
3. While score is not the sentinel
      3.1.   Add score to sum.
      3.2.   Read next score into score.

Step 2 reads in the first score and step 3.1 adds this score to zero (initial value of sum). Step 3.2 reads all remaining scores, including the sentinel. Step 3.1 adds all scores except the sentinel to sum.

The read before the loop (step 2) is often called the *initial read* because it is required prior to entry into the loop. If this read is omitted or misplaced, the loop may not work correctly. The C++ implementation shown in Fig. 5.7 uses -1 as the sentinel because all exam scores should be nonnegative. A sentinel value is best declared as a constant, because its value must not change for the duration of the loop.

Figure 5.7 A sentinel-controlled loop

```cpp
// FILE: SumScore.cpp
// ACCUMULATES THE SUM OF EXAM SCORES

#include <iostream.h>

void main ()
{
    // Local data ...
    const int sentinel = -1;      // sentinel value
    int count;                    // count of scores processed
    int score;                    // each exam score
    int sum;                      // sum of scores
    float average;                // average of scores processed

    count = 0;
    sum = 0;
    cout << "Enter scores one at a time as requested." << endl;
    cout << "When done, enter " << sentinel << " to stop." << endl;
    cout << "Enter the first score: ";
    cin >> score;
    while (score != sentinel)
    {
        count++;
        sum += score;
        cout << "Enter the next score : ";
        cin >> score;
    }  // end while

    cout << endl << endl;
    cout << "Sum of exam scores is " << sum << endl;
    cout << count << " exam scores were processed." << endl;
    cout.setf (ios::showpoint);
    cout.setf (ios::fixed);
    cout.precision (2);
    average = float (sum) / float (count);
    cout << "Average of the exam scores is " << average << endl;
}
```

──────────── Program Output ────────────

```
Enter scores one at a time as requested.
When done, enter -1 to stop.
Enter the first score: 55
Enter the next score : 33
Enter the next score : 77
Enter the next score : -1

Sum of exam scores is 165
3 exam scores were processed.
Average of the exam scores is 55.0
```

You might initially think you can reverse the order of steps 3.1 and 3.2 in an attempt to avoid the need for step 2, which at first might seem like an unnecessary duplication. Be assured that in doing so the sentinel will be added to the sum and sum will be incorrect.   ■

It is usually instructive (and often necessary) to question what happens when there are no data items to process. To test this idea, the sentinel value should be entered as the "first score." Loop exit would occur right after the first and only test of the loop repetition condition, so the loop body would not be executed (that is, it would be a loop with zero iterations), and sum would correctly retain its initial value of zero.

Sentinel-controlled loops have the following general form:

1. Read the first value of input variable.
2. While input variable is not equal to the sentinel
    2.1. Process value just read.
    2.2. Read the next value of input variable.

PROGRAM STYLE

Counting the Number of Data Items Processed in a Program

Keeping track of the number of data items processed in a program is one of the easiest steps to include in your code. The display of such counts can also provide important information to a programmer or to a program user, even sometimes pointing out the presence of a run-time error that might not otherwise be discovered until it is too late. In the program shown in Fig. 5.7, we added the counter initialization, increment, and display steps needed to keep track of and display the number of data items processed in the loop. We also added a step in which we used this count to determine the average of the data processed. We encourage you to keep track of loop repetitions wherever practical and to display this information for the user. It is easy to do and often very helpful.   ■

Loops Controlled by Flags

Type bool variables are often used as *status flags* controlling the execution of a loop. The value of the flag is initialized (usually to false) prior to loop entry and is redefined (usually to true) when a particular event occurs inside the loop. A *flag-controlled loop* executes until the anticipated event occurs and the flag value is changed.

For example, let's assume we are reading various data characters entered at the keyboard and are waiting for the first digit character that is entered. The variable digit_read could be used as a flag to indicate whether a digit character has been entered.

Program Variable

`digit_read` (bool)   status flag—value is true after a digit character has been read; otherwise, value is false.

Because no characters have been read before the data entry loop executes, we should initialize `digit_read` to false. The `while` loop must continue to execute as long as `digit_read` is false because this means that the event "digit character entered as data" has not yet occurred. Therefore, the loop repetition condition should be (`!digit_read`), because this condition is true when `digit_read` is false. Within the loop body, we will read each data item and set the value of `digit_read` to true if that data item is a digit character. The `while` loop follows.

```
digit_read = false;    // assume no digit character has been read
while (!digit_read)
{
    cout << "Enter another data character: ";
    cin >> next_char;
    digit_read = (('0' <= next_char) && (next_char <= '9'));
    // Process digit_read.
    ...
}  // end while
```

The assignment statement

```
digit_read = (('0' <= next_char) && (next_char <= '9'));
```

assigns a value of true to `digit_read` if `next_char` is a digit character (within the range `'0'` through `'9'`); otherwise, `digit_read` remains false. If `digit_read` becomes true, loop exit occurs; if `digit_read` remains false, the loop continues to execute until a digit character is finally read.

We will examine better ways of testing for "digit characters" as well as for other categories of characters (lowercase letters, etc.) in later chapters of the book.

The general form of a flag-controlled loop is shown next.

General Structural Pattern for a Flag-Controlled Loop

1. Set the loop control flag to ensure the loop executes correctly the first time.
2. While loop control condition is still true
   2.1. Perform loop processing.
   2.2. Reset flag to ensure loop exit if the exit event occurs.

In our example, setting `digit_read` to false prior to loop entry ensures that the loop will execute correctly the first time. The statement at the end of the loop that redefines the value of `digit_read`, sets `digit_read` to true the first time a digit character is read in the loop. Reading a digit character is the event that should cause the repetition of the loop to terminate.

EXERCISES FOR SECTION 5.4

Self-Check
1. How would the execution of the program in Fig. 5.7 be affected if we moved the assignment statement in the sentinel-controlled loop to the end of the loop body (as the last statement in the loop body)?
2. How would the execution of the program in Fig. 5.7 be affected if we removed the first `cin >> score` line and moved the second `cin >> score` line to the beginning of the loop body?
3. Change the assignment statement in the flag-controlled loop:

```
digit_read = (('0' <= next_char) && (next_char <= '9'));
```

   to use the C++ function `isdigit` to determine if `next_char` is a digit character.
   a. What would happen if this entire statement were accidentally omitted from the loop?
   b. What is the value of each of the two relational expressions in the preceding assignment statement if the value of `next_char` is '2'? What is the value of the entire logical expression (to be assigned to `digit_read`) if the value of `next_char` is '2'?
4. In the program shown in Fig. 5.7, what value would have been stored in the variable `average` had we used the computation

```
average = sum / count;
```

   rather than the statement shown.
5. What value of count would have been displayed by the program in Fig. 5.7 had the sentinel value been the only value entered by the program user? What would have happened in this case when the program attempted to compute the average?

Programming
1. Modify the counter-controlled loop in Fig. 5.3 so that it is a sentinel-controlled loop. Use a negative value of `hours` as the sentinel.
2. Write a program segment that allows the user to enter values and prints out the number of positive and negative values entered. Use 0 as the sentinel value.
3. Write a `while` loop that displays all powers of an integer, n, less than a specified value, `max_power`. On each line of a table, show the power (0, 1, 2, ...) and the value of the integer n raised to that power.
4. Write a loop that prints a table of angle measures along with their sine and cosine values. Assume that the initial and final angle measures (in degrees) are available in `initial_degree` and `final_degree` (type `float`), respectively, and that the change in angle measure between table entries is given by `step_degree`. (Remember that C++ trigonometric functions perform their computations in radians, so you will have some conversion to do from degrees to radians and vice versa.)
5. Write a flag-controlled loop that continues to read pairs of integers until it reads a pair with the property that the first integer in the pair is evenly divisible by the second.

5.5 ——— USING THE `while` LOOP

We are now ready to put to use what we have learned about the `while` loop and other C++ features introduced so far in this chapter.

CASE STUDY: EFFECT OF GRAVITY ON A FREE-FALLING OBJECT

Problem Statement

Your physics professor has asked you to write a program that displays the effect of gravity on a free-falling object. The program must display a table showing the height of an object dropped from a tower for every second that the object is falling.

Problem Analysis

This is an example of a problem requiring the *simulation* of a physical phenomenon—specifically, the dropping of an object from a tower. Our primary task in this case is to generate a table that shows for accumulated intervals of time (t = 0, 1, 2, 3, etc.) the distance of an object above the ground. To solve this problem, we need first to identify the relevant physical information and formulas that must be known to the program. Clearly, we need to know the height of the tower from which the object is to be dropped. We can treat the tower height as input provided by the program user at the beginning of program execution. Although the time interval is fixed (at one second) by the problem specification, we will also allow the program user to enter this value at the start of program execution in order to make the program useful in more general situations.

Once the tower height and time interval information have been entered by the user, the program must generate the table. Our problem can therefore be decomposed into two basic subproblems, as shown in the structure chart in Fig. 5.8: (1) entry of the two input values and (2) generation of the table. We will solve the table generation subproblem separately and write it as a sepa-

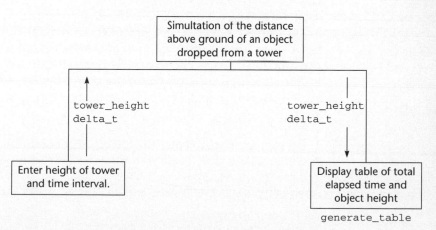

Figure 5.8   Structure chart for the effect of gravity case

rate function. We will see that most of the complexity of the problem solution will be hidden in this lower level function. The data flow illustrated in the structure chart shows that two input values are needed for the function to do its work: the time interval and the tower height.

Given this outline, we can provide the basic data requirements summary needed as the first step in solving the problem. We have chosen the metric system of distance measure for this problem. The choice and documentation of the units of measurement are critical in the solution of any problem, since it can have an effect on the choice of constants and the selection of computational formulas to be used in a program. In this case, had we chosen feet as the unit of distance measure, the value of the gravitational constant (to be considered later) would be different.

DATA REQUIREMENTS

Problem Input

`tower_height` (`float`) — height (in meters) of the tower from which the object is to be dropped

`delta_t` (`float`) — the time interval for which the distance computation is to be done

Problem Output

(not yet considered)

Program Design

The program should begin execution by asking the user to enter the height of the tower and the time interval as program input. The program then can generate the table required by the professor. We will accomplish this second task in a separate function, `generate_table`, which will also print a brief message indicating when the object hits the ground.

The initial algorithm is shown next. To write the main function, we simply need to specify the information that is to be passed from the main program to the function `generate_table`. This specification is provided following the initial algorithm. It is based on the data flow information illustrated in the structure chart in Fig. 5.8.

INITIAL ALGORITHM

1. Prompt the user to enter the tower height and time interval.
2. Generate the table of elapsed times and object height.

DATA REQUIREMENTS FOR `generate_table` (INTERFACE ONLY)

Input Arguments

`tower_height` (`float`)   — height of tower (in meters)

delta_t (float)   — time interval (in seconds)

Function Return Value

(none)

FUNCTION PROTOTYPE

```
// GENERATE TABLE
void generate_table
  (float,        // IN: height of tower (in meters)
   float);       // IN: time interval (in seconds)
```

Analysis for generate_table (step 2)

We must be able to figure out the distance traveled by the dropped object every second from time 0, the time at which the object is dropped. Assuming t is the elapsed time of free fall, we can make the following observations about the height of the object at time t:

- At t equal to 0.0, the height of the object is the same as the height of the tower.
- While an object is falling, its height equals the height of the tower minus the distance that it has traveled.
- Free fall ends when the object height is no longer > 0.0.

The determination of the distance traveled by the object is a function of the gravitational pull on earth. The distance may be computed using the formula

$$Distance = 1/2 \times gt^2$$

where g is the gravitational constant. Since we have chosen to provide the problem solution using meters as the measure of distance and seconds as the measure of time, the value of g that we must use is 9.80665 meters per second squared.

DATA REQUIREMENTS FOR generate_table (local data)

Problem Constants

g = 9.80665   — gravitational constant (in meters per feet squared)

Formula

distance = $1/2 \times gt^2$

Local data

object_height (float)   — used to keep track of the height of the
                          dropped object at any time
t (float)   — used to keep track of the elapsed time
                          since object was dropped

Design for generate_table

We use a while loop to control the generation of the table. The loop will continue executing as long as the distance of the object above the ground is greater than zero. When this condition fails, execution of the loop terminates and a short message is displayed. The elapsed time increases by the value of delta_t. For each new value of total elapsed time (t) until the object hits the ground, the loop generates a display line indicating the total elapsed time and the height of the object above the ground (object_height). The algorithm is shown next.

Algorithm for **generate_table**

1. Initialize object_height to tower_height and elapsed time (t) to 0.
2. While (object_height > 0)
   2.1. display t and object_height.
   2.2. recompute t by adding the time interval (delta_t) to the current value of t.
   2.3. recompute object_height.

Implementation of the Program

The complete program is shown in Fig. 5.9. The algorithm for generate_table forms the basis for the while loop shown in the function. The while condition

```
(object_height > 0.0)
```

ensures that loop exit occurs when the object hits the ground. Within the loop body, the assignment statement

```
object_height = tower_height - 0.5 * g * pow (t,2);
```

recomputes the height of the object.

The number of lines in the table depends on the time interval between lines (delta_t) and the height of the tower (tower_height), both of which are data values. During each loop iteration, the current elapsed time (t) and the current height of the object (object_height) are displayed and new values are assigned to these variables. The message following the table is displayed when the object hits the ground.

Figure 5.9   The descent of an object from a tower

```cpp
// FILE: FreeFall.cpp
// DISPLAY HEIGHT OF A DROPPED OBJECT AT EQUAL INTERVALS
// Displays the height of an object dropped from a tower
//    at user specified intervals, until it hits the ground.

#include <iostream.h>
#include <iomanip.h>
#include <math.h>

    // Function prototypes ...
    // GENERATE TABLE
    void generate_table
      (float,      // INPUT: height of tower from which object dropped
       float);    // INPUT: time interval

void main ()
{

    // Local data ...
    float tower_height;         // height of tower (meters)
    float delta_t;              // time interval

    // Enter tower height and time interval.
    cout << "Enter tower height in meters: ";
    cin >> tower_height;
    cout << "Enter time in seconds between table lines: ";
    cin >> delta_t;
    cout << endl;

    // Display object height until it hits the ground.
    generate_table (tower_height, delta_t);
}


// GENERATE TABLE
void generate_table
    (float tower_height,        // INPUT: height of tower from which
                                //         object dropped
     float delta_t)             // INPUT: time interval
{
    // Local data ...
    const float g = 9.80655;    // gravitational pull in meters per
                                //    second squared
    float object_height;        // height of object at any time t
    float t;                    // total elapsed time

    // Display table header.
    cout << setw (10) << "Time" << setw (9) << "Height" << endl;
    t = 0.0;
    object_height = tower_height;
```

(continued)

Figure 5.9   Dropping an object from a tower

```cpp
// Display table.
cout.setf (ios::showpoint);
cout.setf (ios::fixed);
while (object_height > 0.0)
{
   cout << setw (9) << t << setw (10) << precision (2)
        << object_height << endl;
   t += delta_t;
   object_height = tower_height - 0.5 * g * pow (t, 2);
}  // end while

// Object hits the ground.
cout << endl;
cout << "SPLAT!!!" << endl << endl;
}
```

——————————— Program Output ———————————

```
Enter tower height in meters: 100
Enter time in seconds between table lines: 1

    Time   Height
      0    100.00
      1     95.10
      2     80.39
      3     55.87
      4     21.55

SPLAT!!!
```

Input/Output Manipulators

In the program in Fig. 5.9, we illustrated the use of the *input/output (I/O) manipulators* `setprecision` and `setw`. I/O manipulators behave in the same manner as their corresponding member functions, but they provide a way to reference stream member functions directly in an output statement, following the insertion operator. The ability to embed a manipulator directly in an output statement provides a more convenient mechanism for formatting the information being inserted into the output stream. Without these manipulators, for example, the line

```cpp
cout << setw (10) << "Time" << setw (9) << "Height" << endl;
```

in Fig. 5.9 would have to be replaced by the four lines

```cpp
cout.width (10);
cout << "Time";
cout.width (9);
cout << "Height" << endl;
```

The C++ library header <iomanip.h> is required for the use of manipulators. As illustrated in Fig. 5.9, you will likely find it most convenient to use the setprecision and setw manipulators to control the format of longer lines of output. You may prefer to continue to use the function call forms setf and unsetf.

I/O MANIPULATOR	CORRESPONDING STREAM MEMBER FUNCTION	EXAMPLE USE OF MANIPULATOR	EXPLANATION
setiosflags	setf	setiosflags (ios::showpoint) setiosflags (ios::showpoint || ios::fixed)	Sets designated I/O flags.
setprecision	precision	setprecision (2) *Note.* Remains in effect until next setting encountered.	Specifies number of decimal places of accuracy for floating-point value.
setw	width	setw (7) *Note:* Remains in effect only for the next data item displayed.	Specifies width of next item to be printed.

Program Testing

We should ensure that the program works correctly for a positive value of the tower height and for two or three different values of the time interval. This verification will require some hand calculations to verify that the program is executing correctly. We should also ensure that the program behaves appropriately in cases in which invalid values are entered for the tower height or the time interval (see Self-Check Exercise 1 at the end of this section).

Commentary

Once again, the software design approach first outlined in Chapter 1 has been carefully followed to illustrate how the process works. Of particular importance is the identification of the relevant physical information (data and formulas) needed for the solution of the problem. We have been particularly cautious about introducing unnecessary information before it is needed, as part of the effort to limit such details to the program components that need to know them. In this problem, virtually all of the complexity was associated with the loop generating the table. The main calculations were embedded in this loop as well, so that all specifications of formulas and constants related to this computation were specified only where needed—in the function generate_table.

EXERCISES FOR SECTION 5.5

Self-Check
1. For the program shown in Fig. 5.9, describe a strategy that you might use to verify that meaningful values (greater than zero, for example) had been entered for the tower height and the time interval.
   a. What would happen in the execution of this program if a time interval of 0 were entered?
   b. What would happen in the execution of this program if a negative time interval were entered?
   c. What would happen in the execution of this program if a tower height of 0 were entered?
2. What would change in the first two lines of the table shown in Fig. 5.9 if the statements

   ```
   cout.setf (ios::showpoint);
   cout.setf (ios::fixed);
   ```

   were removed? Would any other part of the output change as a result of removing these two lines of code? Explain your answer.
3. How would we have to change the program shown in Fig. 5.9 if we declare the gravitational constant *g* in the main program rather than the function `generate_table`? Is there any benefit to moving the declaration of *g* to the main program?
4. Rewrite the output statement that appears inside the `while` loop in Fig. 5.9 using only the format function `width` rather than the manipulator `setw`.

5.6 ———— THE for STATEMENT

In addition to the `while` loop, C++ provides another loop form, the `for` statement, that is more convenient for implementing loops, especially those involving *counter-controlled repetition*. The `for` statement enables us to place all loop control operations in one place—the statement header. For example, we can write the `while` loop form of the counter-controlled loops illustrated in Section 5.2 as follows:

Set *lcv* to initial value.
While (*lcv* < *final value*)
    Perform loop processing.
    Update *lcv* to *next value*.

The `for` statement having the same behavior as this `while` statement is shown next:

for   (set *lcv* to *initial value*;   *lcv* < *final value*;   update *lcv* to *next value*)
    Perform loop processing.

There are three loop control operations indicated in the *statement header:*

1. Set the *lcv* to *initial value.*
2. Test *lcv* against *final value* (the *repetition condition test*).
3. Update *lcv* to *next value* before next test.

It is important to understand the order of execution in a `for` loop with executable statements in its body. The lcv initialization is done first and only once. The repetition condition test is performed next. If the condition is false, nothing further in the loop is executed. If the condition is true, the statements in the loop body are executed next. Finally, the lcv is updated, but only if the repetition condition was true and only after the execution of the loop body finishes.

Example 5.8   The statement segments below behave in the same way.

```
// print n blank lines          // print n blank lines
line = 0;                       for (line = 0; line < n; line++)
while (line < n)                    cout << endl;
{
    cout << endl;
    line++;
}   // end while
```

If `line` is declared as an integer variable, the `for` statement on the right causes the `cout` operation to be performed n times. The `while` loop implementation shown on the left is longer because the statements

```
line = 0;
line++;
```

which are needed to initialize and update the loop control variable, appear on separate lines. In a `while` loop, only the repetition condition test appears in the statement header.   ∎

Example 5.9   The `for` statement in Fig. 5.10 reads payroll data for seven employees and computes and displays each employee's weekly pay. Compare it with the `while` statement shown in Fig. 5.1.

The first line of Fig. 5.10 can be interpreted as follows:

a) Initialize loop control variable `employee_count` to 0.
b) Test the repetition condition (`employee_count < 7`).
c) After execution of the loop body, update value of `employee_count` (increment by 1).

Figure 5.10 for loop for seven employees

```
for (int employee_count = 0; employee_count < 7; employee_count++)
{
    cout << "Hours: ";
    cout << hours;
    cout << "Rate : $";
    cin >> rate;
    pay = hours * rate;
    cout << "Weekly pay is " << pay << endl;
}   // end for

cout << "All employees processed" << endl;
```

PROGRAM STYLE

Localized Declarations of Loop Control Variables

This example also illustrates the use of a localized variable declaration—in this case, for the loop control variable employee_count. Because for loop control variables are often relevant only to the loop in which they are specified, we will adopt the convention of declaring these variables at the point of first reference—in the for loop header. ∎

Example 5.10 Function print_I (Fig. 5.11) displays the capital letter I in block form. The for loop prints five lines that contain asterisks in columns 4 and 5. A blank line is printed just before the return from the function.

The program segment in Fig. 5.11 specifies that the loop control variable next_line takes on each of the values in the range 0 to 4 during successive loop repetitions. This means that the value of next_line is 0 during the first loop repetition, 1 during the second loop repetition, and 4 during the last repetition. ∎

The for loops illustrated thus far have exhibited the following similarities:

- the *initial value* was 0.
- the *increment* step was of the form counter++, where counter is the loop control variable.

Figure 5.11 Function print_I

```
// PRINTS THE BLOCK LETTER I
void print_I ()
{
    cout << "********" << endl;
    for (int next_line = 0; next_line < 5; next_line++)
        cout << "   **" << endl;
    cout << "********" << endl << endl;
}
```

■ The *final value* is actually the number of repetitions for the loop—that is, the number of times the loop body is to be repeated.

This is one of the simplest versions of the general C++ for loop. However, it is easy to understand and is by far the most often used. As we will see in many of the remaining examples in this chapter, we are not restricted to this for loop form.

The following example illustrates a for statement in which the loop control variable is referenced in the loop body.

Example 5.11   The program in Fig. 5.12 uses a for loop to print a list of integer values, their squares, and their square roots. During each repetition of the loop body, the statement

```
square = pow (i, 2);
```

Figure 5.12   Table of integers, squares, and square roots

```
// FILE: Squares.cpp
// DISPLAYS A TABLE OF INTEGERS AND THEIR SQUARES

#include <iostream.h>
#include <iomanip.h>          // needed for setw and setprecision
#include <math.h>             // needed for pow() and sqrt()

void main ()
{
    // Local data ...
    const int max_i = 4;      // largest integer in table

    int square;               // output: square of i
    float root;               // output: square root of i

    // Prints a list of integers, their squares, and square roots.
    cout.setf (ios::showpoint);
    cout.setf (ios::fixed);
    cout << setw (5) << "i" << setw (10) << "square" << setw (14)
         << "square root" << endl;
    for (int i = 1; i <= max_i; i++)
    {
        square = pow (i, 2);
        root = sqrt (i);
        cout << setw (5) << i << setw (8) << square;
        cout << setw (11) << setprecision (1) << root << endl;
    }  // end for
}
```

———————————— Program Output ————————————

```
i     square   square root
1        1         1.0
2        4         1.4
3        9         1.7
4       16         2.0
```

calls function `pow` to compute the square of the loop control variable `i`. `pow` takes two arguments, `x` and `y`, and returns x^y. Since we want to compute i^2, we pass in the variable `i` for `x`, and the number 2 for `y`. It would be a good idea to declare 2 as a constant and use it as the second argument to `pow`.

The statement

```
root = sqrt (i);
```

calls function `sqrt` to compute the square root of `i`. Both of these functions require the inclusion of the math header file `math.h`. In the last steps of the loop, the values of `i`, `i` squared, and the square root of `i` are displayed. Table 5.2 traces the execution of the `for` loop.

The hand trace in Table 5.2 shows that the loop control variable `i` is initialized to 1 when the `for` loop is reached. Although most loops generally start with 0, it is not required by C++. In this particular case, starting our loop with 1 has more relevance. After each loop repetition, `i` is incremented by one and tested to see whether its value is still less than or equal to `max_i` (4). If the

Table 5.2   Trace of Program in Fig. 5.12

STATEMENT	i	square	root	EFFECT
	?	?	?	
`for (i = 1; i <= max_i; i++)`	1			Initialize i to 1
`  square = pow (i, 2);`		1		Assign 1 to square
`  root = sqrt (i);`			1.0	Assign 1.0 to root
`  cout << ...`				Print 1, 1, 1.0
Increment and Test i	2			$2 \le 4$ is true
`  square = pow (i, 2);`		4		Assign 4 to square
`  root = sqrt (i);`			1.4	Assign 1.4 to root
`  cout << ...`				Print 2, 4, 1.4
Increment and Test i	3			$3 \le 4$ is true
`  square = pow (i, 2);`		9		Assign 9 to square
`  root = sqrt (i);`			1.7	Assign 1.7 to root
`  cout << ...`				Print 3, 9, 1.7
Increment and Test i	4			$4 \le 4$ is true
`  square = pow (i, 2);`		16		Assign 16 to square
`  root = sqrt (i);`			2.0	Assign 2.0 to root
`  cout << ...`				Print 4, 16, 2.0
Increment and Test i	5			$5 \le 4$ is false
				Exit loop

test result is true, the loop body is executed again, and the next values of i, square, and root are printed. If the test result is false, the loop is exited.

The last loop repetition occurs when i is equal to max_i. After this repetition, the value of i becomes one greater than max_i, and the loop is exited. You can reference the last value of the variable i anytime after leaving the loop. ∎

Example 5.12 The counting loop shown in Fig. 5.13 computes the sum of all integers from 1 to n. The for loop causes the assignment statement

```
sum += i;
```

to be repeated n times. During each repetition, the current value of i is added to the sum being accumulated and the result is saved back in sum. This is illustrated in Fig. 5.14 for n equal to 3. ∎

Example 5.13 The loop shown next displays the characters in your_name, one character per line. It illustrates the use of the string functions length and at. The function getline reads a full name into the string object your_name prior to the execution of the loop. If your_name is Jill, the loop displays the letters J, i, l, l on separate lines.

Figure 5.13 Program for sum of integers from 1 to n

```cpp
// FILE: Sum_Int.cpp
// FINDS AND PRINTS THE SUM OF ALL INTEGERS FROM 1 TO n
#include <iostream.h>

void main ()
{
    // Local data ...
    int n;                          // last integer to be added to sum
    int sum;                        // sum of all integers from 1 to n

    // Read the last integer.
    cout << "Enter the last integer in the sum: ";
    cin >> n;

    // Find the sum of all the integers from 1 to n inclusive.
    sum = 0;
    for (int i = 1; i <= n; i++)
       sum += i;

    // Print the sum.
    cout << "The sum is " << sum << "." << endl;
}
```

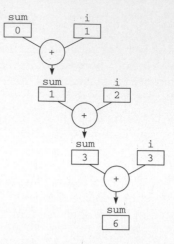

Figure 5.14   Effect of loop repetitions for **n** equal to 3

```
string your_name;
cout << "Enter your name:";
getline (cin, your_name, '\n');
for (int pos_char = 0; pos_char < your_name.length ();
     pos_char++)
   cout << your_name.at (pos_char) << endl;
```

EXERCISES FOR SECTION 5.6

Self-Check

1. Extend the output for the program shown in Fig. 5.12 for max_i = 9.
2. The following for loop is intended to display the values of i from 1 to 10. But the loop does not work correctly. Explain what the problem is and describe how to correct it.

```
for (int i = 0; i < 10; i++)
{
    cout << i++;
}
```

3. What is the result of execution of the program shown in Fig. 5.13 for n = 5? What is the value of sum, as computed by the formula

$$\text{Sum} = \frac{n(n + 1)}{2}$$

Do you think you would get the same result if n = 50? Which approach to computing sum do you think is more efficient? Explain your answer.

Programming

1. Modify the program in Fig. 5.13 so the main function calls a separate function to implement the loop that computes the sum.

5.7 ——— MORE for STATEMENT EXAMPLES

So far, we have used the for loop to implement counting loops—loops that are executed once for each integer value between an initial and a specified final value. In these examples, the loop control is a special variable whose value is increased by 1 each time the loop is repeated. In fact, as shown in the next examples, the for loop may be used in more general ways.

Example 5.14   It is actually possible to specify any positive or negative change to the value of a for loop control variable in the loop header. Thus, the value of the for loop control variable may increase or decrease by any specified amount after each loop repetition. The following for loop computes the sum of all odd integers from 1 to n.

```
// Add the odd integers between 1 and n.
sum = 0;
for (int odd = 1; odd <= n; odd += 2)
    sum += odd;
```

The update expression

```
odd += 2
```

causes the value of the loop control variable odd to increase by 2 instead of 1. In the trace shown in Table 5.3, n is 5 so the values of odd that get summed are 1, 3,

Table 5.3 The trace of Loop for Computing the Sum of Odd Integers

STATEMENT	n	odd	sum	EFFECT
	5	?	?	
sum = 0;			0	Initializes sum to 0.
for (odd = 1;		1		Initializes odd to 1.
odd <= n;				$1 \le 5$ is true
odd += 2)				(no action yet)
sum += odd;			1	adds odd to sum (1 + 0)
Increment odd		3		add 2 to odd (2 + 1)
Test odd <= n;				$3 \le 5$ is true
sum += odd;			4	adds odd to sum (3 + 1)
Increment odd		5		add 2 to odd (2 + 3)
Test odd <= n;				$5 \le 5$ is true
sum += odd;			9	adds odd to sum (5 + 4)
Increment odd		7		add 2 to odd (2 + 5)
Test odd <= n;				$7 \le 5$ is false
				exit loop

and 5. Loop exit occurs when the value of odd *passes* (becomes larger than) n, so the value of odd after loop exit is 7. If the value entered for n is 6 instead of 5, the final values of odd and sum would be the same (7 and 9, respectively). ∎

Decrementing the Loop Control Variable

The examples seen so far showed the `for` loop using an incrementing loop control variable to increase that variable's value. It is just as easy to use a decrementing counter. In the next example, we will demonstrate a loop using decrements of 5.

Example 5.15   The program in Fig. 5.15 prints a table for converting Celsius temperatures to Fahrenheit temperatures. The values of temperature go from +20 degrees Celsius down to −20 degrees. ∎

Figure 5.15   Converting Celsius to Fahrenheit

```
// FILE: Temperat.cpp
// CONVERSION OF CELSIUS TO FAHRENHEIT TEMPERATURE

#include <iostream.h>
#include <iomanip.h>

void main ()
{
   // Local data ...
   const float m = 1.8;
   const float b = 32;
   float fahrenheit;
   // Print the table heading.
   cout << setw (10) << "Celsius" << setw (15) << "Fahrenheit"
        << endl;

   // Print the table.
   cout.setf (ios::showpoint);
   cout.setf (ios::fixed);
   for (int celsius = 20; celsius >= -20; celsius -= 5)
   {
      fahrenheit = m * celsius + b;
      cout << setw (7) << celsius << setw (14) << setprecision (2)
           << fahrenheit << endl;
   }  // end for
}
```

(continued)

Figure 5.15   *(continued)*

――――――――――――― Program Output ―――――――――――――

Celsius	Fahrenheit
20	68.00
15	59.00
10	50.00
5	41.00
0	32.00
-5	23.00
-10	14.00
-15	5.00
-20	-4.00

The for Statement Syntax

Make sure that you place semicolons between the three parts of the for state-ment within the parentheses. You should not place a semicolon after the clos-ing parenthesis or you will create a null loop. The for statement

```
for (i = -5; i <= 5; i++);    // empty statement after parenthesis
    cout << i << endl;
```

executes an empty statement 11 times then prints only the final value of i after loop exit, which will be 6. If the semicolon after the closing parenthesis were removed, the for statement would list the integers from −5 through 5. The syntax display for the general form of the for statement follows.

**C++
SYNTAX**

for Statement

Form: for *(initialization; test expression; update)*
        statement

Examples: for (time = start; time >= 1; time -= interval)

```
    {
        . . .
    }

    sum = 0.0;
    for (i = 0; i < 5; i++)
    {
        cin >> next_number;
        sum += next_number;
    }
```

Interpretation: The for loop header describes the three actions to be per-formed on the loop control variable (normally an integer variable). The *initialization* normally involves assigning an integer value (often a constant) to the lcv and may include a declaration of the lcv. The *test expression* must be a logical expression (have a true or false value) and usually consists of a comparison of two integer-valued expressions, one involving the *lcv*.

The *statement* is executed once for each value of the *lcv*, starting with the value specified in the *initialization*. Before each repetition of *statement* (including the first), the *test expression* is evaluated. If it is false, execution control passes to the first statement following *statement* (loop exit); otherwise, *statement* is executed. After *statement* is executed, the value of *lcv* is updated as specified in the *update* component, and the *test expression* is evaluated once again. ∎

As shown in this display, C++ allows considerable flexibility in the form of the *initialize, test expression,* and *update* parts that can be used in a `for` loop header. As we progress through the text, we will illustrate more of the versatility of the `for` construct.

EXERCISES FOR SECTION 5.7

Self-Check
1. Write the header for a `for` loop that computes successive powers of 1/2 [for example, $(1/2)^0$, $(1/2)^1$, $(1/2)^2$, $(1/2)^3$, ...] until a power p is reached for which $(1/2)^p$ is equal to 0.
2. Correct the errors in the following program segment so that the values of all multiples of 5 between 0 and 100 inclusive are printed.

```
for mult5 = 0; mult5 < 100; mult5 = mult5 + 5);
    cout << mult5;
```

3. Trace the following program segment.

```
j = 10;
for (i = 0; i < 3; i++)
{
    cout << i << "  " << j << endl;
    j -= 2;
}  // end for
```

4. Write `for` loop headers that process all values of Celsius (type `int`) in the ranges indicated below.
   a. −10 through +10
   b. 100 through 1
   c. 15 through 50
   d. 50 through −75

Programming
1. a. Write a program to print a table for converting kilometers to miles (1 km = 0.6 mile). Test your `for` loop with several different start and end values.
   b. Reverse the direction of your loop in part (a) (increasing or decreasing).

5.8 _____ THE do-while STATEMENT

The do-while statement is used to specify a conditional loop that executes at least once. That is, the loop repetition test is specified at the bottom of the loop so that the test cannot be made until at least one execution of the statement has been completed.

Example 5.16   Both program segments in Fig. 5.16 print the powers of 2 whose values lie between 1 and 1000.

The test used in the do-while loop (power < 1000) is the same test used in the while loop; it is just in a different place. The loop body is repeated as long as the value of power is less than 1000. Loop repetition stops when the condition becomes false. The major difference between the two forms is that the do-while loop test is at the bottom of the loop following the execution of the loop body. Thus, do-while loops are guaranteed to execute at least one time. ■

The syntax display for the do-while statement follows. Note that braces are needed, as they are with other loop statements, around multistatement loop bodies.

C++ SYNTAX

do-while Statement

Form:
```
do
    statement
while (expression);
```

Example:
```
do
{
    cout << "Enter a digit: ";
    cin >> ch;
} while ((ch < '0') || ('9' < ch));
```

Interpretation: After each execution of the *statement*, the *expression* is evaluated. If the *expression* is false, loop exit occurs and the next program statement is executed. If the *expression* is true, the loop body is repeated. ■

Figure 5.16   while (left) and do-while (right) statements

```
power = 1;                          power = 1;
while (power < 1000)                do
{                                   {
    cout << power << endl;              cout << power << endl;
    power *= 2;                         power *= 2;
}   // end while                    } while (power < 1000);
```

Figure 5.17   Main control loop for menu-driven program

```
do
{
    display_menu ();      // display the menu choices
    cout << "Enter a number between 1 and " << exit_choice << endl;
    cin >> choice;
    do_choice (choice);   // perform the user's choice
}   while (choice != exit_choice);
```

Example 5.17   A `do-while` statement is often used to control a *menu-driven program* that prints a list of choices from which the program user selects a program operation. For example, the menu displayed for a statistics program might look like this:

1. Compute an average.
2. Compute a standard deviation.
3. Find the median.
4. Find the smallest and largest value.
5. Plot the data.
6. Exit.

The main control routine for such a program would follow the pseudocode below where `exit_choice` represents the constant 6.

do
  Display the menu.
  Read the user's choice.
  Perform the user's choice.
while choice is not exit_choice

The program segment (Fig. 5.17) implements this loop in C++. For each iteration, function `display_menu` displays the menu and reads and performs the user's choice. Function `do_choice` is called with actual argument `choice`. `do_choice` could contain a series of alternatives in a `switch` structure, as suggested in Section 4.18. It is assumed that `do_choice` would carry out the action specified by the `choice` value (between 1 and 5). For any other value of `choice`, `do_choice` does nothing but return control to the loop. Note that the loop continues to repeat for all values of `choice` except `exit_choice`. Therefore, if the user enters improper values (such as a negative value or a value larger than `exit_choice`), the loop provides another chance for entry of a correct value.   ■

Example 5.18   The program in Fig. 5.18 uses a `do-while` loop to find the largest value in a sequence of data items. The variable `item_value` is used to hold each data

Figure 5.18 Finding the largest value

```
// FILE: Largest.cpp
// FINDS THE LARGEST NUMBER IN A SEQUENCE OF INTEGER VALUES

#include <iostream.h>          // needed for cin and cout
#include <limits.h>            // needed for INT_MIN

void main ()
{
   // Local data ...
   int item_value;             // each data value
   int largest_so_far;         // largest value so far
   int min_value;              // the smallest integer

   // Initialize largest_so_far to the smallest integer.
   min_value = INT_MIN;
   largest_so_far = min_value;

   // Save the largest number encountered so far.
   cout << "Finding the largest value in a sequence: " << endl;
   do
   {
      cout << "Enter an integer or " << min_value << " to stop: ";
      cin >> item_value;
      if (item_value > largest_so_far)
         largest_so_far = item_value;    // save new largest number
   } while (item_value != min_value);

   cout << "The largest value entered was " << largest_so_far
        << endl;
}
```

────────────── Program Output ──────────────

```
Finding the largest value in a sequence:
Enter an integer or -32768 to stop: -999
Enter an integer or -32768 to stop: 500
Enter an integer or -32768 to stop: 100
Enter an integer or -32768 to stop: -32768
The largest value entered was 500
```

item, and the variable largest_so_far is used to save the largest data value encountered. Within the loop, the if statement

```
if (item_value > largest_so_far)
   largest_so_far = item_value;   // save new largest number
```

redefines the value of largest_so_far if the current data item is larger than all previous data values. The loop continues to repeat as long as the min_value (a sentinel value in this case) is not read.

The variable min_value, which represents the smallest integer value serves two purposes in the program shown in Fig. 5.18. By initializing largest_so_far to min_value before loop entry, we ensure that the condition (item_value > largest_so_far) will be true during the first loop repetition. Thus, the first data item will be saved as the largest value so far. We are also using min_value as a sentinel because it is unlikely to be entered as a data item for a program that is finding the largest number in a sequence. Note that the library header file limits.h, which defines INT_MIN for a particular system, is included in the program shown in Fig. 5.18. INT_MIN may vary according to the C++ system being used; the value of INT_MIN displayed in the figure may not be the same as the value displayed on your system.   ∎

EXERCISES FOR SECTION 5.8

Self-Check   1. What output is produced by the following do-while loop (m is considered to be of type int)?

```
m = 10;
do
{
    cout << m << endl;
    m = m - 3;
} while (m > 0);
```

2. Redo Exercise 1 for an initial value of m = 12.
3. What is the most significant difference between the while and the do-while loops?
4. a. Write a while loop that prompts a user for a grade between 0 and 100 inclusive and continues to repeat the prompt until a valid entry is provided.
   b. Write a do-while loop that prompts a user for a grade between 0 and 100 inclusive and continues to repeat the prompt until a valid entry is provided.
   c. Do you prefer version (a) or (b) of these loops? Justify your answer.

5.9 ——— REVIEW OF while, for, AND do-while LOOPS

C++ provides three loop control statements: while, for, and do-while. The while loop is repeated as long as its loop repetition condition is true; the do-while loop executes in a similar manner except that the statements in the loop body are always performed at least once. The for loop is normally used where counting is involved, either for loop control, where the number of iterations required can be determined at the beginning of loop execution, or simply when there is a need to track the number of times a particular event has taken place. In such cases, initialization and increment steps are required, and the for

Table 5.4 Three Loop Forms

while	Most commonly used when repetition is not counter controlled; condition test precedes each loop repetition; loop body may not be executed at all
for	Counting loop—when number of repetitions is known ahead of time and can be controlled by a counter; also convenient for loops involving noncounting loop control with simple initialization and update steps; condition test precedes the execution of the loop body
do-while	Convenient when at least one repetition of loop body must be ensured

loop enables us to specify these steps together in one line at the top of the loop. Table 5.4 describes when to use each of these three loop forms. In C++, the for loop is the most frequently used of the three. The generality of the for loop significantly reduces the importance of the while loop in C++.

It is relatively easy to rewrite a do while loop as a while loop by inserting an initial assignment of the conditional variable. However, not all while loops can be conveniently expressed as do-while loops because a do-while loop will always execute at least once, whereas a while loop body may be skipped entirely. For this reason a while loop is preferred over a do-while loop unless it is clear that at least one loop iteration must always be performed.

As an illustration of the three loop forms, a simple counting loop is written in Fig. 5.19. (The dotted lines represent the loop body.) The for loop is the

Figure 5.19 Comparison of three loop forms

```
count = start_value;
while (count < stop_value)
{
   .....
   count++;
}   // end while

for (count = start_value; count < stop_value; count++)
{
   .....
}   // end for

count = start_value;
if (start_value < stop_value)
   do
   {
      .....
      count++;
   } while (count < stop_value);
```

best to use in this situation. The `do-while` loop must be nested in an `if` statement to prevent it from being executed when `start_value` is greater than `stop_value`. For this reason, the `do-while` version of a counting loop is least desirable.

In Fig. 5.19, the assignment statement

```
count++;
```

is used in all three loops to update the loop control variable `count`. `count` will be equal to `stop_value` after the loops are executed; `count` will remain equal to `start_value` if these loops are skipped.

EXERCISES FOR SECTION 5.9

Self-Check   1. What does the `while` statement below display? Rewrite it as a `for` statement and as a `do-while` statement.

```
num = 10;
while (num <= 100)
{
    cout << num << endl;
    num += 10;
}   // end while
```

2. What does the `for` statement below display? Rewrite it as a `while` statement and as a `do-while` statement.

```
for (n = 3; n > 0; n--)
    cout << n << " squared is " << pow (n, 2) << endl;
```

3. When would you make use of a do-while loop rather than a `while` loop in a program?

Programming   1. Write a program fragment that skips over a sequence of positive integer values read as data until it reaches a negative value. Write two versions: one using `do-while` and one using `while`.

2. Write a program fragment that could be used as the main control loop in a menu-driven program for updating an account balance (D = deposit, W = withdrawal, Q = quit). Assume that functions `process_withdrawal` and `process_deposit` already exist and are called with the actual argument `balance`. Prompt the user for a transaction code (D, W, or Q) and call the appropriate function.

5.10 —— NESTED LOOPS

You have seen examples of nested `if` statements in earlier programs. It is also possible to nest loops. Nested loops consist of an outer loop with one or more inner loops. Each time the outer loop is repeated, the inner loops are reentered, their loop control components are reevaluated, and all required iterations are performed.

Example 5.19 Figure 5.20 shows a sample run of a program with two nested `for` loops. The outer loop is repeated four times (for i equals 0, 1, 2, 3). Each time the outer loop is repeated, the statement

```
cout << "Outer" << setw (7) << i << endl;
```

displays the string `"Outer"` and the value of i (the outer loop control variable). Next, the inner loop is entered, and its loop control variable, j, is reset to 0. The number of times the inner loop is repeated depends on the current value of i. Each time the inner loop is repeated, the statement

```
cout << "  Inner" << setw (10) << j << endl;
```

displays the string `"  Inner"` and the value of j.

Figure 5.20 Nested `for` loop program

```
// FILE: NestLoop.cpp
// ILLUSTRATES A PAIR OF NESTED FOR LOOPS

#include <iostream.h>              // needed for cin and cout
#include <iomanip.h>               // needed for setw

void main ()
{
   // print heading
   cout << setw(12) << "i" << setw(6) << "j" << endl;

   for (int i = 0; i < 4; i++)
   {
      cout << "Outer" << setw (7) << i << endl;
      for (int j = 0; j < i; j++)
         cout << "  Inner" << setw (10) << j << endl;
   }  // end for - outer loop

}
```

───────────── Program Output ─────────────

```
                 i    j
Outer            0
Outer            1
   Inner              0
Outer            2
   Inner              0
   Inner              1
Outer            3
   Inner              0
   Inner              1
   Inner              2
```

Figure 5.21   Isosceles triangle program

```cpp
// FILE: Triangle.cpp
// DRAWS AN ISOSCELES TRIANGLE

#include <iostream.h>

void main ()
{
   // Local data ...
   const int number_lines = 5; // number of rows in triangle
   const char blank = ' ';      // output characters
   const char star = '*';       // display character

   // start on new line
   cout << endl;

   // draw each row - outer loop
   for (int row = 1; row <= number_lines; row++)
   {
      // print leading blanks - 1st inner loop
      for (int lead_blanks = number_lines - row; lead_blanks > 0;
           lead_blanks--)
           cout <<  blank;

      // print asterisks - 2nd inner loop
      for (int count_stars = 1; count_stars < 2 * row;
           count_stars++)
        cout << star;

      // terminate line
      cout << endl;
   }  // end for - outer loop
}
```

———————— Program Output ————————

```
    *
   ***
  *****
 *******
*********
```

Table 5.5   Loop Control Variable Values

row	lead_blanks	count_stars	EFFECT
1	4 down to 1	1	Displays 4 blanks and 1 asterisk
2	3 down to 1	1 up to 3	Displays 3 blanks and 3 asterisks
3	2 down to 1	1 up to 5	Displays 2 blanks and 5 asterisks
4	1	1 up to 7	Displays 1 blank and 7 asterisks
5	0	1 up to 9	Displays 0 blanks and 9 asterisks

A compound statement executes each time the outer `for` loop is repeated. This statement displays the value of the outer loop control variable and then executes the inner `for` loop. The body of the inner `for` loop is a single statement displaying the value of the inner loop control variable. This statement executes i times, where i is the outer loop control variable.

The outer loop control variable i determines the number of repetitions of the inner loop, which is perfectly valid. On the other hand, you should not use the same variable as the loop control variable of both an outer and inner `for` loop in the same nest. ■

In this example, we have declared and used each of the two loop control variables directly in their respective `for` loop headers. This is allowed by C++ and is a feature that we find quite convenient. When a loop control variable is declared in this manner, it may be referenced anywhere below the point of declaration in the current function. For a given variable such as i, only one such declaration may be placed in each function.

Example 5.20   The isosceles triangle program in Fig. 5.21 contains an outer loop (lcv row) and two inner loops. Each time the outer loop is repeated, two inner loops are executed. The first inner loop prints the leading blank spaces; the second inner loop prints one or more asterisks.

The outer loop is repeated five times; the number of repetitions performed by the inner loops is based on the value of row. Table 5.5 lists the inner loop control expressions for each value of row. As shown in the table, four blanks and one asterisk are printed when row is 1, three blanks and three asterisks are printed when row is 2, etc. When row is 5, the first inner loop is skipped and nine (2 × 5 − 1) asterisks are printed. ■

EXERCISES FOR SECTION 5.10

Self-Check   1. What is displayed by the following program segments assuming m is 3 and n is 5?

```
a. for (int i = 0; i < n; i++)
   {
       for (int j = 0; j < i; j++)
          cout << "*";
       cout << endl;
   }  // end for i
b. for (int i = n; i > 0; i--)
   {
       for (int j = m; j > 0; j--)
          cout << "*";
       cout << endl;
   }  // end for i
```

2. Show the output printed by the following nested loops:

```
for (int i = 0; i < 2; i++)
{
    cout << "Outer" << setw (5) << i << endl;
    for (int j = 0; j < 3; j++)
        cout << " Inner" << setw (3) << i << setw (3) << j
<< endl;
    for (int k = i; k >= 0; k--)
        cout << " Inner" << setw (3) << i << setw (3) << k
<< endl;
} // end for i
```

3. Describe how you would modify the program in Fig. 5.21 to display a 7-line triangle rather than a 5-line triangle.

4. Describe how you would modify the program in Fig. 5.21 to display a right angle triangle rather than the isosceles triangle shown at the end of the figure. *Note:* In a right angle triangle, each line is left adjusted (displayed beginning at the left margin of the page).

5. Describe how you would modify the program in Fig. 5.21 to display a diamond. Your figure should appear as though the triangle displayed in Fig. 5.21 is turned upside down and placed immediately under itself. Do not duplicate the bottom line of the original triangle (see below). Test your modified program to ensure that it works.

```
        *
       ***
      *****
     *******
    *********
     *******
      *****
       ***
        *
```

Programming   1. Write nested loops that cause the output below to be printed.

```
1
1 2
1 2 3
1 2 3 4
1 2 3
1 2
1
```

5.11 ——— DEBUGGING AND TESTING PROGRAMS

In Section 2.9, we described the general categories of errors that you are likely to encounter: syntax, link, run-time, and logic errors. As you may have already discovered, it is possible for a program to execute without generating any error messages but still produce incorrect results. Sometimes the origin of incorrect results is apparent, and the error can easily be fixed. However, very often the error is not obvious and may require considerable effort to locate.

The first step in attempting to find a hidden error is to examine the program output to determine which part of the program is generating incorrect results. You can then focus on the statements in that section to determine which one(s) are at fault. You may want to insert extra cout statements to trace the values of certain critical variables during program execution. For example, if the loop in Fig. 5.17 is not computing the correct sum, you might want to insert an extra *diagnostic statement*, as shown in the second line of the loop below.

```
cin >> score;
while (score != sentinel)
{
    sum += score;
    cout << "***** score is " << score << " and sum is "
         << sum << endl;
    cout << "Enter the next score : ";
    cin >> score;
}  // end while
```

The diagnostic output statement will display the current value of score and each partial sum that is accumulated. This statement displays a string of asterisks at the beginning of its output line. This makes it easier to identify diagnostic output in the debugging runs and to locate the diagnostic cout statements in the source program.

Take care when inserting extra diagnostic output statements. Sometimes it will be necessary to add an additional pair of braces if a single statement inside an if or while statement becomes a compound statement when a diagnostic cout is added.

Once it appears that you have located an error, you will want to take out the extra diagnostic statements. As a temporary measure, it is sometimes advisable to make these diagnostic statements comments by prefixing them with the double slash (//). If these errors appear again in later testing, it is easier to remove the slashes than to retype the diagnostic statements. (Later you may become comfortable with using special debug flags or *conditional compilation* to control the execution of diagnostic statements. Your instructor can tell you more about these topics if it is desirable for you to use them.)

Off-by-One Errors

A fairly common error in programs with loops is a loop that executes one more time or one less time than it is supposed to. If a sentinel-controlled while loop performs an extra repetition, it may erroneously process the sentinel value along with the regular data.

If a `for` loop performs a counting operation, make sure that the initial and final values of the loop control variable are correct. For example, the loop body below executes n + 1 times instead of n times. In this particular case, the program will hang waiting for an extra entry, and the loop will not exit until you enter one too many items. If your intention is to execute the loop body n times, change the logical condition to (`count < n`).

```
sum = 0;
cout << "Enter " << n << " integers and press return:" << endl;
for(int_count = 0; count <= n; count++)
{
    cin >> item;
    sum += item;
} // end for
```

A general rule of thumb for most C++ loops is to begin with a start value of 0. When the start value is 0, the test will normally involve the relational operator *less than*:

```
count = 0;
(count < n)
```

But if starting with 1 is more convenient for a problem (see Fig. 5.12), the test usually will involve the relational operator *less than or equal to*:

```
count = 1;
(count <= n)
```

You can get a good idea as to whether a loop is correct by checking what happens at the *loop boundaries*—that is, at the initial and final values of the loop control variable. For a `for` loop, you should carefully evaluate the *initial expression* and *final expression* to make sure that these values make sense. Then substitute these values everywhere the loop control variable appears in the loop body and verify that you get the expected result at the boundaries. As an example, in the `for` loop

```
sum = 0;
for (int i = k; i <= n - k; i++)
    sum += i * i;
```

check that the first value of the loop control variable i is supposed to be k and that the last value is supposed to be n - k. Next, check that the assignment statement

```
sum += i * i;
```

is correct at these boundaries. When i is k, sum gets the value of k squared. When i is n - k, the value of n - k squared is added to the previous sum. As a final check, pick some small values of n and k (say, 3 and 1) and trace the loop execution to see that it computes sum correctly for this case.

Using Debugger Programs

Most computer systems have *debugger programs* that can be used to identify problems in a C++ program. The debugger program lets you execute your program one statement at a time (*single-step execution*) so that you can see the effect of each statement. You can select several variables whose values will be automatically displayed after each statement executes. This allows you to trace the program's execution.

You can also separate your program into segments by setting *breakpoints* at selected statements. A breakpoint is like a fence between two segments of a program. You can request the debugger to execute all statements from the last breakpoint up to the next breakpoint. When the program stops at a breakpoint, you can select variables to examine. This allows you to determine whether the program segment executed correctly. If there are no errors, you will want to execute through to the next breakpoint. Otherwise, you may want to set more breakpoints in that segment or perhaps perform single-step execution through that segment.

Testing

After all errors have been corrected and the program appears to execute as expected, the program should be tested thoroughly to make sure that it works in every given situation. In Chapter 4, we discussed tracing an algorithm and suggested that enough sets of test data be provided to ensure that all possible paths are traced. The same suggestion can be made for the completed program. Make enough test runs to verify that the program works properly for representative samples of all possible data combinations.

EXERCISES FOR SECTION 5.11

Self-Check
1. In the subsection entitled "Off-by-One Errors," add debugging statements to the `for` loop to show the value of the loop control variable at the start of each repetition. Also, add debugging statements to show the value of `sum` at the end of each loop repetition.
2. Repeat Self-Check Exercise 1 for the second `for` loop in the same subsection.

5.12 ── COMMON PROGRAMMING ERRORS

- *Confusing the `if` and `while` Statements:* Beginners sometimes confuse `if` and `while` statements because both statements contain a condition. Make sure that you use an `if` statement to implement a decision step and a `while` statement to implement a conditional loop.

- *Writing Loop Exit Conditions:* Be very careful when using tests for inequality to control the repetition of a `while` loop. For instance, the loop below is intended to continue executing as long as the acceleration of a projectile is positive.

```
while (acceleration != 0.0)
{
    . . .
}
```

If the acceleration rate goes from a positive to a negative amount without being exactly 0.0, the loop will not terminate; it will become an infinite loop. The loop below would be safer.

```
while (acceleration > 0.0)
{
    . . .
}
```

- *Using a Sentinel Value:* You should always verify that the repetition condition for a `while` loop will eventually become false. If you use a sentinel-controlled loop, remember to provide a prompt that tells the program user what value to enter as the sentinel. Make sure that the sentinel value cannot be confused with a normal data item.
- *Writing Compound Loop Statements:* If the loop body contains more than one statement, remember to bracket it with a pair of braces `{ }`. Otherwise, only the first statement will be repeated, and the remaining statements will be executed when and if the loop is exited. The loop below will not terminate (an infinite loop), because the step that updates the loop control variable is not considered part of the loop body. The program will continue to print the initial value of power until either it exceeds its time limit or you instruct the computer to terminate its execution.

```
while (power <= 10000)
    cout << "Next power of n is " << setw(6) << power
        << endl;
    power *= n;
```

To avoid the possibility of omitting required braces, some programmers always insert braces even with single-statement loops.
- *Initializing Variables:* Be sure to initialize to zero a variable used for accumulating a sum by repeated addition, and to initialize to one a variable used for accumulating a product by repeated multiplication. Omitting this step will lead to results that are inaccurate. An easy way to determine if a variable needs to be initialized is if the same variable appears on both sides of an assignment statement in a mathematical formula.
- *Writing Loop Entry Conditions:* The value of the loop control variable in a `for` statement either increases or decreases after each repetition. If m is

greater than n (e.g., m is 10, n is 5), the cout statement below will not execute, because the initial value that would be assigned to i (10) is larger than the limiting value (5).

```
for (int i = m; i <= n; i++)
    cout << setw (4) << i << setw (4) << m << setw (4) << n
         << endl;
```

Similarly, the cout statement below will not execute because the initial value that would be assigned to i (5) is smaller than the limiting value (10).

```
for (int i = n; i >= m; i--)
    cout << setw (4) << i << setw (4) << m << setw (4) << n
         << endl;
```

- *Using the* do-while *Loop:* A do-while loop always executes at least once. Use a do-while statement only if you are certain that there is no possibility of zero loop iterations; otherwise, use a while loop.
- *Loop Control Variables:* Be sure to trace each nest of loops carefully, checking the inner loop and outer loop control variables. A loop control variable in a for statement can be altered inside the loop body if you are not careful. This could lead to undesirable results. It is also bad practice to use the same loop control variable for two for statements within the same nest.

CHAPTER REVIEW

In this chapter, we examined the while statement and used it to repeat steps in a program. We learned how to implement counter-controlled loops, or loops where the number of repetitions required can be determined before the loop is entered. The while statement was shown to be useful when we do not know the exact number of repetitions required before the loop begins.

In designing a while loop, we need to consider both the loop control and loop processing operations that must be performed. Separate C++ statements are needed for initializing and updating the loop control variable that is tested in the loop repetition condition.

We discovered a common technique for controlling the repetition of a while loop: using a special sentinel value to indicate that all required data have been processed. In this case, an input variable must appear in the loop repetition condition. This variable is initialized when the first data value is read (the initial read), and it is updated at the end of the loop when the next new data value is read. Loop repetition terminates when the sentinel value is read.

The `for` statement (`for` loop) and `do-while` statement (`do-while` loop) were introduced. The `for` statement was used to implement counting loops in which the exact number of loop iterations can be determined before loop repetition begins. The loop control variable may be increased or decreased by any value after each loop iteration. The `for` loop is also convenient in numerous other situations involving simple loop initialization and update steps. More of these examples are illustrated in later chapters.

The `do-while` statement was used to implement conditional loops. With the `do-while` statement, you can implement a loop that will always execute at least one time.

We also analyzed nested loops. Every inner loop of a nest is reentered and executed to completion each time an outer loop is repeated.

New C++ Constructs

The new C++ constructs introduced in this chapter are described in Table 5.6.

Table 5.6 **Summary of New C++ Constructs**

CONSTRUCT	EFFECT
`while` **Statement**	
| ```cpp
sum = 0;
while (sum <= max_sum)
{
   cout << "Next integer: ";
   cin >> next_int;
   sum += next_int;
}  // end while
``` | A collection of input data items is read and their sum is accumulated in `sum`. The process stops when the accumulated sum exceeds `max_sum`. |
| `for` **Statement** | |
| ```cpp
for (int current_month = 3;
     current_month <= 9;
     current_month++)
{
   cin >> month_sales;
   year_sales += month_sales;
}  // end for
``` | The loop body is repeated for each value of `current_month` from 3 to 9, inclusive. For each month, the value of `month_sales` is read and added to `year_sales`. |
| `do-while` **Statement** | |
| ```cpp
sum = 0;
do
{
   cout << "Next integer: ";
   cin >> next_int;
   sum += next_int;
}  while (sum <= max_sum);
``` | Integer values are read and their sum is accumulated in `sum`. The process terminates when the accumulated sum exceeds `max_sum`. |
```

✔ QUICK-CHECK EXERCISES

1. A while loop is called a _____ loop.
2. It is an error if a while loop body never executes. (True/False)
3. The sentinel value is always the last value added to a sum being accumulated in a sentinel-controlled loop. (True/False)
4. Which loop form (for, do-while, while)
   a. executes at least one time?
   b. is the most general?
   c. should be used to implement a counting loop?
5. What does the following segment display?

```
product = 1;
counter - 2;
while (counter < 6)
    product *= counter;
    counter++;
cout << product;
```

6. What does the segment of Exercise 5 display if the opening and closing braces are inserted where intended?
7. For the program segment below:

```
for (int i = 0; i < 10; i++)
{
    for (int j = 0; j <= i; j++)
        cout << setw (4) << (i * j);
    cout << endl;
}
```

   a. How many times does the first cout statement execute?
   b. How many times does the second cout statement execute?
   c. What is the last value displayed?

Answers to Quick-Check Exercises

1. conditional
2. False
3. False; the sentinel should not be processed.
4. a. do-while   b. while   c. for
5. Nothing; the loop executes "forever."
6. The value of $1 \times 2 \times 3 \times 4 \times 5$ (or 120).
7. a. $1 + 2 + 3 + ... + 9 + 10$ (or 55)   b. 10   c. 81

REVIEW QUESTIONS

1. How does a sentinel value differ from a program flag as a means of loop control?
2. For a sentinel value to be used properly when reading in data, where should the input statements appear?

3. Write a program to sum and print a collection of payroll amounts entered at the terminal until a sentinel value of −1 is entered.
4. Hand trace the program below given the following data:

```
4 2 8 4   1 4 2 1   9 3 3 1   −2 2 10 8 2   3 3 4 5
```

```cpp
// FILE: Slope.cpp
// CALCULATES SLOPE OF A LINE

#include <iostream.h>

void main ()
{
    // Local data ...
    const float sentinel = 0.0;

    float slope;
    float y2;
    float y1;
    float x2;
    float x1;

    cout << "Enter four numbers separated by spaces."
         << endl;
    cout << "The program terminates if the last two"
         << endl;
    cout << " numbers are the same."
         << endl;
    cout << "Numbers entered will be in the order:"
         << "y2, y1, x2, x1." << endl << endl;
    cout << "Enter four floating point numbers: ";
    cin >> y2 >> y1 >> x2 >> x1;

    while ((x2 - x1) != sentinel)
    {
        slope = (y2 - y1) / (x2 - x1);
        cout << "Slope is " << slope << endl;
        cout << "Enter four more floating point numbers: ";
        cin >> y2 >> y1 >> x2 >> x1;
    }  // end while

}
```

5. Rewrite the while loop appearing in the slope program as a
   a. do-while loop.
   b. flag-controlled loop.
6. Consider the following program segment:

```cpp
count = 0;
for (i = 0; i < n; i++)
{
```

```
      cin >> x;
      if (x == i)
         count++;
   } // end for
```

   a. Write a while loop equivalent to the for loop.
   b. Write a do-while loop equivalent to the for loop.
7. Explain when it is appropriate to use semicolons with
   a. an if statement.
   b. a case statement.
   c. a while statement.
   d. a for statement.
   e. a do-while statement.

PROGRAMMING PROJECTS

1. Write a program that will find the product of a collection of data values. Your program should ignore any negative data and should terminate when a zero value is read.
2. Bunyan Lumber Co. needs to create a table of the engineering properties of its lumber. The dimensions of the wood are given as base and height in inches. Engineers need to know the following information about lumber:

   Cross sectional area: (base × height)
   Moment of inertia: (base × height^3) / 12
   Section modulus: (base × height^2) / 6

The owner, Paul, makes lumber with height sizes 2, 4, 6, 8, 10, and 12 inches. The base sizes are 2, 4, 6, 8, and 10 inches. Produce a table with appropriate headings to show these values and the computed engineering properties. Do not repeat your computations and display for boards having the same dimensions. (For example, you may consider a 2-by-6 and a 6-by-2 board to be the same.) Show only computed values for base and height such that the base is always less than or equal to the height.
3. Write a program to read a collection of integer data items and find and print the index of the first occurrence and the last occurrence of the number 12. Your program should print index values of 0 if the number 12 is not found. The index is the sequence number of the data item 12. For example, if the eighth data item is the only 12, then the index value 8 should be printed for the first and last occurrence.
4. Write a program to find the largest, smallest, and average values in a collection of n numbers where the value of n will be the first data item read.
5. a. Write a program to read in a collection of exam scores ranging in value from 0 to 100. Your program should count and print the number of outstanding scores (90 to 100), the number of satisfactory scores (60 to 89), and the number of unsatisfactory scores (0 to 59). It should also display the category of each score as it is read in. Test your program on the following data:

   63   75   72   72   78   67   80   63   0
   90   89   43   59   99   82   12   100   75

b. Modify your program so that it also displays the average exam score (a real number) at the end of the run.

c. Modify your program to disallow out-of-range scores.

6. Write a program to process weekly employee time cards for all employees of an organization. Each employee will have three data items indicating an identification number, the hourly wage rate, and the number of hours worked during a given week. Employees are to be paid time-and-a-half for all hours worked over 40. A tax amount of 3.625 percent of gross salary will be deducted. The program output should show the employee's number and net pay. Display the total payroll and average amount paid at the end of the run.

7. Write a menu-driven savings account transaction program that will process the following sets of data:

Group 1
```
I    1234      1054.07
W               25.00
D              243.35
W              254.55
Z
```

Group 2
```
I    5723      2008.24
W               15.55
Z
```

Group 3
```
I    2814       128.24
W               52.48
D               13.42
W               84.60
Z
```

Group 4
```
I    7234         7.77
Z
```

Group 5
```
I    9367        15.27
W                16.12
D                10.00
Z
```

Group 6
```
I    1134     12900.00
D              9270.00
Z
```

The first record in each group contains the code (I) along with the account number and its initial balance. All subsequent transaction records show the amount of each withdrawal (W) and deposit (D) made for that account, followed by a sentinel value (Z). Display the account number and its balance after processing each record in the group. If a balance becomes negative, print an appropriate message and take whatever corrective steps you deem proper. If there are no transactions for an account, print a message so stating. A transaction code (Q) should be used to allow the user to quit program execution.

8. Suppose you own a soft drink distributorship that sells Coca-Cola (ID number 1), Pepsi (ID number 2), Canada Dry (ID number 3) and Hires (ID number 4) by the case. Write a program to
   a. read in the case inventory for each brand at the start of the week.
   b. process all weekly sales and purchase records for each brand.
   c. print out the final inventory.

   Each transaction will consist of two data items. The first will be the brand identification number (an integer). The second will be the amount purchased (a positive integer value) or the amount sold (a negative integer value). The weekly inventory for each brand (for the start of the week) will also consist of two items: the identification and initial inventory for that brand. For now, you may assume that you always have sufficient foresight to prevent depletion of your inventory for any brand. (*Hint:* Your data entry should begin with eight values representing the case inventory. These should be followed by the transaction values.)

9. Revise Project 8 to make it a menu-driven program. The menu operations supported by the revised program should be (E)nter inventory, (P)urchase soda, (S)ell soda, (D)isplay inventory, and (Q)uit program. Negative quantities should no longer be used to represent goods sold.

6

Program Design and Functions Revisited

In the introduction to functions in Chapter 3, we examined the process of writing the separate program components—the functions—of a program. The functions correspond to the individual steps in a problem solution. The only communication among these functions (if any) is through a single return value and one or more input arguments.

In this chapter we more fully develop the C++ function feature. We begin by examining some fundamental issues related to the documentation and use of functions. We discuss the importance of validating function input and writing "driver programs" to test our functions thoroughly before we integrate them into larger program systems. We then introduce functions with multiple output arguments—that is, functions that return more than one value to the caller. We discuss the concepts of value (input) and reference (output) arguments.

Our goal is to use functions as building blocks of larger systems. As you progress through this book, your programming skills and personal function library will grow. We will continue to emphasize the reuse of your own functions as well as C++ library functions in the development of solutions to new problems.

6.1 ——— FUNCTIONS IN THE DESIGN PROCESS

We begin our expanded discussion of functions with a simple example of a function having a single return value. We will use this function to illustrate several important points concerning function input and output. In particular, we need to ensure that function input argument values are defined and that they make sense in terms of the given problem, and that the function terminates properly and returns correct values.

Example 6.1 The function compute_tax shown in Fig. 6.1 computes and returns the federal income tax for a couple filing a joint return whose income after deductions (adjusted gross income) is given by the input argument adj_income (type money). The function uses a tax rate of 15 percent for the first $34,000 earned, 28 percent for any salary amount in excess of $34,000 but less than $82,150, and 31 percent for any salary amount in excess of $82,150.

Figure 6.1   Function to compute tax amount

```
// FILE: CompuTax.cpp
// COMPUTES TAX OWED ON ADJUSTED GROSS INCOME

money compute_tax
   (money adj_income)        // IN: adjusted gross income
```

(continued)

Figure 6.1 *(continued)*

```
// Pre:  adj_income must be assigned a nonnegative value.
// Post: Tax amount computed based on tax category.
// Returns: Tax owed if adj_income is nonnegative; otherwise -1.0.
{
   // Local data ...
   const money cat1_max = 34000.00;
   const money cat2_max = 82150.00;
   const float cat1_rate = 0.15;
   const float cat2_rate = 0.28;
   const float cat3_rate = 0.31;
   const money min_valid_amount = 0.0;
   const money invalid_input = -1.0;

   money tax_amount;       // computed tax amount to be returned

   // Compute and return tax.
   if (adj_income < min_valid_amount)
      return invalid_input;                  // return for
                                             // invalid input
   else if (adj_income > cat2_max)
      tax_amount = cat1_rate * cat1_max
         + cat2_rate * (cat2_max - cat1_max)
         + cat3_rate * (adj_income - cat2_max);
   else if (adj_income > cat1_max)
      tax_amount = cat1_rate * cat1_max
         + cat2_rate * (adj_income - cat1_max);
   else
      tax_amount = cat1_rate * adj_income;

   return tax_amount;
}  // end compute_tax
```

■

Function Preconditions and Postconditions

A function cannot execute properly and return correct results if it is not given correct input argument values. Furthermore, the parent function of several subordinates will not behave as desired if the subordinates do not return the correct output. The implementor of a function must consider and document carefully the input argument values for which the function can be expected to behave correctly. Also, the implementor must specify clearly the values to be computed and returned by a function.

A *precondition* describes a condition that must be true before the function is called. The precondition for function compute_tax may be described by the following comment:

```
// Pre:  adj_income must be assigned a nonnegative value.
```

A *postcondition* describes what must be true about those data items that have been altered by the time a function completes execution. The postcondition for `compute_tax` is described by the following comment:

```
// Post: Tax amount computed based on tax category.
```

A function's preconditions and postconditions provide valuable information to a programmer who might want to use the function. For example, the preconditions provide the programmer with information about the required values of the function input arguments before the function is called. In this case, a nonnegative data value must be assigned or read into the actual function argument prior to calling `compute_tax`. The postconditions tell the programmer the effect of the function's execution on its output arguments. In this case, a nonnegative tax amount is computed and returned (unless the adjusted income is negative, in which case a value of −1.0 is returned). Occasionally, an argument may be used for both input and output purposes (an input/output, or *inout*, argument). The value of such an argument will normally be prescribed in both the precondition and postcondition.

We have added a third component, the "returns summary," to the function interface documentation. This summary describes the value (if any) returned to the caller through the use of the function `return` statement. It should be kept separate from the postcondition documentation, which describes changes made to data items during the execution of the function.

Validating Input Arguments

The `if` statement in function `compute_tax` tests for an invalid value of the input argument `adj_income` before performing the tax computation. All functions should validate their input arguments; there are no guarantees that the values passed to an input argument will be meaningful.

Driver Functions

The sole purpose of the main function body in Fig. 6.2 is to call and test function `compute_tax`. A function used to call and test another function is called a *driver function*. The driver contains a `while` loop that allows the user to enter several different values for the input argument `my_income` in order to test `compute_tax` fully. The body of the loop accepts a value for `my_income`, calls `compute_tax` (with `my_income` as input), and then prints the function result. You should enter data values that ensure all possible paths through `compute_tax` have been tested (see Self-Check Exercise 1 at the end of Section 6.1).

Figure 6.2   Driver program for function `compute_tax`

```
// FILE: CompuTax.cpp
// DRIVER PROGRAM FOR FUNCTION COMPUTE_TAX

#include <iostream.h>
#include "money.h"

// Functions used ...
// COMPUTES TAX OWED ON ADJUSTED GROSS INCOME
   money compute_tax
      (money);                  // IN: adjusted gross income

void main ()
{
   // Local data ...
   const money sentinel = -1.0;
   money my_income;        // input: adjusted gross income (taxable)
   money my_tax;           // output: computed tax amount

   // Test compute_tax function -- all possible paths.
   cout << "Driver program for function compute_tax." << endl;
   cout << "Enter income greater than zero (or " << sentinel
        << " to stop test): ";
   cin >> my_income;
   while (my_income != sentinel)
   {
      my_tax = compute_tax (my_income);
      if (my_tax >= 0.0)
      {
         cout << "The tax on " << my_income;
         cout << " is " << my_tax << endl;
      }  // end if
      else
      {
         cout << "Income " << my_income << " was negative. ";
         cout << "Try another value." << endl;
      }  // end else

      cout << endl << endl;
      cout << "Enter income greater than zero (or " << sentinel
           << " to stop test): ";
      cin >> my_income;
   }  // end while

   cout << "A " << sentinel << " was entered.  "
        << "Test execution terminated." << endl;
}

// Insert function compute_tax here.
```

Experienced programmers often use driver programs to pretest functions before integrating them into the program system under development. The importance of such a testing process will become clearer in larger and more complicated programs. Generally, the small investment in time and effort required to write a short driver program will result in a noticeable reduction in the total time spent debugging a large program system.

PROGRAM STYLE

Cohesive Functions

Function `compute_tax` only computes the tax. It neither reads in a value for `adj_income` nor displays the computed result. Function `compute_tax` does not display an error message if the value passed to `adj_income` is out of range. It simply returns a special value (−1.0) to indicate this, and the calling function displays the error message.

Functions that perform a single operation are called *functionally cohesive*. It is good programming style to write such single-purpose, highly cohesive functions, as this helps to keep each function relatively compact and easy to read, write, and debug. You can determine whether a function is highly cohesive from the comment describing what the function does. If the comment consists of a short sentence or phrase with no connectives such as "and" or "or," then the function should be highly cohesive. If more than one or two connectives or separate sentences are needed to describe the purpose of a function, this may be a hint that the function is doing too many things and should be further decomposed into subfunctions.   ∎

EXERCISES FOR SECTION 6.1

Self-Check
1. Provide a set of data values that traces each path through the `if` statement in Fig. 6.1. Show the output for these data values.
2. Write the precondition, postcondition, and returns comments for function `compute_gross` in Fig. 4.9.
3. Write the precondition, postcondition, and returns comments for function `compute_net` in Fig. 4.9.

Programming
1. Write a driver function to test function `compute_gross` in Fig. 4.9.
2. Write a driver function to test function `compute_net` in Fig. 4.9.

6.2 ——— OUTPUT ARGUMENTS

So far we know how to write functions that return up to one result. In this section, we will learn how to write functions that use *output arguments* to return more than one result.

Recall that when a function is called, space is allocated locally in the function data area for each of its formal input arguments. The value of each actual input argument is copied into the local memory cell allocated to its corresponding formal argument. The function body manipulates only this local copy; the original data cannot be altered. The function may return a single value to the calling function using a `return` statement. We now turn our attention to a discussion of how a function can return output to the function that called it through the use of output arguments.

Function `compute_sum_ave` in Fig. 6.3 has four arguments: two for input (`num1` and `num2`) and two for output (`sum` and `average`). The symbol `&` (ampersand) in the function header indicates that the arguments `sum` and `average` are output arguments. The function computes the sum and average of its input but does not display them. Instead, these values are assigned to formal arguments `sum` and `average` and returned as function results to the calling function.

To see how this works, assume that the calling function declares `x`, `y`, `sum`, and `mean` as type `float` variables. The function call

```
compute_sum_ave (x, y, sum, mean);
```

sets up the argument correspondence below.

ACTUAL ARGUMENT	FORMAL ARGUMENT
x	num1 (input)
y	num2 (input)
sum	sum (output)
mean	average (output)

The values of `x` and `y` are passed into the function when it is first called. These values are associated with formal input arguments `num1` and `num2`. The statement

```
sum = num1 + num2;
```

Figure 6.3 Function to compute `sum` and `average`

```
// FILE: CmpSumAv.cpp
// COMPUTES THE SUM AND AVERAGE OF NUM1 AND NUM2

void compute_sum_ave
   (float num1, float num2,        // IN:  values used in
                                   //      computation
    float& sum,                    // OUT: sum of num1 and num2
    float& average)                // OUT: average of num1 and num2

// Pre:  num1 and num2 are assigned values.
// Post: The sum and average of num1 and num2 are computed
//       and returned as output arguments.
{
    sum = num1 + num2;
    average = sum / 2.0;
}  // end compute_sum_ave
```

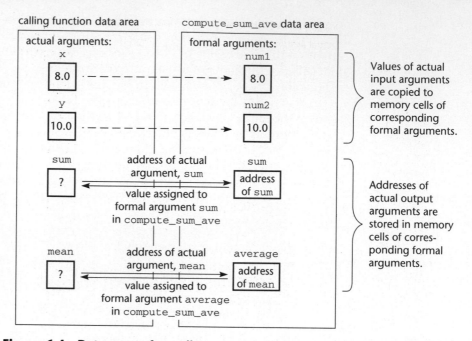

Figure 6.4   Data areas after call to `compute_sum_ave` (but before execution)

stores the sum of the function input arguments in the calling function variable `sum` (the third actual argument). The statement

```
average = sum / 2.0;
```

divides the value stored in the calling function variable `sum` by 2.0 and stores the quotient in the calling function variable `mean` (the fourth actual argument). Figure 6.4 shows the calling function data area and function `compute_sum_ave`'s data area after the function call but before the execution of `compute_sum_ave` begins; Fig. 6.5 shows these data areas just after `compute_sum_ave` finishes execution. The execution of `compute_sum_ave` sets the values of calling function variables `sum` and `mean` to 18.0 and 9.0, respectively. We provide an explanation of the phrases "address of `sum`" and "address of `mean`" next.

Call-by-Value and Call-by-Reference Arguments

As indicated earlier, C++ uses the symbol & immediately following the type of a formal argument in the function header to distinguish between arguments that are used only for input and those that are used for returning a value to the

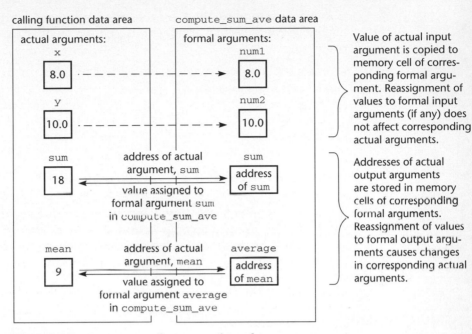

Figure 6.5 Data areas after execution of compute_sum_ave

calling function. Thus, in the function compute_sum_ave in Fig. 6.4, the formal arguments num1 and num2 are used only for input; the arguments sum and average are used for output (to return values to the caller).

This distinction provides important information for the compiler, enabling it to set up the correct *argument passing mechanism* for each function argument. For arguments used only as input, this mechanism is known as *call-by-value* because the *value* of the argument is copied to the called function's data area (see Figs. 6.4 and 6.5, formal argument num1), and there is no further connection between formal argument num1 and its corresponding actual argument. The dashed arrow in Fig. 6.4 indicates this situation, and its arrowhead shows that data flows in one direction only: from the calling function to the called function.

C++ uses *call-by-reference* for formal arguments sum and average because they are listed as type float&. For *reference arguments*, the compiler stores in the called function's data area the memory *address* of the actual variable that corresponds to each reference argument. Through this address, the called function accesses the actual argument in the calling function, which enables the called function to change the actual argument value or use it in a computation. In Fig. 6.4, this relationship is shown by a double-headed arrow connecting each reference argument with its corresponding actual argument. The double-headed arrow indicates that data can flow into the called function and out of the called function through a reference argument.

Remember to place the & for reference arguments in the formal argument list but not in the actual argument list. Also, you must insert it in the function prototype:

```
// COMPUTE SUM AND AVERAGE OF TWO TYPE FLOAT VALUES
void compute_sum_ave
   (float, float,        // IN: values used in computation
    float&,              // OUT: sum of the two input values
    float&);             // OUT: average of two input values
```

Protection Afforded by Value Arguments

Reference arguments are more versatile than value arguments because their values can be used in a computation as well as changed by the function's execution. Why not make all arguments, even input arguments, reference arguments? The reason is that value arguments offer some protection to data integrity. Because copies of value arguments are stored locally in the called function data area, C++ protects the actual argument's value and prevents it from being erroneously changed by the function's execution. For example, if we add the statement

```
num1 = -5.0;
```

at the end of function `compute_sum_ave`, the value of formal argument `num1` will be changed to `-5.0`, but the value stored in x (the corresponding actual argument) will still be `8.0`.

If a programmer neglects to declare an output formal argument as a call-by-reference argument (using the ampersand), then its value (not its address) will be stored locally and any change to its value will not be returned to the calling function. This is a very common error in argument usage.

When to Use a Reference or a Value Argument

How do you decide whether to use a reference argument or a value argument? Here are some rules of thumb:

- If information is to be passed into a function and does not have to be returned or passed out of the function, then the formal argument representing that information should be a value argument (for example, `num1` and `num2` in Fig. 6.4). An argument used in this way is called an *input argument*.
- If information is to be returned to the calling function through an argument, then the formal argument representing that information must be a reference argument (`sum` and `average` in Fig. 6.4). An argument used in this way is called an *output argument*.

■ If information is to be passed into a function, perhaps modified, and a new value returned, then the formal argument representing that information must be a reference argument. An argument used in this way is called an *input/output argument* (or *inout argument*).

Although we make a distinction between output arguments and input/output arguments, C++ does not. Both must be specified as reference arguments (using the ampersand), so that the address of the corresponding actual argument is stored in the called function data area when the function is called. For an input/output argument (as well as for an input argument), we assume there are some meaningful data in the actual argument before the function executes; for an output argument, we make no such assumption.

PROGRAM STYLE

Writing Formal Argument Lists (revisited)

In Fig. 6.3, the formal argument list

```
(float num1, float num2,     // IN: values used in computation
 float& sum,                 // OUT: sum of num1 and num2
 float& average)             // OUT: average of num1 and num2
```

is written on three lines to improve program readability. The value arguments are on the first line with a comment that documents their use as input arguments. The reference arguments are on the next two lines followed by comments that document their use as function outputs.

Generally we follow this practice in writing formal argument lists. We list input arguments first, input-output arguments next, and output arguments last.   ■

Passing Expressions to Value Arguments

Expressions (or variables or constants) can serve as actual arguments corresponding to value arguments. For example, the function call

```
compute_sum_ave (x + y, 10, my_sum, my_ave)
```

calls `compute_sum_ave` to compute the `sum` (returned in `my_sum`) and the `average` (returned in `my_ave`) of the expression `x + y` and the integer 10. However, only variables can correspond to reference arguments, so `my_sum` and `my_ave` must be variables (declared as type `float`) in the calling function. This restriction is imposed because an actual argument corresponding to

Table 6.1   Comparison of Value and Reference Arguments

VALUE ARGUMENTS	REFERENCE ARGUMENTS
• Value of corresponding actual argument is stored in the called function.	• Address of corresponding actual argument is stored in the called function.
• The function execution cannot change the actual argument value.	• The function execution can change the actual argument value.
• Actual argument can be an expression, variable, or constant.	• Actual argument must be a variable.
• Formal argument type must be specified in the formal argument list.	• Formal argument type must be followed by & in the formal argument list.
• Used to pass inputs to a function (input arguments).	• Used to return outputs from a function (output arguments) or to change the value of a function argument (input/output arguments).

a formal reference argument may be modified when the called function executes; it is illogical to allow a function to change the value of either a constant or an expression.

Comparison of Value and Reference Arguments

Table 6.1 summarizes the differences between the two argument passing mechanisms used in C++.

Multiple Calls to a Function

Recall that arguments enable a function to execute the same set of instructions on different sets of data each time it is called. In the next examples, we study two functions that would generally be called more than once in an application program. Both functions illustrate the use of input, output, and input/output arguments.

Example 6.2   Function `make_change` (see Fig. 6.6) determines the quantity of a particular denomination of bills or coins to be given as change. The formal input argument `change_denom` specifies the monetary amount of each change unit (for example, 10.00 for ten-dollar bills, 0.10 for dimes). The formal input/output argument `change_needed` indicates the total amount of money for which

Figure 6.6 Function `make_change`

```
// FILE: MkChange.cpp
// DETERMINES THE NUMBER OF UNITS OF CHANGE OF A PARTICULAR
//    DENOMINATION TO DISPENSE WHEN MAKING CHANGE
//    USES MONEY CLASS

void make_change
   (money change_denom,      // IN:    denomination in which change
                             //           is to be returned
    money& change_needed,    // INOUT: amount for which change needed
    int& num_units)          // OUT:   number of units of specified
                             //           denomination to be returned

// Pre:  Change_denom > 0.0 and change_needed >= 0.0.
// Post: num_units is the number of units of change to dispense
//         and change_needed is reduced by the change amount given.
{
    num_units = int (change_needed / change_denom);
    change_needed = change_needed - (num_units * change_denom);
}   // end make_change
```

change is to be made. The function determines how many units of the given change denomination should be dispensed and returns this value through the formal output argument `num_units`. The value returned through `change needed` is the amount of change remaining after we dispense the calculated units of `change_denom`. For example, if the value passed as `change_needed` is 20.45 and `change denom` is 10.00, the function returns 2 (2 ten-dollar bills) through `num_units` and 0.45 through `change_needed`.

Assume that the calling function for `make_change` declares change as type `money` and `num_tens` as type `int`. The statements

```
change = 20.45;
make_change (10.00, change, num_tens);
cout << "The number of tens dispensed is " << num_tens << endl;
cout << "The change left to dispense is " << change << endl;
```

determine how many ten-dollar bills to dispense and the amount of change remaining after these bills have been given out. They then display the function results:

```
The number of tens dispensed is 2
The change left to dispense is $0.45
```

Figure 6.7 shows the calling and called function data areas just after the call to `make_change`; Fig. 6.8 shows these data areas just after the execution of function `make_change`. These figures show that the function execution

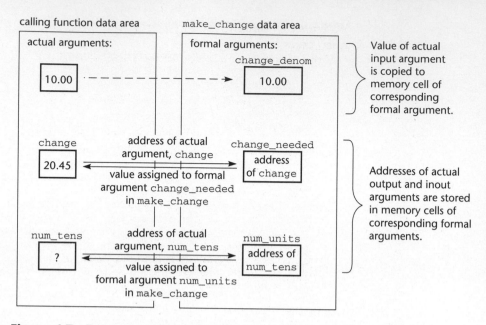

Figure 6.7 Data areas after call to `make_change` (but before execution)

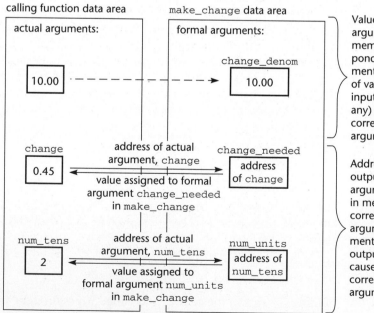

Figure 6.8 Data areas after execution of `make_change`

updates the value of `change` (from 20.45 to 0.45) and defines the value of `num_tens` as 2.

If the calling function continues with the statements

```
make_change (0.10, change, num_dimes);
cout << "The number of dimes dispensed is " << num_dimes
     << endl;
cout << "The change left to dispense is " << change << endl;
```

where `num_dimes` is type `int`, the lines below would be displayed:

```
The number of dimes dispensed is 4
The change left to dispense is $0.05
```
■

Example 6.3   The `main` function in Fig. 6.9 reads three data values into num1, num2, and num3 and rearranges the data so that they are in increasing sequence, with the smallest value in num1. The three calls to function `order` perform this sorting operation.

Figure 6.9   Function to order three numbers

```
// FILE: Sort3Nmb.cpp
// READS THREE FLOATING POINT NUMBERS AND SORTS THEM IN ASCENDING
//      ORDER

#include <iostream.h>

// Functions used ...
// SORTS A PAIR OF FLOATING POINT NUMBERS
void order
    (float&, float&);               // INOUT: numbers to be ordered

void main ()
{

    // Local data ...
    float num1, num2, num3;      // input: holds numbers to be sorted

    // Read and sort numbers.
    cout << "Enter 3 numbers to be sorted separated by spaces:"
         << endl;
    cin >> num1 >> num2 >> num3;
    order (num1, num2);           // order the data in num1 and num2
    order (num1, num3);           // order the data in num1 and num3
    order (num2, num3);           // order the data in num2 and num3

    // Print results.
    cout << "The three numbers in order are:" << endl;
    cout << num1 << " " << num2 << " " << num3 << endl;
}
```

(continued)

Figure 6.9   *(continued)*

```
// SORTS A PAIR OF NUMBERS REPRESENTED BY x AND y
void order
   (float& x, float& y)             // INOUT: numbers to be ordered

// Pre:  x and y are assigned values.
// Post: x is the smaller of the pair and y is the larger.
{
   // Local data ...
   float temp;                      // temp holding cell for number in x

   // Compare x and y and exchange values if not properly ordered.
   if (x > y)
   {                                // exchange the values in x and y
      temp = x;                     // store old x in temp
      x = y;                        // store old y in x
      y = temp;                     // store old x in y
   }  // end if
}  // end order
```

———————————— Program Output ————————————

```
Enter 3 numbers to be sorted separated by spaces:
8.5   10.2   6.3
The three numbers in order are:
6.3 8.5 10.2
```

The body of function order consists of the if statement from Fig. 4.7. The function heading contains the formal argument list

```
(float& x, float& y)             // INOUT: numbers to be ordered
```

which identifies x and y as the formal arguments. x and y are input/output arguments because the function uses the current actual argument values as inputs and may return new values.

After function order executes, the smaller of its two argument values is stored in its first actual argument and the larger is stored in its second actual argument. Therefore, the first function call

```
order (num1, num2);        // order the data in num1 and num2
```

stores the smaller of num1 and num2 in num1 and the larger in num2. In the sample run shown, num1 is 8.5 and num2 is 10.1, so these values are not changed by the function execution. However, the second function call

```
order (num1, num3);        // order the data in num1 and num3
```

switches the values of num1 (initial value is 8.5) and num3 (initial value is 6.3). Table 6.2 traces the program execution.

Table 6.2 Trace of Program to Sort 3 Numbers

STATEMENT	num1	num2	num3	EFFECT
cin >> num1 >> num2 >> num3;	8.5	10.1	6.3	Enters data
order (num1, num2);				No change
order (num1, num3);	6.3		8.5	Switches num1 and num3
order (num2, num3);		8.5	10.1	Switches num2 and num3
cout << num1 << num2 << num3 << endl;				Displays 6.3, 8.5, 10.1

EXERCISES FOR SECTION 6.2

Self-Check   1. Trace the execution of function make_change when change_needed is 5.56 and change_denom is 5.00.
2. Show the output displayed by the function show listed below in the form of a table of values for x, y, w, and z.

```
// Functions used ...
// ???
void sum_diff
  (int, int,                    // IN: ...
   int&, int&);                 // INOUT: ...

void show ()
{
// Local data...
   int w, x, y, z;

// Perform ...
   x = 5;  y = 3;  z = 7;  w  = 9;
   cout << "   x   y   z   w " << endl;
   sum_diff (x, y, z, w);
   cout << "   " << x << "   " << y << "   " << z
        << "   " << w << endl;
   sum_diff (y, x, z, w);
   cout << "   " << x << "   " << y << "   " << z
        << "   " << w << endl;
   sum_diff (z, w, y, x);
   cout << "   " << x << "   " << y << "   " << z
        << "   " << w << endl;
}  // end show

// ???
void sum_diff
  (int num1, int num2,          // IN: ...
   int& num3, int& num4)        // INOUT: ...
{
```

```
        num3 = num1 + num2;
        num4 = num1 - num2;
    }   // end sum_diff
```

a. Show the function output.

b. Briefly describe what function `sum_diff` computes. Include a description of how the input and input/output arguments to `sum_diff` are used.

c. Write the preconditions and postconditions for function `sum_diff`.

3. a. Trace the execution of the three function calls

```
    order (num3, num2);
    order (num3, num1);
    order (num2, num1);
```

for the data sets: 8.0, 10.0, 6.0 and 10.0, 8.0, 60.0.

b. What is the effect of this sequence of calls?

4. A function has four formal arguments: w, x, y, and z (all type `float`). During its execution, it stores the sum of w and x in y and the product of w and x in z. Which arguments are input and which are output?

5. a. What changes would you need to make in function `order` (Fig. 6.9) so that it can be reused to order two integer values rather than two floating-point values?

   b. Given the answers to part (a), what changes would have to be made to the main function for it to work with integers? Make sure you identify all changes required.

Programming

1. Write a main function that reads in an amount of change to make and calls function `make_change` (Fig. 6.8) with different arguments to determine the number of twenties, tens, fives, ones, quarters, dimes, nickels, and pennies to dispense as change.

2. Write the function in Self-Check Exercise 4.

3. Write a function that displays a table showing all powers of its first argument (an integer) from zero through the power indicated by its second argument (a positive integer). The function should also return the sum of all power values displayed. For example, if the first argument is 10 and the second argument is 3, the function should display 1, 10, 100, and 1000 and return 1111 as its result.

6.3 ——— SYNTAX RULES FOR FUNCTIONS WITH ARGUMENT LISTS

The syntax rules for functions with value arguments are presented in Chapter 3; except for the required use of the ampersand, these rules remain the same for reference arguments. Remember that for a reference argument, the function manipulates the corresponding actual argument through a local memory cell that contains the address of the actual argument. For a value argument, a local memory cell is initialized to the corresponding actual argument value, and the function manipulates the local copy without altering the actual argument.

Recall, also, that the formal argument list for a function determines the form of any actual argument list that may be used to call the function. An actual argument list and its corresponding formal argument list must agree in number, order, and type, as described next.

Rules for Argument List Correspondence

1. Correspondence between actual and formal arguments is determined by position in their respective argument lists. These lists must be the same size. The names of corresponding actual and formal arguments may be different.
2. Formal arguments and corresponding actual arguments should agree with respect to type.
3. For reference arguments, an actual argument must be a variable. For value arguments, an actual argument may be a variable, a constant, or an expression.

The compiler finds out about the order, type, and structure of the formal arguments for a function when it processes its prototype. Later, when it reaches a function call, the compiler checks the actual argument list for consistency with the formal argument list.

Be aware that Rule 2 above is a recommendation rather than a requirement. C++ provides some flexibility and will do some type conversion automatically. We show examples in which this is done next and discuss this topic further in Chapter 7. For now, we encourage you to do your own conversion explicitly, using type casting operators, such as int or float, as described in Chapter 3 (Section 3.6).

Example 6.4   Assume that a program begins with the following declarations:

```
// Functions used ...
void test                    // prototype argument names provided
                             //    for illustration ONLY
   (int a, int b,
    float& c, float& d,
    char& e);


void main ()
{...
   // Local data ...
   float x, y;
   int m;
   char next;
```

Function test has two value arguments (a and b) and three reference arguments (c, d, and e). Any of the following function calls would be syntactically correct in the main function.

```
test (m + 3, 10, x, y, next);
test (m, -63, y, x, next);
test (35, m * 10, y, x, next);
```

Table 6.3   Argument Correspondence for `test (m + 3, 10, x, y, next)`

ACTUAL ARGUMENT	FORMAL ARGUMENT	DESCRIPTION
m + 3	a	int, value
10	b	int, value
x	c	float, reference
y	d	float, reference
next	e	char, reference

Table 6.4   Invalid Function Calls

FUNCTION CALL	ERROR
`test (30, 10, m, 19, next);`	Constants not allowed for reference arguments. Note that the integer m will automatically be converted to floating point by the compiler.
`test (m, 19, x, y);`	Not enough actual arguments.
`test (m, 10, 35, y, 'E');`	Constants 35 and 'E' cannot correspond to reference arguments.
`test (m, 3.3, x, y, next);`	This is legal. However, the type of 3.3 is not integer; the value will be truncated—the fractional part will be lost.
`test (30, 10, x, x + y, next);`	Expression x + y cannot correspond to a reference argument.
`test (30, 10, c, d, e);`	c, d, and e are not declared in the main function.

The first actual argument list shows that an expression (e.g., m + 3) or a constant (e.g., 10) may be associated with a reference argument. The correspondence specified by this argument list is shown in Table 6.3.

All the function calls in Table 6.4 contain syntax errors. The last function call points out an error often made in using functions. The last three actual argument names (c, d, e) are the same as their corresponding formal arguments. However, they are not declared as variables in the main function, so they cannot be used as actual arguments. You will be less likely to make this error if you avoid using formal argument names in function prototypes (our normal convention). ∎

When writing relatively long argument lists such as those in this example, be careful not to transpose two actual arguments; this will avoid a possible syntax error. If no syntax is violated, the function execution will probably generate incorrect results.

EXERCISES FOR SECTION 6.3

Self-Check
1. Provide a table similar to Table 6.3 for the other correct argument lists shown in Example 6.4.
2. Correct the syntax errors in the prototype argument lists below.

```
(int&, int&; float)
(value int, char x, y)
(float x + y, int account&)
```

3. Assume that you have been given the following declarations:

```
// Functions used ...
void massage
  (float&, float&,
   int);

// Local data ...
const int maxint = 32767;

float x, y, z;
int m, n;
```

Determine which of the following function calls are invalid and indicate why. If any standard conversions are required, indicate which one(s) and specify the result of the conversion.

```
a. massage (x, y, z);
b. massage (x, y, 8);
c. massage (y, x, n);
d. massage (m, y, n);
e. massage (25.0, 15, x);
f. massage (x, y, m+n);
g. massage (a, b, x);
h. massage (y, z, m);
i. massage (y+z, y-z, m);
j. massage (z, y, x);
k. massage (x, y, m, 10);
l. massage (z, y, maxint);
```

Programming
1. Write a function that accepts a real number as input and returns its whole and fractional parts as outputs. For example, if the input is 5.32, the function outputs should be the integer 5 and the real value .32.

6.4 ——— STEPWISE DESIGN WITH FUNCTIONS

Using argument lists to pass information to and from functions improves problem-solving skills. If the solution to a subproblem cannot be written easily using just a few C++ statements, code it as a function. The case study demonstrates stepwise design of programs using functions.

CASE STUDY: GENERAL SUM AND AVERAGE PROBLEM

Problem Statement

You have been asked to accumulate a sum and to average a list of data values using functions. Because these tasks surface in many problems, design a general set of functions you can reuse in other programs.

Problem Analysis

Let's look again at the loop in Fig. 5.3, which computed a company's total payroll. We can use a similar loop here to compute the sum of a collection of data values. To compute an average, divide a sum by the total number of items, being careful not to perform this division if the number of items is zero.

DATA REQUIREMENTS

Problem Input

num_items (int)   — number of data items to be added
the data items to be read and summed

Problem Output

sum (float)   — accumulated sum of data items
average (float)   — average of all data items

FORMULA

average = sum of data / number of data items

Program Design

INITIAL ALGORITHM

1. Read the number of items to be processed.
2. Compute the sum by reading each data item and accumulating it in the sum (compute_sum).
3. Compute the average of the data items (compute_ave).
4. Print the sum and the average (print_sum_ave).

The structure chart in Fig. 6.10 documents the data flow between the main problem and its subproblems. We will implement each step as a separate function; the label under a step denotes the name of the function that implements that step.

Figure 6.10 clarifies the data flow between the main function and each subordinate function. All variables whose values are set by a function are *function outputs* (indicated by an arrow pointing out of the function). All variables

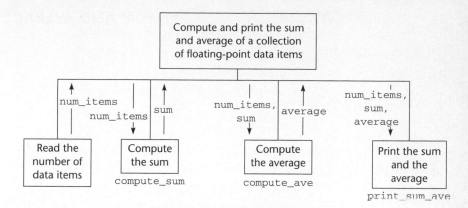

Figure 6.10 Structure chart with data flow information

whose values are used in a computation but are not changed by a function are *function inputs* (indicated by an arrow pointing into the function). The role of each variable depends on its usage in a function and changes from step to step in the structure chart.

Because the step "Read the number of data items" defines the value of num_items, this variable is an output of this step. Function compute_sum needs the value of num_items to know how many data items to read and sum; consequently, num_items is an input to function compute_sum. The variable sum is an output of function compute_sum but is an input to functions compute_ave and print_sum_ave. The variable average is an output of function compute_ave but is an input to function print_sum_ave.

Program Implementation

Using the data flow information in the structure chart, you can write the main function before refining the algorithm. Follow the approach described in Section 3.1 to write function main. Begin by converting the data requirements shown earlier into local declarations for function main. Declare all the variables that appear in the structure chart in the main function because they store data passed to a function or results returned from a function. Omit the declaration for a variable that stores the individual data items since it does not appear in the structure chart. However, remember to declare this variable later in the function that uses it (compute_sum). Next, move the initial algorithm into the main function body, writing each algorithm step as a comment (see Fig. 6.11).

To complete the main function, code each algorithm step *in-line* (as part of the main program code) or as a function call. Code the data entry step in-line because it consists of a simple prompt and data entry operation.

Figure 6.11 Outline and declarations for general sum and average problem

```
// COMPUTES AND PRINTS THE SUM AND AVERAGE OF A COLLECTION
//     OF DATA ITEMS
// Functions used ...
//     (to be completed)

void main ()
{
   // Local data ...
   int num_items;        // input: number of data items to be added
   float sum;            // output: accumulated sum of data items
   float average;        // output: average of all data items

   // Read the number of items to be processed.

   // Compute the sum by reading each data item and accumulating
   //     it in the sum.

   // Compute the average of the data items.

   // Print the sum and the average.
}
```

The data flow information in Fig. 6.10 indicates the actual arguments to use in each function call. It also indicates the name of the main program variable that will hold the function result. For example, use the assignment statement

```
sum = compute_sum (num_items);
```

to call `compute_sum` and set the value of `sum`. In this call, `num_items` is passed as an input argument to function `compute_sum` and the function result (determined by the `return` statement) is assigned to `sum`. Similarly, use the statement

```
average = compute_ave (num_items, sum);
```

to call `compute_ave`. Finally, use the statement

```
print_sum_ave (num_items, sum, average);
```

to call `print_sum_ave`, which has three input arguments and returns no result. Figure 6.12 shows the main function.

Figure 6.12 Main function for general sum and average problem

```
// FILE: CmpSmAvN.cpp
// COMPUTES AND PRINTS THE SUM AND AVERAGE OF A COLLECTION OF DATA
//     ITEMS

#include <iostream.h>
```

(continued)

Figure 6.12   *(continued)*

```
// Functions used ...
// COMPUTES SUM OF DATA
float compute_sum
   (int);                  // IN: number of data items

// COMPUTES AVERAGE OF DATA
float compute_ave
   (int,                   // IN: number of data items
    float);                // IN: sum of data items

// PRINTS NUMBER OF ITEMS, SUM, AND AVERAGE
void print_sum_ave
   (int,                   // IN: number of data items
    float,                 // IN: sum of the data
    float);                // IN: average of the data

void main ()
{
    // Local data ...
    int num_items;         // input: number of items to be added
    float sum;             // output: accumulated sum of data
    float average;         // output: average of data being processed

    // Read the number of items to process.
    cout << "Enter the number of items to process:";
    cin >> num_items;

    // Compute the sum of the data.
    sum = compute_sum (num_items);

    // Compute the average of the data.
    average = compute_ave (num_items, sum);

    // Print the sum and the average.
    print_sum_ave (num_items, sum, average);
}

// Insert definitions for functions compute_sum, compute_ave,
//    and print_sum_ave here.
```

Analysis for `compute_sum`

In specifying the data requirements for `compute_sum`, begin with the function interface information. This function is given the number of items to be processed as an input argument (`num_items`). It is responsible for reading and computing the sum of this number of values. This sum is then returned using the `return` statement.

FUNCTION INTERFACE FOR compute_sum

Input Arguments

num_items (int)   — number of items to be processed

Output Arguments

(none)

Function Return Value

the sum (float) of the data items processed

Design of compute_sum

With the main function complete, you can concentrate on the level-1 functions, starting with compute_sum. Besides a variable to store the sum, compute_sum needs two more local variables: one for storing each data item (item) and one for loop control (count).

Local Data

item (float)   — contains each data item as it is read (read in)
sum (float)   — used to accumulate the sum of each data item as it is read
count (int)   — used to keep track of the count of the number of data items processed at any point

Before accumulating a sum in a loop, initialize the sum to zero prior to loop entry (see Section 5.2). The loop control steps must ensure that the correct number of data items are read and included in the sum being accumulated. Since you know the number of items to sum beforehand (num_items), use a counting loop. Use these steps to write the algorithm for compute_sum; Fig. 6.13 shows the code for compute_sum.

INITIAL ALGORITHM FOR compute_sum

1. Initialize sum to zero.
2. For each value of count from 0, as long as count < num_items
   2.1. Read in a data item.
   2.2. Accumulate data item in sum.
3. Return sum.

Figure 6.13   Function compute_sum

```
// FILE: CmpSmAvN.cpp
// COMPUTES SUM OF DATA

float compute_sum
  (int num_items)      // IN: number of data items
```

(continued)

Figure 6.13   *(continued)*

```
// Pre:  num_items is assigned a value.
// Post: num_items data items read; their sum is stored in sum.
//    Returns: Sum of all data items read if num_items >= 1;
//    otherwise 0.0.
{
    // Local data ...
    float item;        // input:  contains current item being added
    float sum;         // output: used to accumulate sum of data
                       //         items read

    // Read each data item and accumulate it in sum.
    sum = 0.0;
    for (int count = 0; count < num_items; count++)
    {
        cout << "Enter a number to be added: ";
        cin >> item;
        sum += item;
    }   // end for


    return sum;
}   // end compute_sum
```

Analysis for `compute_ave` and `print_sum_ave`

Both `compute_ave` and `print_sum_ave` are relatively straightforward. We list their interface information and algorithms next. Neither function requires any local data, but both algorithms include a test of num_items. If num_items is not positive, it makes no sense to compute or display the average of the data items.

FUNCTION INTERFACE FOR `compute_ave`

> ### Input Arguments
>
> num_items (int)   — the number of data items to be processed
> sum (float)   — the sum of all data processed
>
> ### Output Arguments
>
> (none)
>
> ### Function Return Value
>
> the average of all the data (float)

Design of `compute_ave`

INITIAL ALGORITHM

1. If the number of items is less than 1
    1.1. display "invalid number of items" message.
    1.2. return a value of 0.
2. Return the value of the sum divided by num_items.

FUNCTION INTERFACE FOR `print_sum_ave`

Input Arguments

num_items (int)   — the number of data items to be processed
sum (float)   — the sum of all data processed
average (float)   — the average of all the data

Output Arguments

(none)

Design of `print_sum_ave`

INITIAL ALGORITHM

1. If the number of items is positive
    1.1. display the number of items and the sum and average of the data.
  else
    1.2. display "invalid number of items" message.

Implementation of `compute_ave` and `print_sum_ave`

The implementation of the `compute_ave` and `print_sum_ave` functions is shown in Figs. 6.14 and 6.15.

Figure 6.14 Function `compute_ave`

```
// FILE: CmpSmAvN.cpp
// COMPUTES AVERAGE OF DATA

float compute_ave
   (int num_items,      // IN: number of data items
    float sum)          // IN: sum of data

// Pre:  num_items and sum are defined; num_items must be
//       greater than 0.
// Post: If num_items is positive, the average is computed as
//       sum / num_items;
// Returns: The average if num_items is positive; otherwise, 0.
{
```

(continued)

Figure 6.14 *(continued)*

```
        // Compute the average of the data.
        if (num_items < 1)                        // test for invalid input
        {
            cout << "Invalid value for num_items = " << num_items
                 << endl;
            cout << "Average not computed." << endl;
            return 0.0;                           // return for invalid input
        }  // end if
        return sum / float (num_items);     // recast operand num_items
    }  // end compute_ave
```

Figure 6.15 Function `print_sum_ave`

```
// FILE: CmpSmAvN.cpp.cpp
// PRINTS NUMBER OF ITEMS, SUM, AND AVERAGE OF DATA


void print_sum_ave
    (int num_items,            // IN: number of data items
     float sum,                // IN: sum of the data
     float average)            // IN: average of the data

// Pre:  num_items, sum, and average are defined.
// Post: Displays num_items, sum and average if num_items > 0.
{
    // Display results if num_items is valid.
    if (num_items > 0)
    {
        cout.precision (2);
        cout.setf (ios::fixed);
        cout << "The number of items is " << num_items << endl;
        cout << "The sum of the data is " << sum << endl;
        cout << "The average of the data is " << average << endl;
    }
    else
    {
        cout << "Invalid number of items = " << num_items << endl;
        cout << "Sum and average are not defined." << endl;
        cout << "No printing done.  Execution terminated." << endl;
    }  // end if
}  // end print_sum_ave
```

Program Testing

The program that solves the general sum and average problem consists of four separate functions. In testing the complete program, you should make sure that sum and average are displayed correctly when num_items is positive and that a meaningful diagnostic is displayed when `num_items` is zero or negative. The following is a sample run of the completed program system:

────────── Program Output ──────────

```
Enter the number of items to be processed: 3
Enter a number to be added: 5.0
Enter a number to be added: 6.0
Enter a number to be added: 17.0
The number of items is 3
The sum of the data is 28.00
The average of the data is 9.33
```

Commentary for the General Sum and Average Problem

In the four steps of the general sum-and-average program, all but the first step are performed by separate functions. It was obvious that step 1 could be implemented in just two lines of code. Even though it was relatively easy to implement the step for computing the average, we used a function (`compute_ave`) for this step, too. We want to encourage the use of separate functions even for relatively simple-to-implement algorithm steps. This separation of algorithm step implementations helps keep the details of these steps (no matter how minor) separate and hidden. This in turn makes debugging, testing, and later function modification easier to perform. From this point on, your main functions should consist primarily of a sequence of function calls.

Multiple Declarations of Identifiers in a Program

The identifiers `sum` and `num_items` are declared as variables in the `main` function and as formal arguments in the three subordinate functions. From the discussion of scope of identifiers, you know that each of these declarations has its own scope, and the scope for each formal argument is the function that declares it. The argument lists associate the main function variable `sum` with each of the other identifiers named `sum`. The value of variable `sum` is initially defined when function `compute_sum` executes because variable `sum` is assigned the function result. This value is passed into function `compute_ave` because variable `sum` corresponds to `compute_ave`'s input argument `sum`, and so on.

To avoid the possible confusion of seeing the identifier `sum` in multiple functions, we could have introduced different names in each function (e.g. `total`, `my_sum`). However, the program is easier to read if the name `sum` is used throughout to refer to the sum of the data values. Make sure that you remember to link these separate uses of identifier `sum` through argument lists.

EXERCISES FOR SECTION 6.4

Self-Check

1. Function `compute_ave` returns a single value using a `return` statement. Rewrite this function to return this result through an output argument.
2. Draw the before and after data areas for the main function and revised `compute_ave` (see Self-Check Exercise 1) assuming `compute_ave` is called with `sum` equal to 100.0 and `num_items` equal to 10.
3. Draw the main function and `print_sum_ave` data areas given the data value assumptions in Self-Check Exercise 2.
4. Rewrite function `compute_sum` to return the sum through an output argument rather than through the return statement.
5. Consider the three functions `compute_sum`, `compute_ave`, and `print_sum_ave` as though the code to validate the value of the argument `num_items` had been omitted. For each of these functions, describe what would happen now that the function would be allowed to proceed with its work even if `num_items` were zero or negative.
6. Draw the main function and revised `compute_sum` (see Self-Check Exercise 4) data areas assuming `compute_sum` is called with `num_items` defined to be 10.

Programming

1. Design and implement an algorithm for `read_num_items` that uses a loop to ensure that the user enters a positive value. The loop should execute repeatedly, each time prompting the user for a positive value (the number of items to be processed) until a positive value for the number of items has been entered. Don't forget to write the function interface and interface documentation.

6.5 ———— USING OBJECTS WITH FUNCTIONS

C++ provides two ways that you can use functions to process objects. First, you can apply a member function to an object using dot notation. The member function may modify one or more data attributes of the object to which it is applied. For example, if `test_string` is type `string`, the function call

```
test_string.remove (0, 5);
```

calls member function `remove` to delete the first five characters from `test_string`.

You can also pass objects as function arguments. Figure 6.16 shows function `do_replace`, which replaces a substring in its input/output argument `test_string`. First, `do_replace` calls `string` member function `getline` to read the substring to be replaced (`target`) and the replacement string (`new_string`). We pass both `target` and `new_string` as output arguments to `getline`. Next, `do_replace` calls `string` function `find` to search for `target`, and the `if` statement performs the replacement if `target` is found. This `if` statement is based on the one in Example 4.11.

Figure 6.16   Function `do_replace`

```cpp
// FILE: DoReplac.cpp
// REPLACES A SUBSTRING OF A STRING. USES <string>

void do_replace
   (string& test_string,    // INOUT: string in which replacement
                            //          occurs
    bool& success)          // OUT: indicates success or failure
// Pre:  test_string is assigned a value.
// Post: test_string is modified and success is true or test_string
//       is unchanged and success is false.
{
   // Local data
   string new_string;      // input - new substring to insert
   string target;          // input - substring being deleted
   int pos_target;         // location of target if found

   // Enter string data needed
   cout << "Enter substring to be replaced: ";
   getline (cin, target, '\n');
   cout << "Enter replacement string: "
   getline (cin, new_string, '\n');

   // Locate target string and perform replacement if possible
   pos_target = test_string.find (target);
   if ((0 <= pos_target) && (pos_target < test_string.length ()))
   {
      test_string.replace (pos_target, target.length (),
                           new_string);
      success = true;
   }
   else
      success = false;
}   // end do_replace
```

The `if` statement also sets `success` to indicate whether the replacement was performed.

In the statement

```cpp
test_string.replace (pos_target, target.length (), new_string);
```

member function `replace` is applied to `string` object `test_string`, member function `length` is applied to `string` object `target`, and `string` object `new_string` is passed as an input argument to member function `replace`. We will say more about objects as arguments in Chapter 11.

EXERCISES FOR SECTION 6.5

Self-Check
1. Write a driver function for `do_replace`.
2. Trace the execution of function `do_replace` when `test_string` is `"This is a string"`, `target` is `"str"`, and `new_string` is `"bless"`.

Programming
1. Write a function `do_insert` that performs an insertion into its argument string. The function should read the insertion string and its position. It should also return a success indicator.
2. Write a function `do_remove` that removes the first occurrence of a substring from its argument string. Base it on function `do_replace`.

6.6 ——— DEBUGGING AND TESTING A PROGRAM SYSTEM

As the number of statements in a program or function grows, the possibility of error increases. Keeping each function to a manageable size lowers the likelihood of error and increases the readability and testing of each function.

Just as you can simplify the overall programming process by writing a large program as a set of independent functions, you can simplify testing and debugging a program with multiple functions if you test in stages as the program evolves. Two kinds of testing are used: top-down testing and bottom up testing. You should use a combination of these methods to test a program and its functions.

Top-Down Testing and Stubs

Whether a single programmer or a programming team is developing a program system, not all functions will be ready at the same time. It is possible, however, to test the overall flow of control between the main program and its level-1 functions and to test and debug the level-1 functions that are complete. The process of testing the flow of control between a main program and its subordinate functions is called *top-down testing*.

Because the main function calls all level-1 functions, we need a substitute, called a stub, for all functions that are not yet coded. A *stub* consists of a function header followed by a minimal body, which should display a message identifying the function being executed and should assign simple values to any outputs. Figure 6.17 shows a stub for function `compute_sum` that could be used in a test of the main function in Fig. 6.12. The stub arbitrarily returns a

Figure 6.17   Stub for function `compute_sum`

```cpp
// FILE: SumNStub.cpp
// COMPUTES SUM OF DATA - stub

float compute_sum
   (int num_items)     // IN: number of data items

// Pre:  num_items is assigned a value.
// Post: num_items data items read; their sum is stored in sum.
// Returns: Sum of all data items read if num_items >= 1;
//   otherwise 0.0.
{
    cout << "Function compute_sum entered" << endl;
    return 100.0;
}  // end compute_sum stub
```

value of 100.0, which is reasonable data for the remaining functions to process. Examining the program output tells us whether the main function calls its level-1 functions in the required sequence and whether data flows correctly between the main function and its level-1 functions.

Bottom-Up Testing and Drivers

A completed module can be substituted for its stub, of course, but a preliminary test of a new function should always be performed first. Locating and correcting errors in a single function is easier than in a complete program system. You can test a new function by writing a short driver function similar to the one shown in Fig. 6.2.

Don't spend a lot of time creating an elegant driver function because you will have to discard it as soon as the new module is tested. A driver function should contain only the declarations and executable statements necessary to test a single function. A driver should begin by reading or assigning values to all input arguments and to input/output arguments. Next comes the call to the function being tested. After calling the function, the driver should display the function results.

Once you are confident that a function works properly, substitute it for its stub in the program system. The process of separately testing individual functions before inserting them in a program system is called *bottom-up testing*.

By following a combination of top-down and bottom-up testing, a programming team can be fairly confident that the complete function system will be relatively free of errors when it is finally put together. Consequently, the final debugging sessions should proceed quickly and smoothly. A list of suggestions for debugging a program system follows.

Debugging Tips for Program Systems

- As you write the code, carefully place comments to document each function argument and local identifier. Also use comments to describe the function operation.
- Leave a trace of execution by printing the function name as you enter it.
- Print the values of all input and input/output arguments upon entry to a function. Check that these values make sense.
- Make sure that a function stub assigns a value to each of its output arguments.
- Upon return from a function, print the values of all information returned to the caller (the return value and the values of the actual output and input/output arguments). Verify that these values are correct by hand computation. Make sure that all input/output and output arguments are declared as reference arguments.

You should plan for debugging as you write each function rather than adding debugging statements later. Include any output statements that you might need to help determine that the function is working. When you are satisfied that the function works as desired, you can remove these *debugging statements*. One efficient way to remove them is to change them to comments by preceding them with the symbol //. If you have a problem later, you can remove this symbol, thereby changing the comments back to executable statements.

Another approach to turning debugging statements on and off is to use a special type `bool` constant (say, `debug`). Use the declaration

```
const bool debug = true;              // turn debugging on
```

during debugging runs, and the declaration

```
const bool debug = false;             // turn debugging off
```

during normal runs. Within a function, each diagnostic print statement should be part of an `if` statement with `debug` as its condition. If function `compute_sum` begins with the `if` statement below, the `cout` statements will execute only during debugging runs (`debug` is `true`) as desired.

```
if (debug)
{
    cout << "Function compute_sum entered.";
    cout << "Input argument num_items has value "
        << num_items;
} // end if
```

Using a Debugger to Trace a Function

In many systems a special debugger program is used to generate debugging information while a program is executing. In this section, we describe the debugger that is integrated with Borland C++. Your debugger may operate differently, but its capabilities will be similar.

As an alternative to displaying the initial values of a function's input and input/output arguments using special debugging statements, you can use a debugger and its trace feature to provide this information. If the next statement to be executed is a function call, pressing F7 in Borland C++ causes the function to be entered. The function arguments can then be designated as Watch variables by pressing Ctrl F7. The initial argument values appear in the Watch window. As you execute each statement in the function (by pressing F7), any new values assigned to output arguments or input/output arguments appear in the Watch window.

After the function return occurs, you can use the debugger to see what values were returned to the calling function. This time, designate as Watch variables any actual arguments that correspond to output arguments or to input/output arguments. The values returned by the function appear in the Watch window.

Using the Step Over Option

Whenever the next statement to be executed is a function call statement, you have the option of executing the complete function body as a unit, or of executing each statement individually. If you have thoroughly tested a function before using it in a new program, there is no need to trace through the execution of each individual statement. If you press F8 (Step over), the debugger executes the whole function body, stopping at the first statement after the function call. You should use this option when the function being called is a library function. Tracing through each statement in a library function can be a time-consuming process.

Identifier Scope and Watch Window Variables

The values displayed in the Watch window are determined by the normal scope rules for identifiers. Consequently, a function's local variables and formal arguments will be displayed with the value Undefined symbol until that function begins execution. Upon exit from the function, its local variables and formal arguments will again have Undefined symbol displayed as their value in the Watch window.

When identifiers having the same name are declared in different functions, you can qualify a Watch variable by using dot notation. For example, in the general sum-and-average program, the Watch variable main.sum refers to the main function variable sum and the Watch variable compute_sum.sum refers to the local variable sum in function compute_sum. When function compute_sum executes, the value displayed for main.sum is Undefined symbol, but the value displayed for compute_sum.sum is the accumulating sum of the data items.

Self-Check

EXERCISES FOR SECTION 6.6

1. Show the output you would expect to see using the stub in Fig. 6.17 when num_items is 10.
2. Write a driver program to test the actual function compute_sum.

6.7 ——— RECURSIVE FUNCTIONS (OPTIONAL)

C++ allows a function to call itself. A function that calls itself is a *recursive function*. This ability allows a function to be repeated with different argument values; therefore, recursion can be an alternative to repeating an operation in a loop.

Just as we did for a loop, we need to identify a situation (called a *stopping case*) that stops the recursion; otherwise, the function will call itself forever. Usually a recursive function has the following form:

1. If the stopping case is reached
    1.1. Return a value for the stopping case
  else
    1.2. Return a value computed by calling the function again with different arguments.

The if statement tests whether the stopping case has been reached; if it has not, the recursive function calls itself again with different arguments. The arguments in successive calls should bring us closer and closer to reaching the stopping case.

In this section we describe a recursive function that returns an integer value representing the factorial of its argument. The *factorial of n* is the product of all positive integers less than or equal to n and is written in mathematics as $n!$. For example, 4! is the product $4 \times 3 \times 2 \times 1$ or 24. We provide a recursive definition for $n!$ next.

$$n! = 1 \qquad\qquad \text{for } n = 0 \text{ or } 1$$
$$n! = n \times (n - 1)! \qquad \text{for } n > 1$$

This definition can be translated into pseudocode:

1. If n is 0 or 1
    1.1. Return 1
  else
    1.2. Return $n \times (n-1)!$

Figure 6.18   Recursive function factorial

```
int factorial (int n)
{
   // Pre:  n is >= 0
   // Returns: The product 1 * 2 * 3 * ... * n for n > 1;
   //     otherwise 1.

   if (n <= 1)
      return 1;
   else
      return n * factorial (n-1);
}
```

Figure 6.18 shows function `factorial` rewritten as a recursive function in which the `if` statement implements the recursive definition for n!: The stopping case is reached when n is less than or equal to 1. When n is greater than 1, the statement

```
return n * factorial (n-1);
```

executes, which is the C++ form of the second formula. The expression part of this statement contains a valid function call, `factorial (n-1)`, which calls function `factorial` with an argument that is 1 less than the current argument. This function call is a *recursive call*. If the argument in the initial call to `factorial` is 3, the following chain of recursive calls occurs:

```
factorial (3) -> 3 * factorial (2) -> 3 * (2 * factorial (1))
```

In the last call above, n is equal to 1, so the statement

```
return 1;
```

executes, stopping the chain of recursive calls.

When the last function call has been completed, C++ must return a value from each recursive call, starting with the last one, a process called *unwinding the recursion*. The last call was `factorial (1)` and it returns a value of 1. To find the value returned by each call for n greater than 1, multiply n by the value returned from `factorial (n-1)`. Therefore, the value returned from `factorial (2)` is 2 * the value returned from `factorial (1)` or 2; the value returned from `factorial (3)` is 3 * the value returned from `factorial (2)` or 6 (see Fig. 6.19).

For comparison purposes, Fig. 6.20 shows an iterative factorial function that uses a loop to accumulate partial products in local variable `product_so_far`. The `for` loop repeats the multiplication step when n is greater than 1. If n is 0 or 1, the `for` loop body does not execute, so `product_so_far` retains its initial value of 1. After loop exit, the last value of `product_so_far` is returned as the function result.

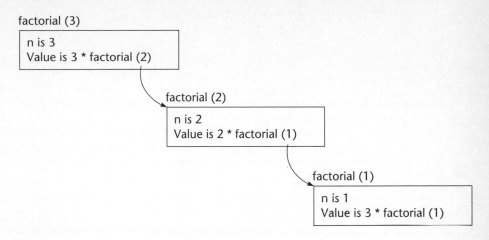

Figure 6.19   **Unwinding the recursion**

Figure 6.20   **Iterative factorial function**

```
int factorial (int n)
{
    // Pre:  n is >= 0
    // Returns: The product 1 * 2 * 3 * ... * n for n > 1;
    //    otherwise 1.

// Local data ...
int product_so_far; // output: accumulated product

// Initialize accumulated product
    product_so_far = 1;

// Perform the repeated multiplication for n > 1.
    for (int i = 2; i <= n; i++)
      product_so_far = product_so_far * i;

    return product_so_far;
}
```

EXERCISES FOR SECTION 6.7

Self-Check   1. Show the chain of recursive calls to function mystery when m is 4 and n is 3. What do you think mystery does?

```
int mystery (int m, int n)
{
    int answer;
```

```
      if (n == 1) then
         return m;
      else
         return m * mystery (m, n-1);
   }
```

Programming   1. Write a recursive function that, given an input value of n, computes n + n−1 + ... + 2 + 1.

2. Write a function c (n, r) that returns the number of different ways *r* items can be selected from a group of *n* items. The mathematical formula for c (n, r) follows. Test c (n, r) using both the recursive and the nonrecursive versions of function factorial.

$$c(n, r) = \frac{n!}{r!(n-r)!}$$

6.8 ——— COMMON PROGRAMMING ERRORS

We have already discussed many of the most common programming errors that arise when using functions in the Common Programming Errors section of Chapter 3. We now focus on two common errors in the use of call-by-reference arguments.

■ *Argument Inconsistencies with Call-by-Reference Arguments:* In Chapter 3, where call-by-value argument passing was discussed, we indicated that argument inconsistencies involving character, integer, and floating-point data usually do not cause even a warning message from the compiler. However, such inconsistencies will cause a warning message if they occur when using reference arguments.

For example, for the function

```
void initiate (char &);
```

the call

```
initiate (sum);
```

where sum is type float will result in a compiler warning such as

```
"Temporary used for parameter 1 in call to 'initiate
   (char &)'"
```

In one sense, this message may be viewed as informational—a report on the usual action taken by the compiler when such an argument-passing inconsistency occurs. Remember that C++ allows some degree of type mixing when passing arguments, so the message may not be an indication of anything illegal. However, at this stage in your programming work, such a warning indicates a possible error. Check the function call carefully to ensure that you have written exactly what you wanted.

■ *Forgetting to use & with Call-by-Reference Arguments:* Make sure you remember to use an & in the function prototype and function header (but not the call) before each output or input/output argument. Forgetting the & does not cause an error message; however, C++ will treat the formal argument as call-by-value instead of call-by-reference. Therefore, any change made to the argument by the called function will not be returned to the calling function.

CHAPTER REVIEW

This chapter completes our presentation of the main concepts of procedural decomposition and abstraction. We began this discussion in Chapter 3, where we introduced the idea of top-down problem decomposition. Here, we first used functions to provide a means of separating and hiding the details for each component of a problem solution. The use of functions made it possible to carry this separation through from the early problem analysis and program design stages to the implementation of a program in C++.

In Chapter 3, our discussion of functions was limited to relatively simple problems and to functions that returned a single value. In this chapter, we introduced another mechanism, the reference argument, for transmitting information between two functions. The reference argument provides an additional means (beyond the use of the `return` statement) for transmitting information from a called function back to its caller.

The argument list provides a highly visible communication path between two functions. By using arguments, we can cause different data to be manipulated by a function each time we call it, making the function easier to reuse within the current program or in another program. We use arguments in three different ways, depending on the direction of communication that is desired. We use input arguments to pass information to a function. We use output arguments to return information to a calling function, and we use input/output arguments when bidirectional communication is required.

C++ uses a call-by-value argument passing mechanism (introduced in Chapter 3) to transmit information as input to a called function. Actual arguments corresponding to a call-by-value formal argument cannot be altered by the called function and therefore cannot be used to return values to the caller. The call-by-reference argument passing mechanism, designated by an ampersand (&) in the specification of a formal argument, is used to return results to a calling function. Thus, formal arguments used to represent output only or input/output data transmission must always be specified as call-by-reference. The actual argument corresponding to a value argument may be an expression, a variable, or a constant; the actual argument corresponding to a reference argument must always be a variable.

The patient, step-by-step practice of procedural abstraction and decomposition is a very important part of the process of building good software. We will continue to emphasize this process throughout the remainder of the book. In Chapter 10, we will augment this procedural approach with an even more powerful idea involving the use of data-oriented abstraction and decomposition.

New C++
Constructs
The new C++ constructs introduced in this chapter are described in Table 6.5.

Table 6.5   Summary of New C++ Constructs (functions with output arguments)

CONSTRUCT	EFFECT
Function Prototype	

`void do_it`
`  (float,`
`   char,`
`   float&,`
`   char&);`
	Prototype for a function having two input and two output arguments

Function Definition	

`void do_it`
`  (float x,`
`   char op,`
`   float& y,`
`   char& sign)`
`{`
`   switch (op)`
`   {`
`      case '+': y = x + x; break;`
`      case '*': y = x * x; break;`
`   } // end switch`
 	
`   if (x >= 0.0)`
`      sign = '+';`
`   else`
`      sign = '-';`
`} // end do_it`
	x and op are input arguments that contain valid values passed in from the calling function. The memory cells corresponding to the output arguments y and sign are undefined upon entrance to function do_it, but contain valid values that are passed back to the calling function upon exit.

Function Call Statement	
`do_it (-5.0, '*', y, my_sign)`	Calls function do_it. −5.0 is passed into x and '*' is passed into op. 25.0 is returned to y, and '-' is returned to my_sign.

✔ QUICK-CHECK EXERCISES

1. Actual arguments appear in a function _____; formal arguments appear in a function _____.

2. Constants and expressions may be used as actual arguments corresponding to formal _____ arguments.

3. In a function header, _____ arguments must be used for function output and are designated by using the special character _____ following the type specifier.

4. A _____ must be used as an actual argument corresponding to a call-by-reference formal argument.

5. For _____ arguments, the argument's address is stored in the called function data area for the corresponding formal argument. For _____ arguments, the argument's value is stored in the called function data area for the corresponding formal argument.

6. Is it a driver or a stub that is used to test a function?

7. Is it a driver or a stub that is used to allow an upper-level function to be tested before all lower-level functions are complete?

8. What are the values of main function variables x and y after the function below executes?

```
   // Functions used ...
   void silly
      (float);



void main ()
{
   // Local data ...
   float x;
   float y;

   // Do something silly.
   silly (x);
}



void silly
      (float x);
{
   // Local data ...
   float y;

   // This is something silly.
   y = 25.0;
   x = y;
} // end silly
```

9. Answer Quick-Check Exercise 8 if argument x of `silly` is a reference argument.
10. Answer Quick-Check Exercise 8 if argument x of `silly` is a reference argument and the function call is changed to

    ```
    silly (y);
    ```

11. In what ways can a function return values to its caller?

Answers to Quick-Check Exercises

1. call; definition
2. value (or call-by-value)
3. reference (or call-by-reference), &
4. variable
5. call-by-reference; call-by-value
6. driver
7. stub
8. both x and y are undefined
9. x is 25.0; y is undefined
10. x is undefined; y is 25.0
11. A function can return values by using a `return` statement or by assigning the values to be returned to reference arguments.

REVIEW QUESTIONS

1. Write the prototype for a function called `script` that has three input arguments. The first argument will be the number of spaces to print at the beginning of a line; the second argument will be the character to print after the spaces; and the third argument will be the number of times to print the second argument on the same line.
2. Write a function called `letter_grade` that has a single integer argument called `score` and that returns the appropriate letter grade using a straight scale (90 to 100 is an A; 80 to 89 is a B; 70 to 79 is a C; 60 to 69 is a D; and 0 to 59 is an F). Be sure to include a validity check for `score` and to specify some appropriate action if `score` is not between 0 and 100 inclusive.
3. Why would you choose to make a formal argument a value argument rather than a reference argument?
4. Explain the allocation of memory cells when a function is called. Illustrate using an example.
5. Write the prototype for a function named `pass` that has two integer arguments. The first argument should be a value argument and the second a reference argument.
6. Explain the use of a stub in the top-down program development process.

PROGRAMMING PROJECTS

1. Write a program that computes and prints the fractional powers of 2 (1/2, 1/4, 1/8, and so on). The function should also print the decimal value of each fraction as shown below.

Power	Fraction	Decimal Value
1	1/2	0.5
2	1/4	0.25
3	1/8	0.125

Print all values through power equal to 10.

2. The assessor in your town has estimated the market value of all of the properties in the town and would like you to write a program that determines the tax owed on each property and the total tax to be collected. The tax rate is 125 mils per dollar of assessed value (a mil is 0.1 of a penny). The assessed value of each property is 28 percent of its estimated market value. (This assessed value is the value to be used in computing the taxes owed for each property.)

   Design and implement a program for the town assessor. First develop the structure chart indicating the functions you will need and the relationships among them. Carefully develop the data tables for these functions, and be sure to add the input and output argument information to the structure chart. Test your program on the following market values:

$50,000	$48,000	$45,500	$67,000	$37,600	$47,100
$65,000	$53,350	$28,000	$58,000	$52,250	
$56,500	$43,700				

   Your program should continue to read and process market values until a zero value is read. A meaningful, readable table of output values should be produced by your program. The table should consist of four columns of information: the initials of the owner of each property (three characters), the market value of each property, the assessed value, and the taxes owed. At the end of the table, the total taxes and the count of the number of properties processed should be printed. Don't forget to print column headers for your column output. Also, be sure to include some other information at the top of the assessor's report, such as the assessor's name, the name of your township, and the date of the report. You should provide separate functions at least for the following subproblems (and maybe more):

   - Display instructions to the user of your program.
   - Display the informational heading (name, date, etc.) at the top of the report.
   - Process all market values (and print table).
   - Display final totals.

3. The trustees of a small college are considering voting a pay raise for their 12 faculty members. They want to grant a 5.5-percent pay raise; however, before doing so, they want to know how much this will cost. Write a program that will print the pay raise

for each faculty member and the total amount of the raises. Also, print the total faculty payroll before and after the raise. Test your function for the salaries:

$42,500	$34,029.50	$46,000	$53,250
$45,500	$32,800	$40,000.50	$38,900
$53,780	$57,300	$54,120.25	$34,100

4. Redo Programming Project 3 assuming that faculty members earning less than $30,000 receive a 7-percent raise, those earning more than $40,000 receive a 4-percent raise, and all others receive a 5.5-percent raise. For each faculty member, print the raise percentage as well as the amount.

5. Patients required to take many kinds of medication often have difficulty in remembering when to take their medicine. Given the following set of medications, write a function that prints an hourly table indicating what medication to take at any given hour. Use a counter variable `clock` to go through a 24-hour day. Print the table based on the following prescriptions:

Medication	Frequency
Iron pill	0800, 1200, 1800
Antibiotic	Every 4 hours starting at 0400
Aspirin	0800, 2100
Decongestant	1100, 2000

6. A monthly magazine wants a program that will print out renewal notices to its subscribers and cancellation notices when appropriate. Using functions when needed, write a program that first reads in the current month number (1 through 12) and year (00 through 99). For each subscription processed, read in four data items: the account number, the month and year the subscription started, and the number of years paid for the subscription.

   Read in each set of subscription information and print a renewal notice if the current month is either the month prior to expiration or the month of expiration. A cancellation notice should be printed if the current month comes after the expiration month. Sample input might be:

10, 97	for a current month of October 1997
1364, 4, 97, 3	for account 1364 whose 3-year subscription began in April 1997

7. The square root of a number N can be approximated by repeated calculation using the formula

$$NG = 0.5 \, (CG + N \, / \, CG)$$

where NG stands for *next guess* and CG stands for *current guess*. Write a function that implements this computation. The first argument will be a positive real number, the second will be an initial guess of the square root of that number, and the third will be the computed result.

   The initial guess will be the starting value of CG. The function will compute a value for NG using the formula above. To control the computation, we can use a `while` loop. Each time through the loop, the difference between NG and CG is checked to see whether these two guesses are almost identical. If so, the function returns *NG* as the square root; otherwise, the next guess (*NG*) becomes the current guess (*CG*) and the process is repeated (i.e., another value is computed for *NG*, the difference is checked, and so forth).

For this problem, the loop should be repeated until the magnitude of the difference between *CG* and *NG* is less than 0.005. Use an initial guess of 1.0 and test the function for the numbers 4.0, 120.5, 88.0, 36.01, and 10,000.0.

8. It is a dark and stormy night. Our secret agent (007) is behind enemy lines at a fuel depot. He walks over to a cylindrical fuel tank that is 20 feet tall and 8 feet in diameter. He opens a circular nozzle that is 2 inches in diameter. He knows that the volume of the fuel leaving the tank is

$$volume\ lost = velocity \times (area\ of\ the\ nozzle) \times time$$

and that

$$velocity = 8.02 \times (height\ of\ fluid\ in\ the\ tank)^{0.5}.$$

How long will it take to empty the tank? Assume velocity measured in feet per second, area in feet squared, time in seconds, and height in feet.

Hint: Although this is really a calculus problem, we can simulate it with the computer and get a close answer. We can calculate the volume lost over a short period of time, such as 60 seconds, and assume that the loss of fluid is constant. We can then subtract the volume from the tank and determine the new height of the fluid inside the tank at the end of the minute. We can then calculate the loss for the next minute. This can be done over and over until the tank is dry.

Print a table showing the elapsed time in seconds, the volume lost, and the height of the fluid. At the very end, convert the total elapsed seconds to minutes. The fluid height can be negative on the last line of the table.

9. Write a program to simulate a hand-held electronic calculator. (In other words, write a program that will cause your computer to behave as though it were a hand-held calculator.) Your program should execute as follows.

- *Step 1:* Display a prompt and wait for the user to enter an instruction code (a single character):

'+' for addition	'-' for subtraction
'*' for multiplication	'/' for division
'p' for power (exponentiation)	's' for square root
'c' to clear the current accumulator value (set the value to 0.0)	'q' for quit

- *Step 2* (if needed): Display a prompt and wait for the user to enter a type float number (which we will call the *left-operand*).

- *Step 3* (if needed): Display a prompt and wait for the user to enter a type float number (which we will call the *right-operand*).

- *Step 4:* Display the accumulated result at any point during processing and repeat steps 1 through 3 (unless, of course, the instruction code 'q' has been entered).

Use a separate function, enter_code, to prompt the user for the instruction code and to ensure that a valid code is entered. Also use a separate function, enter_operand, for the entry of the left-operand and the right-operand. Finally, use another function, compute, to perform the indicated operation (unless 'q' has been entered).

10. Write a text-editor program that reads in a string and edits the string, performing a series of operations listed in Example 4.20. Use the switch statement from that example as the basis of a function perform_edit that accepts a character as input and calls one of the functions listed to perform the selected operation. You will have to implement each of these functions (see Fig. 6.16). Each function will allocate local storage to hold the data that it needs. Your main function will contain a loop that repeatedly reads a character and calls perform_edit to do the operation selected by the user. This menu-driven loop should also display the string after each edit operation is performed.

7

Simple Data Types

So far in your programming experience, you have used four of the *predefined data types* of C++: int, float, char, and bool. In this chapter we take a closer look at these data types and introduce several variants of the integer type, such as long and short integers. The forms in which these data types are stored in computer memory (their internal representations) will be examined and related to the forms that we commonly use (the external representations). Some new operators that can be applied to these types will be introduced. We will also introduce a new data type, the enumeration type. All of these data types (int, the variants on int, float, char, and bool, and enumeration types) are characterized by the fact that only a single value can be stored in a variable of the type. Such types are often referred to as *simple* or *scalar data types*.

7.1 _____ CONSTANTS REVISITED

Additional Representations of Integers

We begin by re-examining the concept of constants in C++. Constant definitions have the form

const *type identifier* = *constant*;

where *constant* is normally of the same type as specified for the identifier.

There are three reasons for using constant identifiers. First, if we are careful in our choice of the identifier we use for a constant, it should be more recognizable than the constant itself. The identifier speed_of_light has more meaning than the value 2.998E+5. Second, declaring a constant identifier tells the compiler not to allow any changes in the value associated with the identifier.

The third reason relates to the concern for writing good programs. It is reasonable to expect that the constant associated with the speed of light will never change (unless the units of measurement or the precision change). However, other constants (such as city wage tax or federal tax bracket maximum and minimum values) may remain fixed for a long period of time but are subject to change when new legislation is passed. Once we associate a constant with an identifier (when we give the constant a name), we can subsequently refer to that constant by its identifier name rather than its value. Any change in the specification of the value of the constant can be handled in the program by changing just one statement—the declaration of the constant. We would not be forced to search through the entire program looking for other uses of the constant value, an exercise that at best can be very time consuming and, at worst, quite prone to mistakes.

Example 7.1 Several sample constant declarations are illustrated below.

```
a.  const int max = 100;
    const float speed_of_light = 2.998E+5;
    const char initial = 'A';
b.  const short int age = 32;
    const long int mask = 8476376;
```

We have seen examples of the declarations shown in (a) in our earlier work; (b) illustrates two integer type declarations to be discussed further in the next section. ∎

The #define Directive

Another feature of C++ is useful in defining important constants in one place in a program. The #define line is a compiler directive that can be used to associate an identifier with a particular sequence of characters called the *replacement-text*. The general form of the #define line follows:

#define *identifier* *replacement-text*

Once this line has appeared in a program, any occurrence of *identifier* (not enclosed in quotes and not part of another name) will be replaced by the associated *replacement-text* during compilation. The *identifier* has the same form as any C++ identifier. The *replacement-text* can be any sequence of characters. It is not a character string and is therefore not enclosed in quotes.

The #define line is the second example (#include was the first) of a compiler directive that we have seen so far.

Example 7.2 In the area and circumference problem (Section 3.1), we could replace the constant declaration

const float pi = 3.14159;

with the #define line

#define pi 3.14159

The remainder of the program would not change; all references to the identifier pi would be textually replaced by the floating-point constant 3.14159 during the compilation process. Note that pi is simply an identifier; it is not treated as a variable and has no storage associated with it. During compilation, the replacement text is substituted for the identifier wherever the identifier appears. A define line must begin with the symbol # and has no equal sign or ending semicolon. ∎

The #define line was the only vehicle available for naming constants in earlier versions of the C language. However, with the addition of the constant declaration and enumerated types in C++, this device is needed only occasionally. In this text, we limit the use of #define to situations in which textual replacement is needed for program clarity or some other specific purpose.

EXERCISES FOR SECTION 7.1

Self-Check 1. Which of the constants declared below are valid and which are invalid? Explain your answers briefly.

```
const int maxint = 32767;
const int minint = -maxint;
const char last_letter = 'Z';

const int max_size = 50;
const int min_size = max_size - 10;
const int id = 4FD6;

const int koffman_age = 47;
const int friedman_age = z59;

const float price = $3,335.50;
const float price = 3335.50;
const float price = "3335.50";
```

2. Why would you declare an identifier as a constant rather than as a variable?
3. Explain the difference between the #define line and the constant declaration.

7.2 —— INTERNAL REPRESENTATIONS OF INTEGER AND FLOATING-POINT DATA TYPES

In this section, we take a closer look at the different data types seen thus far and discuss the differences in their external and internal representations.

Differences Between Numeric Types

The data types int and float are used to represent numeric information. We have used integer variables as loop counters and to represent data, such as exam scores, having no fractional parts. In most other instances we used type float numeric data.

You may be wondering why it is necessary to have two numeric types. Can the data type float be used for all numbers? The answer is yes, but on many computers operations involving integers are faster than those involving type float numbers and less storage space may be needed to store integers.

Also, operations with integers are always precise, whereas there may be some loss of accuracy when dealing with type `float` numbers.

These differences result from the way in which type `float` numbers and integers are represented internally in a computer's memory. All data are represented in memory as strings of *binary digits* or *bits* (0s and 1s). However, the binary string stored for the integer 13 is not the same as the binary string stored for the type `float` number 13.0. The actual internal representation is computer-dependent, but the general forms are consistent in all computers. Compare the sample integer and floating-point formats shown in Fig. 7.1, where integers are represented by a sign and a binary number. The sign is a single binary digit, either a 0 (for a nonnegative integer) or a 1 (for a negative integer).

The internal representation of floating-point data is analogous to scientific notation. Recall that in scientific notation 3.57×10^3 refers to the same number as 3570. Similarly, 3.57×10^{-4} refers to 0.000357.

The storage area occupied by a floating-point number is divided into three sections: the *sign* (a single bit), the *characteristic*, and the *mantissa*. Usually, the mantissa is a binary fraction between 0.5 and 1.0 for positive numbers (and between −0.5 and −1.0 for negative numbers). The characteristic is normally a power of 2. The mantissa and characteristic are chosen to satisfy the formula

$$type\text{-}float\text{-}number = 2^{characteristic} \times mantissa$$

Because the size of a memory cell is finite, not all floating-point numbers (in the mathematical sense) can be represented precisely in the range of type `float` numbers provided on your computer system. We will talk more about this later.

In addition to the capability of storing fractions, the range of numbers that may be represented in type `float` form is considerably larger than for the integer form. For example, positive type `float` numbers might be expected to range between 10^{-37} (a very small fraction) and 10^{+37} (a rather large number), whereas positive type `int` values might range from 1 to +32767 (2^{15}). The actual ranges are dependent on the particular C++ compiler and the computer being used. Specifically, they depend on the number of binary digits that the compiler uses to store these different data types. This variation is caused by the fact that C++ does not specify the number of bits (length) for type `int` or `float` data. These lengths depend on the particular compiler used.

| type `int` format | | | | type `float` format | |
| sign | binary number | | sign | characteristic | mantissa |

Figure 7.1   **Internal forms of representation of type `int` and type `float` data**

Variations of Integer Types

C++ provides three sizes of integers, `short int`, `int`, and `long int`. The actual lengths corresponding to the sizes are implementation-defined. C++ does, however, place some restrictions on the lengths of *short integers* (minimum of 16 bits) and *long integers* (minimum of 32 bits). It also requires that the following must be true:

- short integers may be no longer than type `int` values.
- type `int` values may be no longer than long integers.

On most computers, short integers are 16 bits long and long integers are 32 bits long.

If you are writing a program for which correct execution depends on the number of bits used to store your integer data, use of the type modifiers `long` or `short` provides a greater assurance of consistency across compilers and can help make your program more portable. That is, it can help increase the likelihood that your program, written for one computer using one compiler, will compile and execute correctly on another computer. There are no ironclad guarantees, however.

The use of short integers can save considerable space in programs with large volumes of integer data. However, as we have noted, the largest positive integer that may be stored in a short integer on most computers is $2^{15} - 1$, or 32767. (Remember, one bit is used for the sign of the integer, leaving 15 bits to store the magnitude of the integer. See the Self-Check Exercises at the end of this section for more details.) This may not always be sufficient for storing and manipulating your data.

Variations on Floating-Point Types

C++ provides three sizes of floating-point types: `float`, `double`, and `long double`. As with integers, these are implementation-defined, but with the following restrictions: `double` is no less precise than `float`, and `long double` provides no less precision than `double`. Some C++ compilers provide a `double` with approximately twice the precision of `float` and a `long double` with twice the precision of `double`.

Types of Numeric Literals

The data type of a numeric literal is determined in the following way. If the literal has a decimal point, then it is considered to be of type `float`. For example, `-67.345` and `2.998E+5` (read as 2.998×10^5 or 299800.0) are floating-point literals. A literal written with a decimal *scale factor* is also considered to be a floating-point literal whether or not it has a decimal point. For example, the value `5E2` is considered type `float` (value is 500.0) because it has a scale factor.

Value Ranges for Integer and Floating-Point Types

C++ provides names for the ranges of integer and floating-point types. Some of these names, their interpretations, and the values they represent are shown in Table 7.1. These definitions are included along with many others in the C++ `limits.h` and `float.h` libraries. It is important to note that the values shown in this table are acceptable minimum (or maximum) values for these constant identifiers. The actual values on your computer may be larger (or smaller). You should try to print the values associated with some of the names

Table 7.1   Special C++ Constants

FROM `limits.h`		
Name	**Value**	**Interpretation**
CHAR_BIT	8	Number of bits in a character type item
INT_MAX	32767	Maximum value of `int` (16 bits)
INT_MIN	-32767	Minimum value of `int` (16 bits)
LONG_MAX	+2127483647L	Maximum value of long integer (32 bits)
LONG_MIN	-2127483647L	Minimum value of long integer (32 bits)
SHRT_MAX	+32767	Maximum value of short integer (16 bits)
SHRT_MIN	-32767	Minimum value of short integer (16 bits)

FROM `float.h`		
Name	**Value**	**Interpretation**
FLT_DIG	6	Number of decimal digits of precision (32-bit float type)
FLT_MAX	1E+37	Maximum floating-point number
FLT_MIN	1E-37	Minimum floating-point number
FLT_EPSILON	1E-5	Minimum positive number x such that $1.0 + x$ does not equal 1.0
DBL_DIG	10	Decimal digits of precision for `double`
DBL_EPSILON	1E-9	Minimum positive number x such that $1.0 + x$ does not equal 1.0
LDBL_DIG	10	Decimal digits of precision for `long double`

in this table to learn their values in your computing environment. This will help you determine the sizes used for the various integer and floating-point types just discussed.

Review of Integer Division

In Section 2.8, we discussed the computation of integer quotients and remainders using the C++ division (/) and modulus (%) operators with integer operands only. The division operator / yields the integer quotient of its first operand divided by its second; the modulus operator % yields the integer remainder of its first operand divided by its second (for example, 7 / 2 is 3, and 7 % 2 is 1). The next example illustrates the use of these operators.

Example 7.5   Function `print_digits_reversed` in Fig. 7.2 prints the individual decimal digits of its argument `number` in reverse order (e.g., if number is 738, the digits printed are 8, 3, 7). This is accomplished by printing successive remainders of `number` divided by 10. To preserve the original value of `number`, a local variable, `temp_number`, is used in the computation of these successive remainders. In each loop iteration, the integer quotient of `temp_number` divided by 10 becomes the new value of `temp_number` to be used in the next iteration. The function `abs` computes the absolute value of its integer operand; this function may be found in the libraries `math.h` and `stdlib.h`.   ∎

Figure 7.2   **Printing decimal digits in reverse order**

```
// FILE: DgtsRvrs.cpp

#include <math.h>      // for function abs()
#include <iostream.h>

// PRINTS DIGITS IN A NON-NEGATIVE INTEGER IN REVERSE ORDER
void print_digits_reversed
   (int number)      // IN:  number to be printed digit by digit

// Pre : number is positive or zero (non-negative).
// Post: Each digit of number is displayed, starting with the
//       least significant one.
{

   // Local data ...
   const int base = 10; // number system base

   int temp_number;     // local store for value of number / 10
   int digit;           // contains each digit as computed
```

(continued)

Figure 7.2   *(continued)*

```
// Determine and print each digit beginning with the least
//     significant one.
temp_number = abs(number);
while (temp_number != 0)
{
   digit = temp_number % base;   // get next digit
   cout << digit;
   // Get quotient for next iteration.
   temp_number /= base;
}  // end while
cout << endl;
}  // end print_digits_reversed
```

The local variable `temp_number` is used as the loop control variable. Within the `while` loop, the modulus operator `%` is used to determine the rightmost digit of the number stored in `temp_number`. The division operator is used to compute the rest of the number (with the rightmost digit "tossed away") to be used in the next iteration. The loop is exited when this number (in `temp_number`) becomes 0.

Table 7.2 shows a trace of the execution of `print_digits_reversed` for an actual parameter of 3704. The digits 4, 0, 7, and 3 are displayed in that order.

Numerical Inaccuracies

The representation of floating-point data can cause numerical inaccuracies to occur in floating-point computations. Just as certain numbers cannot be represented exactly in the decimal number system (e.g., the fraction 1/3 is 0.333333...), so some numbers cannot be represented exactly in floating-point form in the computer. The *representational error* will depend on the number of binary digits (bits) used in the mantissa: The more bits, the smaller the error.

The number 0.1 is an example of a number that has such a representational error. The effect of a small error is often magnified through repeated computations. Therefore, the result of adding 0.1 to itself ten times is not exactly 1.0. As a result, some loops, such as the one shown next, may fail to terminate on some computers.

```
trial = 0.0;                          for (int trial = 0.0;
while (trial != 1.0)                      trial != 1.0;
{                                         trial += 0.1)
                          or          {
   ...                                    ...
   trial += 0.1;                       }  // end for
}  // end while
```

Table 7.2 Trace of Execution of `print_digits_reversed`: Initial Value of Number = 3704

temp_number	digit	STATEMENT	EFFECT
3704	?	`temp_number = abs(number);`	
		`while (temp_number != 0)`	3704 != 0 is true
	4	`digit = temp_number % base;`	
		`cout << digit;`	print 4
370		`temp_number /= base;`	
		`while (temp_number != 0)`	370 != 0 is true
	0	`digit = temp_number % base;`	
		`cout << digit;`	print 0
37		`temp_number /= base;`	
		`while (temp_number != 0)`	37 != 0 is true
	7	`digit = temp_number % base;`	
		`cout << digit;`	print 7
3		`temp_number /= base;`	
		`while (temp_number != 0)`	3 != 0 is true
	3	`digit = temp_number % base;`	
		`cout << digit;`	print 3
0		`temp_number /= base;`	
		`while (temp_number != 0)`	0 != 0 is false
			exit loop

If the loop repetition test is changed to `trial < 1.0`, the loop might execute 10 times on one computer and 11 times on another. This is yet another reason why it is best to use integer variables whenever possible in loop repetition tests.

Other problems occur when manipulating very large or very small real numbers. In adding a large number and a small number, the larger number may "cancel out" the smaller number (resulting in a *cancellation error*). If X is much larger than Y, then $X + Y$ may have the same value as X (e.g., 1000.0 + 0.0001234 is equal to 1000.0 on some computers).

If two very small numbers are multiplied, the result may be too small to be represented accurately, so it will be represented as zero. This phenomenon is called *arithmetic underflow*. Similarly, if two very large numbers are multiplied, the result may be too large to be represented. This phenomenon, called *arithmetic overflow,* is handled in different ways by C++ compilers. Arithmetic overflow can occur when processing very large integer values as well.

Mixing Types: Integral Promotions

In Chapter 2 (Section 2.8), we first introduced the notion of mixed-type expressions and assignments as they related to type int and float data. In Chapters 3 and 6, we discussed the correspondence of formal and actual arguments. We suggested that care should be taken to ensure that the types of all actual arguments in a function call exactly match those of the corresponding formal arguments.

C++ allows many uses of mixed types: in expressions, in assignment, and in argument passing. When data values of mixed type are used in expressions, the compiler examines the operands involved with each operation and *converts* (or *promotes*) mixed operands to make them the same. For example, short integers and characters would be promoted to type int, type int to type float, and type float to double. The result of the operation is always the same as the type of the operands involved following promotion.

For example, in the expression

```
3 + x / 2
```

where x is type float, the constant 2 is promoted to float before the division is performed. Because the result of the division is type float, the constant 3 would be promoted to float before the addition is performed.

All such conversions are intended to be *value preserving*. For the most part, whatever integral conversions are performed (char to int, short int to int) will not alter the value of the data. This is also true when integers are converted to floating point, except that some loss of accuracy can occur because not all type float values can be precisely represented in the computer.

Type Conversions

Conversions similar to those just described for expressions are performed whenever mixed assignments are specified. Again the conversions are intended to preserve value. However, value preservation is often not the case with either assignment or argument passing when the type conversion is in the "other direction." In these cases, actual changes in value are likely to occur. For example, the assignment of a type float value to an integer variable will result in the *truncation* (chopping off) of the fractional part of the floating-point value (the assignment of the value 13.78 to the integer variable m stores the integer 13 in m). A few other examples are shown next.

```
i = 3.89;        // Floating-point value 3.89 is truncated.
                 //    The value stored in i is 3.
ch = 64.97;      // Floating-point value 64.97 is truncated.
                 // Character with ASCII value 64 (a '@')
                 //    is stored in ch.
```

```
print_int (27.7);      // Value 27 is printed.
                       // Function print_int has the prototype
                       // void print_int (int);
```

Type Casting

Especially in the early stages of learning to program, we believe it is important for you to avoid mixing data types in expressions, assignments, and argument passing. Casting operators, such as int and float, can be used to ensure the use of matching data types in such cases. For example, to compute the floating-point average (average) of the sum of n floating-point values (where n is an integer), the following assignment might be written:

```
average = sum / float (n);
```

The *cast operator*, float, is applied to n using a functional notation to create a floating-point copy of n for use in the division operation. The floating-point result is then assigned to average. The value of n is not altered by the casting change.

Casting operators can be extremely useful in their own right, as illustrated in the next example.

Example 7.4   *Rounding to the Nearest* n *Decimal Places.* It is sometimes useful to be able to compute the value of a number rounded to the nearest n decimal places. The statements

```
ten_to_n = float (int_power (x, n));
x = float (int ( x * ten_to_n + half)) / ten_to_n;
```

use the casting operators int and float to force *explicit type conversion*. For example, if $x = 7.0862$ and $n = 2$, the evaluation of the second expression would proceed as shown in Fig. 7.3, and x would become 7.09.   ∎

Example 7.5   *Getting the Desired Results.* If $x = 5.9$ and y are type float variables, and $m = 6$ and $n = 2$ are of type int, then execution of the assignment statement

```
y = float (m + int (x) / 2);
```

would result in the assignment to y of the value 8.0. Execution of the statement

```
y = m + x / 2;
```

would result in the assignment to y of the value 8.95 (see Self-Check Exercise 3 at the end of this section).   ∎

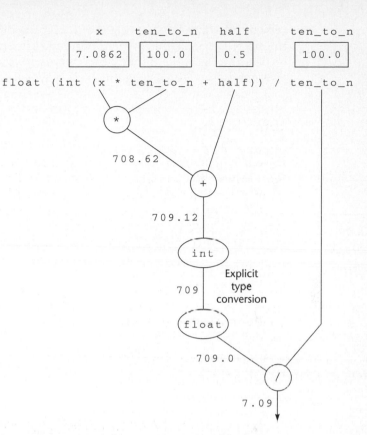

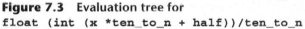

Figure 7.3 Evaluation tree for
`float (int (x *ten_to_n + half))/ten_to_n`

Commentary

Types `float` and `int` and their variants should not be confused with the mathematical structures (integers and real numbers) they model. Rather, they are abstractions of these structures, and, as such, they are not perfect. Because of the limited number of bytes allocated to store type `int` and `float` data, these abstractions can be used to model only a finite (limited) subset of their respective mathematical structures. In addition, as we have seen, the size limitations for type `float` data make it impossible for us to accurately represent some real values (for example 0.1) using this type.

Nonetheless, when it comes to manipulating integer and real data on the computer, the `float` and `int` abstractions provide the data stores and operations sufficient for most of our programming needs. In cases where these language-defined abstractions prove to be inadequate—for example, when we need to manipulate nonnumeric data such as character strings or streams, when we require greater accuracy than provided by type `float` for modeling money—we use either system-defined (`string` or `stream`) or user-defined (`money`) data types. In all cases, whether working with language-defined, system-defined, or user-defined data types, remember that the variables or objects of these types that we manipulate are imperfect, limited models of the problem domain elements they represent.

EXERCISES FOR SECTION 7.2

Self-Check

1. A hypothetical C++ compiler uses 8 bits to store all `int` data. What is the largest positive integer that may be stored (with sign) in a type `int` variable of size 2 bytes (16 bits)?
2. How does a cancellation error differ from a representational error?
3. In Example 7.5, explain why execution of the assignment statement

   ```
   y = m + x / 2;
   ```

   results in the assignment of 8.95 to y.

Programming

1. Write a C++ program to print the largest integer and largest floating-point values that can be used on your computer system.
2. To illustrate machine dependence and the importance of scratching below the surface—at least a little—write a short program to print the value of `FLT_DIG` (see Table 7.1) and then enter a loop to do the following:

   ■ Prompt the user for a floating-point number x and an integer n (greater than or equal to zero)
   ■ Round the floating-point number x to the nearest n digits.

   You might terminate the execution of your loop whenever a negative value of n is read.

   Test your program by rounding several floating-point numbers, some to n_1 digits of accuracy (for any integer n_1 less than or equal to `FLT_DIG`) and some to n_2 digits (where n_2 is any integer value greater than `FLT_DIG`). Describe in English what happens and try to explain why. For example, if `FLT_DIG` is 6 for your computer, try rounding some values of a floating-point number to $n_1 \le 6$ digits; try rounding some other floating-point numbers to $n_2 > 6$ digits.

7.3 _____ CHARACTER DATA AND FUNCTIONS

C++ provides a character data type for storing and manipulating individual characters such as those that comprise a person's name, address, and other personal data. Character variables are declared using the type specifier `char`. A type `char` literal consists of a single character (a letter, digit, punctuation mark, or the like) enclosed in single quotes. A character value may be associated with a constant identifier or assigned to a character variable:

```
const char star = '*';
```

```
char next_letter;
next_letter = 'A';
```

The Internal Representation of Character Values

The number of bits required to store a character value must be sufficient to store any member of the character set being used by your C++ language system. The ASCII (American Standard Code for Information Interchange) character set (see Appendix A), is most often used in C++ systems. The discussion that follows assumes the use of this character set.

In C++, the value of a character is equivalent to the *numeric (integer) code* that represents the character. Thus, the char data type is another example of an integral data type in C++.

We will assume a one-byte (8-bit) representation for character values. For our purposes, the ASCII character set, using only the rightmost seven bits (values 0 to 127), will be considered, and each of the characters—letters, digits, punctuation characters, and special characters (designated using the escape character \)—will have a value within this range.

Using Relational Operators with Characters

In the statement

```
next_letter = 'A';
```

the character variable next_letter is assigned the character value 'A'. A single character variable or value may appear on the right-hand side of a character assignment statement. Character values may also be compared, read, and printed, as illustrated next.

Assuming next and first are type char, the logical expressions

```
next == first
next != first
```

determine whether two character variables have the same or different values. Order comparisons can also be performed on character variables using the relational operators <, <=, >, >=.

To understand the result of an order comparison, you must know something about the way your computer represents characters internally. As discussed earlier, each character has its own unique numeric code representing the value of the character. It is the binary form of this code that is stored in a character memory location.

If you examine the ASCII code shown in Appendix A, you will see that consecutive codes (decimal values 48 through 57) represent the digit characters '0' through '9' respectively. The order relationship shown below holds for the digit characters:

'0'<'1'<'2'<'3'<'4'<'5'<'6'<'7'<'8'<'9'.

For the uppercase letters 'A', 'B', ... 'Z', the following order relationship holds:

'A'<'B'<'C'< ... <'X'<'Y'<'Z'.

In the ASCII code, these characters are also represented using consecutive decimal values (decimal values 65 through 90).

A similar situation is true for lowercase letters. Once again, the expected order relationship holds in the ASCII code:

'a'<'b'<'c'< ... <'x'<'y'<'z'.

In ASCII, the lowercase letters have the consecutive decimal code values 97 through 122.

In ASCII, the *printable characters* have codes from 32 (the code for a blank or space) to 126 (the code for the symbol ~). The other codes represent non-printable *control characters.* Sending a control character to an output device causes the device to perform a special operation, such as returning the cursor to column one, advancing the cursor to the next line, or sounding a beep.

Some Useful Character Functions

The C++ standard library `ctype.h` provides a number of useful character functions. These functions are explained in Table 7.3. The first two of these functions may be used to convert uppercase characters to lowercase (and vice versa). The remaining functions are used for testing characters. All of the test

Table 7.3 Some Character Functions from the Library `ctype.h`

FUNCTION	PURPOSE
tolower (c)	If c is uppercase, this function returns the corresponding lower-case letter. Otherwise, returns c.
toupper (c)	If c is lowercase, this function returns the corresponding upper-case letter. Otherwise, it returns c.
isalnum (c)	Returns true if either isalpha (c) or isdigit (c) is non-zero. Otherwise, returns false.
isalpha (c)	Returns true if either isupper (c) or islower (c) is true. Otherwise, returns false.
iscntrl (c)	Returns true if c is a control character. Otherwise, returns false.

(continued)

Table 7.3 *(continued)*

FUNCTION	PURPOSE
isdigit (c)	Returns true if c is a digit character ('0', '1', '2', ..., '9'). Otherwise, returns false.
isgraph (c)	Returns true if c is a printing character (other than a space). Otherwise, returns false.*
islower (c)	Returns true if c is a lowercase letter. Otherwise, returns false.
isprint (c)	Returns true if c is a printing character (including the space). Otherwise, returns false.
ispunct (c)	Returns true if c is a printing character other than a space, letter, or digit. Otherwise, returns false.
isspace (c)	Returns true if c is a space, newline, formfeed, carriage return, tab, or vertical tab. Otherwise, returns false.
isupper (c)	Returns true if c is an uppercase letter. Otherwise, returns false.

*A printing character is any character in the ASCII table (Appendix A) between the space (ASCII value 32) and the tilde (~, ASCII value 126).

functions have a single character input argument, and all return a bool value (either true or false). The conversion functions (tolower and toupper) also have a single character input argument, but they return a character rather than a bool value.

The following examples illustrate the use of a few of the functions in Table 7.3, as well as the definitions of new functions that return character and bool values. Several of the functions defined in these examples will be used later in solving larger problems.

Example 7.6 The function to_digit in Fig. 7.4 returns the type bool value true if the input argument ch is a digit character (i.e., is one of the characters '0', '1', ..., '9'); otherwise, to_digit returns false. The output argument, i, for this function will be used to return the equivalent integer form of ch, if this character is a digit. Otherwise, i will be assigned a value of −1. Function to_digit is an example of a type bool function—it returns only type bool values. We will have more to say about type bool functions in the next section.

Figure 7.4 Function to_digit

```
// FILE: ToDigit.cpp

#include <ctype.h>          // for isdigit ()
```

(continued)

Figure 7.4 *(continued)*

```
// DETERMINES EQUIVALENT INTEGER FORM OF ITS CHARACTER INPUT
bool to_digit
   (char ch,              // IN: the character to be converted
    int& i)               // OUT: the integer form of ch (or -1)

// Pre : ch must be a digit character.
// Post: converts ch to a decimal digit.
// Returns: true if ch is a digit character and false otherwise.
//          Also returns through the output argument i the
//          integer form of the character input argument
//          (or -1 if this character is not a digit).
{
    // Determine if ch is a digit character.
    if (isdigit (ch))
    {
        i = int (ch) - int ('0');
        return true;
    }
    else
    {
        i = -1;
        return false;
    }

}  // end to_digit
```

The type cast operator int is used in the first assignment statement to show explicitly that integer values are involved in the indicated subtraction operation. Although this particular use of the cast operator has no effect on the internal value of its character operand, it provides for program clarity and complete type consistency in the specified data manipulation. This clarity and consistency is an important aspect of programming in C++, and we will continue to follow this convention in the remainder of the text. We strongly urge you to do the same, even when not required by C++.

The subtraction indicated in the expression

```
int (ch) - int ('0')
```

is required to ensure that the correct integer form of ch is returned through the output argument i. The desired result would not be returned simply by assigning int (ch) to i. For example, if the ch were the digit character '7', the value of int (ch) would be 55 (the ASCII value of the character '7' is 55). On the other hand, the value of the expression int (ch) - int ('0') would be 55 − 48 = 7, which is the desired result. ∎

Example 7.7   A *collating sequence* for characters is the ordering of characters according to their numeric codes. The program in Fig. 7.5 prints part of the C++ collating sequence

Figure 7.5   ASCII collating sequence illustration

```
// FILE: CollSeq.cpp
// PRINTS PART OF THE CHARACTER COLLATING SEQUENCE

#include <iostream.h>

void main ()
{
   // Local data ...
   const int min = 32;    // smallest numeric code
   const int max = 126;   // largest numeric code

   char next_char;        // character form of next_code (to
                          // be printed)

   // Print sequence of characters.
   cout << "Program output ..." << endl;
   for (int next_code =  min; next_code <= max; next_code++)
   {
      next_char = char (next_code);
      cout << next_char;
      if (next_char == 'Z')
         cout << endl;
   }   // end for
}
```

──────── Program Output ────────

```
Program output ...
 !"#$%&`()*+,-./0123456789:;<=>?@ABCDEFGHIJKLMNOPQRSTUVWXYZ
[/]^_'abcdefghijklmnopqrstuvwxyz{|}~.
```

for the ASCII character set. It lists the characters with numeric codes 32 through 126, inclusive. The first character printed is a blank (numeric code 32); the last one is the tilde (numeric code 126). These are precisely the C++ printing characters discussed in the isprint function description in Table 7.3. ∎

EXERCISES FOR SECTION 7.3

Self-Check   1. Evaluate the following C++ expressions using the ASCII character set.

   a. int ('D') - int ('A')
   b. char ((int ('M') - int ('A')) + int ('a'))
   c. int ('m') - int ('a')
   d. int ('5') - int ('0')

2. What is the purpose of the type cast operators int and char used in Self-Check Exercise 1?

3. Briefly explain the result of each of the following function references. (First indicate the type of the result and then its actual value.)

a. `isdigit ('8');`
b. `isdigit ('A');`
c. `isdigit (7);`
d. `toupper ('#');`
e. `tolower ('Q');`
f. `to_digit ('6', i);` (indicate also what value is returned in `i`)

4. In Fig. 7.5, what is the effect of the following lines of code?

```
if (next_char == 'Z')
    cout << endl;
```

Programming

1. Write a short segment of C++ code that prompts the user to type a single-digit integer and repeats this prompt as necessary until the user enters a digit. Your code segment should read the user input as a character and call the function `to_digit` (from Fig. 7.4) to verify that a digit character was indeed typed, and to return its equivalent integer representation.

7.4 —— TYPE bool DATA AND LOGICAL EXPRESSIONS

Type `bool` data was introduced in Chapter 2. Variables of type `bool` can take on just two values, true and false, and there are but two `bool` literals—`true` and `false`. (Contrast this with type `int` and `float` data, each of which may take on an infinite number of values and allows for the representation of an infinite number of different literals). In Chapter 4, we showed that type `bool` data could be used in assignment statements and to form logical expressions. We now turn our attention to some additional issues related to these logical expressions.

Complementing Logical Expressions

We first introduced logical expressions in Chapter 4 as conditions in `if` and `while` statements. In this section, we discuss how to *complement* a logical expression.

The logical operator `!` (not) is used to form the complement or opposite of a condition. If a logical expression is nonzero (true), then its complement is zero (false) and vice versa.

Some facility in determining the complements of conditions may come in handy when you write `if` and `while` statements in C++. For example, certain expressions involving the use of the `!` operator are more difficult to read and think about than an equivalent *complement expression* written without the `!`

operator. We can complement a simple condition just by changing the relational operator as shown below.

Operator	*Operator Used in Complement*
<	>=
<=	>
>	<=
>=	<
==	!=
!=	==

For example, the complement of x <= y is x > y. Thus, if a simple expression such as !(x <= y) is used in a condition, its equivalent condition may be obtained by removing the ! operator and complementing the relational operator. This process would yield the simpler but equivalent condition x > y.

DeMorgan's theorem explains how to complement a compound logical expression:

1. Write the complement of each simple logical expression.
2. Change each && (and) to || (or) and each || to &&, respectively.

DeMorgan's Theorem (viewed in C++)

!(*expression₁* && *expression₂*)   !(*expression₁* || *expression₂*)

is the same as   is the same as

!*expression₁* || !*expression₂*   !*expression₁* && !*expression₂*

Another way to complement a logical expression is to precede the entire expression with the not operator. Table 7.4 shows the complements of some more complicated logical expressions as determined by applying DeMorgan's theorem. We see that flag and swap are integer variables; next is type char; and x, y, m, and n are type int. In the complement of the expression on the first line, the relational operators are reversed (e.g., >= is changed to <)

Table 7.4 Complements of Logical Expressions

EXPRESSION	COMPLEMENT
x >= 1 && x <= 5	x < 1 || x > 5
!flag || x <= y	flag && x > y
flag && !swap	!flag || swap
(n % m == 0) && flag	(n % m != 0) || !flag
next == 'A' || next == 'a'	next != 'A' && next != 'a'
next == 'A' || next == 'a'	!(next == 'A' || next == 'a')

and the operator && (and) is changed to || (or). The last two lines show two complements of the same expression. In the last line, the expression is complemented by simply inserting the logical operator ! (not) in front of the entire condition. Any logical expression can be complemented in this way.

Type bool Functions

Function to_digit illustrated in Fig. 7.4 and most of the functions listed in Table 7.3 are examples of type bool functions—they return either true or false values. Such functions can be quite useful in specifying query operations concerning the state of data stores (variables and objects) declared in a program or a class. We can give these functions meaningful names and write clear and concise conditions consisting of calls to these functions.

Example 7.8   The bool function isdigit described in Table 7.3 was used in Fig. 7.4 to determine whether the contents of the character variable ch was a digit character (a character in the set {'0', '1', '2', ... '9'}). The call to isdigit was embedded directly as the condition in the if statement

```
if (isdigit (ch))
```

Since isdigit returns a type bool value, this is a perfectly correct use of the function and the use by itself comprises a legal C++ condition. We read the if statement in Fig 7.4 as follows:

If isdigit (ch) is true execute the statements
```
    i = int (ch) - int ('0');
    return true;
```
otherwise execute the statements
```
    i = -1;
    return false;
```

■

Example 7.9   If the integer variables dollars and cents were used in the money class to represent the amount of dollars and cents associated with an object of type money, then the addition operator + for this class might contain the statement

```
if (cents_overflow (cents))
{
    cents -= 100;
    dollars++;
}
```

This is a simple example, but it once again illustrates how type bool functions can be written as conditions in if or while statements.

The function `cents_overflow` might be written as

```
bool cents_overflow (int cents)
{
    if  (cents >= 100)
        return true;
    else
        return false;
}
```

■

Input and Output of Type bool Data

The type `bool` literals `true` and `false` cannot be used for the input or output of `bool` data. Normally, when `bool` data are displayed, the value `true` prints as the integer 1 and `false` prints as the integer 0. Similarly, only 0 (`false`) and 1 (`true`) may be read as type `bool` values. These restrictions are not likely to affect you very often, since you will rarely have an occasion to read `bool` data and will mostly display such data only when you are debugging your programs. Should you wish to read or display `true` and `false` as type `bool` literals in the function you are writing, simply insert the following lines of C++ code in the function:

```
cin.setf (ios::boolalpha);   // for reading true/false literals
cout.setf (ios::boolalpha);  // for displaying true/false
                             //     literals
```

Once these function calls have been executed by your program, you can read and display `bool` literals. For example, the statements

```
cout << "Enter a type bool value (true or false):";
cin >> flag;
cout << flag;
```

produce the following display (assuming `flag` is a type `bool` variable):

```
Enter a type bool value (true or false): true
true
```

Note that the word "true" written as any combination of upper- and lowercase characters will be read as the literal `true`. Any other string of characters will be treated as the literal `false`.

EXERCISES FOR SECTION 7.4

Self-Check

1. Write the complements of the conditions below (assume the variables are all of type `int`).

    a. x <= y && x != 15

b. x <= y && x != 15 || z == 7
c. x != 15 || z == 7 && x <= y
d. flag || !(x != 15)
e. !flag && x <= 8

2. What does the following function do:

```
bool is_in_range (score)
{
    if (score >= 0 && score <= 100)
      return true;
    else
      return false;
}
```

Programming 1. Write a function that has two integer input arguments m and n and returns an integer value of true when the value of m is a divisor of n and false otherwise.

7.5 ———— ENUMERATION TYPES

In many programming situations, the int, char, and float data types are inadequate to provide the desired degree of program readability and understandability. Let's assume we have been asked to do a textbook inventory for a local bookstore. This will involve monitoring the status of each book ordered for the courses offered in a given semester. In particular, we must determine if a book is in stock, back ordered, out of stock, or out of print. For each book, we might choose to represent this state information using an integer variable book_state with values of 0, 1, 2, and 3 representing the four states just described. This representation will work just fine, but it is not very readable, since the integer values are not easily associated with the four states. In fact, we may have to continually refresh our memory each time we see one of these state values as to which of the four states the value represents. In this section, we show how to declare a data type that performs this association for us.

Example 7.10 The enumeration type day declared below has the values sunday, monday, and so on.

```
enum day {sunday, monday, tuesday, wednesday,
          thursday, friday, saturday};      // days of the week
```

The first identifier in the *enumerator list* has the value 0; the second, the value 1; the third, the value 2, and so on. Because day is a new data type defined by the programmer, it is sometimes referred to as a *user-defined data type*. ∎

We can alter this *default association* by explicitly specifying a different association for some or all of the identifiers in an enumeration type, as shown in the following example.

Example 7.11 The 12 identifiers in the enumeration type `months` are associated with the constant integer values 1, 2, 3, ..., 12. When an associated value for an identifier in an enumeration type is specified, any unspecified values continue the progression from the last specified value.

```
enum months {jan = 1, feb, mar, apr, may, jun, jul, aug, sep,
              oct, nov, dec};
```

■

Example 7.12 The 12 identifiers in the enumeration type `month_length` have the constant integer values specified. The identifiers `may_len`, `jul_len`, `oct_len`, and `dec_len` all have the value 31. The specification of the value for `sep_len` shows that expressions may be used as values, provided all elements of the expression are constants.

```
enum month_length  {jan_len = 31, feb_len = 28, mar_len = 31,
                     apr_len = 30, may_len, jun_len = 30,
                     jul_len, aug_len = 31, sep_len = feb_len + 2,
                     oct_len, nov_len = 30, dec_len};
```

As this example shows, *enumerator values* used within the same enumeration need not be unique. However, identifiers within the same enumeration must be different, and no identifier may be used more than once in any enumeration within the same scope of definition. Thus, given the declaration for `months` shown in Example 7.11, the declaration

```
enum cold_months {nov, dec, jan, feb, mar};
```

appearing within the same scope as the declaration of `months` would cause a compiler error.

■

The points just illustrated are summarized in the next display.

C++ SYNTAX

Enumeration Type Declarations

Form: enum *enumeration-type* {*enumerator-list*};

Example: enum class_id {freshman, sophomore, junior, senior};

Interpretation: A new, distinct integral data type (an *enumeration-type*) is declared. The values associated with this type are specified in the *enumerator-list*. The enumerators in the list may be either identifiers or of the form

   identifier = constant-expression

Each enumerator is a constant, type `int` identifier defined within the scope containing the type declaration statement. (Normally, for our purposes in this text, this scope will be the function containing the declaration.) Unless explicitly indicated otherwise (using the *identifier = constant-expression* form), these values start at 0 and increase by increments of one. If not all values are specified, unspecified values continue in increments of one from the last specified value. Values in the same enumeration need not be distinct, but a particular identifier can appear in only one enumerator list within its scope of definition and must be distinct from any variable or constant name within that scope.

Example 7.13   You are writing a budget program in which you want to distinguish among several categories of expenditures: entertainment, rent, utilities, food, clothing, automobile, insurance, miscellaneous. Although you could create an arbitrary code that associates entertainment with a character value of `'e'`, rent with a character value of `'r'`, and so on, the use of enumeration types is clearly a preferred way of writing readable code. The declaration shown next defines a new type, expenses, as an enumeration type with eight enumerators. The variable, expense_category, is of type expenses and therefore can contain any of these eight enumerators.

```
enum expenses {entertainment, rent, utilities, food, clothing,
               automobile, insurance, other};
expenses expense_category;
```

These declarations can also be combined as shown below:

```
enum expenses {entertainment, rent, utilities, food, clothing,
               automobile, insurance, other} expense_category;
```

In either case, the following if statement can be used to test the value stored in expense_category.

```
if (expense_category == entertainment)
   cout << "Postpone until after your payday.";
else if (expense_category == rent)
   cout << "Pay before the first of the month!";
...
else if (expense_category == other)
   cout << "Do you really think you needed that?";
```

Characters as Enumerator Values

Because characters also have integer values, character constants may also be used to specify the value of an enumerator. In this case, the value of the identifier in the enumerator is the value of the character's numeric code.

Example 7.14   Although it is fairly easy to remember the character descriptions of many of the special characters that we commonly use, we could define an enumeration type to associate names with each of these special characters, as shown next.

```
enum escape_chars
    {backspace = '\b', bell = '\a', newline = '\n',
     return = '\r',    tab = '\t',  vtab = '\v'};
```
■

The identifiers in an enumerator list have integer values and are considered by C++ as names for type int constants. Thus, each enumeration type declaration you use in a function defines another C++ integral type, in addition to the integer and character data types we have already seen. As with integers and characters, variables of an enumeration type may also be assigned type int values. However, usually only a small subset of these values are meaningful for a given enumeration type. For example, only the integer values 0 through 7 are meaningful for type expenses; 1 through 12 are meaningful for type months, and 0 through 6 are meaningful for type day. Attempts to assign values outside the meaningful range to an enumeration variable (such as assigning 10 to a variable of type day) can produce unpredictable results. Some compilers may produce a warning message when such an assignment is attempted; others may provide no message at all.

Enumeration types behave like integers and thus may be used in C++ in much the same way as variables of the other integral types. For example, they may be used in switch and for statements.

Example 7.15 The switch statement shown next provides a clear and convenient way to represent the multiple decision shown in Example 7.13.

```
switch (expense_category)
{
case entertainment:
    cout << "Postpone until after your payday.";
    break;
case rent:
    cout << "Pay before the first of the month!";
    break;
...
case other:
    cout << "Do you really think you needed that?";
    break;
}
```
■

Comparisons Involving Enumeration Types

The order relationship among the identifiers of an enumeration type is fixed when the enumeration type is declared. For example, for types day, month_len, and expenses, the following ordering relationships are all true:

```
sunday < monday
wednesday != tuesday
wednesday == wednesday
wednesday >= tuesday
entertainment < rent
other >= automobile
utilities != food
```

Distinctions Among Integral Types

When using enumeration types, it is important to remember that each declaration of an integral type is different from all the others (and therefore also different from the int type). These different types cannot be mixed in an expression. Thus the expression

```
entertainment + wednesday
```

and the order relation

```
entertainment < wednesday
```

each would cause a syntax error because the values shown are associated with two different enumeration types. Note, however, that the expression

```
int (entertainment) + int (wednesday)
```

and the order relation

```
int (entertainment) < int (wednesday)
```

are legal, because both involve the use of type int operands. (From a problem point of view, however, it might be difficult to make any sense of either.)

Reading and Writing Enumeration Type Values

Enumeration types are defined by the programmer; thus, their values are not known in advance, and the C++ input/output systems cannot read or write these values. However, you can write your own functions for this purpose. The next example illustrates one approach to displaying the value of an enumeration variable in a readable form.

Example 7.16   Function write_color in Fig. 7.6 prints a character string that represents a value of type color. If the value of eyes is defined, the statement

```
write_color (eyes);
```

displays the value of eyes as a string. This function returns the status back to the calling function, informing the caller of its success or failure in attempting to print the correct string. Make sure you understand the difference between the string literal "blue" and the constant identifier blue, which is one of the type color enumerators in this example.

Figure 7.6 Function to print a value of type color

```cpp
// FILE: DispEnum.cpp

#include <iostream.h>

enum color {red, green, blue, yellow};

// DISPLAYS THE VALUE OF this_color
bool write_color
    (color this_color)        // IN: color to be printed as string

// Pre : this_color is assigned a value.
// Post: The value of this_color is displayed as a string.
// Returns: Status flag indicating if execution successful.
{
    // Local data ...
    bool status;    // indicates if function executes successfully

    // Print correct color as string literal.
    status = true;
    switch (this_color)
    {
        case red:
            cout << "red";
            break;
        case green:
            cout << "green";
            break;
        case blue:
            cout << "blue";
            break;
        case yellow:
            cout << "yellow";
            break;
        default:
            status = false;
            cerr << "*** ERROR: Invalid color for value." << endl;
    }  // end switch
    return status;
}  // end write_color
```

With the case statement shown in Fig. 7.6 (having enumerated constants as case labels), we take this opportunity to remind you not to give in to the temptation to use a character string (such as `"green"`) as a case label. Enumerators are allowed as case labels; character strings are not.

Motivation for Using Enumeration Types

At this point you may have a legitimate concern as to whether it is worth using enumeration types. The fact is that the use of enumeration types in a program can make that program considerably easier to read and understand.

Example 7.17   The `switch` statement

```
switch (day_num)
{
   case 6:
      pay_factor = 1.5;        // time and a half for Saturday
      break;
   case 7:
      pay_factor = 2.0;        // double pay for Sunday
      break;
   default:
      pay_factor = 1.0;        // regular pay
}
```

might appear in a payroll program without enumeration types if `saturday` and `sunday` are "encoded" as the integers 6 and 7, respectively. If we use the enumeration type `day` and variable `today` (type `day`), we can write this statement as

```
switch (today)
{
   case saturday:
      pay_factor = 1.5;
      break;
   case sunday:
      pay_factor = 2.0;
      break;
   default:
      pay_factor = 1.0;        // regular pay
}
```

The second form is obviously more readable because, instead of an obscure code, it uses enumerators (`saturday` and `sunday`) that are meaningful to the problem. Consequently, the comments on the right in the first version of the `switch` statement are not needed.   ■

EXERCISES FOR SECTION 7.5

Self-Check

1. Given the enumeration type expenses as defined in Example 7.12, for which integer values of the type int variable i will the expression

    ```
    expense_category (i)
    ```

    produce a meaningful result?

2. Evaluate each of the following, assuming before each operation that today (type day) is thursday.

    a. int (monday)
    b. int (today)
    c. today < tuesday
    d. day (int (wednesday) + 1)
    e. wednesday + monday
    f. int (today) + 1
    g. today >= thursday
    h. wednesday + thursday

3. Indicate whether each sequence of type declarations below is valid or invalid. Explain what is wrong with each invalid sequence.

    a. enum logical {true, false};
    b. enum letters {A, B, C};
       enum two_letters {A, B};
    c. enum day {sun, mon, tue, wed, thu, fri, sat};
       enum week_day {mon, tue, wed, thu, fri};
       enum week_end {sat, sun};
    d. enum traffic_light {red, yellow, green};
       int green;

Programming

1. Given the enumeration type months, rewrite the if statement below assuming that current_month is type months instead of type int. Also, write the equivalent switch statement.

    ```
    if (current_month == 1)
        cout << "Happy new year." << endl;
    else if (current_month == 6)
        cout << "Summer begins." << endl;
    else if (current_month == 9)
        cout << "Back to school." << endl;
    else if (current_month == 12)
        cout << "Happy holidays." << endl;
    ```

2. Write function write_day for enumeration type day.

7.6 ——— COMMON PROGRAMMING ERRORS

Considerable care is required when writing complicated expressions, especially those involving the use of parentheses. Two kinds of errors are most prevalent: omitting pairs of parentheses and unbalanced parentheses.

■ *Omitting pairs of parentheses:* This error will often go undetected by the compiler because the resulting expression may well be syntactically legal even though it is logically incorrect. For example, the statement

$$m = y_2 - y_1/x_2 - x_1$$

might be intended to compute the slope of a line through two points, (x_1, y_1) and (x_2, y_2), in the xy-plane. Yet because of the missing parentheses, the expression will actually compute m as

$$y_2 - (y_1 / x_2) - x_1$$

rather than

$$\frac{y_2 - y_1}{x_2 - x_1}$$

- *Unbalanced parentheses:* The omission of a single left or right parenthesis is also quite common in programming. This error will be detected by the compiler, causing a message such as `"parse error before )"` or `"parse error before ?"`. The first error usually indicates a missing left parenthesis; the second usually indicates a missing right parenthesis. The part of your program appearing in place of the `?` represents the point in your program code at which the missing right parenthesis was finally detected.

  To help prevent such errors in the use of parentheses, it is important to study the C++ operator precedence rules summarized in Appendix D. In addition, it sometimes helps to break a complicated expression into subexpressions that are separately assigned to *temporary variables,* and then to manipulate these temporary variables. For example, it may be easier to write correctly the three assignment statements

  ```
  temp1 = sqrt (x + y);
  temp2 = 1 + temp1;
  z = temp1 / temp2;
  ```

  than the single assignment statement

  ```
  z = sqrt (x + y) / (1 + sqrt (x + y));
  ```

  which has the same effect. Using three assignment statements is also more efficient because the square root operation is performed only once; it is performed twice in the single assignment statement above.

- *Mixing Operators and Operands of Different Types:* It is easy to make mistakes when writing expressions using mixed data types. To make matters worse, most errors of this nature are not detected by the compiler. Thus, for example, the expressions `'3' + '4'` and `gross_pay != '3'` (`gross_pay` of type `float`) are syntactically correct but will likely yield an unexpected and undesirable result at execution time.

  The best advice we can give for avoiding these problems is not to mix data types in the first place. Instead, use the casting operators discussed earlier in this chapter to ensure that you have explicitly specified all conversions desired.

- *Operator Precedence Errors:* Because of the operator precedence hierarchy in C++, very little use of parentheses is normally required when writing expressions involving relational and equality operators. The one major exception lies in the use of the not operator, !, which has a higher precedence than most of the other operators used up to this point. Care must be taken to ensure that the scope of application of this operator is as desired for your problem. For example, if x is true and y is false, then !x && y is false, but !(x && y) is true.

The precedence of all operators used in this book is summarized in Appendix D. Note that the unary operators have a higher precedence than the others [except the parentheses ()] and that they associate right to left. Expressions such as

```
-5.0 <= x && x <= 5.0
```

may be written correctly without parentheses. You may, however, find such expressions easier to read when parentheses are used:

```
(-5.0 <= x) && (x <= 5.0)
```

■ *Using Enumeration Types:* When declaring enumeration types, remember that only identifiers can appear in the list of values for an enumeration type. Strings, characters, and numbers are not allowed. Make sure that the same constant identifier does not appear in more than one enumeration-type declaration in a given declaration scope. Remember that there are no standard functions available to read or write the values of an enumeration type. You will need to write your own when printing such values is required.

C++ treats enumeration and char data as integral data types (having integer values). Therefore, it is permissible to perform the standard arithmetic and relational operations on values of these data types. You must be careful, however; neither the compiler nor the run-time system will attempt to verify that the results of the arithmetic operations fall within the range of meaningful values for these types. Remember, each enumeration type you define, as well as the char type, are considered to be different integral types. Thus elements of different enumeration types or of char should not be mixed in the same arithmetic or relational expression.

Note that you cannot assign a type int value to an enumeration type without first applying the appropriate type casting operator. Thus for the variable today of type day, the statement

```
today = i;
```

(for an i of type int) must be written as

```
today = day (i);
```

where i is first recast to type day before the assignment takes place.

CHAPTER REVIEW

In this chapter, we reviewed the manipulation of simple data types, including the predefined types—`short int`, `int`, `long int`, `float`, `double`, `bool` and `char`—and user-defined enumeration types. We discussed the internal representation of these simple types as well as the differences between the numeric types, `int` and `float`, and the enumeration types, `bool` and `char`.

The finite capacity of computer memory introduces representational inaccuracies and limitations. Floating-point arithmetic is inherently less precise because not all type `float` numbers can be represented precisely. Other sources of numerical errors, such as cancellation error and arithmetic overflow and underflow, can occur due to the finite nature of computer memory.

More topics related to the character data type were presented, and the character function library `ctype.h` was introduced. The use of the relational and equality operators (`<=, >=, <, >, ==, !=`) and the logical operators (`&&, ||, !`) were elaborated further. DeMorgan's theorem, which describes how to form the complement of a logical expression, was presented. A number of examples illustrating the declaration and use of enumeration types to make programs more readable and understandable were presented.

New C++ Constructs

The new C++ constructs introduced in this chapter are described in Table 7.5.

Table 7.5   Summary of New C++ Constructs

CONSTRUCT	EFFECT
Integer Variants	
`const long int big` `  = 123456789L;`	a long integer constant
`const short int small = 32;`	a short integer constant
Floating-Point Variants	
`double x;`	provides additional accuracy over float
Enumeration Types	
`enum coins {penny, nickel, dime, quarter, half_dollar};`	

✔ QUICK-CHECK EXERCISES

1. a. Evaluate the logical expression

   `true && ((30 % 10) == 0)`

   b. Is the outer pair of parentheses required?

    c. What about the inner pair?

    d. Write the complement of this expression.

2. Assuming m and k are integers (k = 13),

    a. Rewrite the following assignment statement so that there are no mixed data types. What is the value assigned to m?

```
m = 2.5 + k / 2;
```

    b. Rewrite this expression assuming m is type float. What is the value assigned to m now?

    c. Is the statement given in (a) syntactically legal in C++? If so, what value would be assigned to m for this mixed type expression?

3. What is the value of each of the following in ASCII?

    a. `char (int ('a'))`   b. `char (int ('a') + 3)`

    c. `char (int ('z') - 20)`   d. `char (int ('z') - 40)`

    e. `int ('z') - 40`   f. `ch - '0'` (where ch is any digit character)

4. If ch contains the character `'a'`, what is the value of the expression

```
isdigit (ch) || iscntrl (ch)
```

    What kind of an expression is this?

5. Can an enumerator of the enumeration type day be assigned to a variable of another enumeration type? (In other words, is the assignment

```
today - entertainment
```

    valid if today is a variable of type day and entertainment is an enumerator of type expense?)

6. If two variables are not of the same integral type (int, long int, char, enumeration, and so on),

    a. can they be mixed in the same arithmetic expression?

    b. can one be assigned to the other?

7. Under what condition can a type int variable or value be assigned to a variable of an enumeration type?

8. What is wrong with the following enumeration type declaration?

```
enum prime {2, 3, 5, 7, 11, 13};
```

Answers to Quick-Check Exercises

1. a. true

    b. The outer pair is not required.

    c. The inner pair is not required.

    d. `false || !((30 % 10) == 0)`

2. a. `m = int (2.5 + float (k) / 2.0);`

       9; 13.0/2.0 = 6.5; 6.5 added to 2.5 is 9.0 and this result is recast to type int, so 9 is assigned to m.

    b. `m = 2.5 + float (k) / 2.0;`

       9.0; 13.0/2.0 = 6.5; so 6.5 added to 2.5 or 9.0 is assigned to m.

    c. 8; 13/2 is an integer 6; the 6 is converted to float and added to 2.5, yielding 8.5; when 8.5 is stored in the integer m, the fractional part is lost.

3. a. `'a'` b. `'d'` c. `'f'` d. `'R'` e. 82

    f. The result is the integer form of the character—e.g., 7 if ch = `'7'`.

4. false or false is false; this is a logical expression involving calls to two type bool functions.

5. no

6. a. Yes, but carefully. Remember that these data are each considered to be different C++ types and are subject to the C++ conversion/promotion given earlier in the chapter.

   b. The same applies to assignment except that integer type values may not be assigned to variables of enumeration types.

7. This can happen only if the enumerated variable's type cast is applied to the type int variable or value (e.g., today = day (i);).

8. Integers are not allowed as enumerators in enumeration types.

REVIEW QUESTIONS

1. What are the advantages of data type int over data type float?

2. List and explain three computational errors that may occur in type float expressions.

3. a. Write an enumeration type declaration for fiscal as the months from July through June.

   b. Write an enumeration type declaration for winter as December through February.

4. Write functions for writing values for variables of type season:

   ```
   enum season {winter, spring, summer, fall};
   ```

5. Write a bool function is_weekend that returns true if the value of today (of type day—see Example 7.10) is a weekend day. Otherwise the function should return false.

6. Write a switch statement that tests to see if the type day variable today is a working day. Print the message "Workday" or "Weekend".

7. Write an if statement that will write out true or false according to the following conditions: either flag is true or color is red, or both money is plenty and time is up.

8. Write the statement to assign a true value to the integer variable over_time only if a worker's weekly hours are greater than 40.

9. a. Write the C++ instructions to determine whether the value for 'a' is greater than the value for 'Z'.

   b. What is the value of this expression?

10. Write the C++ statements necessary to enter an integer between 0 and 9, inclusive, and convert it to an equivalent character value (e.g., 0 to '0', 1 to '1') to be stored in a character variable dig_char.

PROGRAMMING PROJECTS

1. An integer n is divisible by 9 if the sum of its digits is divisible by 9. Recall that we used the modulus operator % in function print_digits_reversed (Fig. 7.2) to

print the digits in a number one at a time in reverse order. Develop a program to determine whether or not the following numbers are divisible by 9:

$$n = 154368$$
$$n = 621594$$
$$n = 123456$$

2. Redo Programming Project 1 by reading each digit of the number to be tested into the type char variable digit. Form the sum of the numeric values of the digits. (*Hint:* The numeric value of digit is int (digit) - int ('0').)

3. If a human heart beats on an average of once per second (60 beats per minute), how many times does the heart beat in a lifetime of 78 years? (Use 365.25 for the number of days in a year.) Rerun your program for a heart rate of 75 beats per minute. Implement the program first using beats per minute and years as integers and total beats and all constants as type double. Then try changing all type double data to type float and see what happens. Can you explain the difference (if any) in the execution output of the two versions?

4. A number is said to be *perfect* if the sum of its divisors (except for itself) is equal to itself. For example, 6 is a perfect number because the sum of its divisors (1 + 2 + 3) is 6. The number 8 is said to be *deficient* because the sum of its divisors (1 + 2 + 4) is only 7. The number 12 is said to be *abundant* because the sum of its divisors (1 + 2 + 3 + 4 + 6) is 16. Write a program that lists the factors of the numbers between 1 and 100 and classifies each number as perfect, deficient, or abundant.

5. Find out how to access the printer from a C++ program running on your computer system. Write a program for generating a bar graph on the printer summarizing the rainfall in Bedrock for one year. Include the average monthly rainfall and the maximum monthly rainfall during the year as part of the program output.

Prompt the user for the amount of rainfall for a particular month and instruct the computer to send an appropriate output line to the printer. Assume that no one month will have more than 14 inches of rainfall. Your graph should resemble Fig. 7.7.

```
January     | * * * * * * * * * * * * * * * * * *

February    | * * * * * * * * * * * *

March       |

December    | * * * * * * * * * * * * * * * * * * * * * * * * * * * * * * * * * * * *
            | -----1-----2-----3-----4--  5-----6-----7-----8-----9...
                              Inches of Rainfall
```

Figure 7.7   Bar graph for inches of rainfall

Write functions corresponding to the prototypes shown below as part of your solution.

```
// WRITE THE MONTH VALUE AS A STRING
void write_month
   (int);           // IN: month to be written as a string
```

```
// GET RAINFALL FOR MONTH; UPDATE TOTALS
void get_monthly_total
   (int,           // IN: current month
    float&,        // OUT: inches of rain for month
    float&,        // INOUT: max inches of rain
    float&);       // INOUT: total inches of rain

// User is prompted for inches of rainfall during a month.
// Max inches and total inches are updated to contain
//    the maximum and total inches of rainfall input so far.

// DRAW BAR OF LENGTH GIVEN BY INCHES
void draw_bar
   (int,           // IN: the month to be written as a string
    float);        // IN: the inches of rain for the month
// Draw a bar whose length is computed from inches with label
//    determined by the value of month.

// DRAW SCALE AND LABEL AT BOTTOM OF GRAPH
void draw_scale_line ();
```

6. The interest paid on a savings account is compounded daily. This means that if you start with *startbal* dollars in the bank, at the end of the first day you will have a balance of

startbal * (1 + *rate*/365)

dollars, where *rate* is the annual interest rate (0.10 if the annual rate is 10 percent). At the end of the second day, you will have

startbal * (1 + *rate*/365) * (1 + *rate*/365)

dollars, and at the end of n days you will have

startbal * (1 + *rate*/365)^n

dollars. Write a program that processes a set of data records, each of which contains values for `rate`, `startbal`, and n and computes the final account balance.

7. Experiments that are either too expensive or too dangerous to perform are often simulated on a computer when the computer is able to provide a good representation of the experiment. Find out how to call the random-number generator (usually a function returning a floating-point value in the range 0 to 1) for your C++ system. (Look up the functions `rand` and `srand` in the library `stdlib.h`). Write a program that uses the random-number generator to simulate the dropping of glass rods that break into three pieces. The purpose of the experiment is to estimate the probability that the lengths of the three pieces are such that they might form the sides of a triangle.

   For the purposes of this experiment, you may assume that the glass rod always breaks into three pieces. If you use the line segment 0 to 1 (on the real number line) as a mathematical model of the glass rod, a random-number generator (function) can be used to generate two numbers between 0 and 1 representing the coordinates of the breaks. The triangle inequality (the sum of the lengths of two sides of a triangle are always greater than the length of the third side) may be used to test the length of each piece against the lengths of the other two pieces.

To estimate the probability that the pieces of the rod form a triangle, you will need to repeat the experiment many times and count the number of times a triangle can be formed from the pieces. The probability estimate is the number of successes divided by the total number of rods dropped. Your program should prompt the user for the number of rods to drop and allow the experiment to be repeated. Use a sentinel value of -1 to halt execution of the program.

8

Streams, Files, and Formatting

This chapter is devoted to a discussion of the concepts of files and streams in C++. The features presented are part of the input and output facilities provided by the C++ libraries that support stream input. The discussion is partitioned into several main components:

- Files, streams, and the connection between them
- Stream output
- Stream input
- String input and output
- Formatting

We begin with a discussion of streams.

8.1 ————— THE STANDARD INPUT/OUTPUT STREAMS

A *stream* is a sequence of characters. Up to this point in the book, input and output has been implemented using the *standard input stream* (named cin) and the *standard output stream* (named cout). Every C++ program has these streams available automatically (as long as you include the iostream.h header). As indicated when we first introduced streams in Chapter 2, cin and cout are objects of type istream and ostream respectively. The user-defined types istream and ostream are defined by classes in the iostream library and cin and cout are declared as objects of these types. Normally, cin is connected to your keyboard and cout is connected to your display. Reading characters from the standard input stream object cin is equivalent to reading from the keyboard; writing characters to the standard output stream object cout is equivalent to displaying these characters on your screen.

All stream input/output facilities are concerned with converting internal representations of data (variables or objects) to a stream of characters (for output) and converting streams of characters to the correct internal form (for input). This conversion is illustrated in Fig. 8.1 for the streams cin and cout, where each data store appearing as an operand of the output operator, <<, is converted to a stream of characters and "inserted into" the output stream (cout). Conversely, the input operator, >>, specifies the "extraction from" the input stream of a stream of characters. These characters are then converted to the appropriate internal form and stored in the specified storage locations.

Any character, whether printable or not, may be read from or written to a stream. Thus nonprintable characters such as '\a' and '\n' may also be read from or written to streams. As their name suggests, these characters are not printed. Rather, on many computers, they cause special actions to occur, such as sounding a beep ('\a') or moving the cursor to the beginning of the next line ('\n'). In this chapter, we will need to represent only the newline

Output conversion (from internal representation to characters)

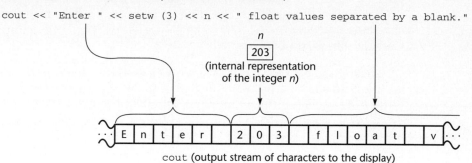

```
cout << "Enter " << setw (3) << n << " float values separated by a blank."
```

cout (output stream of characters to the display)

Input conversion

```
cin >> month >> day >> year;
```

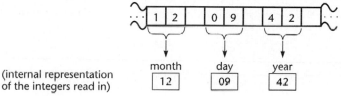

cin (stream of characters entered at the keyboard)

Figure 8.1   Conversion of data to and from streams

character (`'\n'`) in a stream. We will use the symbol <nwln> for this purpose, as shown in the next example.

Example 8.1   *Streams as a Sequence of Lines.* The newline character partitions a stream into a sequence of lines. We call this a *logical partition,* because it reflects the way we often think and talk about a stream. We should not forget, however, that a stream is physically just a sequence of characters with the newline character interspersed. For example, the following represents a stream of two lines of data consisting of letters, blank characters, `'.'` (a period), and `'!'` (an exclamation point).

```
This is a stream!<nwln>It would be displayed as two lines.<nwln>
```

The <nwln> character separates one line of data in the stream from the next. The letter I following the first <nwln> is the first character of the second line. If we were to display this stream, each <nwln> character would cause a *line feed* and a *carriage return,* ensuring that everything that follows it would appear at the beginning of a new line. The displayed stream would appear as follows:

```
This is a stream!
It would be displayed as two lines.
```
∎

A stream has no fixed size. As we write (insert) information to a stream, we are simply adding characters to the end of the stream (increasing its size). We use the C++ stream output library functions to keep track of the size of the stream. As we read (extract) information from a stream, the C++ stream input library functions keep track of the last character read using an *input stream buffer pointer*. Each new attempt to get information from an input stream begins at the current position of this pointer.

Example 8.2   *Reading Data Using* >>. When reading a character data element using the input operator >>, any leading *white space* (blanks, tab, and newline characters, for example) is skipped until the first non–white space character is found. This first character is then read and stored in the designated character variable. The input stream buffer pointer is advanced past all characters processed (all preceding white space and the single non–white space character) and positioned at the next character. For example, given the input stream

```
□□□□□CIS 642 ...
```

the line

```
cin >> ch;  // read one character into the character variable ch
```

causes the five blanks (indicated using the symbols □□□□□) at the start of the stream to be skipped. The character C is then extracted from the stream and stored in the variable ch. The stream buffer pointer then is positioned at the character I.

When reading a numeric value, the input operator skips over any leading whitespace characters until a non–white space character is encountered. Next, all characters that are part of the numeric value (a sign, digits, etc.) are processed until a character that is not legally part of a number in C++ is read. At this point, the number processed is returned to the program. If no digits are read before an illegal numeric character is encountered, the result returned is undefined.

For example, when processing the stream

```
347an old man
```

the line

```
cin >> my_age;  // my_age is an integer variable
```

reads the characters 347 and stops when the character a is encountered. The integer value 347 would be stored in my_age. If the line to be read had been

```
an old man
```

reading would have stopped as soon as the a had been encountered, and the result stored in my_age would be undefined.

As another example, consider the input stream consisting of exam score *records* (three initials and a score) for each of four students, where each record is entered as a single line, with the return key pressed after each score is typed:

```
f l f 78<nwln>e b k 89<nwln>j a s 95<nwln>p a c 66<nwln>
```

Assuming that the variable score is type int, and fst_init, mdl_init, and lst_init are type char, the C++ instructions

```
for (i = 0; i < nmbr_students; i++)
{
    cin >> fst_init >> mdl_init >> lst_init >> score;
    // Process the information just read.
    ...
}
```

may be used to read in this information. If nmbr_students is 4, this loop would extract (read) four data elements (three characters and an integer) at a time from the stream just shown until all four student records have been processed. In each for loop iteration, the next student's initials would be extracted and stored in the character variables, fst_init, mdl_init, and lst_init, and the integer that follows them would be read and stored in score.

The newline character in the stream has no special impact on the processing of the data just shown. Leading white space, including blanks and the newline character, is always skipped when reading a data element using cin. After the score for the first student has been read, the input stream buffer pointer is positioned a little beyond the characters just processed, at the character that stopped the processing (in this case, the white space character <nwln>):

```
f l f 78<nwln>e b k 89<nwln>j a s 95<nwln>p a c 66<nwln>
      ↑
```

When reading for the second student has begun, the white space (<nwln>) that precedes this student's first initial is skipped. If we replace each newline with a blank, as shown in Fig. 8.2, the processing would be the same. In fact, if there were no white-space characters anywhere in the line, the processing of the line would not change. This point is illustrated next.

Figure 8.2 **An input stream without the newline character**

```
f l f 78 e b k 89 j a s 95 p a c 66 d m s 97
```

∎

Example 8.3   The processing of the stream shown in Fig. 8.2 would be the same even if all of the blanks were eliminated from the stream. In this case, the C++ instructions

```
for (i = 0; i < nmbr_students; i++)
{
    cin >> fst_init >> mdl_init >> lst_init >> score;
    // Process the information just read.
    ...
}
```

would process the line

```
flf78ebk89jas95pac66<nwln>
```

as follows:
a. In the first repetition of the loop,
    ■ the characters `flf` are read and stored in `fst_init`, `mdl_init`, and `lst_init`, respectively.
    ■ the integer `78` is read; reading is stopped when the letter `e` is encountered and the value `78` is stored in `score`; the stream buffer pointer is moved to point to the `e`.
b. In the second repetition of the loop,
    ■ the characters `ebk` are read and stored in `fst_init`, `mdl_init`, and `lst_init`, respectively.
    ■ the integer `89` is read; reading is stopped when the letter `j` is encountered and the value `89` is stored in `score`; the stream buffer pointer is moved to point to the `j`.
c. Repetition continues in this fashion until finally,
    ■ the characters `pac` are read and stored in `fst_init`, `mdl_init`, and `lst_init`, respectively.
    ■ the integer `66` is read; reading is stopped when the `<nwln>` is encountered and the value `66` is stored in `score`; the stream buffer pointer is moved to point to the `<nwln>`.   ■

Reading One Character at a Time

There are numerous situations in which it is convenient to read data from a stream one character at a time with white space treated the same way as any other character. The following examples illustrate how this might be done using the stream input and output functions `get` and `put`, which are part of the C++ `iostream` library. Function `put` is the output analog of `get`; `get` is used to read one character at a time; `put` is used to display one character at a time and is included in this example for illustrative purposes.

Example 8.4 The program in Fig. 8.3 counts and displays the number of blanks in a stream of information entered at the keyboard, one line at a time. It also counts and displays the number of lines in the stream. The inner loop terminates each time the `<nwln>` character is detected, marking the beginning of a new line.

Figure 8.3 **Counting blanks in an input stream**

```cpp
// File: CntBlPer.cpp
// COUNTS THE NUMBER OF BLANKS IN EACH LINE OF A FILE

#include <iostream.h>

void main ()
{
    // Local data ...
    const char blank = ' '; // character being counted
    const char nwln = '\n'; // newline character

    char next;              // next character in current line
    int blank_count;        // number of blanks in current line
    int line_count;         // keeps track of number of lines in file

    line_count = 0;
    cin.get (next);              // get first char of new line
    while (!cin.eof ())
    {
        blank_count = 0;  // initialize blank count for new line
        while ((next != nwln) && !cin.eof ())
        {
            cout.put (next);
            if (next == blank)
                blank_count++;       // increment blank count.
            cin.get (next);          // get next character.
        }   // end inner while

        cout.put (nwln);  // marks end of current display line
        line_count++;
        cout << "The number of blanks is " << blank_count << "."
            << endl;
        cin.get (next);     // get next character.
    }   // end outer while
    cout << "The number of lines processed is " << line_count
        << "." << endl;
}
```

The detection of the beginning of a new line is required to count the number of lines appearing in the stream. The `put` function is used to display each character in the stream as it is processed.

The inner loop condition `(next != nwln) && !cin.eof ()` is true as long as the newline character has not been read and we have not run out of characters. Therefore, this inner loop processes all of the characters in the current data line, including the blanks. When the newline character is read by the inner call to `get`, the inner `while` loop expression evaluates to false, and loop exit occurs. At this point, the newline is displayed (marking the end of the current line of output), the line count is incremented, and the number of blanks in the line is printed. This sequence of steps is repeated as long as the outer loop condition is true.

This example illustrates the use of a third `iostream` function, `eof`, which is used to detect the end of the stream of characters entered at the keyboard. This function returns a value of `false` as long as there are more characters to be read in a stream. When the end of the stream has been reached, the value `true` is returned. From the keyboard, the end of a file may be indicated by typing a special character. Exactly which character depends on the computer you are using. For MS-DOS, the character CTRL-Z (typed by pressing the CONTROL and Z keys simultaneously) is used to enter an end of file. On UNIX computers the character CTRL-D is used. Your instructor can tell you which character to use on your computer system to indicate the end of a file.

The dot notation is used to indicate which stream is involved in the designated operation (`get`, `put`, `eof`). We simply precede the function name with the name of the stream to which it is to be applied, followed by a dot:

```
cin.get (next);
```

If you are wondering why two tests for end-of-file are required, remove either test and trace the execution of this program for a short sample of data (see Self-Check Exercise 6 at the end of this section). ∎

The `get`, `put`, and `eof` functions are summarized, together with other stream input/output functions in the syntax display. The `open`, `fail`, and `close` functions are used only with external file streams, described in the next section.

C++
SYNTAX

The File Manipulation Member Functions: `open`, `get`, `put`, `eof`, `fail`, `close`

Requires: `iostream.h` or `fstream.h`

Forms: *fs*.open (*fname*);
        fs.get (*ch*);
        fs.put (*ch*);
        fs.eof ();
        fs.fail ();
        fs.close ();

Examples: ins.open (in_file);
        ins.get (first_init);
        ins.fail ();
        if (ins.eof ()) {... }
        ins.close ();

Interpretation: For each of these functions, the variable name before the period, *fs*, designates the input/output stream affected by the operation. For the function open, the argument *fname* is a string representing the name of the external file to be opened. The open function connects the stream *fs* to the external file designated by *fname*. Function get extracts the next character from the stream and places it in the character variable *ch*. Function put *inserts* (writes or displays) character *ch* into the stream. The close function disconnects the stream and its associated file, and eof tests for the end-of-file condition. The eof function returns true when the end-of-file is reached. Function fail may be used to check if a stream operation such as open failed to execute properly. This function also returns true if the operation fails. ∎

EXERCISES FOR SECTION 8.1

Self-Check
1. Provide a careful and detailed explanation of what would happen in Fig. 8.3 if the function calls cin.get were replaced by the use of the input operator, <<, as in
   cin << next;
2. Let x be type float, n type int, and c type char. Indicate the contents of each variable after each read operation is performed, assuming that the input stream consists of the following lines:

   ```
   123 3,145 XYZ<nwln>
   35 Z <nwln>
   ```

   a. cin >> n >> x; cin >> c;
   b. cin >> n; cin.get (c);
   c. cin >> x; cin.get (c); cin >> n;
   d. cin >> c >> n >> x; cin >> c;
   e. cin >> c >> c >> c >> x >> n;
3. What would happen to the displayed output if the line cout.put (nwln); were omitted from the program in Fig. 8.3?
4. Describe the behavior of the program in Fig. 8.3 if the statement containing the innermost cin.get were omitted.
5. Describe the behavior of the program in Fig. 8.3 if the input stream being processed were empty (contained no data at all).
6. Describe the problems that would occur
   a. if the inner end-of-file test were omitted from the function in Fig. 8.3.
   b. if the outer end-of-file test were omitted in Fig. 8.3.

Programming
1. Write a function that reads a float constant (*not* in scientific notation) typed from the keyboard one character at a time and returns the number of digits to the left of the decimal point and the number digits to the right of the decimal point. This function should call another that ensures that each character read meets the criteria for a type float constant and that asks for another character any time this validation test fails. We will assume that at most one sign is present in a legal float numeric value and that it must appear in front of the value. In addition, if no period is

encountered in the line, then the number of digits appearing to the right of this nonexistent point would be zero.

8.2 —— STREAMS AND EXTERNAL FILES

Interactive Versus Batch Processing

In all of the example C++ code segments, programs, and case studies presented so far, we have used interactive input. Interactive programs read their input data from the `cin` stream associated with the keyboard and display their output to the `cout` stream associated with a display. This mode of operation is fine for small programs. However, as you begin to write larger programs, you will see that there are many advantages to using external data files. These files are stored on a secondary storage device, normally a disk. Except under extreme circumstances, external files are permanent—you can create and save them one day and return to your computer some later day and find them still stored on your disk.

You can create an external data file using a text editor in the same way that you create a program file. Once the data file is entered in computer memory, you can carefully check and edit each line and then save the final data file as a permanent disk file. When you enter data interactively, you do not always have the opportunity to examine and edit the data. Also, the data are processed as they are entered—they are not saved permanently.

After the data file is saved on disk, you can instruct your program to read from the data file rather than from the keyboard. This mode of execution is called *batch processing*. Because the program data are supplied before execution begins, prompting messages are not required for batch programs. Instead, batch programs should contain display statements that print back, or *echo-print*, those data values read by the program that are important to its successful execution. This provides a record of the values read and processed in a particular program run, which can be useful, especially for debugging and testing.

In addition to giving you the opportunity to check for errors in your data, using data files provides another advantage. A data file can be read many times. Therefore, during debugging you can rerun the program as often as you need to without reentering the test data each time.

You can also instruct your program to write its output to a disk file rather than display it on the screen. When output is written to the screen, it disappears when it scrolls off the screen and cannot be retrieved. However, if program output is written to a disk file, you have a permanent copy of it. You can get a *hard copy* (a copy on paper) of the file by sending it to your printer, or you can use an operating system command such as

```
type filename
```

to list file `filename` on the screen.

Finally, you can use the output generated by one program as a data file for another program. For example, a payroll program may compute employee salaries and write each employee's name and salary to an output file. A second program, which prints employee checks, could then be run, using the output from the payroll program as its input data file.

Directory Names for External Files

To access a file in a program, you must know both the name of the file and the *disk directory* in which the file resides. A disk directory lists the names of all files stored on the disk. We need to communicate both pieces of information to the operating system so it can locate the files for processing by the program. The details as to how you provide directory names and information will vary according to the system you are using. Your instructor can give you the proper steps to follow for your particular computer system.

File names must also follow whatever conventions apply on a particular computer system. As an example, some systems limit you to a file name that consists of eight characters, a period, and a three-letter *extension*. Many programmers use the extensions .cpp and .dat to designate C++ program and data files, respectively.

In the discussion that follows, we will not concern ourselves with the details of locating the directory of a file you wish to read or write. We will assume that you already know how to do this or that, for the time being, you do not even need to know in order to proceed. We will therefore confine our attention to the issue of how we tell a C++ program the names of the external files it is to process.

As we mentioned earlier, the input and output stream objects cin and cout are attached to the keyboard and display, respectively, by the C++ language system. To read from or write to any other external data file, however, we must first *attach* a stream object to that file. We will now see how this is done.

Attaching Streams to External Files

Writing programs that manipulate external disk files is complicated by the fact that two different names are involved: the *external file name,* which appears in your directory and is the name by which the operating system knows the file, and the *stream object name,* which is the *internal name* by which your program accesses the file. In C++, the connection between these two names is accomplished through the use of a special function, called the open function. The open function is illustrated in the following example, together with a number of other fstream functions.

Example 8.5 For security reasons, it is a good idea to have a backup or duplicate copy of a file in case the original is lost. Although most operating systems provide a single command for copying a file, we will write our own C++ program to do this. Program `CopyFile.cpp` in Fig. 8.4 copies each character in file `in_data.dat` to file `out_data.dat`.

Figure 8.4 Copying a file

```cpp
// FILE: CopyFile.cpp
// COPIES FILE IN_DATA.DAT TO FILE OUT_DATA.DAT

#include <stdlib.h>           // for the definition of EXIT_FAILURE
                              // and EXIT_SUCCESS
#include <fstream.h>          // required for external file streams

// ASSOCIATE PROGRAM IDENTIFIERS WITH EXTERNAL FILE NAMES
#define in_file "in_data.dat"
#define out_file "out_data.dat"

   // Functions used ...
   // COPIES ONE LINE OF TEXT
   int copy_line
      (ifstream&,              // IN: infile stream
       ofstream&);             // OUT: outfile stream

int main()
{

   // Local data ...
   int line_count;            // output: number of lines processed
   ifstream ins;              // associates ins as an input stream
   ofstream outs;             // associates outs as an output stream

   // Open input and output file, exit on any error.
   ins.open (in_file);        // ins connects to file in_file
   if (ins.fail ())
   {
      cerr << "*** ERROR: Cannot open " << in_file
           << " for input." << endl;
      return EXIT_FAILURE;     // failure return
   } // end if

   outs.open (out_file);       // outs connects to file out_file
   if (outs.fail ())
   {
      cerr << "*** ERROR: Cannot open " << out_file
           << " for output." << endl;
      return EXIT_FAILURE;     // failure return
   } // end if

   // Copy each character from in_data to out_data.
   line_count = 0;
```

(continued)

Figure 8.4 *(continued)*

```
      if (copy_line (ins, outs) != 0) line_count++;
      while (!ins.eof ())
         if (copy_line (ins, outs) != 0) line_count++;

      // Display a message on the screen.
      cout << "Input file copied to output file." << endl;
      cout << line_count << " lines copied." << endl;

      ins.close ();            // close input file stream
      outs.close ();           // close output file stream
      return EXIT_SUCCESS;     // successful return
}


// COPY ONE LINE OF TEXT FROM ONE FILE TO ANOTHER
int copy_line
      (ifstream& ins,          // TN: ins stream
       ofstream& outs)         // OUT: outs stream

// Pre:    ins is opened for input and outs for output.
// Post:   Next line of ins is written to outs.
//         The last character processed from ins is <nwln>;
//         the last character written to outs is <nwln>.
// Returns: The number of characters copied.
{
      // Local data ...
      const char nwln = '\n';          // newline character

      char next_ch;                    // inout: character buffer
      int char_count = 0;              // number of characters copied

      // Copy all data characters from ins file stream to outs file
      //    stream.
      ins.get (next_ch);
      while ((next_ch != nwln) && !ins.eof ())
      {
         outs.put (next_ch);
         char_count++;
         ins.get (next_ch);
      }  // end while

      // If last character read was nwln write it to out_data.
      if (!ins.eof ())
      {
         outs.put (nwln);
         char_count++;
      }
      return char_count;
}  // end copy_line
```

(continued)

Figure 8.4   *(continued)*

—————————— Program Output ——————————
```
Input file copied to output file.
37 lines copied.
```

Before we can read or write an external file in a program, we must first declare a stream variable for each stream to be processed by our program. As shown in Fig. 8.4, the required declarations

```
ifstream ins;
ofstream outs;
```

have the same form as those we have been using to declare variables and string objects, but they involve two new data types, `ifstream` (input file stream) and `ofstream` (output file stream). These two types are defined in the C++ library header `fstream.h`. Once the stream variables have been declared, the files may be opened using the library function `open`:

```
ins.open (in_file);
outs.open (out_file);
```

This function communicates with the operating system we are using and attaches the declared stream (`ins`, for example) to the external file. The connection established by the `open` statement between the external file and associated stream is depicted in Fig. 8.5.

The use of the `#define` compiler directive enables us to associate the name of a stream used by the program (for example, `in_file`) with the actual external name of a file (such as `in_data.dat`). This association enables us to

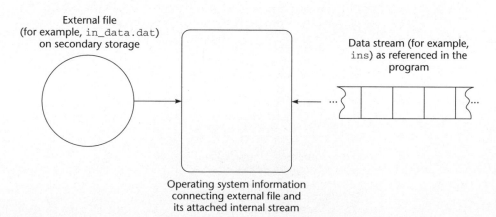

Figure 8.5   Connection between an external file and a stream

easily reuse this program with different input and output files. All we would need to change is the two #define lines in the program, and the program would be ready to run with different files.

Immediately following the call to the open function is an if statement used to determine whether or not the requested open operation was successful. The success or failure of the open operation can be checked via a call to the function fail. It is a good idea always to test whether an open operation is successful and terminate execution of the program if the value returned by fail is nonzero (true). A return with the integer value EXIT_FAILURE may be used to report unsuccessful termination to the C++ system. A return with EXIT_SUCCESS may be used when a program terminates successfully. Note that the function main header line starts with int to reflect the fact that main returns an integer. ■

In addition to the open function, the program in Fig. 8.4 illustrates the use of the get, put, and eof functions plus two new functions in the C++ fstream.h library: fail and close. The new functions are explained in the Syntax Display appearing at the end of the previous section. The use of get and put is essentially the same as shown earlier, except that these versions are applied to external files rather than to the keyboard and display. Similarly, eof and fail apply to the external file ins rather than to a stream of characters entered at the keyboard.

Function copy_line

In the main function in Fig. 8.4, the loop that does the actual copying follows the open instructions. This loop calls the function copy_line to copy one line of information at a time from the input file to the output file and keep a count of the number of lines copied. Copying continues as long as the end of the input file has not been reached. Once the end of this file is encountered, loop execution terminates, a message indicating the number of lines just copied is displayed on the screen, and both files are closed.

Function copy_line copies a single line of the input file to the output file each time it is called. The while loop header in copy_line:

```
while ((next_ch != nwln) && !ins.eof ())
```

controls a loop that copies one character at a time as long as neither a newline character nor the end of the input file has been encountered. When either of these events occurs, the character copy loop terminates. In case this termination is caused by the occurrence of the newline character, this character is copied to the output file before copy_line returns to the calling program:

```
// If last character read was nwln write it to out_data.
if (!ins.eof ())
   outs.put (nwln);
```

The Error Stream `cerr`

In addition to the standard iostreams `cin` and `cout`, there is another standard stream, `cerr`, the *standard error stream,* which is also usually connected to your terminal or workstation. As shown in Fig. 8.4, this stream is used to provide an alert to an error or exception condition that might occur during the execution of a C++ program.

The standard error stream is used throughout this chapter to provide an alert related to stream input or output exceptions such as invalid data, premature end of file, or failure during an attempt to open a file. However, it can also be used to provide an alert for other exceptions such as divide by zero:

```
if (a == 0.0)
  cerr << "+++ Error: attempt to divide by zero.";
else
  x = discr/(2.0 * a);
```

Using `for` Loops in File Processing

In Chapter 5 (Section 5.6) we introduced a general form of the `for` loop construct

`for` (*initialization*; *test-expression*; *update*)

We indicated that there was considerable flexibility in the form of the three *loop parameters,* but we restricted our examples to counting loops with parameters such as

`i = 0; i < n; i++`

Figure 8.6 illustrates the use of the for loop in specifying program repetition controlled by file input actions, in this case using the functions `get` and `eof`. In this loop, the `for` loop parameters are as follows:

<table>
<tr><td>`ins.get (next_ch)`</td><td>Used as both the initialization and update</td></tr>
</table>

Figure 8.6   The `while` loop from copy_line written as a `for` loop

```
for (ins.get (next_ch);
     (next_ch != nwln) && !ins.eof ();
     ins.get (next_ch))
{
  outs.put (next_ch);
  char_count++;
}
```

```
(next.ch != nwln) && !ins.eof ()    Used as the loop repeti-
                                     tion test expression
```

The loop works in exactly the same way as the `while` loop shown in Fig. 8.4. The initialization step, `ins.get (next ch)`, is executed prior to the start of loop repetition. The loop repetition test is carried out at the top of the loop (just prior to the start of the next loop iteration), and the update step is performed at the end of each iteration of the loop.

This use of the `for` loop enables us to keep the initialization, test, and update steps together in a single place—the `for` loop header—and yet maintain the same functionality as provided by the `while` loop. Because the C++ `for` loop provides such flexibility and convenience, we can use it to specify a variety of program repetitions, not just for counter-controlled repetition.

More on the Newline Character

The processing of newline characters in `copy_line` should be clearly understood. Consider the input file shown next:

```
This is a text file!<nwln>It has two lines.<nwln><eof>
```

When the first `<nwln>` is read during the execution of the `while` loop, the input and output files (and their respective stream buffer pointers) would appear as follows:

```
This is a text file!<nwln>It has two lines.<nwln><eof>    (input file)
                     ↑
This is a text file!                                      (output file)
                    ↑
```

If the lines

```
// If last character read was nwln write it to out_data.
if (!ins.eof ())
{
    outs.put (nwln);
    char_count++;
}
```

were omitted from `copy_line`, the `<nwln>` character just read from the input file would not be written to the output file. As this continued throughout the program, the output file `out_data.dat` would contain all the characters in `in_data.dat`, but the line separators would have been lost:

```
This is a text file!It has two lines.
```

The call to function put following the `while` loop in function `copy_line` ensures that a newline character is written to the output file at the end of each complete line. Once the `<nwln>` has been copied to the output file, control is returned to the calling program. When `copy_line` is called the next time, the input and output files would appear as shown below:

```
This is a text file!<nwln>It has two lines.<nwln><eof>    (input file)
                     ↑
This is a text file!<nwln>                                 (output file)
                          ↑
```

The first call to function `get` (just prior to the `while` loop in `copy_line`) causes the next character (the `I` in `It`) to be read. This loop continues copying characters from input to output until the second newline is encountered. This newline then is copied to the output file, and control is returned to the calling function. What happens upon the next call to `copy_line` is left as an exercise at the end of this section (see Self-Check Exercise 1).

Note that reading from and writing to a file stream modifies the file position pointer associated with the stream. For this reason, we must pass all file stream arguments by reference. The streams are otherwise used just like `cin` and `cout`.

EXERCISES FOR SECTION 8.2

Self-Check
1. Consider the following input file (with the file position pointer shown below the information in the file):

   ```
   This is a text file!<nwln>It has two lines.<nwln><eof>
                                                  ↑
   ```

   Examine the file copy program shown in Fig. 8.4 and provide a complete, step-by-step description of the completion of the processing of this line.
2. What is the purpose of the open function?
3. What are some of the advantages to having external (permanent) storage files in which to store program input and output?

Programming
1. Rewrite the program shown in Fig. 8.3 (counting the number of blanks per line in a stream) to read from an external file named `my_txt.dat` (rather than from the keyboard).
2. Rewrite the copy program shown in Fig. 8.4 as a reusable function component with two arguments—specifically, the input and output file streams. The function should return an integer indicating the number of lines copied (0, if the input file is empty).

8.3 ____ USING EXTERNAL FILE FUNCTIONS: AN EXAMPLE

In this section, we provide an illustration of how one program can communicate with another using an intermediate disk file. If one program writes its output to a disk file rather than to the screen, a second program may use this output file as its own data input file. The program we will write illustrates the use of external file functions introduced in the previous section. The development of the program provides still further illustration of the design techniques we have stressed so far.

CASE STUDY: PREPARING A PAYROLL FILE

Problem Statement

You have been asked to write two programs for processing the company pay roll. The first program reads a data file consisting of employee salary data. The data for each employee is stored in a single *data record* containing the employee's first and last names, hours worked, and hourly rate, as shown next for a file consisting of three data records:

```
Jim Baxter      35.5   7.25<nwln>
Adrian Cybriwsky   40.0  6.50<nwln>
Ayisha Mertens    20.0  8.00<nwln><eof>
```

The first program you are asked to write is to read the input for each employee and compute the employee's gross salary as the product of the hours worked and the hourly pay rate. The program must then write the employee's name and gross salary to the output file and accumulate the gross salary amount in the total company payroll. When the processing of all employees has been completed, the total payroll amount should be displayed. The following sample output file corresponds to the previous input file:

```
Jim Baxter          $257.38<nwln>
Adrian Cybriwsky       $260.00<nwln>
Ayisha Mertens         $160.00<nwln><eof>
```

The second program reads the file created by the first program and prints payroll checks based on the contents of this file. For example, the first check issued should be a check for $257.38 made out to Jim Baxter.

Problem Analysis

We will write the first program now and present the second one as Programming Project 1 at the end of this chapter. As already explained, our program reads each employee record, computes the gross salary, and writes the employee's name and salary to the output file. Finally, the gross salary is added to the payroll total.

DATA REQUIREMENTS

Streams Used

eds (ifstream)   — employee data information
pds (ofstream)   — payroll data information

Problem Input (from stream eds)

for each employee:
    first name (string)
    last name (string)
    hours worked (float)
    hourly rate (money)

Problem Output (to stream pds)

for each employee:
    first name (string)
    last name (string)
    salary (money)

Problem Output (to stream cout)

total payroll (money)   — the company payroll total

Program Design

The main function prepares the streams and associated files for input and output. It then calls function process_emp to process the data for the company employees and determine the total company payroll amount. After process_emp is finished, the main function displays the final payroll total. Figure 8.7 shows the structure chart for this problem. The algorithm for the main function is shown next, followed by the interface description for the main program and process_emp.

ALGORITHM FOR FUNCTION main

1. Prepare streams and associated files for processing.
2. Process all employees and compute payroll total.
3. Display the payroll total.

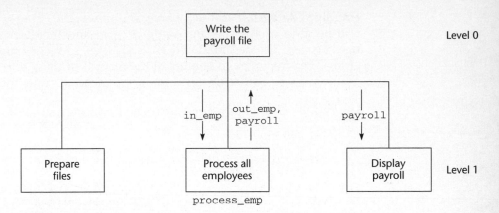

Figure 8.7   Top levels of structure chart for Payroll Problem

DATA REQUIREMENTS FOR process_emp

Input Arguments

eds (input stream)   — employee data stream
pds (output stream)   — payroll data stream

Output Arguments

(none)

Function Return Value

total_payroll (money)   — total company payroll

Function Prototype

```
// PROCESS ALL EMPLOYEES AND COMPUTE TOTAL PAYROLL AMOUNT
money process_emp
   (ifstream&            // IN: employee file stream
    ofstream&);          // IN: payroll file stream
```

Program Implementation

The C++ code for function main is shown in Fig. 8.8. Only the three streams cout, eds (employee data stream), and pds (payroll data stream) and the total payroll variable need to be visible in this function. The individual employee data (first and last name, hours worked, hourly rate, and salary) will be used exclusively in `process_emp` and therefore are not declared until needed. The designation of the data files is known only to the main program. The structure and content of the records of these files is known only to `process_emp`. The main function has no need to know this information.

Figure 8.8   Creating a payroll file (main function)

```
// FILE: Payroll.cpp
// CREATES A COMPANY EMPLOYEE PAYROLL FILE
//    COMPUTES TOTAL COMPANY PAYROLL AMOUNT

#include <fstream.h>              // required for file streams
#include <stdlib.h>              // for definition of EXIT_FAILURE
                                 //     & EXIT_SUCCESS
#include "money.h"               // process employee data

// ASSOCIATE PROGRAM IDENTIFIERS WITH EXTERNAL FILE NAMES
#define in_file "Emp_File.dat" // employee file
#define out_file "Salary.dat"  // payroll file

// Functions used ...
   // PROCESS ALL EMPLOYEES AND COMPUTE TOTAL
   money process_emp
     (ifstream&,               // IN: employee data stream
      ofstream&);              // IN: payroll data stream

int main()
{
   // Local data ...
   ifstream eds;               // input: employee data stream
   ofstream pds;               // output: payroll data stream
   money total_payroll;        // output: total payroll

   // Prepare files.
   eds.open (in_file);
   if (eds.fail ())
   {
      cerr << "*** ERROR: Cannot open " << in_file
           << " for input." << endl;
      return EXIT_FAILURE;      // failure return
   }
   pds.open (out_file);
   if (pds.fail ())
   {
      cerr << "***ERROR: Cannot open " << out_file
           << " for output." << endl;
      eds.close ();
      return EXIT_FAILURE;   // failure return
   }
```

(continued)

Figure 8.8   *(continued)*

```
        // Process all employees and compute total payroll.
        total_payroll = process_emp (eds, pds);

        // Display result.
        cout << "Total payroll is " << total_payroll << endl;

        // Close files.
        eds.close ();
        pds.close ();
        return EXIT_SUCCESS;       //_successful return
    }

    // Insert process_emp here.
```

――――――― Program Output ―――――――

```
Total payroll is $677.38
```

Design of process emp

The function process_emp performs the tasks required for building the output file and determining the total payroll amount. The structure chart outlining the required steps is shown in Fig. 8.9; the algorithm is shown next.

ALGORITHM FOR process_emp

1. Initialize payroll total to 0.0.
2. While there are more employees
    2.1. read employee's first and last names and salary data from eds.
    2.2. compute employee's net pay.
    2.3. write employee's first and last names and salary to pds; add it to payroll total.

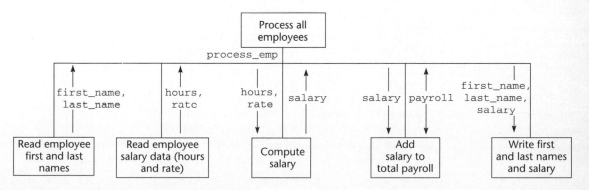

Figure 8.9   Structure chart for process_emp

Implementation for `process_emp`

Figure 8.10 shows function `process_emp`. We declare variables `first_name`, `hours`, `rate`, and `salary` to be local variables in `process_emp` because they are referenced only in this component and are not needed anywhere else. Note that the lines

```
eds >> first_name >> last_name >> hours >> rate;
```

and

```
pds << first_name << last_name << salary << endl;
```

are written in exactly the same form that we have been using since Chapter 2 for doing stream I/O with the streams `cout` and `cin`. We have simply changed the names of the streams involved (to `eds` and `pds`).

Figure 8.10 Implementation of `process_emp`

```cpp
// FILE: Payroll.cpp
// PROCESS ALL EMPLOYEES AND COMPUTE TOTAL PAYROLL AMOUNT

money process_emp
    (ifstream& eds,            // IN: employee file stream
     ofstream& pds)            // IN: payroll file stream

// Pre:  eds and pds are prepared for input/output.
// Post: Employee names and salaries are written from eds to pds
//       and the sum of their salaries is returned.
// Returns: Total company payroll
{
    string first_name;     // input: employee first name
    string last_name;      // input: employee last name
    float hours;           // input: hours worked
    money rate;            // input: hourly rate
    money salary;          // output: gross salary
    money payroll;         // return value - total company payroll

    payroll = 0.0;
    // Read first employee's data record.
    eds >> first_name >> last_name >> hours >> rate;
    while (!eds.eof ())
    {
        salary = hours * rate;
        pds << first_name << last_name << salary << endl;
        payroll += salary;
        // Read next employee's data record.
        eds >> first_name >> last_name >> hours >> rate;
    }   // end while

    return payroll;
}   // end process_emp
```

EXERCISES FOR SECTION 8.3

Self-Check   1. In the payroll program:
a. What would be the effect, if any, of trailing blanks at the end of an employee data record (see Fig. 8.10)?
b. What would be the effect, if any, of leading blanks in an employee record (see Fig. 8.10)?
c. What would be the effect of blank lines (empty data records, shown in Fig. 8.10)?
2. What would happen if we used a single string object, `name`, and attempted to read an employee data record such as

```
Karina Haavik    30.0    7.75<nwln>
```

into this object using the input statement

```
eds >> name >> hours >> rate;
```

Programming   1. Write a program that reads from file `SALARY.DAT` produced by the payroll program and displays a count of the number of employees processed by the payroll program and their average salary.
2. Modify the payroll program `process_emp` function to count the number of records processed and display this value before returning.

8.4 —— STRING INPUT/OUTPUT

Small changes in the specification of a problem can sometimes result in less than minor changes in the problem solution. However, even in these situations, appropriate modularization of a system can keep even significant complications localized, so that changes to the system can be limited to a small number of components, not affecting the other parts of a system.

Limitations of cin

In the case study in the previous section we assumed that the name stored in each employee data record consisted exactly of a first name and a last name. If we wished to provide greater flexibility in the appearance of the employee name, use of the input operator >> would be difficult and alternatives would have to be considered (see Self-Check Exercise 1 at the end of this section).

One possible alternative involves the use the `getline` function first introduced in Chapter 3 (Section 3.7) to read the entire name and store it in a string object. To do this correctly, however, requires that we separate the employee name from the rest of the data in the employee record (see Self-Check Exercise 2). We use the pound character, '#', to mark the end of each employee name and treat this character as the delimiter symbol (the third argument) in the `getline` function call. The pound character must be inserted in each employee record as shown here:

```
Jim Andrew Baxter#      35.5    7.25<nwln>
Adrian Cybriwsky#    40.0   6.50<nwln>
Ayisha W. Mertens#      20.0   8.00<nwln><eof>
```

We can use the statement

```
getline (eds, name, '#');
```

to read each person's name into `string` object `name` and

```
pds << name << salary << endl;
```

to write it to the output file. We describe the effect of the `<nwln>` character in the next section and in self-check exercise 1.

Advancing Past the Newline Character

Usually, the `getline` function is used to extract a sequence of characters up to and including a newline character. In such cases, it is important to remember that `getline` does not skip leading white space, so that if a newline character is encountered prematurely—for example, at the very beginning of the characters to be extracted—`getline` will stop immediately and not complete the expected task.

This situation can arise when the both the extraction operator and the `getline` function are used to extract data from the same input stream. To illustrate, let us return to the payroll problem. In this case, we assume that the data for each employee is entered on two lines, as shown next:

```
Jim Andrew Baxter<nwln>
     35.5    7.25<nwln>
Adrian Cybriwsky<nwln>
   40.0   6.50<nwln>
Ayisha W. Mertens<nwln>
     20.0   8.00<nwln><eof>
```

We then modify the `while` loop in Fig. 8.10 to read two lines for each employee:

```
payroll = 0.0;
// Get name of first employee.
getline (eds, name, '\n');
while (!eds.eof ())
{
```

```
        // Get current employee salary data.
        eds >> hours >> rate;
        salary = hours * rate;
        pds << name << salary << endl;
        payroll += salary;
        // Get name of next employee.
        getline (eds, name, '\n');
    }   // end while
```

Given our six-line data sample, the execution of the first line of code inside the loop

```
eds >> hours >> rate;
```

advances the input stream buffer pointer for stream eds to just beyond the last legal floating-point character in the hourly rate value:

```
35.5    7.25<nwln>
            ↑
```

If we leave the input stream buffer pointer here, the next call to getline (to extract the next employee's name) would cause the loop to exit immediately without reading the name; getline would process the <nwln> and return control to the main function.

At this point, the next character in the stream would be the first letter of an employee's name (the A in Adrian). However, the next input statement to be executed is

```
eds >> hours >> rate;
```

This statement expects numeric information consisting of perhaps a sign, decimal digits, and perhaps a decimal point. When a letter (part of an employee's name) or any other illegal floating-point character is encountered while reading a numeric value, the read terminates and control is returned to the calling function. If this illegal character is the first character in the number to be read, the returned result is unpredictable. If the nonnumeric character appears in the middle of the read operation, the value returned will be computed based only on the preceding numeric characters. Thus an attempt to read the characters 2Q8.5 into the floating-point variable hours would result in the return of the value 2.

One way to skip the newline character is to use the fstream function ignore:

```
eds.ignore (100, '\n');
```

In this example, the ignore function skips up to 100 characters in the specified stream (eds in this case) until the character argument '\n' is encountered. The character argument is also extracted and ignored.

EXERCISES FOR SECTION 8.4

Self-Check

1. If we use `getline (eds, name, '#')` in `process_emp` (Fig. 8.10) to read an employee's name:
   a. What would be the effect, if any, of trailing blanks and the <nwln> character at the end of an employee data record in the input stream?
   b. What would be the effect, if any, of leading blanks in an employee record in the input stream?

2. Describe what would happen during the execution of function `process_emp` (Fig. 8.11) had we neglected to insert the pound character '#' to mark the end of an employee name in the input stream.

3. Change `process_emp` (Fig 8.11) to write the name and salary for a given employee on separate lines. Explain the changes that have to be made.

4. Explain the differences between the input operator << and the `string` class function `getline`.

5. Describe as precisely as possible the effect of the statement

   `eds.ignore (INT_MAX, '\n');`

6. a. In `process_emp` modified as per exercise 1, what does `getline` do with the delimiter '#' that marks the end of each employee's name?
   b. In function `process_emp` (Fig. 8.10), the output (name and salary) for each employee was written on a single line with no pound character to mark the end of the name. Discuss the problems this would cause for the individual writing a program that has to read this file.

Programming

1. Write a function `skip_newline` that, regardless of the current position of a stream buffer pointer, will read one character at a time in the designated stream up to and including the next newline (if any), and then leave the pointer at the next character in the stream (following the newline). Function `skip_newline` should require only one input argument—specifically, the stream for which the skip operation is to be carried out.

2. Rewrite the `copy_line` program (Fig. 8.4) to use the function `getline` rather than function `copy_line` to copy one line of information in the file.

8.5 ———— STREAM I/O MANIPULATOR FUNCTIONS AND FLAGS

The Manipulators

In Chapter 5 (Section 5.3), we introduced four stream member functions (`setf`, `unsetf`, `precision`, and `width`) and showed how these functions could be used to control the format (overall width, number of decimal places, etc.) of data being inserted into an output stream. Then in Section 5.5, we showed how two of these functions could be referenced in a nontraditional way—by embedding the *i/o manipulators* setprecision and setw directly in an output statement (following the insertion operator <<). This use of manipulators provided some convenience in controlling the format of data being inserted to an output file. (Don't forget to include header file iomanip.h.)

In this section, we complete the discussion of i/o manipulators by introducing two other manipulators, setiosflags and unsetiosflags. These four functions and corresponding manipulators are summarized in Table 8.1. An additional manipulator, endl (not shown in the table) was introduced much earlier in the text. This manipulator is used to insert the newline character into an output stream. The four manipulators are defined in the library header iomanip.h.

The Format State Flags

The term *flag* is used to refer to something that can be turned on or off. In C++ programming, we use flags in a similar fashion, setting them on or off, or to 0 or 1 (or true or false), depending on the particular definition of the flag. The manipulators setiosflags and unsetiosflags (functions setf and unsetf) control the formatting of output by setting various *format state flags* associated with stream input and output. The flags are elements of an enumeration type defined for all iostreams. The notation ios::flag_name is used to reference these flags (ios is short for input output stream). Some of

Table 8.1 I/O Manipulators and Functions

MANIPULATOR/ FUNCTION NAME	ARGUMENT	EFFECT	FUNCTION EXAMPLE
setiosflags/ setf	list of flags to be set	Turns on the flag bits corresponding to those in the argument list.	cout.setf (ios::left, ios::adjustfield);
resetiosflags/ unsetf	list of flags to be unset	Turns off the flag bits corresponding to those in the argument list.	cout.unsetf (ios::show point);
setprecision/ precision	an integer	Sets the precision to the argument. The default is 6.	sts.precision (10);
setw/ width	an integer	Sets the width to the argument. Affects only the next output value, after which the width returns to the default of 0.	grs.width (6);

Table 8.2   Format State Flags

FLAG NAME	MEANING IF SET	DEFAULT VALUE
boolalpha	If on, true and false may be extracted from an input stream or inserted into an output stream as values of type bool variables. If off, 0 and 1 are used for stream extraction and insertion	Off
fixed	Use 123.45 floating notation (turns off scientific flag if on)	Off
left	Left-adjust output in field (turns off right-adjust flag if on)	Off
right	Right-adjust output in field (turns off left-adjust flag if on)	On
scientific	Use 1.2345E2 floating notation (turns off fixed flag if on)	Off
showpoint	Force decimal point and trailing zeros (floating output)	Off
skipws	Skip white space on input	On

the flags that must be directly manipulated by setiosflags (setf) are listed in Table 8.2.

Example 8.6   Let a = 55, n = −3074 (both integers), and x = 210.0, y = 16.876 (both floating point). The following illustrate the use of the functions and manipulators just discussed.

a. `cout.setf (ios::fixed, ios::showpoint);`
   `cout << setw (3) << a << setw (7) << x <<  setw (10)`
   `      << "Oops";`

   inserts the following string of characters into the output stream cout:
   ⎕55⎕⎕⎕210.⎕⎕⎕⎕⎕⎕Oops

   The string Oops is right adjusted as are the numeric values 55 and 210 (right justification is the default if not otherwise changed). Since the showpoint flag is turned on but no precision is specified, the floating-point value 210. is inserted into the output stream.

b. `cout << "Oops" << setw (5) << a << n;`

   produces the output
   Oops⎕⎕⎕55-3074

   The string Oops uses only as much space as required for output. Since the field width is reset to 0 after a is inserted into the output stream, a and n appear without separating spaces. The field width for n is expanded to accommodate the five characters to be inserted.

c. `cout.setf (ios::fixed, ios::showpoint);`
`cout << setw (8) << y << endl`
`        << setw (7) << setprecision (2) << y << endl`
`        << setw (4) << setprecision (3) << y << endl;`

produces the following three lines of output

`□□16.876<nwln>`
`□□16.88<nwln>`
`16.876<nwln>`

The second display of y is accurate to two decimal places as required. Insufficient space was allocated for the third display of y (at least six spaces were needed) so the field is automatically expanded to accommodate the number.

d. `cout << setw (5) << a << setw (8)`
`        << setioflags (ios::left) << "Oops";`

produces the following three lines of output

`□□□55Oops□□□□`

The string Oops is displayed left adjusted in a field of width 8 (with four *trailing blanks* used *to right fill* the field).

e. If we let first_name = Felix and last_name = Frankfurter, hours = 20.0 and rate = 7.25, then

`cout.setf (ios::fixed, ios::showpoint, ios::left);`
`cout.setprecision (2);`
`cout << setw (10) << first_name << setw (10) << last_name`
`        << setw (8) << setioflags (ios::right) << hours`
`        << setw (8) << rate;`

produces the following output

`Felix□□□□□Frankfurter□□□20.00□□□□□7.25`

The last name field is expanded to 11 columns to accommodate the 11 characters in the string. The strings are printed left adjusted; the numeric values are printed right adjusted. ∎

8.6 ⎯⎯⎯ COMMON PROGRAMMING ERRORS

■ *Connecting Streams and External Files:* To use an external file in your program, you first must declare a stream object and establish a connection between the name of the file as it is known to the operating system and the name of the stream object known to your program. In C++, this connection is established using the file open function, open. Once this connection has been established, you must use the stream name (for example, ins, outs) in all subsequent references to the file in your program. Normally, you will not receive a compiler or an execution-time diagnostic if a call to the open function fails to open a file successfully. For this reason, you are urged always to check to ensure that all files have been successfully opened (see, for example, the program shown in Fig. 8.4).

■ *Preparing Files for Input and Output:* The C++ cin and get can be used only after a file has been prepared for input. Similarly, cout and put can be used only after a file has been prepared for output. The omission of an open statement will not be detected by the compiler, and the failure of an open to execute properly may not be detected at run time. In either case, your program will simply not execute correctly. For example, if your program contains a while loop with an end-of-file termination condition, the loop could execute without termination as it repeatedly looks for a nonexistent end-of-file. No data will be read and no useful processing will take place, but the program will not terminate.

Always be careful to prefix each call to a file processing function with the correct stream name. For example, accidental use of an output stream name with a file input operation such as get will cause a compiler error message such as "Get is not a member of ofstream". This message indicates that the get function, which you have tried to use with an output file stream, can be used only with input file streams.

■ *Reading Past the End of a File:* An execution time error such as "attempt to read beyond end of file" will occur if a read operation is performed after all data in a file have been processed. The most likely cause for such an error is a loop that has executed once too often.

■ *Matching Data in an Input Stream to Input Data Stores:* When using the extraction operator, it is up to you to ensure that the order and type of the data stores (objects and variables) listed following each occurrence of the operator are consistent with the order and type of the data in the specified stream object (e.g., cin or eds). In general, no execution-time diagnostics will be issued as a direct result of data inconsistencies. Instead, incorrect and sometimes undefined information will be stored. It is imperative that you always check to ensure that the input to your programs is correct. Input failures will guarantee wrong answers; one of the first tasks you should perform in debugging and testing a program is to ensure that your test data are being read correctly.

Remember that any character (not just white space) detected during numeric input that is not a valid numeric character will terminate the reading of the current numeric input value and return the value read to that point (or an undefined value if no digits have been read).

■ *White Space and Input:* Always remember that, for all input involving the extraction operator, leading white space (blanks, tabs, newlines, for example) is ignored—even when reading a single character or character string! If your program requires that white space be considered as any other character, use the function get to read a single character at a time.

Trailing white space also terminates the extraction of characters for strings and for numeric data. You can read an entire string regardless of white space content by using the member functions get (to read one character at a time) or getline (to read an entire string). In either case, however, you must have some character (often the newline) to mark the end of the string to be extracted. Failure to provide the end marker can produce incorrect results that may be difficult to diagnose.

■ *Proper Handling of the Newline Character During Input:* In many situations, the newline character in an input stream has no effect on the input instructions you write in your program. However, when character or string input (using get or getline) is mixed with numeric input (using the extraction operator), considerable care is needed to ensure that the newline character is properly handled. There is one important case to keep in mind.

If the extraction of numeric data is followed by the extraction of character data using an algorithm dependent upon the newline for termination, any newline left in the input stream at the conclusion of numeric input must be skipped. This is the case in the payroll program example in which the getline function extracts an employee's name from the input stream (see Section 8.4). If the newline terminating the extraction of the hourly rate for one employee is not explicitly skipped, the extraction of the name of the next employee will not work properly.

■ *Input/Output Argument and Flag Settings:* Once set, most input/output settings and flags remain in effect until reset. Remember, however, that the field width setting always reverts back to your system default value (usually a 0 field width) if it is not set again prior to the input or output of the next data element. When this occurs, data elements may be inserted into an output stream with no separating blanks and will be hard to read.

CHAPTER REVIEW

In this chapter, we learned more about the input and output features supported by the C++ input/output libraries. We began with the use of functions get and put to extract characters from the keyboard and insert characters into the display. We briefly discussed the differences in the use of these functions and the iostream operators << and >>.

Considerable attention was devoted to the use of *external (permanent) data files*. Two new C++ data types, `ifstream` and `ofstream`, were introduced. A number of examples and one case study illustrated how to declare objects (streams) of these types and how to use the library functions associated with these objects.

1. The operating system keeps a *directory* of all external files associated with your computer. These files are known to the system by an *external file name*.
2. The C++ `iostream` library function `open` is used to *establish a connection* between the external file name and the name of the stream to be processed by your program.
3. The newline character breaks a stream into a sequence of lines. We showed how to test for the presence of a newline character in a file and how to skip past this character, leaving the *input stream buffer pointer* at the beginning of the next line.
4. Finally, we showed how to use the manipulator functions and manipulators introduced in Chapter 5, and we discussed a number of the format flags that can be set using the `setiosflags` manipulator or `setf` function.

New C++ Constructs   Stream manipulator functions and related flags are summarized in Tables 8.1 and 8.2. The other new C++ constructs introduced in this chapter are described in Table 8.3.

Table 8.3   Summary of New C++ Constructs

CONSTRUCT	EFFECT
Stream Declarations	
`ifstream ins;` `ofstream outs;`	Declares `ins` and `outs` as stream variables.
Open and Close Operations on Data File Streams	
`ins.open (in_data);`	Establishes the connection between the external file named `in_data` and the stream `ins`.
`ins.close ();`	Closes or disconnects stream `ins`.
Input and Output Operations for External Data File Streams	
`eds.get (ch);`	Gets the next character from the stream `eds`.
`eds >> i;`	The next integer is read from file `eds` as a string of characters then converted to an integer.
`pds.put (ch);` `pds << i;`	Puts the character in `ch` to the stream `grs`, followed by the integer value of `i` (output is a stream of characters).
`eds.ignore (INT_MAX, '\n');`	Causes the characters in the input stream `eds` up to and including the delimiter (`'\n'` in this case) to be extracted and skipped.

(continued)

Table 8.3 *(continued)*

CONSTRUCT	EFFECT

End-of-File Function
`ins.get (ch);`
`while (!ins.eof ())`
`{`
`    outs.put (ch);`
`    ins.get (ch);`
`}`
	A character is read from stream `ins` and written to the stream `outs` as long as there are more characters to be processed. (Can also be written as a `for` loop.)

✔ QUICK-CHECK EXERCISES

1. The _____ operation prepares a file for input or output by connecting the _____ name of the file to a _____ name.
2. The _____ character separates a stream into lines.
3. What data types can be read or written to a stream?
4. Where are external files stored?
5. Correct the C++ program segment shown below. Explain the changes you make.

    ```
    while (!ins.eof())
    {
        ins.get (...);
        outs.put (...);
    }
    ```

6. What does the symbol `endl` represent? What do we call this symbol in C++?

Answers to Quick-Check Exercises

1. open; external; stream
2. `<nwln>`
3. Any data type can be read or written to a stream.
4. External files are stored in secondary storage or on a disk.
5.
    ```
    ins.get (...);
    while (!ins.eof ())
    {
        outs.put (...);
        ins.get (...);
    }
    ```
    The original version will attempt to insert a character into the stream `outs` even after the end of file has been encountered (and there are no more characters to be processed).
6. `endl` represents the newline character; it is a manipulator.

REVIEW QUESTIONS

1. List three advantages to using files for input and output as opposed to the standard input and output you have used thus far in this course.
2. Explain how `get` and `cin` differ in reading data items from a stream.
3. a. Explain why there are usually two distinct names associated with a file.
   b. What conventions are followed for choosing each name?
   c. What does the name appearing in a program represent?
   d. Which name appears in the stream variable declaration?
   e. Which one of the names is known to the operating system?
4. Let x be type `float`, n and m type `int`, ch type `char`, and `str` of type `string`. Indicate the contents of each variable after each input operation is performed, assuming the file consists of the lines below. Discuss any errors that might arise and indicate what causes them.

   ```
   23 53.2 ABC<nwln>
   145 Z<nwln>
   ```

   a. `cin >> n >> x >> str;`
      `cin >> m;`
   b. `cin >> ch >> n >> x >> ch1 >> ch2 >> ch3;`
      `cin >> m >> ch5;`
   c. `cin >> n >> ch;`
5. Write a loop that reads up to 10 integer values from a data file and displays them on the screen. If there are not 10 integers in the file, the message `"That's all, folks"` should be displayed after the last number.
6. Write a function that copies several data lines typed at the keyboard to an external file. The copy process should be terminated when the user enters a null line (indicated by two consecutive newlines).
7. Explain how the following manipulators or manipulator flags are used in formatting output data. In each case, provide an example to illustrate what happens if the manipulator in question is not used or the flag is not set.
   a. the manipulator flag `left` when inserting a string of length six in a field of size 20;
   b. the manipulator flag `showpoint` when inserting a floating point value such as 65. 0 into an output stream;
   c. the manipulator `precision (3)` when inserting a floating point value such as 25.635248 into an output stream.
   d. the manipulator `width` when inserting an integer value such as 250 into a field of width 10 in an output stream.
   e. the manipulator flag `fixed` when inserting a floating point value such as 25000143.6352 into an output stream.

PROGRAMMING PROJECTS

1. Write a program system that prints payroll checks using the file produced by the payroll program described in Section 8.3. The format of the checks should be similar to the one shown in Fig. 8.11.

```
Temple University                    Check No. 12372
Philadelphia, PA                     Date: 03-17-97

Pay to the
Order of:  William Cosby             $  20000.00

                                     Jane Smith
```

Figure 8.11   **Format of check for Programming Project 1**

2. Each year the state legislature rates the productivity of the faculty of each of the state-supported colleges and universities. The rating is based on reports submitted by the faculty members indicating the average number of hours worked per week during the school year. Each faculty member is rated, and the university receives an overall rating.

The faculty productivity ratings are computed as follows:

a. Highly productive means over 55 hours per week reported.
b. Satisfactory means reported hours per week are between 35 and 55.
c. Overpaid means reported hours per week are less than 35.

Read the following data from a data file (assuming all names are padded with blanks to 10 characters):

Name	Hours
Herm	63
Flo	37
Jake	20
Maureen	55
Saul	72
Tony	40
Al	12

Your program should include functions corresponding to the function prototypes shown below as part of your solution.

```
// DISPLAYS TABLE HEADING
void print_header ();

// DISPLAYS PRODUCTIVITY RANKING GIVEN HOURS WORKED
void display_productivity
    (float);     // IN: hours worked per week

// READS AND DISPLAYS ONE FACULTY NAME FROM A DATA STREAM FILE
void process_name
    (ifstream&);       // IN: stream of names and hours worked

// READS DATA LINES FROM FILE FAC_HOURS AND DISPLAYS BODY OF
//    TABLE. RETURNS NUMBER OF FACULTY AND SUM OF HOURS WORKED.
void process_data
    (ifstream&, // IN: stream containing names and hours
     int&,      // INOUT: count of number of faculty
```

```
        float&);    // INOUT: sum of hours worked by faculty
    // Uses: process_name and display_productivity.
```

3. Write a program system that reads several lines of information from a data file and prints each word of the file on a separate line of an output file followed by the number of letters in that word. Also print a count of words in the file on the screen when done. Assume that words are separated by one or more blanks. Reuse as many functions introduced in the text or in the C++ library as possible.

4. Compute the monthly payment and the total payment for a bank loan, given the following:

   a. amount of loan
   b. duration of loan in months
   c. interest rate for loan

   Your program should read in one loan at a time, perform the required computation, and print the values of the monthly payment and the total payment.

   Test your program with at least the following data (and more if you want).

Loan	Months	Rate
16000	300	12.50
24000	360	10.50
30000	300	9.50
42000	360	9.50
22000	300	8.25
100000	360	9.125

   Hints:

   a. The formula for computing monthly payment is

   $$monthly\_pay = \frac{ratem \times expm^{months} \times loan}{expm^{months} - 1.0},$$

   where

   ```
        ratem = rate / 1200.0,
         expm = (1.0 + ratem).
   ```

   b. The formula for computing the total payment is

   ```
        total = monthly_pay × months.
   ```

   Use type `double` data for all calculations.

5. Use your solution to Programming Project 4 as the basis for writing a program that will write a data file containing a table of the following form:

   ```
   Loan Amount: $1000
   INTEREST        DURATION        MONTHLY         TOTAL
     RATE          (YEARS)         PAYMENT         PAYMENT
    10.00             20
    10.00             25
    10.00             30
    10.25             20
   ```

   The output file produced by your program should contain payment information on a $1000 loan for interest rates from 10 percent to 14 percent with increments of 0.25 percent. The loan durations should be 20, 25, and 30 years.

6. Whatsamata U. offers a service to its faculty in computing grades at the end of each semester. A program will process three weighted test scores and will calculate a student's average and letter grade (A is 90 to 100, a B is 80 to 89, etc.). Read the student data from a file and write each student's name, test score, average, and grade to an output file.

   Write a program system to provide this valuable service. The data will consist of the three test weights followed by three test scores and a student ID number (four digits) for each student. Calculate the weighted average for each student and the corresponding grade. This information should be printed along with the initial three test scores. The weighted average for each student is equal to

   weight1 × score1 + weight2 × score2 + weight3 × score3

   For summary statistics, print the "highest weighted average," "lowest weighted average," "average of the weighted averages," and "total number of students processed." Sample data:

   ```
   0.35   0.25   0.40      (test weights)
   100    76    88   1014  (test scores and ID)
   ```

7. Write a program to read in a string of characters that represent a Roman numeral and then convert it to Arabic form (an integer). The character values for Roman numerals are as follows:

M	1000
D	500
C	100
L	50
X	10
V	5
I	1

   Test your program with the following data: LXXXVII (87), CCXIX (219), MCCCLIV (1354), MMDCLXXIII (2673), MCDLXXVI (1476).

8. Because text files can grow very large, some computer systems supply a handy utility program that displays the head and tail of a file where the head is the first four lines, and the tail is the last four lines. Write a program that asks the user to type in a file name and then displays the head of the file, a line of dots (three or four dots will do), and the tail of the file. If the file is eight lines long or less, just display the entire file.

9. Write a program to manage a dictionary. Your dictionary should be stored on a text file named diction.txt and consist of an alphabetized list of words, one per line. When a user enters a word, scan the dictionary looking for the word. If the word is in the dictionary, say so. If not, display the dictionary word immediately preceding and the word immediately following so the user can see words that are close in spelling. Then ask whether the user wants to add this new word to the dictionary. If the answer is yes, do so and go back to request the next word.

   To insert a word into a file in alphabetical order, simply copy the file to a new, temporary file named diction.tmp and move words one at a time from this temporary file back to the original file, inserting the new word when you reach its correct position alphabetically.

9

Arrays and Structures

Simple data types, whether built-in (`int`, `float`, `bool`, `char`) or user defined (e.g., enumeration type `day`), use a single variable to store a value. To solve many programming problems, it is more efficient to group data items together in main memory than to allocate a different variable to hold each item. A program that processes exam scores for a class of 100 students, for example, would be easier to write if all the scores were stored in one area of memory and were able to be accessed as a group. C++ allows a programmer to group such related data items together into a single composite structured variable. Without such a structured variable, we would have to allocate 100 different variables to hold each individual score. In this chapter, we look at two structured data types: the array and the struct.

9.1 —— THE ARRAY DATA TYPE

An *array* is a collection of variables having the same data type—for example, all the exam scores (type `int`) for a class of students. By using an array, we can associate a single name such as `scores` with the entire collection of data. We can also reference each individual item (called an *element*) in the array. The naming process is like the one used to describe families and their members. The Clinton household refers to all three members of a family, and individual names—Bill Clinton, for example—designate individuals in the family. For an array, we designate individual elements by using the array name and the element's position, starting with 0 for the first array element. Thus, for example, the first element in the array named `scores` is referred to as `scores[0]`, the second element as `scores[1]`, and the tenth element (if it exists) as `scores[9]`. In general, the *k*th element in the array is referred to as `scores[k-1]`.

C++ stores an array in consecutive storage locations in main memory, one item per memory cell. We can perform some operations, such as passing the array as an argument to a function, on the whole array. We can also access individual array elements and process them like other simple variables.

Array Declaration

Arrays in C++ are specified using *array declarations* that specify the type, name, and size of the array:

```
float x[8];
```

C++ associates eight memory cells with the name x. Each element of array x may contain a single floating-point value. Therefore, a total of eight floating-point values may be stored and referenced using the array name x.

C++
SYNTAX

Array Declaration

Form: *element-type array-name* [*size*]

Example: `char my_name[5]`

Interpretation: The identifier *array-name* describes a collection of array elements, each of which may be used to store data values of type *element-type*. The *size*, enclosed in brackets, [ ], specifies the number of elements contained in the array. The *size* value must be a constant expression; that is, it must consist solely of constant values and constant identifiers. This value must be an integer and must be greater than or equal to 1. There is one array element for each value between 0 and the value *size* −1. All elements of an array must be the same type, *element-type*. ∎

Array Subscripts

To process the data stored in an array, we must be able to access its individual elements. We use the array name (a variable) and the array subscript (sometimes called an *index*) to do this. The *array subscript* is enclosed in brackets after the array name and selects a particular array element for processing. For example, if x is the array with eight elements declared earlier, then we may refer to the elements of array x as shown in Fig. 9.1. The *subscripted variable* x[0] (read as "x sub 0") references the first element of the array x, x[1] the second element, and x[7] the eighth element. The number enclosed in brackets is the array subscript.

Example 9.1 Assume x is the array shown in Fig. 9.1. Table 9.1 shows some statements that manipulate the elements of this array. Figure 9.2 shows the array after the statements in Table 9.1 execute. Note that only x[2] and x[3] are changed.

A subscript can be an expression of any integral type (int, long, short, char, or an enumeration type). In the next example, we use integer variables and expressions as subscripts.

x[0]	x[1]	x[2]	x[3]	x[4]	x[5]	x[6]	x[7]
16.0	12.0	6.0	8.0	2.5	12.0	14.0	−54.5

| First element | Second element | Third element | . . . | | | | Eighth element |

Figure 9.1 Array x

Table 9.1 Statements that Manipulate Elements of Array **x** in Fig. 9.1

STATEMENT	EXPLANATION
cout << x[0];	Displays the value of x[0], or 16.0.
x[3] = 25.0;	Stores the value 25.0 in x[3].
sum = x[0] + x[1];	Stores the sum of x[0] and x[1], or 28.0, in the variable sum.
sum += x[2];	Adds x[2] to sum. The new sum is 34.0.
x[3] += 1.0;	Adds 1.0 to x[3]. The new x[3] is 26.0.
x[2] = x[0] + x[1];	Stores the sum of x[0] and x[1] in x[2]. The new x[2] is 28.0.

x[0]	x[1]	x[2]	x[3]	x[4]	x[5]	x[6]	x[7]
16.0	12.0	28.0	26.0	2.5	12.0	14.0	−54.5

First element   Second element   Third element   . . .   Eighth element

Figure 9.2 Array **x** after execution of statements in Table 9.1 ∎

Example 9.2   Table 9.2 shows some simple statements involving the array x shown in Fig. 9.2. In these statements, i is assumed to be an integer variable with value 5. Make sure you understand the effect of each statement.

In Table 9.2 you can see two attempts to display element x[10], which is not in the array. These attempts will result in the display of an unpredictable value. C++ does not provide any run-time checking that an array reference does not exist. ∎

C++ SYNTAX

Array Reference

Form: *name*[*subscript*]

Example: x[3*i-2]

Interpretation: The *subscript* must be an expression with an integral value. If the expression value is not in range between 0 and one less than the array size (inclusive), a memory location outside the array will be referenced. If this reference occurs—for example, on the right side of an assignment statement—the accessed element value is unpredictable. If the reference occurs on the left side of an assignment, a memory location that is not part of the array may be modified unexpectedly or an error may result. ∎

Table 9.2 Some Simple Statements Referencing Array **x** in Fig. 9.2

STATEMENT	EFFECT
`cout << 3 << ' ' << x[3];`	Displays 3 and 26.0 (value of x[3]).
`cout << i << ' ' << x[i];`	Displays 5 and 12.0 (value of x[5]).
`cout << x[i] + 1;`	Displays 13.0 (value of 12.0 + 1).
`cout << x[i] + i;`	Displays 17.0 (value of 12.0 + 5).
`cout << x[i+1];`	Displays 14.0 (value of x[6]).
`cout << x[i+i];`	Value in x[10] is undefined.
`cout << x[2*i];`	Value in x[10] is undefined.
`cout << x[2*i-3];`	Displays −54.5 (value of x[7]).
`cout << x[floor(x[4])];`	Displays 28.0 (value of x[2]).
`x[i] = x[i+1];`	Assigns 14.0 (value of x[6]) to x[5].
`x[i-1] = x[i];`	Assigns 14.0 (new value of x[5]) to x[4].
`x[i] - 1 = x[i-1];`	Illegal assignment statement. Left side of an assignment operator must be an addressable expression.

The last `cout` line in Table 9.2 uses `floor(x[4])` as a subscript expression. Because this evaluates to 2, the value of `x[2]` is displayed. If the value of `floor(x[4])` were outside the range 0 through 7, an unpredictable value would be displayed.

Two different subscripts are used in each of the three assignment statements at the bottom of the table. The first assignment statement copies the value of `x[6]` to `x[5]` (subscripts `i+1` and `i`); the second assignment statement copies the value of `x[5]` to `x[4]` (subscripts `i-1` and `i`). The last assignment statement causes a syntax error because there is an expression to the left of the assignment operator.

Example 9.3 The declarations for a plant operations program shown below include two arrays, `vacation` and `plant_hours`.

```
// Local data ...
const int num_employees = 10; // number of employees

enum day {sunday, monday, tuesday, wednesday, thursday,
          friday, saturday, numdays};

bool vacation[num_employees];
float plant_hours[numdays];
```

vacation[0]	true
vacation[1]	false
vacation[2]	true
vacation[3]	false
vacation[4]	true
vacation[5]	false
vacation[6]	true
vacation[7]	false
vacation[8]	true
vacation[9]	false

Figure 9.3 Array `vacation`

The array `vacation` has 10 elements with subscripts 0 through `num_employees-1`. Each element of array `vacation` can store a type `bool` value. The contents of this array indicate which employees are on vacation (`vacation[i]` is `true` if employee `i` is on vacation). If employees 0, 2, 4, 6, and 8 are on vacation, the array will have the values shown in Fig. 9.3.

Because the enumerator `numdays` is associated with the integer 7, the array `plant_hours` has seven elements (subscripts `sunday` through `saturday`). The array element `plant_hours[sunday]` indicates how many hours the plant was operating during Sunday of the past week. The array shown in Fig. 9.4 indicates that the plant was closed on the weekend, operating single shifts on Monday and Thursday, double shifts on Tuesday and Friday, and a triple shift on Wednesday.

plant_hours[sunday]	0.0
plant_hours[monday]	8.0
plant_hours[tuesday]	16.0
plant_hours[wednesday]	24.0
plant_hours[thursday]	8.0
plant_hours[friday]	16.0
plant_hours[saturday]	0.0

Figure 9.4 Array `plant_hours`

Array Declaration and Initialization

The next example shows how to specify the initial contents of an array as part of its declaration.

Example 9.4 The statements below declare and initialize three arrays (see Fig. 9.5). The list of initial values for each array is enclosed in braces and follows the assignment operator =.

```
const int size = 7;
int scores[size] = {100, 73, 88, 84, 40, 97};
char grades[] = {'A', 'C', 'B', 'B', 'F', 'A'};
char my_name[size] = {'F', 'R', 'A', 'N', 'K'};
```

The length of the list of initial values must not exceed the size of the array as specified in the declaration. If it does exceed the array size, the compiler will generate an error message. If the size of the array is not specified, indicated by an empty pair of brackets [], the compiler sets the array size to match the number of elements in the initial value list. If the list contains fewer elements than the array size allows, then the value of the elements not explicitly initialized is system dependent (indicated by ? in Fig. 9.5).

Array scores (size 7)

100	73	88	84	40	97	?
[0]	[1]	[2]	[3]	[4]	[5]	[6]

Array grades (size 6)

'A'	'C'	'B'	'B'	'F'	'A'
[0]	[1]	[2]	[3]	[4]	[5]

Array my_name (size 7)

'F'	'R'	'A'	'N'	'K'	?	?
[0]	[1]	[2]	[3]	[4]	[5]	[6]

Figure 9.5 Initialization of three Arrays   ■

Example 9.5 So far we used arrays whose elements were predefined types. You can also allocate storage for arrays whose elements are system-defined or user-defined types. The array declaration:

```
string kid_names[] = {"Richard", "Debbie", "Robin", "Shelley",
                      "Dara"};
```

allocates storage for an array of five strings called kid_names, storing the string literals shown in the initialization list in this array. The statement

```
cout kid_names[0] << '/' << kid_names[4] << endl;
```

displays the output line

Richard/Dara   ∎

EXERCISES FOR SECTION 9.1

Self-Check
1. What is the difference between the expressions x3 and x[3]?
2. For the following declarations, how many memory cells are reserved for data and what type of data can be stored there?

   a. int scores[10];
   b. char grades[100];
   c. logical left_diag[8];

3. Write array declarations for each of the following:

   a. subscript type int, element type complex (assuming complex to be a user-defined type), size 100.
   b. subscript type day (enumeration type), element type float, size 7

4. Which of the following array declarations are legal? Defend your answer and describe the result of each legal declaration. Use enumeration type day as defined in Example 9.3.

   a. float payroll[fri];
   b. int workers[3] = {6, 8, 8, 0};
   c. char vowels[] = {'a', 'e', 'i', 'o', 'u'};
   d. int freq[12] = {0, 0, 3, 7, 10, 16, 28, 31,
                              30, 19, 13, 5, 2};
   e. day today[] = {mon, tue, wed, thu, fri};

Programming
1. Provide array type declarations for representing the following:

   a. a group of rooms (living room, dining room, kitchen, etc.) that have a given area
   b. elementary school grade levels (0 through 6, where 0 means kindergarten) with a given number of students per grade
   c. a group of colors with letter values assigned according to the first letter of their name (e.g., 'B' for blue)

9.2 ——— ACCESSING ARRAY ELEMENTS

Random Access

Arrays are *random-access data structures*, which means you can access the elements of an array in arbitrary (or random) order. For example the following fragment begins by reading an array subscript value into int variable sub. If sub is in the range 0 through 9, the statement

```
cin >> x[sub];
```

reads a data value into the array element x[sub]. This process continues until the user enters a value of sub that is outside the range 0 through 9.

```
float x[10];     // array of data
int sub;         // array subscript

// Enter data into elements of array x selected by the
// program user.
cout << "Enter the subscript of an array element: ";
cin >> sub;
while ((0 <= sub) && (sub < 10))
{
    cout << "Enter a number for storage in element "
         << sub << ": ";
    cin >> x[sub];
    cout << "Enter the subscript of an array element: ";
    cin >> sub;
}
```

In this fragment, the order in which the array elements receive their data values is random and is determined by the program user. For example, the following interaction

```
Enter the subscript of an array element: 9
Enter a number for storage in element 9: 5.5
Enter the subscript of an array element: 0
Enter a number for storage in element 0: -5.5
Enter the subscript of an array element: 10
```

stores 5.5 in the last array element and then -5.5 in the first array element. The elements in between receive no data.

Sequential Access

Many programs require processing all the elements of an array in sequential order, starting with the first element (subscript 0). To enter data into an array, print its contents, or perform other sequential processing tasks, use a for loop whose loop-control variable (i) is also the array subscript (x[i]). Increasing the value of the loop-control variable by 1 causes the next array element to be processed.

Example 9.6   The array cube declared below stores the cubes of the first 10 integers (for example, cube[1] is 1, cube[9] is 729).

```
int cube[10];    // array of cubes
int i;           // loop control variable
```

	[0]	[1]	[2]	[3]	[4]	[5]	[6]	[7]	[8]	[9]
	0	1	8	27	64	125	216	343	512	729

Figure 9.6 Array cube

The `for` statement

```
for (i = 0; i < 10; i++)
    cube[i] = i * i * i;
```

initializes this array as shown in Fig. 9.6.   ∎

Example 9.7 In Fig. 9.7, the statements

```
const int max_items = 8;
float x[max_items];                     //array of data
```

allocate storage for an array x with subscripts 0 through 7. The program uses three `for` loops to process the array. The loop-control variable i, with i in the range ($0 \leqslant i \leqslant 7$), is also the array subscript in each loop. The first `for` loop,

```
for (i = 0; i < max_items; i++)
    cin >> x[i];
```

reads one data value into each array element (the first item is stored in x[0], the second item in x[1], and so on). The `cin` line is repeated for each value of i from 0 to 7; each repetition causes a new data value to be read and stored in x[i]. The subscript i determines the array element to receive the next data value. The data shown in the first line of the sample execution of Fig. 9.7 cause the array to be initialized as illustrated in Fig. 9.1.

The second `for` loop

```
sum = 0.0;              // initialize sum
for (i = 0; i < max_items; i++)
    sum += x[i];        // add each element to sum
```

accumulates the sum of all eight elements of array x in the variable sum. Each time the `for` loop is repeated, the next element of array x is added to sum. Table 9.3 traces the execution of this program fragment for the first three loop repetitions.

Figure 9.7 Table of differences

```
// FILE: ShowDiff.cpp
// COMPUTES THE AVERAGE VALUE OF AN ARRAY OF DATA AND PRINTS
//    THE DIFFERENCE BETWEEN EACH VALUE AND THE AVERAGE
```

(continued)

Figure 9.7   *(continued)*

```
#include <iostream.h>
#include <iomanip.h>

void main()
{
   // Local data ...
   const int max_items = 8;

   float x[max_items];          // array of data
   int i;                       // loop control variable
   float average;               // average value of data
   float sum;                   // sum of the data

   // Enter the data.
   cout << "Enter " << max_items << " numbers: ";
   for (i = 0; i < max_items; i++)
      cin >> x[i];

   // Compute the average value.
   sum = 0.0;                   // initialize sum
   for (i = 0; i < max_items; i++)
      sum += x[i];              // add each element to sum
   average = sum / max_items;   // get average value

   // Set i/o flags and precision for output to ensure 1
   //    decimal place for output.
   cout.setf (ios::fixed);
   cout.precision (1);
   cout << "The average value is " << average << endl << endl;

   // Display the difference between each item and the average.
   cout << "Table of differences between x[i] and the average."
        << endl;
   cout << setw (4) << "i" << setw (8) << "x[i]"
        << setw (14) << "difference" << endl;
   for (i = 0; i < max_items; i++)
      cout << setw (4) << i << setw (8) << x[i]
           << setw (14) << x[i] - average << endl;
}
```

——————— Program Output ———————

Enter 8 numbers: **16.0   12.0   6.0   8.0   2.5   12.0   14.0   −54.5**
The average value is 2.0

Table of differences between x[i] and the average.
```
   i     x[i]      difference
   0     16.0          14.0
   1     12.0          10.0
   2      6.0           4.0
   3      8.0           6.0
   4      2.5           0.5
   5     12.0          10.0
   6     14.0          12.0
   7    -54.5         -56.5
```

Table 9.3   Partial Trace of Second `for` Loop in Fig. 9.6

STATEMENT PART	i	x[i]	sum	EFFECT
sum = 0.0;			0.0	Sets sum to zero
for (i = 0; i < max_items; i++)	0	16.0		Sets i to zero
sum += x[i];			16.0	Add x[0] to sum
increment and test i	1	12.0		1 < 8 is true
sum += x[i];			28.0	Add x[1] to sum
increment and test i	2	6.0		2 < 8 is true
sum += x[i];			34.0	Add x[2] to sum

The last `for` loop, displays a table showing each array element, `x[i]`, and the difference between that element and the average value, `x[i]` − `average`. ∎

As shown in the first `for` loop in Fig. 9.7, you must read data into an array one element at a time. In most instances, you will also want to display one array element at time, as shown in the last `for` loop in the figure.

EXERCISES FOR SECTION 9.2

Self-Check   1. If an array is declared to have 10 elements, must the program use all of them?
2. The sequence of statements below changes the initial contents of array x displayed by the program in Fig. 9.7. Describe what each statement does to the array and show the final contents of array x after all statements execute.

```
i = 3;
x[i] = x[i] + 10.0;
x[i-1] = x[2*i-1];
x[i+1] = x[2*i] + x[2*i+1];
for (i = 4; i < 7; i++)
    x[i] = x[i+1];
for (i = 2; i >= 0; i--)
    x[i+1] = x[i];
```

Programming   1. Write program statements that will do the following to array x shown in Fig. 9.1 (see also the program in Fig. 9.7):
a. Replace the third element (subscript 2) with 7.0.
b. Copy the element in the fifth location (subscript 4) into the first one.
c. Subtract the first element from the fourth and store the result in the fifth one.
d. Increase the sixth element by 2.
e. Find the sum of the first five elements.
f. Multiply each of the first six elements by 2 and place each product in the corresponding element of a new array named `answer_array` (of size `max_size`).
g. Display all even-numbered elements on one line.

9.3 ——— ARRAY ARGUMENTS

The C++ operators (for example, <, ==, >, +, -) can be used to manipulate only one array element at a time. Consequently, an array name in an expression will generally be followed by its subscript. One exception to this rule involves the use of arrays as function arguments. Not only can we pass individual array elements to a function (using a subscript to indicate which element to pass), but we can also pass an entire array. In fact, if several elements of an array are being manipulated by a function, it is generally better to pass the entire array of data instead of individual array elements. In the following examples, we illustrate both of these argument passing features. In the first example, we show how to pass individual elements of an array to a function; in the next two, we pass entire arrays to a function. You will see that we always pass arrays as reference arguments; we will explain why later.

Example 9.8   The function exchange shown in Fig. 9.8 may be used to switch the contents of its two floating-point arguments. The arguments a1 and a2 are used for both input and output and are therefore passed by reference.

This function may be used to exchange the contents of any two floating-point variables, such as x and y, with the statement

```
exchange (x, y);
```

When the function has completed the execution specified by the call, the original contents of the floating-point variables x and y will have been switched.

This function may also be used to exchange the contents of any pair of elements of a floating-point array. For example, the function call

```
exchange (s[3], s[5]);
```

Figure 9.8 Function to exchange the contents of two floating point memory locations

```
void exchange
   (float& a1, float& a2)
{
   // Local data ...
   float temp;

   temp = a1;
   a1 = a2;
   a2 = temp;
}  // end exchange
```

s[0]	s[1]	s[2]	s[3]	s[4]	s[5]	s[6]	s[7]
16.0	12.0	28.0	26.0	2.5	12.0	14.0	-54.5

s[0]	s[1]	s[2]	s[3]	s[4]	s[5]	s[6]	s[7]
16.0	12.0	28.0	12.0	2.5	26.0	14.0	-54.5

Figure 9.9 Array s before (top) and after (bottom) exchange of s[3] and s[5]

would cause an exchange of the elements of array s with subscripts 3 and 5, as shown in Fig. 9.9 (assuming, of course, that s has at least six elements).

C++ treats this call to exchange in the same way as the call involving x and y. In both cases, the contents of two floating-point memory locations (x and y in the first case, s[3] and s[5] in the second) are exchanged. The mechanics are the same, whether none, one, or both of the memory cells involved in the exchange are array elements. Of course, the subscripts in the specification of the array elements do not have to be constants, as shown in the following call to exchange, which exchanges two adjacent elements of the array s:

```
exchange (s[k], s[k+1]);
```

If k is equal to 0, this call to exchange would modify array s as shown in Fig. 9.10.

s[0]	s[1]	s[2]	s[3]	s[4]	s[5]	s[6]	s[7]
12.0	16.0	28.0	12.0	2.5	26.0	14.0	-54.5

Figure 9.10   Array s after exchange of s[k] and s[k+1], for k = 0   ■

The next two examples illustrate the use of arrays as function arguments. Because C++ cannot pass all the array element values from one function to another, we must pass arrays as reference arguments (call by reference). C++ passes the address of the first element of an array argument to the called function. This enables the function to access the first element and all elements that follow it in the array storage area. We use three floating-point arrays, x, y, and z, each of size 5, in both illustrations:

```
const int max_size = 5;            // size of arrays
float x[max_size];
float y[max_size],
float z[max_size];
```

Example 9.9   In this example, we illustrate how to write and call a function, add_array, that can be used to add together, element by element, the contents of any two floating-point arrays of the same single dimension and store the result in the corresponding element of a third floating-point array of the same size. If x, y, and z (declared previously) are three such arrays, then the call

```
add_array (max_size, x, y, z);
```

would cause the addition of corresponding elements in arrays x and y with the result stored in the corresponding element of array z. This problem description may be written more compactly as follows:

> For each value of i between 0 and max_size-1,
>   x[i] + y[i] is stored in z[i].

In fact, this statement of the problem provides the main idea in the implementation of the function shown in Fig. 9.11.

Figure 9.12 shows the argument correspondence for arrays established by the function call

```
add_array (max_size, x, y, z);
```

Because C++ always passes arrays by reference, arrays a, b, and c in the function add_array data area are represented by the addresses of the actual arrays x, y, and z used in the call. Thus the values of the elements of x and y used in the addition are taken directly from the arrays x and y in the calling function, and the function results are stored directly in array z in the calling function. After execution of the function, z[0] will contain the sum of x[0]

Figure 9.11   Function add_array

```
// FILE: AddArr.cpp
// STORES THE SUM OF a[i] AND b[i] IN c[i]

void add_array
   (const int size,            // IN: the size of the three arrays
    const float a[],           // IN: the first array
    const float b[],           // IN: the second array
    float c[])                 // OUT: result array

// Array elements with subscripts ranging from 0 to size-1
//     are summed element by element.
// Pre:  a[i] and b[i] are defined (0 <= i <= size-1
// Post: c[i] = a[i] + b[i] (0 <= i <= size-1)
{
    // Add corresponding elements of a and b and store in c.
    for (int i = 0; i < size; i++)
       c[i] = a[i] + b[i];
}   // end add_array
```

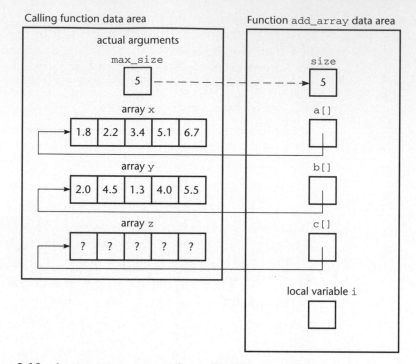

**Figure 9.12   Argument correspondence for function call `add_array`
(max_size, x, y, z);**

and y[0], or 3.8; z[1] will contain 6.7; and so on. Arrays x and y will be unchanged. In fact, the use of the reserved word `const` in front of the formal arguments a and b ensures that the contents of the corresponding actual arguments (x and y) cannot be changed by the function. We use `const` in the declaration of formal argument `size` for the same reason. ■

These and other points about transmitting entire arrays as arguments in function calls are summarized in the following box.

Arrays as Function Arguments

In C++, arrays are passed by reference. Thus a formal array argument in a function (such as c[] in Fig. 9.11) represents the address of the first element of the actual array argument (z in Example 9.9).

Corresponding to each formal array argument, a local memory location is set up in the data area for the called function. When the function is called, the address of the first element of the corresponding actual array argument is placed in this location. All references to the formal array argument are, therefore, actually references to the corresponding actual array argument in the calling program.

When passing arrays as function arguments, it is important to remember the following:

1. A formal array argument in a function is not itself an array but rather is a name that represents an actual array argument. Therefore, in the function definition or its prototype, we need only inform the compiler (using the empty brackets [ ]) that the actual argument will be an array.
2. Formal array arguments that are not to be altered by a function should be specified using the reserved word const as illustrated in the function add_array for formal arguments a and b. When this specification is used, any attempt by the function to alter the contents of the designated array will cause the compiler to generate an error message.

Example 9.10   Function same_array in Fig. 9.13 determines whether two arrays are identical. We consider two arrays to be identical if the first element of one is the same as the first element of the other, the second element of one is the same as the second element of the other, and so forth.

We can determine that the arrays are not identical by finding a single pair of unequal elements. Consequently, the while loop may be executed anywhere from one time (first elements unequal) to max_size - 1 times. Loop exit occurs when a pair of unequal elements is found or just before the last pair is tested.

After loop exit, the statement

```
return (a[i] == b[i]); // define result
```

defines the function result. If loop exit occurs because the pair of elements with subscript i is not equal, the function result is false. If loop exit occurs because the last pair of elements is reached (i equal to max_size), the function result will be true if the elements at i are equal and false if they are not.

As an example of how you might use function same_array, the if statement

```
if (same_array (x, y, max_size))
    cout << "The arrays x and y are equal. No addition" << endl;
else
    add_array (max_size, x, y, z);
```

either displays a message (when x and y are identical) or stores the sum of arrays x and y in array z (when x and y are not identical).

Figure 9.13   Function same_array

```
// FILE: SameArra.cpp
// COMPARES TWO FLOAT ARRAYS FOR EQUALITY BY COMPARING
//     CORRESPONDING ELEMENTS
```

(continued)

Figure 9.13   *(continued)*

```
bool same_array
    (const float a[],            // IN: float arrays to be compared
     const float b[],
     const int size)             // IN: size of the arrays

// Pre:  a[i] and b[i] (0 <= i <= size-1) are assigned
//       values.
// Post: Returns true if a[i] == b[i] for all i in range
//       0 through size - 1; otherwise, returns false.
{
    // Local data ...
    int i;                       // loop control variable and array subscript

    i = 0;
    while ((i < size-1) && (a[i] == b[i]))
        i++;
    return (a[i] == b[i]);       // define result
}   // end same_array
```

EXERCISES FOR SECTION 9.3

Self-Check

1. Give another example (other than those already in the text) of a function to which it is better to pass an entire array of data rather than individual elements.
2. In function `same_array`, what will be the value of `i` when the statement

   ```
   return (a[i] == b[i]);
   ```

   executes if array a is equal to array b? If the third elements do not match?
3. Rewrite the `exchange` and `same_array` functions to work with character operands rather than floating-point operands.
4. Describe how to modify function `add_array` to obtain a new function, `mult_array`, that does a pair-wise, element-by-element multiplication of two floating-point vectors of the same size.

Programming

1. Write a function that assigns a value of 1 to element `i` of the output array if element `i` of one input array has the same value as element `i` of the other input array; otherwise, assign a value of 0.
2. Write a function `scalar_mult_array` that multiplies an entire floating-point array x (consisting of *n* elements) by a single floating-point scalar c, assigning the result to the floating-point array y.

9.4 ——— READING PART OF AN ARRAY

Usually it is not known prior to program execution exactly how many elements will be stored in an array. As an example, let's say you are helping a professor process exam scores. There may be 150 students in one section, 200 in the next, and so on. Because you must declare the array size before program execution begins (at *compile time*), you must allocate enough storage space so that the program can process the largest expected array without error.

When you read the array data into memory, you should begin filling the array starting with the first element (at subscript 0) and be sure to keep track of how many data items are actually stored in the array. The part of the array that contains data is called the *filled subarray*. The *length* of the filled subarray is the number of data items that are actually stored in the array.

Example 9.11   Function read_scores in Fig. 9.14 reads and stores in its array argument scores up to max_size exam scores, where max_size is an input argument that represents the size of the actual array corresponding to scores. The output argument section_size represents the length of the filled subarray and is initialized to zero. Within the loop, the statements

```
scores[section_size] = temp_score;   // save score just read
section_size++;
```

store the score just read (value of temp_score) in the next array element and increment section_size. After loop exit, the value of section_size is the length of the filled subarray array. The if statement displays a warning message when the array is filled (when section_size equals max_size).

Figure 9.14   Function read_scores

```
// FILE: ReadScor.cpp
// READS AN ARRAY OF EXAM SCORES FOR A LECTURE SECTION
//    OF UP TO max_size STUDENTS.

#include <iostream.h>

void read_scores
   (int scores[],            // OUT: array to contain all scores read
    const int max_size,      // IN: max size of array scores
    int& section_size)       // OUT: number of elements read

// Pre:  None
// Post: The data values are stored in array scores.
//       The number of values read is stored in section_size.
//       (0 <= section_size < max_size).
{
   // Local data ...
   const int sentinel = -1;    // sentinel value
   int temp_score;             // temporary storage for each score
                               //   read

   // Read each array element until done.
   cout << "Enter next score after the prompt or enter "
        << sentinel << " to stop." << endl;
   section_size = 0;           // initial class size
```

(continued)

Figure 9.14   *(continued)*

```
    cout << "Score: ";
    cin >> temp_score;
    while ((temp_score != sentinel) && (section_size < max_size))
    {
        scores[section_size] = temp_score;  // save score just read
        section_size++;
        cout << "Score: ";
        cin >> temp_score;
    }  // end while

    // Sentinel was read or array is filled.
    if (section_size == max_size)
        cerr << "Warning: array filled, extra data ignored if any.";
}  // end read_scores
```

Function read_scores is general enough to be reused for reading any collection of integer values into an integer array. For example, the following fragment could be used to read a collection of exam scores into the integer array my_class_scores and to compute the sum and average of these scores. Assume my_class_size is the number of scores processed and max_size is the declared size of array my_class_scores.

```
read_scores (my_class_scores, max_size, my_class_size);
sum = 0;
for (int i = 0; i < my_class_size; i++)
    sum += my_class_scores[i];
average = float (sum) / float (my_class_size);
```

As shown above, use the variable my_class_size to limit the number of array elements processed. Because only the subarray of my_class_scores with subscripts 0 through my_class_size-1 contains meaningful data, array elements with subscripts larger than my_class_size-1 should not be processed.   ∎

EXERCISES FOR SECTION 9.4

Self-Check   1. Describe the changes necessary to use function read_scores for reading floating-point data.
2. Rewrite the while loop in read_scores as a do-while loop.
3. In function read_scores, what prevents the user from entering more than max_size scores?

9.5 ____ SEARCHING AND SORTING ARRAYS

This section discusses two common problems in processing arrays: *searching* an array to determine the location of a particular value and *sorting* an array to rearrange the elements in an ordered fashion. As an example of an array search, we might want to search the array to determine which student, if any, got a particular score. An example of an array sort would be rearranging the array elements so that they are in increasing order by score. This would be helpful if we wanted to display the list in order by score or if we needed to locate several different scores in the array.

Finding the Smallest Value in an Array

We begin by solving a different kind of search problem: finding the smallest value in a subarray.

1. Assume that the first element is the smallest so far and save its subscript as "the subscript of the smallest element found so far."
2. For each array element after the first one
    2.1. If the current element < the smallest so far
        2.1.1. Save the subscript of the current element as "the subscript of the smallest element found so far."

Function find_index_of_min in Fig. 9.15 implements this algorithm for any subarray of floating-point elements. During each iteration of the loop, min_index is the subscript of the smallest element so far and x[min_index] is its value. The function returns the last value assigned to min_index, which is the subscript of the smallest value in the subarray. Arguments start_index and end_index define the boundaries of the subarray, x[start_index] through x[end_index], whose smallest value is being found. Passing these subscripts as arguments results in a more general function. To find the minimum element in the entire array, pass 0 to start_index and the array size - 1 to end_index.

Note that function find_index_of_min returns the subscript (or index) of the smallest value, not the smallest value itself. Assuming small_sub is type int, and y_length is the number of array elements containing data, the following statements display the smallest value in array y.

```
small_sub = find_index_of_min (y, 0, y_length -1);
if (small_sub != -1)
    cout << "Value of smallest element in array y is "
         << y[small_sub] << endl;
else
    cerr << "Error - invalid array range" << endl;
```

Figure 9.15   Function `find_index_of_min`

```
// FILE: FloatMin.cpp
// FIND THE INDEX OF THE SMALLEST VALUE IN A FLOATING-POINT
// SUBARRAY CONSISTING OF ELEMENTS x[start_index] THROUGH
// x[end_index]
int find_index_of_min
    (const float x[],          // IN: array of elements
     int start_index,          // IN: subscript of first element
     int end_index)            // IN: subscript of last element

// Returns the subscript of the smallest element in the subarray.
// Returns -1 if the subarray bounds are invalid.
// Pre:  The subarray is defined and 0 <= start_index <= end_index.
// Post: x[min_index] is the smallest value in the array.
{
    // Local data ...
    int min_index;           // index of the smallest element found
    int i;                   // index of the current element

    // Validate subarray bounds
    if ((start_index < 0) || (start_index > end_index))
    {
        cerr << "Error in subarray bounds" << endl;
        return -1;                          // return error indicator
    }

    // Assume the first element of subarray is smallest and check
    //    the rest.
    // min_index will contain subscript of smallest examined so far.
    min_index = start_index;
    for (i = start_index + 1; i <-end_index; i++)
        if (x[i] < x[min_index])
            min_index = i;

    // All elements are examined and min_index is
    //    the index of the smallest element.
    return min_index;              // return result for valid subarray
} // end find_index_of_min
```

Strings and Arrays of Characters

A `string` object uses an array whose elements are type `char` to store a character string. That is why the position of the first character of a string object is 0, not 1. We can use the string search function `find` (see Table 3.3) to locate the first occurrence of a substring or of an individual character in a string object. For example, given the declarations:

```
const string alphabet = "abcdefghijklmnopqrstuvwxyz";
char ch;
int pos;
```

we can use the following statement to find the position in the alphabet of the character stored in ch:

```
pos = alphabet.find (ch);
```

If ch is a lowercase letter, function find returns a value between 0 and 25; otherwise, it returns a value ≥ 26. If we were attempting to form a *cryptogram*, or coded message, we could use the statement

```
if ((pos >= 0) && (pos < 26))
    ch = code_string.at (pos);
```

to replace the character in ch with its corresponding code symbol (the character in position pos of the 26-character string in code_string).

Array Search

We can write a function like find to search an array. We discuss how to do this next.

We can search an array for a particular element by comparing each array element, starting with the first (subscript 0), to the target, the value we are seeking. If a match occurs, we have found the target in the array and can return its subscript as a search result. Otherwise, we continue searching until we either get a match or test all array elements without success.

DATA REQUIREMENTS FOR A SEARCH FUNCTION

Input Arguments

items (int[])	— array to be searched
size (int)	— number of items to be examined
target (int)	— item to be found

Output Arguments

(none)

Returns

Subscript of the first element of the array containing the target (-1 is returned if no element contains the target)

Local Variables

next (int)   — subscript of the next item to be tested
not_found (bool)   — flag initialized to true (target has not been
                        found); may be reset to false (if target is
                        found)

We use a linear search algorithm to search the input array for the target value.

1. Start with the first array element.
2. Set not_found to true (assume the target has not yet been found).
3. While target is not found and there are more elements
    3.1. If the current element matches the target
        3.1.1. Set not_found to false (will cause the loop to exit at the
        next iteration attempt).
    else
        3.1.2. Try the next element.
4. If the target was not found
    4.1. Return −1.
    else
    4.2. Return the target's subscript.

The while loop in step 3 executes until it finds an array element that contains the target or it has tested all array elements without success. Step 3.1 compares the current array element (selected by the subscript next) to the target and sets not_found to false if they match. If they do not match, the subscript next is increased by 1. After loop exit, the if statement defines the function result as −1 (target was not found) or as the value of next when the match occurred. Figure 9.16 shows the search function.

The program status flag not_found controls loop repetition and communicates the results of the search loop to the if statement that follows the loop. not_found is set to true before entering the search loop and reset to false as soon as a tested element matches the target. The only way not_found can remain true throughout the entire search is if no array element matches the target.

Note that the following statement (called a *loop invariant*) must remain true each time through the while loop:

```
// Invariant: Target was not found in subarray a[0] through
//    a[next-1] and next is less than or equal to size.
```

This means that the target has not yet been found in any of the elements a[0] through a[next - 1] and that next is less than or equal to size. Because next < size also must be true, items[size-1] is the last array element that can be compared to the target.

Figure 9.16   The function `lin_search`

```cpp
// FILE: LnSearch.cpp
// SEARCHES AN INTEGER ARRAY FOR A GIVEN ELEMENT (THE TARGET)

int lin_search
  (const int items[],        // IN: the array being searched
   int target,               // IN: the target being sought
   int size)                 // IN: the size of the array

// Array elements ranging from 0 to size - 1 are searched for
//    an element equal to target.
// Pre:  The target and array are defined.
// Post: Returns the subscript of target if found;
//       otherwise, returns -1.
{

   // Local data ...
   int next;                 // index of the current score
   bool not_found;           // program flag — true if target
                             // not found in elements so far

   next = 0;
   not_found = true;
   while (not_found && (next < size))
   // Invariant: Target was not found in subarray a[0] through
   //    a[next-1] and next is less than or equal to size.
      if (items[next] == target)
         not_found = false;
      else
         next++;

   // Target was found or all elements were tested
   //    without success.
   if (not_found)
      return -1;
   else
      return next;
}   // end lin_search
```

In the sketch of the array `items` shown in Fig. 9.17, the shaded elements are the ones that have already been tested, and the element with the subscript `next` will be tested in the current loop iteration. If `items[next]` does not match the target, the shaded portion of the array will grow by one element and the value of `next` will increase by 1. The invariant is true before the first iteration (`next` is 0) because there are no array elements that precede the element with subscript 0. If the current element matches the target, loop exit will occur without changing `next`, so the invariant will still be true. If `next` becomes `size`, all array elements will have been tested without success and loop exit will occur.

Figure 9.17   Array items

Sorting an Array in Ascending Order

Many programs execute more efficiently if the data they process are sorted before processing begins. For example, a check-processing program executes more quickly if all checks are in order by checking account number. Other programs produce more understandable output if the information is sorted before it is displayed. For example, your university might want your instructor's grade report sorted by student ID number. In this section, we describe one simple sorting algorithm from among the many that have been studied by computer scientists.

Example 9.12   The *selection sort* is a fairly intuitive (but not very efficient) sorting algorithm. To perform a selection sort of an array of n elements (subscripts 0 through $n - 1$), we locate the smallest element in the array and then switch the smallest element with the element at subscript 0, thereby placing the smallest element at location 0. We then locate the smallest element remaining in the subarray with subscripts 1 through $n - 1$ and switch it with the element at subscript 1, thereby placing the second smallest element at location 1. We then locate the smallest element in the subarray with subscripts 2 through $n - 1$ and switch it with the element at subscript 2, and so on.

DATA REQUIREMENTS FOR A SORT FUNCTION

Input Arguments

items (int [])   — array to be sorted
n (int)   — number of items to be sorted

Output Arguments

items (int [])   — original array sorted in ascending order

Local Variables

i (int)   — subscript of first element in each subarray
min_sub (int)   — subscript of each smallest item located by
                          find_index_of_min

ALGORITHM

1. Beginning with the first item in the array (subscript 0) and repeating in steps of 1 through to the next-to-last item:
    1.1. Set i equal to the subscript of the first item in the subarray to be processed in the next steps.
    1.2. Find the subscript (min_sub) of the smallest item in the subarray with subscripts ranging from i through n-1;
    1.3. Exchange the smallest item found in step 1.2 with item i (exchange items[min_sub] with items[i]).

Figure 9.18 traces the operation of the selection sort algorithm on an array with four elements. The first array shown is the original array. Then we show each step as the next smallest element is moved to its correct position. The shaded portion of each array represents the subarray that is sorted. Note that, at most, n-1 exchanges will be required to sort an array with n elements.

We can use function find_index_of_min (see again Fig. 9.15) to perform step 1.2. Function sel_sort in Fig. 9.19 implements the selection sort algorithm. Local variable min_sub holds the index of the smallest value found so far in the current subarray. At the end of each pass, we call function

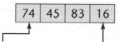

i is 0. Find the smallest element in subarray items[0] through items[3] and swap it with items[0].

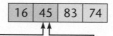

i is 1. Find the smallest element in subarray items[1] through items[3] — no swap needed.

i is 2. Find the smallest element in subarray items[2] through items[3] and swap it with items[2].

Figure 9.18 Trace of selection sort

Figure 9.19   Function `sel_sort`

```
// FILE: SelSort.cpp
// SORTS AN ARRAY (ASCENDING ORDER) USING SELECTION SORT ALGORITHM
//     USES exchange AND find_index_of_min

   // Functions used ...
   // FINDS THE SUBSCRIPT OF THE SMALLEST VALUE IN A SUBARRAY
   int find_index_of_min
      (const int [],  // IN: the array of elements
       int,           // IN: index of first subarray element
       int);          // IN: index of last subarray element

   // EXCHANGES TWO INTEGER VALUES
   void exchange
      (int&,          // INOUT: first item
       int&);         // INOUT: second item

void sel_sort
   (int items[],      // INOUT: array to be sorted
    int n)            // IN: number of items to be sorted (n >= 0)

// Sorts the data in array items (items[0] through items[n-1]).
// Pre:  items is defined and n <= declared size of actual argument
//       array.
// Post: The values in items[0] through items[n-1] are in
//       increasing order.
{
   // Local data ...
   int min_sub;   // subscript of each smallest item located by
                  // find_index_of_min

   for (int i = 0; i < n-1; i++)
   {
      // Invariant: The elements in items[0] through items[i-1] are
      //    in their proper_place and i < n.
      // Find index of smallest element in unsorted section of
      //    items.
      min_sub = find_index_of_min (items, i, n-1);

      // Exchange items at position min_sub and i if different
      if (i != min_sub)
         exchange (items[min_sub], items[i]);
   }  // end for

}  // end sel_sort
```

exchange (see again Fig. 9.8) to exchange the elements with subscripts `min_sub` and i when `min_sub` and i are different. After execution of function `sel_sort`, the array element values will be in increasing order. We must modify function exchange to accept type int arguments.

[0] [1] [2]	. . .	[i-1]	[i]	. . .	[n-1]
elements in their proper place			elements larger than items [i-1]		

Figure 9.20 Array `items`

In the function in Fig. 9.19, the loop invariant

```
// Invariant: The elements in items[0] through items [i-1] are
//    in their proper_place and i < n.
```

summarizes the progress of the selection sort. The subarray whose elements are in their proper place is shown in the shaded part of the array in Fig. 9.20. The remaining elements may not be in place yet and are all larger than `items[i-1]`. During each *pass* of the `for` loop, the shaded portion of the array grows by one element and `i` is incremented to reflect this. When `i` is equal to `n-1`, the first `n-1` elements will be in their proper place, so `items[n-1]` must also be in its proper place. ∎

The selection sort is a good illustration of the importance of component reuse in problem-solving and program engineering. Our goal is always to decompose a complicated problem into simpler subproblems so that as many of these subproblems as possible are solvable using existing and tested components. Occasionally, perhaps, some minimal modification to these components may be needed to tailor them to the current problem. But this is preferable to designing, implementing, and testing a new function from scratch.

EXERCISES FOR SECTION 9.5

Self-Check

1. For the linear search function in Fig. 9.16, what happens if
   a. the last element of the array matches the target?
   b. several elements of the array match the target?
2. Trace the execution of the selection sort on the following list:

   10   55   34   56   76   5

   Show the array after each exchange occurs. How many comparisons are required?
3. How could you modify the selection sort algorithm to arrange the data items in the array in descending order (smallest first)?
4. Modify the `exchange` function (Fig. 9.8) to work for integer data.

Programming

1. Write a function to count the number of items in an integer array having a value greater than 0.
2. Another method of performing the selection sort is to place the largest value in position `n-1`, the next largest in `n-2`, and so on. Write this version.

3. A technique for implementing an array search without introducing a status flag is to use a `while` loop that increments `next` as long as both of the following statements are true:

   ■ The target does not match the current element.
   ■ `next` is less than `size-1`.

   After loop exit, the element at position `next` can be tested again to determine the function result. If the element matches the target, the result is `next`; otherwise, the result is −1. Rewrite the function body for the linear search to reflect this algorithm change.

9.6 _____ THE STRUCT DATA TYPE

Although arrays are useful as data structures for storing related data, they are limited because all the data in an array must be the same type. Many programming problems can be easily solved if we are able to organize related data having different data types. With the *struct* data type, we can store related data of different types in a single data structure. In this section, we show how to declare and process structs.

The individual components of a struct are called *members*. Each member of a struct can contain data of a different type from the other members. For example, we can use a `struct` to store a variety of information about a person, such as name, marital status, age, and date of birth. We reference each of these data items through its *member name*.

Declaring a struct Type and struct Variables

Example 9.13   The manager of a software firm has asked you to keep organized, accessible information about her staff. As part of her plan, she would like certain information about each employee. An example might look like this:

ID: 1234
Name: Noel Goddard
Gender: Female
Number of dependents: 0
Hourly rate: 6.00
Total wages: 240.00

This information can be stored in a struct with six data elements. The struct type declaration describes the format of each struct including the name and type of each data element, or *struct member*. To store the preceding information, you can use the struct type `employee` shown next with

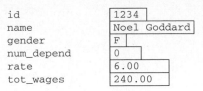

Figure 9.21   The struct variable `organist`

two integer fields, a string field, a character field (for gender), and two `float` fields:

```
struct employee
{
    int id;
    string name;
    char gender;
    int num_depend;
    float rate;
    float tot_wages;
};
```

This sequence of C++ statements defines a new data type named `employee`, a *structured type* consisting of members, each of which has a type associated with it. There is no memory associated with this type. However, once it has been defined, you can declare *structure variables* of this type. The variable declarations

```
employee organist, janitor;
```

cause the allocation of storage space for variables `organist` and `janitor` in the form defined by the structured type `employee`. Thus, the memory allocated for these variables consists of storage space for six distinct values. The variable `organist` (of type `employee`) is shown in Fig. 9.21, assuming that values shown earlier are stored in memory. ∎

As with other identifiers in C++ programs, use member names that describe the information to be stored and select a data type that is appropriate for that kind of information. For example, struct type `employee` uses a string field for storage of an employee's name.

C++
SYNTAX

struct Type Declaration

This is a restricted form and does not show the full generality of the construct.

Form: struct *struct-type*
            {
                type₁ id-list₁;

$$type_2 \; id\text{-}list_2;$$

.
.
.

$$type_n \; id\text{-}list_n;$$

```
};
```

Example: `struct complex`
```
    {
        float real_part, imaginary_part;
    };
```

Interpretation: The identifier *struct-type* is the name of the structure being described. Each *id-list$_i$* is a list of one or more member names of the same type separated by commas, and each *id-list$_i$* is separated from the next *id-list* of a possibly different type by a semicolon. The data type of each member in *id-list$_i$* is specified by *type$_i$*. ∎

You must declare a struct type before you can declare any variables of that type. We recommend that you declare a struct type before the function prototypes in a program system. This placement makes the struct type global, which means that all functions in the program system can use it.

Accessing Members of a struct

We can access a struct member using the *member access operator,* a period. If s is a struct variable and m is a member of that struct, then s.m accesses member m of the struct s.

Example 9.14   The statements below store data in the struct variable `organist`. Refer back to Fig. 9.21 to view the contents of `organist` after these statements execute.

```
organist.id = 1234;
organist.name = "Noel Goddard";
organist.gender = 'F';
organist.num_depend = 0;
organist.rate = 6.00;
organist.tot_wages += organist.rate * 40.0;
```

Once data are stored in a struct, they can be manipulated in the same way as other data in memory. For example, the last assignment above computes the organist's new total wages by adding this week's wages to her previous total wages. The computed result is saved in the struct member `organist.tot_wages`.

The statements

```
cout << "The organist is ";
switch (organist.gender)
{
   case 'F': case 'f':
      cout << "Ms. ";
      break;
   case 'M': case 'm':
      cout << "Mr. ";
      break;
   default:
      cout << organist.gender << " is bad character for gender!"
         << endl;
}
cout << organist.name << endl;
```

display the organist's name after an appropriate title ("Ms." or "Mr."); the output line follows:

```
The organist is Ms. Noel Goddard
```

EXERCISES FOR SECTION 9.6

Self-Check

1. Describe what happens when the following assignment is executed:

   ```
   organist.num_depend += 2;
   ```

2. A catalog listing for a textbook consists of the author's name as well as the title, publisher, and year of publication. Declare a struct `catalog_entry` and a variable `book` and write assignment statements that store the relevant data for this textbook in `book`.

3. Each part in an inventory is represented by its part number, a descriptive name, the quantity on hand, and the price. Define a struct `part`.

9.7 _____ STRUCTS AS OPERANDS AND ARGUMENTS

Besides accessing individual struct members to perform arithmetic operations, logical operations, or input or output operations, programmers often need to write functions that process entire structs. Usually it is more convenient to pass the struct itself as a function argument rather than to pass the individual members. Programmers also need to copy the contents of one struct variable to another. This section describes operations on entire structs.

struct Copy or Assignment

We can copy all of the members of one struct variable to another struct variable of the same type. If `organist` and `janitor` are both struct variables of type `employee`, the statement

```
organist = janitor;   // Copy janitor to organist
```

copies each member of `janitor` into the corresponding member of `organist`.

Passing a struct as an Argument

A struct can be passed as an argument to a function, provided the actual argument is the same type as its corresponding formal argument. The use of structs as arguments can shorten argument lists considerably, because one argument (a struct variable) can be passed instead of several related arguments.

Example 9.15 You have been asked to organize a grading program, which will keep track of a student's name, exam scores, average score on the exams, and letter grade based on the exams. Previously you would have stored these data in separate variables, but now you can group them together as a struct.

```
struct exam_stats
{
    string stu_name;
    int scores[3];
    float average;
    char grade;
};

void main
{
    // Local data
    exam_stats a_student;
```

Struct variable `a_student` (type `exam_stats`) contains all the data regarding the student's exam performance. Notice that the member `scores` is an array of integers. We use the notation `a_student.scores[0]` to access the first element of this array. Figure 9.22 shows a sketch of variable `a_student`.

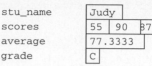

Figure 9.22 Sketch of variable `a_student`

Function `print_stat` (Fig. 9.23) displays the value stored in each member of its struct argument (type `exam_stats`). For the sample data shown, the statement

```
print_stat (a_student);
```

would display the following output:

```
Exam scores for Judy: 55 90 87
Average score: 77.3333
Letter grade : C
```

Figure 9.23 Function `print_stat`

```cpp
// FILE: PrintSta.cpp
// PRINTS THE EXAM STATISTICS

void print_stat
   (exam_stats stu_exams)    // IN: the structure variable to
                             //      be displayed

// Pre:  The members of the struct variable stu_exams are
//        assigned values.
// Post: Each member of stu_exams is displayed.
{
   cout << "Exam scores for " << stu_exams.stu_name << ": "
   cout << stu_exams.scores[0] << ' ' << stu_exams.scores[1]
        << ' ' << stu_exams.scores[2] << endl;
   cout << "Average score: " << stu_exams.average << endl;
   cout << "Letter grade : " << stu_exams.grade << endl;
}  // end print_stat
```

In `print_stat`, the struct argument was declared as a value argument. You can pass a struct as a reference argument, as illustrated in the next example.

Figure 9.24 Function `read_employee`

```cpp
// FILE: ReadEmp.cpp
// READS ONE EMPLOYEE RECORD INTO one_employee

#include <string>
#include <iostream.h>

void read_employee
   (employee& one_employee)      // OUT: The destination for the data
                                 //      read
// Pre:  None
// Post: Data are read into struct one_employee
{
   cout << "Enter a name terminated with the symbol # : ";
   getline (cin, one_employee.name, '#');
   cout << "Enter an id number: ";
   cin >> one_employee.id;
   cout << "Enter gender (F or M): ";
   cin >> one_employee.gender;
   cout << "Enter number of dependents: ";
   cin >> one_employee.num_depend;
   cout << "Enter hourly rate: ";
   cin >> one_employee.rate;
}  // end read_employee
```

Reading a struct

Function `read_employee` in Fig. 9.24 reads data into the first five members of a struct variable of type `employee` represented by reference argument `one_employee`. The function call

```cpp
read_employee (organist);
```

causes the data read to be stored in struct variable `organist`.

PROGRAM STYLE

Efficiency of Reference Arguments

For efficiency reasons, programmers sometimes prefer not to pass structs as value arguments because C++ must copy all members of a struct passed as a value argument into the called function's data area. However, they can still get the protection afforded by value arguments if they use the word `const` in a formal argument declaration. For example, the function header

```cpp
void print_stat
   (const exam_stats& stu_exams)    // IN: the structure variable
                                    //     to be displayed
```

declares `stu_exams` as a reference argument that cannot be changed by the execution of function `print_stat`. Instead of making a local copy of the actual struct argument during a call to `print_stat`, C++ passes the actual argument's address to function `print_stat`. This enables `print_stat` to access the data stored in its actual argument, but C++ does not allow `print_stat` to modify the data in its actual argument.

EXERCISES FOR SECTION 9.7

Self-Check

1. For variables a_student and type exam_stats (Example 9.16) describe the meaning of each of the valid references below. Which are invalid?

   a. `a_student.stu_name`
   b. `exam_stats me`
   c. `exam_stats.stu_name`
   d. `a_student.scores[3]`
   e. `a_student.scores[2]`
   f. `a_name.scores[0]`
   g. `a_name`
   h. `a_student exam_stats`

Programming

1. Write a function to read in the data for a variable of type `catalog_entry`. (See Exercise 2 at the end of Section 9.6.)
2. Write a function that reads in the coordinates of a point on the *x-y* plane where point is defined by

```
struct point
{
    float x;
    float y;
};
```

   The function should return the values read through a single argument of type `point`.
3. Consider the `struct employee` given in Example 9.14.
   a. Write a function `print_employee` to print all the members of a structure variable of type `employee`.
   b. Write a function `assign_employee` that assigns all members of one variable of type `employee` to another.
   c. Write a code segment illustrating how you would call `print_employee` and `assign_employee` (include all necessary declarations).

9.8 ─── COMMON PROGRAMMING ERRORS

■ *(Arrays) Use of Noninteger Subscripts:* Floating-point as well as integral data types are allowed as array subscripts. When characters are used as subscripts, as in `x['A']`, the subscript value is the ASCII value of the character (65 in this case). When floating-point values are used as subscripts, as in `x[3.14159]`, the subscript value (3 in this case) is obtained by truncating the floating-point value. Enumerators may also be used as subscripts; the subscript value for an enumerator is the integer value associated with the enumerator in the enumeration in which it is listed. None of these different subscript types will generate a compiler error, although warnings may be given by some compilers.

■ *(Arrays) Out-of-Range Subscript References:* Array subscript references that are out-of-range (less than zero, or greater than or equal to the array size) will not generate any error messages. Instead, they will cause access to memory locations outside the range of the array, possibly destroying information necessary to the successful execution of the program or retrieving invalid data.

Such errors may be particularly difficult to identify; they may not become readily apparent until the execution of some section of your program that is seemingly unrelated to the point where the problem first occurred. Neither the C++ compiler nor the run-time system detects these errors; it is up to the programmer to build the necessary detection/prevention mechanisms into programs.

■ *(Arrays) Unsubscripted Array References:* Arrays may be used as function arguments. However, unsubscripted array references in expressions are invalid and will generate an error message. For example, if x[20] is an integer array and y is an integer, the expression

```
y = y + x;
```

will generate an error message.

■ *(Arrays) Subscripted References to Nonarray Variables:* Subscripted references to nonarray variables, such as the reference b[10] in

```
a = a + b[10];
```

where a and b are both simple variables, causes an error message to be generated indicating an "Invalid operation."

■ *(Arrays) Mixing Types in Passing Arrays to Functions:* When array arguments are passed to functions, differences between actual and formal array argument types will produce error messages. For example, passing an integer array actual argument when a character array is expected will cause the compiler to generate a message such as

```
"Type mismatch in parameter y in call to find_match".
```

■ *(Structs) References to a struct Member with No Prefix:* The dot notation must always be used when referencing a member, comp, of a variable, v, of some structured type. If the dot notation is omitted, the compiler assumes that your intent is to reference a variable that is not part of a structured variable. If comp is not declared outside a structure, a diagnostic such as "undefined symbol comp" will be issued by the compiler. If a variable named `comp` also happens to be declared in the same function in which the reference occurs, omitting the prefix from a reference to `comp` will not cause an error but will result in a reference to the wrong data element (the variable rather than the structure component).

- *(Structs) Reference to a struct Member with Incorrect Prefix:* If `v` is a structured variable with a member named `comp` and `x` is a structured variable with no member of that name, then the reference `x.comp` will also generate an "Undefined symbol `'comp'`" message. If the prefix used in a reference to a structured member is the name of a `struct` type (such as `coord`) rather than the name of a variable of `struct` type, then a message such as "Improper use of typedef `'coord'`" might be generated. This is a tip that the name of a user-defined type (`coord`, in this case) has been used illegally.

- *(Structs) Missing Semicolon Following a struct Declaration:* If the semicolon required at the end of a `struct` declaration is missing, a variety of error messages might be generated, depending on what follows the declaration. Frequently, another declaration will follow the faulty one. If so, the second declaration is considered part of the struct, and a diagnostic such as "Too many types in declaration." will be produced.

CHAPTER REVIEW

In this chapter, we introduced two structured types: the array and the struct. The array is a convenient facility for naming and referencing a collection of like items, and the struct is convenient for organizing a collection of related data items of different types.

We discussed how to declare arrays and structs and how to reference their elements. You access an array element by placing a subscript in brackets after the array name. For multidimensional arrays, follow the array name with a subscript in brackets for each dimension. You access individual members of a struct by placing the name of the member after the name of the struct, separating the two by the member access operator (a period).

We discussed two common operations involving arrays: searching an array and sorting an array. We wrote a function for searching an array and also described the selection sort function.

The `for` statement enables us to reference the elements of an array in sequence. We can use the `for` statement to initialize arrays, to read and write arrays, and to control the manipulation of individual array elements in sequence.

You must manipulate each individual component of an array or a struct separately in an input or output operation or in an arithmetic expression.

However, you can assign one struct variable to another struct variable of the same type, and you can pass an array or struct as a function argument.

New C++ Constructs   The C++ constructs introduced in this chapter are described in Table 9.4.

Table 9.4   Summary of New C++ Constructs

CONSTRUCT	EFFECT
Array Declaration	
`int cube[10];` `int count[10];`	cube and count are arrays with 10 type int elements.
Array References	
`for (i = 0; i < 10; i++)` `    cube[i] = i * i * i;`	Saves i cubed in the ith element of array cube.

`if (cube[5] > 100)`
`    cout << cube[0]`
`        << cube[1];`
	Compares cube[5] to 100.
	Displays the first two cubes.

struct Declaration	

`struct part`
`{`
`    int id;`
`    int quantity;`
`    float price;`
`};`
 	
`part nuts, bolts;`
	A struct part is declared with data fields that can store two ints and a float number. nuts and bolts are struct variables of type part.

struct References	
`total_cost = nuts.quantity *` `    nuts.price`	Multiplies two members of nuts.
`cout << bolts.id;` `bolts = nuts;`	Displays the id field of bolts. Copies struct nuts to bolts.

✔ QUICK-CHECK EXERCISES

1. What structured data types were discussed in this chapter? What is a structured data type?
2. Which fundamental types cannot be array subscript types? Array element types?

3. Can values of different types be stored in the same array?
4. If an array is declared to have 10 elements, must the program use all 10?
5. When can the assignment operator be used with array elements? With entire arrays? Answer the same questions for the equality operator.
6. The two methods of array access are _____ and _____.
7. The _____ loop allows us to access the elements of an array in _____ order.
8. What is the primary difference between an array and a struct? Which would you use to store the catalog description of a course? Which would you use to store the names of the students in the course?
9. When can you use the assignment operator with struct operands? When can you use the equality operator?
10. For a_student declared as follows, provide a statement that displays the name of a student in the form: *last name, first name.*

```
struct student
{
    string first;
    string last;
    int age;
    int score;
    char grade;
}; // end student


student a_student;
```

11. How many members are there in struct student?
12. Write a function that displays a variable of type student.

Answers to Quick-Check Exercises

1. Arrays and structs. A structured data type is a named grouping of related values.
2. Floating-point types cannot be used for array subscript types; all types can be element types.
3. no
4. no
5. Both the assignment and equality operators may be used with array elements. Neither the assignment operator nor the equality operator may be used with entire arrays.
6. direct (random); sequential
7. for or while, sequential
8. The values stored in an array must all be the same type; the values stored in a struct do not have to be the same type. You would use a struct for the catalog item and use an array for the list of names.
9. The assignment operator may be used between structs of the same type. The equality operator may not be used to compare structs.
10. cout << a_student.last << ", " << a_student.first << endl;
11. five

```
12. void write_student
       (student one_stu)      // IN: The data to be displayed
    {
        cout << "Student is " << one_stu.first << " "
             << one_stu.last << endl;
        cout << "Age is " << one_stu.age << endl;
        cout << "Score is " << one_stu.score << endl;
        cout << "Grade is " << one_stu.grade << endl;
    }
```

REVIEW QUESTIONS

1. Identify the error in the following code segment. When will the error be detected?

```
void main()
{
    int x[8];
    for (int i = 0; i < 9; i++)
        x[i] = i;
}
```

2. Declare an array of floating-point elements called week that can be referenced by using any day of the week as a subscript. Assume sunday is the first subscript.

3. What are the two common ways of selecting array elements for processing?

4. Write a C++ program segment to print out the index of the smallest and the largest numbers in an array x of 20 ints with values from 0 to 100. Assume array x already has values assigned to each element.

5. The arguments for a function are two arrays of type float and an integer that represents the length of the arrays. The function copies the first array in the argument list to the other array using a loop structure. Write the function.

6. How many exchanges are required to sort the following list of integers, using the selection sort? How many comparisons are required?

20 30 40 25 60 80

7. Declare a struct called subscriber that contains the member's name, street_address, monthly_bill (how much the subscriber owes), and which paper the subscriber receives (morning, evening, or both).

8. Write a C++ program to enter and then print out the contents of the variable competition declared as follows:

```
struct olympic_event;
{
    string event;
    string entrant;
    srting country;
    int place;
};

olympic_event competition;
```

9. Identify and correct the errors in the following program:

```
void main ()
{
    struct summer_help
    {
        string name;
        int emp_id;
        string start_date;
        float pay_rate
        int hours_worked;
    }

    summer_help operator;

    summer_help.name = "Stoney Viceroy";
    summer_help.start_date = "June 1, 1992";
    summer_help.hours_worked = 29.3;
    cout << operator << endl;
}
```

10. Declare the proper data structure to store the following student data: `student_name`, GPA, `major`, and `address` (consisting of `street_address`, `city`, `state`, `zip_code`). Use whatever data types are most appropriate for each member.

PROGRAMMING PROJECTS

1. Write a program for the following problem. You are given a file that contains a collection of scores (type `int`) for the last exam in your computer course. You are to compute the average of these scores and assign grades to each student according to the following rule:

> If a student's score is within 10 points (above or below) of the average, assign the grade of satisfactory. If a student's score is more than 10 points above average, assign a grade of outstanding. If a student's score is more than 10 points below average, assign a grade of unsatisfactory.

The output from your program should consist of a labeled two-column list that shows each score and its corresponding grade. As part of the solution, your program should include functions that correspond to the function prototypes that follow.

```
// READS EXAM SCORES INTO ARRAY SCORES
void read_stu_data
    (ifstream &rss,        // IN: Raw scores data stream
     int scores[],         // OUT: The data read
     int &count,           // OUT: Number of students read
```

```
      bool &too_many);            // OUT: A flag to indicate that more
                                  // than max_size scores items are in
                                  // input file.


      // COMPUTES AVERAGE OF COUNT STUDENT SCORES
      float mean (int scores[], int count);


      // PRINTS A TABLE SHOWING EACH STUDENT'S SCORE AND GRADE ON A
      // SEPARATE LINE
      void print_table (int score[], int count);
      // Uses: print_grade


      // PRINTS STUDENT GRADE AFTER COMPARING one_score TO AVERAGE
      void print_grade (int one_score, float average);
```

2. Redo Programming Project 1 assuming that each line of file `raw_scores` contains a student's ID number (an `int`) and an exam score. Modify function `read_stu_data` to read the ID number and the score from the `i`th data line into array elements `id[i]` and `scores[i]`, respectively. Modify function `print_table` to display a three-column table with the following headings:

```
ID            Score          Grade
```

3. Write a program to read n data items into two arrays, x and y, of size 20. Store the products of corresponding pairs of elements of x and y in a third array, z, also of size 20. Print a three-column table that displays the arrays x, y, and z. Then compute and print the square root of the sum of the items in z. Make up your own data, with n less than 20.

4. Another approach to sorting an array is to create an index array, where the index is an array whose element values represent array subscripts. An index will allow you to access the elements of a second array in sequential order without rearranging the second array's element values. After "sorting," the first element of the index array will contain the subscript of the smallest element, the second element of the index array will contain the subscript of the second smallest element, and so on. For example, if the array `scores` contains the exam scores 60, 90, 50, 100, and 75, then the array `scores_index` should contain the subscripts 2, 0, 4, 1, 3. `scores_index[0]` is 2 because `scores[2]` is the smallest score (50); `scores_index[1]` is 0 because `scores[0]` is the second smallest score (60), and so on. Write a function `index_sort` that creates an index array for its input array arguments.

5. The results of a survey of the households in your township are available for public scrutiny. Each record contains data for one household, including a four-digit integer identification number, the annual income for the household, and the number of household members. Write a program to read the survey results into three arrays and perform the following analyses.
   a. Count the number of households included in the survey and print a three-column table displaying the data. (Assume that no more than 25 households were surveyed.)
   b. Calculate the average household income, and list the identification number and income of each household that exceeds the average.

c. Determine the percentage of households that have incomes below the poverty level. Compute the poverty level income using the formula

$$p = \$6500.00 + \$750.00 \times (m - 2)$$

where m is the number of members of each household. This formula shows that the poverty level depends on the number of family members, m, and that the poverty-level income increases as m gets larger. Test your program on the following data.

Identification Number	Annual Income	Household Members
1041	12,180	4
1062	13,240	3
1327	19,800	2
1483	22,458	8
1900	17,000	2
2112	18,125	7
2345	15,623	2
3210	3,200	6
3600	6,500	5
3601	11,970	2
4724	8,900	3
6217	10,000	2
9280	6,200	1

6. Assume that your computer has the very limited capability of being able to read and write only single-integer digits and to add two integers consisting of one decimal digit each. Write a program that can read two integers up to 30 digits each, add these integers together, and display the result. Test your program using pairs of numbers of varying lengths. (*Hint:* Store the two numbers in two int arrays of size 30, one digit per array element. If the number is less than 30 digits in length, enter enough leading zeros (to the left of the number) to make the number 30 digits long.) You will need a loop to add the digits in corresponding array elements. Don't forget to handle the carry digit if there is one!

7. A number expressed in scientific notation is represented by its mantissa (a fraction) and its exponent. Write a function that reads two character strings that represent numbers in C++ scientific notation and stores each number in a struct with two members. Write a function that prints the contents of each struct as a real value. Also write a function that computes the sum, product, difference, and quotient of the two numbers. (*Hint:* The string -0.1234E20 represents a number in scientific notation. The fraction -0.1234 is the mantissa, and the number 20 is the exponent.)

8. A prime number is any number that is divisible only by one and itself. Write a program to compute all the prime numbers less than 2000. One way to generate prime numbers is to create an array of bool values that are true for all prime numbers, but are false otherwise. Initially set all the array entries to true. Then, for every number from 2 to 1000, set the array locations indexed by multiples of the number (but not the number itself) to false. When done, output all numbers whose array location is true. These will be the prime numbers.

9. Write a program that generates the Morse code for a sentence that ends in a period and contains no other characters except letters and blanks. After reading the Morse

code into an array of strings, your program should read each word of the sentence and display its Morse equivalent on a separate line. The Morse code is as follows:

A .- B -... C -.-. D -.. E . F ..-. G --- . H .... I .. J .--- K -.- L .-.. M --
N -. O --- P .--. Q --.- R .-. S ... T - U ..- V ...- W .-- X -..- Y -.-- Z --..

Your program should include functions corresponding to the prototypes shown next.

```
// Stores Morse codes read from code_file in array code.
void read_code (ifstream& code_file, string code_array[]);

// Writes Morse equivalent for a letter.
void write_code (string code_array[], char letter);
```

10. Write an interactive program that plays the game of Hangman. Read the word to be guessed into word. The player must guess the letters belonging to word. The program should terminate when either all letters have been guessed correctly (player wins) or a specified number of incorrect guesses have been made (computer wins). (*Hint*: Use solution to keep track of the solution so far. Initialize solution to a string of symbols '*'. Each time a letter in word is guessed, replace the corresponding '*' in solution with that letter.)

11. Write a program that generates a cryptogram for a sentence that it reads. In a cryptogram, every occurrence of the letter a is replaced by a particular code symbol. The same for the letter b, and so on. *Hint:* See the subsection "Strings and Arrays of Characters" in Section 9.5.

10

Introduction to Software Engineering

The programs you have written and studied thus far have been relatively short and designed to solve specific problems. Many problems, particularly those in industry, require larger, more complex programs. This type of large system programming is called programming in the large, and it is the focus of this chapter.

To implement large programs, professional programmers use a collection of tools and techniques for program design, coding, and maintenance. The study and use of these tools and techniques is called *software engineering.* One technique used to write large programs is to reuse code that accomplished a particular task. In several earlier programs in this book, we have extended problem solutions from one problem to another, but for the most part these programs were not general enough to solve more than one problem. To program a large system efficiently, the problem solution must be modularized so that many different programmers can write and test different components of the program. Quite often a component used in one program can be part of another program. This chapter illustrates the benefits of writing efficient, multicomponent (modular) programs.

In addition to learning how large programs are designed and written, this chapter also introduces testing techniques. Because we describe here the concepts used by software professionals, we conclude with a discussion of professional behavior, ethics, and responsibilities.

10.1 ━━━ PROGRAMMING IN THE LARGE

In order to deal with large-scale programming, we must have some way of attacking a problem in a systematic way and managing its complexity. The techniques professional programmers use to do this are not very different from what you have been practicing so far. They also use the software development method to structure their solution, and they implement their solution by writing a collection of small, well-defined components. Wherever possible, they reuse components that have been written to solve earlier problems. In this section, we describe how professional programmers use the software development method to develop a computer application or software system.

The System/Software Life Cycle

Because the development of a software system proceeds in stages from its initial inception (birth) to its ultimate obsolescence (death), programmers refer to these different stages as the *system/software life cycle* (SLC). The SLC, like the software development method, consists of a series of steps:

1. Requirements specification
   a. Prepare a complete and unambiguous problem statement.
   b. Users and analysts sign the requirements document.

2. Analysis
   a. Understand the problem: develop a system behavior model and determine problem input, output, and other relevant data elements.
   b. Name each identified data element and develop a model of the essential characteristics (attributes and operations) for each element.

3. Design
   a. Using the system and data models developed during requirements analysis, perform a top-down design of the system.
   b. For each system component, identify key data elements and subordinate functions using structure charts.

4. Implementation
   a. Write algorithms and pseudocode descriptions of individual functions.
   b. Code the solution.
   c. Debug the code.

5. Testing and verification
   a. Test the code, verifying that it is correct. Each data modeling component should be tested separately, before all components are tested as an integrated whole.
   b. Involve users and special testing teams in all system tests.

6. Operation, follow-up, and maintenance
   a. Run the completed system.
   b. Evaluate its performance.
   c. Remove new bugs as they are detected.
   d. Make required changes to keep the system up to date.
   e. Verify that changes are correct and that they do not adversely affect the system's operation.

   Problem analysis should always precede problem solution (synthesis). The first two stages of the SLC—requirements specification and analysis—are the analysis part, and the next two stages—design and implementation—are the synthesis part. Program users take the lead in developing the initial requirements specification for a proposed software system. System analysts work closely with program users to understand more thoroughly the problem requirements and to evaluate possible alternative solutions.

   The SLC is iterative. During the design phase (step 3), problems may arise that make it necessary to modify the requirements specification. Similarly, during implementation (step 4) it may become necessary to reconsider decisions made in the design phase. All changes must be approved by both the systems analysts and the users.

Once the system is implemented, it must be thoroughly tested before it enters its final stage (operation and maintenance). System changes identified in these stages may require repetition of earlier stages of the SLC to correct errors found during testing or to accommodate changes required by external sources (for example, a change in federal or state tax regulations).

Estimates vary as to the amount of time necessary for each stage. For example, a typical system may require a year to proceed through the first four stages, three months of testing, then four or more years of operation and maintenance. With these figures in mind you can see why it is so important to design and document software in such a way that it can be easily maintained. This is especially important because the persons who maintain the program may not have been involved in the original program design or implementation.

Requirements Specification

Although we have illustrated most of the phases of the SLC (our software development method) in solving the case studies thus far, we have not really had the opportunity to examine the requirements specification process. Programming problems used as examples for learning a programming language tend to be stated simply so that students can focus on the rudiments of the language and on programming techniques. For these reasons, each case study was preceded by a brief statement of the problem, and we began our solutions with the analysis phase.

As an example of the requirements specification process, let's say you have been given the following problem specification for a telephone directory program.

PROBLEM

Write an interactive telephone directory program that contains a collection of names and telephone numbers. You should be able to insert a new entry into the directory as well as retrieve, change, and delete a directory entry.

Some questions that need to be answered deal with the format of the input data, the desired form of any output screens or printed forms, and the need for data validation.

- Is an initial list of names and numbers to be stored in the directory beforehand, or are all entries to be inserted at the same time? If there is an initial list, is it stored in a data file or will it be entered interactively?
- If a data file is used, what are the formatting conventions (e.g., will the name start in position 1 and the phone number in position 20)? Are the name and number on the same data line or on separate lines?
- Is the final directory printed or stored as a file in secondary memory?
- Can more than one number be associated with a particular name? If so, should the first number, the last number, or all numbers be retrieved?

- Is there a limit on the length of a name? How are the names stored (e.g., *lastname, firstname* or *firstname lastname*)?
- Are phone numbers stored as numbers or as strings of characters? Do they contain area codes? Are there any special characters, such as hyphens and parentheses, in a phone number? Should you check for illegal characters in a number or for numbers that are too short or too long?

As you can see, plenty of questions are left unanswered by the initial problem statement. To complete the requirements specification, you should answer these questions and more. Many of the questions deal with details of input data, the handling of potential errors in input data, and formats of input data and output lists.

Prototyping

An alternative approach to traditional system development is prototyping. In *prototyping*, systems analysts work closely with system users to develop a prototype, or model, of the actual system. Initially, a prototype has few working features and just mimics the input/output interaction of the users with the system. At each stage, the users and the analysts decide what changes should be made and what new features should be added; these changes are then incorporated into the prototype. The process continues until a complete prototype is available that performs all the functions of the final system. The analysts and the users can then decide whether to use the prototype as the final system or as the basis of the design for a new system, which will perform the same operations as the prototype but will be more efficient.

Programming Teams

Another major difference between programming in college and in industry is that in industry it is rare for a large software project to be implemented by a single programmer. Most often, a large project is assigned to a team of programmers after the problem specification and analysis phase are complete. Team members must coordinate the overall organization of the project and communicate on a regular basis to exchange information and report progress.

Normally, one team member acts as "librarian" by assuming responsibility for determining the status of each component in the system. Initially, the library of components consists of a stub for each new component. As a component is completed and tested, its updated version replaces the version currently in the library. The librarian keeps track of the date that each version of a component is inserted into the library and makes sure that all programmers use the latest version of any component.

Each team member is responsible for a set of components, some of which may be accessed by other team members. After the initial organizational meeting, each team member should provide the other members with a specification for each component that he or she is implementing. Such a specification is similar to the documentation provided for each of the C++ functions illustrated thus far in this text. It consists of the name and a brief statement of the purpose of the function, its pre- and postconditions, and its formal argument list. This information is all that a potential user of the component needs to know to use it correctly.

In the following sections of this chapter, we outline some techniques used to modularize a large program and to build our own libraries of C++ program functions. In Chapters 11 and 12, we show how to write our own classes to implement the data element models developed during the analysis and design stage of the software life cycle. We will see how to build, test, and use our own class libraries as part of the software engineering process.

EXERCISES FOR SECTION 10.1

Self-Check

1. Compare the role of the systems analyst and the librarian during the development of a large software system.
2. List the six phases of the software life cycle. Which phase is usually the longest?
3. Explain how a programming team has the potential to complete a large software project more quickly than a single programmer working independently.

10.2 —— PROCEDURAL ABSTRACTION REVISITED: TEMPLATES AND LIBRARIES

Abstraction has been one of the key concepts in managing the complexity of computer software. Although the concept, as it relates to building software, has evolved considerably since its earliest inception in the late 1940s and early 1950s, it has always been an important mechanism for helping us think about and design solutions to large, complex problems in terms of less complicated subproblems. We can in turn apply this concept to each subproblem and try to solve it in terms of still simpler, smaller problems. This process of top-down analysis continues until each subproblem has become small enough that we can successfully work out the lowest-level details of implementation as a single unit.

The dictionary defines *abstraction* as the process of separating the inherent qualities or properties of something from the actual physical object to which they belong. One example of the use of abstraction is representing a program variable (for example, `name` or `tel_number`) by a storage location in memory. We do not have to know anything about the physical structure of memory in order to use variables in programming.

So far in this book we have discussed *procedural abstraction*, a technique guided by the philosophy of separating the concern of *what* is to be achieved by a program component from the details of *how* it is to be achieved. In other words, we have been able to specify what we expect a component to do, then use that component specification in the design of a problem solution before we know how to implement it.

Function Components

We have already discussed many of the software life-cycle benefits of procedural abstraction and top-down design. One benefit of particular importance concerns the ability to reuse parts of a program system that have already been implemented and tested so that we can avoid "reinventing the wheel" as much as possible.

For example, many times we would like to ensure that a given input data value makes sense within the current problem context—that is, that it lies within a specific range of values. We might like to read in a character that is an uppercase letter or to read in an integer within some specified range, such as −10 to +10, or 0 to 100. It is helpful to have at our disposal a collection of working and tested program components responsible for reading a value and verifying that it makes sense. Often, we will want to ignore values that do not fall within the indicated range, as the execution of our program may make no sense given such input. We may also want to alert the program user of the presence of such data, which may be indicative of more serious problems with the input data set.

The interactive function `enter_int` shown in Fig. 10.1 performs the task of ensuring that a type `int` input value falls within a certain range (between `min_n` and `max_n` inclusive). The function displays an error message and terminates execution if the specified range makes no sense (for example, if the minimum range value exceeds the maximum value). Otherwise, it repeatedly asks the program user to enter a value within the indicated range until an appropriate value is entered.

Figure 10.1 Function `enter_int`

```
// File: EnterInt.cpp
// READS AN INTEGER BETWEEN min_n AND max_n INTO n

int enter_int
   (int min_n,            // IN: minimum range value for n
    int max_n)            // IN: maximum range value for n

// Pre:    min_n and max_n are assigned values.
```

(continued)

Figure 10.1   *(continued)*

```
// Post:    If min_n <= max_n, returns the first data value read
//          that has a value between min_n and max_n (inclusive).
//          Otherwise, prints a message and exits.
// Returns: First integer read that has a value between min_n and
//          max_n (inclusive).
{
   // Local data ...
   bool in_range;          // flag—indicates whether in-range
                           //        value was read
   int n;                  // input: each input value

   // Check for nonempty range
   if (min_n <= max_n)
      in_range = false;
   else
   {
      cerr << "*** ERROR: min_n > max_n in enter_int."
           << endl;
      cerr << "Program terminated!" << endl;
      exit (0);                              // Exit indicating failure
   }

   // Keep reading until a valid number is read
   while (!in_range)
   {
      cout << "Enter a value between " << min_n << " and "
           << max_n << ": ";
      cin >> n;
      in_range = (min_n <= n) && (n <= max_n);
   }  // end while
   return n;
}   // end enter_int
```

Function Templates for Procedural Abstraction

The function shown in Fig 10.1 should prove useful in any number of inter-active programs involving the reading of type `int` data elements. Examples of other functions that lend themselves to substantial reuse include the `exchange`, `search`, and `sort` functions shown in Section 9.5. In examining these functions, it may have occurred to you that similar functions written for different data types would be equally as useful. For example, functions that search for, exchange, or sort strings or floating-point values would be nice; functions such as `enter_char` and `enter_float` that ensure type `char` or type `float` data fall within a given range of values might also be helpful. Of course, we could write separate versions of each of these functions simply by editing the original version and changing the base type of the data to be manipulated. However, such changes are error-prone and lead to a proliferation of separate functions, one for each of the huge variety of different data types that might be searched, exchanged, or sorted.

Template functions provide a mechanism for addressing this problem. They allow us to design functions in a manner that is independent of the type of data to be manipulated. The focus of the function is instead on the algorithm (for example, searching, sorting, or entering data). The function user specifies the base type of the data to be manipulated in the program that uses the function. Figure 10.2 illustrates the definition of functions `sel_sort` and `exchange` (see Fig. 9.19) written as templates. The call of the `exchange` function is also illustrated in this figure. The definition of `find_index_of_min` is left as an exercise (see Programming Exercise 4 at the end of this section).

Figure 10.2 Function templates `sel_sort` and `exchange`

```
// FILE: SelSortT.cpp
// SORTS AN ARRAY (ASCENDING ORDER) USING SELECTION SORT ALGORITHM
//     USES exchange AND find_index_of_min

   // Functions used ...
   // FINDS THE SUBSCRIPT OF THE SMALLEST VALUE IN A SUBARRAY
   template<class T>
   int find_index_of_min
      (T[],              // IN: the array of elements to be checked
       int,              // IN: index of first subarray element to be
                         // IN: checked
       int);             // IN: index of last subarray element to be
                         // IN: checked

   // EXCHANGES TWO INTEGER VALUES
   template<class T>
   void exchange
      (T&,               // INOUT: first item
       T&);              // INOUT: second item

template<class T>
void sel_sort
   (T items[],           // INOUT: array to be sorted
    int n)               // IN: number of items to be sorted (n >= 0)

// Sorts the data in array items (items[0] through items[n-1]).
// Pre:  items is defined and n <= declared size of actual
//       argument array.
// Post: The values in items[0] through items[n-1] are in
//       increasing order.
{

   // Local data ...
   int min_sub;      // subscript of each smallest item located by
                     // find_index_of_min
```

(continued)

Figure 10.2   *(continued)*

```
    for (int i = 0; i < n-1; i++)
    {
        // Invariant: The elements in items[0] through items[i-1] are
        //     in their properJplace and i < n.
        // Find index of smallest element in unsorted section of
        //     items.
        min_sub = find_index_of_min (items, i, n-1);

        // Exchange items at position min_sub and i if different
        if (i != min_sub)
            exchange (items[min_sub], items[i]);
    }   // end for
}   // end sel_sort


template<class T>
void exchange
   (T& element1, T& element2)
{
    // Local data ...
    T temp;

    temp = element1;
    element1 = element2;
    element2 = temp;
}   // end exchange

// Insert function template find_index_of_min here.
```

The prototype and definition of a template function begins with the *template prefix* line

```
template<class T>
```

which tells the compiler that the definition that follows is a *template* and that T is a *type parameter* (indicated by the `<class T>` part of the prefix line). Within the parameter lists of the prototype and function definition, as well as in the body of the function definition, T is used just as any other type. Each time a template function is referenced, the compiler substitutes the type of the actual argument corresponding to T in the argument list, effectively creating an instance of the function for that type. For example, given the prototype

```
// SORTS AN ARRAY (ASCENDING ORDER) USING SELECTION SORT
//     ALGORITHM
void sel_sort
   (T [],                // INOUT: array to be sorted
    int);                // IN: number of items to be sorted (n >= 0)
```

and assuming `years_in_service` to be an array of integers, the function call

```
sel_sort (years_in_service, n);
```

causes the compiler to create the versions of `sel_sort` (and `exchange`) shown in Chapter 9 (with `int` replacing the parameter `T`). Notice that you call a template function just like you call an ordinary function.

In a different application containing the prototype for the `sel_sort` template function and an array `name` containing n type string objects, the function reference

```
sel_sort (name, n);
```

would cause the compiler to create a version of `sel_sort` similar to that shown in Fig. 9.19 but with type `string` as the base type of the array, with `string` replacing the type parameter `T`. The function reference

```
exchange (name[i], name[j];
```

would cause the compiler to behave as though it created another instance of the `exchange` function:

```
void exchange (string& element1, string& element2)
{
    string temp;

    temp = element1;
    element1 = element2;
    element2 = temp;
}
```

It is not necessary for you to do anything special when you call a function defined as a template. The compiler does the work of producing the function instance from the template (actually, a separate function instance is not created, but the compiler behaves as though that is what happens). Remember that function templates have prototypes and definitions just like ordinary functions. In addition, these prototypes and definitions are specified in the same place as ordinary functions.

Template Function Prototype and Definition

Form: `template<class T>`

(The remaining portion of a template function definition consists of a typical function definition with the type parameter `T` used in place of a defined type; see again Figure 10.2).

Example: A template function prototype:

```
// SEARCHES AN ARRAY FOR AN GIVEN ELEMENT (THE TARGET)
template<class T>
int lin_search
```

```
(T,                // IN: the target being sought
  const int,       // IN: the size of the array
  T []);           // IN: the array being searched
```

A template function definition:

```
// SEARCHES AN ARRAY FOR AN GIVEN ELEMENT (THE TARGET)
template<class T>
int lin_search
  (T target,         // IN: the target being sought
   const int size,   // IN: the size of the array
   T items[])        // IN: the array being searched
{
    ...
}
```

Interpretation: Template functions may be used to define a form for an entire group of related functions. Each time the template function name is used with matching types in a function call, the compiler effectively creates a specific function (a function *instance*) in this group. The type of each actual argument in the call must match its corresponding formal argument. Actual arguments corresponding to each occurrence of T in the formal argument list must be of the same type. In the linear search example, the types of the first and third actual arguments in a call to lin_search must be the same. This type replaces the placeholder type specifier T in the template; a function instance is created. The third argument must be an array; the second argument must always be of type int and must be a constant expression.

Notes:

1. Most function templates will have just one type parameter. However, more than one parameter is permitted, as in

   ```
   template<class T1, class T2>
   ```

2. The use of the letter T (or T1 or T2) to represent a type parameter is customary but not required in C++.
3. Some C++ compilers may have special requirements for using templates. If you encounter any problems in compiling a program that uses templates, consult your C++ manual or a local expert.   ∎

Building Function Libraries

As you write more and more C++ programs and functions, you should try to keep each new function as general as possible so that it might be reused in other applications. You will eventually build up a sizable library of your own functions. Reusing tried and tested functions is always much more efficient than starting from scratch; each new function that you write will have to be thoroughly tested and debugged and will require a lot of start-up time in every case. The functions in your personal library already will have been tested, so you will save time if you use them over and over again. (And, don't forget about the wealth of functions in the C++ libraries.)

C++ provides facilities to assist you or your team of programmers to write and test functions and function templates separately before integrating them into a larger system of components for more complete testing (testing strategies are discussed later in this chapter). These facilities allow you to place the definition of a function in a file that is separate from the other components of a system, including those components that use the function.

A program, therefore, may be made up of several different C++ code files (usually named with the .cpp extension). For one function to reference the others, the file containing the calling function need only include the prototype for the function to be called. The prototype either can be inserted directly in the text of the calling function file or it can be placed in a separate file (usually called a .h file) and included in the calling program. The net result is the same, whether the prototype is written directly in the file of the caller, or is included. Were we to place the find_index_of_min and exchange template function prototypes in their own .h files, then the compiler directives

```
#include "FindMinT.h"
#include "ExchngT.h"
```

could have been used as shown in Fig. 10.3 to include these prototypes for use by the sel_sort function. The use of quotes in this case rather than the angle brackets < and > is to distinguish these user library function components from C++ system library components. When the header file name is enclosed in double quotes rather than angle brackets, the compiler system looks for the named file in the programmer's directory of files rather than in the C++ system directory.

In Fig. 10.3, we assume that the sel_sort template function itself has been saved in a separate .h file and may be included in any program that requires its use.

If we now assume that the complete implementations for the find_index_of_min and exchange template functions are stored in separate files named FindMinT.cpp and ExchngT.cpp, respectively, then we can compile and test these functions independently (using their own test driver programs). Once this testing has been completed, we can compile and link these components together with a driver program that tests the sel_sort function. This integration process may differ, depending upon the C++ compiler you are using.

An example of this process is illustrated in Fig. 10.4. The test driver program (the main function) is stored in file SortDrvr.cpp. This file and the files SelSortT.cpp, FindMinT.cpp, and ExchngT.cpp are compiled separately, producing the *object files* SortDrvr.obj, SelSortT.obj,

Figure 10.3 Function `sel_sort` with separate prototype and code files for `find_index_of_min` and `exchange`

```cpp
// FILE: SelSrtT.cpp
// SORTS AN ARRAY (ASCENDING ORDER) USING SELECTION SORT ALGORITHM
//    USES exchange AND find_index_of_min

// Functions used ...
#include "FindMinT.h"    // find_index_of_min template
#include "ExchngT.h"     // exchange template

void sel_sort
   (T items[],          // INOUT: array to be sorted
    int n)              // IN: number of items to be sorted (n >= 0)

// Sorts the data in array items (items[0] through items[n-1]).
// Pre:  items is defined and n <= declared size of actual
//       argument array.
// Post: The values in items[0] through items[n-1] are in
//       increasing order.
{
   // Local data ...
   int min_sub;   // subscript of each smallest item located by
                  // find_index_of_min

   for (int i = 0; i < n-1; i++)
   {
      // Invariant: The elements in items[0] through items[i-1] are
      //    in their proper place and i < n.
      // Find index of smallest element in unsorted section of
      //    items.
      min_sub = find_index_of_min (items, i, n-1);

      // Exchange items at position min_sub and i if different
      if (i != min_sub)
         exchange (items[min_sub], items[i]);
   } // end for
} // end sel_sort
```

`FindMinT.obj`, and `ExchngT.obj`. Separate object files cannot, however, be executed by the computer. The system linker program must first bring these four files together to form an executable program file (called `SortDrvr.exe`). The result is a single file of code formed from what was originally four separate components—written, compiled, and tested separately and finally linked together for final testing and use.

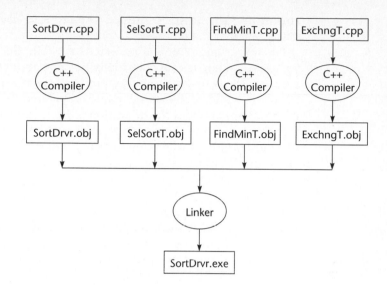

Figure 10.4 Compiling and linking separate program components

Separate Program Components: Role of the Linker

In addition to the life-cycle benefits just discussed, there is another reason for maintaining such a high degree of separation of program components—software modification. Whether caused by errors in the code or changes in the problem specification, it is important that changes in a software system be kept as localized as possible so that they affect a relatively small number of system components. We recall that except for the argument list in a function header and the function name and return value, the remaining details of a function implementation are hidden from all other system components. Thus, changes to a function, unless they affect the argument list or return value specifications, can be expected to have no impact on other system components. Only those functions affected by a change need to be recompiled. The .obj files generated from this recompilation can then be combined by the linker with the existing .obj files from the unchanged components into a new, ready to test and then use executable program.

The use of separately compiled functions provides a good illustration of the use of *externally defined names* (names that are used but not declared) in a program component. In addition to functions, almost every program component contains references to names of data types, constants, variables, flags, etc., that are not defined in that component. We have already seen numerous examples of such externally defined names, such as cin, cout; the string functions `at`, `remove`, and `insert`; and `INT_MAX`, `EXIT_FAILURE`, `setprecision`, and `setw`.

It is important to remember that as the compiler translates one function in a program system, it knows virtually nothing about the other components of the system. The inclusion of `.h` files provides the compiler with information about the file in which each external name is declared. But it provides no information to the compiler about the definition of these names nor where the information represented by the names will be stored during program execution. For example, function prototypes included in another component tell the compiler about the name, arguments, and return value for these components. However, at the point at which the compiler sees the prototype, it has no way of knowing where the function itself will be stored in memory during execution.

In fact, the compiler can do its translation work perfectly well without knowing any more information than what is given in the declarations for the externally referenced names used in a component. Knowledge of function arguments and return values or of the declarations of other externally referenced names is all the compiler needs to carry out the syntax checking and translation it must do. However, for all the components of a program to work together during execution, the location of every function and every data item used must be known. That is, the reference to each and every name used in a component must be *resolved* prior to the start of execution of a program. It is the job of the linker to ensure that all of the external references are resolved prior to the start of program execution. This is a complicated task, and one that often takes even longer than compilation.

Validating a Library Function's Arguments

In Fig. 10.1 function `enter_int` began by checking whether its user correctly entered its input arguments, `min_n` and `max_n`. If the arguments define an empty range, an error message is displayed and the function exits, skipping the read operation. You should make sure that you carefully validate input arguments for functions, especially those functions that are candidates for extensive reuse and inclusion in a library.

Your validation steps should ensure that all program input and function input argument values are defined consistently with the preconditions described in the function comments. In case program or component input data fails to meet required conditions and recovery from the error is not possible, it is important to ensure a *graceful exit* from the affected component. Such an exit normally involves the display of an informative diagnostic message about what went wrong, followed by the return to the calling component. If recovery from an error is not possible (preventing the program from further execution), complete program termination may be required.

Because library functions may be reused many times and by many different programmers, this extra effort can pay valuable dividends. As you may already know from your own experience, the simple failure of a program, with little or no indication as to the cause of the problem, is one of the most frustrating aspects of computer work.

EXERCISES FOR SECTION 10.2

Self-Check
1. List at least three pieces of information that must be known about a library function before it can be called.
2. Why is the validation of function arguments more critical for a library function than for a function that is used in only a single program?
3. Why were the last two arguments of function find_index_of_min (see Fig. 10.3) specified as type int as opposed to unspecified type T arguments?
4. List as many external references as you can find in the function in Fig. 10.3.

Programming
1. Write function enter_float, which returns a data value that lies within a specified range of floating-point values. Your function should display an error message if the specified range is invalid
2. Redo Programming Exercise 1 but provide a function output argument to return a type bool flag indicating whether the specified range of values makes sense. Do not print any diagnostic messages.
3. Write a function my_toupper to convert a lowercase letter to uppercase. The letter to be converted is the input argument; the resulting uppercase letter is returned. If the input argument is not a lowercase letter, simply return the argument itself.
4. Write the function definition for the template function find_index_of_min. The prototype for find_index_of_min is shown in Fig. 10.2.
5. Write a test driver program to test the selection sort function (as well as find_index_of_min and exchange) on a small array (size 10 or so) of strings (such as students' last names).

10.3 ——— DATA ABSTRACTION AND ABSTRACT DATA TYPES: PROGRAM OBJECTS

You may have already noticed in using procedural abstraction (writing and using C++ functions) that it is often helpful to be sure you know exactly how to solve certain subproblems before actually working out the higher-level details of the "parent" problem (the one that depends on these subproblem solutions). There is nothing wrong with this! In fact, as we have seen, implementing, testing, and saving smaller problem solutions for later use is a way of establishing a collection of building blocks or tools that can be reused in designing the solutions to more complicated problems.

Up to this point in the book, our emphasis has been on procedural aspects of problem solving and on structured programming. Yet even with this focus, we have tried not to lose sight of issues related to data analysis: the identification of information that is relevant to the solution of a problem and the representation of that information in a C++ program. We have already illustrated the use of different types of data, such as int, char, and string, and of two different structures, arrays and structs, for representing information in C++. In addition, we have written functions to perform operations on these data in accordance with the problem specifications given.

In this section, we begin to place a far heavier emphasis on data analysis and its impact on the programming process and the software life cycle. By the time we have finished the next few chapters, you will have learned how to develop far more powerful and reusable program components representing problem domain data entities. You will see how to design C++ classes to model these entities and how to use these classes in solving larger and more complex problems.

Limiting Data Access

For several decades, the great majority of programmers have used the *procedure-oriented paradigm* of identifying the types and structures for representing problem data and constructing a program to perform the required operations on these data. The focus of this paradigm has been on the steps to be carried out (the algorithm or procedure) in solving a problem, rather than on the data elements involved in the solution. As this paradigm evolved over time, numerous advances had a profound positive influence on the software development process. Yet as programming systems grew in size and complexity, it became more and more apparent that the procedural paradigm was not adequate to the task.

One of the major flaws in this paradigm concerned the scope of definition and visibility of the data used in their programs. Most languages, and the software development approaches that use them, provide little help in controlling the visibility of or access to data. There has been little methodological incentive or language assistance for programmers to limit data access to only those program components that require such access. This lack of attention to and support for *data access control* is a serious problem in large systems. In the absence of tight access control, program changes to correct or improve one section of code often produce undesirable *side effects* that cause other, apparently unrelated code sections to fail.

Often seemingly simple, highly localized changes ultimately result in modifications to large portions of an existing system. To further exacerbate the situation, many of these ripple-effect changes are not recognized immediately and often show up later during testing, or worse, during the production use of a system. In some cases, the entire original design structure of a system may collapse under the weight of a set of changes, making later changes even more difficult to manage.

Encapsulation and Information Hiding

It is in this connection that the ideas of *information hiding* and *encapsulation* play a major role, providing programmers with a framework within which to view each relevant piece of problem data and the operations on these data as bound together in a single program unit. At the top levels of the design, it is advantageous to be able to take an abstract view of the data to be manipulated and the operations required on this data. For example, we may prefer to think of a string as a sequence of characters of some length that we can copy, read, display, concatenate and insert, delete, and replace. The details of the storage representation of the string and the actual code that implements the operations can be described at a later point (and perhaps taken from an existing library, as is the case with strings).

Even when implemented, these lower-level details should remain hidden from the user. There is no need for the user to know any of these details in order to correctly use the string abstraction properly. From a software engineering viewpoint, this is an advantage rather than a limitation. It allows the designer and implementor of the abstraction to change his or her mind at a later date and possibly to choose a more efficient method of internal representation or implementation. Furthermore, the modules using this abstraction will not have to be rewritten and may not even need to be recompiled when changes are made to the encapsulated component. The process of "hiding" the details of a low-level module's implementation from a higher-level module is called *information hiding*. The programming language implementation mechanism for building information-hiding program components is called an *encapsulation mechanism*.

Data Abstraction

The process of identifying each problem data item, its properties, and its required operations involves another kind of abstraction, *data abstraction*. Data abstraction enables programmers to isolate all concerns related to a particular problem data element and then to implement a model of this element as a separate program component. It is most desirable to begin this isolation during the analysis phase of software development and carry it through to the design stage, and finally, to implementation.

Through *data abstraction,* we specify the data for a problem and the operations to be performed on these data. We need not be overly concerned with how the data will be represented in memory or how the operations will be implemented. In other words, we can describe *what* information must be stored without being specific as to *how* the information is organized and represented. This is the *logical view* of the data as opposed to its *physical view* (the actual internal representation in memory). Once we understand the logical view and we have an *abstract view* of the operations that we need to have performed, we can use the data and their operations in our programs. However, we (or someone else) will eventually have to implement the data and their operations before we can run any program that uses them.

As early as Chapter 2, we began the study of several simple examples of data abstractions. One such example is the C++ data type `float`, an abstraction for the set of real numbers (in the mathematical sense). This set includes the integers (such as −10234, 0, and 7098) as well as other numbers, some being represented as fractions (such as 1/4 or 5/11) and others having no precise fractional representation (such as $\pi = 3.14159$). The computer hardware limits the range of floating-point numbers that can be represented, and not all floating-point numbers within the specified range can be represented (see Section 7.2). Also, the result of manipulating floating-point numbers is often an approximation of the actual result. However, we can generally use the data type `float` and its C++ operators (+, −, *, /, =, <=, <, and so on), as well as the square root, logarithmic, and trigonometric functions, without being concerned with the details of their implementation. `int` and `char` are other examples of the use of data abstraction in C++.

The `string` data type provides another such abstraction consisting of a string of characters, information about the length of string, and a large number of operations for reading and displaying strings, determining string length, and handling typical string manipulations such as assignment, comparison, concatenation, insertion, and replacement.

Collections of data of the same type provide another useful abstraction. The information to be represented consists of the collection itself, a count of the number of items currently in the collection, and perhaps an upper limit or maximum on the number of items allowed in the collection. Given this specification of information to be represented, we must next turn our attention to the operations required on this collection. Clearly, we need to be able to put items into the collection (add an item), remove items from the collection (delete), obtain the value of an item (get an item), and determine the size of the collection. Other operations we might need include sorting the collection, adding all the values in the collection (assuming the elements in the collection are numeric), and displaying the entire collection.

The diagrams shown in Fig. 10.5 provide a quick-reference illustration for the floating-point and string abstractions, summarizing some of the information encapsulated in the abstraction and depicting a few of the operations that may be performed on this information. The operations are shown as *access windows* to the encapsulated information. In fact, only through these windows can information be altered or retrieved.

Ultimately, abstractions such as floating-point numbers or integers, strings, streams, or money, must be implemented in a programming language. In C++, for example, we could choose an array for modeling (or representing) the collection and use integers to represent the number of items and maximum number of items. The operations would each be implemented as functions. The entire set of data structures chosen to model the information, together with the functions, can be encapsulated in a class. The implementation details would be hidden from any other parts of a program that might need to use

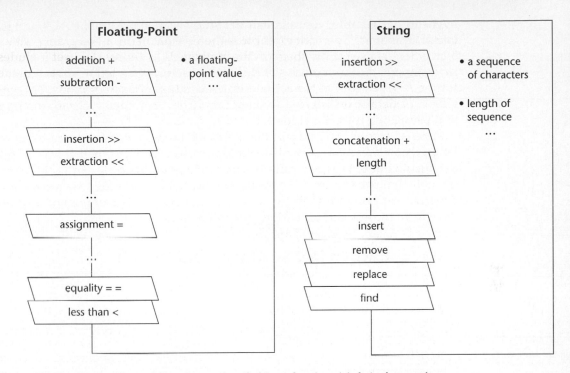

Figure 10.5 Illustration of floating point (left) and string (right) abstractions

this class. This implementation process and the concepts of abstract data types and C++ classes are reviewed in the following sections.

Abstract Data Types

We have already seen how to use libraries of system-defined and user-defined abstract data types—we have been doing so from the beginning, when we wrote programs using the stream, string, and money data types. A primary goal of the remaining chapters of this book is to show you how to design and code your own data types and how to build libraries of these types. As you progress through each chapter, you will create a large collection of abstract data types in your own program library. Because all such abstract data types will already have been coded, debugged, tested, and maybe even compiled, the use of these types will make it much easier for you to design and implement new applications programs.

Normally, an abstract data type (ADT) consists of two parts: (1) its definition, or specification, and (2) its implementation. The *specification part* of an ADT describes the problem domain information (such as a collection of data elements of the same type, and its size) to be encapsulated in the ADT and the capabilities of the operations (add, delete, get, etc.) on this information. This is all a potential user of the abstract data type needs to know. The *implementation part* contains the declarations of the data structures needed to store the data for the ADT, as well as the actual implementation of its operations. This collection of details is intended to be hidden from the other program modules that use the abstract data type.

Most languages that support the use of ADTs also provide separate compilation for software components that contain abstract data types. If we compile the abstract data type, we can then link its executable code with other components that need to use it. If we are careful to include a fairly complete and general set of operators in the abstract data type, this component will not have to be recompiled for each new application.

Data Abstraction in C++: Classes and Objects

Not all modern programming languages provide a mechanism for implementing data abstractions defined during the design stage. C++ is, however, one language that does provide such a mechanism—the `class`—and this is considered to be a major advantage of the language. In C++, we can use classes to define new data types as encapsulations of data and operations. Then, in much the same way that we declare variables, array elements, and structure members of the fundamental types, we can declare program entities as being of the new type defined by the class. In C++, such entities are called *objects.* The programming paradigm that uses objects as the foundational element of the design of programming systems is called *object-oriented programming.*

In this chapter, and in much of the remaining text, we will focus on this object-oriented (o-o) paradigm, developing numerous examples and providing an introduction to a number of important issues related to object-oriented programming in C++. Among other things, we will show how classes can be used to encapsulate information and isolate program details from all but those system components that require them. We will provide some introductory illustrations of the use of classes in designing and implementing new data types to serve as the foundational components of a new system We also will show how these components may be used and reused to serve the needs of a number of different software systems.

Before moving on to this development, however, we need to cover a few more issues of software engineering. These are the subject of the rest of this chapter.

EXERCISES FOR SECTION 10.3

Self-Check   1. In a manner similar to what was done in this section for the fundamental types `float` and `string`, list the C++ operations and functions that should be considered part of the complete specifications for the fundamental data types (a) `int` and (b) `char`

2. What is information hiding? Why is it important to a software engineer?
3. How can the use of C++ functions and classes be of help to the software engineer building a programming system in C++?

10.4   ANALYSIS OF ALGORITHM EFFICIENCY: BIG-O NOTATION

It is often important in programming to be able to provide comparative estimates of the efficiency of algorithms for performing a certain task. In this section, we provide a brief introduction to the topic of algorithm efficiency analysis, with a focus on the searching and sorting algorithms introduced in Section 9.5.

There are many algorithms for searching and sorting arrays. Because arrays can have a large number of elements, the time required to process all of the elements of an array can be significant. Therefore, it is important to have some idea of the relative efficiency of the various algorithms for performing these tasks. Unfortunately, it is difficult to get a precise measure of the efficiency of an algorithm or program. For this reason, we normally try to approximate the effect on an algorithm of a change in the number of items, n, that the algorithm processes. In this way, we can see how an algorithm's execution time increases with n, so we can compare two algorithms by examining their growth rates.

Usually, growth rates in execution efficiency are examined in terms of the *largest contributing factor* as the value of n gets large (for example, as it grows to 1,000 or more). If we determine that the expression

$$2n^2 + n - 5$$

expresses the relationship between the processing time of an algorithm and n, we say that the algorithm is an $O(n^2)$ algorithm, where O is an abbreviation for "the order of magnitude." This notation is known as *big-O notation*. The reason that this is an $O(n^2)$ algorithm rather than an $O(2n^2)$ algorithm or an $O(2n^2+n-5)$ algorithm is that the dominant factor in the relationship is the n^2 term. Efficiency considerations are most relevant for large values of n, because they tend to have the greatest impact on our work for these values. But for large values of n, the largest exponent term has by far the greatest impact on our measurements. For this reason, we tend to ignore the "smaller" terms and constants.

Analysis of a Search Algorithm

To search an array of n elements using the linear search function from Section 9.5, we have to examine all n elements if the target is not present in the array. If the target is in the array, then we have to search only until we find it. However, the target could be anywhere in the array—it is equally as likely to be at the beginning of the array as at the end. So, on average, we have to examine $n/2$ array elements to locate a target value in an array. This means that the linear search is an $O(n)$ process; that is, the growth rate is linear with respect to the number of items being searched. While this might not seem so bad, it is considerably worse, for example, than some other search algorithms that are $O(\log_2 n)$ processes. For example, for a binary search, the worst-case number of examinations, or *probes,* for any given item in a collection of data is $O(\log_2 n)$. For large n, the difference can be significant; for $n = 1,000$, for example, $n/2 = 500$, whereas $\log_2 n$ is approximately equal to 10.

Analysis of a Sort Algorithm

To determine the efficiency of a sorting algorithm, we normally focus on the number of array element comparisons and exchanges that it requires. Performing a selection sort on an array of n elements requires $n - 1$ comparisons during the first pass, $n - 2$ during the second pass, and so on. Therefore, the total number of comparisons is represented by the series

$$1 + 2 + 3 + ... + (n - 2) + (n - 1).$$

The value of this series is expressed in the closed form

$$\frac{n \times (n - 1)}{2} = n^2/2 - n/2$$

The number of comparisons performed in sorting an array of n elements using the selection sort is always the same; however, the number of array element exchanges can vary, depending on the initial ordering of the array elements. During the search for a given smallest element (with subscript min_sub) we can skip the exchange process if the smallest element is already in place. If this condition never occurs, there will be one exchange for each iteration of the main sort loop (*worst-case situation*). If the array happens to be sorted before the sort is called, all its elements will be in the proper place, so there will be zero exchanges (*best-case situation*). Therefore, the number of exchanges for an arbitrary initial ordering is between 0 and $n - 1$, which is $O(n)$.

Because the dominant term in the expression for the number of comparisons shown earlier is $n^2/2$, the selection sort is considered an $O(n^2)$ process and the growth rate is said to be *quadratic* (proportional to the square of the number of elements). What difference does it make whether an algorithm is an $O(n)$ or $O(n^2)$ process? Table 10.1 shows the evaluation of n and n^2 for different values of n. A doubling of n causes n^2 to increase by a factor of 4. Because n^2 increases much more rapidly than n, the performance of an $O(n)$ algorithm is not as adversely affected by an increase in array size as it is in an $O(n^2)$ algorithm. For large values of n (say, 100 or more), the difference in the performances of an $O(n)$ and an $O(n^2)$ algorithm is significant (see the last three lines of Table 10.1).

Table 10.1   Table of Values of n and n^2

n	n^2
2	4
4	16
8	64
16	256
32	1024
64	4096
128	16384
256	65536
512	262144

Other factors besides the number of comparisons and exchanges affect an algorithm's performance. For example, one algorithm may take more time preparing for each exchange or comparison than another. Also, one algorithm might exchange subscripts, whereas another might exchange the array elements themselves. The second process can be more time consuming. Another measure of efficiency is the amount of memory required by an algorithm. Further discussion of these issues is beyond the scope of this book.

EXERCISES FOR SECTION 10.4

Self-Check   1. Determine how many times the cout line is executed in each of the following fragments. Indicate whether the algorithm is $O(n)$ or $O(n^2)$.

```
a. for (i = 0; i < n; i++)
       for (j = 0; j < n; j++)
           cout << i << ' ' << j;
b. for (i = 0; i < n; i++)
       for (j = 1; j <= 2; j++)
           cout << i << ' ' << j;
c. for (i = 0; i < n; i++)
       for (j = n; j > 0; j--)
           cout << i << ' ' << j;
```

Programming   1. Let n be a type integer variable and y1, y2, and y3 be type floating-point. Write a program to compute and print the values of y1, y2, and y3 (below) for n, from 0 to 1,000 inclusive, in increments of 25. Use the function ceil in the math.h library to compute y3. Do the results surprise you?

$y1 = 100n + 10,$
$y2 = 5n^2 + 2,$
$y3 = 1{,}000 \times \text{ceiling} (\log_2 n).$

10.5 —— SOFTWARE TESTING

It does not really matter whether a program is designed carefully and runs efficiently if it does not do what it is supposed to do. One way to gain reasonable assurance that a program does what you want is through testing. However, it is difficult to determine how much testing should be done. Very often errors will appear in a software product after it is delivered, causing great inconvenience. Some notable software errors in operational programs have caused power brownouts, telephone network saturation, and space flight delays. In some situations it is impossible to completely test a software product in advance of its use. Examples would include software that controls a missile and software that prevents a nuclear disaster in the event of malfunction of a nuclear power plant.

Preparing a Test Plan Early

It is best to develop a plan for testing early in the design stage of a new system. Some aspects of a test plan include deciding how the software will be tested, when the tests will occur, and who will do the testing. Under normal circumstances, testing is done by the programmer, by other members of the software team who did not code the module being tested, and by users of the software product. Some companies have special testing experts who find bugs in other programmers' code. If the test plan is developed early in the design stage, testing can take place concurrently with the design and coding. The earlier an error is detected, the easier and less expensive it will be to correct.

Another advantage of deciding on the test plan early is that it should encourage programmers to prepare for testing as they write their code. A good programmer will practice *defensive programming* and include code that detects unexpected or invalid data values. For example, if a function has the precondition

```
Pre: n greater than zero
```

it would be a good idea to place the `if` statement

```
if (n <= 0)
   cout << "Invalid value for argument n -- " << n;
```

at the beginning of the function. This `if` statement will provide a diagnostic message in the event that the argument passed to the function is invalid.

Similarly, if a data value being read from the keyboard is supposed to be between 0 and 40, a defensive programmer would use function `enter_int` shown in Fig. 10.1:

```
cout << "Enter number of hours worked: ";
hours = enter_int (0, 40);
```

The two arguments of `enter_int` define the range of acceptable values for the data element to be read and returned.

Structured Walkthroughs

The *structured walkthrough* is an important testing technique in which the programmer describes, or "walks through," the logic of a new module as part of a presentation to other members of the software team. The purpose of the walkthrough is for the team members to identify design errors or bugs that may have been overlooked by the programmer because he or she is too close to the problem. The goal is to detect errors in logic before they become part of the code.

Black-Box Versus White-Box Testing

There are two basic ways to test a completed module or system: (1) *black-box*, or *specification-based*, testing and (2) *white-box*, or *glass-box*, testing. In black-box testing, it is assumed that the program tester has no information about the code inside the module or system. The tester's job is to verify that the module does what its specification says that it does. For a function, this means ensuring that the function's postconditions are satisfied whenever its preconditions are met. For a system or subsystem, this means ensuring that the system does indeed satisfy its original requirements specification. Because the tester cannot look inside the module or system, he or she must prepare sufficient sets of test data to ensure that the system output is correct for all values of valid system input. The tester should especially check the *boundaries* of the system, or particular values for the program variables where the system performance changes. For example, a boundary for a payroll program would be the value of hours worked that triggers overtime pay. Also, the module or system should not crash when presented with invalid input. Black-box testing is most often done by a special testing team or by program users.

In white-box (or glass-box) testing, the tester has full knowledge of the code for the module or system and must ensure that each section of code has been thoroughly tested. For a selection statement (`if` or `switch`), this means checking all possible paths through the selection statement. The tester must determine that the correct path is chosen for all possible values of the selection variable, taking special care at the boundary values where the path changes.

For a repetition statement, the tester must make sure that the loop always performs the correct number of iterations and that the number of iterations is not off by one. Also, the tester should verify that the computations inside the loop are correct at the boundaries—that is, for the initial and final values of the loop control variable. Finally, the tester should make sure that the module or system still meets its specification when a loop executes zero times and that under no circumstances can the loop execute forever.

Integration Testing

In Section 6.5 we discussed the differences between top-down and bottom-up testing of a single system. In *integration testing,* the program tester must determine whether the individual components of the system, which have been separately tested (using either top-down or bottom-up testing, or some combination), can be integrated with other similar components. Each phase of integration testing deals with larger units, progressing from individual modules, through subsystems, and ending with the entire system. For example, after two subsystems are completed, integration testing must determine whether the two subsystems can work together. Once the entire system is completed, integration testing must determine whether that system is compatible with other systems in the computing environment in which it will be used.

EXERCISES FOR SECTION 10.5

Self-Check

1. Devise a set of data to test function `enter_int` (Fig. 10.1) using:
   a. white-box testing
   b. black-box testing
2. Write the pseudocode algorithms (or the C++ code) to verify that the input values to the functions `compute_gross` and `compute_net` in Fig. 4.9 are meaningful.

Programming

1. Write a function `enter_money` based on the function `enter_int` shown in Fig. 10.1. Your function should have the same behavior as `enter_int`, but it should be written to check for an appropriate range of type `money` data rather than integer data.
2. Write a template function `enter_data` based on the function `enter_int` shown in Fig. 10.1. Your function should have the same behavior as `enter_int`, but it should be written to check for an appropriate range of type `T` data rather than integer data.
3. Write appropriate calls to functions `enter_money` (Programming Exercise 1 in this section) and `enter_float` (Programming Exercise 1 in Sec. 10.2) to ensure that meaningful values of rate and hours are read in by the payroll program in Section 4.5. Indicate where these calls should be inserted in the payroll program. Also write the prototypes for these functions. (Before you can write the function calls, you will first need to decide on the range of values to be considered meaningful for the purposes of this program.)

10.6 _____ FORMAL METHODS OF PROGRAM VERIFICATION

In the last section, we described some aspects of program and system testing. We stated that testing should begin as early as possible in the design phase and continue through system implementation. Even though testing is an extremely valuable tool for providing evidence that a program is correct and meets its specification, it is difficult to know how much testing is enough. For example, how do we know that we have tried enough different sets of test data or that all possible paths through the program have been executed?

For these reasons, computer scientists have developed a second method of demonstrating the correctness of a program. This method is called *formal verification.* By carefully applying formal rules, we can determine that a program meets its specification just as a mathematician proves a theorem using definitions, axioms, and previously proved theorems. This approach has been shown to work well on small programs, but there is some question as to whether it can be used effectively on very large programs or program systems.

In this section, we confine our attention to two fundamental aspects of program verification: the assertion and the loop invariant. The discussion here will be more intuitive and practical than formal. Our goal is to encourage you to think clearly about the purpose of each C++ code segment or function that you write, to insert comments concerning this intent where appropriate, and to check to ensure that your algorithms and C++ code are consistent with this intent.

Assertions

An important part of formal verification involves the use of *assertions,* logical statements about the program that are supposed to be true whenever they are encountered during the execution of a program. The C++ library assert.h provides support for the use of assertions in the form of *logical predicates*: expressions that can have a value of either true or false. If at any point during the execution of your program a predicate is encountered that has the value of false, a suitable error message will be written to the standard error file stderr and your program will terminate execution.

We believe it is premature to introduce the formal use of C++ assertions in this text. Instead, we will illustrate how to write each assertion that we use as a program comment describing what is supposed to be true about the program variables at the point at which it appears. We will focus our attention primarily on the special assertions related to program loops.

Example 10.1 The following program fragment contains a sequence of assignment statements, each followed by an assertion:

```
//  assert: 5 is a constant
a = 5;       // assert: a is equal to 5
x = a;       // assert: x is equal to 5
y = x + a;   // assert: y is equal to 10
```

The truth of the first assertion, a is equal to 5, follows from executing the first statement with the knowledge that 5 is a constant. The truth of the second assertion, x is equal to 5, follows from executing x = a with the knowledge that a is 5. The truth of the third assertion, y is equal to 10, follows from executing y = x + a with the knowledge that x is 5 and a is 5. In the earlier fragment, we used assertions as comments to document the change in a program variable after each assignment statement executes. ■

The task of a person using formal verification is to prove that a program fragment meets its specification. For the fragment above, this means proving that the final assertion, or *postcondition* (y is equal to 10), follows from the initial presumption, or *precondition* (5 is a constant), after the program fragment executes. The assignment rule (presented in the box below) is critical to this process. If we know that a is equal to 5 is true, this rule allows us to make the assertion x is equal to 5 after executing the statement x = a.

The Assignment Rule

```
//   P(a)
x = a;
//   P(x)
```

Explanation: If P(a) (for example, a = 5) is a logical predicate (assertion) about a, the same predicate with x substituted for a will be true after the assignment statement x = a; executes.

Loop Invariants

We stated earlier that loops are a common source of program errors. It is often difficult to determine that a loop body executes exactly the right number of times or that loop execution causes the desired change in program variables. A special type of assertion, a *loop invariant,* is used to help establish the correctness of an iterative algorithm. We introduced loop invariants in Section 9.5. These invariants were written informally as comments using English statements involving program variables. In general, a loop invariant is a logical expression for which the following four points must be shown to be true:

1. The loop invariant must be true initially; that is, it must be true before loop execution begins the first time.
2. The execution of the loop must preserve the loop invariant; that is, if the loop invariant is true prior to the next iteration of the loop, it must still be true after this iteration is complete.
3. The loop must terminate after some finite number of executions.
4. The loop invariant must capture the intent (correctness) of the algorithm. Thus if the invariant is still true when the loop terminates, the algorithm must compute the desired result.

Therefore, the loop invariant defines a relationship among the variables of a loop that remains true as loop execution progresses (hence the name invariant).

As an example of a loop invariant, let's examine the loop below, which accumulates the sum of the integers 1, 2, ... , n where n is a positive integer and sum and n are integers:

```
// Accumulate the sum of integers 1 through n in sum.
// Assert: n >= 1 (precondition)
sum = 0;
i = 1;
while (i <= n)
{
    sum += i;
    i++;
}   // end while
```

In this example, the invariant should be a logical expression about the loop control variable i and the accumulating sum. The best way to gain some insight into how to formulate a loop invariant is to trace the progress of the loop through several iterations. Figure 10.6 sketches this loop's progress for the first three iterations. At the end of the third iteration, i is 4 and sum is $6 = 1 + 2 + 3$, or the sum of all integers less than 4.

When loop repetition finishes, i will be n+1 and sum will contain the desired result $(1 + 2 + 3 + ... + n)$. Therefore, we propose the following as the loop invariant:

```
// Invariant: 1 <= i <= n+1 and sum is equal to the sum of all
//            positive integers less than i.
```

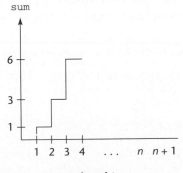

Figure 10.6   Sketch of summation loop for $n = 3$

Based on the four points listed earlier (and repeated below), it can be shown that this invariant is correct for the summation loop:

- *The loop invariant must be true before loop execution begins.* Clearly, this is the case, because before loop entry i is 1. Also, the invariant requires that sum be equal to the sum of all positive integers less than i. Because sum is initialized to 0, this is also the case.
- *The execution of the loop must preserve the loop invariant.* To prove that this is the case, we need to use the technique of *mathematical induction.* To provide a reasonable demonstration that the invariant is preserved, it is usually sufficient to check the values of all variables affected by the loop during the last iteration (or the next-to-last and last iterations). In this example, when the last iteration begins, i is equal to n and

$$sum = 1 + 2 + \dots + (i-1)$$

In the last iteration, i is added to sum. Because i is equal to n at this point, sum is indeed equal to the sum of the integers 1 through n.
- *The loop must terminate.* Following the addition of i to sum, i is incremented (i now equals n+1), the loop repetition test i<=n fails, and loop execution terminates.
- *The loop invariant must capture the intent of the algorithm.* As mentioned above, sum is indeed equal to the sum of the integers 1 through n after loop execution terminates.

In program verification, the loop invariant is used to prove that the loop meets its specification—that it does what it is supposed to do. For our purposes, we will use the invariant to document what we know about the loop's behavior. We will place the invariant just before the code associated with the loop, as shown Fig. 10.7.

Some computer scientists recommend writing the loop invariant as a preliminary step before coding the loop. The invariant can then be used as a guide to help determine the correct repetition condition for a loop. This condition, the loop initialization, and the increment of the loop control variable are the key factors affecting the correct execution of the loop. By hand tracing

Figure 10.7   Summation loop with invariant

```
// Accumulate the sum of integers 1 through n in sum.
// Assert: n >= 1 (precondition)
// Invariant: 1 <= i <= n+1 and sum is equal to the sum of all
//            positive integers less than i.
sum = 0;
i = 1;
while (i <= n)
{
   sum += i;
   i++;
}  // end while
```

the execution of a loop with appropriate *boundary cases* of the variables affected by the loop, we can gain a reasonable assurance that the loop behaves as desired. In the summation example, we checked that i and sum had the correct values in the boundary cases involving the first and last iterations of the loop. This typical loop analysis should be performed for all loops that you write.

Invariants and the `for` Statement

Because the loop invariant states what we know to be true about a loop after each iteration, we should be able to write an invariant for a for loop as well as a while loop. Because the loop control variable in a C++ for loop is incremented just before loop exit and retains its final value, the same preconditions and postconditions and the same loop invariant can be used for both loops:

```
// Accumulate the sum of integers 1 through n in sum.
// Assert: n >= 1 (precondition)
// Invariant: 1 <= i <= n+1 and sum is equal to the sum of all
//            positive integers less than i.
sum = 0;
for (i = 1; i <= n; i++)
    sum += i;
```

Invariants and Sentinel-Controlled Loops

Example 10.2   Figure 10.8 shows a sentinel-controlled while loop that computes the product of a collection of values. Loop exit occurs after reading in the sentinel value. The loop invariant indicates that the variable product is the product of all values read before the current one and that none of these values was the sentinel.

Figure 10.8   Sentinel-controlled loop with invariant

```
cout << "When done, enter: " << sentinel << " to stop.";
// Compute the product of a sequence of data values.
// Assert: sentinel is a constant (precondition).
// Invariant: product is the product of all prior values read
//            into num and no prior value of num was the sentinel.
product = 1;
cout << "Enter the first number: ";
cin >> num;
while (num != sentinel)
{
    product *= num;
    COUT << "Enter the next number: ";
    cin >> num;
}  // end while
```

The analysis of this loop with respect to the four points listed earlier requires some explanation. The invariant is true "by default" before loop execution begins because it makes no statement about the value of the product before any values are read in. After the first iteration of the loop, product is equal to num × 1, as desired. After each subsequent iteration, product is always equal to the product of all values read. Furthermore, because the loop is not repeated once the sentinel has been read, the loop invariant is still preserved.

So far, this seems simple enough. However, two important questions have not yet been considered:

- What if there are no data other than the sentinel value?
- What if there is no sentinel value at the end of the data?

These may seem like silly questions, but they point out two potential errors that can easily occur with the input data to many problems—errors that often are not properly handled by programmers. The first case (no data other than the sentinel value) can be handled in several ways. One way is to state explicitly in the invariant the assumed value of product if there are no data to be processed. The easiest choice for this value of product is 1. This choice yields the following invariant:

```
// Invariant: product is the product of all prior values read
//            into num and no prior value of num was the
//            sentinel. If no values are read in, product is
//            assumed to be 1.
```

If the sentinel value is missing, the program will eventually terminate when an attempt is made to read past the end-of-file. In this case, the value of product may well be correct, but our program will not be able to use it. In such situations, it is better to use the C++ end-of-file test to determine when all data have been read. This option is discussed in Programming Exercise 2 at the end of this section. ∎

Function Preconditions and Postconditions

A function's precondition is a logical statement about its input arguments. The postcondition may be a logical statement about its output arguments (and return value), or it may be a logical statement that describes the change in *program state* caused by the function execution. Any of the following activities represents a change in program state: changing the value of a variable, writing additional program output, reading new input data. It is as important to describe the effect of a function on device input or output and variable or class attributes as it is to indicate the effect on output or input/output arguments.

Example 10.3   The precondition and postcondition for function `enter_int` (see again Fig. 10.1) are repeated next:

```
// READS INTEGER BETWEEN min_n AND max_n INTO n
int enter_int
   (int min_n,        // IN: minimum range value for n
    int max_n)        // IN: maximum range value for n

// Pre:     min_n and max_n are assigned values.
// Post:    If min_n <= max_n, returns the first data value read
//          that has a value between min_n and max_n (inclusive).
//          Otherwise, prints a message and exits.
// Returns: First integer read that has a value between min_n and
//          max_n.

{
   ...
}
```

The precondition tells us that input arguments `min_n` and `max_n` are defined before the function begins execution. The postcondition tells us that the function returns the first data value read in that has a value between `min_n` and `max_n` whenever `min_n <= max_n` is true.   ∎

EXERCISES FOR SECTION 10.6

Self-Check   1. Write the loop invariant and the assertion following the loop for the `while` loop in function `enter_int` in Fig. 10.1.
2. If the sentinel-controlled loop in Fig. 10.8 were rewritten as a flag-controlled loop, what would the new loop invariant look like? Use zero as the sentinel value, and define the flag `no_zero` as the value of the condition `num != sentinel`. The flag should remain true until a zero value is read.
3. Write the loop invariant for the loop in Fig. 5.15 (temperature conversion).
4. In Example 10.2 (involving the sentinel-controlled loop) we chose 1 for the product value in the case in which no data preceded the sentinel value. Although this was an easy choice, it did not enable us to determine whether the missing data condition occurred. Describe one possible change to the loop in Fig. 10.8 that would enable the program to check for missing data following loop execution.
5. Consider the following version of the loop shown in Fig. 10.8:

```
cout << "When done, enter: " << sentinel << " to stop.";
// Compute the product of a sequence of data values.
// Assert: sentinel is a constant (precondition).
// Invariant: product is the product of all prior values
//            read into num and no prior value of num was
//            the sentinel.
```

```
product = 1;
cout << "Enter the first number: ";
while (num != sentinel)
{
    cin >> num;
    product *= num;
    cout << "Enter the next number: ";
} // end while
```

Does the invariant still hold true for this loop? Carefully explain your answer.

Programming   1. Write a function that returns the count of the number of nonzero digits in an arbitrary integer number. Your solution should include a while loop for which the following is a valid loop invariant:

```
// Invariant: 0 <= count; number > 0 and number has been
//            divided by 10 count times.
```

The assertion below should be valid following the loop:

```
// Assert: number = 0
```

2. Rewrite the product computation loop shown in Fig. 10.8 to terminate on end-of-file. Be sure to include the appropriate invariant as a comment.

10.7 ——— PROFESSIONAL ETHICS AND RESPONSIBILITIES

Software engineers and computer programmers are professionals and should always act that way. As part of their jobs, programmers may be able to access large data banks containing sensitive personnel information, information that is classified "secret" or "top secret," or financial transaction data. Programmers should always behave in a socially responsible manner and not retrieve information that they are not entitled to see. They should not use information to which they are given access for their own personal gain or do anything that would be considered illegal, unethical, or harmful to others.

You may have heard stories about "computer hackers" who have broken into secure data banks by using their own computer to call (by telephone) the computer that controls access to the data bank. Some individuals have sold classified information retrieved in this way to intelligence agencies of other countries. Other hackers have tried to break into computers to retrieve information for their own amusement or as a prank, or just to demonstrate that they can do it. Regardless of the intent, this activity is illegal, and the government will prosecute anyone who does this. Your university now probably addresses this kind of activity in your student handbook. The punishment is probably similar to that for other criminal activity, because that is exactly what it is.

Another illegal activity sometimes practiced by hackers is the insertion of special code, called a *virus*, in a computer's disk memory. A virus will cause sporadic activities to disrupt the operation of the host computer. For example, unusual messages may appear on the screen at certain times. Viruses can also cause the host computer to erase portions of its own disk memory, thereby destroying valuable information and programs. Viruses are spread from one computer to another when data are copied from the infected disk and processed by a different computer. Certainly, these kinds of activity should not be considered harmless pranks; they are illegal and should not be done under any circumstances.

A programmer who changes information in a database containing financial records for his or her own personal gain is guilty of *computer theft* or *computer fraud*. This is a felony that can lead to fines and imprisonment.

Another example of unprofessional behavior is using someone else's programs without permission. Although it is certainly permissible to use modules in libraries that have been developed for reuse by your own company's programmers, you cannot use another programmer's personal programs or programs from another company without getting permission beforehand. Doing this may lead to a lawsuit, and you or your company may have to pay damages.

Another fraudulent practice is submitting another student's code as your own. This, of course, is plagiarism and is no different from copying paragraphs of information from a book or journal article and calling it your own. Most universities have severe penalties for plagiarism, which may include failing the course and/or dismissal from the university. You should be aware that even if you modify the code slightly or substitute your own comments or different variable names, you are still guilty of plagiarism if you are using another person's ideas and code. To avoid any question of plagiarism, find out beforehand your instructor's rules with respect to working with others on a project. If group efforts are not allowed, make sure that you work independently and submit only your own code.

Many commercial software packages are protected by copyright laws and cannot be copied or duplicated. It is illegal to make additional copies of protected software that you may be using at work in order to use this software at home on your computer or on someone else's computer. Besides the fact that this is against the law, using software copied from another computer increases the possibility that your computer will receive a virus. For all these reasons, you should act ethically and honor any copyright agreements that pertain to a particular software package.

Computer system access privileges or user account codes are also private property. Such privileges are usually granted for a specific purpose. For example, you may be given a computer account for work to be done in a particular course or, perhaps, for work to be done during the time you are a student at your institution. The privilege is to be protected; it should not be loaned to anyone else and should not be used for any purpose for which it was not intended. When you leave the institution, this privilege is normally terminated and any accounts associated with the privilege will be closed.

Computers, computer programs, data, and access (account) codes are like any other property. If they belong to someone else and you are not explicitly given use privileges, then do not use them. If you are granted a usage privilege for a specific purpose, do not abuse the privilege—so that it will not be taken away.

We often tend forget the significance of information and security devices as they relate to the computer. We tend to view information privacy, intellectual property, and access privileges differently when the computer is involved. But electronic mail, personal programs and documents, and computer passwords demand the same privacy as U.S. mail, term papers, and keys to personal lock boxes.

Legal issues aside, it is important that we apply the same principles of right and wrong to computerized property and access rights as to all other property and privileges. If you are not sure about the propriety of something you are thinking about doing, ask first. As students and professionals in computing, we need to be aware of the example we set for others. As a group of individuals who are most dependent on computers and computer software, we must respect both the physical and the intellectual property rights of others. If we set a bad example, others are sure to follow.

CHAPTER REVIEW

Software engineering is an area of study and practice encompassing a broad range of topics. In this chapter we focused on several of these topics, including the system software life cycle (SLC), algorithm and program efficiency, program testing and verification, and ethics and social responsibility. Special emphasis was placed on the use of abstraction as an important tool in the analysis and design of large, complex programs.

We began our discussion with a description of the phases of the software life cycle:

1. Requirements specification
2. Analysis
3. Design
4. Implementation
5. Testing and verification
6. Operation, follow-up, and maintenance

We then reviewed the limitations of procedural abstraction. The concept of data abstraction was introduced and the advantages of practicing data abstraction in performing systems analysis and design were summarized.

We discussed the importance of identifying the problem domain information to be represented and manipulated in a program and introduced the idea of encapsulating the representations and manipulations for each problem domain entity in a single, encapsulated unit. The fact that C++ provides a feature (the `class`) for implementing such encapsulations was cited as a major advantage and one of the reasons for using C++ in the beginning course of a computer science curriculum.

Additional issues related to software testing and validation were introduced. We discussed planning for testing, selection of test teams, structured walkthroughs, black-box testing, white-box testing, and integration testing. We also introduced program verification as an alternative to testing and described the use of assertions and loop invariants in this process. In this book, we will use informal versions of these logical statements about programs and loops to aid our understanding of our code and of the demonstration that it does what it is intended to do.

Finally, because we geared the discussion in this chapter to techniques practiced by software professionals, we included a discussion of ethics and professional behavior. We described the special responsibilities that programmers have because of their ability to access sensitive information. We discussed computer viruses and how they are spread. We also described how using another programmer's code or ideas is plagiarism and carries severe penalties in industry as well as in the classroom.

✔ QUICK-CHECK EXERCISES

1. The six phases of the software life cycle are listed below in arbitrary order. Place them in their correct order.

   - testing and verification
   - design
   - requirements specification
   - operation and maintenance
   - implementation
   - analysis

2. In which phases are the users of a software product likely to be involved?
3. In which phases are the programmers and analysts likely to be involved?
4. Which phase lasts the longest?
5. _____ testing requires the use of test data that exercise each statement in a module.
6. _____ testing focuses on testing the functional characteristics of a module.
7. Which of the following may be false?

   - loop invariant
   - `while` condition
   - assertion

8. The use of loop invariants is useful for which of the following?

- loop control
- loop design
- loop verification

9. Write a loop invariant for the following code segment:

```
product = 1;
counter = 2;
while (counter < 5)
{
    product *= counter;
    counter++;
}
```

Answers to Quick-Check Exercises

1. requirements specification, analysis, design, implementation, testing and verification, operation and maintenance
2. requirements specification, testing and verification, operation and maintenance
3. all phases
4. operation and maintenance
5. white-box
6. black-box
7. `while` condition
8. loop design, loop verification
9. ```
// Invariant: counter <= 5 and product contains product of all
//   integers < counter
```

# REVIEW QUESTIONS

1. Explain why the principle of information hiding is important to the software designer.
2. Define the terms *procedural abstraction* and *data abstraction*.
3. Which of the following are likely to occur in a programmer's library of functions? Explain your answers.

   a. A function that raises a number to a specified power
   b. A function that writes the user instructions for a particular program
   c. A function that displays the message HI MOM in block letters
   d. A function that displays the block letter M

4. Which of the following statements is incorrect?

   a. Loop invariants are used in loop verification.
   b. Loop invariants are used in loop design.
   c. A loop invariant is always an assertion.
   d. An assertion is always a loop invariant.
```

5. Write a function that computes the average number of characters found in the lines of a text file. Include loop invariants and any other assertions necessary to verify that the function is correct.

PROGRAMMING PROJECTS

1. Write a set of library functions that can be used to determine the following information for an integer input argument:

   a. Is it a multiple of 7, 11, or 13?
   b. Is the sum of the digits odd or even?
   c. What is the square root value?
   d. Is it a prime number?

   Write a driver program that tests your library functions, using the input values 104 3773 13 121 77 3075

2. Each month, a bank customer deposits $50 into a savings account. Assume that the interest rate is fixed (does not change) and is a problem input. The interest is calculated on a quarterly basis. For example, if the account earns 6.5 percent interest annually, it earns one-fourth of 6.5 percent every 3 months. Write a program to compute the total investment, the total amount in the account, and the interest accrued for each of the 120 months of a 10-year period. Assume that the rate is applied to all funds in the account at the end of a quarter, regardless of when the deposits were made.

   Print all values accurate to two decimal places. The table printed by your program when the annual interest rate is 6.5 percent should begin as follows:

MONTH	INVESTMENT	NEW AMOUNT	INTEREST	TOTAL SAVINGS
1	50.00	50.00	0.00	50.00
2	100.00	100.00	0.00	100.00
3	150.00	150.00	2.44	152.44
4	200.00	202.44	0.00	202.44
5	250.00	252.44	0.00	252.44
6	300.00	302.44	4.91	307.35
7	350.00	357.35	0.00	357.35

   Carefully design your system in terms of separate functional modules, and use either C++ library functions or your own in writing your program.

3. Redo Programming Project 2, adding columns to allow comparison of interest compounded monthly (one-twelfth of annual rate every month) with continuously compounded interest. The formula for continuously compounded interest is

   $$amount = principle \times e^{rate \times time},$$

   where *rate* is the annual interest rate and *time* is expressed in years. Carefully design your system in terms of separate functional modules, and use either C++ library functions or your own in writing your program.

4. An employee time card is represented as one long string of characters having the following form:

Positions	Data
1–10	Employee last name
11–20	Employee first name
21	Contains C for city office or S for suburban office
22	Contains U (union) or N (nonunion)
23–26	Employee identification number
27	Blank
28–29	Number of regular hours (a whole number)
30	Blank
31–36	Hourly rate (dollars and cents)
37	Blank
38–39	Number of dependents
40	Blank
41–42	Number of overtime hours (a whole number)

Write a program that processes a collection of these strings stored in a data file and writes the results to an output file.

a. Compute gross pay using the formula

gross = regular hours × rate + overtime hours × 1.5 × rate.

b. Compute net pay by subtracting the following deductions:

federal tax = 0.14 × (*gross* − 13 × *dependents*)
social security = 0.052 × *gross*
city tax = 4% × *gross* if employee works in the city
union dues = 6.75% × *gross* for union member

All information read and all values computed in parts (a) and (b) should be written to the output file.

Carefully design your system in terms of separate functional modules, and use either C++ library functions or your own in writing your program.

5. Write a menu-driven program that contains options for creating a data file to be processed by the payroll program described in Programming Project 4. (The user should be prompted to enter several time "cards" from the keyboard.) Your program should allow the user to display the time cards in the file, add new time cards to the end of the existing file, delete time cards from an existing file based on their ordinal position within the file (e.g., delete the seventh time card), and quit the program.

Carefully design your system in terms of separate functional modules, and use either C++ library functions or your own in writing your program.

6. For any one of the previous programming projects, identify and list all of the problem domain data entities relevant to the problem solution. For each such entity, list the information about the entity needed to solve the problem and provide a list of the operations on this information required in the problem solution.

11 User-Defined Classes

In this chapter, we expand our capability to practice data abstraction and object-oriented programming by further study of the C++ class. The C++ class provides a mechanism to encapsulate, or build a protective wall around, its data and function members. A class contains a public and private section, and only the information provided in the public section of the class is accessible from the outside—everything else is hidden. The class construct enables you to build truly self-contained program components that may be designed, implemented, and tested separately and then integrated into a larger program system. You should follow the techniques illustrated in this chapter and the rest of the book to design and build large program systems.

We show how to use classes to define our own user-defined data types as encapsulations of data and operations. Then, we show how to declare and manipulate objects that are instances of the new class type. We implement a variety of classes, including a class for a counter, circle, simple string, and bank account.

11.1 ____ CLASS DEFINITION

From the very beginning of this book, we have been using a number of abstract data types as the foundation elements in our programming. The types int, float, double, and char are examples of data abstractions that are *built into* the C++ language. We have also studied string and stream types that are provided through C++ class libraries, and we have seen how to implement a user-defined money class. Section 7.5 presented a definition of simple data types called *enumeration types.* All of these abstract data types consist of data items and a collection of operations that can be performed on those items. For example, the type float abstraction might consist of 4 bytes (32 bits) of memory. The leftmost bit indicates the sign of the number, and the remaining bits are divided into two parts, the *characteristic* and the *mantissa.* The operations defined on variables of type float include addition, multiplication, subtraction, and division. These operations manipulate the sign, characteristic, and mantissa of their operands to produce type float results. In actuality, we rarely need to concern ourselves with the details of either the storage of type float values or their manipulation—these details are hidden from the view of most programs that we write. We simply declare variables of this type and use the operations defined on them.

With this in mind, we now turn our attention to the definition of *user-defined data types.* This journey will extend through the remainder of this book. We will illustrate how to define our own data types as extensions to the C++ language, tailoring them as necessary to the particular problem to be solved, while at the same time making them general enough so that they can be reused repeatedly. The C++ feature that will enable us to do this is the class.

Although beyond the scope of this book, the C++ class also enables experienced C++ programmers to derive new classes from existing classes through a process called *inheritance.* Using inheritance, a programmer creates new classes from an existing class by adding additional data members or new member functions, or by redefining member functions. Inheritance enhances reusability because it allows a programmer to modify existing classes easily to fit new situations, rather than having to start from scratch (see Appendix E).

Class Definition for the `counter` Class

Figure 11.1 shows an example of a class definition for a simple abstract data type, which we have called a `counter`. The class contains two single integer variables `value` and `max_value`, declared at the bottom of Fig. 11.1. The variable `value` represents the current counter value; the variable `max_value` represents the maximum counter value where 0 is always the minimum counter value. The value of `max_value` is set when we allocate storage for a counter object (more on this later). The variables `value` and `max_value` represent the counter *state* at a particular time. Just like any variable you used as a counter in an earlier program, a `counter` object can be set to an initial value in its range (use function `set_value`) and its value can be increased (use function `increment`) or decreased (use function `decrement`) by 1. Functions `access_value` and `access_max_value` retrieve the data stored in a `counter` object.

The class definition begins with the line

```
class counter
```

and consists of everything between the opening brace { through the semicolon following the closing brace }. Later, we will explain the purpose of the compiler directives that precede and follow the class definition.

The public definition part of a class (beginning with `public:`) describes the interface of the class with other program components that use the class. This interface consists of the specification of any variables, types, constants, and function prototypes that a programmer needs to know about in order to use the class successfully. This information is also all the compiler needs to know about to compile a program that uses the class. Identifiers such as `set_value`, `increment`, and `decrement` (in Fig. 11.1) that are declared in the public section of a class may be accessed inside or outside of the class. The public section for class counter contains seven function prototypes. We define these functions in Section 11.2.

The class definition also contains a *private section* (beginning with `private:`) in which the variables, constants, data types, and function prototypes to be hidden from other program components are specified. Identifiers declared in the private section, such as the variable `value`, can be accessed only within the class itself.

Figure 11.1   The abstract data type `counter`

```
// FILE: Counter.h
// COUNTER CLASS DEFINITION

#ifndef COUNTER_H_            // used to avoid multiple definitions
#define COUNTER_H_           //    not part of class

class counter
{
   public:
       // Member Functions...
       // Constructors
       counter ();
       counter (int);

       // SET COUNTER VALUE
       void set_value (int);

       // INCREMENT COUNTER
       void increment ();

       // DECREMENT COUNTER
       void decrement ();

       // RETURN CURRENT COUNTER VALUE
       int access_value () const;

       // RETURN MAXIMUM COUNTER VALUE
       int access_max_value () const;

   private:
       // Data Members (Attributes)...
       int value;
       int max_value;

}; // NOTE -- a class definition must end with a semicolon

#endif // COUNTER_H_
```

The functions specified in a class definition section are referred to as the *member functions* of the class. The variables, constants, and data types are referred to as the *data members* or *storage attributes* of the class (we use these last two terms interchangeably in the text).

Normally, we place the data members in the private section of the class because the user does not need to know their names or internal representations. This allows us to change their representations at a later time (for example, from type `float` to type `money`) without affecting the programs that use the class. The member functions provide the interface between the user and the data, so they are normally found in the public section of the class.

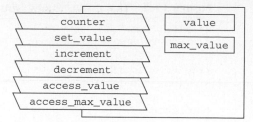

Figure 11.2 Class diagram for `counter` class

Figure 11.2 shows a diagram for the `counter` class. As shown in this *class diagram,* the member functions declared in the public section of the class are accessible outside of the class. The variables declared as private, `value` and `max_value`, are protected and may not be accessed from outside the class.

Compiler Directives in File `counter.h`

The purpose of the first two lines in the `Counter.h` file

```
#ifndef COUNTER_H_        // used to avoid multiple definitions -
#define COUNTER_H_        //     not part of class
```

is to prevent multiple definitions of the identifiers defined in class `counter` during compilation of a project (program system) in which more than one file includes the `counter` class. These lines precede the class definition and cause the compiler to skip all lines through the last line in the file

```
#endif // COUNTER_H_
```

during the second and subsequent processings of

```
#include "counter.h"
```

The line beginning with `#ifndef` (`if not defined`) tests whether identifier `COUNTER_H_` has been defined yet. If it has not, the second line defines `COUNTER_H_` giving it the value `NULL`. Then the compiler processes the rest of the lines in file `Counter.h`. If your compiler attempts to include this file at a later time, it will determine that `COUNTER_H_` is defined, so all lines through `#endif` will be skipped, thereby preventing multiple definitions of the identifiers in the class. There is nothing magical about the name `COUNTER_H_`; we formed it by adding `_H_` to the end of the class name.

Using the `counter` Class

To help us understand the `counter` class, let us look at an example program that uses it (see Fig. 11.3). This class declares two counters, one with range 0

Figure 11.3 Test program and sample output for user of `counter` class

```
// FILE: CntrTest.cpp
// TEST PROGRAM FOR Counter CLASS

#include <iostream.h>
#include "Counter.h"

void main ()
{
   // Local data ...
   counter c_1;          // variable of type counter - maximum value
                         //    INT_MAX
   counter c_2 (10);     // variable of type counter - maximum value
                         //    10

   // Test set_value, increment, decrement, and access_value
   //    functions.
   c_1.set_value (50);          // Set_value of c_1 to 50
   c_1.decrement ();
   c_1.decrement ();
   c_1.increment ();
   cout << "Final value of c_1 is " << c_1.access_value () << endl;

   c_2.increment ();
   c_2.increment ();
   c_2.decrement ();
   cout << "Final value of c_2 is " << c_2.access_value () << endl;
}
```

───────────── Program Output ─────────────

```
Final value of c_1 is 49
Final value of c_2 is 1
```

through INT_MAX (a system constant) and one with range 0 through 10. It performs several operations on each counter and displays the final counter value.

The first two lines of code in the main function

```
counter c_1;
counter c_2 (10);
```

declare two objects of type `counter`. These declarations resemble those that we have used previously for the C++ built-in data types, and they have a similar effect. The first `counter` object, c_1, can have a maximum value of INT_MAX, which is the largest integer value on your C++ system (defined in `<limits.h>`). The second `counter` object, c_2, can have a maximum value of 10. Both c_1 and c_2 have an initial value of 0.

The legal operations on the objects c_1 and c_2 are defined by the member functions declared in the public section of the counter class. These are the only operations allowed on the counter variables.

The statement

```
c_1.set_value (50);              // Set_value of c_1 to 50
```

sets the value of counter c_1 to 50. Because c_1 is an object, we use dot notation to apply the member function set_value to it. Next, we decrement c_1 twice and increment it once. The function call c_1.access_value (in the first line beginning with cout) retrieves its final value (49), which is then displayed. The counter object c_2 has an initial value of 0. We increment c_2 twice and decrement it once. The last program line retrieves and displays the final value of c_2, which is 1.

Compiler Directives in File CntrTest.cpp

We need the #include line

```
#include "Counter.h"
```

in file CntrTest.cpp because the counter class definition is stored in file Counter.h. You do not need to store classes in separate files, but it is highly advisable. Doing so enables you to keep each file fairly small and makes it easier to locate and reuse classes as the need arises. In fact, in this book, most C++ classes are stored in two separate files, a .h file and a .cpp file. The .h, or *header*, file contains the *header part* of the class, including the public and private sections, down to and including the semicolon following the right brace. The .cpp file (shown in Section 11.2) normally contains all member function implementations. Note that the .h and .cpp *file extensions* are not standard and may be compiler-dependent.

File CntrTest.cpp also contains the line

```
#INCLUDE <iostream.h>
```

because it accesses operator << and stream cout, both defined in class iostream.

EXERCISES FOR SECTION 11.1

Self-Check   1. Explain why the prefixes c_1 and c_2 are required in references to the functions set_value, increment, decrement, and access_value as shown in Fig. 11.3.

Programming   1. A for loop header that uses a counter variable has the form

```
for (i = 0; i < n; i++)
```

where i is type int. Declare a counter variable i and rewrite the for loop header using the operators for the counter class.

11.2 —— CLASS IMPLEMENTATION

The implementation section of the `counter` class (Fig. 11.4) contains the implementation of the class member functions. This information, provided in file `counter.cpp`, is also hidden from the class users, which do not need to know these details. An important aspect of this section is the use of the *scope resolution operator* `::` as a prefix to the function name in each function header. This operator tells the compiler that the function being defined is a member of the class (`counter` in this case) named just preceding the operator. The scope resolution operator applies to all identifiers in the function definition through the closing `}`.

When you call a member function, you specify through dot notation to which object the function is being applied. Therefore, you do not need to use an object name and period before data member `value` in the member function definitions.

A class member function can access all the data members of the class directly. Therefore, you should not use member functions `set_value` or `access_value` inside the member function definitions to process the `value` attribute of an object. However, you must use these functions outside the class.

Figure 11.4   Implementation file for `counter` class

```
// FILE: Counter.cpp
// COUNTER CLASS DEFINITION

#include "Counter.h"

#include <iostream.h>
#include <limits.h>          // For INT_MAX

// DEFAULT CONSTRUCTOR
counter::counter ()
{
    value = 0;
    max_value = INT_MAX;     // Set max_value to default maximum
}  // end default constructor


// CONSTRUCTOR WITH ARGUMENT
counter::counter (int m_v)   // IN: maximum integer value
{
    value = 0;
    max_value = m_v;         // Set max_value to maximum integer
                             // value
}  // end constructor with argument
```

(continued)

Figure 11.4 *(continued)*

```
// SET COUNTER VALUE
void counter::set_value (int val)
{
   if (val >= 0  &&  val <= max_value)
      value = val;
   else
      cerr << "New value is out of range. Value not changed."
           << endl;
}  // end set_val


// INCREMENT COUNTER
void counter::increment ()
{
   if (value < max_value)
      value++;
   else
      cerr << "Counter overflow. Increment ignored." << endl;
}  // end increment


// DECREMENT COUNTER
void counter::decrement ()
{
   if (value > 0)
      value--;
   else
      cerr << "Counter underflow. Decrement ignored." << endl;
}  // end decrement


// RETURN CURRENT COUNTER VALUE
int counter::access_value () const
{
   return value;
}  // end access_value


// RETURN MAXIMUM COUNTER VALUE
int counter::access_max_value () const
{
   return max_value;
}  // end access_max_value
```

Constructors

The file begins with *constructors,* two special member functions with the same
name as the class. A constructor automatically executes each time an object of
type counter is declared. Its purpose is to initialize one or more of the
object's data members. The constructor without an argument is the *default*

constructor and is the one that normally executes. It sets the initial state of the object (value is 0, max_value is INT_MAX). The second constructor executes whenever the declaration ends with an argument list. For example, the declaration of object c_2 in Fig. 11.3

```
counter c_2 (10);
```

causes the second constructor to execute, setting value to 0 and max_value to 10.

A constructor cannot specify a return type or explicitly return a value. For this reason, you should not precede the constructor name with either void or a data type when writing its prototype or definition.

Accessor Functions

You should be able to read and understand the remaining member functions. Functions set_value, increment, and decrement *modify* the counter value; functions access_value and access_max_value *retrieve* the counter data and are called *accessor functions.* This classification of the operations of an abstract data type into those that modify data and those that retrieve a data value is typical. Most of the member functions that you write for a class will fall into one of these two categories.

The accessor function headings end with the word const, which indicates to C++ that the function execution does not change the state of the object to which it is applied. You should do this whenever you define a member function that does not change an object's state. Examples of such functions would be member functions that display or test an object's data.

Compiler Directives in File **Counter.cpp**

Notice that both files CntrTest.cpp and Counter.cpp contain the line

```
#include "Counter.h"
```

You must place this directive in both files, so that C++ can access the class definition when compiling these files. Again, the line beginning with #ifndef in file Counter.h prevents multiple definitions of identifiers. File Counter.cpp also accesses identifier INT_MAX (from file limits.h), so it must include that file. Similarly, file Counter.cpp accesses operator << and cerr, so it must include file iostream.h.

EXERCISES FOR SECTION 11.2

Self-Check   1. Explain how the *scope resolution operator* :: is used in the counter class shown in Fig. 11.4. Why is this operator needed?

2. Explain why no prefix is required in references to the attribute `value` in functions `set_value`, `increment`, `decrement`, and `access_value`, as shown in Fig. 11.4.

Programming 1. Write a type `bool` member function called `at_max` that returns a value of true when the value of a `counter` object has reached its maximum value. Discuss how you would have to modify the class definition to include `at_max`.

11.3 ⎯⎯ SUMMARY OF RULES FOR USE OF CLASSES AND OBJECTS

Objects as Class Instances

The declaration

```
counter c_1;
```

creates a new object `c_1` which is called an *instance* of the class `counter`. The declaration causes a constructor (the default constructor in this case) to execute and to initialize the data members of object `c_1`. As we pointed out earlier, this declaration is conceptually the same as declarations involving standard data types, such as

```
int value;
```

All of these declarations associate a name with a region of computer memory. We will continue to refer to names associated with the fundamental types and enumeration, array, and struct types as variables. We will refer to names associated with types defined using the class construct as *objects*. Thus `c_1` is an object (of type `counter`) in the test program for the `counter` class; `value` and `max_value`, variables (of type `int`), are attributes of the `class`.

The member functions of the class should include at least one constructor that has the same name as the class. A constructor automatically executes each time a `counter` object is created, and the constructor initializes one or more of the object's data members. The default constructor takes no argument and executes when the object declaration does not end with an argument list. A constructor does not have a result type and cannot return a value.

Public Versus Private Access

Any user program component may apply member functions, `set_value`, `increment`, `decrement`, `access_value`, and `access_max_value`, as operations on object `c_1`. In this example, the member functions for the `counter` class are all publicly accessible. This sometimes is not the case, as classes may have member functions that are private and therefore not directly accessible outside the class. For example, if the member functions of a class needed to call another function that was not part of the class interface, we would declare this function in the private section to restrict its availability.

Similarly, not all class attributes must appear in the private section of a class. However, you should have a very good reason for cases in which an attribute is made public and hence not protected from outside reference. You also do not need to maintain separate function prototype declarations and definitions. In fact, for functions that have simple implementations, such as those in the `counter` class, this can be more inconvenient than useful. We do it here because it is important at this stage in the learning process to develop and maintain a clear view of what should be kept private and what should be kept public in a class.

A program that uses a class is called a *client* of the class, and the class itself is referred to as the *server*. The client program may declare and manipulate objects of the data type defined by the class. It may do so without knowing the details of the internal representation of the data or the implementation of its operators and without affecting the server program code. Thus, the details of the server are hidden from the client. As we proceed through the rest of the book, we will illustrate, among other things, the benefits of this information-hiding capability and its impact in all phases of the software development process.

Syntax for Class and Member Function Definitions

A summary of the syntax rules for defining a class and its operations is shown in the following two displays.

C++ SYNTAX

Class Definition

Form:

```
class class_name
{
    public:
        List of class attributes (variables, types, constants, and so
            on) that may be accessed by name from outside the class
        List of prototypes for each member function that may be
            accessed by name from outside the class

        ...
    private:
        List of class attributes (variables, types, constants, and so
            on) that are intended to be hidden for reference from
            outside the class
        List of prototypes for each member function intended to
            be hidden from outside of the class

        ...
```

```
                };


Example: class checking_account
         {
            public:
                // Member functions ...
                // DEPOSIT INTO CHECKING ACCOUNT
                void make_deposit
                  (int);              // IN: number of account to
                                      //     receive deposit

                // SET SERVICE CHARGE FOR ACCOUNT
                void set_service_charge
                  (int,               // IN: number of account to
                                      //     be charged
                   float);            // IN: amount of service
                                      //     charge

            private:
                // Data members ...
                char init_first, init_middle, init_last;
                                      // initials
                int this_account_number;    // account
                                            //     number
                float balance;              // balance in
                                            //     account
                float service_charge_amount;  // amount of
                                              //     service
                                              //     charge
         };
```

Interpretation: The functions, variables, types, and constants that are declared in the class definition are accessible to all class member functions (see next display). However, only those declared as public may be accessed by name from outside the class. ∎

C++
SYNTAX

Class Member Function Definition

Form: *type class_name* : : *fname*
    (list of formal argument types and names)
    {

```
        . . .
    function body
        . . .
    }
```

Example:
```
// CONSTRUCTOR
checking_account::checking_account ();
{
    this_account_number = 0;
    balance = 0.0;
}


// DEPOSIT INTO CHECKING ACCOUNT
void checking_account::make_deposit
  (int account_number)  // IN: number of account
                        // to receive deposit
{
    // Local data ...
    money amount;

    // Make deposit.
    if (account_number == this_account_number)
    {
        . . .
    }
    else
        cout << "Wrong account number specified."
            << endl;
}
```

Interpretation: The function `make_deposit` is a member of the class `check-ing_account`. It is like any other C++ function except that it has access to all class data and function members. To ensure that C++ knows that the functions are associated with a class, the function names must be preceded by the name of the class followed by the scope resolution operator `::`.

Reminder: Note carefully that all data members (variables, constants, and so on) of a class are directly accessible to the class member functions.   ■

Comparing the struct and the class

Both the struct and the class define a data type that is a collection of related data elements that may be of different types. Both may also contain function prototype declarations, although we have not illustrated their use with structs, and both provide the capability to specify three levels of access control to the functions and data: public, protected (not discussed in this text), and private. In fact, the only difference between structs and classes is that with structs, the default access is public; with classes, the default is private. We will use structs in this book only when no functions are involved in the structure definition and when all data are to be publicly accessible within the scope of the defining function; otherwise, we will use classes.

Project Files and Separate Compilation

In many C++ systems, you will need to create a project file to facilitate compiling and linking the separate `.cpp` files for your client and server. The details of doing this are system dependent. However, your project file must contain all the `.cpp` files (but not the `.h` files) that comprise your program system. As a first step, you should designate as the active window the client program (the one that contains the main function) and attempt to compile it. If you are successful, select a command such as Build which will complete the compilation of the other `.cpp` files and then link the object files together. When this step completes successfully, you can run the `.exe` file created by the Build operation.

Combining Arrays, Structs, and Classes

We will illustrate a class that has an array as one of its data members in Section 11.6. You can combine arrays, structs, and classes in many different ways in C++. For example, the declaration

```
counter counts[10];
```

allocates storage for an array of ten counter objects named `counts[0]` through `counts[9]`. The default constructor sets the `value` attribute of each `counter` object to 0 and the `max_value` attribute to `INT_MAX`. We will provide many examples of combinations of different kinds of data structures in Chapter 12.

Function Overloading and Polymorphism

There are two constructors in the `counter` class. When translating a `counter` object declaration, the C++ compiler determines which constructor function to use based on the presence or absence of an actual argument. Having multiple functions with the same name is called *function overloading*. The ability of a function to perform different operations based on its actual arguments is called *polymorphism*.

Another example of function overloading and polymorphism would be the use of the same function name in different classes. For example, several classes might declare a function named `display` that displays the class attributes. For a particular call of function `display`, C++ determines which `display` function to use by the data type of the object to which it is applied. This capability frees the programmer from having to ensure that each function name is unique and does not appear in another class.

EXERCISES FOR SECTION 11.3

Self-Check   1. For the array of counters declared in this section, write a function call to increment the contents of `counts[3]`. Write a statement that displays the value stored in `counts[4]`.

11.4 —— CLASSES AS OPERANDS AND ARGUMENTS

In Chapter 9, we discussed rules for using arrays and structs as function arguments and as operands of assignment, equality, relational, and arithmetic operators. We saw that, with the exception of assignment of structs, you were not permitted to use familiar operators with these data structures.

You can use the assignment operator with two objects of the same class type; however, you cannot use the other familiar operators with classes unless you explicitly define them as operators for the class (a process called *operator overloading*). We will show you how to do this in Section 12.7.

Normally you do not need to pass objects as member function arguments, because you use dot notation to specify the object to which the function is being applied. If you need to specify an operation that involves two objects, you can apply the member function to one and pass the other one as an argument. The rules for using objects as formal arguments follow.

Rules for Using Objects as Formal Arguments

- If `C` is a class type, use `C& ob_1` to declare `ob_1` as a formal reference argument.
- If `C` is a class type, use `const C& ob_1` to specify that formal argument `ob_1` cannot be changed by the function's execution.

Rule 2 is for efficiency but is not a requirement of C++. You can declare an object as a value argument in a function header, but that requires storing a local copy of the object argument each time the function is called. We illustrate the second rule in the following example.

Example 11.1   Figure 11.5 shows a function called `compare_counter` written as a member function for the class `counter`. The function compares two counter objects and returns −1, 0, or 1 depending on whether the `value` attribute of the counter object to which it is applied is less than (−1), equal to (0), or greater than (1), the `value` attribute of its counter argument. If `c_1` and `c_2` are counters, you can use either statement below to call `compare_counter`. Both function calls return the same value (0) when the counter objects have the same `value` attribute; they return different results when the `value` attributes of the counter objects are not equal.

```
c_1.compare_counter (c_2)       or       c_2.compare_counter (c_1)
```

Figure 11.5   Function `compare_counter`

```
int counter::compare_counter (const counter& a_counter) const
{
    IF (value <= a_counter.value)
        result = -1;
    else if (value == a_counter.value)
        result = 0;
    else
        result = 1;

    return result;
}
```

Each condition compares the `value` attribute of the object to which the function is applied (denoted by just `value`) to the `value` attribute of the function argument (denoted by `a_counter.value`). The function result is based on this comparison.

Some programmers dislike the lack of symmetry in the definition and use of function `compare_counter` and would prefer to use a function call such as

```
compare_counter (c_1, c_2)
```

in which both objects being compared (not just one) are passed as arguments to function `compare_counter`. We will see how to do this in Section 12.7.   ■

EXERCISES FOR SECTION 11.4

Self-Check   1. What value is returned by the function call `c_1.compare_counter (c_2)` when `c_1.value` is 5 and `c_2.value` is 7? Answer the same question for `c_2.compare_counter (c_1)`.

Programming   1. Rewrite function `compare_counter` to base its result on both attributes of a counter object: `value` and `max_value`.
2. Write a function `less_than` that returns a value of true when the `counter` object to which it is applied has a smaller value than its `counter` argument.

11.5 ——— A CIRCLE CLASS

In a graphics program, we need to represent simple graphical objects such as circles, squares, rectangles, and triangles. We want to be able to position these objects anywhere on the screen and draw them in various sizes and colors. Besides drawing the objects themselves, we want to display the object's characteristics, including its center coordinates, area, and perimeter. In this section, we design a class that could be used to represent circle objects.

Design of `circle` Class

Our `circle` class should have data members to represent the *x*- and *y*-coordinates of a circle object's center as well as its radius, color, area and perimeter. Normally a user of this class would set values for all of a circle object's attributes except its area and perimeter, These attributes can be computed (using member functions) after its radius is set by the class user.

Since our purpose is to represent objects for display on a screen, we will use type `int` attributes for the circle's center coordinates and radius. We will declare an enumeration type `color` with eight values for the circle color. We summarize these design decisions next and Fig. 11.6 shows the class definition.

Specification for `circle` Class

Public Data Type for `circle` Class

`color`   An enumeration type with 8 color values

Attributes for `circle` Class

`x_coord` (`int`)	*x*-coordinate of the circle
`y_coord` (`int`)	*y*-coordinate of the circle
`radius` (`int`)	Radius of the circle
`c_color` (`color`)	Color of the circle
`area` (`float`)	Area of the circle
`perimeter` (`float`)	Perimeter of the circle

Member Functions for `circle` Class

`circle`	A constructor
`set_coord`	Sets the *x*- and *y*-coordinates
`set_radius`	Sets the circle radius
`set_color`	Sets the circle color

compute_area	Computes the area of the circle: $area = \pi \times radius^2$
compute_perimeter	Computes the perimeter of the circle: $perimeter = 2.0 \times \pi \times radius$
display_circle	Displays circle attributes
get_x_coord	Returns x-coordinate value
get_y_coord	Returns y-coordinate value
get_color	Returns circle color
get_area	Returns circle area
get_perimeter	Returns circle perimeter

Figure 11.6 Class Definition for `circle`

```cpp
// File Circle.h
// Circle class definition

#ifndef CIRCLE_H_
#define CIRCLE_H_

class circle
{
    public:
        // enumeration type
        enum color {black, blue, green, cyan, red,
                    magenta, brown, lightgray, nocolor};

        // Member Functions...
        // CONSTRUCTOR
        circle ();

        // SET CENTER COORDINATES
        void set_coord (int, int);

        // SET_RADIUS
        void set_radius (int);

        // SET COLOR
        void set_color (color);

        // COMPUTE THE AREA
        void compute_area ();

        // COMPUTE THE PERIMETER
        void compute_perimeter ();

        // DISPLAY ATTRIBUTES
        void display_circle () const;

        // ACCESSOR FUNCTIONS
        int get_x_coord () const;
        int get_y_coord () const;
```

(continued)

Figure 11.6   *(continued)*

```
        int get_radius () const;
        color get_color () const;
        float get_area () const;
        float get_perimeter () const;

    private:
        // Data members (attributes) ...
        int x_coord;
        int y_coord;
        int radius;
        color c_color;
        float area;
        float perimeter;
};

#endif // CIRCLE_H_
```

We declare the enumeration type `color` in the public section of the class, so that a user of the class can access its values. The ninth color value, `nocolor`, indicates that a color value has not yet been assigned. Rather than define the enumeration type here, another approach is to define a separate class `color` and to include this class (using `#include "color.h"`) in class `circle`. This modification is left as Programming Project 1 at the end of the chapter.

Notice that we declare member functions `compute_area` and `compute_perim` as `void` functions. You might be tempted to declare them as type `float` because they each compute a floating-point value. However, that value is stored in a class attribute and is not returned as a function result. You can call accessor functions `get_area` and `get_perimeter` (both type `float`) to retrieve the attribute values.

Using Class `circle`

Figure 11.7 shows a small driver function (with program output) that tests the operation of several member functions of class `circle`. First, it stores values in attributes `x_coord`, `y_coord`, `radius`, and `c_color` (value is `magenta`) Next, it computes the values for attributes `area` and `perimeter`. Finally, it displays the circle's attributes. Notice that in the call to function `set_color` (in the middle of Fig. 11.7), we must use the scope resolution operator `circle::` to inform the compiler that `magenta` is defined in class `circle`.

Implementation File for Class `circle`

Figure 11.8 shows the implementation file for class `circle`. The file begins by declaring the constant `pi`, which is used by member functions `compute_area`

Figure 11.7   A driver function to test class `circle`

```
// File CirDrivr.cpp
// Tests the Circle class

#include <iostream.h>
#include "circle.h"

void main ()
{
    // Local data ...
    circle my_circle;

    // Set circle attributes.
    my_circle.set_coord (150, 100);
    my_circle.set_radius (10);
    my_circle.set_color (circle::magenta);

    // Compute area and perimeter
    my_circle.compute_area ();
    my_circle.compute_perimeter ();

    // Display the circle attributes.
    cout << "The circle attributes follow:" << endl;
    my_circle.display_circle ();
}
```

───────────────── Program Output ─────────────

```
The circle attributes follow:
x-coordinate is 150
y-coordinate is 100
radius is 10
color is 5
area is 314.159
perimeter is 62.8318
```

and `compute_perimeter`. When a `circle` object is declared, the constructor initializes the numerical attributes to zero and the object's color to `nocolor`. Notice that `display_circle` casts the value of `c_color` to type `int` before displaying it.

In the definition of accessor function `get_color`, we must precede the result type `color` with the scope resolution operator `circle::`. We do this to inform the compiler that `color` is declared inside class `circle`. We did not need to do this for the identifier `color` (the formal argument type) in member function `set_color` because the scope resolution operator `circle::` precedes the argument declaration. We leave the other accessor functions as Programming Exercise 1 at the end of this section.

Figure 11.8   Implementation file for class `circle`

```cpp
// File circle.cpp
// Circle class implementation

#include <iostream.h>
#include "circle.h"

const float pi = 3.14159;

// Member Functions...
// CONSTRUCTOR
circle::circle ()
{
   x_coord = 0;
   y_coord = 0;
   radius = 0;
   c_color = nocolor;
   area = 0.0;
   perimeter = 0.0;
}

// SET CENTER POSITION
void circle::set_coord (int x, int y)
{
   x_coord = x;
   y_coord = y;
}


// SET_RADIUS
void circle::set_radius (int r)
{
   radius = r;
}


// SET COLOR
void circle::set_color (color c)
{
   c_color = c;
}


// COMPUTE THE AREA
void circle::compute_area ()
{
   area = pi * radius * radius;
}
```

(continued)

Figure 11.8   *(continued)*

```
// COMPUTE THE PERIMETER
void circle::compute_perimeter ()
{
    perimeter = 2 * pi * radius;
}


// DISPLAY ATTRIBUTES
void circle::display_circle () const
{
    cout << "x-coordinate is " << x_coord << endl;
    cout << "y-coordinate is " << y_coord << endl;
    cout << "color is " << int (c_color) << endl;
    cout << "area is " << area << endl;
    cout << "perimeter is " << perimeter << endl;
}


// ACCESSOR FUNCTIONS
circle::color circle::get_color () const
{
    return c_color;
}

//      Insert definitions for rest of accessor functions here.
//         ...
```

EXERCISES FOR SECTION 11.5

Self-Check
1. Draw a class diagram for the circle class.
2. Why is it not necessary to pass `radius` as an argument to functions `get_area` and `get_perimeter`?
3. Explain how you would have to modify the class `circle` to form a class `rectangle`.

Programming
1. Write the accessor functions.
2. Write a private member function `write_color` to display a color value as a string instead of as an integer (see Fig. 7.6) Modify `display_circle` to use this function.

11.6 —— A SIMPLE STRING CLASS

If C++ did not provide a `string` class in its system library, we would need to write our own. In this section we discuss a simple string class that has an array of characters as one of its data members.

Design of Class `simple_string`

We do not have the programming expertise to build a string class that has all the capability of library `string`, but we would like to be able to at least read a sequence of characters from a stream into a simple string object and display the sequence that we stored. Our class should have a data member for storing the characters in a string and a data member that is a count of the number of characters stored. It should also have a constant data member that specifies the maximum number of characters that may be in a string.

We will provide a minimal set of member functions for our class: a function to read in a string (`read_string`), a function to display a string (`write_string`), and a function to retrieve a character at a particular position (`at`). In addition, we provide accessor functions to retrieve the string length and string capacity. We summarize these decisions next.

Specification for Class `simple_string`

Attributes for `simple_string` **Class**

`capacity`	Constant 255
`contents`	string data
`length (int)`	string length

Member Functions for `simple_string` **Class**

`simple_string`	Constructor
`read_string`	Reads the string data
`write_string`	Writes the string data
`at`	Retrieves a character at a specified position
`get_length`	Returns the string length
`get_capacity`	Returns the string capacity

Definition of Class `simple_string`

Figure 11.9 shows the definition for class `simple_string`. The class definition shows that attribute `capacity` is an enumerator with value 255. This is how we define constant class attributes because C++ does not permit us to ini-

Figure 11.9   Class Definition for `simple_string`

```
// File SimplStr.h
// Simple string class definition

#ifndef SIMPLE_STRING_H_
#define SIMPLE_STRING_H_
```

(continued)

Figure 11.9   *(continued)*

```
class simple_string
{
    public:
        // Member Functions...
        // CONSTRUCTOR
        simple_string ();

        // READ A SIMPLE STRING
        void read_string ();

        // DISPLAY A SIMPLE STRING
        void write_string () const;

        // RETRIEVE THE CHARACTER AT A SPECIFIED POSITION
        //    Returns the character \0 if position is out of bounds
        char at (int) const;

        // RETURN THE STRING LENGTH
        int get_length () const;

        // RETURN THE STRING CAPACITY
        int get_capacity () const;

    private:
        // Data members (attributes) ...
        enum {capacity = 255};       // Capacity of a string
        char contents[capacity];     // string data
        int length;                  // string length
};

#endif //SIMPLE_STRING_H_
```

tialize a class attribute (using `const int capacity = 255;`) except inside a class constructor. The string data is stored in data member `contents`, which is an array of characters whose size is `capacity`.

Figure 11.10 shows how the character string `Philly cheesesteak` would be stored in object `food` (type `simple string`). Table 11.1 lists some calls to member functions applied to object `food` and their effect.

Testing Member Functions of Class `simple_string`

Figure 11.11 shows a small driver function that tests the operation of the member functions of class `simple_string`. First, it reads a character string typed at the keyboard (terminated by pressing RETURN) and displays the string on the next line. It then displays each character on a separate line by executing the `for` statement

```
for (int pos = 0; pos < a_string.get_length (); pos++)
    cout << a_string.at (pos) << endl;
```

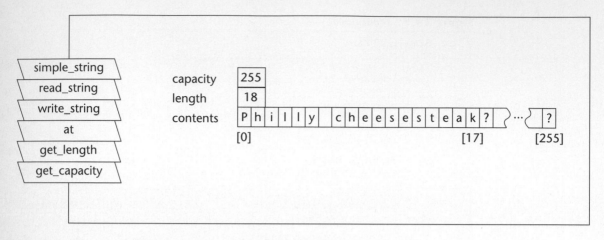

Figure 11.10 Diagram for `simple_string` object `food`

Table 11.1 Sample calls to member functions of class `simple_string`

CALL	EFFECT
`food.get_length ()`	returns 18
`food.at (0)`	returns P
`food.at (17)`	returns k
`food.at (18)`	returns `'\0'`, the null string
`food.get_capacity ()`	returns 255
`food.write_string ()`	Displays `Philly cheesesteak`

The loop body executes once for each character in the data string, retrieving and displaying that character. The loop repetition test compares the current character position (starting at 0) to the string length.

Figure 11.11 A driver function to test class `simple_string`

```
// File StrDrivr.cpp
// Tests the simple string class

#include <iostream.h>
#include "SimplStr.h"

void main ()
{
   // Local data ...
   simple_string a_string;   // input - data string
```

(continued)

Figure 11.11 *(continued)*

```
    // Read in a string.
    cout << "Enter a string and press RETURN: ";
    a_string.read_string ();

    // Display the string just read.
    cout << "The string read was: ";
    a_string.write_string ();
    cout << endl;

    // Display each character on a separate line.
    cout << "The characters in the string follow:" << endl;
    for (int pos = 0; pos < a_string.get_length (); pos++)
        cout << a_string.at (pos) << endl;
}
```

───────── Program Output ─────────

```
Enter a string and press RETURN: Philly cheesesteak
The string read was: Philly cheesesteak
The characters in the string follow:
P
h
i
l
l
y

c
h
e
e
s
e
s
t
e
a
k
```

Implementation File for Class `simple_string`

Figure 11.12 shows the implementation file for class `simple_string`. When a `simple_string` object is declared, the constructor initializes the object to an empty string by setting its data member `length` to 0.

Figure 11.12 Implementation file for class `simple_string`

```
// File SimplStr.cpp
// Simple string class implementation

#include <iostream.h>
#include "SimplStr.h"
```

(continued)

Figure 11.12   *(continued)*

```
// Member Functions...
// CONSTRUCTOR
simple_string::simple_string ()
{
   length = 0;    // Denotes an empty string
}


// READ A SIMPLE STRING
void simple_string::read_string ()
{
   // Local data...
   char next;                // input - next data character
   int pos = 0;              // subscript for array contents

   cin.get (next);           // Get first character from cin
   while ((next != '\n') && (pos < capacity))
   {
      // Insert next in array contents
      contents[pos] = next;
      pos++;
      cin.get (next);        // Get next character from cin
   }

   length = pos;             // Define length attribute
}


// WRITE A SIMPLE STRING
void simple_string::write_string () const
{
   for (int pos = 0; pos < length; pos++)
      cout << contents[pos];
}


// RETRIEVE THE CHARACTER AT A SPECIFIED POSITION
//    Returns the character \0 if position is out of bounds
char simple_string::at (int pos) const   // IN: position of
                                         // character to get
{
   // Local data...
   const char null_character = '\0';

   if ((pos < 0) || (pos >= length))
   {
      cerr << "Character at position " << pos
           << " not defined." << endl;
      return null_character;
   }
```

(continued)

Figure 11.12 *(continued)*

```
    else
        return contents[pos];
}


// RETURN THE STRING LENGTH
int simple_string::get_length () const
{
    return length;
}

// RETURN THE STRING CAPACITY
int simple_string::get_capacity () const
{
    return capacity;
}
```

Member function read_string (compare with read_scores in Fig. 9.14) uses a while loop to read each data character from the keyboard and store it in the next element of data member contents. Loop repetition terminates when the newline character '\n' is read or the array is filled (length equals capacity). Notice that the newline character is not stored in contents or counted in the string length.

Member function write_string displays each character in data member contents, starting with the character at position 0 (the first character) and ending with the character at position length - 1 (the last character). If length is zero (the case for an empty string), the for loop body does not execute because pos < 0 is false. Therefore, no characters are displayed for an empty string.

Member function at begins by testing whether the value of its argument pos is in bounds for the string stored in array contents. If so, the character selected by its argument is returned; otherwise, an error message is printed and a special character called the *null character* ('\0') is returned.

EXERCISES FOR SECTION 11.6

Self-Check

1. Does read_string store leading blanks in a string object? If your answer is yes, how could you change it to skip leading blanks?
2. What happens if the user presses the return key before typing any characters when reading in a string?
3. Compare the for loop in the driver function for simple_string with the one in member function write_string. Explain why the loop repetition condition in the driver function uses member function get_length but the loop in member function write_string does not.

Programming
1. Modify the constructor to store the null character (`'\0'`) in every character position of a new object of type `simple_string`.
2. Write a member function `concat` that stores the string formed by concatenating its two argument strings in the string object to which it is applied.

11.7 ——— A SAVINGS ACCOUNT CLASS

In this section, we consider how to develop a class for representing a savings account. The following case illustrates the use of a private member function to validate the account identification.

CASE STUDY: USING THE SAVINGS ACCOUNT CLASS

Problem Statement

You have been asked to define a savings account class that will enable you to represent a savings account and perform all necessary operations on a savings account object.

Analysis

Your experience in maintaining your own bank account should help you determine what attributes and member functions to include. Associated with each account is the account holder's name, an account identification number, the account balance, and the annual interest rate. The operations performed on a savings account include: opening the account, making a deposit, making a withdrawal, checking the balance, adding interest, getting the balance, and closing the account. The specification for our savings account class follow.

SPECIFICATION FOR SAVINGS ACCOUNT CLASS

> **Attributes for Savings Account Class**
>
> | | |
> |---|---|
> | `name` (`string`) | The account holder's name |
> | `id` (`int`) | Account identification |
> | `interest_rate`/`float` | The annual interest rate (%) |
> | `balance` (`money`) | The account balance |
>
> **Member Functions for Savings Account Class**
>
> | | |
> |---|---|
> | `savings` | A constructor |
> | `open_account` | Opens an account |

change_name	Changes the account name
add_interest	Adds quarterly interest
deposit	Processes a deposit
withdraw	Processes a withdrawal
close_account	Closes the account
get_balance	Gets the account balance

Private Member Function for Savings Account Class

valid_id	Validates the account identification before performing an operation

The class will include a private member function valid_id that will be called by other member functions to validate the user identification before performing a critical operation such as processing a withdrawal or deposit, changing the account name, or closing the account.

Design

The class definition (Fig. 11.13) provides all the information that a user of the class needs to know.

Figure 11.13   Definition for class savings

```
// File Savings.h
// Savings account class definition

#include <string>          // access string class
#include "money.h"         // access money class

#ifndef SAVINGS_H_
#define SAVINGS_H_

class savings
{
   public:
      // Member Functions...
      // CONSTRUCTOR
      savings ();

      // OPEN A NEW ACCOUNT
      void open_account ();

      // CHANGE ACCOUNT NAME
      void change_name (int, string);

      // ADD QUARTERLY INTEREST
      void add_interest ();
```

(continued)

Figure 11.13   *(continued)*

```
    // PROCESS A DEPOSIT
    void deposit (int, money);

    // PROCESS A WITHDRAWAL
    void withdraw (int, money);

    // CLOSE AN ACCOUNT
    void close_account (int);

    // GET ACCOUNT BALANCE
    money get_balance () const;

  private:
    // Data members (attributes) ...
    int id;
    string name;
    money balance;
    float interest_rate;

    // Member functions...
    // VALIDATE USER IDENTIFICATION
    bool valid_id (int) const;
};

#endif // SAVINGS_H_
```

Implementation

Next, we implement the member functions. Figure 11.14 shows the `.cpp` file for the savings account class.

Figure 11.14   File `Savings.cpp`

```
// File Savings.cpp
// Savings account implementation file

#include <iostream.h>
#include "savings.h"
#include <string>
#include "money.h"

// Member Functions...
// CONSTRUCTOR
savings::savings ()
{
   name = "";
   id = 0;
   balance = 0.0;
```

(continued)

Figure 11.14 *(continued)*

```
   interest_rate = 0.0;
}


// OPEN A NEW ACCOUNT
void savings::open_account ()
{
   cout << "Account name: ";
   getline (cin, name, '\n');
   cout << "Account ID: ";
   cin >> id;
   cout << "Initial balance: $";
   cin >> balance;
   cout << "Annual interest rate percentage: %";
   cin >> interest_rate;
}


// VALIDATE USER ID
bool savings::valid_id (int ident) const
{
   if (id == ident)
      return true;
   else
   {
      cerr << "Error - ID's do not match! "
      return false;
   }
}


// CHANGE ACCOUNT NAME
void savings::change_name (int ident, string na)
{
   if (valid_id (ident))
   {
      name = na;
      cout << "Changing account name to " << na << endl;
   }
   else
      cerr << "Reject name change request." << endl;
}


// ADD QUARTERLY INTEREST
void savings::add_interest ()
{
   // Local data
   float quarter_rate_frac;        // quarterly rate as a decimal
                                   //    fraction
```

(continued)

Figure 11.14 *(continued)*

```cpp
      quarter_rate_frac = interest_rate / 400.0;
      balance += balance * quarter_rate_frac;
}

// PROCESS A DEPOSIT
void savings::deposit (int ident, money amount)
{
   if (valid_id (ident))
   {
      balance += amount;
      cout << "Depositing " << amount << endl;
   }
   else
      cerr << "Reject deposit of " << amount << endl;
}

// PROCESS A WITHDRAWAL
void savings::withdraw (int ident, money amount)
{
   if ((valid_id (ident)) && (amount <= balance))
   {
      balance -= amount;
      cout << "Withdrawing " << amount << endl;
   }
   else
      cerr << "Reject withdrawal of " << amount << endl;
}


// CLOSE AN ACCOUNT
void savings::close_account (int ident)
{
   if (valid_id (ident))
   {
      cout << "Final balance for account number " << id
           << " is " << balance << endl;
      cout << "Account has been closed" << endl;
      balance = 0.0;
      id = 0;
      name = "";
   }
   else
      cerr << "Account not closed" << endl;
}


// GET ACCOUNT BALANCE
money savings::get_balance () const
{
   return balance;
}
```

Functions add_interest, deposit, and withdraw all assign a new value to attribute balance. Function add_interest divides the annual interest rate (a percentage) by 400.0 to convert it to a decimal fraction. Then it adds the interest amount for the quarter to the current balance.

Functions deposit and withdraw call valid_id to verify that the transaction ID (ident) and the account ID match before updating the balance attribute. Function withdraw also rejects a withdrawal that would lead to a negative balance. Functions close_account and change_name also check for an ID match before performing their operations. This extra check guards against invalid occurrences of these critical operations.

Testing

To test this class, we should create a driver function that allocates a type savings object and then performs several of the operations provided in the class. You should try calling member functions with valid and invalid account identification. Figure 11.15 shows a program with sample output that accomplishes this task.

Figure 11.15   A driver function to test class savings

```
// File SavDrivr.cpp
// Tests the savings class

#include <iostream.h>
#include "savings.h"
#include "money.h"

void main ()
{
    // Local data ...
    savings my_account;

    // Open a savings account.
    my_account.open_account ();
    cout << endl;

    // Make valid and invalid deposit.
    my_account.deposit (1234, 500.00);
    my_account.deposit (1111, 300.00);

    // Get and display balance.
    cout << endl << "Current balance is "
        << my_account.get_balance () << endl;
```

(continued)

Figure 11.15   *(continued)*

```
    // Make valid and invalid withdrawal.
    my_account.withdraw (1234, 750.00);
    my_account.withdraw (1234, 15000.00);

    // Add interest.
    my_account.add_interest ();

    // Close the account.
    my_account.close_account (1234);
}
```

——————— Program Output ———————

Account name: **John P. Getty**
Account ID: **1234**
Initial balance: **$1000.00**
Annual interest rate percentage: **%5**

Depositing $500.00
Error - IDs do not match! Reject deposit of $300.00

Current balance is $1,500.00
Withdrawing $750.00
Reject withdrawal of $15,000.00
Final balance for account number 1234 is $759.38
Account has been closed

EXERCISES FOR SECTION 11.7

Self-Check   1. Assume you have written a client program that creates two different bank account objects. Explain why it will not be possible to place a deposit intended for one of these accounts in the other.
2. Trace the following code fragment assuming the account is opened with an ID of 1234 and an initial balance of $500.

```
savings a_1;
int ident = 1234;

a_1.open_account ();
a_1.deposit (ident, 500);
a_1.withdraw (ident, 200);
a_1.get_balance (ident);
a_1.close_account (ident);
```

Programming   1. Write a code fragment for a client program that reads transaction data and then calls withdraw or deposit to update the balance based on whether the transaction type is W (for withdrawal) or D (for deposit). Assume the account ID is stored in variable my_id.

11.8 ___ DEFINING AND USING FUNCTIONS AND CLASSES: A SUMMARY OF RULES AND RESTRICTIONS

As you may have realized by now, C++ provides a wealth of program components (functions and classes) that all programmers can use in designing and building their own programs. C++ also provides mechanisms for programmers to build their own program component libraries. Your instructor or lab manager can tell you more about how to build and refer to such user-defined libraries on your operating system and for your version of the C++ language system. Our purpose here is to describe the reuse mechanism as it relates to your C++ programs. We will not go into those issues related to the particular computer system or C++ version you are using.

We can reuse the components in C++ or user-provided libraries by including the following library header files in our programs:

```
#include <iostream.h>
#include "Counter.h"
```

Once this has been done, however, we must be careful to follow the rules and restrictions for using functions (and argument consistency) and for defining and using classes. Failure to use the correct syntax or to follow the other rules that apply can cause significant headaches, especially when you are starting out. The following is an annotated list of the rules and restrictions described in this chapter for using library functions and for defining and using classes.

■ *Using Library Components—Functions:* When using a component from a library, you must know the name of the library in which the component is found and you must have a description of the component interface. Functions and classes that are stored in separate files must be either included in your program or separately compiled and linked with your program at execution time. The commands used in either case may vary according to the computer system you are using. Your instructor can give you the commands for your system.

Certain factors must be clear for any function you wish to use: what the function does (but not necessarily how); what value (if any) it returns; and the number, order, and type of the function's arguments. When you write a call to a function, you should ensure that there is a one-to-one correspondence and agreement in type between the actual and the formal arguments. You should also ensure that all preconditions for a function's arguments (as listed at the beginning of the function) are satisfied before the function call executes. Calls to member functions of an abstract data type must be prefixed by the name of the object being manipulated by the function, followed by a period, as in

```
my_account.open_account ();
```

You should be consistent in writing the definitions of any classes you may need. Normally, only the prototypes of the member functions required by the user in manipulating the data of an abstract data type should appear in the public section of the definition. Rarely, if ever, will you need to make public a class attribute (variable, constant, or type) declaration; these belong in the private section of your class. Additional functions, not required by the user but perhaps called by the class methods, may also appear in the private section of a class. Be sure to add the semicolon required after the right brace at the end of a class definition and after each function prototype included in the class definition.

- *Defining a Class:* The definition of a class should always follow the same form. The class should have a header such as

```
class savings
```

and it should have a public section (normally containing the prototypes of those functions that any client program may need to use). Most classes will also have a private section (normally containing the class attributes—variables, types, and constants). Some function prototypes may also appear in the private section, but these will be accessible only within the class and not to any client. Remember that all prototypes must end with a semicolon.

- *Defining Member Functions of a Class:* The definitions of the member functions of a class are usually placed in a separate file having the same name as the class header file but with the extension `.cpp` rather than `.h`. This file is compiled separately from the client program and linked with the program after compilation. The implementation header for each function must include the class name and scope resolution operator preceding the function name, as in

```
void counter::increment () or
circle::color circle::get_color ()
```

This identifies the function as a member of the class and allows it to reference the class attributes and other member functions. Functions not preceded by a class name will not be considered members of a class by the compiler and will not be allowed to reference class attributes. Function result types must also be preceded by the scope resolution operator (as in `circle::color`).

- *Using Classes:* When using classes, you must always remember to do the following:

1. Include the `.h` file for the class in the program that uses it.

2. Be sure to declare all objects of the class that will be used in the program. These declarations should be local to the program components that have a need to know about the object and hidden from those that do not have this need.
3. For member functions of a class, be sure to prefix the name of the function with the name of the object to which it is to be applied, as in

```
c_1.counter ();
```

11.9 ____ COMMON PROGRAMMING ERRORS

In Section 11.8, we provided a number of reminders concerning the rules and restrictions to be followed in using functions and classes. In this section, we describe a number of the different error messages you may see when errors occur in your C++ programs. All of the examples used for illustration involve the counter class described in Sections 11.1–11.3.

- *Function Argument and Return Value Errors* (see also Common Programming Errors in Chapters 3 and 6): Return value or argument mismatches involving class member functions may cause the compiler not to recognize the function as a member of the class. For example, if the prototype for the function access_value (defined in the counter class) specifies a return value of int but the function definition specifies a return value of float, the message

```
"'counter::access_value ()' is not a member function
of 'counter'"
```

will appear when the compiler attempts to compile the function definition. Even though the name of the function is the same, the return value inconsistency causes the compiler to treat the defined function as different from the prototype. Having the same name is not sufficient—return values and arguments are also used to distinguish among functions.

- *Failure to Define a Function as a Member of a Class:* This error can be caused in several ways:

1. Failure to prefix the function definition by the name of its class and the scope operator (two colons)
2. Failure to spell the function name correctly
3. Complete omission of the function definition from the class

In any case, the result is the same—a compiler error message indicating that the function you called

```
"is not a member"
```

of the indicated class. Thus, if `c_1` is an object of type `counter` and the C++ statement

```
c_1.print ();
```

appears in a client program, the message

```
"'print' is not a member of 'counter'"
```

will be displayed.

■ *Prefixing a Class Member Function Call:* Any reference (using the dot notation) to a class member function must be prefixed by the name of an object to be manipulated. For example, for function `increment` defined in class `counter`, the function call

```
c_obj.increment ();
```

is legal only if `c_obj` is declared as an object of type `counter`. If `c_obj` has a different type, the message

```
"Structure required on left side of ."
```

appears; if the identifier is not defined at all, an

```
"undefined symbol"
```

error will occur.

■ *Referencing a Private Attribute of a Class:* Identifiers declared as private attributes or functions in a class cannot be referenced from outside the class. Any such reference attempt will produce an

```
"undefined symbol"
```

error. Even if the correct prefix for such a reference is used—for example, `c_1.counter::value`—an error message will appear:

```
"'counter::value' is not accessible".
```

This message simply says that the identifier `value` declared in the class `counter` cannot be accessed from outside the class.

■ *Failure to Include a Required Header File:* Numerous messages will be generated by this programming error. Because the header file most likely contains the definitions for a number of the identifiers used in your program, perhaps the most common of these errors will be the

```
"undefined symbol"
```

■ *Missing Semicolon Following a Class Definition:* Failure to place a semicolon at the end of a class definition (after the right brace) will cause a number of errors when the definition is included in and compiled with another file. The semicolon is required to terminate the class definition and separate it from the function implementations (if these are included in the same file as the definition). Error messages that might appear as a result of this syntax error include

```
"Declaration right brace won't stop declaration",
"Declaration occurs outside of class"
```

and,

```
"class_name may not be defined",
```

where `class_name` is the name of the class in which the missing semicolon was detected.

- *Semicolons in a Function Header and Prototypes:* A missing semicolon at the end of a function prototype may cause a

```
"Statement missing ;"
```

or

```
"Declaration terminated incorrectly"
```

diagnostic (a prototype is a declaration and must be terminated with a semicolon). However, the accidental inclusion of a semicolon separating a function header from its definition will cause numerous compiler errors following the header.

CHAPTER REVIEW

In this chapter we focused attention on the definition and implementation of C++ classes. We showed how to define four data abstractions using classes: `counter`, `circle`, `simple_string`, and `bank_account`. In addition, we showed how to declare data objects (instances) of these new types and how to reference the operations defined on these objects.

We also discussed the ideas of function overloading and polymorphism in Section 11.3. Because C++ supports function overloading, we can use the same function name in different classes (and even the same class). C++ determines which version of the function to call based on the object it is applied to and the function's actual arguments.

 ## QUICK-CHECK EXERCISES

1. Why is an object prefix name required before the function name when referencing a member function of a class?

2. How does the C++ compiler know which + operation (`int`, `float`, `double`, etc.), to use when it evaluates an operator-operand-operator triple?
3. A class is an encapsulation of _____ and _____ in a single data structure.
4. A _____ declaration is needed to declare an object of a class type. It causes a _____ to execute.
5. The declared items in the _____ part of a class may not be directly accessed outside the class. Those in the _____ part are accessible outside the class.
6. Write a type declaration for an array of 12 objects of type `counter`; write an expression to increment the sixth element of your array.
7. Arrays and structs may not be used in the declarations of class attributes. True or false?
8. Why would you declare a private member function?
9. Where do you use member functions to access a class attribute? Where can you access the attribute directly?

Answers to Quick-Check Exercises

1. The prefix is required to specify the object to which the member function is applied.
2. The correct operation is chosen solely on the basis of the type of operands used in the triple.
3. data members (attributes), member functions
4. type, constructor
5. private; public
6. `counter my_counts[12];`

   `my_counts[5].increment ();`

7. false—they may be used
8. To provide a function that may be used inside of the class by other member functions but not outside of the class.
9. Use member functions in a client program. Access the attributes directly in the declaration of a member function of that class.

REVIEW QUESTIONS

1. Explain why each of the notions of information hiding, separation of concerns, and language extension is important to the software designer.
2. Write a C++ class definition for an abstract data type describing a bookstore inventory consisting of the attributes and methods given. The following attributes apply to a collection of eight books, each having the characteristics listed:

   ■ Book title (character string of maximum length 32)
   ■ Book author (character string of maximum length 20)
   ■ Book price (floating-point number having two decimal places)
   ■ Count of books on hand (integer)

The member functions are as follows:

- A constructor that is used to initialize all eight elements of the array (to any values you want)
- A function that displays in a readable tabular form the contents of the entire book collection
- A modify function that, once called, prompts the user first for a book number (1 through 8) and then for a code (T, A, P, or C) indicating which attribute (title, author, price, or count) of the indicated book is to be changed; finally, the function should provide a prompt for the new value of the attribute being altered.

Reasonable tests for valid input should be performed in the modify function. Write the declaration for an object named inventory of the type described by this class.

3. Redo the previous question assuming the following:

- Your attributes are simply the title, author, price, and count of one book.
- Your constructor is replaced by an explicit initialization function that initializes the contents of the book objects in your inventory.
- Your display function displays the information for a single book in your inventory.
- Your modify function no longer needs the number of the book to be changed (why not?) and begins by prompting for the attribute to be changed.

(*Hint:* You will need to declare an array of objects, size 8, of your book type.) Write a call to your modify function to change an attribute of one book.

4. Which of the following statements is incorrect?

a. All class attributes must appear in the private part of a class.
b. All class member functions must appear in the public part of a class.
c. The attributes of a class are allocated memory each time a member function of the class is called; this memory is deallocated when the called function returns control to its caller.
d. Classes may be used in C++ to model problem domain entities.

PROGRAMMING PROJECTS

1. Write a C++ class for an abstract data type color with a public enumeration type color_type, that has the color values shown in Figure 11.6. Your abstract data type should have an attribute for storing a single value of type color_type and member functions for reading (read_color) and writing (write_color) a color value, setting a color value, and accessing a color value. The function read_color should read a color as a string and store the corresponding color value in the value attribute of a type color object. The function write_color should display as a string the value stored in the value attribute of a type color object (See Fig. 7.6). Modify class circle and the driver function in Fig. 11.7 to include and use this class. You will need to remove the declaration for color in class circle. Test your modified driver function with the new color and circle classes.

Note: Programming Projects 2–6 are very similar to problems 1–5 in Chapter 10. These problems, however, require the use of the C++ class feature for complete program implementation.

2. Define a class `my_int` that has as its single attribute an integer variable and that contains member functions for determining the following information for an object of type `my_int`:

   a. Is it a multiple of 7, 11, or 13?
   b. Is the sum of the digits odd or even?
   c. What is the square root value?
   d. Is it a prime number?
   e. Is it a perfect number? (*Reminder:* The sum of the factors of a perfect number is equal to the number itself—for example, $1 + 2 + 4 + 7 + 14 = 28$, so 28 is a perfect number.) Write a client program that tests your methods, using the input values 104, 3773, 13, 121, 77, 3075.

3. Each month, a bank customer deposits $50 into a savings account. Assume that the interest rate is fixed (does not change) and is a problem input. The interest is calculated on a quarterly basis. For example, if the account earns 6.5 percent interest annually, it earns one-fourth of 6.5 percent every three months. Write a program to compute the total investment, the total amount in the account, and the interest accrued for each of the 120 months of a ten-year period. Assume that the rate is applied to all funds in the account at the end of a quarter, regardless of when the deposits were made.

   Print all values accurate to two decimal places. The table printed by your program when the annual interest rate is 6.5 percent should begin as follows:

MONTH	INVESTMENT	NEW AMOUNT	INTEREST	TOTAL SAVINGS
1	50.00	50.00	0.00	0.00
2	100.00	100.00	0.00	100.00
3	150.00	150.00	2.44	152.44
4	200.00	202.44	0.00	202.44
5	250.00	252.44	0.00	252.44
6	300.00	302.44	4.91	307.35
7	350.00	357.35	0.00	357.35

   Design a class to model the customer bank account, including the attributes for each account and at least five methods needed to initialize, update, and display the information in each account.

4. Redo Programming Project 3, adding columns to allow comparison of interest compounded monthly (one-twelfth of annual rate every month) with interest compounded continuously. The formula for continuously compounded interest is

   $$amount = principle \times e^{rate \times time}$$

   where *rate* is the annual interest rate and *time* is expressed in years.

5. An employee time card is represented as one long string of characters. Write a program that processes a collection of these strings stored in a data file and writes the results to an output file.

a. Compute gross pay using the formula

$gross = regular\ hours \times rate + overtime\ hours \times 1.5 \times rate$

b. Compute net pay by subtracting the following deductions:

$federal\ tax = 0.14 \times (gross - 13 \times dependents)$
$social\ security = 0.052 \times gross$
$city\ tax = 4\% \times gross$ if employee works in the city
$union\ dues = 6.75\% \times gross$ for union member

The data string for each employee has the following form:

Positions	Data
1–10	Employee last name
11–20	Employee first name
21	Contains C for city office or S for suburban office
22	Contains U (union) or N (nonunion)
23–26	Employee identification number
27	Blank
28–29	Number of regular hours (a whole number)
30	Blank
31–36	Hourly rate (dollars and cents)
37	Blank
38–39	Number of dependents
40	Blank
41–42	Number of overtime hours (a whole number)

Declare the attributes of the class and define and implement five class methods.

6. Write a menu-driven program that contains the following options:

- Creating a data file to be processed by the payroll program described in Programming Project 5 (the user should be prompted to enter several time "cards" from the keyboard)
- Displaying the time cards in the file on a printer
- Adding new time cards to the end of an existing file
- Deleting time cards from an existing file based on their ordinal position within the file (e.g., deleting the seventh time card)
- Quitting the program.

To add or delete lines from a text file requires copying the original data file to a scratch, or temporary, file and then back to the original file. During the copy process, time cards to be deleted are simply not copied to the scratch file. New time cards are added to the end of the file after all the time cards from the original file have been copied to the scratch file. Use classes as you see fit to model the additional abstract data types.

7. Your university runs many hundreds of courses each semester and needs to keep track of key information on each one. Among the data needed for each course would be the following:

- University course identification number
- Department course id and section number (for multiple sections of the same course)
- Number of credits for the course

- Days and times the course meets
- Room in which the course meets (building id and room number)
- Maximum course enrollment
- Campus on which the course is held
- Name of course instructor
- Number of students currently enrolled and the student id of each such student
- Course status: open (for additional enrollment), closed, or canceled

You must be able to change the value of each of these ten data items and, upon request, print all of this information. Initially, the values of the first seven items are known—the last three are not. Design and implement an abstract data type that can be used to model this university course entity. List the attributes that you expect to model and how, and list any assumptions that you have made about these attributes. Choose whatever 12 methods defined on objects of this type that you wish to implement as part of the class, and illustrate calls to several of these methods.

8. Write a C++ class definition for an abstract data type money that allows you to do basic arithmetic operations (addition, subtraction, multiplication, and division) on floating-point numbers having exactly two digits to the right of the decimal point. You need not write the implementations for the operations but be sure to include the prototypes for all member functions that would be needed in this class, including any that might be private to the class.

12

Modeling Data with Arrays, Structs, and Classes

The focus in this chapter is on modeling data with combinations of arrays, structs, and classes. We begin by studying the multidimensional array, which is an array whose elements are arrays. Next, we discuss arrays whose elements are structs and classes.

In the last chapter, we saw that a class is an improvement over a struct because it encapsulates data (class attributes) and operators (member functions). In this chapter, we study a data abstraction, the indexed list, which is an improvement over the array data structure. Like an array, you can use an indexed list object to provide storage for a collection of elements of the same data type, including array types, struct types, or classes. However, unlike an array, you cannot accidentally access storage space outside of an indexed list. We also include member functions for reading, displaying, searching, and sorting an indexed list object. We study a case that uses an indexed list object for storing a personal telephone directory.

The chapter concludes with a discussion of the stack, a data abstraction that has many applications in computer science. Like the indexed list, the stack implementation uses an array data member for information storage.

12.1 ____ MULTIDIMENSIONAL ARRAYS

The array data structure allows a programmer to organize information in arrangements that are more complex than the linear or one-dimensional arrays discussed so far. We can declare and use arrays with several dimensions of different sizes.

C++ SYNTAX

Multidimensional Array Declaration

Syntax: *element-type aname* [*size*$_1$] [*size*$_2$] ... [*size*$_n$] ;

Example: `double table[NROWS][NCOLS];`

Interpretation: The array declaration allocates storage space for an array *aname* consisting of *size*$_1$ $\times$ *size*$_2$ $\times$ ... $\times$ *size*$_n$ memory cells. Each memory cell can store one data item whose data type is specified by *element-type*. The individual array elements are referenced by the subscripted variables *aname*[0][0] ... [0] through *aname*[*size*$_1$-1] [*size*$_2$-1] ... [*size*$_n$-1]. An integer constant expression is used to specify each *size*$_i$. ∎

Declaring Two-Dimensional Arrays

Two-dimensional arrays, the most common multidimensional arrays, store information that we normally represent in tabular form. Let's first look at some examples of two-dimensional arrays—game boards, seating plans, and matrixes.

Example 12.1   The array declaration

```
char tic_tac_toe[3][3];
```

allocates storage for a two-dimensional array (`tic_tac_toe`) with three rows and three columns. This array has nine elements, each of which must be referenced by specifying a row subscript (0, 1, or 2) and a column subscript (0, 1, or 2). Each array element contains a character value. For the array shown in Fig. 12.1, the character O is stored in the subscripted variable

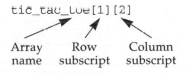

■

Example 12.2   Your instructor wants to store the seating plan (Fig. 12.2) for a classroom on a computer. The declarations

```
const int num_rows = 11;
const int seats_in_row = 9;
string seat_plan[num_rows][seats_in_row];
```

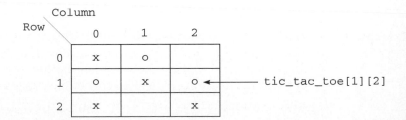

Figure 12.1   A tic-tac-toe board stored as array `tic_tac_toe`

allocate storage for a two-dimensional array of strings called `seat_plan`. Array `seat_plan` could be used to store the first names of the students seated in a classroom with 11 rows and 9 seats in each row. The statement

```
seat_plan[0][8] = "Gerry";
```

stores the string `"Gerry"` in the last seat of the first row. ∎

Initializing Two-Dimensional Arrays

Example 12.3 The statements

```
const int num_rows = 2;
const int num_cols = 3;
float matrix[num_rows][num_cols] = {{5.0, 4.5, 3.0},
                                    {-16.0, -5.9, 0.0}};
```

allocate storage for the array `matrix` with 2 rows and 3 columns. In the initialization list enclosed in braces, each inner pair of braces contains the initial values for a row of the array `matrix`, starting with row 0, as shown below.

	col 0	col 1	col 2
row 0	5.0	4.5	3.0
row 1	-16.0	-5.9	0.0 ← matrix[1][2]

∎

Nested Loops for Processing Two-Dimensional Arrays

You must use nested loops to access the elements of a two-dimensional array in row-order or column-order. If you want to access the array elements in row-order (the normal situation), use the row subscript as the loop control variable for the outer loop and the column subscript as the loop control variable for the inner loop.

Example 12.4 The nested `for` statements that follow display the seating plan array from Fig. 12.2 in tabular form. The top row of the table lists the names of the students sitting in the last row of the classroom; the bottom row of the table lists the names of the students sitting in the first row of the classroom (closest to the teacher).

```
for (int row = num_rows - 1; row >= 0; row--)
{
    for (int seat = 0; seat < seats_in_row; seat++)
        cout << setw (10) << seat_plan[row][seat];
    cout << endl;
}
```

∎

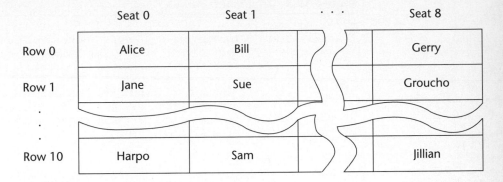

Figure 12.2 **A classroom seating plan**

Two-Dimensional Arrays as Function Arguments

You can pass two-dimensional arrays as function arguments. In the function call, simply list the actual array name, just as you would for one-dimensional arrays. In the formal argument list, you must list the column dimension, but the row dimension is optional. For example, you could use the function prototype

```
float sum_matrix
  (float table[][num_cols],     // IN: array to be summed
   int rows)                    // IN: number of rows in array
                                //      (rows > 0)
```

for a function sum_matrix (see Fig. 12.3), which calculates the sum of all the elements in an array of floating-point values with num_cols (a constant) columns. The second function argument represents the number of rows to be included in the sum. You can use the statement

```
total = sum_matrix (matrix, num_rows)
```

to assign to total the sum of the element values in the array matrix from Example 12.3.

Figure 12.3 **Function sum_matrix**

```
// FILE: SumMatrx.cpp
// CALCULATES THE SUM OF THE ELEMENTS IN THE FIRST rows ROWS
//    OF AN ARRAY OF FLOATING POINT VALUES
//    WITH num_cols (A CONSTANT) COLUMNS.
```

(continued)

Figure 12.3   *(continued)*

```
float sum_matrix
   (float table[][num_cols],      // IN: array to be summed
    int rows)                     // IN: number of rows in array
                                  //         (rows > 0)

// Pre:   The type int constant num_cols is defined (num_cols > 0)
//        and the array element values are defined and rows > 0.
// Post: sum is the sum of all array element values.
// Returns:  Sum of all values stored in the array.
{
    // Local data ...
    float sum = 0.0;      // sum of all element values - initially 0.0

    // Add each array element value to sum.
    for (int r = 0; r < rows; r++)
       for (int c = 0; c < num_cols; c++)
          sum += table[r][c];

    return sum;
}
```

You may be wondering why you only need to specify the column dimension (num_cols) in the declaration of the formal array argument table. Because the array elements are stored in row order, starting with row 0, C++ must know the number of elements in each row (value of num_cols) in order to access a particular array element. For example, if num_cols is 3, the first row is stored in array positions 0, 1, and 2, the second row is stored in array positions 3, 4, and 5, and so on. C++ uses the formula

```
num_cols * r + c
```

to compute the array position for array element table[r][c]. For example, array element table[1][0], the first element in the second row, is stored at array position 3 * 1 + 0 (array position 3).

Arrays with Several Dimensions

C++ does not limit the number of dimensions an array may have, although arrays with more than three dimensions are rare. The array sales declared here

```
const int people = 10;
const int years = 5;
money sales[people][years][12];
```

is a three-dimensional array with 600 (value of $10 \times 5 \times 12$) elements that may be used to store the monthly sales figures for the last five years for the ten sales representatives in a company. Thus `sales[0][2][11]` represents the dollar amount of sales for the first salesperson (person subscript is 0) during December (month subscript is 11) of the third year (year subscript is 2). As you can see, three-dimensional and higher arrays consume memory space very quickly.

Example 12.5 The following fragment finds and displays the total dollar amount of sales for each of the ten sales representatives.

```
// Find and display the total dollar amount of sales by
//    person
for (int person = 0; person < people; person++)
{
    total_sales = 0.0;

    // Find the total sales for the current person.
    for (int year = 0; year < years; year++)
        for (int month = 0; month < 12; month++)
            total_sales += sales[person][year][month];

    cout << "Total sales amount for salesperson "
         << person << " is " << total_sales << endl;
}
```

Because we are displaying the total sales amount for each person, we use the salesperson subscript as the loop control variable in the outermost loop. We set the value of `total_sales` to zero before executing the inner pair of nested loops. This pair accumulates the total sales amount for the current salesperson. The statement beginning with `cout` displays the accumulated total for each individual. ∎

EXERCISES FOR SECTION 12.1

Self-Check
1. Assuming the following declarations

```
const int max_row = 5;
const int max_col = 4;
float matrix[max_row][max_col];
```

answer these questions:

a. How many elements in array `matrix`?
b. Write a statement to display the element in row 2, column 3.
c. How would you reference the element in the last column of the last row?

2. Write the declarations for a multidimensional array used to store the course enrollment data for a school with five campuses and 20 subject areas, and up to ten courses per subject area.

3. Explain why it is not necessary to specify the first dimension (number of salespeople) when you declare a formal argument that is an array with the same form as the

one in Example 12.5. Describe the storage order for elements of this array in memory. Give a formula that will compute the position of array element `sales[i][j][k]`.

Programming   1. For the array `matrix` declared in Self-Check Exercise 1, do the following:
   a. Write a loop that computes the sum of the elements in row 4.
   b. Write a loop that computes the sum of the elements in column 3.
   c. Write nested loops that compute the sum of all the array elements.
   d. Write nested loops that display the array elements in the following order: display column 3 as the first output line, column 2 as the second output line, column 1 as the third output line, and column 0 as the fourth output line.

2. For the array `sales` in Example 12.5, do the following:
   a. Write a program fragment that displays the total sales amount in a table whose rows are years and whose columns are months.
   b. Write a program fragment that displays the total sales amount for each year and the total for all years.

12.2 —— ARRAYS OF STRUCTS AND CLASSES

Earlier we showed that you can declare a struct with an array component. You can also declare an array of structs.

Example 12.6   The declaration

```
employee company[10];
```

allocates storage for an array with ten elements of struct type `employee` (see Fig. 12.4). We use the subscripted variable `company[0]` to access the first element (a struct) of this array. We use the notation `company[9].name` to access the `name` component (a string) of the last employee.   ∎

Example 12.7   Array `company` provides storage for ten elements of type `employee`, and function `read_employee` (see again Fig. 9.24) reads data into a single type `employee` variable. Function `read_company` (Fig. 12.5) reads data into all ten elements of array `company`. The statement

```
read_employee (company[i]);
```

reads employee data into the array element with subscript `i`. Because `i` goes from 0 through 9, all ten elements receive data.   ∎

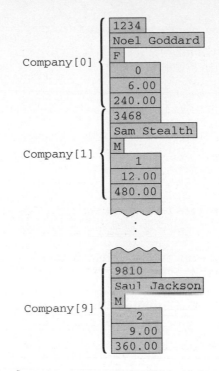

	1234
Company[0]	Noel Goddard
	F
	0
	6.00
	240.00
	3468
	Sam Stealth
Company[1]	M
	1
	12.00
	480.00

⋮

	9810
	Saul Jackson
Company[9]	M
	2
	9.00
	360.00

Figure 12.4 Sketch of array **company**

Figure 12.5 Function **read_company**

```
// FILE: ReadComp.cpp
// READS 10 EMPLOYEE RECORDS INTO ARRAY company

void read_company
   (employee company[])    // OUT: The destination for data being
                           //      read

// Pre:  None
// Post: Data are read into array company
{
   // Read 10 employees.
   for (int i = 0; i < 10; i++)
   {
      cout << "Enter data for employee " << i+1 << ":" << endl;
      read_employee (company[i]);
   }
}
```

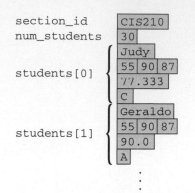

section_id

num_students

students[0]

students[1]

Figure 12.6   Sketch of variable `my_section`

Example 12.8   C++ provides a great deal of flexibility in the use of arrays and structs. The struct type `grade_book` declared next has three components. The last component is an array of 100 structs of type `exam_stats` (see Example 9.16) containing exam data for each student. Figure 12.6 shows a sketch of variable `my_section` (type `grade_book`).

```
struct grade_book
{
    string section_id;
    int num_students;           // Count of students in
                                //     section
    exam_stats students[100];   // Storage for 100 students
};
```

```
grade_book my_section;
```

You use `my_section.section_id` to access the section id number, and use `my_section.num_students` to access the count of students. You use `my_section.students[0]` to access the data for the first student (struct type `exam_stats`). You use `my_section.students[0].stu_name` to access the first student's name and `my_section.students[0].scores[0]` to access her first exam score. You use `my_section.students[num_students-1]` to access the data for the last student in the section. ∎

EXERCISES FOR SECTION 12.2

Self-Check   1. For array `company`, describe the meaning of each of the valid references below. Which are invalid?

a. `company[1].gender`   e. `company[1].employee`
b. `id.company[0]`   f. `company[1].employee.gender`
c. `company[9]`   g. `company[9].name`
d. `company[10]`   h. `company[2].company[1]`

2. For variable `my_section`, write the correct way to reference each data item described below.

   a. the first student's name
   b. the section ID
   c. all data for the last student
   d. the first student's letter grade
   e. the first student's score on the first exam
   f. the number of students in the section
   g. the last student's average
   h. the last student's score on the last exam

Programming   1. Write a function that displays the data in variable `my_section`. Use function `print_stats` (Fig. 9.23) to display each student's data.

12.3 ——— TEMPLATE CLASSES

In Section 10.2 you saw how to write a function template. Just as you used the template prefix line

```
template <class T>
```

before a function definition, you can use this prefix line before a class definition to allow the class to be used with any data type `T`. This makes the class definition much more versatile.

Definition of a Template Class

As an example, Fig. 12.7 provides a header file and definition for a template class `dummy` that provides storage for a data member, `value`, of type `T`. The type `bool` data member `defined` indicates whether a data item is stored in `value` (yes, if `defined` is true). Parameter `T` is a placeholder for an actual data type. You can use any of the C++ predefined data types (`int`, `char`, and so on) for type `T`, or any other user-defined or system-defined data type.

Figure 12.7   Header file for template class **dummy**

```
// FILE: dummy.h
// HEADER FILE FOR TEMPLATE CLASS DUMMY

#ifndef DUMMY_H_
#define DUMMY_H_

template <class T>
class dummy
{
public:
    // CONSTRUCTOR
    dummy ();
```

(continued)

Figure 12.7 *(continued)*

```
        // STORES A VALUE OF TYPE T
        void set_value (const T&);  // IN: the value to be stored

        // RETRIEVES A VALUE OF TYPE T
        void get_value (T&) const;  // OUT: returns the value stored
private:
   T value;                // Storage for a value of type T
   bool defined;           // Indicates whether value is defined
};

#endif  // DUMMY_H_
```

Parameter T appears in the formal argument list for both member functions:

```
void set_value (const T&);   // IN: the value to be stored
void get_value (T&) const;   // OUT: the value returned
```

Because T may be any previously defined data type, including a struct or class type, we use const T& for formal arguments that cannot be modified.

The data type corresponding to T is determined when we declare an instance of class dummy. For example, the declaration

```
dummy<int> day_num;
```

creates an object day_num with storage for a type int attribute (value). It also causes automatic generation of the function prototypes:

```
void set_value (const int&);  // IN: the value to be stored
void get_value (int&) const;  // OUT: the value returned
```

In case you are wondering, we have no real purpose for introducing template class dummy other than to provide a simple example for illustrating the definition and use of template classes.

C++
SYNTAX

Template Classes

Form: `template <class T>`
        `class class_name`
        `{`
            `public:`

- List of class variables, types, constants, etc. (if any) that may be accessed by name from outside the class
- Prototype for each function that may be accessed by name from outside the class

        . . .

```
        private:
```

- List of class variables, types, constants, etc., that are intended to be hidden from reference from outside the class
- Prototype for each function (if any) to be hidden from outside the class

```
        ...
        };
```

C++
SYNTAX

Object Definitions Using Template Classes

Form: *class-template-name<type> an-object* ;

Example: `index_list<int> int_list;`

Interpretation: *Type* may be any defined data type. *class-template-name* is the name of a template class. The object *an-object* is created when the arguments specified between the symbols <> replace their corresponding parameters in the template class.

Example 12.9   Figure 12.8 shows a main function that uses template class dummy. The declarations

```
dummy<int> num_depend;        // object num_depend
dummy<string> spouse_name;    // object spouse_name
```

allocate storage for two objects, num_depend and spouse_name, that are instances of template class dummy. We store a type int value in object num_depend and a type string value in object spouse_name. Then we retrieve and display the two values stored.

Figure 12.8   Driver function for template class dummy

```
// FILE: DumyDriv.cpp
// TESTS FUNCTION DUMMY

#include <iostream.h>
#include <string>
#include "dummy.h"

void main ()
{
   // Local data ...
   dummy<int> num_depend;        // object num_depend
   dummy<string> spouse_name;    // object spouse_name
```

(continued)

Figure 12.8 *(continued)*

```
    int num;
    string name;

    // Store data in objects num_depend and spouse_name
    num_depend.set_value (2);
    spouse_name.set_value ("Caryn");

    // Retrieve and display values stored
    num_depend.get_value (num);
    spouse_name.get_value (name);
    cout << num << endl;
    cout << name << endl;
}
```

———————————— Program Output ————————————

```
2
Caryn
```

Implementation of a Template Class

We can implement a template class in two ways. The first method involves inserting the member function definitions directly in the class definition. In Fig. 12.9, we rewrite the definition for template class dummy by replacing each function prototype with a complete function definition.

Figure 12.9 Template class dummy with member function definitions inserted

```
// FILE: DummyFun.h
// DEFINITION FILE FOR TEMPLATE CLASS DUMMY WITH FUNCTIONS

#include <iostream.h>
#ifndef DUMMY_FUN_H
#define DUMMY_FUN_H

template <class T>
class dummy                 // with function definitions
{
public:
  // CONSTRUCTOR
  dummy ()
  {
      defined = false;     // No value stored yet
  }


  // STORES A VALUE OF TYPE T
  void set_value (const T& a_val)  // IN: the value to be stored
  {
```

(continued)

Figure 12.9 *(continued)*

```
      value = a_val;
      defined = true;
   }


   // RETRIEVES A VALUE OF TYPE T
   void get_value (T& a_val) const   // OUT: returns the value
                                     //      stored
   {
      if (defined)
         a_val = value;
      else
         cerr << "Error - no value stored!" << endl;
   }

private:
   T value;               // Storage for a value of type T
   bool defined;          // Indicates whether value is defined
};

#endif                    // DUMMY_FUN_H_
```

The advantage of this approach is its simplicity. Because the function definitions appear inside the class definition, we do not need to precede each function name with a scope resolution operator. However, a disadvantage is that we no longer have a clear separation between the class interface and the class implementation. We would prefer to place the class definition in an interface file (dummy.h) that contains only the information needed by a class user and to hide the implementation details in a separate implementation file (dummy.cpp). Figure 12.10 shows such an implementation file which includes the original class definition from Fig. 12.7 (file dummy.h).

Figure 12.10   Implementation file for template class **dummy**

```
// FILE: dummy.cpp
// IMPLEMENTATION FILE FOR TEMPLATE CLASS DUMMY

#include "dummy.h"
#include <iostream.h>

// CONSTRUCTOR
template <class T>
dummy<T>::dummy ()
{
   defined = false;     // No value stored yet
}
```

(continued)

Figure 12.10   *(continued)*

```
// STORES A VALUE OF TYPE T
template <class T>
void dummy<T>::set_value (const T& a_val)   // IN: the value to be
                                            //     stored
{
   value = a_val;
   defined = true;
}

// RETRIEVES A VALUE OF TYPE T
template <class T>
void dummy<T>::get_value (T& a_val) const   // OUT: the value
                                            //      returned
{
   if (defined)
      a_val = value;
}
```

In Fig. 12.10, we place the template prefix line

```
template <class T>
```

before each function header, and we precede each function name with

```
dummy<T>::
```

to tell the compiler that the function being defined is a member of template class dummy with parameter T. We use the same function bodies that were used in Fig. 12.9.

Compiler Instructions to Support Separate Compilation

Some C++ compilers require special instructions from the programmer when attempting separate compilation of template class header and implementation files. For example, Borland C++ requires the programmer to insert a special compiler directive

```
#pragma option -Jgd
```

at the end of the implementation file. Also, the programmer must follow this line with typedef declarations showing the template classes with actual parameters as they will appear in the client:

```
typedef dummy<int>    fake_int;
typedef dummy<string> fake_string;
```

The names fake_int and fake_string are synonyms for the actual data type (the template class with parameter) listed first in the typedef.

Also, the programmer must insert the compiler directive

```
#pragma option -Jgx
```

in the client file, before the main function.

C++
SYNTAX

Type Definitions for Template Classes

Form: typedef *class-template-name*<*type*> *new-type-name*;
             new-type-name an-object;

Example: typedef vector<int> int_vector;
              int_vector my_data;

Interpretation: The prefix typedef indicates that a synonym or new type name is being defined (in the example, the new type name is int_vector). *Type* may be any defined data type. *new-type-name* is the name of a new data type that is created when the parameters specified between the symbols <> replace their corresponding parameters in the template class.   ∎

EXERCISES FOR SECTION 12.3

Self-Check   1. Write a driver function that allocates storage for three objects of type dummy<float>. Your function should read two numbers, store them in two of the objects, and then retrieve these values and store their sum in the third object. Finally, retrieve and display the sum.
2. What function prototypes are generated by the object declarations in Fig. 12.8?

Programming 1. Write member functions read and display for template class dummy. Assume stream operators << and >> are defined for all data types that will be used as class parameters.

12.4 ——— THE INDEXED LIST ABSTRACT DATA TYPE

In this section we describe a very versatile data structure called the *indexed list*. We will implement an indexed list as a template class, so that the elements of an indexed list object can be any data type, including a struct or a class.

Although the C++ array has proven to be a useful data structure for storing a collection of elements of the same type, it has some deficiencies:

- You can access (or overwrite) data outside of an array if you use a subscript that is too small (< 0) or a subscript that is larger than the maximum allowed for the array.
- If an array has some empty or unfilled storage locations, your program must keep track of how many elements actually contain data, increasing or

decreasing the count of filled elements when an array element is inserted or deleted. When processing the array, you must be careful to access only the filled portion of the array.

■ You need to write your own functions to perform operations such as finding the smallest and largest values in the array, searching an array, sorting an array, and reading and displaying an array. You may need different versions of these functions for different array element types.

Analysis and Design of an Indexed List Class

We will design our own abstract data type, the indexed list class, as an alternative to the array structure. Besides being safer to use than an array, our indexed list class will be more versatile because it can include as methods most of the common array operations that we listed above and coded in Chapter 9.

An indexed list is a collection of data items of the same type. We access the elements of an indexed list through an index, an integral expression with value between 0 and size-1, where size is the actual number of elements stored in the indexed list.

Specification for Indexed List Class

Attributes for Indexed List Class

elements[]	Array of data items
size(int)	Count of items

Member Functions for Indexed List Class

indexed_list	Constructor
append	Appends a new item to the indexed list (i.e., insert at the end).
insert	Inserts a new item at a specified index.
retrieve	Retrieves the value stored at a specified index.
remove	Deletes the value stored at a specified index.
find_min	Locates the smallest value in a portion of an indexed list.
find_max	Locates the largest value in a portion of an indexed list.
search	Searches for a target value in an indexed list.
sort	Sorts an indexed list.
read	Reads data into an indexed list, starting at element 0.
display	Displays the items in the indexed list.
get_size	Gets the size of the indexed list.

Figure 12.11 shows the template class `index_list`. In the template prefix line

```
template <class T, int max_size>
```

parameter `T` is a placeholder for the data type of each element stored in an indexed list and `max_size` (type `int`) represents the maximum size of an indexed list object.

Figure 12.11   Class `indexed_list`

```
// FILE: IndxList.h
// DEFINITION OF INDEXED_LIST TEMPLATE CLASS

#ifndef INDEX_LIST_H_
#define INDEX_LIST_H_

template <class T, int max_size>
class index_list
{
public:
   // Constructor
   index_list ();

   // Add an item to the end of an indexed list
   bool append (const T&);    // IN: item appended

   // Insert an element at a specified index
   bool insert (int,          // IN: insertion index
                const T&);    // IN: item inserted

   // Retrieve an element at a specified index
   bool retrieve (int,        // IN:  index
                  T&) const;  // OUT: value retrieved

   // Delete an element at a specified index
   bool remove (int);         // IN: index

   // Find index of smallest value in a sublist
   int find_min (int,         // IN:  start index
                 int) const;  // OUT: end index

   // Find index of largest value in a sublist
   int find_max (int,         // IN:  start index
                 int) const;  // OUT: end index

   // Find index of a target item
   //    Returns -1 if target item not found
   int search (const T&) const;  // IN: target item

   // Sort an indexed list
   void sel_sort ();
```

(continued)

Figure 12.11   *(continued)*

```
   // Read data into the list
     void read ();

   // Display the list contents
   void display () const;

   // Get the current size
   int get_size () const;
private:
   T elements[max_size]; // Storage for elements
   int size;                // Count of elements in list
};

#endif   // INDEX_LIST_H_
```

The data member `elements` is an array of type `T` values. Because the size of the array, `max_size`, is passed as the second template parameter, we can allocate storage for indexed lists with different storage capacities and different element types in the same program. The declaration

```
index_list<int, 50> my_list;   // my_list is an indexed list of
                               //     integers
```

creates an indexed list object, `my_list`, that can hold up to 50 integer values. The data member `size` (0 <= `size` <= `max_size`) is a count of elements in the indexed list.

The public part in Fig. 12.11 declares all the member functions described earlier. We use type `T` to represent the element type and type `int` to represent an index. Because `T` may be a class type, we use `const  T&` for formal arguments that cannot be modified. For example, in the prototype for function `insert`

```
bool insert (int,          // IN: insertion index
             const T&);    // IN: item inserted
```

the first argument represents the index (type `int`) where the second argument (type `T`) will be inserted.

Functions `append`, `insert`, `remove`, and `retrieve` return a type `bool` result to indicate success or failure of the operation. For `insert`, `remove`, and `retrieve`, the operation succeeds if the index passed to the function is valid. For `append`, the operation succeeds if there is room to store the new element.

The arguments for functions `find_min` and `find_max` define the starting and ending points of a sublist:

```
int find_min (int,          // IN:  start index
              int) const;   // OUT: end index
```

Function find_min returns the index of the smallest value in the sublist and find_max returns the index of the largest value. Both functions return −1 if the sublist boundaries are invalid.

Using the indexed_list Class

You can think of an object of class indexed_list as a user-friendly array. You do not need to keep track of the number of elements currently filled with data as this will be done automatically. You also do not need to be concerned about accessing storage locations outside the array, because the class member functions will not allow it.

Finally, you do not need to know anything about arrays or subscripts in order to use an indexed list. The member functions perform all array accesses. If you want to retrieve a particular item, you simply pass its index and the variable that will store the item to member function retrieve; the function does the rest. For example, to retrieve the element in location 2 of indexed list my_list and store it in me, you write

```
my_list.retrieve (2, me);
```

Example 12.10   Function main in Fig. 12.12 performs a number of operations using the indexed list class. The declarations

```
index_list<int, 10>   my_int_data;     // indexed list of ints
index_list<string, 5> my_string_data;  // indexed list of
                                       //    strings
```

allocate storage for an indexed list of ten type int values (my_int_data) and an indexed list of five type string values (my_string_data), showing that main can process two different kinds of indexed lists at the same time. Function main next stores data items in both lists and sorts them. It then retrieves and displays the first value in each list after sorting. Finally, it displays the number of elements in each list and the sorted lists.   ■

Figure 12.12   Using class indexed_list

```
// FILE: IndxDrvr.cpp
// TESTS MEMBER FUNCTIONS OF INDEXED_LIST CLASS

#include <iostream.h>
#include <string>
#include "IndxList.h"
```

(continued)

Figure 12.12   *(continued)*

```
void main ()
{
  index_list<int, 10>   my_int_data;    // indexed list of ints
  index_list<string, 5> my_string_data; // indexed list of strings
  string a_string;
  int an_int;
  bool a_bool;

  // Store the integer data.
  my_int_data.append (5);
  my_int_data.append (0);
  my_int_data.append (-5);
  my_int_data.append (-10);

  // Store the string data.
  cout << "Read a list of strings:" << endl;
  my_string_data.read ();

  // Sort the indexed lists.
  my_int_data.sel_sort ();
  my_string_data.sel_sort ();

  // Retrieve and display the first value in each list.
  a_bool = my_int_data.retrieve (0, an_int);
  if (a_bool)
     cout << "First integer value after sorting is "
          << an_int << endl;

  a_bool = my_string_data.retrieve (0, a_string);
  if (a_bool)
     cout << "First string value after sorting is "
          << a_string << endl << endl;

  // Display each list size and contents
  cout << "The indexed list of integers contains "
       << my_int_data.get_size () << " values." << endl;
  cout << "Its contents follows:" << endl;
  my_int_data.display ();

  cout << endl << "The indexed list of strings contains "
       << my_string_data.get_size () << " values." << endl;
  cout << "Its contents follows:" << endl;
  my_string_data.display ();
}


Read a list of strings:
Enter number of list items to read: 3
Enter next item - Robin
Enter next item - Beth
```

(continued)

Figure 12.12 *(continued)*

```
Enter next item - Koffman
First integer value after sorting is -10
First string value after sorting is Beth

The indexed list of integers contains 4 values.
Its contents follows:
-10
-5
0
5

The indexed list of strings contains 3 values.
Its contents follows:
Beth
Koffman
Robin
```

EXERCISES FOR SECTION 12.4

Self-Check

1. Trace the following fragment showing the list contents after each statement.

```
index_list<float, 5> small_list;
small_list.append (3.5);
small_list.append (5.7);
small_list.remove (0);
cout << small_list.retrieve (0) << endl;;
small_list.insert (0, 15.5);
small_list.append (5.5);
cout << small_list.search (5.5) << endl;
small_list.sort ();
small_list.display ();
```

Programming

1. Write a client program that allocates three indexed lists, each containing up to ten type `float` values. Read (using member function `read`) data into all ten elements of two of the lists and sort them. Then write a function that stores the sum of corresponding elements of these two lists in the third list. Finally display all three lists, one after the other.

12.5 ⎯⎯ IMPLEMENTING THE INDEXED LIST CLASS

Figure 12.13 shows several member functions for the indexed list class. Every function begins with the template prefix line

```
template <class T, int max_size>
```

In every function header, we use the parameterized class name and scope resolution operator

```
index_list<T, max_size>::
```

to tell the compiler that the function being defined is a member of the template class index_list with parameters T and max_size. Type T, max_size, and any members of the class may be referenced directly within each function body.

The constructor sets data member size to zero. Function append checks whether the list is full. If it is not full, append inserts a new element at the list position with subscript size and then increments size, thereby placing the new element at the end of the list. Function insert overwrites the element at the list position specified by its first argument with the type T item passed as its second argument. Function retrieve accesses the list element at the position specified by its first argument and returns that list element to its second argument.

Function remove overwrites the element at the list position specified by its argument with the last list element, making a copy of the last list element. It then decrements size to remove the copy at the end of the list. By always deleting the last list element, we prevent the formation of gaps, or empty spaces, in the middle of the list.

Function read sets data member size to zero and then reads and stores one data item at a time in the indexed list, starting with the first element. It stores the number of items read in size. It calls member function append to insert each item at the end of the list. Notice there is no need to use dot notation in the call to append.

Figure 12.13   Some member functions for class `indexed_list`

```
// FILE: IndxList.cpp
// INDEXED_LIST CLASS IMPLEMENTATION

#include "IndxList.h"    // file containing class definition
#include <iostream.h>
#include <string>        // required for typedef at end of file

template <class T, int max_size>
index_list<T, max_size>::index_list ()               // constructor
{
   size = 0;            // list is empty
}

// Add an item to the end of an indexed list
template <class T, int max_size>
bool index_list<T, max_size>::append (const T& item)

// Pre:  item is defined
// Post: if size < max_size, item is appended to list
// Returns: true if item was appended; otherwise, false
{
   bool result;
```

(continued)

Figure 12.13   *(continued)*

```
    // Add item to the end of the list if list is not full.
    if (size < max_size)
    {
          elements[size] = item;
          size++;
          result = true;
    }
    else
    {
          cerr << "Array is filled - can't append!" << endl;
          result = false;
    }
    return result;
}


// Insert an item at a specified index.
template <class T, int max_size>
bool index_list<T, max_size>::insert (int index, const T& item)

// Pre:  item and index are defined
// Post: item is inserted at position index if valid
// Returns: true if item was inserted; otherwise, false
{
   bool result;

   // Overwrite a list element if index is valid.
   if (index >= 0  &&  index < size)
   {
          elements[index] = item;
          result = true;
   }
   else
   {
          cerr << "Index " << index << " not in filled part"
               << " - can't insert!" << endl;
          result = false;
   }
   return result;
}


// Retrieve an item at a specified index
template <class T, int max_size>
bool index_list<T, max_size>::retrieve (int index, T& item) const

// Pre:  item and index are defined
// Post: if index is valid, elements[index] is returned
// Returns: true if item was returned; otherwise, false
{
   bool result;
```

(continued)

Figure 12.13   *(continued)*

```
      // Return a list element through item if index is valid.
      if (index >= 0  &&  index < size)
      {
              item = elements[index];
              result = true;
      }
      else
      {
              cerr << "Index " << index << " not in filled part"
                  << " - can't retrieve!" << endl;
              result = false;
      }
      return result;
}


// Delete an element at a specified index
template <class T, int max_size>
bool index_list<T, max_size>::remove (int index)

// Pre:  index is defined
// Post: if index is valid, elements[index] is replaced
//       with elements[size] and size is decremented.
// Returns: true if item was deleted; otherwise, false
{
   bool result;

   // Copy last list item to position index and delete last item.
   if (index >= 0  &&  index < size)
   {
           // Overwrite elements[index] with last item
           elements[index] = elements[size - 1];
           size--;                 //   Ignore old last element
           result = true;
   }
   else
   {
           cerr << "Index " << index << " not in filled part"
               << " - can't delete!" << endl;
           result = false;
   }
   return result;
}


// Read data into the list
template <class T, int max_size>
void index_list<T, max_size>::read ()

// Pre:  none
// Post: All data items are stored in array elements
//       and size is the count of items
{
```

(continued)

Figure 12.13 *(continued)*

```
    int num_items;        // input - number of items to read
    T next_item;          // input - next data item

    cout << "Enter number of list items to read: ";
    cin >> num_items;

    // If num_items is valid, read each list element, starting
    // with first element.
    size = 0;                    // The list is empty.
    if (num_items >= 0  &&  num_items < max_size)
       for (int i = 0; i < num_items; i++)
       {
           cout << "Enter next item - ";
           cin >> next_item;
           append (next_item);
       }
    else
       cerr << "Number of items " << num_items << " is invalid"
            << " - data entry is cancelled!" << endl;
}

// Display the list contents
template <class T, int max_size>
void index_list<T, max_size>::display() const

// Pre:  none
// Post: Displays each item stored in the list
{
  // Display each list element.
  for (int i = 0; i < size; i++)
        cout << elements[i] << endl;
}


template <class T, int max_size>
int index_list<T, max_size>::get_size () const
{
  return size;
}
```

Functions find_min, find_max, search, and sel_sort are similar to functions shown in Chapters 9 and 10, so we leave them as an exercise (see Programming Exercise 3). Function display uses the extraction operator << to display each item stored in the list, and function read uses the insertion operator >>. Functions find_min, find_max, search, and sel_sort work only if the operators ==, <, and > are defined for class T. We discuss these requirements further in Section 12.7.

Self-Check   1. What does the following member function return?

```
template <class T, int max_size>
int index_list<T, max_size>::mystery() const
{
   int count;

   count = 0;
   for (int i = 0; i < size-2; i++)
      if (elements[i+1] > elements[i])
         count++;
   return count;
}
```

2. Write a member function that returns true if its indexed list object is all filled up.

Programming   1. Assume that you have declared data member size as a counter type (See Fig. 11.1) with max_size as its largest value instead of declaring size to be type int. You will thus have to use the counter operators to manipulate size in the indexed_list member functions. Show the declaration for size as it would appear in the indexed_list class definition. Indicate which functions would change and write the new statements for each function.

2. Write a member function that returns true if its indexed list object is all filled up.

3. Write member functions find_min, find_max, search, and sel_sort.

12.6 ⎯⎯ ILLUSTRATING OBJECT-ORIENTED DESIGN

In this section, we solve a programming problem using *object-oriented design (OOD).* A complete discussion of this topic is beyond the scope of this book, but a summation of the steps involved in object-oriented design methodology can be briefly summarized:

1. Identify the objects and define the services to be provided by each object.
2. Identify the interactions among objects in terms of services required and services provided.
3. Determine the specification for each object.
4. Implement each object.

Unlike traditional software design, there is no sharp division between the analysis phase and the design phase. In fact, in object-oriented design programmers often follow the prototyping design practice of designing a little, implementing a little, and testing a little, rather than attempting to build a complete piece of software all at once.

CASE STUDY: A TELEPHONE DIRECTORY PROGRAM

Problem

We have been asked to design a program to store and retrieve a growing collection of names and telephone numbers in a telephone directory. The directory will be created by reading a list of names and numbers of people called frequently. The directory program should also be able to insert new names and numbers, change numbers, retrieve selected telephone numbers, and delete names and numbers.

Analysis and Design

In OOD, we focus on the data objects and the services (operators) that they provide. There are really two distinct data objects to consider: the directory as a whole and each individual entry. We focus on a directory entry first.

Each directory entry should contain a person's name and telephone number, and it should have a unique name that distinguishes it from the other entries. The specification for a directory entry follows.

SPECIFICATION FOR A DIRECTORY ENTRY

Attributes for a Directory Entry

```
name (string)      — person's name
number (string)    — person's number
```

Member Functions for a Directory Entry

```
entry              — a constructor
set_entry          — stores a name and number in the entry
get_name           — retrieves the name attribute
get_number         — retrieves the number attribute
```

Operators for a Directory Entry

```
==                 — equality operator
<                  — less than
>                  — greater than
<<                 — insertion operator
>>                 — extraction operator
```

As shown above, we will use two string objects for storing a directory entry's attributes. In our specification for a directory, we include a list of operators which are familiar symbols. We plan to overload some of the C++ equality, relational, and input/output operators, so that a client program can use them to compare two type `entry` objects or to perform input/output operations on a type `entry` object. We will show how to do this in Section 12.7. Figure 12.14 summarizes the design decisions so far in the header file for class `entry`.

Figure 12.14   Header file for a directory entry

```
// FILE: entry.h
// DEFINITION FOR A DIRECTORY ENTRY CLASS

#include <iostream.h>
#include <string>

#ifndef ENTRY_H_
#define ENTRY_H_

class entry
{
public:
    // Member functions

    // CONSTRUCTOR
    entry ();

    // STORE DATA IN AN ENTRY
    void set_entry (const string&, const string& nr = "");

    // ACCESSOR FUNCTIONS
    string get_name () const;
    string get_number () const;

    // Operators
    friend bool operator == (const entry&, const entry&);
    friend bool operator <  (const entry&, const entry&);
    friend bool operator >  (const entry&, const entry&);
    friend ostream& operator << (ostream&, const entry&);
    friend istream& operator >> (istream&, entry&);

private:
    string name;       // Person's name
    string number;     // and phone number
};

#endif  // ENTRY_H_
```

We list the second argument in the prototype for member function `set_entry` as `nr = ""`. This means that the default value for `nr` is the empty string if a second argument is not explicitly passed. This allows us to call function `set_entry` with either one or two arguments. There can be no default for the first argument.

Next we turn our attention to the services provided by a directory object. We should be able to read in an initial directory and add a new entry, delete an entry, and update an entry when a phone number changes. We also should be able to locate a particular name in the directory and retrieve that person's number. After we update the directory through multiple insertions and deletions, we should be able to sort the entries so they are in alphabetical order by name. Finally, we should be able to display the directory entries. This list of operations may sound familiar to you. It should because these are precisely the operations that can be performed on an indexed list. Therefore, we will use an indexed list object for storing our directory.

Using a Telephone Directory

We can now write a client program that maintains our telephone directory. We will write a menu-driven program that enables the user to select the operations to be performed in any order, although the *read directory operation* must be performed first.

DATA REQUIREMENTS

Problem Input

tel_direc   — telephone directory
choice (char)   — each operation selected

Problem Output

tel_direc   — updated telephone directory

ALGORITHM

1. Read the initial directory.
2. do
 2.1. Display the menu.
 2.2. Read the user's selection.
 2.3. Perform the operation selected.
 while the user is not done

The main function consists of a do-while loop that calls function select to perform each operation (step 2.3). The telephone directory and user's selection are passed as arguments to function select.

Analysis and Design for select (step 2.3)

Function select is a decision structure (a switch statement) in which each case performs a different operation on the indexed list. For each case, we must read any required data and call the appropriate member functions from class entry or class indexed_list. We show the design for function select next and show the complete program in Fig. 12.15.

DATA REQUIREMENTS FOR select

Input Argument

choice (float)   — operation selected

Input/Output Argument

tel_direc   — telephone directory

Local Variables

an_entry (entry)   — input—data for an entry
a_name (string)   — input—a name to be found
index (int)   — index for a particular name

ALGORITHM FOR select

Choose one of the cases listed below:

Case 'A': // Add

Read the entry to add.
Append it to the directory.

Case 'C': // Change an entry

Read the modified entry.
Search for its name in the directory.
if the name is found

insert modified entry at the index position.
else
    Append the entry to the directory if user approves.

Case 'D': // Delete an entry

Read the name of entry to delete.
Search for the name in the directory.
if the name is found

delete the entry.

Case 'G': // Get a number

Read the name of the entry to retrieve.
Search for the name in the directory.
if the name is found

Retrieve the entry.
Retrieve and display the entry's number attribute.

Case 'S': // Sort

   Call the sort function.

Case 'P': // Print

   Call the display function.

Case 'Q': // Do nothing

Figure 12.15 **Menu-driven program for telephone directory**

```cpp
// FILE: TeleMenu.cpp
// MENU DRIVEN TELEPHONE DIRECTORY UPDATE PROGRAM

#include <iostream.h>
#include <string>
#include "IndxList.h"
#include "entry.h"
#include <ctype.h>                 // For toupper

typedef index_list<entry, 100> tel_index_list;

// Function prototype
   // PERFORMS USER SELECTION
   void select (tel_index_list&, char);

void main ()
{
   // Local data
   tel_index_list tel_direc;           // telephone directory
   char choice;                        // menu choice

   // Read the initial directory.
   cout << "Enter the initial directory entries -";
   tel_direc.read ();

   // Keep reading and performing operations until user enters Q
   do
   {
      // Display the menu.
      cout << "Enter your choice -" << endl;
      cout << "A(Add), C(Change), D(Delete)," << endl;
           << "G(Get), S(Sort),   P(Print), Q(Quit): ";

      cin >> choice;

      // Perform the operation selected.
      select (tel_direc, choice);
   }
   while (toupper (choice) != 'Q');
}
```

(continued)

Figure 12.15 *(continued)*

```cpp
// PERFORMS USER SELECTION
void select (tel_index_list& tel_direc,   // INOUT : directory
             char choice)                  // IN: selection
{
   // Local data
   entry an_entry;       // one entry
   string a_name;        // input - entry name
   int index;            // index of name in directory
   char answer;          // input - indicates whether to add
                         //            entry for missing name

   switch (toupper (choice))
   {
      case 'A':    // Add an entry
         cout << "Enter entry to add - ";
         cin >> an_entry;
         tel_direc.append (an_entry);
         break;

      case 'C':    // Change an entry
         cout << "Enter entry to change - ";
         cin >> an_entry;
         index = tel_direc.search (an_entry);
         if (index >= 0)
            tel_direc.insert (index, an_entry);
         else
         {
            cout << "Name not in directory. "
                 << "Do you wish to add it (Y or N): ";
            cin >> answer;
            if (toupper (answer) == 'Y')
               tel_direc.append (an_entry);
         }
         break;

      case 'D':    // Delete an entry
         cout << "Enter name of entry to delete: ";
         cin.ignore (1, '\n');
         getline (cin, a_name, '\n');
         an_entry.set_entry (a_name);
         index = tel_direc.search (an_entry);
         if (index >= 0)
            tel_direc.remove (index);
         else
            cout << "Entry not found - no deletion" << endl;
         break;

      case 'G':    // Get a number
         cout << "Enter name of entry to get: ";
         cin.ignore (1, '\n');
```

(continued)

Figure 12.15 *(continued)*

```
            getline (cin, a_name, '\n');
            an_entry.set_entry (a_name);
            index = tel_direc.search (an_entry);
            if (index >= 0)
            {
                tel_direc.retrieve (index, an_entry);
                cout << "The number you requested is "
                     << an_entry.get_number () << endl;
            }
            else
                cout << "Not in directory." << endl;
            break;

        case 'S':   // Sort directory
            tel_direc.sel_sort ();
            break;

        case 'P':   // Print directory
            tel_direc.display ();
            break;

        case 'Q':   // Quit directory
            cout << "Exiting program" << endl;
            break;

        default:
            cout << "Choice is invalid - try again" << endl;
            cin.ignore (80, '\n');
    }
}  // end select
```

By using classes `index_list` and `entry`, we can accomplish this substantial programming task with minimal effort. The resulting client program is very concise and readable. Figure 12.16 shows a sample run of our program. We discuss the implementation of class `entry` in the next section.

Figure 12.16 **Sample run of telephone directory program**

```
Enter the initial directory entries -
Enter number of list items to read: 1
Enter next item - Enter name: Maria Sanchez
Enter number: 215-555-1234

Enter your choice -
A(Add), C(Change), D(Delete),
G(Get), S(Sort),   P(Print), Q(Quit): A
Enter entry to add - Enter name: Tom Brown
Enter number: 301-555-5643
```

(continued)

Figure 12.16   *(continued)*

```
Enter your choice -
A(Add), C(Change), D(Delete),
G(Get), S(Sort),   P(Print), Q(Quit): c
Enter entry to change - Enter name: Maria Sanchez
Enter number: 215-555-9876

Enter your choice -
A(Add), C(Change), D(Delete),
G(Get), S(Sort),   P(Print), Q(Quit): G
Enter name of entry to get: Maria Sanchez
The number you requested is 215-555-9876

Enter your choice -
A(Add), C(Change), D(Delete),
G(Get), S(Sort),   P(Print), Q(Quit): D
Enter name of entry to delete: Maria Sanchez

Enter your choice -
A(Add), C(Change), D(Delete),
G(Get), S(Sort),   P(Print), Q(Quit): p
Name   is Tom Brown
Number is 301-555-5643

Enter your choice -
A(Add), C(Change), D(Delete),
G(Get), S(Sort),   P(Print), Q(Quit): q
Exiting program
```

EXERCISES FOR SECTION 12.6

Self-Check
1. Explain how the C++ compiler knows whether a function in Fig. 12.15 is a member function of class `entry` or class `indexed_list`.
2. List all changes that would be needed if function `select` were a member function of `indexed_list`.

Programming
1. Add a case to function `select` that determines whether there is more than one entry for a particular name. (*Hint:* You will have to sort the indexed list first and see whether the name in the entry following the one selected by `search` matches the name in the entry selected by `search`.)

12.7 ——— FRIENDS OF A CLASS AND OPERATOR OVERLOADING

From our discussion of the telephone directory program, we know that the data members of a directory entry consist of two string components: `name` and `number`. We also need to provide member functions `set_entry`, `get_name` and get_number and operators ==, <, >, >> and << (insertion). From our earlier work, we know C++ supports operator overloading, a process we examine next.

Friends of a Class

First let's consider how we might write a function to determine whether one data entry was less than another. Figure 12.17 shows a first attempt at member function less_than, which compares the name attributes of two type entry objects.

If a and b are two objects of type entry, we can use the expression

a.less_than (b)

to compare them. However, rather than applying the function to one object and passing the other as an argument, we would prefer to use an expression such as

less_than_2 (a, b)

which treats both objects in the same way. We can use a friend function to do this. Figure 12.18 shows the definition of the friend function less_than_2, which directly accesses the private data members of both its arguments.

Notice that the function name less_than_2 is not preceded by entry:: because function less_than_2 is not a member function of class entry, but rather a friend function of the class. Its prototype must appear in the public section of the class definition, and it must begin with the word friend.

Figure 12.17   Function less_than

```
// RETURNS TRUE IF THE NAME ATTRIBUTE OF THE OBJECT IT IS APPLIED
// TO IS LESS THAN THE NAME ATTRIBUTE OF ITS ARGUMENT OBJECT
bool entry::less_than (const entry& an_entry) const
{
    return (name < an_entry.name);
}
```

Figure 12.18   Friend function less_than_2

```
// RETURNS TRUE IF THE NAME ATTRIBUTE OF ITS FIRST ARGUMENT
// IS LESS THAN THE NAME ATTRIBUTE OF ITS SECOND ARGUMENT
bool less_than_2 (const entry& entry_1,
                  const entry& entry_2)
{
    return (entry_1.name < entry_2.name);
}
```

Also, a friend function cannot be a `const` function. The prototype for `less_than_2` follows.

```
// Prototype for friend function less_than_2
// RETURNS TRUE IF THE NAME ATTRIBUTE OF ITS FIRST ARGUMENT
// IS LESS THAN THE NAME ATTRIBUTE OF ITS SECOND ARGUMENT
friend bool less_than_2 (const entry& const entry&;
```

A friend has all the access privileges of a member function; it may access directly the private data members of its object arguments or operands, and it may also call any private member functions. We use friend functions when we want to allow a function to access the private members of two or more objects of the same class or of two or more different classes.

Although function `less_than_2` is better than the original, it is still not ideal. It would be better if we could use the expression a < b to compare the name fields of objects a and b. We can do this by defining < as a friend operator for class `entry`:

```
friend bool operator <  (const entry&, const entry&);
```

This prototype is like the one for `less_than_2` shown earlier, except we substitute `operator` for the function name.

The public part of class `entry` in Fig. 12.14 declares five friend operators

```
// Operator prototypes
friend bool operator == (const entry&, const entry&);
friend bool operator <  (const entry&, const entry&);
friend bool operator >  (const entry&, const entry&);
friend ostream& operator << (ostream&, const entry&);
friend istream& operator >> (istream&, entry&);
```

The operands for each operator appear in parentheses. For example, the first prototype indicates that the left and right operands of operator == are type `entry` objects that are not changed by the equality operator.

Example 12.11   If d_e1 and d_e2 are type `entry` objects, the expression

```
d_e1 == d_e2
```

compares objects d_e1 and d_e2 and evaluates to true or false depending on how we define operator == for this class. We provide the operator definitions in file `entry.cpp`. ∎

The prototype for the insertion operator << shows that it takes two operands, an output stream and a type `entry` object. The insertion operator returns a modified output stream as its result (result type is `ofstream&`). We must define operator << as a friend of class `entry` because its operands are objects of two different classes.

Example 12.12   The statement

```
cout << d_e1;
```

displays d_e1 and in the process modifies stream cout. The statement

```
cout << d_e2 << endl;
```

first displays d_e2, modifying cout. The new cout becomes the left operand for the second insertion operator (<< endl), which places a newline character in stream cout. ■

C++
SYNTAX

Friend Function (Operator) Declaration

Form: friend *result-type function-name* (*argument_list*);
            friend *result-type* operator *op-symbol* (*argument_list*);

Example: friend bool equal_to (const entry&, const entry&);
            friend bool operator == (const entry&,
                                        const entry&);

Interpretation: The friend function indicated by *function-name* or the friend operator indicated by *op-symbol* returns a value of type *result-type*. The argument list should contain one or more arguments of the class type in which the friend is defined. The friend can access all private data members and function members of the class. Instead of using dot notation to apply a friend function to an object, you pass the object through its argument list. You place a friend operator between its left- and right-operands. ■

Implementing The Directory Entry Class

Figure 12.19 shows the implementation file (entry.cpp) for class entry.

Figure 12.19   File entry.cpp

```
// FILE: entry.cpp
// IMPLEMENTATION FILE FOR CLASS ENTRY

#include <iostream.h>
#include <string>
#include <entry.h>

// CONSTRUCTOR
entry :: entry ()
{
    name = "";
    number = "";
}
```

(continued)

Figure 12.19   *(continued)*

```cpp
// STORE DATA IN AN ENTRY
void entry :: set_entry (const string& na,        // IN: name
                         const string& nr)        // IN: number
{
   name = na;
   number = nr;
}

// GET NAME
string entry :: get_name () const
{
   return name;
}

// GET NUMBER
string entry :: get_number () const
{
   return number;
}


// Operators - friends of the class
bool operator == (const entry& d_e1,     // IN: left-operand
                  const entry& d_e2)     // IN: right-operand
{
   return (d_e1.name == d_e2.name);
}


bool operator <  (const entry& d_e1,     // IN: left-operand
                  const entry& d_e2)     // IN: right-operand
{
   return (d_e1.name < d_e2.name);
}


bool operator >  (const entry& d_e1,     // IN: left-operand
                  const entry& d_e2)     // IN: right-operand
{
   return (d_e1.name > d_e2.name);
}


ostream& operator << (ostream& outs,     // INOUT: stream
                      const entry& d_e)  // IN: entry displayed
{
   outs << "Name   is " << d_e1.name << endl;
   outs << "Number is " << d_e2.number << endl;

   return outs;
}
```

(continued)

Figure 12.19 *(continued)*

```
istream& operator >> (istream& ins,    // INOUT: stream
                      entry& d_e)       // OUT: entry read
{
    cout "Enter name: ";
    cin.ignore (1, '\n');
    getline (ins, d_e1.name, '\n');
    cout << "Enter number: ";
    ins >> d_e1,number;

    return ins;
}
```

The equality and relational operators base their result only on the name attribute of a directory entry, which is what we desire. The definition of operator == enables us to determine if an entry currently in our list has the same name as a target entry. Assuming target and elements[i] are the same data type, the condition

```
(target == elements[i])
```

in function search of class index_list is true (a match) if target and elements[i] have the same name component. Similarly, the definition of operator < enables us to sort the directory entries by name. The condition

```
(elements[i] < elements[min_index])
```

in function find_min of class index_list is true if the name in elements[i] is alphabetically less than the name in elements[min_index].

EXERCISES FOR SECTION 12.7

Self-Check
1. In the definition of friend operator >>, we use the operators << and >>. How can we do this? Explain which insertion or extraction operator C++ associates with each occurrence of these operators in the function body.
2. Explain why we used getline in friend operator >> instead of the string extraction operator to read the person's name.

Programming
1. Write definitions for friend operators <=, >=, and !=.
2. Write an extraction operator that can be used with an ifstream object. Do the same thing for an insertion operator and an ofstream object.

12.8 ___ THE STACK ABSTRACT DATA TYPE

A *stack* is a data structure in which only the top element can be accessed. To illustrate, the plates stored in the spring-loaded device in a buffet line perform like a stack. A customer always takes the top plate; when a plate is removed,

Figure 12.20 A stack of characters

the plate beneath it moves to the top. Also, when a clean plate is returned to the stack, it is always placed on the top of the stack.

The diagram in Fig. 12.20 shows a stack s of four characters. The symbol * is the character at the top of the stack and is the only character that we can access. We must remove the symbol * from the stack in order to access the letter C. Removing a value from a stack is called *popping the stack.* Storing a data item in a stack is called *pushing* it onto the stack.

Compilers use stacks to store procedure and function arguments. Compilers also use stacks for data storage while translating expressions. In general, we use stacks in a program to remember a sequence of data objects or actions in the reverse order from that in which they were encountered.

We begin with a description of the information that any user of our stack abstract data type needs to know. We will implement the stack as a *template* class stack<stack_el_type, max_size> (see Fig. 12.21).

Figure 12.21 stack<stack_el_type, max_size> template class specification

```
// FILE: stack.h
// DEFINITION FOR A TEMPLATE CLASS STACK

// Structure:      A stack consists of a collection of elements
//                 that are all of the same type, stack_el_type.
//                 The elements of a stack are ordered according
//                 to when they were placed on the stack. Only
//                 the element that was last inserted onto the
//                 stack can be removed or examined. New elements
//                 are inserted at the top of the stack. Space for
//                 max_size elements is allocated, default 100.


#ifndef STACK_H_
#define STACK_H_

template <class stack_el_type, int max_size = 100>
class stack
{
```

(continued)

Figure 12.21   *(continued)*

```
public:
    // Member functions ...
    // CONSTRUCTOR TO CREATE AN EMPTY STACK
    stack ();

    // PUSH AN ELEMENT ONTO THE STACK
    bool push
        (const stack_el_type& x);      // IN: item to be pushed onto
                                       //         stack
    // Pre : The element x is defined.
    // Post: If the stack is not full, the item is pushed onto
    //       the stack and true is returned. Otherwise, the stack
    //       is unchanged and false is returned.

    // POP AN ELEMENT OFF THE STACK
    bool pop
        (stack_el_type& x);    // OUT: Element popped from stack
    // Pre : none
    // Post: If the stack is not empty, the value at the top
    //       of the stack is removed, its value is placed in
    //       x, and true is returned. If the stack is empty, x
    //       is not defined and false is returned.

    // GET TOP ELEMENT FROM STACK WITHOUT POPPING
    bool get top
        (stack_el_type& x) const; // OUT: Value returned from top
                                  //             of stack
      // Pre : none
      // Post: If the stack is not empty, the value at the top
      //       is copied into x and true is returned. If the
      //       stack is empty, x is not defined and false is
      //       returned. In either case, the stack is not
      //       changed.

    // TEST TO SEE IF STACK IS EMPTY
    bool is empty () const;
        // Pre : none
        // Post: Returns true if the stack is empty; otherwise,
        //       returns false.

    // TEST TO SEE IF STACK IS FULL
    bool is full () const;
        // Pre : none
        // Post: Returns true if the stack is full; otherwise,
        //       returns false.

private:
    // The data members are explained in Section 12.9
    int top;                                 // index of element at
                                             // the top of the stack
```

(continued)

Figure 12.21   *(continued)*

```
        stack_el_type items[max_size];        // Array storage for
                                              // stack elements
};

#endif //STACK_H_
```

The template declaration

```
template <class stack_el_type, int max_size = 100>
class stack
```

declares that template class `stack` takes two parameters, `stack_el_type` (which may be any data type) and `max_size` (which must be an integer). If the second template argument is omitted, the default value of 100 is used for `max_size`. The declaration

```
stack<int> integer_stack;
```

allocates storage for a stack of integers of the default size 100. The declaration

```
stack<char, 10> small_character_stack;
```

allocates storage for a stack of characters of size 10.

We can illustrate how stacks and their operators work and use them in a client program without worrying about the details of how the stack is represented in memory. Multiple stacks containing different types can be defined in a client program. A given stack, however, can hold variables only of a single type.

As with all variables, a stack must be declared before it can be used. The declaration creates an empty stack. For example, the following allocates storage for a stack of 100 integers and displays the message `Stack is empty`:

```
stack<int, > s;
if (s.is_empty ())
   cout << "Stack is empty" << endl;
```

Example 12.13   In stack s shown on the left in Fig. 12.22, the first element placed on the stack was `'2'`, and the last element placed on the stack was `'*'`. For this stack, the value of `s.is_empty()` is `false`. The value of `s.is_full()` is `false` if stack s can store more than four elements; otherwise, the value of `s.is_full()` is `true`. The function call

```
s.get_top (x)
```

stores `'*'` in x (type `char`) without changing s. The function call

```
s.pop (x)
```

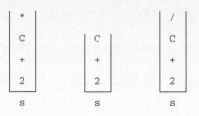

Figure 12.22   Stack s (left) after pop (middle) and push (right) operations

removes ' * ' from s and stores it in x. The new stack s contains three elements, as shown in the middle of Fig. 12.22.

The function call

```
s.push ('/')
```

pushes ' / ' onto the stack; the new stack s, which contains four elements, is shown on the right of Fig. 12.22. The value returned from each operation should be true.   ■

Example 12.14   The program in Fig. 12.23 calls fill_stack to read a collection of data strings ending with the sentinel string ("***"). Function fill_stack pushes each string read except the last onto a stack. Then it calls display_stack to pop each string from the stack and display it, thereby displaying the strings in reverse order.

Figure 12.23   Using a stack of characters

```cpp
// FILE: UseStack.cpp
// USE A STACK TO STORE STRINGS AND DISPLAY THEM IN REVERSE ORDER

#include <string>
#include <iostream.h>
#include "stack.h"          // Uses stack template class

typedef stack<string, 20> string_stack;

int fill_stack (string_stack& s);
void display_stack (string_stack& s);

void main()
{
    // Local data
    stack<string> s;

    // Read data into the stack.
    fill_stack (s);

    // Display the stack contents
    display_stack (s);
}
```

(continued)

Figure 12.23   *(continued)*

```
int fill_stack (string_stack& s)    // OUT: stack to fill
//    Reads data characters and pushes them onto stack s.
//    Pre : s is an empty stack.
//    Post: s contains the strings read in reverse order.
//    Returns the number of strings read not counting the sentinel.
{
   // Local data
      string next_str;            // next string
      int num_strings;            // count of strings read
      const string sentinel = "***";   // sentinel string

   // Read and push strings onto stack until done.
   num_strings = 0;
   cout << "Enter next string or " << sentinel << "> ";
   cin >> next_str;
   while ((next_str != sentinel) && (!s.is_full ()))
   {
      s.push (next_str);   // Push next string on stack S.
      num_strings++;
      cout << "Enter next string or " << sentinel << "> ";
      cin >> next_str;
   }

   return num_strings;
}  // end fill_stack


void display_stack (string_stack& s)  // IN: stack to display
//    Pops each string from stack s and displays it.
//    Pre : Stack s is defined.
//    Post: Stack s is empty and all strings are displayed.
{
   // Local data
   string next_str;

   // Pop and display strings until stack is empty.
   while (!s.is_empty ())
   {
      s.pop (next_str);   // Pop next string off.
      cout << next_str << endl;
   }
}  // end display_stack
```

──────────── Program Output ────────────

```
Enter next string or ***> Here
Enter next string or ***> are
Enter next string or ***> strings!
Enter next string or ***> ***
strings!
are
Here
```

The line

```
typedef stack<string, 20> string_stack;
```

associates the data type stack<string, 20> (a stack of up to 20 strings) with the identifier string_stack. Therefore, we can use stack_string as the stack type in the formal argument lists for fill_stack and display_stack.   ∎

EXERCISES FOR SECTION 12.8

Self-Check   1. Assume that stack s is defined as in Fig. 12.22 (left). Perform the sequence of operations shown below. Show the result of each operation and the new stack if it is changed. Rather than draw the stack each time, use the notation |2 + C * to represent the stack. (The bar "|" represents the bottom of the stack.)

```
s.push ('$')
s.push ('-')
s.pop (next_ch)
s.top (next_ch)
s.is_empty ()
s.is_full ()
```

2. Declare a stack that can store up to ten values of type entry from Section 12.6.

Programming   1. Write a method copy_stack that uses the stack operators to make a copy of an existing stack. The new stack will contain a duplicate of each node in the original stack. (*Hint:* You will need to pop each node and store its data in a temporary stack.)

12.9 ─── IMPLEMENTING THE STACK CLASS

Data Members

This section will discuss how to implement the stack class. Let's begin by looking again at the private part for the template class stack first shown in Fig. 12.21 and repeated below.

```
private:
    // The data members are explained in Section 12.9
    int top;                            // index of element at
                                        //    the top of the stack
    stack_el_type items[max_size];      // Array storage for stack
                                        //    elements
```

There are two data members: an integer (top), which is the index of the top item of the stack, and an array (items), which holds the items. The array items is declared to be of size max_size, which has a default value of 100.

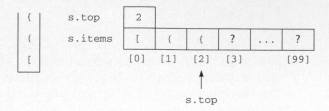

Figure 12.24   Stack s of characters

Storage is not allocated until a variable of type `stack` is declared. The declaration

```
stack<char> s;
```

allocates storage for a stack, s, of up to 100 characters. All the storage space is allocated at one time, even though there will not be any items on the stack initially.

In Fig. 12.24, abstract stack s (on the left) would be represented in memory as shown on the right. `s.top` is 2, and the stack consists of the subarray `s.items[0]` through `s.items[2]`; the subarray `s.items[3]` through `s.items[99]` is currently undefined.

The array element `s.items[s.top]` contains the character value `'{'`, which is the value at the top of the stack.

Example 12.15   Figure 12.25 shows the effect of the statement

```
s.push('(')
```

where the initial stack s is shown in Fig. 12.24. Before push is executed, `s.top` is 2, so `s.items[2]` is the element at the top of the stack. Function push must increment `s.top` to 3 so that the new item (`'('`) will be stored in `s.items[3]`, as shown in the figure.   ■

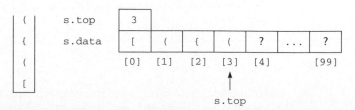

Figure 12.25   Effect of push operation

Stack Operators

The stack operators manipulate the array member items using the integer member top as an index to the array. Their implementation is fairly straightforward. You should be able to read and understand the stack operators shown in the implementation section of the template class stack (Fig. 12.26).

Figure 12.26 Implementation of template class stack using an array

```cpp
// FILE: stack.cpp
// IMPLEMENTATION OF TEMPLATE CLASS STACK

#include "stack.h"

// CONSTRUCTOR TO CREATE AN EMPTY STACK
template <class stack_el_type, int max_size>
stack<stack_el_type, max_size>::stack ()
{
   top = -1;                 // A value of -1 indicates empty
}  // end stack


// PUSH AN ELEMENT ONTO THE STACK
template <class stack_el_type, int max_size>
bool stack<stack_el_type, max_size>::push
   (const stack_el_type& x)      // IN: item to be pushed onto stack

// Pre:  The element x is defined.
// Post: If the stack is not full, the item is pushed onto
//       the stack and true is returned. Otherwise, the stack
//       is unchanged and false is returned.
{
   bool success;         // flag: true indicates successful push

   if (top < max_size - 1)      // If there is room
   {
      top++;                       // increment top
      items[top] = x;              // insert x
      success = true;              // indicate success
   }
   else
      success = false;    // no room, indicate failure

   return success;
}  // end push


// POP AN ELEMENT OFF THE STACK
template <class stack_el_type, int max_size>
bool stack<stack_el_type, max_size>::pop
   (stack_el_type& x)     // OUT: Element popped from stack
```

(continued)

Figure 12.26   *(continued)*

```
// Pre:  none
// Post: If the stack is not empty, the value at the top of
//       the stack is removed, its value is placed in x, and
//       true is returned. If the stack is empty, x is not
//       defined and false is returned.
{
   bool success;          // flag: true indicates successful pop

   if (top >= 0)                   // if not empty
   {
      x = items[top];              // remove top element
      top--;                       // decrement top
      success = true;              // indicate success
   }
   else
      success = false;             // indicate failure

   return success;
}  // end pop


// GET TOP ELEMENT FROM STACK WITHOUT POPPING
template <class stack_el_type, int max_size>
bool stack<stack_el_type, max_size>::get_top
   (stack_el_type& x)// OUT: Value returned from top of stack
   const
// Pre:  none
// Post: If the stack is not empty, the value at the top is
//       copied into x and true is returned. If the stack is
//       empty, x is not defined and false is returned. In either
//       case, the stack is not changed.
{
   bool success;          // flag: true indicates successful get
   if (top >= 0)                   // if not empty
   {
      x = items[top];              // retrieve top element, do not pop
      success = true;              // indicate success
   }
   else
      success = false;             // indicate failure

   return success;
}  // end get_top
```

(continued)

Figure 12.26   *(continued)*

```
// TEST TO SEE IF STACK IS EMPTY
template <class stack_el_type, int max_size>
bool stack<stack_el_type, max_size>::is_empty () const
// Pre:  none
// Post: Returns true if the stack is empty; otherwise,
//       returns false.
{
   return top < 0;
}  // end is_empty


// TEST TO SEE IF STACK IS FULL
template <class stack_el_type, int max_size>
bool stack<stack_el_type, max_size>::is_full () const

// Pre:  none
// Post: Returns true if the stack is full; otherwise,
//       returns false.
{
   return top >= max_size-1;
}  // end is_full
```

EXERCISES FOR SECTION 12.9

Self-Check   1. Declare a stack of 50 student records, where each record is represented by struct type exam_stats (See Fig. 9.26). Can you use the stack operators to manipulate this stack?

Programming   1. Write a member function depth that returns the number of elements currently on the stack.

12.10 ____ COMMON PROGRAMMING ERRORS

You should review the common programming errors sections for Chapters 9 (arrays and structs) and 11 (classes) because many of the same errors can occur when you process combinations of these data structures. When you use multidimensional arrays, make sure the subscript for each dimension is always in range. If you use nested for loops to process the array elements, make sure that loop control variables used as array subscripts are in the correct order. The order of the loop control variables determines the sequence in which the array elements are processed. Also, be careful not to make the mistake of writing all subscripts inside one pair of brackets (e.g., `sales[1, 2, 3]` instead of `sales[1][2][3]`).

For arrays of structs or arrays of classes, use the array name followed by a subscript to access the entire array element. To reference an individual data item stored in an array of structs, you must specify both the array subscript and the name of the struct component using the notation `x[i].comp` where `x[i]` is the `i`th element of array `x` and `comp` is a structure component.

For template classes, you must provide the template class prefix before the header of each member function that is defined in a separate `.cpp` file. Also, the class name with arguments and the scope resolution operator `::` must precede the function name in the function header. If you have difficulty linking the components of a program that uses a template class whose member functions are defined in a separate `.cpp` file, you should determine whether any special compiler directives or `typedef` declarations are required on your system. As an alternative, you can consider placing the function definitions directly in the header file. If you do this, do not forget to remove the template class prefix line and the class name and scope resolution operator from the function header.

For friend functions or operators, also remove the class name and scope resolution operator from the function definition and begin the function prototype with the word `friend`. Remember that friends cannot be `const` functions or operators.

CHAPTER REVIEW

This chapter discussed modeling data using combinations of C++ data structures: arrays, structs, and classes. We saw how to model tables and board games with two-dimensional arrays. We also saw how to represent a company's sales volume for many salespeople, over several years, using a three-dimensional array.

The chapter also focused on examples of modeling data using arrays of structs and arrays of classes. We introduced the indexed list, a safe array, and showed how to implement several of its member functions. We made this a template class so we could allocate storage for indexed lists of different kinds and sizes. Finally, we showed how to model and maintain a telephone directory stored as an indexed list.

We discussed friend functions and friend operators. We used friend operators in a class to write definitions for the equality, relational, and I/O operators.

Finally, we discussed the stack abstraction and showed how to implement a template class for storing a stack. In the next chapter, you will see that the stack plays an important role in implementing recursion.

New C++ Constructs   The C++ constructs introduced in this chapter are described in Table 12.1.

Table 12.1   Summary of New C++ Constructs

CONSTRUCT	EFFECT
Two-Dimensional Array	
`int matrix[10][5];`	`matrix` is a two-dimensional array with 10 rows and 5 columns
```sum = 0;` `for (int i = 0; i < 10; i++)` ` for (int j = 0; j < 5; j++)` ` sum += matrix[i][j];```	Stores the sum of all elements of array `matrix` in `sum`.
Array of Structs	
```struct city` `{` ` string name;` ` string state;` `};```	Declares a struct type `city` with storage for two string components, `name` and `state`.
`city capitals[50];`	Allocates storage for an array `capitals` whose 50 elements are structs of type `city`.
`capitals[49].name = "Juno";`	Stores `"Juno"` in the `name` field of `capitals[49]`.
Array of Objects	
```class point` `{` ` public:` ` void read ();` ` void print ();` ` private:` ` float x;` ` float y;` `};```	Each `point` object has two private data members, `x` and `y`. The class has two public member functions: `read` and `print`.
`point coords[5];`	Allocates storage for an array `coords` whose 5 elements are objects of type `point`.
`coords[0].print ();`	Applies `print` to the first object in array `coords`.
Template Class	
```template<class T, int N>` `class vector` `{` ` public:` ` void read ();```	Template class `vector` has one private data member `stuff` that provides storage for an array of `N` elements of type `T`. Both `T` and `N` are parameters. There are two public member functions: `display` and `read`.

(continued)

Table 12.1   *(continued)*

```
      void display ();
   private:
      T stuff[N];
};
```

`template<class T, int N>` `void vector<T, N>::read ()`	Function header for definition of member function `read` of template class `vector` in a separate implementation file.
`vector<point, 3> triangle;`	Object `triangle` is an instance of template class `vector` that provides storage for 3 objects of type `point`.
`triangle.display ();`	Applies member function `display` to object `triangle`.

Friend Operator Prototype

`friend bool operator >` `   (const El&, const El&);`	Declares a friend operator > for comparing objects of class `El`. Overloads the > operator for class `El`.

✔ QUICK-CHECK EXERCISES

1. What control structure can be used to process sequentially all the elements in a multidimensional array?
2. List the storage sequence for elements of the two-dimensional array `matrix` with 3 rows and 2 columns.
3. Write a program segment to display the sum of the values in each column of a 5 × 3 array `table` with base type `float` elements. How many column sums will be displayed? How many elements are included in each sum?
4. Write a type declaration for a data structure that stores a baseball player's name, salary, position (pitcher, catcher, infielder, outfielder, utility), batting average, fielding percentage, number of hits, runs, runs batted in, and errors.
5. Write the type declaration for a data structure that stores the information in Quick-Check Exercise 4 for a team of 25 players.
6. If the elements of the array `team` have the structure described in Quick-Check Exercise 4, write a program segment that displays the first two structure members for the first five players.
7. Write a type declaration for an array of 12 objects of type `counter` (see Fig. 11.1). Write an expression to increment the sixth element of your array.
8. Write a declaration that allocates storage for an indexed list of 25 players from Quick-Check Exercise 4.
9. Assuming that the variable `a_player` contains a player's data, write a statement to add `a_player` to the end of your indexed list.
10. Write statements to place `a_player` in the first position of the indexed list but first move the player currently in the first position to the end of the list.

11. Draw the array representation of the following stack. What is s.items[0]? What is the value of s.top? What is the value of s.items[s.top-1]?

12. Why should the statement s.top = s.top - 1 not appear in a client program that uses the stack class?
13. Can you have two stacks of float numbers in the same client program? Can you have a stack of integers and a stack of characters in the same client program?
14. Write a program segment that removes from the stack the element just below the top of the stack. Use the stack member functions.
15. Write a member function pop_next_top that performs the operation in Quick-Check Exercise 15. (Use the array implementation of the stack class.)

Answers to Quick-Check Exercises

1. nested for loops
2. matrix[0][0], matrix[0][1], matrix[1][0], matrix[1][1], matrix[2][0], matrix[2][1]
3.
```
for (int c = 0; c < 3; c++)
{
    column_sum = 0.0;
    for (int r = 0; r < 5; r++)
        column_sum += table[r][c];
    cout << "Sum for column " << c << " is " << column_sum
        << "." << endl;
}  // end for c
```
   three column sums; five elements added per column
4. The data elements are of different types:
```
enum position {pitcher, catcher, infielder, outfielder,
                utility};
struct player
{
    string name;
    float salary;
    position place;
    float batting_ave, field_pct;
    int hits, runs, rbis, errors;
}  // end player
```
5. player team[25];
6.
```
for (int i = 0; i < 5; i++)
    cout << team[i].name << "    " << team[i].salary << endl;
```
7. counter counters[11];
   counters[5].increment ();
8. indexed_list<player, 25> team;

```
 9. team.append (a_player);
10. team.retrieve (0, b_player);
    team.insert (0, a_player);
    team.append (b_player);
```

11. &, 2, *

s.top		2	
s.items	&	*	$

     `s.items[0]` is &, `s.top` is 2, `s.items[s.top-1]` is *.

12. Because the member `top` is not visible to the client program, this statement will result in an error message. The member `top` should be part of the private part of the class because the client programs should not be aware of and should not manipulate the internal representation of the data type defined by the class.

13. yes; yes

```
14. success = s.pop (x);
    success = s.pop (y);
    success = s.push (x);
15. bool pop_next_top
    (stack_element &x)
    {
        if (top > 1)
        {
            x = items[top-1];
            items[top-1] = items[top];
            top--;
            return true;
        }
        else
            return false;
    }
```

REVIEW QUESTIONS

1. Write the declarations for the array `cpu_array` that will hold 20 records of type `cpu`. The structure `cpu` has the following fields: `id_number` (a string), `make` (a string), `location` (a string), and `ports` (integer).

Use the following declarations for Review Questions 2 through 4:

```
const int nmbr_employees = 20;

struct employee
{
    int id;
```

```
        float rate;
        float hours;
  };   // end employee
```

```
  employee all_employees[nmbr_employees];
```

2. Write the function `total_gross` that will return the total gross pay given the data stored in the array `all_employees`.
3. Write a program fragment that displays the ID number of each employee who works between 10.0 and 20.0 hours per week.
4. Write a program fragment that displays the ID number of the employee who works the most hours.
5. Write the declarations for an array of structs that can be used to store all the `top40` hits for one week of the year. Assume that the data stored for each hit is the title, artist, production company, cost, and month of issue (an enumerator).
6. Answer Review Question 5 for a data structure that stores the same data for each of the 52 weeks of a year.
7. Provide the definition for a class whose attributes store the information described in Review Question 5. Declare member functions that perform operations analogous to the ones for class `entry` in Fig. 12.14.
8. Provide declarations for indexed lists (not arrays) that store the data described in Review Questions 5 and 6 using the class from Review Question 7 to store data for each hit.
9. Explain the advantages of using an indexed list instead of an array to store the data about the top 40 hits.
10. Describe two circumstances when you would use a friend function instead of a member function.
11. Provide an implementation file with definitions for each member function of the class in Review Question 5. Base the results of a comparison on the title attribute.
12. Show the effect of each of the operations below on `stack<char>` s. Assume that y (type char) contains the character '&'. What are the final values of x and `success` and the contents of stack s? Assume that s is initially empty.

```
  success = s.push ('+');
  success = s.pop (x);
  success = s.pop (x);
  success = s.push ('(');
  success = s.push (y);
  success = s.pop ('&');
```

13. Answer Review Question 12 by showing the values of the data members `top` and `items` after each operation.

PROGRAMMING PROJECTS

1. Write a program that generates the Morse code for a sentence that ends with a period and contains no other characters except letters and blanks. After reading the Morse code into an array of strings, your program should read each word of the sen-

tence and display its Morse code equivalent on a separate line. The Morse code is as follows:

```
A .-    B -...   C -.-   D -..   E .     F ..-.  G --.   H ....  I ..    J .---
K -.-   L .-..   M --    N -.    O ---   P .--.  Q --.-  R .-.   S ...   T -
U ..-   V ...-   W .--   X -..-  Y -.--  Z --..
```

Each letter and its Morse code equivalent should be stored in an indexed list of structs, and an appropriate set of methods should be defined for this data abstraction.

2. Develop a C++ class to model the mathematical notion of a matrix. At a minimum, your class should include methods for addition, subtraction, and multiplication of two matrices, plus at least three other matrix operations that you know about. (If you don't know much about matrices, find a mathematics book that can help.) Before performing the required data manipulation, each method you write should validate its input arguments. In particular, the dimensions of the matrices involved in an operation must be compatible for that operation.

3. The voting district in which you live is partitioned into five precincts. Write a program that reads the election results from each of these precincts and tabulates the total vote in your district for all of the candidates running for election. The program should begin by asking the user to enter the number of candidates, nmbr_candidates, running for office. It should then read the election returns for each precinct for each candidate, compute the total vote for each candidate, and print the input and the results in the form shown in the table below.

For each candidate, the program should also compute and display the percentage of the total vote. If there is one candidate whose percentage is better than 50 percent, print out a message declaring that candidate to be the winner of the election. If there is no such candidate, print out a message indicating the names of the top two vote-getters and indicate that a run-off election will be required. The voting data should be stored in an indexed collection of structured elements, each of which contains the name of a candidate, the number of votes in each precinct for that candidate, and the vote total. The relevant information about each candidate should be modeled by a class containing the definitions of the necessary attributes and methods required for one candidate.

Test your program for the data shown below and also when candidate C receives only 108 votes in precinct 4.

PRECINCT	CANDIDATE A	CANDIDATE B	CANDIDATE C	CANDIDATE D	TOTAL VOTE
1	192	48	206	37	483
2	147	90	312	21	570
3	186	12	121	38	357
4	114	21	408	39	582
5	267	13	382	29	691
TOTALS	906	184	1429	164	2683

4. Modify Programming Project 3 to make it an interactive, menu-driven program. Menu options should include the following:

- Initializing the vote table (prompt the user for the number of candidates, their names, and the number of votes in each precinct)
- Displaying the candidates' names and votes received (raw count and percentage of votes cast)
- Displaying the winner's name (or names of the top two vote-getters in the case of a run-off)
- Exiting the program

5. The HighRisk Software Company has employed us to develop a general sales analysis program that they can market to a number of different companies. The program will be used to enter monthly sales figures for a specified range of years and display these values and some simple statistical measures as requested by the user. The user is to be given a menu from which to choose one of the options shown in the table below.

OPTIONS	DESCRIPTION
0	*Display help information*—presents more detailed information about the other options available.
1	*Display sales data*—provides sales data for the entire range of years using two tables, one covering January–June and the other covering July–December.
2	*Compute annual sales totals*—computes the sum of the monthly sales for each year in the specified range.
3	*Display annual sales totals*—presents the sum of the monthly sales for each year in the specified range.
4	*Display largest monthly sales amount*—finds and displays the largest monthly sales amount for a specified year.
5	*Graph monthly sales data*—provides a histogram for the 12 months of sales for a specified year.
6	*Exit*—exits from the program.

The program is to run interactively and should begin by asking the user to enter the range of years involved. Next it should prompt the user for the sales data for each of the specified years. From this point on, the program should display the options menu, allow the user to make a choice, and carry out the user's selection. This process should continue repeatedly until the user enters option 6.

6. Design and implement a C++ class to model a telephone directory for a company. The directory should contain space for up to 100 names, phone numbers, and room numbers. You should have operators to do the following:

- Create an empty directory (all names blank)
- Read in the telephone directory from a file
- Retrieve the entry corresponding to a given name

- Display the telephone directory
- Add a new entry to the directory.

Also design and implement a class with attributes and methods required to model an individual telephone entry.

7. Write a menu-driven program that tests the operators in Programming Project 6.

8. Design and implement a C++ class to model a building (floors 1 to 3, wings A and B, and rooms 1 to 5). Each entry in the array will be a `struct` containing a person's name and phone number. Provide operators to do the following:

- Create an empty building (all names are blank)
- Read data into the building
- Display the entire building
- Display a particular floor of the building
- Retrieve the entry for a particular room
- Store a new entry in a particular room

To designate a particular room, the program user must enter a floor number, wing letter, and room number as data. Also design and implement a class with attributes and methods required to model a single room in the building.

9. Many supermarkets use computer equipment that allows the checkout clerk to drag an item across a sensor that reads the bar code on the product container. After the computer reads the bar code, the store inventory database is examined, the item's price and product description are located, counts are reduced, and a receipt is printed. Your task is to write a program that simulates this process.

　　Your program will read the inventory information from the data file on disk into an array of records. The data in the inventory file is written one item per line, beginning with a 2-digit product code, followed by a 30-character product description, its price, and the quantity of that item in stock. Your program will copy the revised version of the inventory to a new data file after all purchases are processed.

　　Processing customers' orders involves reading a series of product codes representing each person's purchases from a second data file. A zero product code is used to mark the end of each customer's order. As each product code is read, the inventory list is searched to find a matching product code. Once located, the product price and description are printed on the receipt, and the quantity on hand is reduced by 1. At the bottom of the receipt, print the total for the goods purchased by the customer.

10. Write a program that simulates the movement of radioactive particles in a 20×20-foot two-dimensional shield around a reactor. Particles enter the shield at some random position in the shield coordinate space. Once a particle enters the shield, it moves 1 foot per second in one of four directions. The direction for the next second of travel is determined by a random number from 1 to 4 (forward, backward, left, right). A change in direction is interpreted as a collision with another particle, which results in a dissipation of energy. Each particle can have only a limited number of collisions before it dies. A particle exits the shield if its position places it outside the shield coordinate space before K collisions occur. Determine the percentage of particles that exit the shield, where K and the number of particles are input as data items. Also, compute the average number of times a particle's path crosses itself during travel time within the

shield. (*Hint:* Mark each array position occupied by a particle before it dies or exits the shield.)

11. Write a program to monitor the flow of an item into and out of a warehouse. The warehouse will have numerous deliveries and shipments for this item (a widget) during the time covered. A shipment out is billed at a profit of 50 percent over the cost of a widget. Unfortunately, each shipment received may have a different cost associated with it. The accountants for the firm have instituted a last-in, first-out system for filling orders. This means that the newest widgets are the first ones sent out to fill an order. This method of inventory can be represented using a stack. The push operator will insert a shipment received. The pop operator will delete a shipment out. Input data should consist of the following:

- S or O: shipment received or an order to be sent
- the quantity received or shipped out
- cost: cost per widget (for received shipments only)
- vendor: a character string that names the company sent to or received from

For example, the data fragment below indicates that 100 widgets were received from RCA at $10.50 per widget and 50 were shipped to Boeing:

```
S 100 10.50 RCA
O 50 Boeing
```

Output for an order will consist of the quantity and the total price for all the widgets in the order. (*Hint:* Each widget price is 50 percent higher than its cost. The widgets to fill an order may come from multiple shipments with different costs.)

12. Write a program that can be used to compile a simple arithmetic expression without parentheses. For example, the expression

A + B * C − D

should be compiled as shown in the table below.

OPERATION	OPERAND 1	OPERAND 2	RESULT
*	B	C	Z
+	A	Z	Y
−	Y	D	X

The table shows the order in which the operations are performed (*, +, −) and the operands for each operator. The result column gives the name of an identifier (working backward from Z) chosen to hold each result. Assume the operands are the letters A through F and the operators are +, −, *, and /.

Your program should read each character and process it as follows. If the character is a blank, ignore it. If it is an operand, push it onto the operand stack. If the character is not an operator, display an error message and terminate the program. If it is an operator, compare its precedence with that of the operator on top of the operator stack (* and / have higher precedence than + and −). If the new operator has higher precedence than the one currently on top (or if the operator stack is empty), it should be pushed onto the operator stack.

If the new operator has the same or lower precedence, the operator on the top of the operator stack must be evaluated next. This is done by popping it off the operator stack along with a pair of operands from the operand stack and writing a new line of the output table. The character selected to hold the result should then be pushed onto the operand stack. Next, the new operator should be compared to the new top of the operator stack. Continue to generate output table lines until the top of the operator stack has lower precedence than the new operator or until the stack is empty. At this point, push the new operator onto the top of the operator stack and examine the next character in the data string. When the end of the string is reached, pop any remaining operator along with its operand pair as just described. Remember to push the result character onto the operand stack after each table line is generated.

13

Recursion

A recursive function is able to call itself, an ability that allows this type of function to be repeated with different argument values. You can use recursion as an alternative to iteration (looping). A recursive solution is generally less efficient in terms of computer time than an iterative one due to the overhead for the extra function calls; however, in many instances the use of recursion enables programmers to specify natural, simple solutions to problems that would otherwise be difficult to solve. For this reason, recursion is an important and powerful tool in problem solving and programming.

13.1 ——— THE NATURE OF RECURSION

Problems that lend themselves to a recursive solution have the following characteristics:

- One or more simple cases of the problem (called *stopping cases*) have a straightforward, nonrecursive solution.
- For the other cases, there is a process (using recursion) for substituting one or more reduced cases of the problem that are closer to a stopping case.
- Eventually the problem can be reduced to stopping cases only, all of which are relatively easy to solve.

The recursive algorithms that we write will generally consist of an `if` statement with the form shown below.

> If the stopping case is reached
>   Solve the problem.
> else
>   Reduce the problem using recursion.

Figure 13.1 illustrates this approach. Let's assume that for a particular problem of size *n*, we can split the problem into two subproblems—a problem of

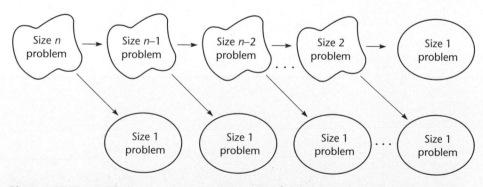

Figure 13.1   **Splitting a problem into smaller problems**

size 1, which we can solve (a stopping case), and a problem of size $n - 1$ that involves recursion. We can split the problem of size $n - 1$ into another problem of size 1 and a problem of size $n - 2$, which we can split further. If we split the problem n times, we will end up with n problems of size 1, each of which can be solved directly.

Example 13.1 As a simple example of this approach, let's consider how we might solve the problem of multiplying 6 by 3, assuming that we know our addition facts but not our multiplication tables. The problem of multiplying 6 by 3 can be split into the two subproblems:

1. Multiply 6 by 2.
2. Add 6 to the result of subproblem 1.

Since we know how to add, we can solve subproblem 2 but not subproblem 1. However, subproblem 1 is simpler than the original problem. We can split it into the two problems 1.1 and 1.2 below, leaving us three problems to solve, two of which involve addition.

1.1 Multiply 6 by 1.
1.2 Add 6 to the result of subproblem 1.1.

Even though we do not know our multiplication tables, we are familiar with the simple rule that for any integer m, m × 1 is m. By solving subproblem 1.1 (the answer is 6) and subproblem 1.2, we get the solution to subproblem 1 (the answer is 12). Solving subproblem 2 gives us the final answer (18).

Figure 13.2 shows the implementation of this solution in the form of the recursive function `multiply`. This function returns the product, m × n, of its

Figure 13.2 Recursive function `multiply`

```
// FILE: Multiply.cpp
// RECURSIVE MULTIPLY FUNCTION

// PERFORMS MULTIPLICATION USING THE + OPERATOR
int multiply
   (int m, int n)       // IN: values to be multiplied

// Pre:      m and n are defined and n > 0.
// Post:     Returns m * n.
// Returns:  Product of m x n.
{
   // Multiply m and n.
   if (n <= 1)
      return m;                              // stopping step
   else
      return m + multiply (m, n - 1);        // recursive step
}  // end multiply
```

two arguments. The stopping case is reached when n finally equals 1 (the condition n <= 1 is true). In this case, the statement

```
return m;                                  // stopping case
```

executes, returning the answer m. If n is greater than 1, the statement

```
return (m + multiply (m, n - 1));          // recursive step
```

executes, splitting the original problem into the two simpler problems:

1. Multiply m by n - 1.
2. Add m to the result of subproblem 1.

The first of these subproblems is solved by calling multiply again with n - 1 as its second argument. If the new second argument is greater than 1, there will be additional calls to function multiply.   ■

For now, we will assume that function multiply performs as desired. We will see how to trace the execution of a recursive function in the next section.

The next example illustrates how we might solve a more difficult problem by splitting it into smaller problems. We will provide a complete case study solution to this problem after you have more experience using recursion.

Example 13.2   The Towers of Hanoi problem involves moving a specified number of disks that are all of different sizes from one tower to another. Legend has it that the world will come to an end when the problem is solved for 64 disks. In the version of the problem shown in Fig. 13.3, there are 5 disks (numbered 1 through 5) and 3 towers (lettered A, B, C). The goal is to move the 5 disks from tower A to tower C, subject to the following rules:

- Only one disk may be moved at a time, and this disk must be the top disk on a tower.

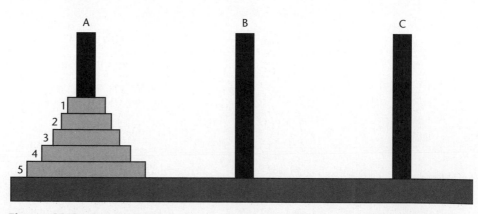

Figure 13.3   Towers of Hanoi

■ A larger disk can never be placed on top of a smaller disk.

The stopping case of the problem involves moving 1 disk only (for example, "move disk 1 from tower A to tower C"). A simpler problem than the original would be to move 4 disks subject to the conditions above, or to move 3 disks, and so on. Therefore, we want to split the original 5-disk problem into one or more subproblems involving fewer disks. Let's consider splitting the original problem into the three subproblems shown below:

1. Move 4 disks (numbered 1 through 4) from tower A to tower B.
2. Move disk 5 from tower A to tower C.
3. Move the four disks (1 through 4) from tower B to tower C.

In subproblem 1, we move all disks but the largest to tower B, an auxiliary tower. In subproblem 2, we move the largest disk to the goal tower, tower C. Finally, we move the remaining disks from B to the goal tower, where they will be placed on top of the largest disk.

Perhaps you are concerned that we have not really solved the original problem because we have not indicated how to perform subproblems 1 and 3. If so, please keep reading—the pieces will fit together shortly.

Let's assume that we can simply "follow the directions" indicated in problems 1 and 2 (a stopping case); Fig. 13.4 shows the status of the 3 towers after the completion of the tasks described in these subproblems. We can now solve the original 5-disk problem by following the directions indicated for subproblem 3. The resulting change to Fig. 13.4 should be fairly obvious.

Unfortunately, we still do not know how to perform subproblems 1 or 3. Both, however, involve 4 disks instead of 5, and so they are in some sense easier than the original problem. We should be able to split them into simpler problems in the same way that we split the original problem. For example, subproblem 3 involves moving 4 disks from tower B to tower C. We split this problem into two 3-disk problems and a 1-disk problem, as follows:

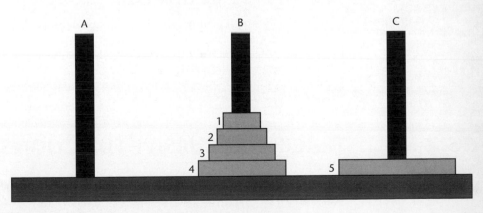

Figure 13.4 Towers of Hanoi after steps 1 and 2

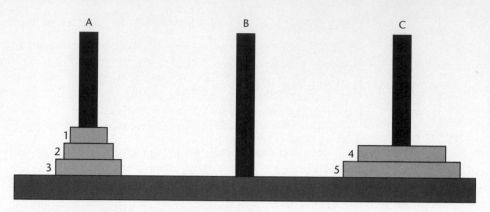

Figure 13.5   Towers of Hanoi after steps 1, 2, 3.1, and 3.2

3.1. Move 3 disks from tower B to tower A.
3.2. Move disk 4 from tower B to tower C.
3.3. Move 3 disks from tower A to tower C.

Figure 13.5 shows the status of the towers after the tasks described in sub-problems 3.1 and 3.2 have been completed. We now have the 2 largest disks on tower C. Note that tower A was the auxiliary disk for this sequence of moves. Once we complete subproblem 3.3, all 5 disks will be on tower C as required.   ■

By repeatedly splitting each n-disk problem into two problems involving n-1 disks and a 1-disk problem, we will eventually reach all cases of 1 disk, which we know how to solve. We will write a C++ program that later solves the Towers of Hanoi problem.

EXERCISES FOR SECTION 13.1

Self-Check   1. Draw a diagram depicting Fig. 13.4 after step 3 (move disks (1–4) from tower B to tower C) has been carried out.
2. Show the subproblems that are generated by the function call `multiply (5, 4)`. Use a diagram similar to Fig. 13.1.
3. Show the subproblems that are generated by attempting to solve the problem "move three disks from tower A to tower C."

13.2 ____ TRACING RECURSIVE FUNCTIONS

Hand tracing the execution of an algorithm provides us with valuable insight as to how that algorithm works. This is particularly true for recursive functions, as shown next.

Tracing a Recursive Function

In the last section, we wrote the recursive function multiply (see Fig. 13.2). We can trace the execution of the function call multiply (6, 3) by drawing an *activation frame* corresponding to each function call. An activation frame shows the argument values for each call and summarizes its execution.

The three activation frames generated to solve the problem of multiplying 6 by 3 are shown in Fig. 13.6. The part of each activation frame that executes before the next recursive call is shaded; the part that executes after the return from the next call has no shading. The darker the shading of an activation frame, the greater the depth of recursion.

The value returned from each call is shown alongside each upwardly directed arrow. The return arrow from each function call points to the operator + because the addition is performed just after the return.

When n is 1 in the third and last activation frame (corresponding to the call multiply (6, 1)), the value of m (6) is returned to the second activation frame (corresponding to the call multiply (6, 2)). This returned value is added to m (also 6) and their sum (12) is returned to the first activation frame (corresponding to the call multiply (6, 3)). This returned value is added

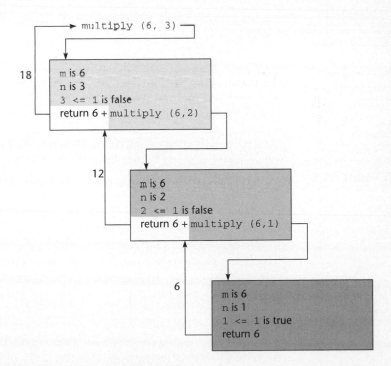

Figure 13.6 Trace of function multiply

to m (6) and their sum (18) is returned to the point of the original function call, multiply (6, 3).

Hand tracing the execution of a recursive function can sometimes be cumbersome. We can easily implement a function to provide a trace of itself by inserting display statements at the points of entry to and exit from the function. For example, we could modify the multiply function in Fig. 13.2 to include

```
cout << "Entering multiply with m = " << setw (2) << m
     << " and n = " << setw (2) << n << endl;
```

as the first executable line of the function and

```
cout << "multiply (" << setw (2) << m << ", " << setw (2) << n
     << ") returns " << setw (2) << answer << endl;
return answer;
```

as the last two lines in the function. Here, answer is assumed to be a variable local to multiply that always must be set to the value to be returned regardless of which alternative is selected. Function multiply is currently not written using such a local variable and would have to be further modified to accommodate the trace (see Self-Check Exercise 2 at the end of this section). Once these modifications have been completed, the output from the revised function multiply with actual arguments (8, 3) appears as follows:

```
Entering multiply with m =   8 and n =   3
Entering multiply with m =   8 and n =   2
Entering multiply with m =   8 and n =   1
multiply ( 8,   1) returns   8;
multiply ( 8,   2) returns  16;
multiply ( 8,   3) returns  24;
```

Tracing a Recursive Function with No Return Value

Example 13.3 Recursive function reverse_string in Fig. 13.7 reads in a string of length n and prints it out backward. If the function call

```
reverse_string (5)
```

is executed, the five characters entered at the screen are printed in reverse order. If the characters abcde are entered when this function is called, the characters edcba are displayed on the next line. If the function call

```
reverse_string (3);
```

is executed instead, only three characters are read, and the output cba is displayed.

As with most recursive functions, the body of function reverse_string consists of an if statement that evaluates a *stopping condition*, n <= 1. When

Figure 13.7   Recursive function `reverse_string`

```
// FILE: RvrsStrg.cpp
// RECURSIVE FUNCTION TO REVERSE THE ORDER OF A CHARACTER STRING

// DISPLAYS A STRING IN REVERSE ORDER
void reverse_string
   (int n)                  // IN: length of the string to be processed

// Pre:  n is defined and is greater than or equal to 1.
// Post: Displays n characters in reverse order.
{
   // Local data ...
   char next;            // contains current character being processed

   // Read string and display in reverse order.
   if (n <= 1)
   {                     // stopping step
      cin >> next;
      cout << next;
   }
   else                  // recursive step
   {
      cin >> next;
      reverse_string (n - 1);
      cout << next;
   }
   return;
}   // end reverse_string
```

the stopping condition is true, the problem has reached a *stopping case:* a data string of length 1. If n <= 1 is true, the input and output lines (cin and cout) are executed. If the stopping condition is false (n greater than 1), the recursive step (following else) is executed. The cin line reads in the next data character. However, before this character can be printed, function reverse_string is called again, with the argument value decreased by 1. When this call occurs, the character just read is saved in the current copy of the local variable next. It is not displayed until after the return from the recursive call, when control is returned to the line immediately following the function call (in this case, the cout line). For example, the character that is read when n is 3 is not displayed until after the function execution for n equal to 2 has completed.

   To help you fully understand this sequence of events, we will trace the execution of the function call

```
reverse_string (3);
```

This trace is shown in Fig. 13.8, assuming the letters abc are entered as data. The trace shows three activation frames for function reverse_string. Each

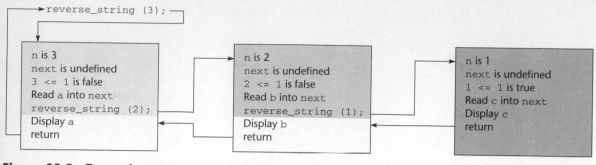

Figure 13.8   Trace of `reverse_string (3);`

activation frame begins with a list of the initial values of n and next for that frame. The value of n is passed into the function when it is called; the value of next is initially undefined.

The statements that are executed for each frame are shown in Fig. 13.9. Each recursive call to reverse_string results in a new activation frame, as indicated by the arrows pointing to the right. The arrows pointing to the left indicate the statement that executes immediately following the return from the recursive call. Tracing the right-directed arrows and then the left-directed arrows gives us the sequence of events listed in Fig. 13.9. To help you understand this list, all the statements for a particular activation frame are indented to the same column.

As shown, there are three calls to function reverse_string, each with a different argument value. The function returns always occur in the reverse order of the function calls; that is, we return from the last call first, then we return from the next to last call, and so on. After the return from a particular execution of the function, the character that was read into next just prior to that function call is displayed.   ▪

Figure 13.9   Sequence of events for trace of `reverse_string (3)`

```
Call reverse_string with n equal to 3.
  Read the first character (a) into next.
  Call reverse_string with n equal to 2.
    Read the second character (b) into next.
    Call reverse_string with n equal to 1.
      Read the third character (c) into next.
      Display the third character (c).
      Return from third call.
    Display the second character (b).
    Return from second call.
  Display the first character (a).
  Return from original call.
```

Argument and Local Variable Stacks

You may be wondering how C++ keeps track of the values of n and next at any given point. The answer is that C++ uses a special data structure, called a *stack* (see Section 12.8), that is analogous to a stack of dishes or trays. In a cafeteria, clean dishes are placed on top of a stack of dishes. When we need a dish, we normally remove the one most recently placed on the stack. Thus, the top dish is removed, and the next to the last dish put on the stack moves to the top.

Similarly, whenever a new function call occurs, the argument value associated with that call is placed on top of the argument stack. Also, a new memory location that represents the local variable next and whose value is initially undefined is placed on top of the stack. Whenever n or next is referenced, the value at the top of the corresponding stack is always used. When a function return occurs, the value currently at the top of each stack is removed, and the value just below it moves to the top.

As an example, let's look at the two stacks right after the first call to reverse string.

After First Call to reverse string There is one memory location on each stack, as shown below.

```
n     next
3     ?    ← top
```

As we trace the execution of reverse_string, we see that the letter a is read into next just before the second call to the function.

```
n     next
3     a    ← top
```

After Second Call to reverse_string After the second call to reverse_string, the number 2 is placed on top of the stack for n, and the top of the stack for next becomes undefined again, as shown below.

```
n     next
2     ?    ← top
3     a
```

The letter b is read into next just before the third call to reverse_string:

```
n     next
2     b    ← top
3     a
```

After Third Call to reverse_string Then next becomes undefined again right after the third call:

```
n     next
1     ?    ←top
2     b
3     a
```

During this execution of the function, the letter c is read into next. This value of c is printed immediately because n is 1 (the stopping case):

```
n     next
1     c    ←top
2     b
3     a
```

After First Return The function return causes the value at the top of each stack to be removed, as shown next:

```
n     next
2     b    ←top
3     a
```

Because control is returned to the cout line that follows the third call to reverse_string, the value of next (b) at the top of the stack is then displayed.

After Second Return Another return occurs, causing the values currently at the top of the stack to be removed:

```
n     next
3     a    ←top
```

Again, control is returned to the cout line that follows the second call to reverse_string, and the value of next (a) at the top of the stack is displayed.

After Third Return The third and last return removes the last values from the stack.

```
n     next
?     ?
```

Because these steps are all done automatically by C++, we can write recursive functions without needing to worry about the stacks. We saw how to declare and manipulate our own stacks in Section 12.8.

Implementation of Argument Stacks in C++

For illustrative purposes, we have used separate stacks for n and next in our discussion. The compiler, however, actually maintains a single stack. Each time a call to a function occurs, all its arguments and local variables are pushed onto the stack along with the memory address of the calling statement. This memory address gives the computer the return point after execution of the function. Although multiple copies of a function's arguments may be saved on the stack, only one copy of the function body is in memory.

EXERCISES FOR SECTION 13.2

Self-Check
1. In the `reverse_string` function (Fig. 13.7), n was passed in as a call-by-value argument. Discuss what happens to the current value of n each time `reverse_string` recursively calls itself. What happens to the current value of n whenever `reverse_string` returns to its calling function?
2. Modify function `multiply` (Fig. 13.2) to print the values of m and n immediately upon entry and to print the value to be returned just prior to exit. You will want to introduce a local variable as a temporary store for the result to be returned.
3. Explain why the six output trace statements shown at the beginning of Section 13.2 for function `multiply` (see also Self-Check Exercise 2) appeared in the order they did. For example, be sure to explain why the three entry displays (`"Entering multiply ..."`) appeared before any of the exit displays (`"multiply ... returns ..."`) and why the exit displays appeared as they did.
4. Assume the characters *+-/ are entered for the function call statement

   `reverse_string (4);`

   What output line would appear on the screen? Show the contents of the stacks immediately after each function call and return.
5. Trace the execution of `multiply (5, 4)` and show the stacks after each recursive call.

13.3 ——— RECURSIVE MATHEMATICAL FUNCTIONS

Many mathematical functions are defined recursively. An example is the factorial, $n!$, of a number n.

$$0! = 1$$
$$n! = n \times (n - 1)!, \text{ for } n > 0$$

Thus $4!$ is $4 \times 3 \times 2 \times 1$, or 24. It is quite easy to implement this definition as a recursive function in C++.

Figure 13.10   Recursive factorial function

```
// FILE: RcsvFact.cpp
// RECURSIVE FACTORIAL FUNCTION

// COMPUTES THE FACTORIAL OF N
int fact
   (int n)         // IN: value used in calculation

// Pre:      n is defined and n >= 0.
// Post:     None
// Returns:  n!
{
   if (n <= 0)
      return 1;
   else
      return n * fact (n-1);
}  // end fact
```

Example 13.4   Function `fact` in Fig. 13.10 computes the factorial of its argument n. The recursive step

```
return n * fact (n - 1);
```

implements the second line of the definition above. This means that the result of the current call (argument n) is determined by multiplying the result of the next call (argument n - 1) by n.

A trace of a call to `fact`,

```
result = fact (3);
```

is shown in Fig. 13.11. The value returned from the original call, `fact (3)`, is 6, and this value is assigned to the variable `result`. Be careful when using the factorial function; the value computed increases rapidly and could lead to an integer-overflow error (for example, 10! may come out as 24320 on your computer instead of the correct value, 3628800).

Although the recursive implementation of function `fact` follows naturally from its definition, this function can be implemented easily using iteration. The iterative version is shown in Fig. 13.12.

Note that the iterative version contains a loop as its major control structure, whereas the recursive version contains an `if` statement. Also, a local variable, `factorial`, is needed in the iterative version to hold the accumulating product. ∎

Example 13.5   The Fibonacci numbers are a sequence of numbers that have many varied uses. They were originally intended to model the growth of a rabbit colony.

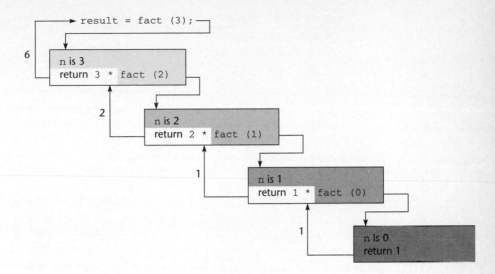

Figure 13.11 Trace of `result = fact (3)`

We will not go into details of the model here, but you can see that the Fibonacci sequence 1, 1, 2, 3, 5, 8, 13, 21, 34, . . . increases rapidly. The fifteenth number in the sequence is 610, and that's a lot of rabbits!

The Fibonacci sequence is defined using the following *recurrence relations*:

- fib_1 is 1
- fib_2 is 1
- fib_n is $fib_{n-2} + fib_{n-1}$, for $n > 2$.

Figure 13.12 Iterative factorial function

```
// FILE: IterFact.cpp
// ITERATIVE FACTORIAL FUNCTION

// COMPUTES THE FACTORIAL OF N
int fact
   (int n)        // IN: value used in calculation

// Pre:     n is defined and n >= 0.
// Post:    None
// Returns: n!
{
   // Local data ...
   int factorial;    // resulting value

   factorial = 1;
   for (int i = 2; i <= n; i++)
      factorial *= i;
   return factorial;
} // end fact
```

Figure 13.13   Recursive Fibonacci number function

```
// FILE: Fibonacc.cpp
// RECURSIVE FIBONACCI NUMBER FUNCTION

// COMPUTES THE NTH FIBONACCI NUMBER
int fibonacci
   (int n)                    // IN: value used in calculation

// Pre:     n is defined and n > 0.
// Post:    None
// Returns: The nth Fibonacci number.
{
   if (n <= 2)
      return 1;
   else
      return fibonacci (n - 2) + fibonacci (n - 1);
}   // end fibonacci
```

Simply stated, n is the sum of the two preceding numbers. Verify for yourself that the above sequence of numbers is correct.

A recursive function that computes the nth Fibonacci number is shown in Fig. 13.13. Although easy to write, the Fibonacci function is not very efficient because each recursive step generates two calls to function Fibonacci.   ■

Example 13.6   Euclid's algorithm for finding the greatest common divisor of two positive integers, GCD (m, n), is defined recursively below. The *greatest common divisor* of two integers is the largest integer that divides them both.

- GCD (m, n) is n if n <= m and n divides m
- GCD (m, n) is GCD (n, m) if m < n
- GCD (m, n) is GCD (n, remainder of m divided by n) otherwise

This algorithm states that the GCD is n if n is the smaller number and n divides m. If m is the smaller number, then the GCD determination should be performed with the arguments transposed. If n does not divide m, the answer is obtained by finding the GCD of n and the remainder of m divided by n. The C++ function GCD is shown in Fig. 13.14.

Figure 13.14   Euclid's algorithm for the greatest common divisor

```
// FILE: FindGCD.cpp
// PROGRAM AND RECURSIVE FUNCTION TO FIND GREATEST COMMON DIVISOR

#include <iostream.h>
```

(continued)

Figure 13.14   *(continued)*

```
    // Functions used ...
    // RECURSIVE FUNCTION TO FIND GREATEST COMMON DIVISOR
    int gcd
       (int,        // IN: first input item
        int);       // IN: second input item

void main ()
{
    // Local data ...
    int m, n;       // the two input items

    cout << "Enter two positive integers separated by a space: ";
    cin >> m >> n;
    cout << endl;
    cout << "Their greatest common divisor is " << gcd (m, n)
         << endl;
}


// RECURSIVE GCD FUNCTION
// FINDS THE GREATEST COMMON DIVISOR OF TWO INTEGERS
int gcd
   (int m, int n)   // IN: the integer values

// Pre:     m and n are defined and both are > 0.
// Post:    None
// Returns: The greatest common divisor of m and n.
{
    if (n <= m && m % n == 0)
       return n;
    else if (m < n)
       return gcd (n, m);
    else
       return gcd (n, m % n);
}  // end gcd
```

──────────── Program Output ────────────

```
Enter two positive integers separated by a space: 24 84
Their greatest common divisor is 12
```

EXERCISES FOR SECTION 13.3

Self-Check   1. Complete the following recursive function, which calculates the value of a number (base) raised to a power (power). Assume that power is positive.

```
int power_raiser
   (int base,
```

```
        int power)
{
    if (power == _____)
        return _____;
    else
        return _____ * _____;
}
```

2. What is the output of the following program? What does function `strange` compute?

```
// STRANGE PROGRAM
// Functions used ...
int strange
   (int n);
main ()

{
    // Do whatever it is that I do.
    cout << strange (8);
}


// DOES STRANGE THINGS
int strange
(int n)
{
   if (n == 1)
      return 0;
   else
      return 1 + strange (n / 2);
}  // end strange
```

3. Explain what would happen if the stopping condition for the Fibonacci number function were (n <= 1).

Programming   1. Write a recursive function, `find_sum`, that calculates the sum of successive integers starting at 1 and ending at n (i.e., `find_sum (n)` $= (1 + 2 + ... + (n-1) + n)$.
2. Write an iterative version of the Fibonacci function. Compare this version to the recursive version shown in Fig. 13.13. Which is simpler? Which is more efficient?
3. Write an iterative function for the greatest common divisor problem.
4. Write a recursive function to compute the sequence of squares sqn, of a nonnegative integer n using the following recurrence relations:

$$\left. \begin{array}{l} sq_0 = 0, \\ d_0 = 1, \end{array} \right\} \quad \text{for } n = 0$$

$$\left. \begin{array}{l} sq_n = sq_{n-1} + d_{n-1}, \\ d_n = d_{n-1} + 2, \end{array} \right\} \quad \text{for } n > 0$$

Note that dn always represents the difference between the nth and $n-1$st squares and that for each n, d_n increases by a constant amount, 2.

13.4 —— RECURSIVE FUNCTIONS WITH ARRAY ARGUMENTS

In this section, we examine a familiar problem and implement a recursive function to solve it. The problem involves array processing.

CASE STUDY: RECURSIVE SELECTION SORT

Problem Statement

We discussed the selection sort and implemented an iterative version of this sort function in Section 9.5. Because the selection sort first finds the largest element in an array and places it where it belongs, and then finds and places the next largest element, and so on, it is a good candidate for a recursive solution.

Program Design

The selection sort algorithm follows from the preceding description. The stopping case is an array of length 1, which is sorted by definition.

RECURSIVE ALGORITHM FOR SELECTION SORT

1. If n is 1
    1.1. The array is sorted.
  else
    1.2. Place the largest array element in x[n-1].
    1.3. Sort the subarray with subscripts 0, ..., n−2.

Program Implementation

This algorithm is implemented as a recursive function in Fig. 13.15. Function place_largest performs step 1.2 of the algorithm. The recursive function select_sort is simpler to understand than the one shown in Fig. 9.19 because it contains a single if statement instead of nested for loops. However, the recursive solution will execute more slowly because of the extra overhead due to the recursive function calls. If n is 1, function select_sort returns without doing anything. This behavior is correct because a one-element array is always sorted.

Figure 13.15 Functions select_sort and place_largest

```
// FILE: RcsvSort.cpp
// RECURSIVE SELECTION SORT FUNCTION

// SELECTION SORT: SORTS ARRAY OF INTEGERS IN ASCENDING ORDER
```

(continued)

Figure 13.15   *(continued)*

```
    // Functions used ...
    // MOVES LARGEST ELEMENT TO END OF SUBARRAY
    void place_largest
       (int[],                    // IN: subarray to be sorted
        int);                     // IN: number of elements

void selection_sort
   (int x[],                      // IN: array to be sorted
    int n)                        // IN: number of elements

// Pre:  Array x and size n are defined and n >= 0.
// Post: x[n-1] >= x[n-2] >= ... >= x[1] >= x[0]
{
    if (n > 1)
    {                             // begin recursive step
        place_largest (x, n);
        selection_sort (x, n - 1);
    }  // end recursive step
}  // end selection_sort



// MOVES LARGEST ELEMENT TO END OF SUBARRAY
void place_largest
   (int x[],                      // IN: subarray to be sorted
    int n)                        // IN: number of elements

// Pre:  x and n must be defined; n >= 0
// Post: Largest element in x[0],..., x[n-1] is placed in x[n-1].
{
    // Local data ...
    int temp;
    int max_index;

    max_index = n - 1;
    for (int j = n - 2; j >= 0; j--)
        if (x[j] > x[max_index])
            max_index = j;

    if (max_index != (n - 1))
    {
        temp = x[n - 1];
        x[n - 1] = x[max_index];
        x[max_index] = temp;
    }
}  // end place_largest
```

EXERCISES FOR SECTION 13.4

Self-Check   1. Trace the execution of select_sort on an array that has the integers 5, 8, 10, 1
stored in consecutive elements.

2. What does the following recursive function do? Trace its execution using the data from Self-Check Exercise 1.

```
int mystery
  (int x[],
   int n)
{
    // Local data ...
      int temp;

    // Do whatever I do now.
    if (n == 1)
        return x[0];
    else
    {
        temp = mystery (x, n-1);
        if (x[n-1] > temp)
            return x[n-1];
        else
            return temp;
    }  // end outer else
}  //end mystery
```

Programming
1. Write a recursive function that reverses the elements in an array x[n]. The recursive step should shift the subarray x[1..n-1] down one element into the subarray x[0..n-2] (for example, x[0] gets x[1], x[1] gets x[2], ..., x[n-2] gets x[n-1]), store the old x[0] in x[n-1], and then reverse the subarray x[0..n-2].
2. Write a recursive function that finds the index of the smallest element in an array.

13.5 ____ PROBLEM SOLVING WITH RECURSION

This case study is considerably more complicated than the preceding ones. It leads to a recursive function that solves the Towers of Hanoi problem introduced in Section 13.1.

CASE STUDY: THE TOWERS OF HANOI

Problem Statement

Solve the Towers of Hanoi problem for *n* disks, where *n* is the number of disks to be moved from tower A to tower C.

Problem Analysis

The solution to the Towers of Hanoi problem consists of a printed list of individual disk moves. We need a recursive function that can be used to move any number of disks from one tower to another, using the third tower as an auxiliary.

DATA REQUIREMENTS

Problem Input

n (int)	— the number of disks to be moved
from_tower (char)	— the *from* tower
to_tower (char)	— the *to* tower
aux_tower (char)	— the *auxiliary* tower

Problem Output

a list of individual disk moves

Program Design

ALGORITHM

1. If n is 1
     1.1. Move disk 1 from the from_tower to the to_tower.
   else
     1.2. Move n−1 disks from the from_tower to the auxiliary tower using the *to* tower.
     1.3. Move disk n from the from_tower to the to_tower.
     1.4. Move n−1 disks from the auxiliary tower to the to_tower using the from_tower.

If n is 1, a stopping case is reached. If n is greater than 1, the recursive step (following else) splits the original problem into three smaller subproblems, one of which is a stopping case. Each stopping case displays a move instruction. Verify that the recursive step generates the three subproblems (3.1, 3.2, 3.3) listed in Example 13.2 when n is 5, the *from* tower is A, and the *to* tower is C.

Program Implementation

The implementation of this algorithm is shown as function towers in Fig. 13.16. Function towers has four arguments, from_tower, to_tower, aux_tower, and n. The function call

```
towers ('A', 'C', 'B', 5);
```

solves the problem posed earlier of moving five disks from tower A to tower C, using tower B as an auxiliary.

In Fig. 13.16, the stopping case (move disk 1) is implemented as a cout statement. Each recursive step consists of two recursive calls to towers

Figure 13.16   Recursive function `towers`

```cpp
// FILE: Towers.cpp
// RECURSIVE TOWERS OF HANOI FUNCTION

// RECURSIVE FUNCTION TO MOVE DISKS FROM from_tower TO to_tower
//      USING aux-tower

void towers
   (char from_tower,       // IN: from_tower
    char to_tower,         // IN: to_tower
    char aux_tower,        // IN: aux_tower
    int n)                 // IN: number of disks

// Pre:  The from_tower, to_tower, aux_tower, and n are defined.
// Post: The disks are moved from from_tower to to_tower.
{
   if (n == 1)
      cout << "Move disk 1 from tower " << from_tower
           << " to tower " << to_tower << endl;
   else
   {
      towers (from_tower, aux_tower, to_tower, n - 1);
      cout << "Move disk " << n << " from tower " << from_tower
           << " to tower " << to_tower << endl;
      towers (aux_tower, to_tower, from_tower, n - 1);
   }
}  // end towers
```

with a `cout` line sandwiched between them. The first recursive call solves the problem of moving n−1 disks to the *auxiliary* tower. The `cout` line displays a message to move disk n to the *to* tower. The second recursive call solves the problem of moving the n−1 disks from the *auxiliary* tower to the *to* tower.

Program Testing

The function call statement

```cpp
towers ('A', 'C', 'B', 3);
```

solves a simpler 3-disk problem: Move 3 disks from tower A to tower C. Its execution is traced in Fig. 13.17; the output generated is shown in Fig. 13.18. Verify for yourself that this list of steps does indeed solve the three-disk problem.

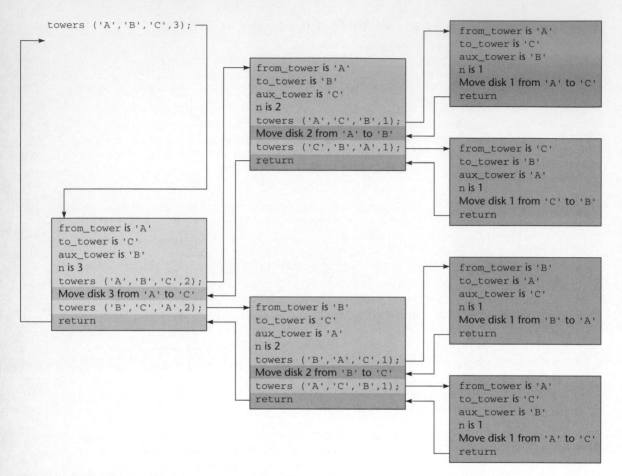

Figure 13.17 Trace of towers (`'A'`, `'C'`, `'B'`, 3);

Figure 13.18 Output generated by towers ('A', 'C', 'B', 3);

```
Move disk 1 from tower A to tower C
Move disk 2 from tower A to tower B
Move disk 1 from tower C to tower B
Move disk 3 from tower A to tower C
Move disk 1 from tower B to tower A
Move disk 2 from tower B to tower C
Move disk 1 from tower A to tower C
```

Comparison of Iteration and Recursive Functions

It is interesting to consider that function towers in Fig. 13.16 will solve the Towers of Hanoi problem for any number of disks. The 3-disk problem results in a total of 7 calls to function towers and is solved by 7 disk moves. The 5 disk problem would result in a total of 31 calls to function towers and is solved in 31 moves. In general, the number of moves required to solve the n-disk problem is $2^n - 1$. Because each function call requires the allocation and initialization of a local data area in memory, the computer time increases exponentially with the problem size. For this reason, be careful about running this program with a value of n that is larger than 10.

The dramatic increase in processing time for larger towers is a function of this problem, not a function of recursion. However, in general, if there are recursive and iterative solutions to the same problem, the recursive solution will require more time and space because of the extra function calls.

Although recursion was not really needed to solve the simpler problems in this section, it was extremely useful in formulating an algorithm for the Towers of Hanoi problem. For certain problems, recursion leads naturally to solutions that are much easier to read and understand than their iterative counterparts. In these cases, the benefits gained from increased clarity far outweigh the extra cost (in time and memory) of running a recursive program.

EXERCISES FOR SECTION 13.5

Self-Check
1. How many moves are needed to solve the 6-disk problem?
2. Write a main function that reads in a data value for n (the number of disks) and calls function towers to move n disks from A to B.

13.6 ——— COMMON PROGRAMMING ERRORS

- *Stopping Condition for Recursive Functions:* The most common problem with a recursive function involves the specification of the stopping condition. If this condition is not correct, the function may call itself indefinitely or until all available memory is used up. Normally, a "stack overflow" run-time error is an indication that a recursive function is not terminating. Make sure that you identify all stopping cases and provide the correct condition for each one. Also be sure that each recursive step leads to a situation that is closer to a stopping case and that repeated recursive calls will eventually lead to stopping cases only.
- *Missing Return Statements:* It is critical that every path through a function that returns a value function lead to a return statement. When multiple

returns are warranted in a function, it is easy to omit one of these returns. Such an omission will not be detected by the compiler but will result in an incorrect return value whenever the sequence of statements requiring the return is executed.

■ *A Few Optimizations for Recursive Functions:* The recopying of large arrays or other large data structures inside a recursive function can quickly consume large amounts of memory. Such recopying should be done only when data protection is required. Even in this case, if only a single copy is required, a nonrecursive function can be created to make the necessary copy and pass this copy and other arguments to the recursive function (and return any computed result to the caller).

It is also a good idea to introduce a nonrecursive function to handle preliminaries of a recursive function call when error checking is involved. Checking for errors inside a recursive function is extremely inefficient if the error is such that it would be detected only in the first of a sequence of recursive calls.

It is sometimes difficult to observe the result of a recursive function's execution. If each recursive call generates a large number of output lines and there are many recursive calls, the output will scroll down the screen more quickly than it can be read. On most systems, it is possible to stop the scrolling temporarily by pressing a special key or control character sequence (e.g., control-s). If this cannot be done, it is still possible to cause your output to stop temporarily by printing a prompting message such as

```
cout << "Press the space bar to continue.";
```

followed by a keyboard input operation such as

```
cin >> next_char;
```

(where next_char is a character data type). Your program will resume execution when you enter a character data item.

CHAPTER REVIEW

This chapter has provided several examples of recursive functions. Studying them should give you some appreciation of the power of recursion as a problem-solving and programming tool and provide you with valuable insight regarding its use. It may take you some time to feel comfortable thinking in this new way about programming. However, as you study a wider variety of more complex problems, you will see that in certain cases (such as the Towers of Hanoi problem) recursion provides a clear, concise, and easy-to-understand solution. In these cases, we are confident that you will view the work in this chapter to have been worth the effort.

Aside from the Towers of Hanoi problem, the shorter examples and case study illustrate different aspects of the use of recursion. The multiply and factorial functions (Examples 13.1 and 13.4, respectively) provide illustrations of recursive functions involving simple mathematical computations that return the result of these computations. Although there are clearly more direct and efficient algorithms for these computations, the simplicity of the recursive solutions provides a good illustration of the trace of execution of recursive functions that return values.

The `reverse_string` example (Example 13.3) does not involve a return value. It was included to show how local data processed in a recursive function are saved at each point of call and then returned in reverse order to complete processing.

The Fibonacci and greatest common divisor examples (Examples 13.5 and 13.6, respectively) illustrate somewhat more complicated mathematical functions. The Fibonacci function (Fig. 13.13) illustrates the use of recursion in computations involving recurrence relations, where the computation of the nth value in a sequence is specified in terms of values computed earlier in the sequence.

The GCD function (Fig. 13.14) has a slightly more complicated stopping condition and involves conditional recursive calls based on the relationship of its arguments.

The recursive sort function (Fig. 13.15) illustrates the processing of an array of data, one element at a time. The basic idea behind the algorithm is typical of all of the other recursive algorithms we have examined.

To sort an array of size n in ascending order,

- place the largest element in the array in the nth array cell;
- sort an array of size $n-1$ in ascending order.

When n becomes equal to 1, the sort is complete.

✔ QUICK-CHECK EXERCISES

1. Explain the use of a stack in recursion.
2. Which is generally more efficient, recursion or iteration?
3. Which control statement do you always find in a recursive function?
4. How do you specify a recursive call to a function?
5. Why would a programmer conceptualize a problem solution using recursion and implement it using iteration?
6. In a recursive problem involving n items, why must n be a call-by-value argument?

7. What kind of a programming error could easily cause a "stack overflow" message?

8. What can you say about a recursive algorithm that has the following form?

    if (condition)
        Perform recursive step.

Answers to Quick-Check Exercises

1. The stack is used to hold all argument and local variable values and the return point for each execution of a recursive function.
2. Iteration is generally more efficient than recursion.
3. The if statement is always found in a recursive function.
4. By writing a call to the function in the function itself.
5. When its solution is much easier to conceptualize using recursion but its implementation would be too inefficient.
6. If n were a call-by-reference argument, its address, not its value, would be saved on the stack, so it would not be possible to retain a different value for each call.
7. Too many recursive calls.
8. Nothing is done when the stopping case is reached.

REVIEW QUESTIONS

1. Explain the nature of a recursive problem.
2. Discuss the efficiency of recursive functions.
3. Differentiate between stopping cases and a terminating condition.
4. Write a recursive function that returns the accumulating sum of the ASCII values corresponding to each character in a character string. For example, if the string value is "a boy", the first value returned would be the ASCII value of a, then the sum of ASCII values for a and the space character, then the sum of the ASCII values for a, space, b, and so on.
5. Write a recursive function that returns the accumulating sum of ASCII values corresponding to each character in a character string (as in Review Question 4). However, this time exclude any space characters from the sum.
6. Convert the following iterative function to a recursive one. The function calculates an approximate value for e, the base of the natural logarithms, by summing the series

    $1 + 1/1! + 1/2! + ... + 1/n!$

    until additional terms do not affect the approximation (at least not as far as the computer is concerned).

```
float elog ()
{
    // Local data ...
    float enl, delta, fact;
```

```
    int n;

    enl = 1.0;
    n = 1;
    fact = 1.0;
    delta = 1.0;
    do
    {
        enl += delta;
        n++;
        fact *= n;
        delta = 1.0 / fact;
    } while (enl != enl + delta);
    return enl;
}   // end elog
```

PROGRAMMING PROJECTS

1. The expression for computing $C(n, r)$, the number of combinations of n items taken r at a time is

$$C(n, r) = \frac{n!}{r!(n-r)!} .$$

   Write and test a function for computing $C(n, r)$ given that $n!$ is the factorial of n.

2. A palindrome is a word that is spelled exactly the same when the letters are reversed. Words such as *level*, *deed*, and *mom* would be examples of palindromes. Write a recursive function that returns a value of 1 (true) if a word, passed as an argument, is a palindrome and that returns 0 (false) otherwise.

3. Write a recursive function that returns the value of the following recursive definition:

   $F(X, Y) = X - Y$ if X or $Y < 0$;
   $F(X, Y) = F(X - 1, Y) + F(X, Y - 1)$ otherwise.

4. Write a recursive function that lists all of the two-letter subsets for a given set of letters. For example:

   ['A', 'C', 'E', 'G'] → ['A', 'C'], ['A', 'E'], ['A', 'G'], ['C', 'E'], ['C', 'G'], ['E', 'G']

5. Write a function that accepts an 8-by-8 array of characters that represents a maze. Each position can contain either an 'X' or a blank. Starting at position [0][0], list any path through the maze to get to location [7][7]. Only horizontal and vertical moves are allowed (no diagonal moves). If no path exists, write a message indicating this. Moves can be made only to positions that contain a blank. If an 'X' is encountered in a path, that path is to be considered blocked and another must be chosen. Use recursion.

6. The Eight Queens problem is a famous chess-related problem that has as its goal the placement of eight queens on a single chessboard so that no queen will be able to attack any other queen. A queen may move any number of squares vertically, horizontally, or along either diagonal on the chessboard (an 8-by-8 grid of squares). Write a program that contains a recursive routine to solve the Eight Queens Problem.

Hint: Work across the board, column by column. Begin in column 1 and arbitrarily choose a row in this column for the placement of the first queen. Then move to the next column and attempt to place a second queen safely in one of the rows of that column. Continue this process as long as it is possible to place a queen in the next column (as long as a row can be found for which a placement of a queen is safe). If a dead end is reached (no safe row can be found in a given column), the last-placed queen (in the column to the immediate left of the current one) is removed from the board and repositioned. To do this, the algorithm will need to backtrack to a previous call of the recursive routine, undo the placement of the queen in this column, and attempt to place it in a different row. This process of moving left to right across the board, backtracking as needed, continues until all eight queens have been successfully (safely) placed, one per column. The determination of whether a placement of a queen (in a given row of the current column) is safe is the critical component of this algorithm. Note that a safe placement requires that no previously placed queen is in the same row or in the same diagonal. There are two diagonals to be considered in addition to each row, as shown in Fig. 13.19. You need to find an easy and simple way to verify that a proposed placement of a queen is indeed safe.

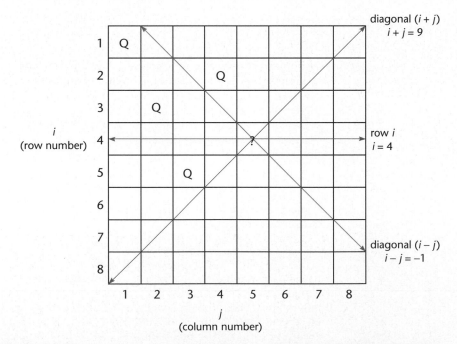

Figure 13.19 Checking row i(column$j$) and diagonals $(i + j)$ and $(i - j)$ for safety

14

Pointers and Dynamic Data Structures

In this chapter we shift our attention from static structures, such as arrays and structs, to dynamic data structures. Unlike static structures, in which the size of the data structure is established during compilation and remains unchanged throughout program execution, dynamic data structures expand and contract as a program executes.

The first dynamic data structure we will study is the *linked list*—a collection of elements (called *nodes*) that are structs. Each node has a special field called a *pointer* that connects it to the next node in the list.

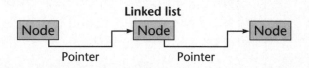

Linked list

Linked lists are extremely flexible. It is easy to add new information by creating a new node and inserting it between two existing nodes. It is also relatively easy to delete a node.

We will also examine several other dynamic data structures, including lists, stacks, queues, and trees. We will create C++ classes for each of these data abstractions and learn how to process information stored in objects of these classes.

14.1 ———— POINTERS AND THE new OPERATOR

The nodes in a linked list are joined by pointers. This section discusses what pointers are and how to use them.

The declaration

```
float *p;
```

identifies p as a pointer variable of type "pointer to float." This means that we can store the *memory address* of a type float variable in p. The statement

```
p = new float;
```

calls the C++ operator new, which creates a variable of type float and places the address of this variable in the pointer variable p. Once storage is allocated for the type float value pointed to by p, we can store a value in that memory cell and manipulate it. *Dynamic allocation* is the process of allocating new storage during program execution.

The actual memory address stored in pointer variable p is a number that has no meaning for us. Consequently, we represent the value of p by drawing an arrow to a memory cell:

The ? in the memory cell pointed to by p indicates that its contents are undefined just after p = new float is executed. In the next section, we will see how to write C++ instructions to store information in the memory cell pointed to by p.

C++ allocates storage at different times for the memory cells shown in the preceding diagram. Storage is allocated for pointer variable p during compilation when its variable declaration is reached. Storage is allocated for the cell pointed to by p when the new statement is executed.

C++
SYNTAX

Pointer Type Declaration

Form: *type *variable;*

Example: float *p;

Interpretation: The value of the pointer variable p (a pointer) is a memory address. A data element whose address is stored in this variable must be of the specified *type*. ∎

C++
SYNTAX

new Operator

Form: new *type*;
          new *type* [*n*] ;

Example: new float;

Interpretation: Storage for a new data element is allocated, and a pointer to this element is returned. The amount of storage allocated is determined by the type specified. With the second form shown, n elements of the specified *type* are allocated. If sufficient storage is not available, a C++ exception is raised and the program will terminate. ∎

Accessing Data with Pointers

The asterisk symbol * is called the *indirection operator.* The assignment statement

```
*p = 15.5;
```

stores the float value 15.5 in memory location *p (the location pointed to by p), as shown next.

The statements

```
float *p;
p = new float;
*p = 15.5;
cout << "The contents of the memory cell pointed to by p is "
     << *p << endl;
```

produce the result

```
The contents of the memory cell pointed to by p is 15.5
```

Pointer Operations

A pointer variable can contain only a memory address. If p is the pointer variable declared above, the following statements are invalid; you cannot assign a type int or a type float value to a pointer variable:

```
p = 1000;    // invalid assignment
p = 15.5;    // invalid assignment
```

If p and q are pointer variables of the same type, they can be manipulated with the assignment operator and the equality operators (== and !=). For example, the *pointer assignment statement*

```
q = p;
```

copies the address stored in pointer variable p to pointer variable q. As a result both p and q point to the same memory area.

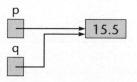

In this instance, the condition p == q is true and p != q is false.

Pointers to Structs

We can declare pointers to structured data types as well as to simple data types. Often, we declare pointers to structs or to objects. The declarations

```
struct electric
{
    string current;
    int volts;
};
electric *p, *q;
```

identify the variables p and q to be of type "pointer to electric." Type electric is a struct type with two members: current and volts.

Variables p and q are pointer variables that can be used to reference variables of type electric (denoted by *p and *q). The statement

```
p = new electric;
```

allocates storage for a struct of type electric and stores its memory address in pointer p. The data components of the struct pointed to by p are initially undefined.

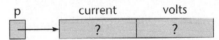

Recall that we use student.name to reference the name field of struct variable student. We can use the member access operator . to reference a member of a struct pointed to by a pointer variable. For example, we use (*p).current to reference the current field of the struct pointed to by p (struct *p). The assignment statements

```
(*p).current = "AC";
(*p).volts = 115;
```

define the fields of the struct pointed to by p as shown in the diagram below.

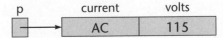

The form (*p).volts first applies the indirection operator to the variable p of type "pointer to node," yielding an expression of type node, and then applies the member access operator to this expression, yielding an expression of type int. If you omit the parentheses, C++ would apply the member access operator first (p.volts), which would be an invalid operation.

Because accessing members of structures through pointers is a common operation, C++ provides a special notation. You can write the statements above as

```
p->current = "AC";
p->volts = 115;
```

Structure Member Access Through a Pointer

Form: $p \rightarrow m$

Example: p->volts

Interpretation: If p is a pointer to a struct (or class), and if *m* is a member of that struct, then $p \rightarrow m$ accesses the member, *m*, of the struct pointed to by p.   ∎

The statement

```
cout << p->current << p->volts << endl;
```

displays the data components of the struct pointed to by p. For the struct in the preceding diagram, the statement displays the line

```
AC115
```

The statement

```
q = new electric;
```

stores the address of a new struct of type electric in q. The next statements copy the contents of the struct pointed to by p to the struct pointed to by q, and change the volts field of the struct pointed to by q.

```
*q = *p;
```

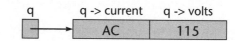

```
q->volts = 220;
```

Finally the pointer assignment statement

```
q = p;
```

resets pointer q to point to the same struct as pointer p. The old struct pointed to by q still exists in memory but can no longer be accessed. Such a struct is called an *orphan*.

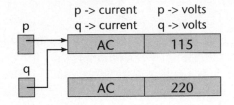

EXERCISES FOR SECTION 14.1

Self-Check 1. If p and q are pointers to structs of type electric, explain the effect of each valid assignment statement. Which are invalid?

a. p->current = "CA";   b. p->volts = q->volts;
c. *p = *q;   d. p = q;
e. p->current = "HT";   f. p->current = q->volts;
g. p = 54;   h. *q = p;

2. If a, b, and c are pointers to structures of type electric, draw a diagram of pointers and memory cells after the following operations. Indicate any orphaned data areas.

a. a = new electric;   d. a = b;
b. b = new electric;   e. b = c;
c. c = new electric;   f. c = a;

Programming 1. Write a program fragment that creates a collection of seven pointers to the struct type below, allocates memory for each pointer, and places the musical notes do, re, mi, fa, so, la, and ti in the data areas.

```
struct music_note
{
    note : string;
};
```

14.2 ——— MANIPULATING THE HEAP

When new executes, where in memory is the new struct stored? C++ maintains a storage pool of available memory cells called a *heap*; memory cells from this pool are allocated whenever procedure new is executed.

Effect of the new Operator on the Heap

If p is a pointer variable of type "pointer to electric" (declared in the last section), the statement

```
p = new node;
```

allocates memory space for a struct that stores a string and an int variable. The memory cells in this struct are originally undefined (they retain whatever data were last stored in them), and the memory address of the first cell allocated is stored in p. Allocated cells are no longer considered part of the heap. The only way to reference allocated locations is through a pointer variable (for example, p->current or p->volts).

Figure 14.1 shows the pointer variable p and the heap (as a collection of bytes with addresses 1000, 1001, ..., etc.) before and after the execution of p = new node. The *before* diagram shows pointer variable p as undefined before the execution of p = new node. The *after* diagram shows p pointing to the first of four memory cells allocated for the new struct (assuming that four memory locations can accommodate a struct of type electric). The cells still considered part of the heap are shaded.

For example, if the memory cells with addresses 1000 through 2000 were originally in the heap, after the execution of p = new electric; the memory cells with addresses 1000 through 1003 are no longer part of the heap. The address 1000 would be stored in pointer variable p, and that cell would contain the first byte of p->current; memory cell 1002 would contain the first byte of p->volts.

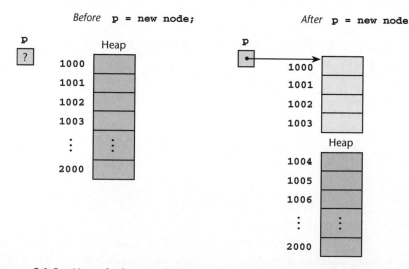

Figure 14.1   Heap before and after execution of p = new node

Returning Cells to the Heap

The operation

```
delete p;
```

returns the memory cells pointed to by p to the heap, restoring the heap to the state shown on the left of Fig. 14.1. At this point, the value of pointer variable p becomes undefined and the data formerly associated with *p are no longer accessible. The four cells that are returned to the heap can be reused later when another new operator is executed.

Often, more than one pointer variable points to the same structure. For that reason, be careful when you return the storage occupied by a struct to the heap. If cells are reallocated after they are returned, errors may result if they are later referenced by another pointer that still points to them. Make sure that you have no need for a particular structure before you return the storage occupied by it. Also make sure that only pointer variables that were set with values returned by the new operator are used as an argument to the delete operator.

C++
SYNTAX

The **delete** Operator

Form: delete *variable*;

Example: delete p;

Interpretation: The memory pointed to by p (which was set from the invocation of the new operator) is returned to the heap. This memory can be reallocated when the new operator is next called.

EXERCISES FOR SECTION 14.2

Self-Check

1. In a program that is allocating memory space for temporary data items, what would be the consequences of failing to use delete when the data items are no longer needed?

14.3 ——— LINKED LISTS

We can arrange groups of dynamically allocated structs into a flexible data structure called a *linked list*. Linked lists are like chains of children's "pop beads," where each bead has a hole at one end and a plug at the other (see Fig. 14.2). We can connect the beads in the obvious way to form a chain and easily modify it. We can remove the grey bead by disconnecting the two beads at both its ends and reattaching this pair of beads, add a new bead by

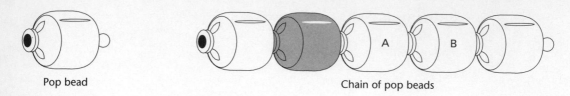

Pop bead   Chain of pop beads

Figure 14.2   Children's pop beads in a chain

connecting it to the bead at either end of the chain, or break the chain somewhere in the middle (between beads A and B) and insert a new bead by connecting one end to bead A and the other end to bead B. We show how to perform these operations to rearrange the items in a linked list next.

In this section we use pointers to create linked lists. We can add a pointer member to a struct and then build a linked list by connecting structs with pointer members. We call a struct in a linked list a *node*.

Declaring Nodes

We can connect two nodes if we include a pointer member in each node. The declarations

```
struct node
{
    string word;
    int count;
    node *link;
};
node *p, *q, *r;
```

allocate storage for three pointer variables. Each pointer variable can point to a struct of type `node` that has three components: `word`, `count`, and `link`. The first two components store a string and an integer value; the third component, `link` (type `node *`-pointer to node), stores an address, as shown in the following diagram:

Struct of type node

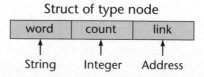

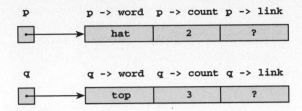

Figure 14.3   Nodes pointed to by p and q

Connecting Nodes

The statements

```
p = new node;
q = new node;
```

allocate storage for two structs of type node. The assignment statements

```
p->word = "hat";
p >count = 2;
q->word = "top";
q->count = 3;
```

define two fields of each node, as shown in Fig. 14.3. The link fields are still undefined.
   The statement

```
p->link = q;
```

stores the address of the struct pointed to by q in the link field of the struct pointed to by p, thereby connecting these two nodes (see Fig. 14.4).
   The link field of the first node, p->link, points to the second node in the list and contains the same address as pointer q. We can therefore use either member accessor q->word or p->link->word to access the word field (contents is "top") of the second node in the list.

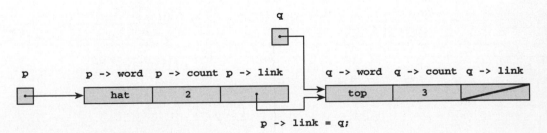

Figure 14.4   List with two elements

We normally store a special pointer value, NULL, in the pointer field of the last element in a list. We can use either of the following statements to accomplish this result. We usually represent the value NULL by drawing a diagonal line in a pointer field.

```
q->link = NULL;                    |              p->link->link = NULL;
```

Inserting a Node in a List

To insert a new node between the nodes pointed to by p and q, we start with the statements

```
r = new node;
r->word = "the";
r->count = 5;
```

They allocate and initialize a new node, which is pointed to by r. The statements

```
// Connect node pointed to by p to node pointed to by r
p->link = r;
// Connect node pointed to by r to node pointed to by q
r->link = q;
```

assign new values to the link fields of the node pointed to by p and the node pointed to by r. The first statement connects the node pointed to by p to the new node; the second statement connects the new node to the node pointed to by q. Figure 14.5 shows the effect of these statements. The gray arrow shows the old values of p->link. Notice that we no longer need pointer variables q and r to access the list nodes because we can reach each node by following a trail of pointers from pointer variable p. The first node is called the

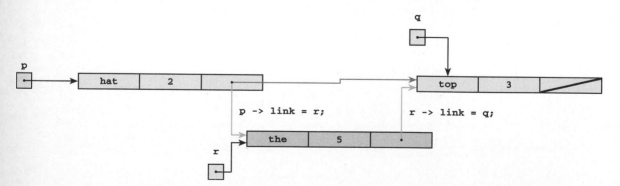

Figure 14.5   Inserting a new node in a list

Table 14.1 References to List Nodes in Fig. 14.5

LIST REFERENCES	DATA ACCESSED
p->word	hat
p->link	link field of first node
p->link->word	the
p->link->link	link field of second node
p->link->link->count	3

list head. Table 14.1 shows some valid references to the list data, starting from the list head.

Insertion at the Head of a List

Although we usually insert new data at the end of a data structure, it is easier and more efficient to insert a new item at the head of a list. The following program fragment allocates a new node and inserts it at the head of the list pointed to by p. Pointer old_head points to the original list head. After the insertion, p points to the new list head which is linked to the old list head, as shown in Figure 14.6. The gray arrow shows the old value of pointer p:

```
// Save pointer to old list head
old_head = p;
// Point p to a new node
p = new node;
// Connect new list head to old list head
p->link = old_head;
```

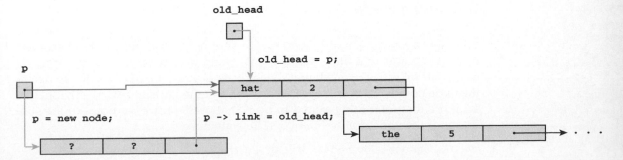

Figure 14.6 Insertion at the head of a list

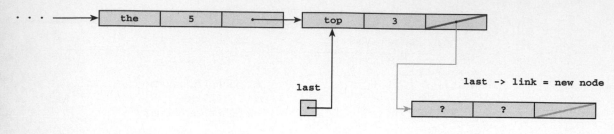

Figure 14.7   Insertion at the end of a list

Insertion at the End of a List

Inserting an item at the end of a list is less efficient because we usually do not have a pointer to the last list element, and so we must follow the pointer trail from the list head to the last list node and then perform the insertion. When last is pointing to the last list node (Fig. 14.7), the statements

```
// Attach a new node to list end.
last->link = new node;
// Mark new list end.
last->link->link = NULL;
```

insert a node at the end of the list. The first statement allocates a new node that is pointed to by the link field of the last list node (before the insertion), so the new node is now the last node in the list. The second statement sets the link field of the new last node to NULL.

Deleting a Node

To delete a node from a linked list, we simply change the link field of the node that points to it (its *predecessor*). We want the predecessor to point to the node that follows the one being deleted (its *successor*). For example, to delete the node pointed to by r from the three-element list in Fig. 14.8, we change the link field of the node pointed to by p (the predecessor) to point to the successor of the node pointed to by r. The statement

```
// Disconnect the node pointed to by r.
p->link = r->link;
```

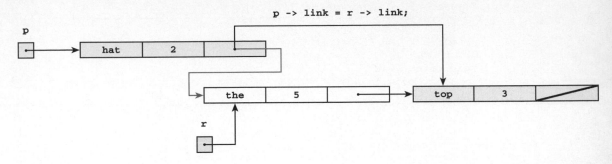

Figure 14.8 Deleting a list node

copies the address of the successor node to the `link` field of the predecessor node, thereby deleting the node pointed to by r from the list. The statements

```
// Disconnect the node pointed to by r from its successor.
r->link = NULL;
// Return the node pointed to by r to the heap.
delete r;
```

are then used to disconnect the node pointed to by r from the list and return its storage to the heap.

Traversing a List

In many list-processing operations, we must process each node in the list in sequence, a procedure called *traversing a list*. We start at the list head and follow the trail of pointers.

One typical operation performed on most data structures is to display the data structure's contents. To display the contents of a list, we must display only the values of the information fields, not the link fields. Function `print_list` in Fig. 14.9 displays the information fields of each node in the list shown in Fig. 14.8 (after the deletion). The function call statement

```
print_list (p);
```

displays the output lines

```
hat 2
top 3
```

The `while` condition

```
(head != NULL)
```

Figure 14.9   Function `print_list`

```
// FILE: PrintLst.cpp
// DISPLAY THE LIST POINTED TO BY head

void print_list
   (list_node *head)      // IN: pointer to list to be printed

// Pre:  head points to a list whose last node has a pointer
//       member of NULL
// Post: The word and count members of each list node
//       are displayed and the last value of head is NULL
{
   while (head != NULL)
   {
      // Invariant: No prior value of head was NULL.
      cout << head->word << " " << head ->count << endl;
      head = head->link;      // Advance to next list node.
   }
}  // end print_list
```

is common in loops that process lists. If the list to be displayed is empty, this condition is true initially and the loop body is skipped. If the list is not empty, the loop body executes and the last statement in the loop,

```
head = head->link;        // Advance to next list node
```

advances the pointer `head` to the next list element, which is pointed to by the `link` field of the current list element. After the last data value in the list is printed, this statement assigns the address NULL to `head` and loop exit occurs.

Because `head` is a value argument, a local copy of the pointer to the first list element is established when the function is entered. This local pointer is advanced, but the corresponding pointer in the calling function remains unchanged. What would happen to our list if `head` was a reference argument?

PROGRAM STYLE

Warning About Reference Arguments for Pointers

Consider the effect of parameter `head` being a reference argument instead of a value argument. This would allow the function to change the corresponding actual argument, regardless of your intentions. In `print_list` and many similar functions, the last value assigned to the pointer argument is NULL. If `head` is a reference argument, the corresponding actual argument would be set to NULL, thereby disconnecting it from the list to which it pointed before the function call.

Passing a pointer as a value argument protects that pointer from being changed by the function. However, you should realize that any changes made to other pointers in the list during the function's execution will remain. ∎

Circular Lists and Two-Way Lists (Optional)

You can traverse a list in only one direction, and you cannot move past the last element. To get around these restrictions, programmers sometimes use either circular or two-way lists.

Circular Lists A *circular list* is one in which the last list node points back to the list head. In the following circular list, you can start anywhere in the list and still access all list elements.

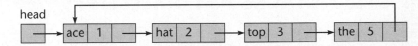

Two-Way Lists In a *two-way* or *doubly-linked list,* each node has two pointers: one to the node's successor (right) and one to the node's predecessor (left). For the node pointed to by next shown here

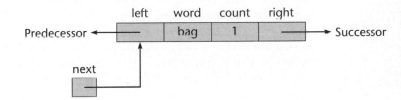

the statement

```
next = next->right;
```

moves pointer next to the successor node, and the statement

```
next = next->left;
```

moves pointer next to the predecessor node.

EXERCISES FOR SECTION 14.3

Self-Check 1. For the three-element list in Fig. 14.5, explain the effect of each fragment. Assume the list is restored to its initial state before each fragment executes.

```
a. r->link = p;                      b. p->link = NULL;
c. p->link = r;                      d. p->link = q->link;
e. p = p->link;                      f. p->word = r->word;
g. p->count = p->link->link->count;  h. p->link->link = NULL;
i. q->link = new node;               j. while (p != NULL)
   q->link->word = "zzz";               {
   q->link->count = 0;                     (p->count)++;
   q->link->link = NULL;                   p = p->link;
                                         }
```

2. How would you delete the node at the head of a list? How would you delete a node if you were given only a pointer to the node to be deleted and a pointer to the list head?

Programming 1. Write a function that finds the length of a list.
2. Write a fragment to advance pointer `last` to the last node of a list whose head is pointed to by p, then insert a new list node at the end of the list. Make sure you consider the special case of an initially empty list (p is NULL).

14.4 ——— STACKS AS LINKED LISTS

In Chapter 12 we studied the stack abstract data type, and in Chapter 13 we showed how to use a stack to store the actual arguments passed in each call to a recursive function. Because the number of elements in a stack may vary considerably, it makes good sense to implement this data structure as a dynamically allocated linked list. Think of a stack as a linked list in which all insertions and deletions are performed at the list head. A linked list representation of a stack s is shown at the top of Fig. 14.10. The first element of the list, pointed to by s.top, is at the top of the stack. If a new node is pushed onto the stack, it should be inserted in front of the node that is currently at the head of the list. Stack s after insertion of the symbol '*' is shown at the bottom of the figure.

If we pop the stack shown in Fig. 14.10 (bottom), we will remove the character * that we just inserted. For this reason, a stack is called a Last-In-First-Out (LIFO) structure.

Each element of a stack can be stored in a node with the data member (type `stack_element`). By defining a `struct` to hold the data element and a pointer to the next node, the private part of the template class `stack` can be declared as shown in Fig. 14.11. The public part is unchanged from that shown in Fig. 12.21.

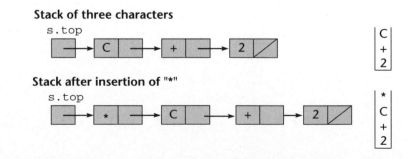

Figure 14.10 Physical stack **s** (left) and abstract stack (right)

Figure 14.11 `stack_list<stack_element>` template class specification

```
// FILE: StackLis.h
// DEFINITION OF A TEMPLATE CLASS STACK_LIST USING A LINKED LIST

#ifndef STACK_LIST_H
#define STACK_LIST_H

template <class stack_element>
class stack_list
{
   public:
      // Member functions ...
      // CONSTRUCTOR TO CREATE AN EMPTY STACK
      stack_list ();

      // PUSH AN ELEMENT ONTO THE STACK
      bool push
         (const stack_element& x);      // IN: item to be pushed onto
                                        //       stack
      // Pre : The element x is defined.
      // Post: If the stack is not full, the item is pushed onto
      //       the stack and true is returned. Otherwise, the stack
      //       is unchanged and false is returned.

      // POP AN ELEMENT OFF THE STACK
      bool pop
         (stack_element& x);     // OUT: Element popped from stack
         // Pre : none
         // Post: If the stack is not empty, the value at the top
         //       of the stack is removed, its value is placed in
         //       x, and true is returned. If the stack is empty, x
         //       is not defined and false is returned.

      // GET TOP ELEMENT FROM STACK WITHOUT POPPING
      bool get_top
         (stack_element& x) const; // OUT: Value returned from top
                                   //        of stack
         // Pre : none
         // Post: If the stack is not empty, the value at the top
         //       is copied into x and true is returned. If the
         //       stack is empty, x is not defined and false is
         //       returned. In either case, the stack is not
         //       changed.

      // TEST TO SEE IF STACK IS EMPTY
      bool is_empty () const;
         // Pre : none
         // Post: Returns true if the stack is empty; otherwise,
         //       returns false.
```

(continued)

Figure 14.11   *(continued)*

```
    // TEST TO SEE IF STACK IS FULL
    bool is_full () const;
        // Pre : none
        // Post: Returns true if the stack is full; otherwise,
        //       returns false.

  private:
    struct stack_node
    {
        stack_element item;    // storage for the node data
        stack_node* next;      // link to next node
    };

    // Data member
    stack_node* top;              // pointer to node at top of stack
};

#endif  // STACK_LIST_H
```

Compare the private part of template class `stack_list<class stack_element>` to the private part of template class `stack<class stack_element, int max_size>` shown in Fig. 12.21. In class `stack_list` (Fig. 14.11), data member `top` is type `stack_node*` (pointer to struct `stack_node`). In class `stack` (Fig. 12.21), `top` is an integer data member containing the subscript of the last filled element of data member `items`, an array with `max_size` elements for storage of the stack data. In template class `stack_list`, we assume dynamic allocation of the stack nodes, so we do not need to allocate an array data member to hold the stack data. Also for this reason, we do not need the template parameter `max_size`.

Example 14.1   The declaration

```
stack_list<char> s;
```

declares s to be an initially empty stack of characters, as shown here.

Assuming that the function `push` has been written for the linked list implementation of a stack, the statements

```
success = s.push ('+');
success = s.push ('A');
```

should redefine stack s, as shown next.

Two new nodes will be allocated to create stack s. Assuming pop has also been modified for the list implementation, the statement

```
success = s.pop (next_ch);
```

should return the character value 'A' to next_ch (type char) and redefine stack s, as shown next.

Stack Operators

Figure 14.12 shows the implementation file for class stack_list. The constructor stack_list sets top to NULL, creating an empty stack. Function push allocates a new node (pointed to by top), stores its argument x in the new node's data member (top->item), and connects the new node to the rest of the stack (pointed to by old_top). Function get_top returns the item at the top of the stack without changing the stack.

Function pop first checks to see if the list is empty. If the list is empty, false is returned. Otherwise, the first element is removed and true is returned, indicating success. Function is_empty checks to see if the class data member top is NULL. Function is_full always returns false. No check is made on available heap space.

Figure 14.12 Implementation of template class `stack_list`

```
// FILE: StackList.cpp
// IMPLEMENTATION OF TEMPLATE CLASS STACK AS A LINKED LIST

#include "stacklis.h"
#include <stdlib.h>                    // for NULL

// Member functions ...
// CONSTRUCTOR TO CREATE AN EMPTY STACK
template <class stack_element>
stack_list<stack_element>::stack_list ()
{
   top = NULL;
}  // end stack_list
```

(continued)

Figure 14.12   *(continued)*

```
// PUSH AN ELEMENT ONTO THE STACK
template <class stack_element>
bool stack_list<stack_element>::push
  (const stack_element& x)    // IN: Element to be pushed onto stack

// Pre:  The element x is defined.
// Post: If there is space on the heap, the item is pushed
//       onto the stack and true is returned. Otherwise, the
//       stack is unchanged and false is returned.
{
    // Local data ...
    stack_node* old_top;
    bool success;                // program flag - indicates success or
                                 // failure

    old_top = top;               // save old top
    top = new stack_node;        // allocate a new node at top of stack
    if (top == NULL)             // check to see if new was successful
    {
        top = old_top;           // if not, restore top
        success = false;         // indicate push failed
    }
    else
    {
        top->next = old_top;     // link new node to old stack
        top->item = x;           // store x in new node
        success = true;          // indicate success
    }
    return success;
}  // end push


// POP AN ELEMENT OFF THE STACK
template <class stack_element>
bool stack_list<stack_element>::pop
  (stack_element& x)    // OUT: Element popped from stack
// Pre:  none
// Post: If the stack is not empty, the value at the top
//       of the stack is removed, its value is placed in
//       x, and true is returned. If the stack is empty, x is
//       not defined and false is returned.
{
    // Local data ...
    stack_node* old_top;
    bool success;                // program flag - indicates success or
                                 // failure

    if (top == NULL)
        success = false;
    else
    {
```

(continued)

Figure 14.12   *(continued)*

```
            x = top->item;          // copy top of stack into x
            old_top = top;          // save old top of stack
            top = old_top->next;    // reset top of stack
            delete old_top;         // return top node to the heap
            success = true;         // indicate success
        }
        return success;
    }   // end pop


// GET TOP ELEMENT FROM STACK WITHOUT POPPING
template <class stack_element>
bool stack_list<stack_element>::get_top
    (stack_element& x) const   // OUT: Value returned from stack top
// Pre:  none
// Post: If the stack is not empty, the value at the top is
//       copied into x and true is returned. If the stack is
//       empty, x is not defined and false is returned. In either
//       case, the stack is not changed.
{
    // Local data
    bool success;               // program flag - indicates success or
                                // failure

    if (top == NULL)
        success = false;
    else
    {
        x = top->item;
        success = true;
    }
    return success;
}   // end get_top


// TEST TO SEE IF STACK IS EMPTY
template <class stack_element>
bool stack_list<stack_element>::is_empty () const
// Pre : none
// Post: Returns true if the stack is empty; otherwise,
//       returns false.
{
    return top == NULL;
}   // end is_empty


// TEST TO SEE IF STACK IS FULL
template <class stack_element>
bool stack_list<stack_element>::is_full () const
// Pre : none
```

(continued)

Figure 14.12   *(continued)*

```
// Post: Returns false. List stacks are never full. (Does not
//       check heap availability.)
{
   return false;
}  // end is_full
```

EXERCISES FOR SECTION 14.4

Self-Check   1. Provide an algorithm for a linked list member function `copy_stack` that makes a copy of an existing stack.

Programming   1. Implement `copy_stack` in C++.

14.5 ———— THE QUEUE ABSTRACT DATA TYPE

A *queue* (pronounced "Q") is a listlike structure in which items are inserted at one end and removed from the other. In contrast, stack elements are inserted and removed from the same end (the top of the stack).

In a queue, the element that has been stored the longest is removed first, so a queue is called a *first-in, first-out (FIFO)* structure. A queue can be used to model a line of customers waiting at a checkout counter or a stream of jobs waiting to be printed by a printer.

Figure 14.13 (a) shows a queue of three customers waiting for service at a bank. The name of the customer who has been waiting the longest is McMann (pointed to by `front`); the name of the most recent arrival is Carson (pointed to by `rear`). The customer pointed to by `front` will be the first one removed from the queue when a teller becomes available, and pointer `front` will be reset to point to Wilson. Any new customers will be inserted after Carson in the queue, and pointer `rear` will be adjusted accordingly. Fig. 14.13 (b) shows the queue after removing customer McMann, and Fig. 14.13 (c) shows the queue after inserting customer Perez at the end of the queue.

Implementing a Queue ADT

If we implement a queue as a linked list, removing elements from a queue is no different from removing them from a stack—the element at the front of the queue is removed next. Because new elements are inserted at the rear of the queue, however, we need a pointer to the last list element as well as the first. We can represent a queue as an object with two data members, `front` and `rear`. Pointer `front` points to the node at the front of the queue, and pointer `rear` points to the node at the rear of the queue. Because we might also want

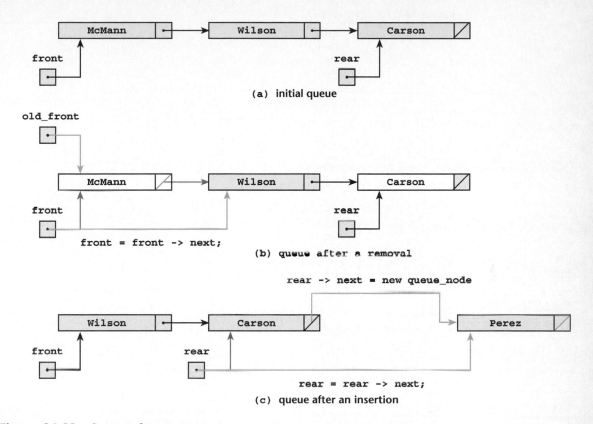

Figure 14.13 Queue of customers

to know how many elements are in a queue, we will add a third data member, num_items. Each queue node is a struct with an information part and a link to the next queue node. Fig. 14.14 shows the specification and definition for template class queue<class queue_element>.

Figure 14.14 Template class specification for **queue<queue_element>**

```
// FILE: Queue.h
// DEFINITION OF A TEMPLATE CLASS QUEUE USING A LINKED LIST

#ifndef QUEUE_H_
#define QUEUE_H_

// Specification of the class queue<queue_element>
// Elements:      A queue consists of a collection of elements
//                that are all of the same type, queue_element.
// Structure:     The elements of a queue are ordered according
//                to time of arrival. The element that was first
```

(continued)

Figure 14.14   *(continued)*

```
//              inserted into the queue is the only one that
//              may be removed or examined. Elements are
//              removed from the front of the queue and
//              inserted at the rear of the queue.

template<class queue_element>
class queue
{
   public:
      // Member functions ...
      // CREATE AN EMPTY QUEUE
      queue ();

      // INSERT AN ELEMENT INTO THE QUEUE
      bool insert
        (const queue_element& x);    // IN: Element to be inserted

      // REMOVE AN ELEMENT FROM THE QUEUE
      bool remove
        (queue_element& x);          // OUT: element removed

   private:
      // Data members ...
      struct queue_node
      {
         queue_element item;
         queue_node* next;
      };

      queue_node* front;      // the front of the queue
      queue_node* rear;       // the back of the queue
      int num_items;          // the number of items currently
                              // in the queue
};

#endif   // QUEUE_H_
```

Next we implement the queue member functions. Constructor `queue` (Fig. 14.15) sets pointer fields `front` and `rear` to `NULL`.

Figure 14.15   Implementation file for template class `queue<queue element>`

```
// FILE: Queue.cpp
// IMPLEMENTATION OF TEMPLATE CLASS QUEUE

#include "Queue.h"
#include <stdlib.h>          // for NULL
```

(continued)

Figure 14.15 *(continued)*

```
// Member functions ...
// CREATE AN EMPTY QUEUE
template<class queue_element>
queue<queue_element>::queue ()
{
   num_items = 0;
   front = NULL;
   rear = NULL;
}


// INSERT AN ELEMENT INTO THE QUEUE
template<class queue_element>
bool queue<queue_element>::insert
   (const queue_element& x)    // IN: Element to be inserted

// Pre : none
// Post: If heap space is available, the value x is inserted
//       at the rear of the queue and true is returned.
//       Otherwise, the queue is not changed and false is
//       returned.
{
   if (num_items == 0)             // Test for empty queue
   {
      rear = new queue_node;       // Allocate first queue node
      if (rear == NULL)            // Check to see that new was
                                   //    successful
         return false;
      else
         front = rear;             // Queue with one element
   }
   else                            // Add to existing queue
   {
      rear->next = new queue_node; // Connect new last node
      if (rear->next == NULL)
         return false;             // new was not successful
      else
         rear = rear->next;        // Point rear to last node
   }
   rear->item = x;                 // Store data in last node
   num_items++;
   return true;
}  // end insert


// REMOVE AN ELEMENT FROM THE QUEUE
template<class queue_element>
bool queue<queue_element>::remove
   (queue_element& x)    // OUT: element removed
```

(continued)

Figure 14.15   *(continued)*

```
// Pre : none
// Post: If the queue is not empty, the value at the front of
//       the queue is removed, its value is placed in x, and
//       true is returned. If the queue is empty, x is not
//       defined and false is returned.
{
    // Local data
    queue_node* old_front;

    if (num_items == 0)        // Test for empty queue
    {
        return false;          // Queue was empty
    }
    else                       // Remove first node
    {
        old_front = front;     // Point old_front to first
                               //    node
        x = front->item;       // Retrieve its data
        front = front->next;   // Bypass old first node
        old_front->next = NULL;  // Disconnect it from rest of
                               //    queue
        delete old_front;      // Return its storage
        num_items--;           // Decrement queue size
        return true;
    }
}
```

In operator insert, the statements

```
rear = new queue_node;
if (rear == NULL)        // Check to see that new was successful
    return false;
else
    front = rear;
```

execute when the queue is empty. These statements create a new node and set both rear and front to reference it. If the queue is not empty, the statements

```
rear->next = new queue_node;
if (rear->next == NULL)
    return false;
else
    rear = rear->next;
```

append a new list node at the end of the queue and then reference rear to this new node.

If the queue is not empty, operator `remove` uses the statements

```
x = front->item;        // Retrieve its data
front = front->next;    // Bypass old first node
```

to retrieve the data stored in `front->item` and reset `front` to point to the successor of the node whose data is retrieved (Fig. 14.13 (b)). Next, `remove` disconnects the old front of the queue (pointed to by `old_front`) and return its storage to the heap.

EXERCISES FOR SECTION 14.5

Self-Check
1. Redraw the queue in Fig. 14.13 (a) after the insertion of customer `Harris` and the removal of one customer from the queue. Which customer is removed? How many customers are left? Show pointers `first` and `rear` after each operation.
2. Trace operators `insert` and `remove` as the operations in exercise 1 are performed. Show before and after values for all pointers.
3. What changes would be made to member function `insert` to create a new `rude_insert` operator which inserts at the front of the queue rather than the end?
4. A circular queue is a queue in which the node at the rear of the queue points to the node at the front of the queue (see circular lists in Section 14.3). Draw the queue in Fig. 14.13 as a circular queue with just one pointer field named `rear`. Explain how you would access the queue element at the front of a circular queue.

Programming
1. Write operator `get_size`.
2. Add a new operator `display`, which presents the data stored in a queue.
3. Is it possible to simulate the operation of a queue using two stacks? Write an ADT for the queue object assuming that two stacks are used for storing the queue. What performance penalty do we pay for this implementation?

14.6 —— BINARY TREES

We can extend the concept of linked data structures to structures containing nodes with more than one pointer component. One such structure is a *binary tree* (or *tree*) whose nodes contain two pointer components. Because one or both pointers can have the value NULL, each node in a binary tree can have 0, 1, or 2 successor nodes.

Figure 14.16 shows two binary trees. For the tree (a), each node stores a three-letter string. The nodes on the bottom of the tree have 0 successors and are called *leaf nodes*. All other nodes have two successors. For tree (b), each node stores an integer. The nodes containing 40 and 45 have a single successor; all other nodes have 0 or 2 successors. A binary tree can be defined recursively: A *binary tree* is either empty (no nodes) or it consists of a node, called the *root*, and two disjoint binary trees called its *left subtree* and *right subtree*, respectively.

In the definition for binary tree, the phrase *disjoint subtrees* means that a node cannot be in both a left and right subtree of the same root node. For the

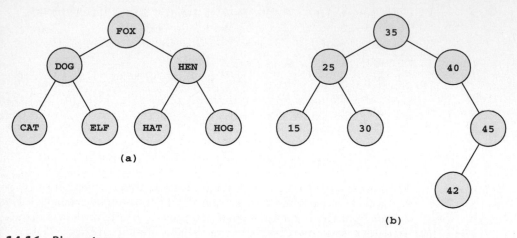

(a)

(b)

Figure 14.16   Binary trees

trees shown in Fig. 14.16, the nodes containing FOX and 35 are the root nodes for each tree. The node containing DOG is the root of the left subtree of the tree whose root is FOX; the node containing CAT is the root of the left subtree of the tree whose root is DOG; the node containing CAT is a leaf node because both its subtrees are empty trees.

A binary tree resembles a family tree and the relationships among the members of a binary tree are described with the same terminology as a family tree. In Fig. 14.16 the node containing HEN is the *parent* of the nodes containing HAT and HOG. Similarly, the nodes containing HAT and HOG are *siblings*, because they are both *children* of the same parent node. The root of a tree is an *ancestor* of all other nodes in the tree, and they in turn are *descendants* of the root node.

For simplicity, we did not show the pointer components in Fig. 14.16. Be aware that each node has two pointer components and that the nodes in (b) containing integers 45 and 42 are stored as follows:

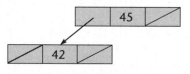

Binary Search Tree

In the rest of this chapter, we focus our attention on the *binary search tree*—a particular kind of binary tree structure that stores data in such a way that it can be retrieved very efficiently. Every item stored in a binary search tree has a special data component (called a *key*) whose value is unique to that item.

A binary search tree is a binary tree that is either empty or has the property that the item in its root has a larger key than each item in its left subtree and a smaller key than each item in its right subtree. Also, its left and right subtrees must be binary search trees.

The trees in Fig. 14.16 are examples of binary search trees; each node has a single data component which is its key. For tree (a), the string stored in every node is alphabetically larger than all strings in its left subtree and alphabetically smaller than all strings in its right subtree. For tree (b), the number stored in every node is larger than all numbers in its left subtree and smaller than all numbers in its right subtree. Notice that this must be true for every node in a binary search tree, not just the root node. For example, the number 40 must be smaller than both numbers stored in its right subtree (45, 42).

Searching a Binary Search Tree

Next we explain how to search for an item in a binary search tree. To find a particular item, say el, we compare el's key to the root item's key. If el's key is smaller, we know that el can only be in the left subtree so we search it. If el's key is larger, we search the root item's right subtree. We write this recursive algorithm in pseudocode below; the first two cases are stopping cases.

Algorithm for Searching a Binary Search Tree

1. if the tree is empty
      The target key is not in the tree.
   else if the target key is in the root item
      The target key is found in the root item.
   else if the target key is smaller than the root's key
      Search the left subtree.
   else
      Search the right subtree.

Figure 14.17 traces the search for 42 in a binary search tree containing integer keys. The pointer root indicates the root node whose key is being compared to 42 at each step. The darker lines show the search path. The search proceeds from the top (node 35) down to the node containing 42.

Building a Binary Search Tree

Before we can retrieve an item from a binary search tree, we must, of course, build the tree. To do this, we must process a collection of data items which is in no particular order and insert each one individually, making sure that the expanded tree is a binary search tree. We build a binary search tree from the

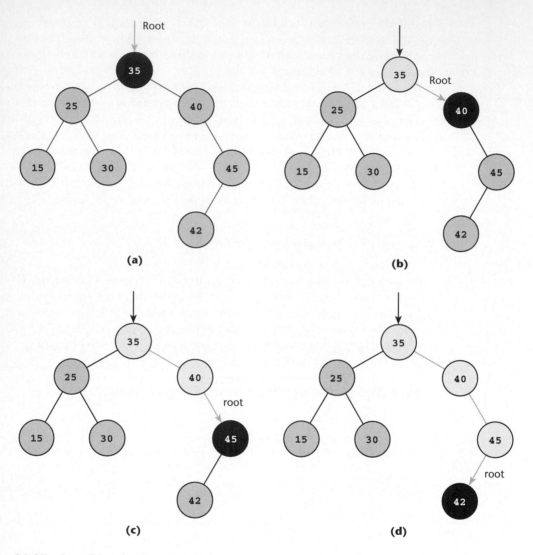

Figure 14.17   Searching for key 42

root node down, so we must store the first data item in the root node. To store each subsequent data item, we must find its parent node in the tree, attach a new node to the parent, and then store that data item in the new node.

When inserting an item, we must search the existing tree to find that item's key or to locate its parent node. If our search is successful, the item's key is already in the tree, so we will not insert the item. (Duplicate keys are not allowed.) If the search is unsuccessful, it will terminate at the parent of the item. If the item's key is smaller than its parent's key, we attach a new node as the parent's left subtree and insert the item in this node. If the item's key is larger than its parent's key, we attach a new node as the parent's right subtree and insert the item in this node. The recursive algorithm below maintains the binary search tree property; the first two cases are stopping cases.

Algorithm for Insertion in a Binary Search Tree

1. if the tree is empty
    Insert the new item in the tree's root node.
   else if the root's key matches the new item's key
    Skip insertion—duplicate key.
   else if the new item's key is smaller than the root's key
    Insert the new item in the tree's left subtree.
   else
    Insert the new item in the tree's right subtree.

Figure 14.18 builds a tree from the list of keys: 40, 20, 10, 50, 65, 45, 30. The darker lines show the search path followed when inserting each key.

The last node inserted (bottom right diagram) contains the key 30 and it is inserted in the right subtree of node 20. Let's trace how this happens using the tree just to the left of the bottom-right tree. Target key 30 is smaller than 40, so we insert 30 in the left subtree of node 40; this tree has 20 in its root. Target

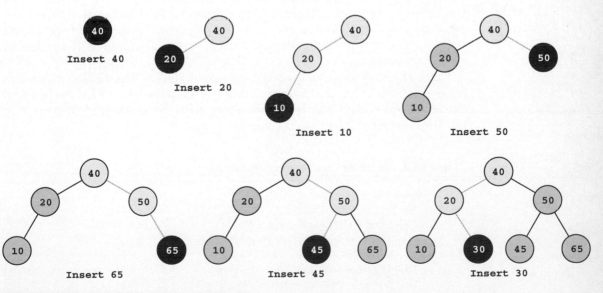

Figure 14.18 Building a binary search tree

key 30 is greater than 20, so we insert 30 in the right subtree of node 20, an empty tree. Because node 20 has no right subtree, we allocate a new node and insert target 30 in it; the new node becomes the root of 20's right subtree.

Be aware that we would get a very different tree if we changed the order in which we inserted the keys. For example, if we inserted the keys in increasing order (10, 20, 30, ...), each new key would be inserted in the right subtree of the previous key and all left pointers would be NULL. The resulting tree would resemble a linked list. We will see later (Section 14.8) that the insertion order also affects search efficiency.

Displaying a Binary Search Tree

To display the contents of a binary search tree so that its items are listed in order by key value, use the recursive algorithm below.

Algorithm for Displaying a Binary Search Tree
1. if the tree is not empty
   2. Display left subtree.
   3. Display root item.
   4. Display right subtree.

For each node, the keys in its left subtree are displayed before the key in its root; the keys in its right subtree are displayed after the key in its root. Because the root key value lies between the key values in its left and right subtrees, the algorithm displays the items in order by key value as desired. Because the nodes' data components are displayed in order, this algorithm is also called an *inorder traversal.*

Table 14.2 traces the sequence of calls generated by the display algorithm for the last tree in Fig. 14.18. Completing the sequence of calls for the last step shown "Display right subtree of node 40." is left as an exercise. The trace so far displays the item keys in the sequence: 10, 20, 30, 40.

Table 14.2   Trace of Tree Display Algorithm

Display left subtree of node 40.
    Display left subtree of node 20.
        Display left subtree of node 10.
            Tree is empty—return from displaying
            left subtree of node 10.
        Display item with key 10.
        Display right subtree of node 10.

(continued)

Table 14.2 *(continued)*

Tree is empty—return from displaying
right subtree of node 10.
 Return from displaying left subtree of node 20.
 Display item with key 20.
 Display right subtree of node 20.
  Display left subtree of node 30.
   Tree is empty—return from displaying
   left subtree of node 30.
  Display item with key 30.
  Display right subtree of node 30.
   Tree is empty—return from displaying
   right subtree of node 30.
  Return from displaying right subtree of node 20.
 Return from displaying left subtree of node 40.
Display item with key 40.
Display right subtree of node 40.

EXERCISES FOR SECTION 14.6

1. Are the trees below binary search trees? Show the list of keys as they would be displayed by an inorder traversal of each tree. If the trees below were binary search trees, what key values would you expect to find in the left subtree of the node containing key 50?

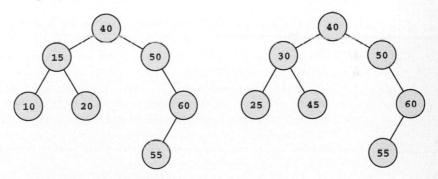

2. Complete the trace started in Table 14.2.
3. Show the binary search trees that would be created from the lists of keys below. Which tree do you think would be the most efficient to search? What can you say about the binary search tree formed in parts (b) and (c)? What can you say about the binary search tree formed in part (d)? How do you think searching it would compare to searching a linked list with the same keys?

 a. 25, 45, 15, 10, 60, 55, 12
 b. 25, 12, 55, 10, 15, 45, 60
 c. 25, 12, 10, 15, 55, 60, 45
 d. 10, 12, 15, 25, 45, 55, 60

4. What would be displayed by an inorder traversal of each tree in exercise 3?

14.7 ——— BINARY SEARCH TREE ABSTRACT DATA TYPE

Next, we design and implement a binary search tree abstract data type.

Design of Binary Tree Class

The pointer to the tree root is the only attribute of a binary tree. Besides the member functions discussed so far (`search`, `insert`, and `display`), we include a function `retrieve` to get the tree item whose key matches a target key. We provide the specification for a binary tree class next.

Specification for Binary Search Tree

Attributes for Binary Tree Class

`root`   — a pointer to the tree root

Member Functions for Binary Tree Class

`bin_tree`   — a constructor
`insert`   — inserts an item into the tree
`retrieve`   — retrieves all the data for a given key
`search`   — locates the node for a given key
`display`   — displays a binary tree

We declare these member functions in the public part of the class definition (see Fig. 14.19). The function prototypes show that all of them, except for `display`, return a type `bool` result which indicates whether the function was able to perform its task.

The private part shows that each binary search tree node (struct `tree_node`) contains a data component, `info`, which is type `tree_element`, and two pointers, `left` and `right`, that connect it to its children. These internal pointers cannot be accessed by a user of the binary tree class.

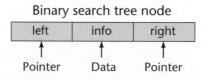

Binary search tree node

A binary tree object contains storage for a single pointer component, `root`, which points to the root node of that tree.

There are three private member functions, `do_search`, `do_insert`, and `do_retrieve`. We will explain the reason for these when we discuss the corresponding public functions.

Figure 14.19 Template class specification for `tree<tree_element>`

```cpp
// FILE: BinTree.h
// DEFINITION OF TEMPLATE CLASS BINARY SEARCH TREE

#include <stdlib_h>        // for NULL


#ifndef BIN_TREE_H_
#define BIN_TREE_H_

// Specification of the class bin_tree<tree_element>
// Elements:       A tree consists of a collection of elements
//                 that are all of the same type, tree_element.
// Structure:      Each node of a binary search tree has zero, one,
//                 or two subtrees connected to it. The key value in
//                 each node of a binary search tree is larger than
//                 all key values in its left subtree and smaller
//                 than all key values in its right subtree.

template<class tree_element>
class bin_tree
{
   public:
       // Member functions ...
       // CREATE AN EMPTY TREE
       bin_tree ();

       // INSERT AN ELEMENT INTO THE TREE
       bool insert
         (const tree_element& el ),   // IN: Element to be inserted

       // RETRIEVE AN ELEMENT FROM THE TREE
       bool retrieve
         (const tree_element& el) const;   // OUT: element retrieved

       // SEARCH FOR AN ELEMENT IN THE TREE
       bool search
         (const tree_element& el) const;   // IN: element being
                                           //      searched for

       // DISPLAY A TREE
       void display () const;

   private:
       // Data type ...
       struct tree_node
       {
           tree_element info;       // the node data
           tree_node* left;         // pointer to left-subtree
           tree_node* right;        // pointer to right-subtree
       };
```

(continued)

Figure 14.19 *(continued)*

```
      // Data member ....
      tree_node* root;              // the root of the tree

      // Member functions ...
      // Searches a subtree for a key
      bool do_search (tree_node*,             // root of a subtree
                  const tree_element&) const; // key being
                                              // searched for
        const;
      // Inserts an item in a subtree
      bool do_insert (tree_node*&,            // root of a subtree
                  const tree_element&);   // item being inserted

      // Retrieves an item in a subtree
      bool do_retrieve (tree_node*,                   // root of a
                                                      // subtree
                    tree_element&) const;             // item being
                                                      // retrieved

      // Displays a subtree
      bool do_display (tree_node*) const;
};

#endif   // BIN_TREE_H_
```

Implementation of Binary Tree Class

We will write the member function definitions for the implementation file in stages. As shown in Fig. 14.20, the constructor bin_tree sets the root pointer of its object instance to NULL, thereby creating an empty tree.

Figure 14.20 Member functions bin_tree, search, and do_search

```
// FILE: BinTree.cpp
// IMPLEMENTATION OF TEMPLATE CLASS BINARY SEARCH TREE

#include "BinTree.h"
#include <iostream.h>

   // Member functions ...
   // CREATE AN EMPTY TREE
   template<class tree_element>
   bin_tree<tree_element>::bin_tree ()
   {
      root = NULL;
   }
```

(continued)

Figure 14.20   *(continued)*

```
// Searches for the item with same key as el
//  in a binary search tree.
template<class tree_element>
bool bin_tree<tree_element>::search
  (const tree_element& el)// IN: Element to search for
  const

// Pre : el is defined.
// Returns true if el's key is located,
//   otherwise, returns false.
{
  return do_search (root, el); // Start search at tree root.
} // search

// Searches for the item with same key as el in the
// subtree pointed to by a_root. Called by search.
template<class tree_element>
bool bin_tree<tree_element>::do_search
   (tree_node* a_root,       // IN: Subtree to search
    const tree_element& el) // IN: Element to search for
   const

// Pre : el and a_root are defined.
// Returns true if el's key is located,
//   otherwise, returns false.
{
  if (a_root == NULL)
    return false;                  // Tree is empty.
  else if (el == a_root->info)
    return true;                   // Target is found.
  else if (el <= a_root->info)
    return do_search (a_root->left, el); // Search left.
  else
    return do_search (a_root->right, el);// Search right.
} // do_search
```

Member function search initiates a search for the tree node with the same key as item el, the target item, by calling private member function do_search. Normally, only the key component of el would be defined. Member function do_search implements the recursive search algorithm illustrated in Fig. 14.17, beginning at the root of the tree to be searched. The operators == and < compare the keys of item el and the root node in the normal way. Both operators must be defined for type tree_element.

Member function retrieve (see Programming Exercise 1 at the end of this section) returns the tree element with the same key as el. Normally, only the key component of el would be defined. Its implementation would be

similar to that of search. When do_retrieve (like do_search) locates
item el's key, use the statements

```
el = a_root-> info;          // Return tree element with same key.
success = true;              // Target is found and retrieved.
```

to return the tree data through el (a reference argument) and to indicate the
result of the retrieval operation.

Figure 14.21   Member functions `do_insert` and `insert`

```
// Inserts item el into a binary search tree.
template<class tree_element>
bool bin_tree<tree_element>::insert
  (const tree_element& el)   // IN

// Pre : el is defined.
// Post: Inserts el if el is not in the tree.
//       Returns true if the insertion is performed.
//       If there is a node with the same key value as el,
//       returns false.
{
    return do_insert (root, el);
} // insert


// Inserts item el in the tree pointed to by a_root.
// Called by insert.
template<class tree_element>
bool bin_tree<tree_element>::do_insert
  (tree_node*& a_root,       // INOUT : Insertion subtree
   const tree_element& el) // IN     : Element to insert

// Pre : a_root and el are defined.
// Post: If a node with same key as el is found,
//       returns false. If an empty tree is reached,
//       inserts el as a leaf node and returns true.
{
  // Check for empty tree.
  if (a_root == NULL)
  { // Attach new node
    a_root = new tree_node;    // Connect a_root to new node.
    a_root->left = NULL;       // Make new node a leaf.
    a_root->right = NULL;
    a_root->info = el;         // Place el in new node
    return true;
  }
  else if (el == a_root->info)
    return false;              // Duplicate key.
  else if (el <= a_root->info)
    return do_insert (a_root->left, el); // insert left.
  else
    return do_insert (a_root->right, el);// insert right.
} // do_insert
```

Member function `insert` (see Fig. 14.21) calls private member function `do_insert` to perform the actual insertion, beginning at the root of the tree receiving the insertion message. Member function `do_insert` implements the insertion algorithm illustrated in Fig. 14.18.

In `do_insert` if `a_root` is NULL, the statements

```
a_root = new tree_node;      // Connect a_root to new node.
a_root->left = NULL;         // Make new node a leaf.
a_root->right = NULL;
a_root->info = el;   // Insert el in node pointed to by a_root.
```

allocate a new tree node that is pointed to by `a_root` and store `el`'s data in it. The new node is a leaf node because its pointers are NULL. The node that has `a_root` as its left or right pointer is the parent of the new node. Fig. 14.22 illustrates this for the insertion of 30 in a binary search tree. The right pointer of node 20 is NULL before the insertion takes place.

Member function `display` (Fig. 14.23) calls recursive member function `do_display` to display the tree items in order by key. Member function `do_display` assumes that the insertion operator `<<` is defined for type `tree_element` and uses it to display each item.

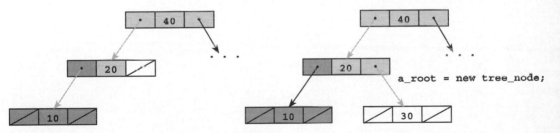

Figure 14.22   Inserting a node in a tree

Figure 14.23   Procedure `display` and `do_display`

```
// Displays a binary search tree in key order.
template<class tree_element>
void bin_tree<tree_element>::display () const

// Pre : none
// Post: Each element of the tree is displayed.
//       Elements are displayed in key order.
```

(continued)

Figure 14.23   *(continued)*

```
{
    do_display (root);
} // display


// Displays the binary search tree pointed to
// by a_root in key order. Called by display.
template<class tree_element>
void bin_tree<tree_element>::do_display
    (tree_node* a_root)          // IN : Subtree to display
    const

// Pre : a_root is defined.
// Post: displays each node in key order.
{
    if (a_root != NULL)
    { // recursive step
        do_display (a_root->left);          // display left subtree.
        cout << a_root->info << endl;        // display root item.
        do_display (a_root->right);          // display right subtree.
    }
} // do_display

// Insert member functions retrieve and do_retrieve.
```

EXERCISES FOR SECTION 14.7

Self-Check

1. Explain the effect of the following program segment if `my_tree` is type `bin_tree` and `tree_element` is type `int`. Draw the tree built by the sequence of insertions. What values would be displayed?

```
bin_tree<int> my_tree;
int my_data;
bool success;

success = my_tree.insert (3000);
success = my_tree.insert (2000);
success = my_tree.insert (4000);
success = my_tree.insert (5000);
success = my_tree.insert (2500);
success = my_tree.insert (6000);
success = my_tree.search (2500);
success = my_tree.search (1500);
my_data = 6000;
success = my_tree.retrieve (my_data);
my_tree.display ();
```

2. Deleting an entry in a binary tree is more difficult than insertion. Given any node in a tree that is to be deleted, what are the three cases for deletion and what must be done in each case. Be sure your approach preserves the binary search tree order.

Programming	1.	Write member functions `retrieve` and `do_retrieve`.
	2.	Write a member function that reads a list of data items from a binary file into a binary search tree. Use member function `insert` to place each item where it belongs.

14.8 ——— EFFICIENCY OF A BINARY SEARCH TREE

Searching for a target data value in an array or in a linked list is an $O(N)$ process. This means that the time required to search a list or array increases linearly with the size of the data. Searching a binary search tree can be a much more efficient process. If the left and right subtrees of every node are the exact same size, each move to the left or the right during a search eliminates the nodes of the other subtree from the search process. Since one subtree need not be searched, the number of nodes we do have to search is cut in half in each step. This is a *best-case analysis*, since, in reality, it is unlikely that a binary search tree will have exactly the same number of nodes in the left and right subtrees of each node. Nevertheless, this best-case analysis is useful for showing the power of the binary search tree.

As an example, if N is 1023 it will require searching ten trees ($N = 1023, 511, 255, 127, 63, 31, 15, 7, 3, 1$) to determine that a target is missing. It should require fewer than 10 probes to find a target that is in the tree. The number 1024 is a power of 2 (1024 is 2 raised to the power 10), so searching such a tree is an $O(\log_2 N)$ process ($\log_2 1024$ is 10). (Keep in mind that not all binary search trees will have equal size left and right subtrees!)

Does it matter whether an algorithm is an $O(N)$ process or an $O(\log_2 N)$ process? Table 14.3 evaluates $\log_2 N$ for different values of N. A doubling of N causes $\log_2 N$ to increase by only 1. Since $\log_2 N$ increases much more slowly with N, the performance of an $O(\log_2 N)$ algorithm is not as adversely affected by an increase in N.

Table 14.3   Values of N versus $\log_2 N$

N	$\log_2 N$
32	5
64	6
128	7
256	8
512	9
1,024	10

EXERCISES FOR SECTION 14.8

Self-Check   1. Given the binary tree below, how many comparisons are needed to find each of the
following keys or to determine that the key is not present? List the keys compared
to the target for each search.

a. 50   b. 65
c. 55   d. 52
e. 10   f. 48

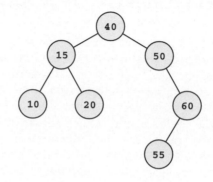

2. Why is it unlikely that a given binary tree will have exactly the name number of elements in the left and right subtrees of every node? For what numbers of nodes is
this possible?
3. If the elements of a binary tree are inserted in order, what will be resulting tree look
like? What is the big-O notation for searching in this tree?

14.9 —— COMMON PROGRAMMING ERRORS

Syntax Errors

- Make sure that you use the dereferencing operator * and the member
access (with pointer) operator -> whenever needed. For example, if p is a
pointer variable pointing to a node defined as a struct, then *p refers to
the whole node and p->x refers to the member x.
- The new operator allocates storage and returns a pointer. The results
should be assigned to a pointer variable having the same type as specified
in using the new operator. The delete operator deallocates storage. It
takes a pointer variable as its argument. For example, p = new node is
correct, but *p = new node is not; delete p is correct, but delete *p
is not.

Run-Time Errors

- There are some typical run-time errors that can occur in writing list traversal code. For example, the `while` loop

```
while (next != NULL)
    cout << next->word;
    next = next->link;
```

will repeatedly display the `word` member of the same node because the pointer assignment statement is not included in the loop body, so `next` is not advanced down the list.
- The `while` loop

```
while (next->id != 9999)
    next = next->link;
```

may execute "beyond the last list node" if a node with `id == 9999` is not found. The statement should be coded as

```
while ((next != NULL) && (next->id != 9999),
    next = next->link;
```

- If a pointer `next` is a function argument that corresponds to a list head pointer, make sure it is a value argument. Otherwise, the last value assigned to `next` will be returned as a function result. This may cause you to lose some of the elements originally in the linked list.
- Problems with heap management can also cause run-time errors. If your program gets stuck in an infinite loop while you are creating a dynamic data structure, it is possible for your program to consume all memory cells on the heap. It is important to check the results of `new` to make sure it is not the `NULL` pointer. If `new` returns a `NULL` pointer, all of the cells on the heap have been allocated.
- Make sure that your program does not attempt to reference a list node after the node is returned to the heap. Such an error is difficult to debug because the program may appear to function correctly under some circumstances. Also, returning a node to the heap twice can cause "strange" results on some systems.

CHAPTER REVIEW

This chapter introduced several dynamic data structures. We discussed the use of pointers to reference and connect elements of a dynamic data structure. The `new` operator allocates additional elements, or nodes, of a dynamic data structure; the `delete` operator returns memory cells to the storage heap.

We also covered many different aspects of manipulating linked lists. We showed how to build or create a linked list, how to traverse a linked list, and how to insert and delete elements of a linked list.

We revisited the stack and showed how to implement it as a linked list. A stack is a LIFO (last-in, first-out) structure in which all insertions (push operations) and deletions (pop operations) are done at the list head. Stacks have many varied uses in computer science, including saving parameter lists for recursive modules and translation of arithmetic expressions.

A queue is a FIFO (first-in, first-out) structure in which insertions are done at one end and deletions (removals) at the other. Queues are used to save lists of items waiting for the same resource (e.g., a printer).

A binary tree is a linked data structure in which each node has two pointer fields leading to the node's left and right subtrees. Each node in the tree belongs to either the left or right subtree of an ancestor node, but it cannot be in both subtrees of an ancestor node.

A binary search tree is a binary tree in which each node's key is greater than all keys in its left subtree and smaller than all keys in its right subtree. Searching for a key in a binary search tree is an $O(\log_2 N)$ process.

New C++ Constructs   The C++ constructs that were introduced in this chapter are described in Table 14.4.

Table 14.4   Summary of New C++ Constructs

CONSTRUCT	EFFECT
Pointer Variable Declaration	
```struct node { int info; node *link; };```	node is a struct that contains a member link, which is of type pointer to node.
```node *head;```	head is a pointer variable of type pointer to node.
new Operator	
```head = new node;```	A new struct of type node is allocated. This struct is pointed to by head and is referenced as *head.
delete Operator	
```delete head;```	The memory space occupied by the struct *head is returned to the storage pool.

(continued)

Table 14.4 *(continued)*

CONSTRUCT	EFFECT
Pointer Assignment	
`head = head->link;`	The pointer head is advanced to the next node in the dynamic data structure pointed to by head.

✔ QUICK-CHECK EXERCISES

1. Operator _____ allocates storage space for a data object that is referenced through a _____ ; operator _____ returns the storage space to the _____ .
2. When an element is deleted from a linked list represented using pointers, it is automatically returned to the heap. True or false?
3. All pointers to a node that is returned to the heap are automatically reset to NULL so that they cannot reference the node returned to the heap. True or false?
4. Why do you need to be wary of passing a list pointer as a reference argument to a function?
5. If a linked list contains three elements with values "Him", "Her", and "Its", and h is a pointer to the list head, what is the effect of the following statements? Assume that each node in the list is a struct with data member pronoun and link member next, and that p and q are pointer variables.

   ```
   p = h->next;
   p->pronoun = "She";
   ```

6. Answer Quick-Check Exercise 5 for the following segment:

   ```
   p = h->next;
   q = p->next;
   p->next = q->next;
   delete q;
   ```

7. Answer Quick-Check Exercise 5 for the following segment:

   ```
   q = h;
   h = new node;
   h->pronoun = "His";
   h->next = q;
   ```

8. Write a single statement that will place the value NULL in the last node of the three-element list in Quick-Check Exercise 5.
9. Draw the list representation of the following stack.

   ```
   $
   *
   &
   ```

10. If A, B, and C are inserted into a stack and a queue, what would be the order of removal for the stack? For the queue?

11. Often computers allow you to type characters ahead of the program's use of them. Should a stack or a queue be used to store these characters?

12. Assume that the left pointer of each node in the tree below is NULL. Is it a binary search tree? What would be displayed by its inorder traversal? Write a sequence for inserting these keys that would create a binary search tree whose NULL pointers were all at the lowest level. Is there more than one such sequence?

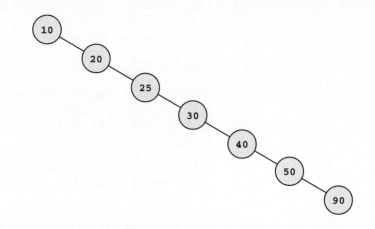

13. If a binary search tree has an inorder traversal of 1, 2, 3, 4, 5, 6, and the root node contains 3 and has 5 as the root of its right subtree, what do we know about the order that numbers were inserted in this tree?

14. What is the relationship between the left child and the right child in a binary search tree? Between the left child and the parent? Between the right child and the parent? Between a parent and all descendants in its left subtree?

Answers to Quick-Check Exercises

1. new; pointer; delete; heap
2. false; delete must be called
3. false
4. The value of the actual argument could be advanced down the list as the function executes, changing the value of the pointer that was originally passed to the function, and part of the list will be lost.
5. "Her", the pronoun member of the second node, is replaced by "She".
6. Detaches the third list element and then deletes it.
7. Inserts a new list value "His" at the front of the list.
8. h->next->next->next = NULL;
9.

s.top

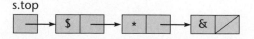

10. for stack: C, B, A; for queue: A, B, C
11. queue

12. yes; 10, 20, 25, 30, 40, 50, 90;
    30, 20, 10, 25, 50, 40, 90; yes
13. 3 was inserted first and 5 was inserted before 4 and 6.
14. left child < parent < right child; parent > all of its descendants

REVIEW QUESTIONS

1. Differentiate between dynamic and nondynamic data structures.
2. Describe a simple linked list. Indicate how the pointers are used to establish a link between nodes. Also indicate any other variables that would be needed to reference the linked list.
3. Give the missing type declarations and show the effect of each of the following statements. What does each do?

```
p = new node;
p->word = "ABC";
p->next = new node;
q = p->next;
q->word = "abc";
q->next = NULL;
```

Assume the following type declarations:

```
struct list_node
{
    string name;
    list_node *next;
};
list_node *the_list;
```

4. Write a program segment that places the names Washington, Roosevelt, and Kennedy in successive elements of the list the_list.
5. Write a program segment to insert the name Eisenhower between Roosevelt and Kennedy in Review Question 4.
6. Write a function to delete all nodes with the data value "Smith" from an argument of type list_node* as defined in Review Question 4.
7. Write a function delete_last that deletes the last node of the_list (defined following Review Question 3).
8. Write a function copy_list that creates a new list that is a copy of another list.
9. Show the effect of each of the operations below on queue<char> q. Assume that y (type char) contains the character '&'. What are the final values of x and success and the contents of queue q? Assume that q is initially empty. Show the queue contents after each operation.

```
success = q.insert ('+');
success = q.remove (x);
success = q.remove (x);
success = q.insert ('(');
success = q.insert (y);
success = q.remove ('&');
```

10. Write a member function `move_to_rear` that moves the element currently at the front of a queue to the rear of the queue. The element that was second in line in the queue will then be at the front of the queue. Use the member functions `insert` and `remove` from the queue template class.

11. Write a member function `move_to_front` that moves the element currently at the rear of a queue to the front of the queue. Use member functions `insert` and `remove` from the queue template class.

12. Discuss the differences between a simple linked list and a binary tree. Consider such things as the number of pointer fields per node, search technique, and insertion algorithm.

13. How can you determine if a binary tree node is a leaf?

14. Trace an inorder traversal of the following tree as it would be performed by member function `display` of class `bin_tree`.

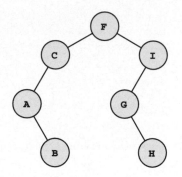

15. What happens when all the elements in a binary search tree are inserted in order? In reverse order? How does this affect the performance of programs that use the tree?

PROGRAMMING PROJECTS

1. Write a client program that uses the queue class to simulate a typical session for a bank teller. `queue_element` should represent a customer at a bank. Define a class `bank_customer` that contains the customer's name, transaction type, and amount. Include operators to read and write customers in the class. After every five customers are processed, display the size of the queue and the names of the customers who are waiting. As part of your solution, your program should include functions that correspond to the following function prototypes:

```
// SIMULATE ARRIVAL OF A SINGLE CUSTOMER
void arrive
   (queue& waiting_line,          // INOUT
    bool success);                // OUT


// SIMULATE DEPARTURE OF A SINGLE CUSTOMER
void depart
```

```
      (queue& waiting_line,          // INOUT
       bool success);                // OUT


// DISPLAY THE SIZE AND CONTENTS OF THE CUSTOMER QUEUE
void show
      (queue& waiting_line);         // IN
```

2. Write a program to monitor the flow of an item into and out of a warehouse. The warehouse will have numerous deliveries and shipments for this item (a widget) during the time covered. A shipment out is billed at a profit of 50 percent over the cost of a widget. Unfortunately, each shipment received may have a different cost associated with it. The accountants for the firm have instituted a last-in, first-out system for filling orders. This means that the newest widgets are the first ones sent out to fill an order. This member function of inventory can be represented using a stack. The push operator will insert a shipment received. The pop operator will delete a shipment out. Input data should consist of the following:

   ■ S or O: shipment received or an order to be sent
   ■ the quantity received or shipped out
   ■ cost: cost per widget (for received shipments only)
   ■ vendor: a character string that names the company sent to or received from

   For example, the data fragment below indicates that 100 widgets were received from RCA at $10.50 per widget and 50 were shipped to Boeing:

```
S 100 10.50 RCA
O 50 Boeing
```

   Output for an order will consist of the quantity and the total price for all the widgets in the order. (*Hint:* Each widget price is 50 percent higher than its cost. The widgets to fill an order may come from multiple shipments with different costs.)

3. Write a program that can be used to compile a simple arithmetic expression without parentheses. For example, the expression

```
A + B * C - D
```

   should be compiled as shown in the table below.

OPERATION	OPERAND 1	OPERAND 2	RESULT
*	B	C	Z
+	A	Z	Y
-	Y	D	X

   The table shows the order in which the operations are performed (*, +, -) and the operands for each operator. The result column gives the name of an identifier (working backward from Z) chosen to hold each result. Assume that the operands are the letters A through F and the operators are +, -, *, and /.

   Your program should read each character and process it as follows. If the character is a blank, ignore it. If it is an operand, push it onto the operand stack. If the character is not an operator, display an error message and terminate the program. If it is an operator, compare its precedence with that of the operator on top of the operator stack (* and / have higher precedence than + and -). If the new operator has higher precedence than the one currently on top (or if the operator stack is empty), it should be pushed onto the operator stack. If the new operator has the same or lower precedence, the operator on the top of the operator stack must be evaluated next. This is done by popping it off the operator stack along with a pair of operands from the operand stack and writing a new line of the output table. The character selected to hold the result should then be pushed onto the operand stack. Next, the new operator should be compared to the new top of the operator stack. Continue to generate output table lines until the top of the operator stack has lower precedence than the new operator or until the stack is empty. At this point, push the new operator onto the top of the operator stack and examine the next character in the data string. When the end of the string is reached, pop any remaining operator along with its operand pair as just described. Remember to push the result character onto the operand stack after each table line is generated.

4. A polynomial can be represented as a linked list, where each node contains the coefficient and the exponent of a term of the polynomial. The polynomial

$$4x^3 + 3x^2 - 5$$

would be represented as the linked list shown in Fig. 14.24.

Figure 14.24 $4x^3 + 3x^2 - 5$ as a linked list

Write a class polynomial that has operators for creating a polynomial, reading a polynomial, and adding and subtracting a pair of polynomials. *Hint:* To add or subtract two polynomials, traverse both lists. If a particular exponent value is present in either one, it should also be present in the result polynomial unless its coefficient is zero.

5. Each student in the university takes a different number of courses, so the registrar has decided to use a linked list to store each student's class schedule and an array of structs to represent the whole student body. A portion of this data structure is shown in Fig. 14.25.

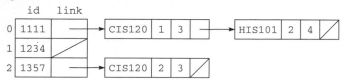

Figure 14.25 Class schedule as an array of structs

These data show that the first student (ID 1111) is taking section 1 of CIS120 for three credits and section 2 of HIS1001 for four credits; the second student is not enrolled; and so on. Write a class for this data structure. Provide operators for creating the original array, inserting a student's initial class schedule, adding a course, and dropping a course. Write a menu-driven program that uses the class.

6. The radix sorting algorithm uses an array of queues (numbered 0 through 9) to simulate the operation of a card-sorting machine. The algorithm requires that one pass be made for every digit of the numbers being sorted. For example, a list of three-digit numbers would require three passes through the list. During the first

pass, the least significant digit (the ones digit) of each number is examined and the number is added to the rear of the queue whose subscript matches the digit. After the numbers have been processed, the elements of each queue, beginning with q[0], are copied one at a time to the end of an eleventh queue prior to beginning the next pass. Then the process is repeated for the next most significant digit (the tens digit) using the order of the numbers in the eleventh queue. The process is repeated again, using the third most significant digit (the hundreds digit). After the final pass, the eleventh queue will contain the numbers in sorted order. Write a program that implements the radix sort using the queue class.

7. A deque is a double-ended queue—that is, a structure in which elements can be inserted or removed from either end. Write a deque class that is similar to the stack and queue classes.

8. Use a binary search tree to maintain an airline passenger list. Each passenger record should contain the passenger name (record key), class (economy, business, first class), and number of seats. The main program should be menu driven and allow the user to display the data for a particular passenger, and for the entire list, create a list, insert or delete a node, and replace the data for a particular passenger. When deleting a node, simply change the number of assigned seats to zero and leave the passenger's node in the tree.

9. Save each word appearing in a block of text in a binary search tree. Also save the number of occurrences of each word and the line number for each occurrence. Use a stack for the line numbers. After all words have been processed, display each word in alphabetical order. Along with each word, display the number of occurrences and the line number for each occurrence.

10. The fastest binary tree is one that is as close to balanced as possible. However, there is no guarantee that elements will be inserted in the right order. It is possible to build a balanced binary tree if the elements to be inserted are in order in an array. Write a procedure and test program that, given a sorted array of elements, builds a balanced binary tree. Augment the binary tree ADT to count the number of nodes that are searched to find an element and display the number of nodes that are searched to find each item in the tree. (*Hint:* The root of the tree should be the middle (median) of the array. This project is easier to do if you use recursion.)

11. Write a function that performs an inorder traversal of a binary tree without using recursion. It will be necessary to use a stack. Write a suitable test program for your function.

Appendix A   Character Sets

The following chart shows the numeric values used to represent each character in the ASCII (American Standard Code for Information Interchange) character set. Only the printable characters are shown. The numeric (ordinal) value for each character is shown in decimal (base 10). For example, in ASCII, the numeric (ordinal) value for 'A' is 65 and the ordinal value for 'z' is 122. The blank character is represented using a □.

Left Digit(s) \ Right Digit	0	1	2	3	4	5	6	7	8	9
							ASCII			
3			□	!	"	#	$	%	&	'
4	(	)	*	+	,	–	.	/	0	1
5	2	3	4	5	6	7	8	9	:	;
6	<	=	>	?	@	A	B	C	D	E
7	F	G	H	I	J	K	L	M	N	O
8	P	Q	R	S	T	U	V	W	X	Y
9	Z	[	/	]	^	–	'	a	b	c
10	d	e	f	g	h	i	j	k	l	m
11	n	o	p	q	r	s	t	u	v	w
12	x	y	z	{			}	~			

Codes 00–31 and 127 are nonprintable control characters.

Appendix B   Reserved Words and Special Characters

The following identifiers are reserved for use as C++ language keywords and may not be used except as intended.

asm	continue	float	new	signed	try
auto	default	for	operator	sizeof	typedef
break	delete	friend	private	static	union
case	do	goto	protected	struct	unsigned
catch	double	if	public	switch	virtual
char	else	inline	register	template	void
class	enum	int	return	this	volatile
const	extern	long	short	throw	while

NOTES

1. Identifiers containing a double underscore (_ _) are reserved for use by C++ implementations and standard libraries and should be avoided by users.

2. The following characters are used for operators or for punctuation in ASCII representations of C++ programs:

   ```
   !    %    ^    &    *    (    )    -    +    =    {    }    |    ~
   [    ]    \    :    "    ;    '    <    >    ?    ,    .    /
   ```

3. The following character combinations are used as operators in C++ :

   ```
   ->   ++   --   .*   ->*  <<   >>   <=   >=   ==   !=   &&
   ||   *=   /=   %=   +=   -=   <<=  >>=  &=   ^=   |=   ::
   ```

4. The tokens # and ## are used by the C++ preprocessor.

Appendix C   Selected C++ Library Facilities[1]

FUNCTION NAME	DESCRIPTION	NUMBER OF ARGUMENTS	TYPE(S) OF ARGUMENTS	RETURN TYPE	HEADER FILE	SECTION NUMBER
abs	integer absolute value	1	int	int	math.h stdlib.h	—
acos	arc cosine	1	double	double	math.h	3.2
asin	arc sine	1	double	double	math.h	3.2
at	returns character in position i (the argument) in source string object (call using dot notation)	1	size_t[2]	char	string	3.7
atan	arc tangent	1	double	double	math.h	3.2
atan2	arc tangent	2	double	double	math.h	3.2
atoi	converts character string to an integer	1	char*[3]	int	stdlib.h	—
atol	converts character string to a long integer	1	char*	long int	stdlib.h	—
atof	converts character string to a double	1	char*	double	stdlib.h math.h	—
bad	returns nonzero (true) if designated stream is corrupted and recovery is not likely	0	(none)	int	iostream.h	—
ceil	smallest integer not less than the argument	1	double or long double	double or long double	math.h	3.2
clear	sets error state of designated stream; argument represents the state to be set	1	int	void	iostream.h	—
close	closes file and disassociates it from stream; flushes buffer	0	(none)	returns 0 on error	iostream.h	8.1
cos	cosine	1	double	double	math.h	3.2
cosh	hyperbolic cosine	1	double	double	math.h	—
eof	returns non-zero (true) if end-of-file has been encountered in designated stream	0	(none)	int	iostream.h	8.1

(continued)

[1]Some functions listed in this table, particularly those in the fixed length string library string.h, are not discussed in the text.
[2]size_t is an unsigned integer type; it is the type of the result returned by the size_of operator (see Appendix D).
[3]Type char* is a pointer to a character string represented in C format.

Appendix C   *(continued)*

FUNCTION NAME	DESCRIPTION	NUMBER OF ARGUMENTS	TYPE(S) OF ARGUMENTS	RETURN TYPE	HEADER FILE	SECTION NUMBER
exit	program termination; same as a `return` statement in function `main` (closes files, flushes buffers, etc.); 0 argument usually means successful termination; nonzero indicates an error	1	int	void	stdlib.h	—
exp	exponential function (calculates *e* to the x power, where x is the argument)	1	double	double	math.h	3.2
fabs	double absolute value	1	double	double	math.h	3.2
fail	returns nonzero (true) if an operation on a stream has failed; recovery still possible and stream still usable once fail condition cleared; also true if `bad` is true	0	(none)	int	iostream.h	8.1
find	returns starting position of string target (the argument) in source string object (call using dot notation).	1	string	size_t	string	3.7
floor	largest integer not greater than the argument	1	double or long double	double or long double	math.h	3.2
get	single character input (extracts single character from stream and stores it in its argument)	1	char	int (zero at eof; else nonzero)	iostream.h	8.1
get	string input (reads from designated stream until n-1 characters are extracted or until delimiter is read or eof encountered; null character is placed at end of string; delimiter not extracted but is left in stream); fails only if no characters extracted	3	char* int n char delim = '\n'	int (zero at eof; else nonzero)	iostream.h	—
getline	extracts data characters up to but not including the delimiter (3rd argument, often newline) in source stream (1st argument) and stores them in a string (2nd argument). The first occurrence of the delimiter is extracted but not stored (call with dot notation).	3	stream string char	(none)	string	3.7

(continued)

Appendix C *(continued)*

FUNCTION NAME	DESCRIPTION	NUMBER OF ARGUMENTS	TYPE(S) OF ARGUMENTS	RETURN TYPE	HEADER FILE	SECTION NUMBER
getline	string input (reads from designated stream until n characters extracted or until delimiter is read or end of file encountered; null character is placed at end of string; delimiter removed from stream but is not stored in string)	3	char* int n char delim = '\n'	int	iostream.h	3.7
ignore	causes the number of characters specified (1st argument) in the input stream object to be ignored. If the delimiter (2nd argument) is encountered first, all characters up to and including the delimiter are ignored.	2	size_t	pointer to stream		8.4
insert	inserts new string (2nd argument) at position start (1st argument) in source string (call with dot notation).	2	size_t string	pointer to object modified by insert	string	3.7
isalnum	checks for alphabetic or base-10 digit character	1	char	int	ctype.h	7.3
isalpha	checks for alphabetic character	1	char	int	ctype.h	7.3
iscntrl	checks for control character (ASCII 0–31 and 127)	1	char	int	ctype.h	7.3
isdigit	checks for base-10 digit character ('0', '1', '2', . . ., '9')	1	char	int	ctype.h	7.3
islower	checks for lowercase letter ('a', . . ., 'z')	1	char	int	ctype.h	7.3
ispunct	checks for punctuation character (ispunct is true if iscntrl or isspace are true)	1	char	int	ctype.h	7.3
isspace	checks for white space character (space, tab, carriage return, newline, formfeed, or vertical tab)	1	char	int	ctype.h	7.3
isupper	checks for uppercase letter ('A', . . ., 'Z')	1	char	int	ctype.h	7.3
length	returns count of charcters in string (call with dot notation)	0	(none)	size_t	string	3.7
log	natural logarithm (ln)	1	double	double	math.h	3.2
log10	base-10 logarithm	1	double	double	math.h	3.2

(continued)

Appendix C   *(continued)*

FUNCTION NAME	DESCRIPTION	NUMBER OF ARGUMENTS	TYPE(S) OF ARGUMENTS	RETURN TYPE	HEADER FILE	SECTION NUMBER
open	opens a file given as first argument and associates it with designated stream	varies	char* ...	void	fstream.h	8.1
peek	returns next character in designated stream without extracting it; returns EOF if no character present in stream	0	(none)	int	iostream.h	—
pow	exponentiation; first argument raised to the power of the second	2	double	double	math.h	3.2
precision	sets the number of significant digits to be used when printing floating-point numbers and returns the previous value	1	int n = 6	int	iomanip.h	5.3
put	inserts a single character to the designated stream	varies	char	int	iostream.h	8.1
random	pseudo-random number generator; returns an integer between 0 and n-1	1	int n	int	stdlib.h	—
remove	starting at position start (1st argument) in source string remove the next count (2nd) argument) characters (call with dot notation).	2	size_t size_t	pointer to object modified by remove	string	3.7
replace	starting at position start (1st argument) in source string replace the next count (2nd) argument) characters (call with dot notation).	3	size_t size_t string	pointer to object modified by replace	string	3.7
seekg	moves position of "get" pointer to a file; move is relative either to the beginning, current position, or end of the file	1 or 2	long int	int	iostream.h	—
setf	turns on the format flags and returns the previous flags	1	long (bitflags)	long (bitflags)	iomanip.h	5.3
setf	clears the specified bit field and then turns on the format flags; returns previous flags	2	long (bitflags) long (bitfield)	long (bitflags)	iomanip.h	5.3
sin	sine	1	double	double	math.h	3.2
sinh	hyperbolic sine	1	double	double	math.h	—
sqrt	square root	1	double or long double	double long double	math.h	3.2

(continued)

Appendix C   *(continued)*

FUNCTION NAME	DESCRIPTION	NUMBER OF ARGUMENTS	TYPE(S) OF ARGUMENTS	RETURN TYPE	HEADER FILE	SECTION NUMBER
srand	random number generator (RNG) seed function; the RNG is reinitialized (to same start point) if the seed is 1; the RNG can be set to a new starting point if any other seed is used	1	`unsigned int` (the seed)	`void`	`stdlib.h`	—
strcat	string concatenation (appends a copy of the string pointed to by from to the end of the string pointed to by to	2	`char* to` `const char *from`	`char*`	`string.h`	—
strchr	search for first occurrence of character in string (returns pointer to first occurrence if found or the null pointer otherwise); any character may be used as the source character (to be found)	2	`const char*` `char`	`char*`	`string.h`	—
strcmp	lexical string comparison (returns <0, 0, >0 if s1 is less than, equal to, or greater than s2, respectively)	2	`const char* s1` `const char* s2`	`int`	`string.h`	—
strcpy	string copy (copies the string pointed to by from to the string pointed to by to up to and including the null character)	2	`char* to` `const char* from`	`char*`	`string.h`	—
strlen	string length (not counting null character, `'\0'`)	1	`const char*`	`size_t`[a]	`string.h`	—
strncat	string concatenation of up to lim characters (same as strcat except that a maximum of lim characters are concatenated; the to string is always terminated by `'\0'`)	3	`char* to` `const char* from` `size_t lim`	`char*`	`string.h`	—
strncmp	lexical string comparison of at most lim characters (same as strcmp except at most lim characters are compared)	3	`const char* s1` `const char* s2` `size_t lim`	`int`	`string.h`	—
strncpy	string copy of up to lim characters (see strcpy) padded by `'\0'` if `'\0'` is found in from string before lim characters copied	3	`char* to` `const char* from` `size_t lim`	`char*`	`string.h`	—

(continued)

Appendix C *(continued)*

FUNCTION NAME	DESCRIPTION	NUMBER OF ARGUMENTS	TYPE(S) OF ARGUMENTS	RETURN TYPE	HEADER FILE	SECTION NUMBER
`strpbrk`	searches for first occurrence in s of any character in `set`; returns pointer to first character in s matched by a character in `set`	2	`const char* s` `const char* set`	`char*`	`string.h`	—
`strrchr`	reverse search for first occurrence of character in string (otherwise, same as `strchr`)	2	`const char*` `char`	`char*`	`string.h`	—
`strstr`	searches for first occurrence in s1 of the substring s2; returns pointer to start of s2 in s1 or the null pointer if s2 not found in s1	2	`const char* s1` `const char* s2`	`char*`	`string.h`	—
`system`	calls operating system	1	`const char*`	`int`	`stdlib.h`	—
`tan`	tangent	1	`double` or `long double`	`double` `long double`	`math.h`	3.2
`tanh`	hyperbolic tangent	1	`double` or `long double`	`double` `long double`	`math.h`	—
`time`	returns time measured in seconds since 00:00:00 Greenwich Mean Time, January 1, 1970	1	`long int` `(time_t)`[4]	`long int*` `(time_t*)`	`time.h`	—
`tolower`	converts uppercase letter to lowercase	1	`int`	`int`	`ctype.h`	7.3
`toupper`	converts lowercase letter to uppercase	1	`int`	`int`	`ctype.h`	7.3
`unsetf`	turns off the format flags and returns the previous flags	1	`long` (bitflags)	`long` (bitflags)	`iomanip.h`	5.3
`width`	sets the minimum field width to the given size and returns the previous field width (zero means no minimum); the minimum field width is reset to zero after each insertion or extraction	1	`int`	`int`	`iomanip.h`	5.3

[4] `time_t` is a `long int` type.

Appendix D   Operators

Table D.1 shows the precedence and associativity of those C++ operators discussed in the text. In this table, the horizontal lines partition the list of operators into groups. All operators in one group have equal precedence. Those in the next group down have a lower precedence. The precedence table is followed by Table D.2, which contains a listing of each operator along with its name, the number of operands required, and the first section of the text that explains the operator.

Table D.1   Precedence and Associativity of Operations

PRECEDENCE	OPERATION	ASSOCIATIVITY
highest (evaluated first)	*scope resolution operator:* : :	left
	member selection operators: . ->	right
	subscripting: a [. .]	right
	function call: f (. .)	right
	post increment and decrement: ++ --	right
	sizeof	right
	logical not: !	right
	pre increment and decrement: ++ --	right
	unary +; unary -	right
	address of: &	right
	dereference: *	right
	new delete delete [ ]	right
	casts (type conversion)	right
	multiplicative binary operators: * / %	left
	additive binary operators: + -	left
	relational operators: < > <= >=	left
	equality operators: == !=	left
	logical and: &&	left
	logical inclusive or: | |	left
	assignment operators: = += -= *= /= %=	right
lowest (evaluated last)	*comma:* ,	left

Table D.2 Where to Find Operators in Text

OPERATOR	NAME	NUMBER OF OPERANDS	WHERE FOUND	
`a[..]`	subscript	1	9.1	
`f(..)`	function call	varies	3.2	(also 3.3; 6.2)
`.`	direct member selection	2	9.7	(also 12.2)
`->`	indirect member selection	2	14.1	
`++`	increment	1	5.1	
`--`	decrement	1	5.1	
`!`	logical negation	1	4.2	
`&`	address of	1	6.2	
`*`	indirection	1	14.1	
	or multiplication	2	2.4	(also 2.6)
type name	cast	1	3.7	(also 7.2)
`/`	division	2	2.4	(also 2.6)
`%`	remainder	2	2.4	(also 2.6)
`+`	unary plus	1	2.4	
	or addition	2	2.4	(also 2.6)
`-`	unary minus	1	2.6	
	or subtraction	2	2.4	(also 2.6)
`<`	less than	2	4.2	(also 7.3)
`<=`	less than or equal	2	4.2	
`>`	greater than	2	4.2	
`>=`	greater than or equal	2	4.2	
`==`	equality	2	4.2	
`!=`	inequality	2	4.2	
`&&`	logical and	2	4.2	
`||`	logical or	2	4.2	
`=`	assignment	2	2.4	
`+=  -=  *=` `/=  %=`	compound arithmetic assignment	2	5.2	
`, (comma)`	sequential evaluation	—	—	
`::`	scope resolution operator	1	11.5	(also 5.3)
`new`	dynamically allocates space in free store	varies	14.1	
`delete`	deallocates dynamically allocated space in free store		14.2	
`sizeof`	returns size, in bytes, of its operand	1	—	

Appendix E   A Brief Introduction to Inheritance and Polymorphism

In this appendix we introduce *inheritance* and *polymorphism*, which are very powerful features of object-oriented languages such as C++. Inheritance allows us to define new classes by extending and adapting existing classes. The new class *inherits* the characteristics of the *parent class*, and it may extend or adapt these features to meet the specific needs of an application. Several classes may be *derived* in this way from a common parent. Each such class represents a different *specialized adaptation* of the parent class. Whenever an object of a derived class is declared, the data members associated with the parent class can be used in the derived class and member functions of the parent are applicable in the derived class. This is often described by saying that the derived class and the parent are bound by the *is-a* relationship, as in "A circle is a specialization of a shape."

SUBCLASSING FOR SPECIALIZATION

There are at least a half-dozen forms of inheritance that have been identified. The first form is called *subclassing for specialization.* In this form, we begin with a complete parent class (a working software component) and develop modified or extended child classes (subclasses). The indexed list class first introduced in Section 12.4 provides a good example of the utility of this kind of subclassing. The class template described contains several member functions, such as `append`, `insert`, `retrieve`, `remove`, and `get_size`, that would be useful in almost any application involving the manipulation of objects of the indexed list data type. The class template also contains several functions that are far less universally used with indexed list objects: `find_min`, `find_max`, `search`, and `sort`.

Subclassing for specialization allows the programmer to begin work by defining a *base* or *parent* class containing the most common attributes (such as the array of elements and the size of the array) and member functions (such as `append`, `insert`, `retrieve`, `remove`, and `get_size`). Once this class has been defined and tested, we *specialize on the class* by adding features (attributes and/or functions) that might be useful in specific applications. A few applications may require the data to be sorted. In other applications it might be useful to be able to compute the sum and average of the data in an indexed list. Applications involving the computation of statistical measures such as the average, standard deviation, range, and median of a collection of numeric values might require sum and average functions combined with functions such as sort, find_min, and find_max.

In each case of specialization, we can use the C++ inheritance feature to *derive* new data types from existing types, adding the required functions, and in some cases, additional attributes (for example, sum and ave). The derivation process requires only that we specify the new attributes and functions, as shown in Fig. E.1. The parent class (referred to as index_list_base in Fig. E.1) remains as shown in Fig. 12.11, but without some of the less commonly used attributes and functions, while the derived class (called index_list_spec) can be specified solely in terms of the added features required for the particular application. We have rewritten the modified specification for class index_list_base; it is the same as class index_list shown in Fig. 12.11, but without functions find_min, find_max, search, sel_sort, read, and display. One other change was made to the Fig. 12.11 code: the word private (as applied to the class attributes) has been changed to protected. We will have more to say about this change in the display that follows Fig. E.1.

Subclassing for specialization saves considerable programming effort because the features of the parent class do not have to be respecified or tested as exhaustively. Yet we also retain the capability of defining and using classes designed to meet the needs of each application, without excess, unused features.

Figure E.1   Class index_list_spec derived from index_list_base parent class

```
// FILE:IndxBase.h
// Index list base class

#ifndef INDEX_LIST_BASE_H_
#define INDEX_LIST_BASE_H_

template <class T, int max_size>
class index_list_base
{
public:
    // Constructor
    index_list_base ();

    // Add an element to the end of an indexed list
    bool append (const T&);         // IN: element appended

    // Insert an element at a specified index.
```

(continued)

Figure E.1 *(continued)*

```
bool insert (int,              // IN: insertion index
             const T&);        // IN: element inserted

// Retrieve an element at a specified index.
bool retrieve (int,            // IN: index of element to be
                               //     retrieved
               T&)const;       // OUT: value to be retrieved

// Remove (delete) an element at a specified index.
bool remove (int);             // IN: index of element to be
                               //     removed

// Get the current number of data elements in the list.
int get_size () const;

protected:
   T elements[max_size];       // Storage for data
   int size;                   // Count of number of elements in list
};

#endif    // INDEX_LIST_BASE_H_



// FILE:IndexSpc.h
// Index list class specialized from index list parent
//     Includes sum and average attributes and functions
//     Definition and Implementation

#ifndef INDEX_LIST_SPEC_H_
#define INDEX_LIST_SPEC_H_

template <class T, int max_size>
class index_list_spec : public index_list_base
{
public:
   // Public member functions inherited from parent class:
   //    append, insert, retrieve, remove, get_size

   // Constructor
   index_list_spec ();

   // Compute sum of all data in the list
   T compute_sum ();

   // Compute average of all data in the list
   T compute_average ();
```

(continued)

Figure E.1   *(continued)*

```
protected:
    // Protected data inherited from parent class:
    //      list of data elements and the count of elements in the
    //      list
    T sum;          // sum of the data elements in the list
    T ave;          // average of the data elements in the list
};
#endif   // INDEX_LIST_SPEC_H_
```

The syntax for defining a derived class is shown in the following display.

C++
SYNTAX

Defining a Derived Class

Form: class *derived* : *access base*
                  { ... };

Example: class circle : public figure
                  { ... };

Interpretation: The class *derived* is derived from the class *base*. The access specifier may be public, private, or protected. If it is public, then public (or protected) members of the base class are public (or protected) in the derived class. If it is private or (protected), then the public and protected members of the base class become private (or protected) members of the derived class. The reserved word protected indicates a level of protection between public and private. Recall that items defined after the reserved word public are accessible by any function and that items defined after the reserved word private are accessible by member functions of the class in which they are declared. Items defined after the reserved word protected are accessible by member functions of both the class in which they are declared and classes derived from this class.

Note: Constructors are not inherited. The base class constructor (in this case, for index_list_base) is executed before the derived class constructor for each declaration of an object of the derived class.   ∎

SUBCLASSING FOR SPECIFICATION

In Section 11.5 we constructed a class for the geometric shape of a circle. Included in this class were attributes to represent the x and y coordinates, color, radius, and the area and perimeter of the circle. Then we specified functions for defining the coordinates, radius, and color of a circle, for computing the area and the perimeter of a circle, and for displaying a circle. Also included were six accessor functions, one for each of the attributes of a circle. The circle class specification is shown in Fig. 11.6 and a driver program illustrating how to use this class is given in Fig. 11.7.

We could easily devise classes for other shapes, patterned after the circle class. A similar class for a rectangle might contain the same attributes and functions as that for the circle class. We would expect to replace the radius attribute (not applicable to a rectangle) with a pair of attributes representing the height and width of the rectangle. With the corresponding changes in the rectangle class functions (replacing set_radius and get_radius with similar functions for height and width), we would have the specification for the new class. To obtain a similar class for a square, we would simply substitute the length of the side of the square for the radius of the circle.

This process of developing a separate class for each figure is workable and leads to the definition of three new data types (circle, rectangle, and square). However, given the substantial degree of commonality among these three classes, there is a significant amount of redundant code in each class. In addition, as shown in the driver program in Fig. 11.7, the manipulation of objects of these new data types requires the use of a different object prefix such as:

```
my_circle.compute_area ();
my_rectangle.compute area ();
my_square.compute_area ();
```

Thus, in any program requiring extensive manipulation of geometric shapes, the required use of separate prefixes for each shape makes the code cumbersome—full of statement sequences that are identical except for the designation of object names. Furthermore, if we wish to add new shapes to the list of those to be manipulated, extensive changes would be required in the user program.

What we would really like is to find a way to reduce, if not eliminate, the code redundancies in the shapes classes as well as in any program that might use these classes. At the same time, we would like a solution that would enable us to add new shapes to our collection with minimal effort and with as little impact as possible on any program that would use our shapes data types. To realize such a solution, we examine a second form of inheritance, called subclassing for specification.

In *subclassing for specification,* the parent class provides a specification of some attributes (perhaps) as well as a list of the member functions common to all (or most) of the subclasses. However, no description of the behavior of these functions is provided. The purpose of the parent class in subclassing for specification is to describe *what must be done* but not *how the listed tasks are to be carried out.* In this case, the member functions specified in each subclass *override* the member function specifications in the parent class and provide a description of exactly how the task is to be carried out for the particular subclass in question.

Subclassing for specification is useful in situations where many different subclasses inherit data and function members from a parent and where we would like to have the same function protocol (return and argument types), terminology, and behavior used for the attributes and functions in all of the subclasses. The following case study provides an illustration of subclassing for specification.

CASE STUDY: AREAS AND PERIMETERS OF DIFFERENT FIGURES

Problem Statement

The problem to be addressed has been outlined in the section preceding the case study. Rather than illustrate the subclassing for specification process with the complete circle class shown in Chapter 11, we use a simplified version, which will allow us to focus on the key aspects of the process. Therefore, we will limit our discussion to the area and perimeter attributes and to those attributes required to compute the area and perimeter. We also provide functions to compute the area and perimeter and a function to display the attribute values of each class. Finally, we add a function that will allow the program user to enter in the values of the attributes required to compute the area and perimeter.

Problem Analysis

Figure E.2 provides a graphical representation of the attributes and operations just described for each of the three classes, `circle`, `square`, and `rectangle`. Recall that the width and height measurements of a rectangle are required to compute its area and perimeter, while the radius and side are required to perform these computations for a circle and a square (respectively).

The subclassing process requires that we be able to abstract the common attributes and functions of these classes into a parent class from which the

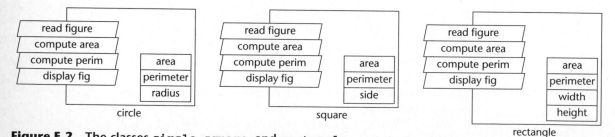

Figure E.2   The classes `circle`, `square`, and `rectangle`

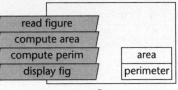

figure

Figure E.3 The class `figure`

individual shapes can be derived. From Fig. E.2, it is clear that two attributes (area and perimeter) and all four of our functions are common to each class. We can therefore define a class figure that contains the common elements of the three classes as shown in Fig. E.3. The member functions in Fig. E.3 are shaded. This indicates that while these functions are common to all three figures, the particular implementation details are specific to each kind of figure.

Figure E.4 shows the C++ definition of the class figure. The reserved word virtual that precedes the specifications of the four functions indicates that these *virtual functions* can have different versions for each of the derived classes. When a virtual function is called during execution, the C++ run-time system decides which of the actual (derived class) functions is to be executed.

Fig. E.4 C++ definition of the class figure

```cpp
// FILE: figure.h
// ABSTRACT CLASS FIGURE CONTAINS OPERATORS AND ATTRIBUTES COMMON
//      TO ALL FIGURES.
#ifndef FIGURE_H_
#define FIGURE_H_

class figure
{
    // Member functions (common to all figures) ...
    public:
        // READ FIGURE ATTRIBUTES
        virtual void read_figure () = 0;

        // COMPUTE THE AREA
        virtual void compute_area () = 0;

        // COMPUTE THE PERIMETER
        virtual void compute_perim () = 0;

        // COMPUTE INFORMATION ABOUT THE FIGURE
        virtual void display_fig ();
```

(continued)

Fig. E.4   *(continued)*

```
    // Attributes common to all figures ...
    protected:
        float area;                     // The area of the figure
        float perimeter;                // The perimeter of the figure
};
#endif       // FIGURE_H_
```

Function specifications such as

```
virtual prototype = 0;
```

indicate the declaration of a *pure virtual function*—a virtual function with an undefined body. We use pure virtual functions instead of virtual functions in situations where the steps to be carried out by the function are known only to the derived class, not to the parent. For example, in the shapes problem, we cannot prescribe the computation of the area or perimeter of a figure until we know which figure is involved (the computation of the area of a circle is different from that of a rectangle or a square). The same applies to function `read_fig`, since it is not possible to know what value(s) need to be read (radius of a circle, length of the side of a square, or the height and width of a rectangle) without knowing which figure is involved. In cases such as these, where there is no other computation to be specified in the function, we leave the body of the function unspecified as shown in Fig. E.4. Note that function `display_fig` is different from the others since the portion of its task that is common to all derived classes (the display of the area and perimeter of a shape) may be specified in the base class (see Fig. E.11).

A class that contains at least one pure virtual function is called an *abstract base class*. Such a class can have no instances; it is used only as the basis for derived classes. An abstract base class, such as the class `figure`, is intended to be used to describe the specification of the attributes and functions common to these derived classes.

Figure E.5 shows unique elements of the classes `circle`, `square`, and `rectangle`. If you were to overlay each of these on Fig. E.3 you would get

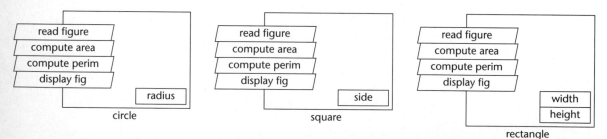

Figure E.5   **The classes `circle`, `square`, and `rectangle`**

Figure E.6   The class `circle`

```
// FILE: Circle.h
#ifndef CIRCLE_H_
#define CIRCLE_H_

#include "Figure.h"

// THE CLASS CIRCLE
class circle : public figure          // a circle is a figure
{
    // Overriding member functions (unique for circles) ...
    public:
        // READ A CIRCLE
        void read_figure ();

        // COMPUTE THE AREA OF A CIRCLE
        void compute_area ();

        // COMPUTE THE PERIMETER (CIRCUMFERENCE) OF A CIRCLE
        void compute_perim ();

        // DISPLAY CHARACTERISTICS UNIQUE TO A CIRCLE
        void display_fig ();

    // Data members (unique to a circle) ...
    private:
        float radius;                          // radius
};
#endif        // CIRCLE_H_
```

the full classes as shown in Fig. E.2. Figures E.6, E.7, and E.8 show the C++ definitions for each of the classes `circle`, `square`, and `rectangle`, as derived from `figure`.

Figure E.7   The class `square`

```
// FILE Square.h
#ifndef SQUARE_H_
#define SQUARE_H_

#include "Figure.h"

// THE CLASS SQUARE
class square : public figure          // A square is a figure
{
```

(continued)

Figure E.7 *(continued)*

```
    // Overriding member functions (unique for squares) ...
    public:
        // READ A SQUARE
        void read_figure ();

        // COMPUTE AREA OF A SQUARE
        void compute_area ();

        // COMPUTE PERIMETER OF A SQUARE
        void compute_perim ();

        // DISPLAY CHARACTERISTICS UNIQUE TO SQUARES
        void display_fig ();

    // Attributes (unique to squares) ...
    private:
        float side;                  // length of side of square
};
#endif      // SQUARE_H_
```

Figure E.8 The class `rectangle`

```
// FILE Rectangl.h
#ifndef RECTANGLE_H_
#define RECTANGLE_H_

#include "Figure.h"

// THE CLASS RECTANGLE
class rectangle : public figure  // a rectangle is a figure
{
    // Overriding member functions (unique for rectangles) ...
    public:
        // READ A RECTANGLE
        void read_figure ();

        // COMPUTE THE AREA OF A RECTANGLE
        void compute_area ();

        // COMPUTE THE PERIMETER OF A RECTANGLE
        void compute_perim ();

        // DISPLAY CHARACTERISTICS UNIQUE TO RECTANGLES
        void display_fig ();
```

(continued)

Figure E.8   *(continued)*

```
    // Data members (unique to rectangles) ...
    private:
       float width;              // width of rectangle
       float height;             // height of rectangle
};
#endif       // RECTANGLE_H_
```

Program Design

Given the parent class figure and the derived classes circle, square, and rectangle, we can now design the program for solving the shapes problem. The initial algorithm follows.

INITIAL ALGORITHM

1. Determine the type of the figure.
2. Read in the figure characteristics (read_figure).
3. Compute the area of the figure (compute_area).
4. Compute the perimeter of the figure (compute_perimeter).
5. Display the complete data for the figure (display_fig).

Program Implementation

We use the parent class figure and the derived classes circle, square, and rectangle as shown in Figs. E.4, E.6, E.7, and E.8. These classes contain the member functions required to perform steps 2 through 5.

CODING THE MAIN FUNCTION

The main function (Fig. E.9) declares a variable (my_fig) of type pointer to figure. The function get_figure returns a pointer to figure. The main function for loop calls get_figure, which carries out step 1 of the algorithm. Depending upon the input received, the pointer returned by get_figure (and stored in my_fig) will point to a particular kind of figure (circle, square, or rectangle). This object, indicated by *my_fig, is passed to the function process_figure (Fig. E.9). The member functions of the class figure are called by process_figure to perform steps 2 through 5 of our initial algorithm. The main function then deletes the object pointed to by my_fig so that another figure may be defined. The program exits when a zero pointer is returned from get_figure. Notice that these functions know only about the class figure and not any of the particular figures derived from it; there are simply no references to the derived classes here.

Figure E.9   Figures program `main` function

```
// FILE: Figures.cpp
// MAIN PROGRAM TO ILLUSTRATE THE FIGURES CLASS

#include <iostream.h>
#include <stddef.h>

#include "Circle.h"
#include "Square.h"
#include "Rectangl.h"


#include "Figure.h"

    // Functions called ...
    // GET THE TYPE OF FIGURE
    figure* get_figure ();

    // PROCESS ONE FIGURE
    void process_figure
        (figure&);                 // INOUT: figure to be processed

void main()
{
    // Local data ...
    figure* my_fig;        // a pointer to a figure

    // Process a selected figure until no more figures selected.
    for (my_fig = get_figure(); my_fig != 0; my_fig = get_figure ())
    {
        process_figure (*my_fig);
        delete my_fig;    // delete this figure
    }
}

// PROCESS ONE FIGURE
void process_figure
    (figure& fig)                  // INOUT: The figure to be processed
{
    fig.read_figure ();   // get characteristics of figure
    fig.compute_area ();  // compute its area
    fig.compute_perim (); // compute its perimeter
    fig.display_fig ();   // display characteristics
}
```

CODING THE FUNCTIONS

All that remains to be done at this point is to code the function `get_figure`, and the member functions of the classes `figure`, `circle`, `square`, and rectangle. The function `get_figure` is shown in Fig. E.10. This function

Figure E.10 Function `get_figure`

```
// FILE Figures.cpp
// FUNCTION TO READ THE KIND OF FIGURE AND RETURN A POINTER TO
//    AN OBJECT OF THE APPROPRIATE TYPE

figure* get_figure ()
// Pre:  None.
// Post: A pointer to the type of figure desired is returned
{
    // Local data ...
    char fig_char;      // a character to indicate the type
                        //    of figure

    do                  // loop until a valid entry is made
    {
        cout << "Enter the kind of object" << endl;
        cout << "Enter C (Circle), R (Rectangle), or S (Square)"
             << endl;
        cout << "Enter X to exit program" << endl;
        cin >> fig_char;
        switch (fig_char)
        {
            case 'c': case 'C':
                return new circle;
            case 'r': case 'R':
                return new rectangle;
            case 's': case 'S':
                return new square;
            case 'x': case 'X':
                return 0;
        } // end switch
    } while (true);
} // end get_figure
```

prompts for an input character and calls the new operator to allocate memory for the particular kind of figure specified. If the letter x is input, the function returns a zero pointer to indicate that no figure was specified. If a letter that is not recognized is entered, the function asks for another input.

Figures E.11, E.12, E.13, and E.14 show the implementations of the classes figure, circle, square, and rectangle. With the exception of the function display_fig, the functions in the parent class figure have little work to do. The function figure::display_fig (the function display_fig which is a member of the class figure) displays the perimeter and area of a shape, attributes that are common to all of the kinds of figures. The implementation of the other member functions is straightforward. Notice that each class implementation need know only about itself and not the other classes.

Figure E.11   Implementation of the class `figure`

```cpp
// FILE: Figure.cpp
// IMPLEMENTATION OF THE BASE CLASS FIGURE

#include <iostream.h>

#include "Figure.h"


// FUNCTIONS read_figure, compute_area, AND compute_perimeter ARE
//      PURE VIRTUAL FUNCTIONS AND HAVE NO BODIES.

// DISPLAY THE COMMON CHARACTERISTICS OF FIGURES
void figure::display_fig ()
{
    cout << "Area is " << area << endl;
    cout << "Perimeter is " << perimeter << endl;
}
```

Thus `figure.cpp` needs to include `figure.h`, `circle.cpp` needs to include `circle.h`, and so on, but they do not need to include the definitions for the other classes.

Figure E.12   Implementation of the class `circle`

```cpp
// FILE: Circle.cpp
// IMPLEMENTATION OF THE CLASS CIRCLE

#include <iostream.h>

#include "Circle.h"
const float pi = 3.1415927;


// READ DATA UNIQUE TO A CIRCLE
void circle::read_figure ()
{
    cout << "Enter radius > ";
    cin >> radius;
}


// COMPUTE THE PERIMETER (CIRCUMFERENCE) OF A CIRCLE
void circle::compute_perim ()
{
    perimeter = 2.0 * pi * radius;
}
```

(continued)

Figure E.12   *(continued)*

```cpp
// COMPUTE THE AREA OF A CIRCLE
void circle::compute_area ()
{
    area = pi * radius * radius;
}



// DISPLAY THE CHARACTERISTICS OF A CIRCLE
void circle::display_fig ()
{
    // Display the type of figure and its radius.
    cout << "Figure Shape is Circle" << endl;
    cout << "Radius is " << radius << endl;
    // Call the base function to display common characteristics.
    figure::display_fig ();
}
```

Figure E.13   Implementation of the class `square`

```cpp
// FILE Square.cpp
// IMPLEMENTATION OF THE CLASS SQUARE

#include <iostream.h>

#include "Square.h"


// READ DATA UNIQUE TO A SQUARE
void square::read_figure ()
{
    cout << "Enter side > ";
    cin >> side;
}



// COMPUTE THE PERIMETER OF A SQUARE
void square::compute_perim ()
{
    perimeter = 4.0 * side;
}



// COMPUTE THE AREA OF A SQUARE
void square::compute_area ()
{
    area = side * side;
}
```

(continued)

Figure E.13   *(continued)*

```
// DISPLAY THE CHARACTERISTICS OF A SQUARE
void square::display_fig ()
{
   // Display the type of figure and its size.
   cout << "Figure shape is Square" << endl;
   cout << "Side is " << side << endl;
   // Call the base function to display common characteristics.
   figure::display_fig ();
}
```

Figure E.14   Implementation of the class `rectangle`

```
// FILE Rectangl.cpp
// IMPLEMENTATION OF THE RECTANGLE CLASS

#include <iostream.h>

#include "Rectangl.h"


// READ DATA UNIQUE TO A RECTANGLE
void rectangle::read_figure()
{
   cout << "Enter width: ";
   cin >> width;
   cout << "Enter height: ";
   cin >> height;
}

// COMPUTE THE PERIMETER OF A RECTANGLE
void rectangle::compute_perim ()
{
   perimeter = 2.0 * (width + height);
}


// COMPUTE THE AREA OF A RECTANGLE
void rectangle::compute_area ()
{
   area = width * height;
}


// DISPLAY THE CHARACTERISTICS OF A RECTANGLE
void rectangle::display_fig ()
{
```

(continued)

Figure E.14   *(continued)*

```
    // Display the type of figure and its height and width.
    cout << "Figure shape is Rectangle" << endl;
    cout << "Height is " << height << endl;
    cout << "Width is " << width << endl;
    // Call the base function to display common characteristics.
    figure::display_fig ();
}
```

Commentary

Had we not used inheritance in solving the shapes problem we would have had to explicitly code the references to each of the member functions of our shapes classes as well as the decisions required to select which functions are to be called (based on the designation of the shape being processed). For example, the simple step of processing one figure, shown in Figure E.9, might have been written as shown next (assuming fig_shape to be of type char):

```
switch (fig_shape)
{
    case 'c' : case 'C' :
        circle.read_figure ();
        circle.compute_area ();
        circle.compute_perim ();
        circle.display_fig ();   break;
    case 'r' : case 'R' :
        rectangle.read_figure ();
        rectangle.compute_area ();
        rectangle.compute_perim ();
        rectangle.display_fig ();   break;
    case 's' : case 'S' :
        square.read_figure ();
        square.compute_area ();
        square.compute_perim ();
        square.display_fig ();   break;
    default:
        cerr << "Incorrect character for shapes designation."
            << "Re-run program." << endl;
}  // end switch
```

Extending this kind of code to include additional figures is not conceptually difficult, but it can become a relatively boring, time-consuming, and error-prone exercise.

Compare this with the `process_figure` function of Fig. E.11. This function contains no `switch` statement. The `switch` statement is in the function `get_figure`, and it simply determines which kind of figure is to be created given the user's input. To extend this new version of the `figures` program for other kinds of figures is very easy. We merely need to define a new class for our new kind of figure and to modify `get_figure` to recognize an input that designates it. (As an exercise, you might try to extend the figures program to include the figure class `right_triangle`. Use the following formulas:

$$area = \frac{1}{2} \; base \times height$$

$$hypotenuse = \sqrt{base^2 + height^2}$$

where *base* and *height* are the two sides that form the right triangle and *hypotenuse* is the side opposite the right angle.)

Polymorphism

A function which is only concerned with the common characteristics of a group of objects may operate on different specialized instances without knowing about the specific instance. As illustrated in Fig. E.11, a pointer, such as `my_fig`, to an object of the parent type can point to an object of any of the derived types. Operations, such as `compute_area`, which are common in function to the derived classes, may be accessed through such a pointer, as in `fig.compute_area()`, even though the implementation details of these operations may vary. This is called *polymorphism* (meaning "many forms").

In this example, we have illustrated one form of polymorphism, known as *overriding through the use of a virtual function.* An overridden function name, such as `compute_area`, is polymorphic in the sense that it can be used to refer to many different functions (five, in our example).

The operator + is also polymorphic; it may be *overloaded.* That is, it can be used to specify integer addition, as in

```
19 + 32
```

or floating-point addition, as in

```
6.1 + 8.8
```

or concatenation, as in

```
first_name_string + " " + last_name_string
```

To the underlying computer, these are three totally distinct operations. To the programmer, + can be viewed as a single operation that allows the use of different types of arguments. The specific underlying computer operation to be performed is determined by the compiler, based upon the operands involved.

The use of inheritance and polymorphism permits us to define a foundation upon which others can build specialized applications. Commercial software vendors provide such foundation classes for a variety of application domains. Two popular domains are in *graphics user interfaces* and in *database management*.

Answers

Chapter 1

Section 1.2
1. Hardware

Section 1.2
1. Contents of memory cell   0: -27.2.
   Contents of memory cell 999: 75.62.

   Memory cell 998 contains the letter x.
   Memory cell 2 contains the fraction 0.005.
3. bit, byte, memory cell, main memory, secondary memory.

Section 1.3
1. `x = a + b + c;`   Add the contents of variables a, b, c. Store the results in variable x.

   `x = y / z;`   Divide the contents of variable y by the contents of variable z. Store the results in variable x.

   `d = c - b + a;`   Subtract the contents of variable b from the contents of variable c. Add the contents of variable a to this. Store the final result in variable d.

   `z = z + 1;`   Add 1 to the contents of variable x. Store the result in variable z.

   `kelvin = celsius + 273.15;`   Add 273.15 to the contents of variable celsius. Store the results in variable kelvin.
3. Assembly language has instructions such as ADD X.
   Machine language has instructions that are binary numbers.

Section 1.4
1. Source program. The compiler.
3. The source program is written in a high-level language. An object code program is the machine code translation of a source program. An executable program is a combination of your object program and other object files. The programmer (you) creates the source program. The compiler creates the object program. The linker/loader creates the executable program.

Section 1.5
1. The three steps/stages of the software development method are:
   - Problem analysis
   - Program design
   - Program implementation
3. Stage 2—Program Design

5. Object-oriented programming is a disciplined approach to programming that results in programs that are easy to read and understand and less likely to contain errors. Programs are constructed from well-designed, largely independent data and procedural components which provide natural models of the properties and behaviors of the problem data objects.

Section 1.6

1. A stand-alone computer system is a single-user system that is not connected in any way to any other computer facilities. In a timeshared system, many users are connected to one central computer. All of these users must share the central facilities, including the CPU, secondary and main memory, and the input/output devices. In a networked system, a number of computers are linked together. Each computer usually has the full capability of a personal computer—its own secondary and main memory, its own CPU, and possibly its own input/output devices (in addition to a keyboard and a screen). Check with your instructor or lab assistant to determine which system your class is using.

Chapter 2

Section 2.1

1. problem input: pound_weight (weight in pounds)
   problem out[put: kilo_weight (weight in kilograms)
   formula: 1 pound equals .453 kilograms
3. During the program design stage, the problem is decomposed into smaller, relatively independent subproblems, each of which is considerably easier to solve than the original. A list of steps, called an algorithm, is then developed to solve each subproblem. Once it has been verified that the algorithm solves the problem, the program implementation stage can begin. Here the algorithm is actually implemented as a program. This implementation requires that each step in the algorithm be converted into statements in a particular programming language.
5. An algorithm is an outline of the steps that a program needs to perform. The program consists of instructions telling the computer how to execute these steps. The algorithm is converted into instructions which are dependent on the programming language being used.

Section 2.2

1. The special pair of symbols // denotes a program comment.
3. Comments can make a program more readable by describing the purpose of a program and by describing the use of each identifier in the program. Comments can also be used to describe the purpose of each major step in a program.
5. The #include is a compiler directive. It instructs the compiler to insert the indicated C++ instructions into the program in place of the directive. For example,
   #include <iostream.h>
   instructs the compiler to get the file iostream.h and insert its contents in place of the #include line during compilation.
7. main   valid
   const   reserved
   y=z   invalid
   cin   valid
   xyz123   valid
   Prog#2   invalid
   Bill   valid
   123xyz   invalid

```
ThisIsALongOne      valid
Sue's               invalid
'Maxscores'         invalid
so_is_this_one      valid
start               valid
int                 reserved
two-way             invalid
return              reserved
go                  valid
```

Section 2.3

1. The value of pi (3.14159) should be stored in a constant because this value never changes.
3. a. Type int data can have no fractional part; type float data can have a fractional part.
   b. We can do arithmetic on type int data; type char data is used to represent individual character values; although the representations are decimal values between 0 and 127, arithmetic operations on type char data produce meaningless results.
5. A string literal is enclosed in double quotes: " ";
   A character literal is enclosed in apostrophes or single quotes: ' ';
   A single character such as an exclamation point is written in double quotes as with "!".
7. shape triangle
   shape rectangle
   shape square

Section 2.4

1. variables are instances of language-defined data types such as int or char; objects are instances of system-defined or user-defined data types such as string or money.
3. class member function—an operation performed on the attributes of a class.
   class data member—an attribute of a class (characteristic or feature modeled by the class)

Section 2.5

1. data 5.0   7.0
   a = 10.0
   b = 21.0
3. My name is: Doe, Jane
   I live in Ann Arbor, MI, and my zip code is 48109

Section 2.6

1.
```
#include <iostream.h>  // tells compiler to include this file
void main ( )          // denotes the start of this program
{
    float x, y, z;     // declares three floating-point variables

    y = 15.0;          // assigns the value 15.0 to variable y
    z = y + 3.5;       // adds the value 3.5 to variable y; stores the
                       //    result in z
    x = y + z;         // adds the contents of y and z; stores the
                       //    result in x
    cout >> x, y, z;   // displays the results
}
```

Values printed will be 33.5   15.0   18.5.

```
3. m = (m / n) * n + (m % n)
   m = 45    n = 5
   45 = (45 / 5) * 5 + (45 % 5)
   45 =   9 * 5 + 0
```

5. a. `i = a % b;`   i is assigned 3
   b. `i = (max_i - 990 / a);`   i is assigned 670
   c. `i = a % y;`   invalid: y must be type int
   d. `i = (990 - max_i) / a;`   i is assigned −3
   e. `i = pi * a;`   i is assigned 9
   f. `x = pi * y;`   x is assigned −3.14159
   g. `x = pi / y;`   x is assigned −3.14159
   h. `i = (max_i - 990) % a;`   i is assigned 1
   i. `x = a % (a / b);`   runtime error: cannot divide by 0
   j. `i = a % 0;`   runtime error: cannot divide by 0
   k. `i = b / 0;`   runtime error: cannot divide by 0
   l. `i = a % (max_i - 990);`   i is assigned 3
   m. `x = a / y;`   x is assigned −3.0
   n. `i = a % (990 - max_i);`   i is assigned −3
   o. `x = a / b;`   x is assigned 0

7. a. `white = color * 2.5 / purple;`   white is assigned 1.0
   b. `green = color / purple;`   green is assigned 0
   c. `orange = color / red;`   orange is assigned 0
   d. `blue = (color + straw) / (crayon + 0.3);`   blue is assigned −3
   e. `lime = red / color + red % color;`   lime is assigned 2
   f. `purple = straw / red * color;`   purple is assigned 0

Section 2.7

1. `15`   int
   `'XYZ'`   invalid: only single character permitted
   `'*'`   char
   `$`   invalid: missing single quotes
   `25.123`   float
   `15.`   float
   `-999`   int
   `.123`   float
   `'x'`   char
   `"x"`   invalid: must use single quotes
   `'9'`   char
   `'-5'`   invalid: only single character permitted
   `'x"`   invalid: second quote must be single quote
   `$4.79`   invalid: no $ permitted for float
   `6.3E-2`   float
   `.0986E3.0`   invalid: the exponent must be an integer

Section 2.8

1. In interactive programs, the cout line is used to prompt the user to enter input. In a batch program, there is no need for this prompt because the data are obtained from a data file. The cout line is used in a batch file to echo the data. This lets the user know what data values were read.

Chapter 3

Section 3.1

1. Input: `hrs_worked`, `pay_rate`
   Output: `pay`
   Initial Algorithm:
   1. Read hours worked, pay rate
   2. Calculate pay
         2.1. Assign hours worked pay rate to pay
   3. Display pay

Section 3.2

1. Note: The following function calls assume that all arguments are valid for their respective functions.
   a. `sqrt (u + v ^ w * w)`
   b. `log10 (pow (x, y))`
   c. `sqrt ((x - y) * (x - y))`
   d. `fabs ((x * y) - (w / z))`

3. a. `disc = square_float (b) - 4.0 * a * c;`   613
      `disc = square_float (b) -(4.0 * a) * c;`   613
   b. `x1 = (-b + sqrt (disc)) / (2.0 * a);`   .04
      `x1 = (-b + sqrt (disc)) / 2.0 * a;`   .36   Results differ because division is done prior to multiplying `2.0` by `a`.

   c. `x2 = (-b - sqrt (disc)) / (2.0 * a);`   8.29
      `x2 =  -b - sqrt (disc)  / (2.0 * a);`   −29.13   Results differ because division is done prior to subtracting `sqrt (disc)` from `-b`.

Section 3.3

1.

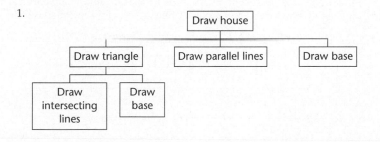

3.

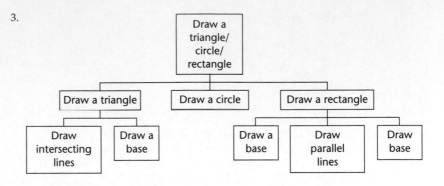

Section 3.4

1. The 5 by 5 letter O prints.
   On the next line, the 5 by 5 letter H prints.
   Three lines are skipped.
   On the next line, the 5 by 5 letter H prints.
   On the next line, the 5 by 5 letter I prints.
   On the next line, the 5 by 5 letter M prints.

Section 3.5

1. The purpose of function arguments is to transmit data back and forth between functions.
3. pass 2.0 to `compute_area`; pass value of 2.0 to `square_float`; value of 4.0 is returned to `compute_area`; value of 12.56636 is returned to the main program

Section 3.6

1. a. The top-down design process allows us to focus initially on the overall problem rather than have our attention distracted by details. The details are handled at a lower level, specifically, in a function. By declaring the function prototype, we can write the main program as a series of function calls prior to actually writing the functions themselves.
   b. The C++ function prototype provides the type information needed by the compiler to check the consistency of all input arguments and of the returned type for our functions.

3.

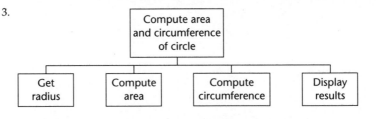

Chapter 4

Section 4.2

1. x = 15, y = 25

x != y	True
x < x	False
x > (y - x)	True
x == (y + x - y)	True

3. Both expressions are correct. In the first, x is compared to 5.1, y to 22.3 and the results are combined using the && (and) operator. In the second, p, q are combined using &&, q, r are combined using && and then the results are combined using || (or).

5. ((x > y) || ((y + 2) >= (x - z)))

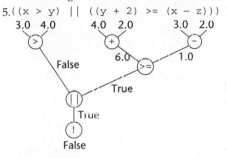

Section 4.3

1. a. Always
   b. O.K.
3. a. "the" is located at position 8 (value of pos_targ) and is replaced by "that". test_string becomes "Here is that string".
   b. "Here" is located at position 0 (value of pos_targ) and replaced by "There". test_string becomes "There is the string".
   c. "Where" is not located so the condition involving pos_targ is false and the error message is displayed.

Section 4.4

1.
```
if (x > y)
{
    x = x + 10.0;
    cout << "x bigger" << endl;
}
else
    cout << "x smaller" << endl;

cout << "y is " << y << endl;
```

3. Placing brackets around the last two lines in the answer to Question 1 would cause the value of y to be displayed only when y <= x.

Section 4.5

1. Program is more readable and easier to modify.
3. We would have to change the definition for constant dues (new value is 17.5) defined in the main function.

Section 4.6

1. hours is 41, rate is 2.10.

Section 4.7

1.

STATEMENT PART	salary	tax	EFFECT
	13500.00	?	
`if (salary < 0.0)`			13500.00 < 0.0 is false.
`else if (salary < 1500.00)`			13500.00 < 1500.00 is false.
`else if (salary < 3000.00)`			13500.00 < 3000.00 is false.
`else if (salary < 5000.00)`			13500.00 < 5000.00 is false.
`else if (salary < 8000.00)`			13500.00 < 8000.00 is false.
`else if (salary < 15000.00)`			13500.00 < 15000.00 is true.
`tax = (salary - 8000.00)`			Tax evaluates to 5500.00.
`* .25`			Tax evaluates to 1375.00.
`+ 1425.00`			Tax evaluates to 2800.00.

3. x = 6, y = 7

  a. `(x > 5) && (y / x <= 10)` evaluates to true.
  b. `(x <= 10) || (x / (y - 7) > 3)` evaluates to true.

In this example, because the left-hand side of the expression evaluates to true, it is not necessary to evaluate the right-hand side. Only one side must be true for an OR to evaluate to true. If the right side was evaluated in this example, a runtime error would occur as a result of division by 0.

Section 4.8

1. red
3. In Section 4.7, the selection is determined based on a sizable range of values rather than a specific value. With the `switch` statement, selection is based on a single value or a small, easily listable set of values.

Chapter 5

Section 5.1

1. a. If the increment operation were omitted, the loop would execute "forever" because `employee_count` would always be zero.
  b. If the increment operation were omitted, the loop would execute "forever" because `employee_count` would always be zero. If the initialization statement were omitted, whatever value was stored in `employee_count` would be used as the starting value.
3. The loop body is repeated three times. Each time, the value of x is printed.
  Output: 9
            81
         6561
5. If the last statement in the loop is omitted, the loop will execute forever because the value of count will never reach 3. If x is type int, the value displayed will be incorrect after the correct value becomes larger than MAX_INT.

Section 5.2

1.   5
    25
    125
    625

3. The segment should read:
```
count = 0;
sum = 0;
while (count < 5)
{
    cout << "Enter data item: ";
    cin >> item;
    cout << endl;
    sum += item;
    count++;
}

cout << count << " data items were added" << endl;
cout << "their sum is " << sum << endl;
```

5. The loop body would not execute because the condition 0 < 0 is false.

Section 5.3

1. The least number of times that the body of a while loop may execute is 0. This will occur when the condition tests false the first time.
3. a. Output: 9.45
              5.6
   b. Output: 5.58
              5.58
5. a. Output: The value of pi is 3.141590
      Output: The value of radius is 4.500000
   b. If the variables are type int, the result would be
      Output: 416
      Output: 10100
   b. If the variables are type float, the result would be
      Output: 4.00000016.000000
      Output: 10.000000100.000000

Section 5.4

1. The first score would not be included in the sum but the sentinel would be.
3. digit_read = isdigit (next_char);
   a. The loop would execute "forever" because digit_read would remain false and !digit_read would be true.
   b. both subexpressions and the complete condition would be true.
5. The value of count would be 0 and a run-time error would result when average was computed (division by zero).

Section 5.5

1. You could add if statements to test each value and report an error and return if they were incorrect.

a. The loop would execute "forever" because `object_height` would not change and would be greater than zero.

b. The value of `t` would decrease from zero instead of increase, but the rest of the table would look the same as for `delta_t` positive. The function call `pow (t, 2)` returns the same value if `t` is negative or positive (e.g., -1.5^2 equals 1.5^2).

c. The loop body would not execute because `0 > 0` would be false.

3. We would have to pass g as an argument to the table generation function. The only advantage is it would be easier to locate g if we needed to change it, but that is outweighed by the disadvantage of not declaring it locally where it is needed.

Section 5.6

1. Add the output lines:

```
 5      25      5.0
 6      36      2.4
 7      49      2.6
 8      64      2.8
 9      81      3.0
10     100     10.0
```

3. Result: 15.

Value of sum as computed by the formula

$$sum = \frac{n(n+1)}{2}$$

is 15. If *n* were 50, the result would be 1275.

Using the formula is a much more efficient means of obtaining the result. There are always three calculations required in the formula. Using the loop, there are *n* calculations.

Section 5.7

1. ```
for (power_p = 1.0; power_p > 0.0; power_p = 0.5 * power_p)
                cout << power_p << endl;
```

3. It displays the following lines:

```
0 10
1 8
2 6
```

Section 5.8

1. It displays the following lines:

```
10
7
4
1
```

3. The `do-while` loop body always executes at least one time. It is possible for a `while` loop body not to execute at all.
```

Section 5.9

1. Output: 10
                20
                30
                40
                50
                60
                70
                80
                90
               100

```
for (num = 10; num <= 100; num += 10)
   cout << num << endl;

num = 10;
do
{
   cout << num << endl;
   num += 10;
}
while (num <= 100);
```

3. The do-while loop should be used only in situations where it is certain that the loop should execute at least once.

Section 5.10

1. a. Output: *
              **
              ***
              ****

   b. Output: *****
              *****
              *****

Section 5.11

1.
```
count = 0;
sum = 0;
cout << "Enter "  << n <<  " integers and press return:" << endl;
for (int count = 0; count <= n; count++)
{
   cout << "count " << count << endl; // debug
   cin >> item;
   sum += item;
   cout << "sum " << sum << endl;     // debug
} // end for
```

The addition of these debug statements should show that the loop has an "off by 1" error. The prompt is requesting n data items. The loop is expecting n+1 data items. This can be corrected by changing the condition test from <= to <.

Chapter 6

Section 6.1

1. You would need to provide salaries in each of the three categories listed: First category is salary < 34,000 (result would be 15% of that salary). Second category is a salary between 34,000 and 82,150 (result would be 15% of 34,000 + 28% of amount over 34,000). The third category is a salary > 82,150 (result would be 15% of 34,000 + 28% of (82,150 − 34,000) + 31% of amount over 82,150). You should also check salaries < 0 (result should be −1). Finally, check the boundary values, 34,000 and 81,250. For the former, the result should be 15% of 34,000. For the latter, add 18% of (81,250 − 34,000) to 15% of 34,000.

3. Pre: gross and rate are defined (both > 0)
   Post: Computes net as gross - 15.00 if
         gross > 100.00; otherwise, net = gross.
   Returns: net

Section 6.2

1.

STATEMENT	change_denom	change_needed	num_units	EFFECT
	5.00	5.56	?	
num_units = int(change_needed / change_denom);			1	Assign num_units the integer value of change_needed / change_denom.
change_needed = change_needed - (num_units * change_denom);		.56		Assign change_needed the decimal portion of the original value of change_needed.

3. a. Assuming data 8.0, 10.0, 6.0 are read into num1, num2, and num3, respectively:

STATEMENT	num1	num2	num3	x	y	temp	EFFECT
	8.0	10.0	6.0	?	?	?	
order (num3, num2);				6.0	10.0		x and y are assigned the values of num3 and num2.
if (x > y)							If 6.0 > 10.0 is false: no change.
order (num3, num1);				6.0	8.0		x and y are assigned the values of num3 and num1.
if (x > y)							If 6.0 > 8.0 is false: no change.

STATEMENT	num1	num2	num3	x	y	temp	EFFECT
order (num2, num1);				10.0	8.0		x and y are assigned the values of num2 and num1.
if (x > y) temp = x;						10.0	If 10.0 > 6.0 is true: temp assigned the value of x.
x = y; y = temp;				8.0	10.0		x assigned the value of y. y assigned the value of temp.
	10.0	8.0					num2 and num1 are now reversed.

Assuming data 10.0, 8.0, 60.0 are read into num1, num2, num3, respectively:

STATEMENT	num1	num2	num3	x	y	temp	EFFECT
	10.0	8.0	60.0	?	?	?	
order (num3, num2)				60.0	8.0		x is assigned 60.0, y is assigned 8.0.
if (x > y) temp = x;						60.0	If 60.0 > 8.0 is true: temp is assigned 60.0.
x = y;				8.0			x is assigned 8.0.
y = temp;					60.0		y is assigned 60.0.
		60.0	8.0				num3 is assigned 8.0 (x) num2 is assigned 60.0 (y). (the contents of num3 and num2 are reversed)
order (num3, num1)				8.0	10.0		x is assigned 8.0. y is assigned 10.0.
if (x > y)							If 8.0 > 10.0 is false: no change.
order (num2, num1)				60.0	10.0		x is assigned 60.0. y is assigned 10.0.
if (x > y) temp = x;						60.0	If 60.0 > 10.0 is true: temp is assigned 60.0.
x = y;				10.0			x is assigned 10.0.
y = temp;					60.0		y is assigned 60.0.
	60.0	10.0					num2 is assigned 10.0 (x). num1 is assigned 60.0 (y) (the contents of num2 and num1 are reversed).

b. As a result of this sequence of calls, the largest value is stored in variable num1, the smallest value is stored in variable num3, and the middle value is stored in variable num2.

5. a. In function `order`, variables `x`, `y`, and `temp` must all be declared type `int` rather than type `float`. The statements:

```
void order
   (float &x, float &y)

float temp;
```

become

```
void order
   (int &x, int &y)

int temp;
```

   b. The prototype for function `order` has to be changed. In addition, the variables being used in the function call should also be declared type `int`. The statements:

```
void order
   (float &,  float &);

float num1, num2, num3;
```

become

```
void order
   (int &, int &);

int num1, num2, num3;
```

Section 6.3

1. Argument correspondence for `test (m, -63,  y,  x, next)`:

ACTUAL ARGUMENT	FORMAL ARGUMENT	DESCRIPTION
-m	a	int, value
-63	b	int, value
-y	c	float, reference
-x	d	float, reference
-next	e	char, reference

Argument correspondence for `test (35, m * 10, y, x, next)`:

ACTUAL ARGUMENT	FORMAL ARGUMENT	DESCRIPTION
35	a	int, value
m * 10	b	int, value
y	c	float, reference
x	d	float, reference
next	e	char, reference

3. Invalid function calls:

   e. must use variable for call by reference
   g. a, b, not declared
   i. must use variable for call by reference
   j. too many arguments

Calls requiring standard conversion:

   a. z becomes `int`
   d. m becomes `float`
   j. x becomes `int`

Section 6.4

```
1. void compute_area (int num_items,          // IN: number of data items
                      float sum,              // IN: sum of data
                      float & ave)            // OUT: average of data

   // Pre:    num_items and sum are defined; num_items must be > 0.0
   // Post:   If num_items is positive, the average (variable ave) is
   //         computed as sum / num_items; otherwise ave is set to 0.0
   // Return: The average (variable ave) if num_items is positive;
   //         otherwise variable ave is set to 0.0

   {
      if (num_items < 1)
      {
         cout << "Invalid value for num_items = " << num_items << endl;
         cout << "Average not computed." << endl;
         ave = 0.0;
      }  // endif
      ave = sum / float (num_items);
   }  // end compute_avc
```

3. Data areas after call but before function execution:

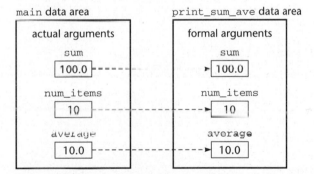

main **data area**   print_sum_ave **data area**

In this example the data areas will contain the same values after print_sum_ave executes (but before it returns to main). No values are changed during execution.

5. If num items were 0 or negative:

- In compute_sum the for loop would attempt to execute. Since count would be greater than or equal to num_items, control would pass to the statement following the for loop. A value of sum = 0 would be returned.
- In compute_ave a runtime error would occur if num_items were 0. If num_items were negative, compute_ave would return with a negative average.
- In print_sum_ave if num_items were 0, the program would previously have failed due to the runtime error in compute_ave caused by an attempt to divide by 0. If num_items were negative, num_items would be displayed as that negative number, sum would be displayed as 0, and average would be displayed as a negative number.

Section 6.5

```
1. void main_()
   {
       string a_string;
       bool success;

       cout << "Enter a source string to edit: "
       getline (cin, a_string, '\n');
       do_replace (a_string, success);
       if (success)
          cout << "Modified string is " << a_string << endl;
       else
          cout << "String " << a_string << " not changed."
               << endl;
   }
```

Section 6.6

```
1. Enter the number of items to be processed: 10
   Function compute_sum entered
   The number of items is 10
   The sum of the data is 100.00
   The average of the data is 10.00
```

Section 6.7

1. mystery (4, 3) -> 4 * mystery (4, 2) -> 4 * (4 * mystery (4, 1)). The result would be 4^3. The function raises its first argument to the power indicated by its second argument.

Chapter 7

Section 7.1

```
1. const int maxint = 32767;                    valid integer
   const int minint = -maxint;                  valid integer
   const char last_char = 'z';                  valid character

   const int max_size = 50;                     valid integer
   const int min_size = max_size - 10;          valid integer
   const int id = 4FD6;                         invalid: integer cannot contain letters

   const int koffman_age = 47;                  valid integer
   const int friedman_age = z59;                invalid: integer cannot contain letters

   const float price = $3,335.50;               invalid: float cannot contain $
   const float price = 3335.50;                 valid: float
   const float price = "3335.50";               invalid: float cannot contain quotes
```

3. The difference between the #define and the const declaration is that the identifier used in the #define has no storage associated with it. The #define is a compiler directive that tells the compiler to associate a constant with a particular identifier. Using a const declaration

involves placing the constant value in a storage location. The contents of this storage location cannot be changed during program execution.

Section 7.2

1. $2^{15} - 1$ (32767)
3. The value of x / 2 is 2.95. Adding 2.95 to 6 (value of m) yields 8.95 which is assigned to y. The smallest value is 23, when x is .1.

Section 7.3

1. a. `int ('D') - int ('A')`
    68 − 65 = 3
   b. `char ((int ('M') - int ('A')) + int ('a'))`
    `char (77 - 65 + 97) = char (109) = 'm'`
   c. `int ('m') - int ('a')`
    109 − 97 = 12
   d. `int ('5') - int ('0')`
    53 − 48 = 5

	TYPE	VALUE	EXPLANATION
3. a. `isdigit ('0'),`	int	true	'8' is the character representation of a digit.
b. `isdigit ('A');`	int	false	'A' is not the character representation of a digit.
c. `isdigit (7);`	int	false	7 is not the character representation of a digit.
d. `toupper ('#');`	char	'#'	# has no upper- or lowercase.
e. `tolower ('Q');`	char	'q'	'Q' is uppercase; returns corresponding lowercase.
f. `to_digit ('6', i);`	int	true, i = 6	'6' is the character representation of a digit; returns the digit equivalent in i.

Section 7.4

CONDITION	COMPLEMENT
1. a. `x <= y && x != 15`	`x > y || x = 15`
b. `(x <= y && x != 15) || z == 7.5`	`(x > y || x == 15) && z != 7.5`
c. `x != 15 || (z == 7.5 && x <= y)`	`x == 15 && (z != 7.5 || x > y)`
d. `flag || ! (x != 15.7)`	`!flag && x != 15.7`
e. `!flag && x <= 8`	`flag || x > 8`

Section 7.5

1. Integer values 0, 1, 2, 3, 4, 5, 6, and 7 for variable i will provide a meaningful result in `expense_category (i)`.
3. a. `enum logical {true, false};`   invalid: `true` and `false` are values of type `bool`.

   b. `enum letters {A, B, C, D};`   valid
    `enum two_letters {A, B};`   invalid: no identifier may be used more than once in any enumeration within the same scope of definition.

```
c. enum day {sun, mon, tue, wed, thur, fri, sat};     valid
   enum week_day {mon, tue, wed, thu, fri};           invalid: see reason in part
                                                       b above.

   enum week_end {sat, sun};                           invalid: see reason in part
                                                       b above.

d. enum traffic_light {red, yellow, green};            valid
   int green; invalid:                                 see reason in part b above.
```

Chapter 8

Section 8.1

1. Using `cin` instead of `cin.get` in Fig. 8.3 would cause the program to wait indefinitely for input because `cin` skips over the newline character.
3. If `cout.put (nwln)` were omitted from the program, the output after the end of the inner loop (`"The number of blanks ..."`) would appear on the same line as the last character output.
5. If there are no data in the input stream, the loops will not execute. If an end-of-file is entered, `line_count` will display as 0 and the program will terminate. If no end-of-file is entered, the program will wait indefinitely for data to be entered.

Section 8.2

1. The e is read in the loop in function `copy_line`. It is written to the output file. The s is read next and written to the output file. The . is read next and written to the output file. The `<nwln>` is read next, causing control to drop out of the loop. `<nwln>` is written to the output file. Control passes back to main. `line_count` is incremented. Since end-of-file is true, control drops out of the loop. Statistics are displayed on the screen, files are closed, and execution is terminated.
3. Some advantages of using external (permanent) files for program input and output are:
   a. The input data can be reused without being reentered. This is especially helpful while you are debugging your program.
   b. The input data can be examined and edited.
   c. The output information can be printed and examined as often as needed.
   d. The output information can be used as input data for another program.

Section 8.3

1. a. Trailing blanks at the end of a record (except for the last one) would cause no problem because they would be skipped when scanning for the first name of the next employee. However, trailing blanks at the end of the last record could cause a problem because the `eof` function would return false (instead of true), so the `while` loop would execute an extra time. One way to get around this is to call the `ignore` function (discussed in Section 8.4). Adding `eds.ignore (1000, '\n');` as the last line of the loop would cause up to 1000 extra characters at the end of a line (through the newline) to be ignored.
   b. Leading blanks are ignored when each employee's first name is read so they cause no problem.
   c. Blank lines in the middle of the data stream would cause no problem because they would be skipped when reading the next employee's first name. A blank line at the end would cause the while loop to execute an extra time.

Section 8.4

1. a. The newline character at the end of each record would be stored as the first character of the next employee's name. If there were any trailing blanks before the newline, they would be stored before the newline character. To prevent this, we can insert eds.ignore (1000, '\n'); after reading hours and rate. This statement skip trailing blanks and the newline character at the end of the line.

   b. Leading blanks are read as part of the employee's name. They are not skipped by getline.

3. To write the name and salary on separate lines use the statement:

   ```
   pds << name << endl << salary << endl;
   ```

5. This statement extracts and ignores (skips) all characters in the input stream through the next newline character. If there are more than 100 characters before the next newline character, it will only skip the first 100 characters.

Chapter 9

Section 9.1

1. x3 is a simple variable. A single value is associated with this single memory location. x[3] is a part of a collection of variables, called an array, all having the same data type. An array is a structured variable. x[3] refers to the fourth element in this array.

3. a. complex x[100];
   b. float x[saturday + 1];

Section 9.2

1. No, it is not necessary to use all of the array elements. If the array is initialized at the time of its declaration, any array elements not explicitly initialized through the list will be assigned a value of 0.

Section 9.3

1. When several items in an array of data are to be processed, it is generally better to pass that entire array to a function rather than to call the function with one array element at a time. For example, to print an array of test scores, the entire array of scores, rather than each individual score, could be passed to a function that would then print each score.

3.
```
void exchange
    (char& a1,        // item to exchange with a2
     char& a2)        // item to exchange with a1

// Pre: a1, a2 are defined.
// Post: contents of a1 are exchanged with the contents of a2.

{
    // Local data ...
    char temp;        // stores (saves) contents of a1 prior to moving
                      //    contents of a2 into a1

    temp = a1;
    a1 = a2;
    a2 = temp;
}   // end exchange
```

```
int same_array
    (int size,           // IN: size of the arrays
     const char a[],     // IN: char array to be compared to array b
     const char b[])     // IN: char array to be compared to array a

// Pre:  a[i] and b[i]  (0 <= i <= size-1) are assigned values.
// Post: Returns 1 (true) if a[i] == b[i] for all i in range 0..
//       size-1; otherwise, returns 0 (false).

    for (int i = 0;
         i < size - 1 && a[i] == b[i];
         i++);

    return a[i] == b[i];

}  // end same_array
```

Section 9.4

1. In read_scores, the int array scores must be changed to float. Local data sentinel and temp_score must be changed from int to float.
3. The condition section_size < max_size in the while loop prevents the user from entering more than max_size scores.

Section 9.5

1. a. not_found is set to 0. The array subscript of the item matching target is returned to the calling function.
   b. not_found is set to 0. The array subscript of the *first* item matching target is returned to the calling function.
3. We could use a function find_index_of_max to arrange the data items in the array in descending order. We should also change the variable min_sub to max_sub to improve readability.

Section 9.6

1. The value of the num_depend component of organist becomes 2.
3. struct part
   ```
   {
       int part_num;          // part number
       string description;    // description of part
       int qoh;               // quantity of part on hand
       float price;           // price of part
   };
   ```

Section 9.7

1. a. References the stu_name component of a_student.
   b. Allocates a struct named me.
   c. invalid, exam_stats is a type, not a variable.
   d. invalid, scores[2] is the last one.
   e. The last score of a_student.

f. The first score of a_student.
g. invalid, need to specify a struct variable.
h. invalid, transpose exam_stats and a_student.

Chapter 10

Section 10.1

1. The librarian, normally one of the programmers, assumes the responsibility for determining the status of each module in the system. The librarian must keep track of the date that each new version of a module is inserted in the library. It is also the librarian's job to make sure that all programmers are using the latest version of any module. The systems analyst is responsible for developing the specifications for the software needed by an organization. The analyst must then be sure the software is developed and performs according to these specifications.
3. A programming team has more manpower to apply to a job. As long as the job can be apportioned into subsystems that can be implemented independently, the programming team will proceed much faster than a lone individual.

Section 10.2

1. Before a library function can be called, the calling function must know the function name, the number and type of arguments, and the return value expected.
3. These arguments represent the bounds of the subarray being examined.

Section 10.3

1. a. With type int, we can use the arithmetic (including %), relational, and equality operators and stream insertion and extraction.
   b. With type char, we can use the relational and equality operators and stream insertion and extraction operators, but should not use the arithmetic operators (although permitted by C++). We can use all the functions in the library with header ctype.h.
3. Both promote reusability. Functions also facilitate modularization. Classes enable a programmer to declare new data types and build abstract data types.

Section 10.4

1. a. Executes n times for each i, or n^2 times; O(n^2).
   b. Executes 2 times for each i, or $2n$ times; O(n).
   c. Executes n times for each i, or n^2 times; O(n^2).

Section 10.5

1. a. Whitebox test data:

min_n	max_n	n
0	100	100
0	100	0
0	100	50
0	100	101
0	100	−1
100	0	
0	0	0

b. Blackbox test data:

min_n	max_n	n
0	100	100
0	100	0
0	100	50
0	100	101
0	100	−1
100	0	
0	0	0

The test data are the same for both white- and blackbox testing due to the simplicity of the function. The interactive information essentially describes the workings of this function.

Section 10.6

1. `assert: min_n <= max_n`
   invariant: n is the first data value read that has a value between `min_n` and `max_n` (inclusive)
3. `invariant: -20 <= celsius <= 20; fahrenheit = 1.8 * celsius + 32`
5. No, the invariant no longer holds true. Since the initial read is not performed prior to testing the loop condition, it is possible for the sentinel value to be processed in the loop body. This would invalidate the invariant.

Chapter 11

Section 11.1

1. These are all member functions of class `counter`. To call them, we must associate them with a particular object of this class using dot notation.

Section 11.2

1. The scope resolution operator `::` is used as a prefix to the function names of each member function header. This operator tells the compiler that the function being defined is a member of the class named just preceding the operator.

Section 11.3

1. `counts[3].increment ();`
   `cout << counts[4].access_value ();`

Section 11.4

1. −1, 1

Section 11.5

1.

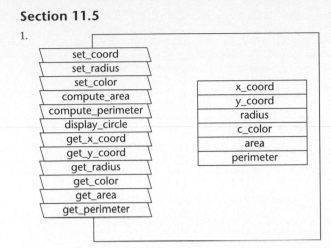

3. To form a rectangle class, substitute the attributes width and length (type float), for the attribute radius. Replace member function set_radius with set_dimensions. The function set_dimensions would have two arguments, representing the width and length of a rectangle. Replace member function get_radius with two accessor functions: get_width and get_length. Replace display_circle with display_rectangle. The bodies of the new member functions would process the new attributes. Functions compute_area and compute_perimeter would do the calculations for a rectangle instead of a circle. The five member functions that set and retrieve the object's coordinates and color would be unchanged.

Section 11.6

1. It does store leading blanks. One way to change it would be to use the extraction operator >> to get the first character only instead of function get.
3. The for loop in write_string can access the attribute length directly, but a client function (including a driver) must use get_length to access this value.

Section 11.7

1. The id validation that is performed by function deposit would not permit a deposit intended for one account to be made in the other.
3. The for loop in write_string can access the attribute length directly, but a client function (including a driver) must use get_length to access this value.

Chapter 12

Section 12.1

1. a. 20
   b. cout << matrix[2][3];
   c. matrix[4][3]

3. The compiler can compute the offset of any element from the first knowing just the size of the second and third dimensions. The array element order is sales[0][0][0] ... sales[0][0][11], sales[0][1][0] ... sales[0][1][11] ... sales[0][4][0] ... sales[0][4][11]. Then the same sequence for the first subscript 1, the first subscript 2 ... the first subscript 9. The last element is sales[9][4][11]. The offset for sales[i][j][k] is computed by the formula

$offset = i \times 5 \times 12 + j \times 12 + k$

For the last element, this gives $9 \times 60 + 4 \times 12 + 11$ or 599.

Section 12.2

1. a. `gender` attribute of 2nd employee
   b. invalid
   c. the last employee (a struct)
   d. invalid
   e. invalid
   f. invalid
   g. the last employee's name
   h. invalid

Section 12.3

1. ```
   dummy<float> a, b, c;
   float num_1, num_2, n_1, n_2;
   cout << "Enter two numbers: ";
   cin >> num_1 >> num_2;
   a.set_value (num_1);
   b.set_value (num_2);
   a.get_value (n_1);
   b.get_value (n_2)
   c.set_value (n_1 + n_2);
   ```

Section 12.4

1. array attribute `small_list.items` has room for 5 `float` values. `small_list.size` is 0.
   contents of `items` is 3.5, `small_list.size` is 1
   contents of `items` is 3.5, 5.7, `small_list.size` is 2
   contents of `items` is 5.7, `small_list.size` is 1
   display 5.7, `items` and `size` are not changed.
   contents of `items` is 15.5, `small_list.size` is 1
   contents of `items` is 15.5, 5.5, `small_list.size` is 2
   display 1, index of 5.5
   contents of `items` is 5.5, 15.5, `small_list.size` is 2
   display array `items`: 5.5, 15.5, `small_list.size` is 2.

Section 12.5

1. It returns the count of array elements that are larger than the array element they follow. For example, if `items` contains 3.5, 5.6, 4.6, 7.7, the value returned would be 2 because 5.6 and 7.7 are larger than the array element they follow.
   ```

Section 12.6

1. The compiler determines which class a member function belongs to by the type of the object it is applied to.

Section 12.7

1. In the definition of friend operator >>, all three occurrences of operators << and >> in the body have a stream as the left operand and a string object as the right operand. C++ has defined >> and << for stream and string objects.

Section 12.8

1. |$
   |$-
   |$ next_ch is -
   |$ next_ch is $
   returns false
   returns true

Section 12.9

1. `stack<exam_stats, 50> my_class;`
   You can use the stack operators with this class.

Chapter 13

Section 13.1

1.

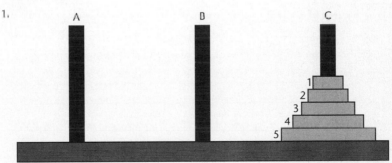

3. 1. Move 2 disks from A to B.
   2. Move 1 disk from A to C.
   3. Move 2 disks from B to C.

Section 13.2

1. The current value of n is placed on the stack each time `reverse_string` recursively calls itself. Upon return to its calling function, whether this is another function or itself, the current value gets popped off the stack. The value of n in the calling function becomes the new current value.

3. The entry displays appear in the order in which the function is recursively called. They appear prior to any exit displays because of the location of the exit displays in the function. Since the exit display is coded to occur after the recursive call to the function, it isn't executed until the stopping step is performed.

5. Trace of `multiply (5, 4)`:

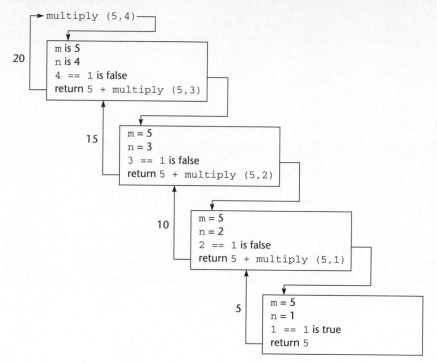

Immediately after each function call, the stacks will appear as:

CALL 1		CALL 2		CALL 3		CALL 4	
m	**n**	**m**	**n**	**m**	**n**	**m**	**n**
5	4	5	3	5	2	5	1
		5	4	5	3	5	2
				5	4	5	3
						5	4

Section 13.3

```
1. int power_raiser
      (int base,
       int power)
{
   if (power == 0)
      return 1;
   else
      return base * power_raiser (base, power-1);
}
```

3. If the stopping condition for the Fibonacci number function were just (n == 1), the function would call itself indefinitely. This occurs because not testing for (n == 2) allows n to become less than the stopping value of 1, for example, n - 2 = 0. Since the stopping value of 1 is passed over and can never be reached, 2 is continually subtracted from n, and the function continues indefinitely.

Section 13.4

1. Trace of recursive function selection_sort:

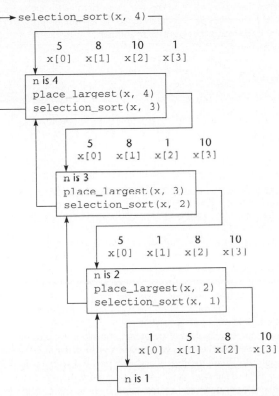

Note that the actual arrangement of values is done each time place_largest is called. No manipulation of array elements takes place at return from selection_sort.

Section 13.5

1. Sixty-three moves are needed to solve the six-disk problem. The number of moves required to solve the n-disk problem is $2^n - 1$.

Chapter 14

Section 14.1

1. a. The string "CA" is stored in the current field of the struct pointed to by p.
   b. Copies the volts member of the struct pointed to by q to the volts member of the struct pointed to by p.
   c. The contents of the struct pointed to by q is copied into the struct pointed to by p.
   d. p now contains the same memory address as q; i.e., it points to the same node.
   e. Copies the string "HT" to the current field of the struct pointed to by p.
   f. Invalid, the current field cannot be assigned an integer value.
   g. Invalid, p cannot be assigned an integer.
   h. Invalid

Section 14.2

1. The memory is not returned to the heap so it is unavailable for other programs and/or operations that could use it.

Section 14.3

1. a. Assigns the link field of the struct pointed to by r to point to the same node as p. Node pointed to by q is deleted from this new circular list of 2 nodes.
   b. Assigns NULL to the link field of the struct pointed to by p thereby denoting that this node is the last (as well as the first) node in the list.
   c. Assigns the link field of the struct pointed to by p to point to node pointed to by r. The list is unchanged.
   d. Causes the link field of the struct pointed to by p to point to the node pointed to by the link field of the node pointed to by q, NULL. Effectively disconnects the rest of the list from the node pointed to by p.
   e. Assigns p to point to the struct pointed to by p's link field (node pointed to by r). The original first list node is deleted from the list.
   f. Copies the word field "the" from the struct pointed to by r to the word field of the node that p points to.
   g. Assigns the count field of the struct pointed to by p to the same value as the count field of the struct pointed to by q (p's count field is assigned the value 3).
   h. Assigns the link field of the struct pointed to by r to NULL by following the chain of pointers starting from p. The node pointed to by q is deleted.
   i. Creates a new node and stores its address in the link field of the struct pointed to by q. Initializes the fields of the newly created node to "zzz", 0, and NULL for word, count, and link. Thus, a new node is added to the end of the linked list.
   j. Traverses through the list, incrementing the count field of each node by one until all nodes have been processed.

Section 14.4

1. Algorithm for copy_stack:
   1.0. Allocate storage for a temporary stack.
   2.0. While the existing stack is not empty
       2.1. Pop the next item from the existing stack.
       2.2. Push the item onto a temporary stack.
   3.0. While the temporary stack is not empty.
       3.1. Pop the next item from the temporary stack.
       3.2. Push the item onto the original stack and onto the copy stack.

Section 14.5

1.

ORIGINAL QUEUE	QUEUE AFTER INSERTION OF HARRIS
McMann	McMann
Wilson	Wilson
Carson	Carson
	Harris

After insertion, front points to McMann and rear points to Harris.

ORIGINAL QUEUE	QUEUE AFTER REMOVAL OF MCMANN
McMann	Wilson
Wilson	Carson
Carson	Harris

After removal of McMann, front points to Wilson and rear points to Harris. There are three passengers left.

2.
```
template <class queue_element>
bool queue<queue_element>::rude_insert
   (const queue_element& el)      // IN - to insert
{
  // Local data...
  queue_node* old_front;         // pointer to old front

  if (front == NULL)
  {  // empty queue
     front = new queue_node;
     if (front == NULL)
       return false;             // no node available
     else
       rear = front;             // one node in queue
  }
  else
  {
     old_front = front;          // save old front
     front = new queue_node;     // new first element
     front->link = old_front;    // connect up
  }

  front->item = el;
  num_items++;
  return true;
}
```

Section 14.6

1. The first tree is a binary search tree whereas the second is not.
   Inorder traversal of first tree: 10, 15, 20, 40, 50, 55, 60
   Inorder traversal of second tree: 25, 30, 45, 40, 50, 55, 60
   In the left subtree of the node containing 50, one would expect to find key values that are less than 50.

3. a.
```
     25
    /  \
  15    45
  /       \
10         60
  \        /
   12     55
```

   b.
```
       25
      /  \
    12    55
   / \   / \
  10 15 45  60
```

   c.
```
       25
      /  \
    12    55
   / \   / \
  10 15 45  60
```

   d.
```
10
  \
   12
     \
      15
        \
         25
           \
            45
              \
               55
                 \
                  60
```

Trees (b) and (c) are the most efficient to search.

The binary search trees in (b) and (c) are full binary search trees. Every node, except the leaves, has a left and a right subtree. Searching the tree is an O(log N) process.

For the binary search tree in (d), each node has an empty left subtree. Searching (d) is an O(N) process just as in searching a linked list with the same keys.

Section 14.7

1. `bin_tree<int> my_tree;`
   Creates an empty binary search tree by setting the data member `root` to NULL.

   `success = my_tree.insert (3000);` Inserts 3000 into the binary search tree returning true in success. This is the root since it is the first value inserted.

   `success = my_tree.insert (2000);` Inserts 2000, in the left subtree of the node containing 3000, returning true in `success`.

   `success = my_tree.insert (4000);` Inserts 4000, in the right subtree of the node containing 3000, returning true in `success`.

   `success = my_tree.insert (5000);` Inserts 5000, in the right subtree of the node containing 4000, returning true in `success`.

   `success = my_tree.insert (2500);` Inserts 2500, in the right subtree of the node containing 2000, returning true in `success`.

   `success = my_tree.insert (6000);` Inserts 6000, in the right subtree of the node containing 5000, returning true in `success`.

   `success = my_tree.search (2500);` Searches the binary search tree for the key value of 2500. Takes the left subtree of the node containing 3000 (since 2500 < 3000), and then the right subtree of the node containing 2000 (since 2500 > 2000). Sets `success` to true indicating that the search key was found.

   `success = my_tree.search (1500);` Searches the binary search tree for the key value of 1500. Searches the left subtrees of the nodes containing 3000 and 2000 respectively. Sets `success` to false (since the left subtree of the node containing 2000 is NULL) indicating that the search key was not found.

   `success - my_tree.retrieve (my_data);` Searches the binary search tree for the key value of 6000 (value of my_data). Searches the right subtrees of the nodes containing 3000, 4000, and 5000 respectively. Sets success to true indicating that the key value was found and returns this element of the tree in my_data.

   `my_tree.display ();` Displays the binary search tree in key order.
   The tree built by the sequence of insertions is:

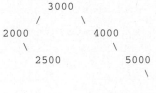

The values displayed are: 2000, 2500, 3000, 4000, 5000, 6000

Section 14.8

1. Excluding the pointer comparisons (testing for NULL):
   a. With a target key of 50, two comparisons are necessary to find the target:

Key	Result	Subtree taken
40	40 < 50	Right
50	50 = 50	None

b. With a target key of 55, four comparisons are necessary to find the target:

Key	Result	Subtree taken
40	40 < 55	Right
50	50 < 55	Right
60	60 > 55	Left
55	55 = 55	None

c. With a target key of 10, three comparisons are necessary to find the target:

Key	Result	Subtree taken
40	40 > 10	Left
15	15 > 10	Left
10	10 = 10	None

d. With a target key of 65, three comparisons are necessary to determine that 65 is not present:

Key	Result	Subtree taken
40	40 < 65	Right
50	50 < 65	Right
60	60 < 65	None

e. With a target key of 52, four comparisons are necessary to determine that 52 is not present:

Key	Result	Subtree taken
40	40 < 52	Right
50	50 < 52	Right
60	60 > 52	Left
55	55 > 52	None

f. With a target key of 48, two comparisons are necessary to determine that 48 is not present:

Key	Result	Subtree taken
40	40 < 48	Right
50	50 > 48	None

3. There will be no left subtree for each node, only a right subtree. The big-O notation for searching a tree like this is O(N).

Index